Sport and Exercise Physiology Testing Guidelines: Volume I – Sport Testing

Since its first published edition more than 30 years ago, the BASES (British Association of Sport and Exercise Sciences) Physiological Testing Guidelines have represented the leading knowledge base of current testing methodology for sport and exercise scientists. Sport and exercise physiologists conduct physiological assessments that have proven validity and reliability, both in laboratory and sport-specific contexts. A wide variety of test protocols have been developed, adapted and refined to support athletes of all abilities reach their full potential. This book is a comprehensive guide to these protocols and to the key issues relating to physiological testing.

With contributions from leading specialist sport physiologists and covering a wide range of mainstream sports in terms of ethical, practical and methodological issues, this volume represents an essential resource for sport-specific exercise testing in both research and applied settings. This new edition draws on the authors' experience of supporting athletes from many sports through several Olympic cycles to achieve world leading performances. While drawing on previous editions, it is presented in a revised format matching the sport groupings used in elite sport support within the UK sport institutes. Building on the underpinning general procedures, these specific chapters are supported by appropriate up-to-date case studies in the supporting web resources.

R. C. Richard Davison, PhD, FBASES, CSci, is Professor of Exercise Physiology in the School of Health and Life Sciences at the University of the West of Scotland, UK.

Paul M. Smith, PhD, FBASES, FHEA, is Senior Lecturer in Exercise Physiology in the School of Sport and Health Sciences at Cardiff Metropolitan University, UK.

James Hopker, PhD, is Professor of Sport and Exercise Science and Deputy Director of the Division of Natural Sciences at the University of Kent, UK.

Michael J. Price, PhD, FBASES, is Reader in Exercise Physiology at Coventry University, UK.

Florentina Hettinga, PhD, FACSM, FECSS, SFHEA, is Professor of Sport, Exercise and Rehabilitation at Northumbria University, UK.

Garry Tew, PhD, FBASES, FHEA, is Professor of Clinical Exercise Science in the Department of Sport, Exercise and Rehabilitation at Northumbria University, UK.

Lindsay Bottoms, PhD, FBASES, is Reader in Exercise and Health Physiology at the University of Hertfordshire, UK and the Director of the Research Centre for Psychology and Sports Sciences.

Sport and Exercise Physiology Testing Guidelines: Volume I – Sport Testing

The British Association of Sport and Exercise Sciences Guide

Fifth Edition

Edited by R. C. Richard Davison, Paul M. Smith, James Hopker, Michael J. Price, Florentina Hettinga, Garry Tew, and Lindsay Bottoms

LONDON AND NEW YORK

Cover image: © metamorworks/Getty Images

Fifth edition published 2022
by Routledge
2 Park Square, Milton Park, Abingdon, Oxon OX14 4RN

and by Routledge
605 Third Avenue, New York, NY 10158

Routledge is an imprint of the Taylor & Francis Group, an informa business

© 2022 Taylor & Francis

The right of R. C. Richard Davison, Paul M. Smith, James Hopker, Michael J. Price, Florentina Hettinga, Garry Tew, and Lindsay Bottoms to be identified as the authors of the editorial material, and of the authors for their individual chapters, has been asserted in accordance with sections 77 and 78 of the Copyright, Designs and Patents Act 1988.

All rights reserved. No part of this book may be reprinted or reproduced or utilised in any form or by any electronic, mechanical, or other means, now known or hereafter invented, including photocopying and recording, or in any information storage or retrieval system, without permission in writing from the publishers.

Trademark notice: Product or corporate names may be trademarks or registered trademarks, and are used only for identification and explanation without intent to infringe.

First edition published by BASES 1988
Fourth edition published by Routledge 2009

British Library Cataloguing-in-Publication Data
A catalogue record for this book is available from the British Library

Library of Congress Cataloging-in-Publication Data
A catalog record for this book has been requested

ISBN: 978-0-367-49246-5 (hbk)
ISBN: 978-0-367-49133-8 (pbk)
ISBN: 978-1-003-04528-1 (ebk)

DOI: 10.4324/9781003045281

Typeset in Baskerville
by Apex CoVantage, LLC

Access the Support Material: www.routledge.com/9780367491338

Contents

List of figures xii
List of tables xv
List of contributors xviii
Foreword xxii

Introduction 1
R. C. RICHARD DAVISON AND PAUL M. SMITH

PART I
Professional best practice 3

1.1 **Professional competency and working with others** 5
MICHAEL J. PRICE, ANDREW M. MILES, AND PAUL M. SMITH

1.2 **Physiological exercise testing: ethical considerations** 10
STEVE R. BIRD AND ANDREW SMITH

1.3 **Health and safety in duty of care: evaluating and stratifying risk** 19
S. ANDY SPARKS, KELLY MARRIN, AND CRAIG A. BRIDGE

1.4 **Safeguarding in physiological testing** 25
EMMA KAVANAGH AND DANIEL RHIND

PART II
Analysis and reporting 29

2.1 **Data intelligence and feedback to the coach** 31
SARAH GILCHRIST AND MARK HOMER

vi Contents

2.2 Reliability and measurement error   36
SHAUN J. MCLAREN

2.3 Scaling: adjusting physiological and performance measures for differences in body size   42
EDWARD WINTER AND SIMON JOBSON

PART III
General procedures   49

3.1 Pre-participation evaluation for athletes   51
RACHEL N. LORD AND DAVID OXBOROUGH

3.2 Equipment maintenance and calibration standards   55
DAVID GREEN AND GLYN HOWATSON

3.3 Lung and respiratory muscle function   61
JOHN DICKINSON AND KARL SYLVESTER

3.4 Surface anthropometry   69
SUSAN C. LENNIE

3.5 Functional screening   76
MIKE DUNCAN, STUART ELWELL, AND MARK LYONS

3.6 Respiratory gas analysis   81
SIMON MARWOOD AND RICHIE P. GOULDING

3.7 Metabolic threshold testing, interpretation and its prognostic prescriptive value   86
MARK BURNLEY AND MATTHEW I. BLACK

3.8 Ratings of perceived exertion   96
JOHN BUCKLEY AND ROGER ESTON

3.9 Strength testing   106
DALE CANNAVAN AND KATIE THRALLS BUTTE

3.10 Blood sampling   112
RONALD J. MAUGHAN AND SUSAN M. SHIRREFFS

Contents vii

3.11 Skeletal muscle biopsy: techniques and applications   118
RICHARD A. FERGUSON AND NATALIE F. SHUR

3.12 Non-invasive assessment of the neuromuscular system   125
GLYN HOWATSON, KEVIN THOMAS, PAUL ANSDELL, AND
STUART GOODALL

3.13 Field-based testing   136
BARRY DRUST AND MARK NOON

3.14 Application of dual energy x-ray absorptiometry   142
KAREN HIND

PART IV
Racing sports (endurance, middle-distance and sprint)   157

4.1 Middle- and long-distance running   159
BRIAN HANLEY AND ANDY SHAW

4.2 Triathlon   168
LAURA NEEDHAM AND BEN STEPHENSON

4.3 Swimming   173
BENJAMIN E. SCOTT, ADRIAN CAMPBELL, AND CLARE LOBB

4.4 Rowing   184
RICHARD J. GODFREY, CRAIG A. WILLIAMS, SARAH GILCHRIST,
AND R. C. RICHARD DAVISON

4.5 Cycling   188
LEN PARKER SIMPSON, JAMES G. HOPKER, AND R.C. RICHARD
DAVISON

4.6 Canoeing and kayaking   197
CIARA SINNOTT-O'CONNOR AND CAROLINE MACMANUS

4.7 Speed skating (long-track and short-track)   202
FLORENTINA HETTINGA, MARTHA BROUWER MUÑOZ, AND
ANDREW HEXT

4.8 Cross-country skiing and biathlon 208
THOMAS W. JONES AND KERRY MCGAWLEY

PART V
Invasion games 219

5.1 Soccer 221
LIAM ANDERSON, CHRIS BARNES, AND BARRY DRUST

5.2 Field hockey 227
CAROLINE SUNDERLAND AND HANNAH MACLEOD

5.3 Rugby 234
CRAIG TWIST AND JAMIE HIGHTON

5.4 Netball 238
SARAH WHITEHEAD AND CAMERON OWEN

5.5 Basketball 244
ANNE DELEXTRAT, MARK WILLIAMS, AND ANDY HOWSE

PART VI
Racket sports 251

6.1 Squash 253
CARL JAMES, TIMOTHY JONES, AND OLIVIER GIRARD

6.2 Table tennis 260
TERUN DESAI, GORAN MUNIVRANA, AND IRENE R. FABER

PART VII
Bat and ball sports 267

7.1 Cricket 269
WILL VICKERY AND JAMIE TALLENT

PART VIII
Target sports 275

8.1 Golf 277
MARK F. SMITH

8.2	**Curling**	283
	DAVID LEITH, HELEN M. COLLINS, AND AUDREY DUNCAN	

PART IX
High-intensity skill sports 289

9.1	**Motorsports**	291
	PETE MCKNIGHT AND JOHN NOONAN	
9.2	**Sport climbing**	297
	EDWARD GIBSON-SMITH, DAVID GILES, SIMON FRYER, AND MAYUR RANCHORDAS	

PART X
Aesthetic physical sports 307

10.1	**Artistic gymnastics**	309
	MONÈM JEMNI	

PART XI
Combat sports 313

11.1	**Judo**	315
	KYLE WALLACE AND EMERSON FRANCHINI	
11.2	**Amateur and professional boxing**	321
	ALAN RUDDOCK AND LAURA NEEDHAM	
11.3	**Fencing**	325
	LINDSAY BOTTOMS, ROBERT CAWDRON, STEVE KEMP, AND LUKE OATES	

PART XII
Paralympic specific 331

12.1	**Ambulant para-athletes**	333
	BEN STEPHENSON, MICHAEL HUTCHINSON, AND VICKY L. GOOSEY-TOLFREY	
12.2	**Wheeled para-sport**	339
	MICHAEL HUTCHINSON, TOM O'BRIEN, CONNOR MURPHY, AND VICKY L. GOOSEY-TOLFREY	

12.3	**Intellectual impairment**	347
	JAN BURNS, MOHAMMED KHUDAIR, AND FLORENTINA J. HETTINGA	

PART XIII
Specific populations 353

13.1	**Testing the master athlete**	355
	R. C. RICHARD DAVISON AND PAUL M. SMITH	
13.2	**Testing considerations for children**	361
	CRAIG A. WILLIAMS, MELITTA MCNARRY, AND KEITH TOLFREY	
13.3	**Testing the female athlete**	368
	KIRSTY M. HICKS, ANTHONY C. HACKNEY, MICHAEL DOOLEY, AND GEORGIE BRUINVELS	

PART XIV
Environmental-specific issues 373

14.1	**Performing at altitude**	375
	MIKE STEMBRIDGE AND CHARLES R. PEDLAR	
14.2	**Performing in the heat**	380
	NEIL S. MAXWELL, CARL A. JAMES, AND ASH G. B. WILLMOTT	
14.3	**Performing in cold environments**	385
	CLARE EGLIN, MICHAEL TIPTON, AND HEATHER MASSEY	
14.4	**Swimming in aquatic environments**	390
	MITCH LOMAX AND HEATHER MASSEY	

PART XV
Athlete health and wellbeing 395

15.1	**The travelling athlete**	397
	SARAH GILCHRIST AND LUKE GUPTA	
15.2	**Athlete wellbeing**	401
	SARAH GILCHRIST AND EMMA NEUPERT	

15.3	**Training load**	405
	SHAUN J. MCLAREN, FRANCO M. IMPELLIZZERI, AARON J. COUTTS, AND MATTHEW WESTON	
15.4	**Overreaching and overtraining**	413
	LEE BELL AND ALAN RUDDOCK	
15.5	**Exercise testing for the pregnant athlete**	418
	VICTORIA L. MEAH, AMAL HASSAN, LIN FOO, CHRISTOPH LEES, AND MARLIZE DE VIVO	
15.6	**Methods in exercise immunology**	430
	NICOLETTE C. BISHOP AND NEIL P. WALSH	

Index 438

Figures

2.2.1	Test and retest 10-m linear sprint times in soccer players. Black points and error bars in the left plot are the mean ± standard deviation.	39
3.2.1	Considerations for determining the frequency of calibration.	58
3.7.1	Schematic representation of the blood [lactate] response during incremental exercise and the methods subsequently applied to determine the metabolic thresholds.	89
3.7.2	Schematic representation of methods used to determine the heavy-severe boundary during non-incremental exercise tests.	91
3.8.1	Eston-Parfitt (E-P) scale.	100
3.11.1	Professor Eric Hultman performing a muscle biopsy of the vastus lateralis using a Bergström needle.	119
3.12.1	Neuromuscular function studied through acquisition of force and electromyographic signals.	127
3.12.2	Techniques combined in a single applied scenario.	128
3.12.3	Potentiated twitch force obtained immediately after the maximal contraction.	132
3.13.1	Six-step process underpinning the development of field-testing protocols.	137
3.14.1	Lumbar spine vertebral deformities indicating requirement for vertebral exclusion.	148
3.14.2	DXA total body scan image and region of interest placements.	149
3.14.3	Mid-prone (A – recommended) and prone hand positioning (B) for DXA scans.	150
4.1.1	The range of running speeds found in men's and women's middle- and long-distance championship racing.	160
4.1.2	A schematic example of a 1500-m athlete's full physiological profile based on the testing outlined in this chapter, their relation to exercise intensity domains and commonly prescribed training zones for distance runners.	161
4.3.1	Some key considerations for the selection of a swimming assessment.	174
4.3.2	A schematic diagram of the fully tethered swimming system.	176

4.5.1	Example short-term power output capabilities from a 'climber' (blue circles) and a 'sprinter' (red circles) with an APR 'predicted' power capability line visible for each rider (climber = solid blue line; sprinter = solid red line).	190
4.5.2	Relative APR for the 'climber' and the (sprinter) from Figure 4.5.1.	192
4.5.3	Theoretically achievable power output, above CP, for cyclists with W' of magnitudes 10 kJ (red), 15 kJ (orange), 20 kJ (blue) and 30 kJ (green) for different durations of trials.	193
4.8.1	An illustration of the sub-techniques employed across speeds and inclines in classic and skate skiing.	209
4.8.2	A laboratory set-up for roller-ski assessments in cross-country skiers and biathletes.	212
4.8.3	An experimental set-up for the 'Wingate'-style double-poling test on the SkiErg.	215
5.2.1	The shuttle sprint and dribble test course (A) and the slalom sprint and dribble test course (B).	231
5.4.1	Isometric mid-thigh pull performed using a dynamometer.	240
6.1.1	Gold, silver and bronze physical qualities for squash performance profiling.	254
6.1.2	Overview of the squash-specific aerobic fitness test (SPPT – Panel A) and squash-specific repeated sprint ability (RSA) and change of direction speed (COD) tests (both Panel B).	257
6.1.3	Example of squash-specific physical profile.	258
6.2.1	Interval shuttle run test course.	262
6.2.2	Modified Edgren side-step test set-up.	263
7.1.1	Set-up for the run-2 test.	272
8.2.1	A. Modified Thomas test position. B. FABER test position.	286
9.2.1	Illustration of recommended four-finger open and half-crimp hand positions.	299
9.2.2	Exemplar of the calculation of critical force for an elite climber calculated as the slope and W' of the intercept of linear fit of the force multiplied by time (Limit work, y axis) plotted against time (T_{lim}, x axis).	301
9.2.3	The end position of the powerslap test, recording the maximal slap height to the nearest centimetre.	303
12.2.1	Schematic for (A) agility test, (B) box test and (C) fan drill.	344
13.3.1	The implementation and interpretation of screening and monitoring tools.	369
14.1.1	Panel A shows the change in race pace oxygen consumption at sea level vs. high altitude, with the most and least desaturated athlete highlighted with a circle.	376
14.2.1	Criteria for administering physiological tests in the heat.	381
15.1.1	Components of measuring 'travel wellness'.	399
15.4.1	Schematic representation of performance outcomes.	414

15.5.1 Physiological adaptation to healthy pregnancy at rest and altered responses or considerations for acute, submaximal physical activity in pregnant individuals. 419

15.6.1 Cell morphology can be used to identify the three main immune cell populations in whole blood. 435

Tables

1.3.1	Classification and explanation of hazard types relevant to physiological testing	20
1.3.2	Example risk quantification guidance assessment tool based on the probability and severity of the outcome impact	23
1.4.1	International Safeguards for Children in Sport	26
2.1.1	Key considerations in data management and analysis	33
2.2.1	Reliability of 10-m linear sprint time in soccer players	40
3.2.1	Calibration and control check list	57
3.2.2	Example: checking the speed of a treadmill	57
3.3.1	Abnormal respiratory function	62
3.4.1	Skinfold measurements	72
3.4.2	Girth measurements	73
3.6.1	Effect of measurement precision on the determined $\dot{V}O_2$ for typical heavy-intensity exercise with 45-s expirate collection	83
3.7.1	The validity, reliability and sensitivity of the metabolic thresholds used to demarcate the exercise intensity domains (EIDs) and the abbreviations commonly used to describe these in the scientific literature	88
3.8.1	Summary of the relationship between the percentages of maximal aerobic power (%$\dot{V}O_2$max), maximal heart rate reserve (%HRRmax), maximal heart rate (%HRmax) and Borg's RPE (6–20) and CR-10 scales	97
3.9.1	Estimated 1-RM formulas from multiple repetition tests	108
3.12.1	Non-invasive techniques available for the assessment of neuromuscular function, a brief description of outcome variables and recommended reading for introductory texts and training	129
3.14.1	Indications for DXA scans in sport and exercise sciences	144
3.14.2	Standardising DXA body composition scans	146
3.14.3	Interpretation of DXA scans: bone density	147
4.1.1	Typical values for running economy (RE) in oxygen cost, lactate threshold (LT), lactate turnpoint (LTP), maximal oxygen uptake	

	($\dot{V}O_2$max) and maximal sprint speed (MSS) in endurance runners based on testing of UK athletes	163
4.3.1	Validity and reliability of key parameters measured using a selection of pool-based swimming tests	177
4.6.1	Canoeing/kayak laboratory incremental test protocol	198
4.8.1	Proposed submaximal roller-ski assessment protocols for experienced cross-country skiers and biathletes	214
4.8.2	Proposed maximal self-paced time trial roller-ski assessment protocols for experienced cross-country skiers and biathletes	214
5.1.1	Selected reference values for a battery of fitness tests	225
5.2.1	Selected performance data from field hockey field tests for elite senior and youth players (mean ±SD)	228
5.2.2	Selected performance data from field hockey field tests for sub-elite senior and youth players (mean ±SD)	229
5.4.1	Netball testing standards	241
5.5.1	Basketball testing standards	248
6.2.1	Average temporal characteristics of table tennis matches (men's singles, best of seven games)	261
6.2.2	Normative values for elite table tennis athletes collated from published and unpublished data	264
7.1.1	Recommended standards for male and female elite cricketers	269
8.1.1	Physiological assessments for golf	279
8.2.1	Normative test data provided courtesy of British Curling	284
8.2.2	Scoring data provided courtesy of British Curling	285
9.2.1	Normative data for forearm strength, rate of force development and critical force	301
9.2.2	Representative data for two-repetition max pull-up, power-slap and bent-arm hangs	303
10.1.1	Summary of the most common lab and field-based tests for artistic gymnastics	311
11.1.1	Normative data for dynamic and isometric strength endurance chin-up gripping in the judogi tests for judo athletes from different sexes and age groups	317
11.1.2	Normative data for the Special Judo Fitness Test for judo athletes from different sexes and age groups	318
11.2.1	Target standards for physiological assessments	323
11.3.1	Mean ± SD isokinetic data for club-level fencers	327
11.3.2	Mean ± SD unpublished data (from British Fencing) for male and female (16–20 yr) fencers	327
12.2.1	Sport-specific starting workload	341
12.2.2	Sport-average reference values for laboratory-based tests	341
12.2.3	Sport-average reference values for field-based tests	343
13.2.1	Sex, maturity and ethnic-specific equations for estimation of percent body fat (%BF) from skinfolds	363

14.2.1	Traffic light system for the rating of heat tolerance	383
14.3.1	Suggested exclusion and withdrawal criteria for testing undertaken in cold environments	386
14.4.1	Example maximal oxygen uptake ($\dot{V}O_2$max) assessment protocols used in swimming	392
14.4.2	Example swimming economy and blood lactate ([La$^-$]) assessment protocols used in swimming	393
15.5.1	Physical reasons to stop antenatal activity and consult a healthcare provider	421
15.5.2	Heart rate ranges and corresponding intensities of physical activity in individuals with uncomplicated pregnancies	424
15.6.1	Case study example of a completed Jackson Common Cold Questionnaire	432

Contributors

Liam Anderson
University of Birmingham, UK

Paul Ansdell
Northumbria University, UK

Chris Barnes
CB Sports Performance Ltd, UK

Lee Bell
Sheffield Hallam University, UK

Steve R. Bird
Royal Melbourne Institute of Technology, Australia

Nicolette C. Bishop
Loughborough University, UK

Matthew I. Black
University of Exeter, UK

Lindsay Bottoms
University of Hertfordshire, UK

Craig A. Bridge
Edge Hill University, UK

Georgie Bruinvels
St Mary's University, UK

John Buckley
University of Chester, UK

Mark Burnley
University of Kent, UK

Jan Burns
Canterbury Christ Church University, UK

Adrian Campbell
SportScotland Institute of Sport, UK

Dale Cannavan
Seattle Pacific University, USA

Robert Cawdron
British Fencing, UK

Helen M. Collins
University of Dundee, UK

Aaron J. Coutts
University of Technology, Sydney, Australia

R. C. Richard Davison
University of the West of Scotland, UK

Marlize de Vivo
Canterbury Christ Church University, UK

Anne Delextrat
Oxford Brookes University, UK

Terun Desai
University of Hertfordshire, UK

John Dickinson
University of Kent, UK

Michael Dooley
The Poundbury Clinic Dorset & King Edward VII Hospital London, UK

Barry Drust
University of Birmingham, UK

Audrey Duncan
University of Dundee, UK

Mike Duncan
Coventry University, UK

Clare Eglin
University of Portsmouth, UK

Stuart Elwell
Dudley Physiotherapy Clinic, UK

Roger Eston
University of South Australia, Australia

Irene R. Faber
International Table Tennis Federation, Switzerland, and Carl von Ossietzky University, Germany

Richard A. Ferguson
Loughborough University, UK

Lin Foo
Imperial College London, UK

Emerson Franchini
University of São Paulo, Brazil

Simon Fryer
University of Gloucestershire, UK

Edward Gibson-Smith
Sheffield Hallam University, UK

Sarah Gilchrist
Gilchrist Performance, UK

David Giles
University of Derby, UK

Olivier Girard
The University of Western Australia, Australia

Richard J. Godfrey
Brunel University, UK

Stuart Goodall
Northumbria University, UK

Vicky L. Goosey-Tolfrey
Loughborough University, UK

Richie P. Goulding
Kobe Design University, UK

David Green
English Institute of Sport, UK

Luke Gupta
English Institute of Sport, UK

Anthony C. Hackney
University of North Carolina, USA

Brian Hanley
Leeds Beckett University, UK

Amal Hassan
University College Healthcare NHS Trust and University College London, UK

Florentina J. Hettinga
Northumbria University, UK

Andrew Hext
Sheffield Hallam University, UK

Kirsty M. Hicks
Northumbria University, UK

Jamie Highton
University of Chester, UK

Karen Hind
Durham University, UK

Mark Homer
Buckinghamshire New University, UK

James G. Hopker
University of Kent, UK

Glyn Howatson
Northumbria University, UK

Andy Howse
Basketball England, UK

Michael Hutchinson
English Institute of Sport, Loughborough University, UK

Franco M. Impellizzeri
University of Technology, Australia

Carl A. James
National Sports Institute, Malaysia

Monèm Jemni
Hartpury University, UK

Simon Jobson
University of Winchester, UK

Thomas W. Jones
Northumbria University, UK

Timothy Jones
Institut Sukan Negara (National Sports Institute), Malaysia

Emma Kavanagh
Bournemouth University, UK

Steve Kemp
British Fencing, UK

Mohammed Khudair
Northumbria University, UK

Christoph Lees
Imperial College London, UK

David Leith
British Curling, UK

Susan C. Lennie
Newcastle University, UK

Clare Lobb
Sport Scotland Institute of Sport, UK

Mitch Lomax
University of Portsmouth, UK

Rachel N. Lord
Cardiff Metropolitan University, UK

Mark Lyons
University of Limerick, Ireland

Hannah MacLeod
Great Britain Hockey, Track Record, UK

Caroline MacManus
High Performance Sport, New Zealand

Kelly Marrin
Edge Hill University, UK

Simon Marwood
Liverpool Hope University, UK

Heather Massey
University of Portsmouth, UK

Ronald J. Maughan
St Andrews University, UK

Neil S. Maxwell
University of Brighton, UK

Kerry McGawley
Mid Sweden University, Sweden

Pete McKnight
Hintsa Performance, UK

Shaun J. McLaren
Durham University, UK

Melitta McNarry
Swansea University, UK

Victoria L. Meah
University of Alberta, Canada

Andrew M. Miles
Cardiff Metropolitan University, UK

Goran Munivrana
University of Split, International Table Tennis Federation, Switzerland

Martha Brouwer Muñoz
Vrije Universiteit Amsterdam, Netherlands

Connor Murphy
Loughborough University, UK

Laura Needham
English Institute of Sport, UK

Emma Neupert
University of Portsmouth, UK

Mark Noon
Coventry University, UK

John Noonan
Hintsa Performance, UK

Luke Oates
Middlesex University, UK

Tom O'Brien
Loughborough University, UK

Cameron Owen
Leeds Beckett University and Leeds Rhinos Netball, UK

David Oxborough
Liverpool John Moores University, UK

Charles R. Pedlar
St Mary's University, UK

Michael J. Price
Coventry University, UK

Mayur Ranchordas
Sheffield Hallam University, UK

Daniel Rhind
University of Loughborough, UK

Alan Ruddock
Sheffield Hallam University, UK

Benjamin E. Scott
English Institute of Sport, University of Brighton, UK

Andy Shaw
English Institute of Sport, UK

Susan M. Shirreffs
St Andrews University, UK

Natalie F. Shur
University of Nottingham, UK

Len Parker Simpson
Japan Cycling, Japan

Ciara Sinnott-O'Connor
Sport Ireland Institute, Ireland

Andrew Smith
Former BASES Chair, UK (retired)

Mark F. Smith
University of Lincoln, UK

Paul M. Smith
Cardiff Metropolitan University, UK

S. Andy Sparks
Edge Hill University, UK

Mike Stembridge
Cardiff Metropolitan University, UK

Ben Stephenson
English Institute of Sport, Loughborough University, UK

Caroline Sunderland
Nottingham Trent University, UK

Karl Sylvester
Cambridge University Hospitals NHS Foundation Trust, UK

Jamie Tallent
St Mary's University, UK

Kevin Thomas
Northumbria University, UK

Katie Thralls Butte
Seattle Pacific University, USA

Michael Tipton
University of Portsmouth, UK

Keith Tolfrey
Loughborough University, UK

Craig Twist
University of Chester, UK

Will Vickery
Deakin University, Australia

Kyle Wallace
Ulster University, UK

Neil P. Walsh
Liverpool John Moores University, UK

Matthew Weston
Teeside University, UK

Sarah Whitehead
Leeds Beckett University and Leeds Rhinos Netball, UK

Craig A. Williams
University of Exeter, UK

Mark Williams
Basketball England, UK

Ash G. B. Willmott
Anglia Ruskin University, UK

Edward Winter
Sheffield Hallam University, UK

Foreword

I write this foreword as the current and first female chair of the British Association of Sport and Exercise Sciences and am delighted to offer support for these Exercise Testing Guidelines. These separate textbooks epitomise the work of the association, through professional collaboration, keeping BASES at the forefront of world-leading science and achieving considerable reach and impact.

The clear expansion of the textbooks, evidenced by overall scale, variety and quality of content, as well as the number and diversity of contributors, is commendable. The contributors are highly respected academics and/or practitioners (many of whom are BASES fellows), and many have collaborated with emerging, early career colleagues. The quality of these textbooks, combined with the process employed by contributors and the editorial team, reflects a commitment to ensure that the standards for sport and clinical physiological testing remains exemplary. This timely project has produced a model of excellent practice, which other disciplines may consider emulating in the future.

Professor Zoe Knowles FBASES, FHEA,
HCPC Practitioner Psychologist
BASES Chair
Liverpool John Moores University, UK

*****

I write as a two-time and first chair of BASES and commend the editors and authors on the completion of the latest edition of the Exercise Testing Guidelines. This new edition is a true reflection on the development of BASES and the profession since the very first Physiological Testing Guidelines were produced in 1986. In the first edition the authors produced recommendations that provided the foundations for 'best practice' for physiological testing of athletes. Before its publication there was no consensus on testing methodologies and often scant regard for the principles of scientific rigour.

Over the ensuing 35 years, each subsequent edition has extended the range of topics and addressed new challenges without compromising the principles of scientific rigour and relevance. In this new edition, the coverage and depth of information are again a significant step forward, providing an exceptional resource for sport and exercise physiologists, particularly for those progressing towards BASES accreditation. This series of guidelines has helped establish and consolidate the association's reputation as a world leader for physiological testing in health and disease. Therefore, it is with great pride and gratitude that I commend the new Exercise Testing Guidelines to all who study, teach and research in sport and exercise sciences.

Professor Clyde Williams OBE, DSc, PhD, FBASES, FFSEM
Professor of Sports Science (emeritus)
Loughborough University, UK

Introduction

R. C. Richard Davison and Paul M. Smith

The origins of the BASES Physiological Testing Guidelines date back to 1986, when the Sports Physiology Section of the British Association of Sports Sciences (BASS) created a working group of Neil Armstrong, Adrianne Hardman, Philip Jakeman, Craig Sharp and Edward Winter. Together, they produced a BASS Position Statement on the Physiological Assessment of the Elite Competitor (Hale et al., 1988). As the study of sport science began to grow, BASS established accreditation schemes for individual practitioners and exercise testing laboratories. In 1998, a second edition of the exercise testing guidelines made reference to both accreditation schemes.

Some nine years later, BASS had evolved into the British Association of Sport and Exercise Sciences (BASES) to acknowledge that not all exercise scientists were exclusively interested in sport. In 1997, Steve R. Bird and R. C. Richard Davison took over the responsibility of editing the third edition of the BASES 'Physiological Testing Guidelines'. This consisted of 19 chapters organised in four sections: General issues and procedures; Generic testing procedures; Sport-specific testing guidelines; and Specific considerations for the assessment of the young athlete (Bird and Davison, 1997).

A further gap of ten years elapsed before the fourth edition was published in 2006 (Winter et al., 2006a, 2006b), and this represented a significant expansion of the coverage of the guidelines, resulting in two volumes: one with an emphasis on sport, while the other focused on clinical practices. Although both volumes shared chapters linked to common principles of physiological exercise testing, remaining chapters related to either sport or clinical topics. The expansion and creation of distinct textbook volumes reflected the growing number of BASES members and accredited practitioners in respective areas.

Since the last edition the number of students studying sport and exercise science in the UK has continued to grow, with more than 17,500 students accepted on to a sport and exercise science course in 2018/19. At that time, the total number of students studying a higher education course in the UK related to sport and exercise science was just under 49,000 and continues to grow. Mirroring this growth has been the increase in vocational applications of sport and exercise science, and many enjoy careers in diverse settings. These settings include sport and exercise support work with national governing bodies, professional clubs, the

DOI: 10.4324/9781003045281-1

Home Countries' Sport Institutes and public and private healthcare providers. Employment opportunities also exist in private enterprises, governmental, voluntary and local authority organisations engaged in the provision of exercise and physical activity for people with or at high risk of developing a myriad of diseases and associated disabilities.

In line with this significant increase of student numbers and applied professions has been the expansion of research in the sport and exercise sciences, which now provides a significantly expanded evidence base that underpins the physiological assessments in the current two volumes.

This edition provides a reference guide for sport and exercise scientists in training (BASES supervised experience), practitioners, researchers and teachers in sport and exercise science. During very challenging times, members of the editorial team have worked with a wide range of contributors, including many of the United Kingdom's leading sport and exercise scientists and/or practitioners. The two volumes of the BASES Exercise Testing Guidelines provide a comprehensive resource, which is underpinned by the latest research and practice in elite sport and the clinical sciences.

Sadly, since 2006, we have lost several giants of our discipline, who were authors/editors of previous editions: Craig Sharp, Tom Reilly and Edward Winter. Each of these individuals were passionate about BASES and the development of the subject area to whom we owe a great debt.

We would like to pay a particular tribute to Edward Winter, who led the editorial team for the last edition and has contributed to every edition of the guidelines, including a chapter in this edition that was completed before his death.

References

Bird, S. and Davison, R. C. R. (1997). *Physiological Testing Guidelines* (3rd ed.). Leeds: The British Association of Sport and Exercise Sciences.

Hale, T., Armstrong, N., Hardman, A., Jakeman, P., Sharp, C. and Winter, E. (1988). *Position Statement on the Physiological Assessment of the Elite Competitor* (2nd ed.). Leeds: White Line Press.

Winter, E. M., Jones, A. M., Davison, R. C. R., Bromley, P. D. and Mercer, T. (2006a). *Sport and Exercise Physiology Testing Guidelines: Volume 1: Sport Testing: The British Association of Sport and Exercise Sciences Guide*. Abingdon, UK: Routledge.

Winter, E. M., Jones, A. M., Davison, R. C. R., Bromley, P. D. and Mercer, T. (2006b). *Sport and Exercise Physiology Testing Guidelines: Volume 2: Clinical Testing: The British Association of Sport and Exercise Sciences Guide*. Abingdon, UK: Routledge.

Part I
Professional best practice

1.1 Professional competency and working with others

Michael J. Price, Andrew M. Miles, and Paul M. Smith

Introduction

Achieving and maintaining a *minimum standard of professional competency* is an important aspect of many careers, and sport and exercise science is no exception. Careers such as medicine, nursing and physiotherapy require practitioners to record and evidence their ongoing professional development, and the relevant professional bodies conduct regular audits in order for practitioners to retain their registration. Whilst BASES does not currently require ongoing evidence of continued development, it does have a strong ethos of achieving and maintaining high standards and professional development, as evidenced in its accreditation and re-accreditation pathways. These require practitioners to meet minimum standards to achieve initial accreditation and to evidence continued professional development and sustained growth to secure re-accreditation.

Within the UK, whether as part of a research role, clinical (or sport) service provision or learning and teaching sport and exercise science, practitioners must abide by the BASES Code of Conduct. This code encompasses specific elements of research ethics, personal and professional conduct and competence. Indeed, there are many linked chapters within this textbook, which relate to these specific issues to help you ensure your practice is consistent with good practice.

Members, at all times, must have regard for the following principles:

a) all Clients have the right to expect the highest standards of professionalism, consideration and respect.
b) the pursuit of scientific knowledge requires that research and testing is carried out with utmost integrity.
c) the law requires that working practices are safe, that the welfare of the Client is paramount, and that data is used and stored in accordance with the law.

BASES Code of Conduct (Paragraph 4.3) March 2017

NB: In anticipation of the publication date of this textbook, note that the BASES code of conduct is currently under review, with a new version available by early 2022.

DOI: 10.4324/9781003045281-3

Maintaining and extending professional competency

The premise underpinning professional competency suggests that an individual achieves some initial baseline, or minimum threshold standard in the form of a measure of his or her *'fitness to practice'* or a *'license to practice'*. In some professions, this criterion requirement is associated with formal, professional body–endorsed academic training at either the undergraduate or postgraduate level (e.g., British Association of Sport Rehabilitators and Trainers [BASRaT]). In other professions, demonstration of professional competency may be attached to evidencing competence through professional practice or training after graduation to achieve professional body recognition through an *accreditation scheme* or similar (e.g., BASES or British Psychological Society). Having achieved this initial baseline, there is an expectation that practitioners maintain and extend their competency and knowledge base through ongoing training and continuous professional development. An employer, a professional organisation and/or private providers can provide ongoing training. Responsibility for maintaining and extending competence lies with the practitioner, but is typically regulated or mandated by the profession.

Employers require minimum knowledge and standards, often identified as 'essential' or 'desirable' skills and knowledge, within person specifications and job descriptions. Many identify that a candidate or applicant must have professional body endorsement/accreditation or similar. This is imperative and ensures an employee can 'hit the ground running' with the minimum acceptable professional knowledge and skills. By ensuring recruits have the required professional skillsets at the outset, employers can focus any initial induction on job- and employer-specific training such as health and safety, data handling and internal policies and practices, some of which are included in chapters of this textbook immediately following this.

Safeguarding and welfare are relevant in all contexts of a client-based industry, but special consideration is required when working with either young or vulnerable populations. In the UK, anyone working with minors (i.e., participants under 18 years of age) or vulnerable groups (e.g., clinical patients or some individuals with physical and/or learning disabilities) must gain formal clearance through the disclosure and barring service (DBS). Sport and exercise practitioners should thus be aware and informed of such areas, referring to policies of their own organisation, BASES's governance documents or policy documents (e.g., Safeguarding and Welfare Policy). In the context of applied sport and exercise science practices, we also refer readers to a wealth of sport- and exercise science–specific information and applied recommendations within a repository of BASES Expert Statements.

Once a practitioner is 'skilled' in both a professional and internal organisational capacity, she or he then needs to *remain up-to-date on emerging developments* in both contexts. There is a shared responsibility between the employer, the profession and an individual to ensure that practitioners are able to access continued professional development (CPD) opportunities. As alluded to earlier, employers and practitioners should be proactive in seeking training opportunities which extend beyond compulsory in-house requirements. Practitioners should be able to clearly demonstrate the retention of their 'fitness to practise' through accessing CPD opportunities such as external (professional) training events, conferences, peer-reviewed publications and opportunities to shadow/observe other practitioners/supervisors, engaging in professional networks and remaining aware of evolving professional regulatory standards. Engagement with a suitable (academic or clinical) mentor (or supervisor) can prove beneficial, helping to ensure a practitioner remains abreast of area-specific requirements, identifying and capitalising upon gainful CPD opportunities.

A fundamental activity to help practitioners recognise those areas of their professional practice in need of improvement is *reflective practice* (Huntley et al., 2019). Reflective practice is a cognitive process that allows practitioners to examine their own professional practice by asking themselves questions about how and why they do things and considering the impact of their actions and decisions on their practice and on the experiences of their clients. Although many reflective practice articles within sport and exercise science appear biased towards sport and exercise psychology (Huntley et al., 2014), reflective practice is key to all applied practice disciplines. However, a study of coach education noted a lack of confidence in understanding reflective practice and thus limited engagement with it (Cropley et al., 2012). Although it is beyond the scope of this chapter to discuss models of reflective practice and the process per se, it is important to note the range of reflective practice models available – each with associated pros and cons (Knowles et al., 2014).

Working in multi- and inter-disciplinary teams

An important requirement in the context of BASES-supervised experience is the consideration and appreciation that working as a component of an integrated, multidisciplinary (or inter-disciplinary) team is a factor that is key for sporting, exercise and health arenas. As a specialist within a particular field of study, you will typically find yourself working alongside others to achieve a common goal, whether evaluating a patient's pre-operative fitness or the impact of a specific intervention on an elite athlete's performance.

Within the sport and exercise sciences, a subtle difference exists between the terms multi- and inter-disciplinarity. With a client at the centre of a wheel (the hub), a multidisciplinary approach would have professions within their individual silos on the rim, all heading towards the centre with no interaction – a parallel provision of support. However, inter-disciplinary work infers there is some interaction between professional areas. For example, a change in sporting equipment and/or technique (i.e., biomechanics), or improvements in strength (i.e., strength and conditioning) might improve exercise efficiency/economy (i.e., exercise physiology), thus leading to an improvement in situation-specific confidence (i.e., training and/or competition) and an improvement in performance. Likewise, in a clinical setting, an improvement in physiological/metabolic fitness and function (i.e., physiology), resulting from behaviour change (i.e., health psychology; see West et al., 2019) will lead to improved self-efficacy (i.e., psychology), leading to greater independence and improvement in overall quality of life.

Within the clinical sciences, many good examples of the workings of multi- and inter-disciplinary teams exist, but the extent of the literature pertaining to such an approach in the sport and exercise sciences remains somewhat scant. This situation continues despite Burwitz et al. (1994) raising the importance of this approach more than a quarter of a century ago. In the context of the sport and exercise community, some good examples exist of multidisciplinary approaches to the support and preparation of individual elite athletes and/or squads.

There will always be limitations to research endeavours and/or programmes of clinical provision/sport science support. A frequent shortfall is the poor translation of existing knowledge to applied practice. While the concept of 'evidence-based practice' is broadly accepted, a paradox exists where a practitioner may turn to 'practice-based evidence'. To contextualise this point, an example relates to the broad topic of coaching or sport science support of elite athletes. While a vast amount of scientific literature exists for well-trained groups of athletes, little exists for truly elite, international competitors. In this example, Ross et al. (2018) describe a need to adopt a blended approach to the collection and assimilation of knowledge to create often novel and unique solutions and practical applications. Here one might draw on all available knowledge, gaining insight from a scientific, professional experience and anecdotal perspectives.

This chapter provides the reader with a general overview of professional practice, competency and the concept of multi- and inter-disciplinary teams. Your challenge is to seek subject-specialist information to help you become more informed and the most competent and effective practitioner possible. Consulting the considerable array of information contained within the BASES policy documents, guidelines and expert statements is highly recommended.

References

Burwitz, L., Moore, P. M. and Wilkinson, D. M. (1994). Future directions for performance-related sports science research: An interdisciplinary approach. *Journal of Sport Sciences*, 12, 93–109.

Cropley, B., Miles, A. and Peel, J. (2012). Reflective practice: Value of, issues, and developments within sports coaching. Sports Coach UK Original Research.

Huntley, E., Cropley, B., Gilbourne, D., Sparkes, A. and Knowles, Z. (2014). Reflecting back and forwards: An evaluation of peer-reviewed reflective practice research in sport. *Reflective Practice*, 15, 863–876.

Huntley, E., Cropley, B., Knowles, Z. and Miles, A. (2019). BASES expert statement: Reflective practice: The key to experimental learning. *The Sport and Exercise Scientist*, 60(Summer), 6–7.

Knowles, Z., Gilbourne, D., Cropley, B. and Dugdill, L. (2014). *Reflective Practice in the Sport and Exercise Sciences: Contemporary issues*. Edited By Zoe (1st ed.). Abingdon, UK: Routledge.

Ross, E., Gupta, L. and Sanders, L. (2018). When research leads to learning, but not action in high performance sport. In *Progress in Brain Research*, pp. 201–217. (Textbook series Chapter 12).

West, R., Michie, S., Chadwick, P., Atkins, L. and Lorencatto, F. (2019). Achieving behaviour change: A guide for local government and partners. *Public Health England: Protecting and Improving the Nation's Health*. www.gov.uk/government/publications/behaviour-change-guide-for-local-government-and-partners (accessed 12 May 2021).

Useful resources

BASES Code of Conduct. www.bases.org.uk/imgs/bases_code_of_conduct872.pdf

The BASES Expert Statement on Ethics and Participation in Research of Young People (2011). www.bases.org.uk/imgs/ethics_and_participation_in_research_of_young_people625.pdf

BASES Safeguarding and Welfare Policy. https://bases.org.uk/imgs/bases_safeguarding__welfare_policy215.pdf (accessed 21 April 2021).

BASES Safeguarding Statement. www.bases.org.uk/imgs/expert_statement_1__pages_380.pdf (accessed 21 April 2021).

General Data Protection Regulations. www.gov.uk/government/publications/guide-to-the-general-data-protection-regulation (accessed 21 April 2021).

1.2 Physiological exercise testing
Ethical considerations

Steve R. Bird and Andrew Smith

The ethics of physiological testing is an important consideration, whether one is conducting tests for research, sport science support, clinical health assessments or teaching. It is an expectation that BASES members will undertake their work in an ethical manner and adhere to the principles of professional practice. This chapter will consider what this means in the context of physiological testing and provide some guidelines on what considerations one must take to ensure that one conducts physiological testing in an ethical manner.

As regulations and legislation change over time and vary across nations, it is important that readers cross reference this chapter with the frameworks in the place when and where they are testing. It is the responsibility of the sport and exercise scientist to identify what approvals they need and which regulations they must adhere to before commencing any test battery.

The application of ethical principles to physiological testing

In relatively recent times, there has been a cultural shift away from the viewpoint that all-knowing experts perform tests on passive subjects, and instead the activity is now recognised as a partnership between assessors and participants, as well as other potential stakeholders. This is reflected in a change in the terminology from the previous vocabulary of referring to those being tested as 'subjects' and instead to now referring to them as 'participants', which is how they will be referred to throughout this chapter. Likewise, for clarity, those responsible for running tests and collecting data will be referred to as 'assessors' from this point onwards.

This partnership of rights, roles and respect is one of many considerations when determining whether the activity is 'ethical'. Within professional practice the conduct of physiological testing in an ethical manner is an expectation, whether it be in research, sport science support, clinical health or teaching, so the conduct of physiological tests in an ethical manner is a principal concern for everyone undertaking this work, regardless of the setting.

Today, research that involves human participants; human organs, tissues, cells, fluids or other biological material; or human data requires approval by a constituted and recognised human research ethics committee. With human samples,

DOI: 10.4324/9781003045281-4

there are also strict codes of conduct and practices set out by the Human Tissue Authority (www.hta.gov.uk). In this context, for example, UK Higher Education Institutions apply for an HTA licence and are subject to ongoing scrutiny to ensure all registered workers abide by the ethical framework set out.

The purpose of human research ethics committees is to ensure that colleagues conduct research ethically and adhere to key principles. The exact wording may differ between codes, but the following directives encapsulate core principles:

1. *Respect* the participants and others involved in the activity;
2. Be fully *transparent* to ensure that all involved are aware of the objectives of the activity, what the activity entails, how data will be managed and any conflicts of interest and be clear about any risks – large or small;
3. Be scientifically *rigorous* in terms of the methods and protocols used (including the calibration of equipment) to ensure the collection of valid, reliable and accurate data;
4. Only be conducted by people who conform to the highest *professional* standards and who are demonstrably competent assessors holding the appropriate qualifications, certification and insurance;
5. Uphold the highest standards of *honesty* and *integrity*;
6. Put the health and safety of all those involved as the top priority and always act to *minimise any risks*;
7. Ensure proposed research outcomes are *meaningful and purposeful* for participants involved; and
8. *Comply* with legal and other regulatory frameworks, including those of the insurer.

The physiological testing of human participants for other purposes, such as fitness testing for sport or health-related assessments and teaching, should also adhere to these principles, regardless of whether the assessment is physiological, biomechanical, psychological, clinical health or medical. The ethical conduct of these activities not only ensures the protection and minimisation of risk to participants and assessors but also to any organisations linked to the work, as well as determining that the activity is of benefit to the individual and/or wider community.

In a research context, a consideration of the numerous ethics principles of working with human participants is formalised, itemised and clearly communicated through the completion of an ethics application form. A relevant ethics committee will then review the application, and an assessment will be made in accordance with the values and guidelines of the code and culture in which the research is taking place.

These same principles should apply to physiological testing in other contexts, with a constituted panel reviewing the submission and providing feedback to the assessors – without such approval, the physiological testing must not proceed. These formalised procedures and the input from a group with diverse experiences will ensure that the proposed physiological testing activity is undertaken in compliance with recognised ethics requirements and, in doing so, will help to safeguard all involved – participants, assessors, professional organisations and institutions. Forms for physiological testing in 'non-research' contexts can be developed and used to help prevent unethical practice, avoid adverse events and reduce the frequency of complaints, all of which may have detrimental consequences to the participant, assessors, employers of assessors and others.

Where physiological or other testing activity is approved, it is then beholden upon the assessors to comply with the approved procedures and to not deviate from the approved procedures or undertake testing that differs from the approved details. Where there be a need to make subsequent changes, a relevant person, such as the chief investigator (CI) must apply to the relevant ethics committee for an amendment to the previously approved physiological testing activity.

This chapter will deal with the broad principles of ethics for physiological testing, regardless of its context, and highlight any specific issues relating to sport and/or clinical exercise testing as they arise.

Ethical issues relating to physiological testing

The following paragraphs consider some of the ethical issues that the assessor needs to address when planning to undertake physiological testing.

Why are you testing: do foreseen benefits outweigh the risks?

Before undertaking any physiological testing, it is important to weigh up the risks versus likely benefits. To do this, the person responsible for the testing, such as the CI in a research study, or the head of sport and sciences services or the clinical expert in the health field, needs to make explicit the purpose of the testing and, from this, the benefit that would be derived from the findings. In some cases, these benefits will directly affect the participant, such as identifying a health concern or generating a fitness profile to inform their training programme. In other circumstances – indeed in the case of most research – the findings may be of little or no immediate benefit to the research participant, but will contribute to knowledge that, when published, may benefit others.

An assessor must consider likely benefits against potential risks for any participant and, in some cases, the assessor(s) and/or their institution or employing organisation. Assessors can view certain risks as being 'negligible' or 'carrying low risk', such as inconvenience and the investment in time by participants, through to discomfort. Other risks may be categorised as 'more than low risk', such as the risk of distress, physical injury or psychological harm. In research, it is the responsibility of the CI to weigh the merits of the potential benefits against the potential risks. At this stage, if intending to proceed, a relevant ethics committee should consider a formal application. At this point, the ethics committee may ask the CI to provide further clarification or to consider alternative approaches in order to reduce risk. In non-research assessments, other suitable experts within the organisation may fulfil this role if there is no formalised procedure or advisory committee.

Minimisation of risk

Assessors can minimise risk through careful consideration of the intended procedures. These include aspects relating to the participant, the assessors, the exercise protocol, the equipment, the environment and the inclusion of specific safety measures.

- To minimise risks, participants should be screened for contraindications to the exercise or other assessment that they will be asked to undertake, typically using a validated screening tool.
- Those conducting the assessment must be appropriately qualified and have the relevant expertise in the techniques they are using, as well as possessing suitable qualifications in first aid and cardiopulmonary resuscitation (CPR). Furthermore, the assessors should know the appropriate way to respond in the case of any 'adverse event'. It is highly recommended that all assessors complete some form of basic ethics awareness training.
- The protocols used in the testing need to be justified and ideally supported by evidence from previously published work that they are safe, valid and reliable, since collecting data that are not valid or reliable may be deemed unethical, as this wastes the participants' time. Many testing protocols will have elements of safety built in, such as the inclusion of electrocardiographic (ECG) monitoring for some forms of exercise and participant groups, or use of a harness if exercising maximally on a treadmill.
- Additionally, assessors must adhere to safety procedures for cleaning and sterilising equipment. Electrical equipment used must have undergone relevant safety checks, including electrical tests, which will generate safety certificates as required by the work environment.
- For the safety of participants and assessors, appropriate personal protective equipment (PPE) should be worn, which, depending on the nature of the testing, may include protective gloves, laboratory coats, safety glasses, masks and other items.

Any potential risks associated with testing procedures need to be articulated clearly to the participant, usually as part of a clear and detailed 'Participant Information Sheet' (PIS) and associated 'Informed Consent Form' (ICF). This ensures participants are appropriately informed and can thereby provide genuine informed consent for their participation.

Recruitment and power relationships

When undertaking physiological testing as part of a research study, there is usually a clear process of recruitment. This may range from a broad advertisement to the general population to a specific targeting of individuals with specific characteristics, such as particular sporting expertise or health condition. In such circumstances, those volunteering to participate are clearly volunteers who have responded to an advertisement without any inherent obligation to do so. However, when undertaking fitness testing for a team or squad, the extent of 'volunteerism' may be compromised if it is the coach or manager who deems that all members of a squad should undergo fitness testing. In such cases, the assessor needs to consider very carefully their involvement and whether participation is truly voluntary. A scenario within many professional teams is that the requirement to participate in such activities is part of the participants' contracts, and the assessor needs to consider these issues carefully. In a clinical exercise testing context, the assessor has to be aware of the potential power balance that may exist if the potential participant's doctor, physiotherapist, allied health therapist or pharmacist is involved in the recruitment process. Their involvement in recruitment does not make this process unethical, *per se*, but some scrutiny and careful consideration of how they are involved is required.

Other unbalanced power relationships may exist between university staff and their students, whereby it is important that there should be no perceived obligation for a student to participate in a research study conducted by one of their lecturers. It should be clear that a student's professional relationship with the lecturer and the institution remain unaffected, whether they volunteered or declined to participate. In the context of teaching, those responsible for the physiological testing within academic courses need to carefully consider the ethics of proposed testing, which is likely to involve justifying the inclusion of physiological testing as part of the educational experience. This should always be for the students' benefit of developing their knowledge, understanding, relevant practical skills and awareness through personal experience, but tutors need to consider this matter in light of the students' rights and possible risks.

Power relationships can also influence safeguarding aspects of physiological testing, covered in Chapter 1.4.

Information, consent and the capacity to provide consent or assent (children)

Before participating in any data collection, an assessor must inform all participants of testing procedures and objectives. Participants should know what they will be required to do, how much time may be involved and what, if any, risks they will encounter. Assessors should declare any sources of funding, as a prospective participant may have concerns about potential conflicts of interest. The information given to the participant should also include how the data will be stored securely and who will have access to stored data. This may include the participant, assessor, coach or health/medical practitioner, as well as the intention to publish (usually anonymised group data or de-identified data) in research publications or reports. Regardless of the final intentions of the use of the data, the participant needs to be made aware of this. Additionally, the assessors should state for how long the data will be stored. Research ethics codes and guidelines specify minimum durations, as do some publications. These may be of the order of 5 years, but typically 7–10 years for health-related data, and often there is no stated maximum. Thus, provided data are stored securely and can be maintained far longer, something that may be useful if longitudinal comparisons are sought in the future.

This information would normally be in the form of written participant information that is given to them, using language that can be clearly understood and without confusing technical and/or scientific jargon. It should also be in a language that they understand, so translated copies may be required in some circumstances. Without this information, participants cannot provide 'informed consent'. The provision of consent would normally be in writing using an approved 'Participant Information and Consent Form' (PICF), which would include statements saying that the participant understands what the testing entails, any risks, what will happen to the data and that they've had the opportunity to have any questions or concerns addressed. The PIS and ICF would normally be signed by the participant, assessor and witness. In some cases, there may be a clause that states that if the results indicate a health concern for the participant, test results may be forwarded to a relevant health/medical practitioner or a medical referral will be made; however, this must be clearly stated to participants and agreed by all, at the outset.

It should be noted that if the participant is a child, consent would be provided by their parent or guardian but that this should then be affirmed by the child giving their 'assent' to their participation.

Confidentiality, privacy, security, data access and usage of data

Data would typically be on secure institution/organisation property in locked cabinets in the case of hard copies and/or secure password-protected computers or servers. Increasingly data are stored on cloud-based servers, which also must follow good security practice in password protection and encryption (where possible). In research contexts, data may be collected and stored using coded identifiers, for which only the assessors are able to match the codes to individuals, as this adds further privacy and confidentiality. With research studies, data normally remain confidential, with any identifying data excluded from publications. However, in some cases this may be difficult, if, for example, the research involves elite sports people, such as Olympic medallists, where the population of individuals is so small that it enables accurate deductions about the identity of participants simply from the nature of the research. In such cases, this would need to be made clear to the participants within their PIS and ICF.

In sports physiological testing or clinical health exercise testing, data should be made available to the participant, coach or other relevant staff, health or medical practitioner, and the participant would need to agree to this in the PIS and ICF. In a sporting context, this may cause some concern for the participant if they perceived that their data may be used in the context of 'team selection' or other means of discrimination. This needs to be clearly established with all concerned, and the assessor must comply with the signed agreements. So, for example, if a coach or selection manager asked for the data at a later date but the participant had not agreed to their having access to the data, then the assessor is not permitted to give it to other persons. Hence clarity on such matters needs to be established in writing prior to any physiological testing activity, and participants may have this access to data included in their contracts.

In some circumstances, photographic images may be taken to illustrate the physiological testing procedures. If this is part of the procedure, the participant must be made aware of what images will be taken and what they would be used for and agree to this. Furthermore, if any images are to be used in subsequent publications, specific permission must be attained from the participant, and this may or may not involve de-identifying those in the images, for example, using pixilation of the face or obscuring the face with a 'black box'. Most institutions will have specific forms that address the publication of images, and these would need to be signed by the participant in addition to the standard PICF or equivalent 'non-research' form.

It should be stated that acquired data can only be used for the purposes that the participant has agreed to within the PIS and ICF. If the assessors perceive that they may wish to use the data for secondary purposes at a later date, such as writing a research paper on previously collected fitness or health data, this must have been specified and stated in the PIS and ICF and the participant knowingly agreed to this possibility.

In some clinical areas, particularly in rare diseases, new models of consent have been developed to enable the collation of data where individual data are scarce. While this wider sharing of data would seem to compromise some aspects of privacy, modified consent clauses have been developed and researched with participants understanding the need for large-scale data sharing and expect their data to be distributed and reused but require, nonetheless, that they be informed of such activities to maintain a level of protection and control. However, despite this wider sharing, the underlying principle must be the possible benefit for participants and others like them and must surpass the potential consequences for their privacy (Nghuyen et al., 2019).

Withdrawal of participant and their data

Within a research ethics submission, there would normally be a clause stating that participants are free to withdraw from the study at any stage without it affecting their relationship with the assessors or their organisation. If the participant has already completed the physiological assessments, a further clause may say that they can withdraw their data, provided it is identifiable as their data, prior to it being included in any data analyses or publication, again, without this affecting their relationship with the assessors or their institution. This option should be clearly stated on the PIS and ICF that they sign, along with whom they should contact in these circumstances.

Monitoring and reporting of activities: annual reports, adverse events and complaints

Ethics committees require regular, typically annual, reporting of the research projects for which they have given ethics approval. This regular monitoring provides those responsible with information on how an approved research project is progressing, and eventually a final report would be required that outlines the outcomes of research undertaken and, where applicable, intended publications. In sports testing or health/clinical testing, there will be similar requirements for regular reporting, and these will be audited at intervals.

In addition to this, even with the best planned physiological testing procedures, there remains a risk, and this should be included in the PIS and ICF so that the participant is aware of the risk before agreeing to participate. As part of the establishment of the physiological testing activity, there must be a clear procedure for reporting adverse events. This may be both internal and external in the case of clinical trials. Where the physiological testing is for sport science support or health/medical assessments, there must be a clear procedure for reporting these events promptly – this means immediate reporting, rather than waiting to include the information in an annual report. When reported, such occurrences will be investigated by the relevant authorities, and the activity may be suspended during the investigation. The findings of the investigation will then determine whether the physiological testing may be resumed or terminated.

Clear procedures must also exist to deal with formal complaints. In the case of research, there will be an established committee, often composed of experts from an institution's research ethics and research governance bodies. The risk of complaints is minimised if the assessors adhere to stated and approved procedures. Complaints often stem from ambiguities, which an assessor can avoid if participants receive comprehensive and clear information within the PIS and signed ICF. Other complaints may relate to the nature of recruitment strategies used where, for example, an assessor has randomly displayed unapproved recruitment posters and signs in public areas. Similar organisations and procedures for dealing with complaints must be established within organisations that undertake sports-, health- and medical-related exercise testing.

Other considerations

If the participants are members of particular cultural groups or vulnerable populations, the assessors will need to consider the implications and undertake recruitment, attainment of consent and testing in a way that complies with the expectations of the ethical collection of data with these participants. For example, where children and minors under the age of 18 years are concerned, both participant informed consent and parent/guardian assent must be obtained. Within the UK, it is obligatory for assessors working with minors to have undergone, and be able to present evidence of, a formal, context-specific and up-to-date disclosure and barring service check (see: https://dbscheckonline.org.uk/).

Assessors should not seek ethics approval retrospectively. Situations whereby research may be undertaken on existing data sets are a specific scenario, with specific issues that are considered by the research ethics committee, including whether the participants had agreed to their data being used for research or teaching purposes when they were collected.

An assessor cannot recruit participants and collect research until an ethics committee has granted approval; this has to fall within the approval period. If the assessors wish to continue collecting data beyond this point, an assessor must request an extension to ethics approval.

Policies and regulations

American College of Sports Medicine Pre-Participation Screening. www.acsm.org/docs/default-source/default-document-library/read-research/acsm-risk-stratification-chart.pdf?sfvrsn=7b8b1dcd_6

Australian Code for the Responsible Conduct of Research. (2018). *National Health and Medical Research Council, Australian Research Council and Universities Australia.* Commonwealth of Australia, Canberra. www.nhmrc.gov.au/about-us/publications/australian-code-responsible-conduct-research-2018

British Association of Sport and Exercise Sciences (BASES) Code of Conduct. www.bases.org.uk/imgs/bases_code_of_conduct872.pdf

Exercise and Sport Science Australia. *Adult Pre-Exercise Screening System (APSS).* www.essa.org.au/Public/ABOUT_ESSA/Adult_Pre-Screening_Tool.aspx?WebsiteKey=b4460de9-2eb5-46f1-aeaa-3795ae70c687

National Health Service. *Health Research Authority.* www.hra.nhs.uk/about-us/committees-and-services/res-and-recs/research-ethics-service/

Nghuyen, M. T., et al. (2019). Model consent clauses for rare disease research. *BMC Medical Ethics*, 20(1), 55.

NHS Health Research Authority. www.hra.nhs.uk/

NHS Research Ethics Service. www.hra.nhs.uk/about-us/committees-and-services/res-and-recs/

UK Government, General Data Protection Regulations. www.gov.uk/government/publications/guide-to-the-general-data-protection-regulation

UK Research and Innovation. www.ukri.org/about-us/policies-and-standards/research-integrity/

1.3 Health and safety in duty of care

Evaluating and stratifying risk

S. Andy Sparks, Kelly Marrin, and Craig A. Bridge

The processes involved in data collection and participant, patient or client assessment in exercise physiology present unique challenges for researchers, clinicians and practitioners – collectively referred to as assessors from this point onwards. The need to collect data in diverse environments that are often less controlled than a traditional laboratory setting but relevant to the assessment and/or research question can further complicate matters. During any physiological testing, an assessor has a duty of care to the individual(s) under his or her supervision. In this context, duty of care represents a formalisation of the social responsibilities that individuals, laboratories and organisations have to research participants, patients or clients in their care. It requires assessors to adhere to standards of reasonable care whilst supervising or conducting any laboratory or field-based procedure that may foreseeably cause harm. Consequently, a key priority is the duty of care for the participant or patient, along with the health and safety of the individuals involved in the data collection itself. Therefore, in order to act reasonably and foresee the possible causes of harm, assessors need to formally identify hazards or risks and implement risk mitigation strategies before any data collection procedures take place. This chapter is intended to provide clear guidelines and suggestions for the processes of hazard identification, risk assessment and mitigation. Assessors and organisations responsible for the physiological assessment of human participants should consider the contents and associated recommendations within this chapter.

Professional obligations

Safe practices and procedures should underpin all laboratory and field-based activities for several vital reasons. Firstly, many assessors will be working either for an organisation, fan employer or as self-employed individuals; in these contexts, assessors and places of work must adhere to the requirements set out in the Health and Safety at Work Act (1974). This outlines the legal requirement for safe practices and environments, along with the paramount importance of client welfare. These principles form the foundation of the BASES Code of Conduct; this framework insists that members use the utmost integrity and concern for their participants, patients or clients and act without jeopardising any individual's safety. Under appropriate assessor supervision, the BASES Code of Conduct ensures that undue risk is avoided (BASES, 2017) – these issues are also covered in some detail in the chapter relating to ethics. It is essential that all aspects of data collection and client sport and exercise science support are assessed for appropriateness and safety before anyone is exposed to unnecessary harm. It is also imperative that there is an appropriate procedure to gain a client's informed consent and that data management occurs in accordance with relevant data protection legislation. Furthermore, the practitioner must recognise their limitations in terms of qualifications, experience, expertise and competence and operate safely within these limits. The following sections detail the chronological order in which processes should occur to ensure assessors meet these key considerations.

Hazard identification

The first key step in duty-of-care-based risk mitigation is the identification of hazards. This should focus not only on research participants or client(s) but also on individuals working with these individuals or, indeed, in isolation. This is especially relevant where anyone may be exposed to potential risks as part of normal working activities and should be addressed within an organisation's lone working policy. In this context, a hazard represents anything that has the potential to harm the health and safety of any person involved in the process of assessing a client or participant, preparing and/or using equipment or anyone in proximity to the testing area. Such hazards can typically be categorised into five types (Table 1.3.1). Unless and until an assessor identifies potential hazards, the rest of

Table 1.3.1 Classification and explanation of hazard types relevant to physiological testing

Hazard Type	Explanation/Example
Physical	This is the most common hazard and may include trips, slips, falls, noise or extremes of ambient temperature and changes in physiological state in response to exertion.
Ergonomic/ mechanical	These factors might result in damage to the musculoskeletal system or skin. Such hazards are common with the use of ergometry or sports equipment, but may also be caused by manual handing or repetitive movements.
Chemical	These hazards include exposure to hazardous substances, most likely in wet laboratories or when using cleaning products for hygiene. They may also include the ingestion of substances/ supplements used in nutrition-based experimental trials.
Biological	These hazards are common where there is either close contact between individuals or the exposure to human biological samples such as blood, urine or saliva.
Psychological	This form of hazard is possible where either severe exercise is needed, participants are exposed to mental fatigue or during exposure to confined spaces, such as during some forms of body composition assessment. Risks may also be present where potentially sensitive information is collected (body composition, nutritional analysis, assessments of disordered eating, fitness assessments).

the risk management process cannot begin. Hazards should also be recorded and reviewed at least annually following an accident or 'near miss', if something in the environment has changed or if modifications occur to a standard operating procedure.

Risk assessment

The assessment of risk is the key component of health and safety practice and management. It is about taking reasonable and logical steps to prevent ill health (HSE, 2012). Furthermore, there is also a legal requirement that all activities are risk assessed and documented in order to ensure what is reasonably practicable has been done to mitigate risks (Health and Safety at Work Act, 1974). This essentially means that there needs to be a balance of the level of risk with the cost, time and practicality of the measures needed to control the risk (HSE, 2016); there is no expectation for an assessor to anticipate unforeseeable risks, nor where mitigation measures are grossly disproportionate to the level of risk (HSE, 2014).

Five steps to risk assessment (HSE, 2014)

1. Identify potential hazards:
   - List the activity in steps, and consider the equipment or materials within the specific environment it is to be used in.
   - List the hazards for each of the steps and/or pieces of equipment.

2. Identify who might be harmed and how:
   - This is likely to be those in immediate contact or presence of the procedure or equipment, but not always.
   - Think carefully about the five types of hazards. This is particularly important for those exposed to potentially harmful substances that are chemical, nutritional or biological in nature.
   - Where exposure is to biological hazards, such as viruses and microorganisms, careful consideration regarding the method of transmission is vital and may require specialised considerations (Tipton et al., 2020). Consultation of the Health and Safety Executive's resources on blood-borne viruses (HSE, 2001), prevention of infection in laboratories (HSE, 2010) and control of substances hazardous to health (COSHH) (HSE, 2012) are recommended.

3. Evaluate the risks – consider the existing controls and assess the extent of the risks which remain:
   - List the existing risk controls.
   - Use the example (or similar) risk matrix (Table 1.3.2) to calculate the level of risk (the product of the outcome impact and its probability) and then again to calculate the risk with the controls in place.
   - List the residual hazards.

- List the additional risk controls required to reduce the residual risk.
- Evaluation should also be done in conjunction with evidence from the literature. This is particularly important for scenarios that involve the ingestion of a substance because safe consumption thresholds may be subject to change with emerging evidence.

4 Record the findings of the assessment – including the controls necessary and any further action needed to reduce risk sufficiently:

- Use a standardised proforma for the recording of this process. These are often stipulated by institutions or can be adapted from the HSE (2014) examples.
- Document that those affected have been consulted.
- Participant pre-exercise screening is a good example of a risk evaluation process that enables assessment and mitigation of potential risks specific to populations – Warburton et al. (2011) provide a comprehensive set of recommendations for this.

5 Review, revise and modify the assessment – this is especially important if the nature of the procedures or equipment changes or if developments suggest existing risk assessment may no longer be valid.

Ensure a risk assessment has a suitable title, details the name of the person completing it and is dated. Further, the person with overall responsibility, for example, the laboratory manager or head of department, should review all risk assessments and counter-sign them.

Key resources for risk assessment

How to control risks (HSE, 2016).
A brief guide to COSHH (HSE, 2012).
Examples of risk assessment documents (HSE, 2014).

Other key considerations

Hygiene

One underpinning risk mitigation strategy that is essential to exercise physiology is to ensure measures are in place to optimise hygiene via effective handwashing and/or use of alcohol gel, cleaning surfaces regularly, sterilising equipment, using disposable equipment where appropriate and performing after-use decontamination (Tipton et al., 2020).

Incidents and accidents

Appropriate provision for first aid equipment and a suitably qualified first aid– trained individual are minimum requirements. Given the nature of much of the work in sport and exercise physiology, it may also be a reasonable expectation that there is access to an automated external defibrillator (AED). A full assessment of the first aid needs of specific locations and procedures should be part of a risk assessment. Any event or 'near miss' should be formally documented under the regulations of the Reporting of Injuries, Diseases and Dangerous Occurrences Regulations (RIDDOR: www.hse.gov.uk/riddor), and the current risk assessments should then be reviewed to ensure they are effective.

Emergency procedures

In data collection or client support situations, which may be in a field or laboratory setting, an assessor should consider what to do in an emergency and create a clear emergency plan. The plan should consider what to do in the case of an emergency; how to communicate with others, including the emergency services; and how to evacuate, for example. A more detailed list of such considerations is available in the Health and Safety Toolbox (HSE, 2016).

Table 1.3.2 Example risk quantification guidance assessment tool based on the probability and severity of the outcome impact.* Cells denote likely risk with example interpretations in parentheses.

Outcome Impact	Severe	Medium (Moderate)	Medium (Moderate)	High (Substantial)	Extreme (Intolerable)	Extreme (Intolerable)
	Major	Low (Acceptable)	Medium (Moderate)	Medium (Substantial)	High (Substantial)	Extreme (Intolerable)
	Moderate	Low (Acceptable)	Low (Acceptable)	Medium (Moderate)	Medium (Substantial)	High (Substantial)
	Minor	Low (Trivial)	Low (Acceptable)	Low (Acceptable)	Medium (Moderate)	Medium (Moderate)
	Minimal	Low (Trivial)	Low (Trivial)	Low (Acceptable)	Low (Moderate)	Low (Moderate)
		Rare	Unlikely	Possible	Likely	Probable

Probability

Risk Rating	Risk Interpretation
Trivial	No action required.
Acceptable	No preventative action, but consider cost-effective measures. Continued monitoring required.
Moderate	Implement measures to reduce risk. The speed of implementation should be proportional to the number of people exposed.
Substantial	Do not commence procedures until extent of risk is reduced. If this outcome occurs during a review of existing processes, seek to mitigate risk as soon as possible.
Intolerable	The level of risk must be reduced before work can either start or progress. If this is not possible, procedures are prohibited.

*One should use a risk classification matrix as a guide and interpret outcomes with caution. Use of such a matrix should only form part of the risk assessment process (Peace, 2017).

Insurance and personal indemnity

The BASES Code of Conduct (BASES, 2017) requires members working with clients to ensure that suitable insurance indemnity coverage is in place. This needs to be with an authorised insurer (a list of these is available from the Financial Conduct Authority: www.fca.org.uk). In many cases, if activities form part of the work of an organisation, public liability insurance coverage may be in place, but it is worth checking that this coverage includes all proposed activities, location(s) and individuals involved.

Standard operating procedures

Many institutions that have physiology laboratories will also have a set of standard operating procedures, such as for the procurement of capillary and venous blood samples. Where such documents exist, they should also be used in the development and review of risk assessments.

References

The British Association of Sport and Exercise Sciences. (2017). *Code of Conduct*. www.bases.org.uk/imgs/bases_code_of_conduct872.pdf (accessed 16 April 2020).

Health and Safety at Work Act. (1974). www.legislation.gov.uk/ukpga/1974/37/contents (accessed 15 May 2020).

Health and Safety Executive. (2001). *Blood-Borne Viruses in the Workplace: Guidance for Employers and Employees*. HSE Books. ISBN 978 0 7176 20623.

Health and Safety Executive. (2010). *Safe Working and the Prevention of Infection in Clinical Laboratories and Similar Facilities*. HSE Books. ISBN 978 0 7176 25130. www.hse.gov.uk/pubns/clinical-laboratories.pdf (accessed 4 May 2020).

Health and Safety Executive. (2012). *Working with Substances Hazardous to Health: A Brief Guide to COSHH*. www.hse.gov.uk/pubns/indg136.htm (accessed 4 May 2020).

Health and Safety Executive. (2014). *Risk Assessment: A Brief Guide to Controlling Risks in the Workplace*. www.hse.gov.uk/pubns/indg163.htm (accessed 4 May 2020).

Health and Safety Executive. (2016). *The Health and Safety Toolbox: How to Control Risks at Work*. HSE Books. ISBN 978 0 7176 65877.

Peace, C. (2017). The risk matrix: Uncertain results? *Policy and Practice in Health and Safety*, 15(2), 131–144. doi: 10.1080/14773996.2017.1348571

Tipton, M., Wilkes, M., Long, G., Morgan, P., Roiz de Sa, D., Corbett, J., Montgomery, H., Mekjavic, I. and Friedl, K. (2020). Returning to the laboratory for human testing. *The Physiological Society*. www.physoc.org/covid19/returning-to-the-lab/ (accessed 14 May 2020).

Warburton, D. E., Gledhill, N., Jamnik, V. K., Bredin, S. S. D., McKenzie, D. C., Stone, J., Charlesworth, S. and Shephard, R. J. (2011). Evidence-based risk assessment and recommendations for physical activity clearance: Consensus Document. *Applied Physiology, Nutrition and Metabolism*, 36(Suppl 1): S266–S298. doi: 10.1139/h11-062

1.4 Safeguarding in physiological testing

Emma Kavanagh and Daniel Rhind

The British Association of Sport and Exercise Sciences (BASES) aims to promote a culture whereby the importance of safeguarding and welfare within sport and exercise sciences is a priority (Kavanagh et al., 2016). Physiologists working in a variety of settings must be cognisant of their duty of care toward clients, participants and co-workers. Traditionally, a legal duty of care amounts to risk: whether reasonable steps to prevent foreseeable risk have been identified and action(s) are taken to reduce such risks. A duty of care further relies upon the moral obligation placed upon an individual to understand their role in the prevention of foreseeable harm to others in order to ensure their safety or wellbeing (Kavanagh et al., 2020). As a physiologist there is an obligation both to maintain legal standards of care and to act in accordance with professional standards set out by your regulatory body. The duty of care thus assumes your responsibility for the care of another individual and necessitates the actions you take in order to mitigate foreseeable risk(s).

Safeguarding serves to promote the welfare and wellbeing of *everyone* in sport and is central in fostering a duty of care (Kavanagh et al., 2020). Safeguarding is of primacy in physiological practice, whether it be during research, applied practice, clinical practice or teaching and learning. Safeguarding concerns a professional obligation to protect all parties (for example, the client, athlete and/or self) from maltreatment or harm (Mountjoy et al., 2016). Everyone is potentially involved in the management of safeguarding concerns as a perpetrator, victim or bystander. This includes all stakeholders from athletes, peers and coaches through to parents, sport scientists or other members of the athlete entourage.

The range of potential threats that an individual can be exposed to are recognised to occur across three levels: the individual level, whereby there is a potential risk to self (e.g., depression, self-harm, substance abuse and disordered eating); the relational level, a risk that occurs between individuals (e.g., sexual, physical and emotional abuse, discrimination or harassment); and organisational level, between an individual and a performance system or organisation (e.g., systems which promote overtraining or competing with an injury, institutional doping or an unhealthy organisational culture). Physiologists should be aware of these levels in order to prioritise the safety and wellbeing of participants and to identify or mitigate risks which may arise at each of these levels (Mountjoy et al., 2016).

DOI: 10.4324/9781003045281-6

Table 1.4.1 International Safeguards for Children in Sport

Safeguard	Description	Action
1: Developing your policy	Any organisation providing or with responsibility for sports activities should have a safeguarding policy. This is a statement of intent that demonstrates a commitment to safeguard everyone involved in sport from harm and provides the framework within which procedures are developed. A safeguarding policy makes clear to all what is required. It also helps to create a safe and positive environment and to show that the organisation is taking its duty of care seriously.	You should be familiar with the related policies for the organisations and contexts in which you work. In addition to these safeguarding policies, you should be familiar with any other relevant policies concerning equity, working with vulnerable groups and health and safety. It is good practice to save links to these policies such that they are easily accessible. Be mindful that there may be a number of policies at any given time, including those regulations that govern being a BASES-accredited practitioner (e.g., BASES Safeguarding and Welfare Policy) and/or those in place for the organisation(s) in which you are working.
2: Procedures for responding to safeguarding concerns	Procedures describe the operational processes required to implement organisational policy and provide clear, step-by-step guidance on what to do in different circumstances. They clarify roles and responsibilities and lines of communication. Procedures help to ensure a prompt response to concerns about a person's safety or wellbeing.	You should be familiar with the procedures required to report and manage any safeguarding concerns. There may also be relevant complaints and disciplinary procedures. It is good practice to make contact with the person to whom you should report concerns after reading this guidance. This should mean that you are more comfortable making a disclosure should a concern arise.
3: Advice and support	Arrangements made to provide essential information and support to those responsible for safeguarding. People should be advised on where to access help and support. An organisation has a duty to ensure advice and support are in place to help people play their part in safeguarding such that they know who they can turn to for help.	You should identify the people and resources which can support you to effectively fulfil the safeguarding aspects of your role (e.g., welfare officer or safeguarding manager). The Child Protection in Sport Unit provide a range of helpful resources on their website (www.thecpsu.org.uk).
4: Minimising risks (to children)	The measures which are taken to assess and minimise the risks to people in the organisation. Minimise risks by putting safeguards in place.	Safeguarding should be a part of the planning in physiological testing; make a safeguarding plan. Aim to mitigate risk and work in a matter which prioritises the safety of participants. Key factors to assess may include ages of participants, additional needs or potential vulnerabilities, the nature of the activity being conducted and how the place or space of the activity may increase vulnerability of participants.

5: Guidelines for behaviour	An organisation should have codes of conduct to describe what an acceptable standard of behaviour is and promote current best practice. Standards of behaviour set a benchmark of what is acceptable for all, and codes of conduct can help to remove ambiguity and clarify the grey areas around what is viewed as acceptable behaviour.	You should be familiar with the BASES Code of Conduct and ensure that this is embedded in your practice, for example, the BASES Safeguarding and Welfare Policy (2017a) and the BASES Code of Conduct (2017b). You should also check for any other codes of conduct within the various contexts in which you work.
6: Recruiting, training and communicating	Everyone within an organisation has a role to play in safeguarding. Ensure that you are up to date with safeguarding knowledge and continue to re-educate yourself in this area to identify any changes in legislation or guidance.	You should attend the BASES Safeguarding Welfare in Sport and Exercise Sciences workshop to ensure you are familiar with current legislative, organisational and professional requirements and are aware of relevant reporting and/or referral requirements.
7: Working with partners	Where organisational partnership, membership, funding or commissioning relationships exist or develop with other organisations, the individual and/or organisation should use its influence to promote the implementation of safeguarding measures.	You should be a champion for safeguarding and demonstrate this through your practice. You should work with other physiologists, stakeholders and organisations to identify, share and embed good practice with respect to safeguarding.
8: Monitoring and evaluating	It is essential that there is on-going monitoring of compliance and effectiveness involving all key stakeholders. This is necessary because organisations need to know whether safeguarding is effective and where improvements and adaptations are needed or how to recognise patterns of risk.	You should conduct an audit of your current knowledge, confidence and behaviours in relation to each of these safeguards. This can help you to identify gaps and set goals to work towards. This can be repeated on an annual basis to ensure that you keep up to date.

Source: Adapted with permission from Rhind and Owusu-Sekyere (2018).

Safeguarding responsibilities

As a physiologist you occupy a position of power and authority, particularly when working with children or young people. In this role it is essential to demonstrate moral and ethical standards throughout your practice toward safeguarding the self and others. Physiologists should be able to recognise and mitigate risks posed to others while understanding how to report or manage safeguarding concerns that they may observe or have disclosed to them during their practice. The International Safeguards (Rhind and Owusu-Sekyere, 2018) outline a number of measures that should be put in place by any organisation providing sports activities. The eight safeguards are outlined in Table 1.4.1 along with their application to physiological testing.

Following the recommendations of the international safeguards will help to safeguard you as a physiologist, the people with whom you work and your organisation and profession as a whole.

References

British Association of Sport and Exercise Science (BASES). (2017a). *Safeguarding and Welfare Policy.* www.bases.org.uk/imgs/bases_safeguarding___welfare_policy215.pdf (accessed 23 June 2020).

British Association of Sport and Exercise Science (BASES). (2017b). *Code of Conduct,* www.bases.org.uk/imgs/bases_code_of_conduct872.pdf (accessed 23 June 2020).

Kavanagh, E. J., Knowles, Z. R., Rhind, D., Brady, A., Miles, A., Gervis, M. and Davison, R. (2016). The BASES expert statement in safeguarding in the sport sciences. *The Sport and Exercise Scientist*, 49, 20–21.

Kavanagh, E. J., Rhind, D. J. A. and Gordon-Thompson, G. (2020). Duties of care and welfare practices in sport. In R. Arnold and D. Fletcher (eds.), *Stress, Wellbeing and Performance in Sport*. London: Routledge. Chapter 14.

Mountjoy, M., Brackenridge, C., Arrington, M., Blauwet, C., Carska-Sheppard, A., Fasting, K., Kirby, S., Leahy, T., Marks, S., Martin, K., Starr, K., Tiivas, A. and Budgett, R. (2016). The IOC consensus statement: Harassment and abuse (non-accidental violence) in sport. *British Journal of Sports Medicine*, 50, 1019–1029. http://dx.doi.org/10.1136/bjsports-2016-096121

Rhind, D. J. A. and Owusu-Sekyere, F. (2018). *International Safeguards for Children in Sport: Developing and Embedding a Safeguarding Culture*. London, UK: Routledge.

Part II
Analysis and reporting

2.1 Data intelligence and feedback to the coach

Sarah Gilchrist and Mark Homer

The information now available to athletes, coaches and practitioners that can inform an athlete's training and performance has increased exponentially during the recent 'data revolution' that has impacted all aspects of our lives. Images of practitioners leaning from car windows with Douglas bags have been replaced with wrist-based super-computers that provide circa 1000 data points per second that can potentially explain and predict multiple components of performance.

The advancements in technology and available information are often considered synonymous with athletes achieving physical, mental and performance improvements which were previously very difficult or seemingly impossible. However, whilst more accurate, reliable and relevant information is undoubtably useful, factors underpinning its use can influence how impactful it can be and, in some cases, additional information can be detrimental to performance.

This chapter will focus on the processes involved in impactful data intelligence, including collection and management. Finally the chapter will discuss how to present or visualise information and provide suggestions for feeding back to the coach and athlete.

Data intelligence

Data intelligence is the ability to collect, understand and use information for effective performance impact. It is easy to become fixated on the quantity of information when discussing 'data', and practitioners should be wary of 'overload' (see later in the chapter). However, in many cases, data intelligence involves better connecting previously unrelated smaller pieces of information. The accessibility of such information is also crucial; if collection, processing and analysis are slow, their impact can be diminished.

In sport, data intelligence can impact all areas of health, wellbeing, training and performance. Topics where an increase in data quantity, quality and variety have had an impact on sport include but are not limited to assessing physiological demands, training load monitoring, match statistics and opponent analysis and injury and illness prevention. As with other industries where multiple factors explain performance, the effective use of data intelligence in sport is dependent on asking the right questions, robust collection, accurate interpretation and impactful feedback

DOI: 10.4324/9781003045281-8

Data collection, management and feedback

Performance questions

When seeking strategies to improve performance, practitioners and coaches should consider the precise challenge being raised and how it can be addressed effectively. Planning should involve all relevant parties, with clear understanding and agreement on what is needed to answer the question and how success will be defined. This stage should identify how to ensure any data collected are valid, reliable and accurate. The impact of any intervention and subsequent data collection on the training or competition process should not be ignored. A defined time frame should be arranged with appropriate analysis, monitoring and evaluation considered throughout the process.

Data collection

Quality assurance of the information you are providing to coaches and athletes is paramount. Processes to ensure data are reliable, valid and repeatable should be the cornerstone of a practitioner's practice. Table 2.1.1 highlights some important considerations for data collection in a sporting context. Take the time to ensure the equipment calibrations are current, regularly performed and producing correct data. A large part of the relationship between the scientist and coach/athlete is based on trust. If there is confidence that the data provided are consistent, accurate and reproducible, this will help build strong relationships and enhance confidence during the feedback process.

Finally, ensure you adhere to data protection regulations. Breaches of the government laws designed to safeguard individuals from which any kind of information is collected and stored are severely punishable. Refer to the Data Protection Act (2018) for further information (Data protection – GOV.UK: www.gov.uk).

Data interpretation and visualisation

Data visualisation is an important consideration when dealing with large volumes of information, particularly when balanced with the need to provide feedback succinctly and efficiently. Effective data visualisation techniques are varied, but their shared aim is to communicate data (large or small) in a constructive manner, increase the ease of understanding and highlight key messages. It can also encourage interaction with the data from coaches, athletes and other members of the support team. Consider the methods that best explain the data set in question, and ensure appropriate scientific rigour in the presentation of information (e.g., report descriptive statistics and typical error of measurements where appropriate). Further, recent advances in data visualisation tools that provide interactive dashboard-style reports allow for accessible interrogation of large volumes of information in a wide variety of flexible tables and charts.

Table 2.1.1 Key considerations in data management and analysis

Considerations	Definition	Practical Example
Accuracy	The degree to which the result of a measurement or calculation relates to the actual value.	A sprint time collected using photocell technology measures the actual time from the starter's gun to the finish line by taking 10,000 images per second.
Reliability	Synonymous with accuracy, the consistency of a result or measurement. Data can be reliably accurate or reliably inaccurate.	Collecting two blood lactate samples at the same time and achieving the same result. Results that are repeatedly 0.2–1.0 mmol/L higher than the true value are reliable but not accurate.
Validity	The appropriateness of a measurement. Is the information being collected applicable to the question being asked?	Using a treadmill rather than a bike protocol to measure the aerobic capacity of a track athlete.
Analysis	Examination and interpretation of information in order to provide a balanced representation of findings.	Descriptive statistics Traditional statistical analysis Meaningful change
Visualisation	The use of tables, charts, diagrams and the written word to interpret information that is suitable for the audience in question.	Tables and charts used in research papers and presentations, infographics, written reports, etc.
Bias	Consciously or unconsciously collecting, interpreting and presenting information in an unbalanced way that prevents a fair evaluation and decision-making process.	Having a pre-existing belief about the effectiveness of an intervention and unfairly presenting results in a way that favours or overexaggerates its success.

In line with quality-assured valid and reliable data, it is important to remain objective in analysing and presenting information. Consciously presenting data to highlight particular patterns or holding an unconscious bias towards particular results and opinions is important to recognise and avoid. This can be achieved by remaining neutral and being evidence based when presenting data and the inferences that can be drawn from it.

Feedback

A vital component of a sport scientist's work is their relationship with the coach and athlete(s). Providing information that can be used to potentially inform training and ultimately improve performance is a common scenario and one that can play a key role in the future influence that a practitioner can have.

The process by which practitioners, coaches and athletes use information to make decisions is unique to the situation and individuals involved. In the authors' experience, it is the sports scientist's role to ensure scientific rigour throughout the whole (previously described) process, while making allowances for the art and intuition that are a crucial part of coaching and should not be ignored. How accurate this can be is determined largely by a coach's experience and the length of time supporting the athlete in question (Crowcroft et al., 2020). Therefore, the practitioner's relationship with the coach should be collaborative when considering adjustments that ensure an athlete is adapting and responding to training appropriately. The skill of the coach and practitioners involved is to combine quantitative and qualitative information when making decisions.

Regardless of the dynamic between practitioner and coach, data and information should be used to augment the decision-making process rather than lead it. Practitioners should recognise that the coach needs data to either tell them something they can't see or provide evidence to support what they can. A practitioner's role is to manage this process and provide the *right* information to help with their coaching process, from talent identification through to training, assessing, selecting then ultimately competing and, hopefully, winning. Without such information, there's no hope of creating success (Williams, 2020).

Common pitfalls

Data fatigue

In using data to supplement the coaching process, it is vital that practitioners are conscious not to fall into the pattern of collecting data 'for the sake of it' as it is 'what has always been done'.

A scenario where data are collected but not used can waste time and resources, potentially leading to inaccurate measurements in the case of subjective data. It can also damage an athlete's commitment to the process.

Similarly, be cautious when there is a mass of data from various support disciplines and technical data. It can be easy to succumb to 'death by data' in the sense that practitioners are just 'seeing' numbers, so be wary of large data sets and don't observe the data in isolation. Remember that a human being, the athlete, is producing the data. Always consider the performance question and the impact of the data intelligence on it. This highlights the importance of setting time frames for data collection and review to ensure interventions remain impactful over time.

Coach engagement

Coaches may choose not to engage with new data and analysis. This can often be hard to accept, but originates in the relationship, trust and respect fostered with the coach before launching into providing them with masses of information they may, or may not, feel or recognise they would benefit from. Of course, an awareness of the stumbling block is derived from the practitioner's experience and the relationship with the coach. Consider a staged approach to using new information and introduce new metrics or feedback one at a time to avoid overwhelming those who are less comfortable with technology, change or both.

Summary

The accuracy and interpretation of 'data' have become an unavoidable influence on modern life. We have access to almost limitless information, but few are trained to properly understand it. With more technology available than ever before, using data and information to scrutinise training and performance is now common practice within sport. Therefore, crucial to this is establishing an effective platform for data management (Williams, 2020). Ensuring practitioners and coaches manage the whole process in the right way, with insight and purpose, employ good data visualisation for understanding and have excellent insight, experience and communication around the data's meaning will all benefit the collective pursuit of athletic success.

References

Crowcroft, S., Slattery, K., McCleave, E. and Coutts, A. J. (2020). Do athlete monitoring tools improve a coach's understanding of performance change? *International Journal of Sports Physiology and Performance*, 15(6), 847–852.

Williams, R. (2020). *The Importance of Data in the Role of a Sports Coach.* https://ludum.com/blog/coaching/the-importance-of-data-in-the-role-of-a-sports-coach/ (accessed October 2020).

2.2 Reliability and measurement error

Shaun J. McLaren

Overview

Reliability refers to the degree of repeatability, reproducibility or consistency in a measure. In sport and exercise science, data obtained from individuals are influenced by both measurement error (associated with equipment and protocols) and the normal, biological variation within systems of the body (or associated functional/performance outputs).

Quantification of reliability has several uses, such as precision of measures and monitoring change within an individual, setting the target sample size for an experimental trial, determining the variability of performance and guiding decisions where measurement error is an important factor (e.g., purchasing equipment).

The purpose of this chapter is to provide a practical guide to reliability analyses and use within sport and exercise science. It is particularly focused on the error of interval and ratio-level quantitative data measured from individuals in sport and exercise. Some of these concepts are also applicable to method agreement but will not be discussed or elaborated in this regard.

Reliability designs

Reliability can be assessed by taking repeated measures of an outcome when, in theory, it should not change or vary substantially. The purpose of subsequent analysis is to determine the extent of change and variation in the measure. Depending on the goal and use of data, repeated observations can be taken over both short- and long-term periods, such as between repetitions, sets, times within a day, days within a week, between weeks or between months and longer (Hurst et al., 2018). Usually, any factors that may reasonably influence the outcome measure will be controlled for or concurrently measured when control is not possible.

Test-retest designs are commonly used for reliability assessment and can be analysed using a consecutive pairwise analysis. The following section shall discuss key statistics from such designs; that is, a two-trial (test-retest) study. When two or more retests are present (i.e., three or more trials) or the outcome measure is observed over a longitudinal period, general and mixed effects linear models (and subsequent use of the sum of squares, or variance parameter estimates) can be used as alternatives (with different calculations).

DOI: 10.4324/9781003045281-9

Key statistics

Statistics from reliability analyses can be used to describe both systematic and random error. For the latter, both absolute reliability (the degree to which repeated measurements vary for individuals) and relative reliability (the degree to which individuals maintain their position in a group during repeated measures) may be quantified (Atkinson and Nevill, 1998).

Mean change

The change in mean between consecutive trials can be used to determine if any systematic (group-level) bias may have influenced change in the outcome measure. This could include, for example, familiarisation effects or changes in the external environment, including test instructions and subsequent communication with subjects during the test (verbal encouragement, etc.). In a two-trial test-retest design, the mean change is identical to that derived from a comparison of paired (dependent) means and can be analysed as such. The most appropriate way to determine this is the mean of individual change scores (test 1 – test 2).

Standard error of measurement (SEM)

Sometimes referred to as the typical error (TE), the SEM is an estimate of within-subject random variability (absolute reliability). It provides an intuitive and important approximation of how subjects may be expected to vary within their own (test) performance over repeated trials, regardless of any systematic bias. The SEM can be used to calculate additional statistics, such as the minimum detectable change (MDC) and confidence/compatibility limits (CL) for an observed value or an individual change. When expressed in percentage units (see the Reliability Estimate Uncertainty and Magnitude Interpretation section), the SEM is referred to as the coefficient of variation (CV).

In a two-trial test-retest design, the SEM can be calculated by dividing the standard deviation (SD) of paired changes scores (SD_Δ) by the square root of 2:

$$SEM = \frac{SD_\Delta}{\sqrt{2}}$$

This is because the variance of the difference scores is equal to the sum of the variances representing the SEM in each trial (Hopkins, 2000). Alternatively, if the intraclass correlation coefficient (ICC) is known, the SEM can be calculated as:

$$SEM = SD \times \sqrt{1 - ICC}$$

where SD is the observed, pooled (averaged), between-subject standard deviation from trial 1 and trial 2.

Intraclass correlation coefficient

The ICC is another measure of random error and represents reproducibility in the rank order of subjects over two or more trials (relative reliability). It should be used over Pearson's retest correlation coefficient, which can only determine how paired measures vary together, not the extent of agreement between them.

There are several variations of the ICC that depend on the model (one-way random effects, two-way random effects, two-way mixed effects), type (single or multiple measurements) and definition (absolute agreement or consistency). These factors are all determined by the reliability goals and design. For a detailed overview of these ICCs and their calculation, the reader is referred to Koo and Li (2016).

In a pairwise analysis of consecutive trials (test-retest), the most relevant ICC measure is that from a two-way mixed effects model for consistency in a single measure ($ICC_{3,1}$). That is, the testing equipment or protocols are fixed and subjects are random (Hopkins, 2000). In this design, the usual $ICC_{3,1}$ (Koo and Li, 2016) can be simplified (Hopkins, 2015) such that:

$$ICC_{3,1} = 1 - \left(\frac{SEM^2}{SD^2}\right)$$

Reliability estimate uncertainty and magnitude interpretation

Values for CL should accompany all reliability estimates as measures of uncertainty. For the mean change, CL can be derived using a t or z distribution. Further, CL for the SEM and ICC should be derived from a chi-squared and F-distribution, respectively.

Sometimes it may be appropriate to express the mean change and SEM in percentages or standardised units, as well as raw units. This can be achieved post-hoc by dividing reliability estimates and their CLs by the appropriate denominator (the overall mean for a percentage and the CV, and the between-subject SD for standardised units). Alternatively, one can make appropriate transformations of data prior to analysis, followed by post-hoc back-transformation (the natural, Napierian logarithm for percentage change and the CV and the between-subject SD for standardised units).

The magnitude of systematic bias (mean change) can be evaluated by scaling its estimate and CL against so-called thresholds of importance. Reference terms include the smallest worthwhile change (SWC), the region of practical equivalence (ROPE), the smallest effect size of interest (SEOI) and the minimum practically or clinically important difference (MPID/MCID), among others. A brief overview of these distribution- and anchor-based concepts is provided in the online supplementary material to this chapter. The SEM can also be interpreted in this manner, but the estimate (and its CL) must be doubled before being evaluated (Smith and Hopkins, 2011). The magnitude of any ICC can be interpreted as follows: >0.99, extremely high; 0.99 to 0.90, very high; 0.75 to 0.90, high; 0.50 to 0.75, moderate; 0.20 to 0.50, low; <0.20, very low (Malcata et al., 2014).

Practical applications

An example reliability analysis from a 10-m linear speed in professional soccer players is presented in Table 2.2.1. Supporting descriptive plots are shown in

Reliability and measurement error 39

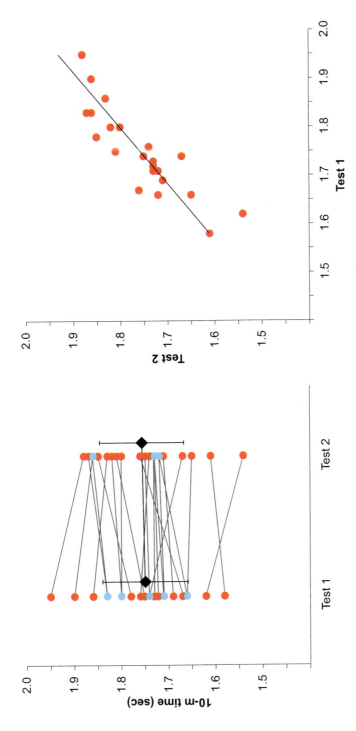

Figure 2.2.1 Test and retest 10-m linear sprint times in soccer players. Black points and error bars in the left plot are the mean ± standard deviation.

Table 2.2.1 Reliability of 10-m linear sprint time in soccer players. Consecutive pairwise analysis was performed on test-retest data measured 7 days apart.

Statistic	Raw Units		%*		Standardised (d)	
	Est.	90% CL	Est.	90% CL	Est.	90% CL
Mean Change	0.01	−0.01; 0.03	0.4	−0.6; 1.4	0.08	−0.12; 0.28
SEM	0.03#	0.03; 0.04	1.9	1.5; 2.5	0.38	0.31; 0.52
$ICC_{3,1}$	0.88	0.77; 0.94	-	-		

*SEM as a % is the CV.
#To 3 dp = 0.032 (0.026; 0.043)
CL: Confidence Limits, SEM: Standard Error of Measurement, ICC: Intraclass Correlation Coefficient.

Figure 2.2.1. This sample of 22 players were tested twice, 7 days apart, at the same time of day and on the same indoor artificial turf pitch. Each testing day was preceded by 48 hours of complete rest, and 4 days of light technical-tactical training were performed between sessions. In each testing session, following a standardised warm-up, players performed five maximal 10-m linear sprint efforts. Sprint time was measured via during dual-beam photocell timing gates, with the average time from the final three trials retained for analysis.

The $ICC_{3,1}$ of 0.88 suggests a high reproducibility (Table 2.2.1). The change in speed required for a soccer player to reach the ball with their shoulders −2% in front of the opposition during a one-on-one duel over 10 m is approximately − (Haugen and Buchheit, 2016). Therefore, the mean bias of 0.4% is trivial, whereas the SEM of 1.9% is compatible with practically significant values (Table 2.2.1). Despite this, the within-player change required to be clearly meaningful is approximately −5.5%, or −0.10 s in this sample. Collectively, these findings support 10-m linear speed as a reliable profiling and monitoring tool, in soccer players.

The online supplementary information to this chapter provides examples of how this reliability analysis can be used in practice, such as monitoring changes in individuals and setting the target sample size for group-based changes or an experimental trial. The raw test-retest data are also provided, along with a step-by-step walkthrough of the reliability analysis.

Summary

Sport scientists and exercise physiologists need to make an informed choice of the most appropriate measurement tool before they start collecting data from athletes or research participants. The degree of test-retest measurement error is one factor that should guide these decisions. Statistics such as the mean change, SEM and ICC can be used to quantify systematic and random variation from retest designs. Practitioners and researchers can use these data to monitor changes in individuals and set the appropriate sample size target for research investigations.

References

Atkinson, G. and Nevill, A. M. (1998). Statistical methods for assessing measurement error (reliability) in variables relevant to sports medicine. *Sports Medicine*, 26(4), 217–238.

Haugen, T. and Buchheit, M. (2016). Sprint running performance monitoring: Methodological and practical considerations. *Sports Medicine*, 46(5), 641–656.

Hopkins, W. G. (2000). Measures of reliability in sports medicine and science. *Sports Medicine*, 30(1), 1–15.

Hopkins, W. G. (2015). Spreadsheets for analysis of validity and reliability. *Sportscience*, 19, 36–42.

Hurst, C., Batterham, A. M., Weston, K. L. and Weston, M. (2018). Short-and long-term reliability of leg extensor power measurement in middle-aged and older adults. *Journal of Sports Sciences*, 36(9), 970–977.

Koo, T. K. and Li, M. Y. (2016). A guideline of selecting and reporting intraclass correlation coefficients for reliability research. *Journal of Chiropractic Medicine*, 15(2), 155–163.

Malcata, R. M., Vandenbogaerde, T. J. and Hopkins, W. G. (2014). Using athletes' world rankings to assess countries' performance. *International Journal of Sports Physiology and Performance*, 9(1), 133–138.

Smith, T. B. and Hopkins, W. G. (2011). Variability and predictability of finals times of elite rowers. *Medicine and Science in Sports and Exercise*, 43(11), 2155–2160.

2.3 Scaling

Adjusting physiological and performance measures for differences in body size

Edward Winter and Simon Jobson

It is well established that measures of performance and physiological characteristics are influenced by the size of the body as a whole or of its principal exercising segments in particular (Åstrand and Rodahl, 1986; Schmidt-Nielsen, 1984). Consequently, if the qualitative properties of tissues are to be explored meaningfully, differences in size have to be partitioned out by adjusting scores. Scaling is the technique that is used to make these adjustments. However, unverified use of ratio standards whereby, for example, a measure is divided simply by body mass continues to predominate.

It has been suggested that in sport and the physiology of exercise, there are four main uses of scaling techniques (Winter, 1992):

1 To compare an individual against standards for the purpose of assessment;
2 To compare groups;
3 In longitudinal studies that investigate the effects of growth or training;
4 To explore possible relationships between physiological characteristics and performance.

There is enthusiastic debate about when scaling might be appropriate and, in particular, how it should be done. In heavyweight rowing, for instance, in which the body is supported, absolute measures either of performance or physiological characteristic are key and hence do not require adjustment. Conversely, in activities such as running where body mass is unsupported and has to be carried, some form of scaling might be informative.

However, there is an intuitive attraction to adjust measures so as to develop insight into underlying metabolism and other physiological mechanisms. It is at this point that consideration can be given to possible methods.

Ratio standards

Traditionally, physiological characteristics such as oxygen uptake ($\dot{V}O_2$) have been scaled simply by dividing them by an anthropometric variable, for instance, body mass (BM). This produces a ratio standard, and the particular standard $\dot{V}O_2/\text{BM}$ expressed as ml·kg^{-1}·min^{-1} is probably the most widely used value in the physiology of exercise. However, it was suggested just over 70 years ago by Tanner (1949) and confirmed by Winter et al. (1991) that these standards can be misleading. Tanner (1949) stated that the ratio standard should be applied only when a 'special circumstance' has been satisfied.

For an outcome physiological or performance measure y and a predictor body size variable x, the special circumstance that allows the legitimate use of a ratio standard is given by:

$$\upsilon_x/\upsilon_y = r$$

Where: υ_x = coefficient of variation of x, i.e., $(SDx/\bar{x}) \times 100$
υ_y = coefficient of variation of y, i.e., $(SDy/\bar{y}) \times 100$
r = Pearson's product-moment correlation coefficient

Rarely is this special circumstance tested, and arguably it is even rarer for it to be satisfied. As the disparity between each side of the equation increases, the ratio standard becomes increasingly unstable and distorts measures under consideration.

An effect of the unchallenged use of ratio standards is an apparent favourable economy in submaximal exercise in large individuals compared with those who are diminutive, whereas for maximal responses, the opposite occurs. This latter observation has bedevilled researchers in the field of growth and development who see children's endurance performance capabilities increase during adolescence while, simultaneously, their aerobic capabilities seemingly deteriorate. The bedevilment is most likely the result of inappropriate scaling (Welsman and Armstrong, 2018).

Allometry

The preferred form of scaling is non-linear allometric modelling (Schmidt-Nielsen, 1984; Nevill et al., 1992). This modelling is based on the relationship:

$$y = ax^b$$

Where: y = a performance or physiological outcome measure
x = an anthropometric predictor variable
a = the constant multiplier
b = the exponent

The terms a and b can be identified by taking natural logarithms (ln) of both the predictor variable and outcome measure and then regressing ln y on ln x (Schmidt-Nielsen, 1984; Winter and Nevill, 2001). Groups can be compared either by analysis of covariance on the log-log regression lines (Amara et al., 2000; Amara et al., 2003; Johnson et al., 2000) or via power function ratios, i.e., y/x^b (Nevill et al., 2003). These types of ratio are created, first, by raising x to the power b to create a power function and then, second, by dividing y by this power function. The power function ratio presents y independent of x. As a note of caution, it should be acknowledged that this simple type of regression is not without its problems, and Ricker (1973) provides a useful introduction to some of the vagaries of linear modelling.

The surface law

The surface area of a body is related to its volume raised to the power 0.67. The relationship between these two measures illustrates what is called the *surface law* (Schmidt-Nielsen, 1984). This means that as a body increases in mass and hence volume, there is a disproportionate reduction in the body's surface area. Conversely, as a body reduces in mass, its surface area becomes relatively greater. This is a fundamental principle which underpins, for instance, the action of enzymes during digestion and partly explains differences in thermoregulation in children and adults. Heat exchange with the environment occurs at the surface of a body, so thermogenesis, and hence energy expenditure, must occur to replace heat lost. The precise rate of thermogenesis is dependent on the temperature differences involved. For bodies that are isometric, i.e., they increase proportionally, surface area increases as volume is raised to the power by two-thirds.

It has been suggested (Åstrand and Rodahl, 1986) and demonstrated (Nevill, 1995; Welsman et al., 1996; Nevill et al., 2003) that maximal oxygen uptake ($\dot{V}O_2$max) and related measures of energy expenditure can be scaled for differences in BM by means of the surface law; BM can be raised to the two-thirds power and then divided into absolute values of $\dot{V}O_2$. This produces a power-function ratio that describes the aerobic capabilities of a performer with units of $ml \cdot kg^{-0.67} \cdot min^{-1}$. Typical values for elite athletes are presented by Nevill et al. (2003). They range from (mean ± SD) 192 ± 19 $ml \cdot kg^{-0.67} \cdot min^{-1}$ for women badminton players to 310 ± 31 $ml \cdot kg^{-0.67} \cdot min^{-1}$ for elite standard heavyweight men rowers. When their aerobic capabilities are expressed as ratio standards, the characteristics of the heavyweight men rowers appear to be less than those of other groups, yet their event demands high aerobic capability.

Elastic similarity

An alternative approach has been to use the power of three-quarters. This is based on McMahon's (1973) model of elastic similarity, which acknowledges that growth in most living things is not isometric; body segments and limbs grow at different rates and hence relative proportions change. In addition, buckling loads and other elastic properties, for instance, of tendons, are not accounted for in a simple surface-law approach. Moreover, in interspecies studies, animals that differ markedly in size seem to be described by a BM exponent that approximates 0.75.

Non-isometric growth

McMahon (1973) identified a key complication to simple surface-law considerations and elasticity: the change in relative size of segments that occurs during growth and development (Medawar, 1944). As humans grow and increase absolutely in BM and other anthropometric dimensions, the relative sizes of each of the body's segments change. For example, the head of an infant is proportionally larger than that of an adult. Conversely, the length of adult legs is a greater proportion of stature than a child's. This change in relative proportions is allometric, but unlike for regular objects such as cubes and spheres, it is termed non-isometric.

Non-isometric change has implications both for locomotion on land and in water and on physiological characteristics. This adds to the complexity of effects on exercise capability that aggregate during adolescence. Nevill et al. (2004) attempted to model limb circumference for different size adults and concluded that fixed scaling exponents can mislead. While ratio standards also mislead and allometric modelling is a distinct improvement, non-isometric growth is probably a key reason why there is still no universally accepted way in which allometry can be applied to investigate human exercise capabilities (Welsman and Armstrong, 2018).

Allometric cascade

However, yet another approach has been advanced: the allometric cascade model for metabolic rate (Darveau et al., 2002). This model acknowledges two important considerations: first, the non-isometric changes in the body's segments that accompany growth and development and training-induced hypertrophy, and second, the tripartite nature of $\dot{V}O_2$ and, in particular, $\dot{V}O_2$max. $\dot{V}O_2$max is the global outcome of the rate at which the body can extract oxygen from the atmosphere via the cardiopulmonary system, transport it via the cardiovascular system and use it in skeletal muscle. The ability to release energy is as strong as the weakest part of this three-link chain.

Darveau et al. (2002) ascribed a weighting to each of these three facets and predicted an exponent for maximal and submaximal metabolic rate. For the former, the exponent was between 0.82 and 0.92. For the latter, equivalent values were 0.76–0.79. Seemingly successful attempts have been made to validate these exponents in exercising humans (Batterham and Jackson, 2003), but without accounting for non-isometric change in the size of body segments.

Recommendations

In the light of these considerations and the possible confusion they create, how should the results of exercise tests be expressed? To report the results of laboratory and field-based tests that meaningfully reflect the performance and physiological status of athletes and exercisers, investigators should:

- Report absolute values of performance measures and physiological characteristics;
- Report ratio standards only when Tanner's special circumstance has been satisfied;
- For expediency, use the surface-law exponent of 0.67 to scale $\dot{V}O_2$ or other related assessments of energy expenditure for differences in BM or the size of exercising segments;

- As appropriate, consider and adjust measures for non-isometric growth;
- Verify the choice of a particular exponent, but acknowledge that because of sampling errors, comparisons between groups might be compromised;
- For $\dot{V}O_2$ and $\dot{V}O_2$max consider applying the allometric cascade model.

References

Amara, C. E., Koval, J. J., Johnson, P. J., Paterson, D. H., Winter, E. M. and Cunningham, D. A. (2000). Modelling the influence of fat-free mass and physical activity on the decline in maximum oxygen uptake with age in older humans. *Experimental Physiology*, 85, 877–885.

Amara, C. E., Rice, C. L., Koval, J. J., Paterson, D. H., Winter, E. M. and Cunningham, D. A. (2003). Allometric scaling of strength in an independently living population aged 55–86 years. *American Journal of Human Biology*, 15, 48–60.

Åstrand, P.-O. and Rodahl, K. (1986). *Textbook of Work Physiology* (3rd ed.). New York: McGraw-Hill.

Batterham, A. M. and Jackson, A. S. (2003). Validity of the allometric cascade model at submaximal and maximal metabolic rates in men. *Respiratory Physiology and Neurobiology*, 135, 103–106.

Darveau, C.-A., Suarez, R. K., Andrews, R. D. and Hochachka, P. W. (2002). Allometric cascade as a unifying principle of body mass effects on metabolism. *Nature*, 417, 166–170.

Johnson, P. J., Winter, E. M., Paterson, D. H., Koval, J. J., Nevill, A. M. and Cunningham, D. A. (2000). Modelling the influence of age, body size and sex on maximum oxygen uptake in older humans. *Experimental Physiology*, 85, 219–225.

McMahon, T. (1973). Size and shape in biology. *Science*, 179, 1201–1204.

Medawar, P. B. (1944). The shape of a human being as a function of time. *Journal of the Royal Statistical Society*, 132B, 133–144.

Nevill, A. M. (1995). The need to scale for differences in body size and mass: An explanation of Kleiber's 0.75 mass exponent. *Journal of Applied Physiology*, 77, 2870–2873.

Nevill, A. M., Brown, D., Godfrey, R., Johnson, P. J., Romer, L., Stewart, A. D. and Winter, E. M. (2003). Modelling maximum oxygen uptake of elite endurance athletes. *Medicine and Science in Sports and Exercise*, 35, 488–494.

Nevill, A. M., Ramsbottom, R. and Williams, C. (1992). Scaling physiological measurements for individuals of different body size. *European Journal of Applied Physiology*, 65, 110–117.

Nevill, A. M., Stewart, A. D., Olds, T. and Holder, R. (2004). Are adult physiques geometrically similar? The danger of allometric scaling using body mass power laws. *American Journal of Anthropology*, 124, 177–182.

Ricker, W. E. (1973). Linear regressions in fishery research. *Journal of Fisheries Research Board, Canada*, 30, 409–434.

Schmidt-Nielsen, K. (1984). *Scaling: Why Is Animal Size So Important?* Cambridge: Cambridge University Press.

Tanner, J. M. (1949). Fallacy of per-weight and per-surface area standards and their relation to spurious correlation. *Journal of Applied Physiology*, 2, 1–15.

Welsman, J. and Armstrong, N. (2018). Interpreting aerobic fitness in youth: The fallacy of ratio scaling. *Pediatric Exercise Science*, 31, 184–190.

Welsman, J., Armstrong, N., Nevill, A., Winter, E. and Kirby, B. (1996). Scaling peak O_2 for differences in body size. *Medicine and Science in Sports and Exercise*, 28, 259–265.

Winter, E. M. (1992). Scaling: Partitioning out differences in size. *Pediatric Exercise Science*, 4, 296–301.

Winter, E. M., Brookes, F. B. C. and Hamley, E. J. (1991). Maximal exercise performance and lean leg volume in men and women. *Journal of Sports Sciences*, 9, 3–13.

Winter, E. M. and Nevill, A. M. (2001). Scaling: Adjusting for differences in body size. In R. Eston and T. Reilly (eds.), *Kinanthropometry and Exercise Physiology Laboratory Manual: Tests, Procedures and Data* (2nd ed.). *Volume 1: Anthropometry*, pp. 321–335. London: Routledge.

Part III
General procedures

3.1 Pre-participation evaluation for athletes

Rachel N. Lord and David Oxborough

Regular physical activity is associated with numerous health benefits, including lower all-cause mortality and lower risk of cardiovascular and metabolic disease (Kohl et al., 2012). Despite the well-established long-term beneficial effects of exercise, the risk of an acute cardiovascular event, including sudden cardiac death (SCD) and/or acute myocardial infarction (AMI), is transiently elevated during and just after vigorous physical exertion (Mittleman et al., 1993). Exercise testing is a cornerstone of exercise physiology, which provides invaluable information about physiological variables that influence performance and allows one to track the effectiveness of training programmes. However, these tests often involve vigorous-intensity exercise, which can trigger an adverse cardiac event in athletes with underlying disease.

Occurrence of SCD in an athletic individual is a rare, but a catastrophic event occurring in what are the healthiest of our population has a far-reaching impact. The data pertaining to the incidence of SCD in young athletes are equivocal but in the region of 1 in 14,000 to 1 in 100,000 (Malhotra et al., 2018) with a 5 to 10 times higher risk in master athletes (>35 years of age; Harmon et al., 2014, see Chapter 13.1). There is a modest but increased risk in male athletes and those of black African/Afro Caribbean ethnicity (Sheikh et al., 2014). The causes of SCD in young athletes are more likely to be secondary to an undiagnosed inherited cardiomyopathy or ion channelopathy, whilst acquired disease such as coronary artery disease (CAD) is more prevalent in older athletes (La Gerche et al., 2013; Finocciaro et al., 2016). Cardiac pre-participation evaluation (PPE) has become an important tool in reducing the risk of SCD (Vessella et al., 2020) by identifying underlying disease and allowing for individualised risk management strategies.

Young athletes and PPE

There is general agreement for the use of PPE as a means of identifying those athletes at risk of SCD; however, the specific protocol that is implemented can vary across sporting organisations and countries (Mont et al., 2017). Most protocols will include a physical examination and a health questionnaire to identify overt abnormalities, cardiac symptoms or a family history of SCD/cardiomyopathy. By combining this with a 12-lead electrocardiogram (ECG), the diagnostic yield increases

DOI: 10.4324/9781003045281-12

significantly with increased sensitivity and specificity. The ECG can detect conditions such as ion channelopathies and cardiomyopathy that would not be detectable with a physical examination alone. One should interpret an ECG recording in accordance with the International Recommendations for Electrocardiographic Interpretation in Athletes (Sharma et al., 2016). Hence, this procedure provides the cornerstone of PPE.

Some sporting organisations employ echocardiographic techniques alongside the 12-lead ECG, a physical examination and a questionnaire. This allows for direct assessment of chamber size and function, blood flow and valvular function, as well as being able to identify the ostia and course of the coronary arteries (coronary anomalies represent up to 11% of SCD in young athletes) (Finocchiaro et al., 2016). That aside, echocardiography, when used as a primary investigation, does not significantly increase the sensitivity or specificity of PPE in young athletes, but does when used as a targeted tool onsite; that is, in response to a positive ECG/physical examination or questionnaire, it has been shown to reduce referral rates by up to 60% (Mont et al., 2017).

Masters athletes and PPE

Evidence suggests that masters-class athletes have a higher prevalence of CAD than non-athletes (Merghani et al., 2017) and therefore may be at higher risk of SCD. Details on recommendations for PPE for master athletes is covered in detail in Chapter 13.1.

PPE protocols should aim to detect underlying cardiomyopathy but also evaluate the risk of existing CAD. Although the resting 12-lead ECG has a high sensitivity for detection of inherited disease, its predictive capacity to detect sub-clinical CAD is poor. In light of this, one should also implement validated questionnaires. Such self-reported inventories include the American Heart Association/American College of Sport Medicine Health/Fitness Facility Pre-participation Screening Questionnaire, or the Physical Activity Readiness for Everyone (PAR-Q). In addition, the inclusion of a risk score such as the Framingham Risk Score or the European Society of Cardiology Systemic Coronary Risk Evaluation (SCORE) improves the diagnostic yield in masters-class athletes (Morrison et al., 2018). The risk scores utilise multiple factors, including age, sex, lipid profile, diabetes and smoking history. Other factors are pertinent, such as resting blood pressure, whether or not an individual is using medication to modify blood pressure, if any family history of cardiovascular disease is evident or if an individual presents a high sensitivity for detection of sub-clinical CAD (D'Agostino et al., 2001). There are some data to suggest that the inclusion of a maximal exercise ECG may provide additional value in identifying those athletes with pre-existing CAD (Gervasi et al., 2018); however, it is important to note the relatively intermediate sensitivity and specificity, particularly in an athletic individual. In conjunction with the resting 12-lead ECG, these additional investigations provide evidence for subsequent referral for further investigations.

Although athletes are overtly 'healthy', there is a small but significant risk of SCD in this population, and PPE is fundamental in identifying those individuals at risk. It is extremely important to understand the information gained from the available protocols and to implement the appropriate protocols dependent on the age of the athlete. It is vital to ensure experts with experience working with athletic populations interpret diagnostic evidence. This approach will go some way to protect individuals from experiencing adverse events and help reduce the risk of false-positive and false-negative findings.

References

D'Agostino, R. B., Sr., et al. (2001). Validation of the Framingham coronary heart disease prediction scores: Results of a multiple ethnic groups investigation. *JAMA*, 286(2), 180–187.

Finocchiaro, G., Papadakis, M., Robertus, J.-L., Dhutia, H., Steriotis, A. K., Tome, M., Mellor, G., Merghani, A., Malhotra, A., Behr, E., Sharma, S. and Sheppard, M. N. (2016). Etiology of sudden death in sports: Insights from a United Kingdom regional registry. *Journal of the American College of Cardiology*, 67(18), 2108–2115.

Gervasi, S. F., et al. (2018). Coronary atherosclerosis in apparently healthy master athletes discovered during pre-participation screening: Role of coronary CT angiography (CCTA). *International Journal of Cardiology*, 1(282), 99–107.

Harmon, K. G., Drezner, J. A., Wilson, M. G. and Sharma, S. (2014). Incidence of sudden cardiac death in athletes: A state-of-the-art review. *British Journal of Sports Medicine*, 48(15), 1185–1192. https://doi.org/10.1136/bjsports-2014-093872

Kohl, H. W., 3rd, Craig, C. L., Lambert, E. V., Inoue, S., Alkandari, J. R., Leetongin, G. and Kahlmeier, S. (2012). The pandemic of physical inactivity: Global action for public health. *Lancet*, 380, 294–305.

La Gerche, A., Baggish, A. L., Knuuti, J., Prior, D. L., Sharma, S., Heidbuchel, H. and Thompson, P. D. (2013). Cardiac imaging and stress testing asymptomatic athletes to identify those at risk of sudden cardiac death. *JACC: Cardiovascular Imaging*, 6(9), 993–1007. https://doi.org/10.1016/j.jcmg.2013.06.003

Malhotra, A. and Sharma, S. (2018). Outcomes of cardiac screening in adolescent soccer players. *New England Journal of Medicine*, in press. https://doi.org/10.1056/NEJMoa1714719

Merghani, A., Maestrini, V., Rosmini, S., Cox, A. T., Dhutia, H., Bastiaenan, R., David, S., Yeo, T. J., Narain, R., Malhotra, A., Papadakis, M., Wilson, M. G., Tome, M., Alfakih, K., Moon, J. C. and Sharma, S. (2017). Prevalence of subclinical coronary artery disease in masters endurance athletes with a low atherosclerotic risk profile running title: Merghani et al.: Coronary disease in master endurance athletes. *Circulation*. https://doi.org/10.1161/CIRCULATIONAHA.116.026964

Mittleman, M. A., Maclure, M., Tofler, G. H., Sherwood, J. B., Goldberg, R. J., and Muller, J. E. (1993). Triggering of acute myocardial infarction by heavy physical exertion: Protection against triggering by regular exertion: Determinants of myocardial infarction onset study investigators. *New England Journal of Medicine*, 329, 1677–1683.

Mont, J. L., Pelliccia, A., Sharma, S., Biffi, A., Borjesson, M., Terradellas, J. B., Carre, F., Guasch, E., Heidbuchel, H., La Gerche, A., Lampert, R., McKenna, W., Papadakis, M., Priori, S. G., Scanavacca, M., Thompson, P., Sticherling, C., Viskin, S., Wilson, M.,

Corrado, D., Gregory, L. Y. H., Gorenek, B., Lundqvist, C. B., Merkely, B., Hindricks, G., Hernandez-Madrid, A., Lane, D. A., Boriani, G., Narasimhan, C., Marquez, M. F., Haines, D. E., Mackall, J., Marques-Vidal, P. M., Corra, U., Halle, M., Tiberi, M., Niebauer, J. and Piepoli, M. F. (2017). Pre-participation cardiovascular evaluation for athletic participants to prevent sudden death: Position paper from the EHRA and the EACPR, branches of the ESC. Endorsed by APHRS, HRS, and SOLAECE. Europace, 19(1), 139–163. https://doi.org/10.1093/europace/euw243

Morrison, B. N., McKinney, J., Isserow, S., Lithwick, D., Taunton, J., Nazzari, H., De Souza, A. M., Heilbron, B., Cater, C., Macdonald, M., Hives, B. A. and Warburton, D. E. R. (2018). Assessment of cardiovascular risk and preparticipation screening protocols in masters athletes: The Masters Athlete Screening Study (MASS): A cross-sectional study. *BMJ Open Sport and Exercise Medicine*, 4(1), 1–10.

Sharma, S., Drezner, J. A., Baggish, A., Papadakis, M., Wilson, M. G., Prutkin, J. M., La Gerche, A., Ackerman, M. J., Borjesson, M., Salerno, J. C., Asif, I. M., Owens, D. S., Chung, E. H., Emery, M. S., Froelicher, V. F., Heidbuchel, H., Adamuz, C., Asplund, C. A., Cohen, G., Harmon, K. G., Marek, J. C., Molossi, S., Niebauer, J., Pelto, H. F., Perez, M. V., Riding, N. R., Saarel, T., Schmied, C. M., Shipon, D. M., Stein, R., Vetter, V. L., Pelliccia, A. and Corrado, D. (2016). International Recommendations for Electrocardiographic Interpretation in Athletes. *Journal of the American College of Cardiology*, 69(8), 1057–1075.

Sheikh, N. and Sharma, S. (2014). Impact of ethnicity on cardiac adaptation to exercise. *Nature Reviews: Cardiology*, 11(4), 198–217. https://doi.org/10.1038/nrcardio.2014.15

Vessella, T., Zorzi, A., Merlo, L., Pegoraro, C., Giorgiano, F., Trevisanato, M., Viel, M., Formentini, P., Corrado, D. and Sarto, P. (2020). The Italian preparticipation evaluation programme: Diagnostic yield, rate of disqualification and cost analysis. *British Journal of Sports Medicine*, 54(4), 231–237.

3.2 Equipment maintenance and calibration standards

David Green and Glyn Howatson

Introduction

Effective maintenance and calibration of laboratory and field equipment are fundamental for ensuring the reliability and validity of testing procedures. By understanding these processes, it is possible to ascertain the error associated with the instrument and hence detect meaningful physiological (biological) changes. Poor practice and user errors during these processes can be detrimental on the quality of data produced and hence have serious implications for research, consultancy and other applied practice. Laboratory accreditation schemes exist, such as that provided by the British Association of Sport and Exercise Sciences (BASES: www.bases.org.uk/spage-organisations-laboratory_accreditation.html).

Such schemes provide external quality assurance of laboratory practices. This external validation is critical in upholding good practice, creating a culture of quality assurance and ensuring acceptable standards are adhered to not just within but also between laboratories. The aim of this chapter is to provide some guiding principles central to the BASES Laboratory Accreditation process that can be employed as good practice for the calibration and maintenance of laboratory or field-testing equipment in the domain of sport and exercise science.

It is important to note that commercial availability does not guarantee the validity, reliability or suitability of a piece of equipment for any given purpose. In this chapter it is assumed due diligence has been performed in the acquisition of any equipment and that, if fully functional, it is fit for purpose. Furthermore, validity and reliability of a testing procedure are influenced by factors other than equipment functionality, such as user competence and biological variation. Therefore, users of all laboratories should make every effort to understand the factors that influence testing validity and reliability and, where appropriate, be able to report these variables to support data.

Calibration

The function of diagnostic equipment within the sport and exercise community is to measure the value of a specific sample or parameter based upon a pre-determined method of measurement. During production, manufacturers

DOI: 10.4324/9781003045281-13

assess methods of measurement against pre-existing criterion values for reliability and validity; during this process, fine adjustments occur until the manufacturer achieves appropriately equivalent results. This process of adjusting the method of measurement to attain a more accurate result is calibration. The requirement for re-calibration arises when a method of measurement is unstable over time. In this instance, any 'drift' in previous calibration procedures may result in inaccurate measures. Re-calibrating the equipment ensures alignment with the manufacturer's original and acceptable tolerances.

Control

A control test differs from a calibration; a control test uses either known criterion values or a measuring device to establish accuracy of an instrument. When running a control test, no adjustment is made to the method of measurement; it is simply a test of accuracy based on the equipment's current calibration. Manufacturers often dictate calibration and control values to ensure optimal performance of a piece of equipment. However, when modifiable, users should prioritise calibration and control values that correspond to an expected testing range. For example, when using controls for blood lactate analysers, the use of a $12 \cdot mmol \cdot L^{-1}$ control (standard) would not be suitable for testing athletes that are expected to range between $0.5\ mmol \cdot L^{-1}$ and $6\ mmol \cdot L^{-1}$. Appropriate ranges should be determined on a laboratory-by-laboratory basis by the technical staff in consultation with the laboratory director or other appropriately qualified laboratory users. Where a piece of equipment calculates results using a non-linear method, multiple calibration values should be considered to determine an appropriate calibration curve that fits within the expected range of values. Using a range of control tests can be useful in assessing the efficacy of different calibration values and thus help to identify the most appropriate calibration protocol.

Quality of calibration and control samples

A calibration sample that does not accurately reflect its designated value will have a detrimental effect on the method of measurement, leading to inaccurate results. A control sample or criterion measure that no longer reflects or measures its designated value will prevent an accurate assessment of equipment functionality and could lead to unnecessary or detrimental follow-up adjustments. The degree of certainty about the value of any individual calibration or control sample can never be 100%. Ultimately, an individual's judgement on the quality and acceptability of a calibrator/control for any given situation must be based on several criteria (see Tables 3.2.1 and 3.2.2 for examples).

How often should I calibrate?

Manufacturers usually advise on the frequency of calibration; however, laboratory-specific knowledge should always complement this fundamental information to

Table 3.2.1 Calibration and control check list

- Can we trust the supplier?
- Does it have official certification?
- Mechanical degradation (e.g., wear and tear)
- Chemical degradation (e.g., check 'use by' dates and storage conditions)
- Effect of environment conditions (e.g., cold, hot, humid, hypoxic)
- Does user competence affect its quality?
- Manufacturer's error limits
- Is this error acceptable for the equipment's intended use?

Table 3.2.2 Example: checking the speed of a treadmill

Method 1 – Contact tachometer:
The wheel of the contact tachometer is applied on the treadmill and speed is determined via on-board software.

Considerations:
A tachometer requires specialist calibration, and assessing its functionality 'in-house' is not possible; thus, guaranteeing there has been no degradation in the tachometer since the previous calibration is not possible. An instant-read tachometer would be very sensitive to slight perturbations in treadmill belt speed.

Method 2 – Counting belt revolutions:
Using a stopwatch, belt velocity can be calculated from the total distance (belt revolutions × belt length) covered in a given time.

Considerations:
If measured appropriately, you could have high confidence in the length of the belt and, provided the belt length is accurate, error in the calculated speed would decrease as the number of counted revolutions increases. Therefore, it is advisable to use no fewer than 100 revolutions at a range of velocities. Errors in the calculation of speed can be determined based on possible inaccuracies of belt length and revolution count. Using this method, it is easy to determine treadmill speed within an error of <1%.

Verdict:
A tachometer is more responsive to changes in treadmill speed and therefore may be the more appropriate tool for assessing instantaneous changes in speed when a load is added to the treadmill (e.g., a foot strike). However, counting revolutions is a more transparent method and has a likely error well within an acceptable level for most treadmill uses.

N.B. Aside from the method of checking belt speed, consideration should be given to the validity of checking the belt when unloaded when the requirement for confidence in its speed is highest when being loaded (i.e., run on). Importantly, a variety of body masses should be considered across a range of treadmill velocities that are most likely to align with the people exercising in the device. This provides excellent task-specific validity to your instrument.

arrive at a best practice protocol for each piece of equipment, its current use and environment. Some considerations (Figure 3.2.1) for determining the frequency of calibration include:

- The equipment does not return a satisfactory result from a control test;

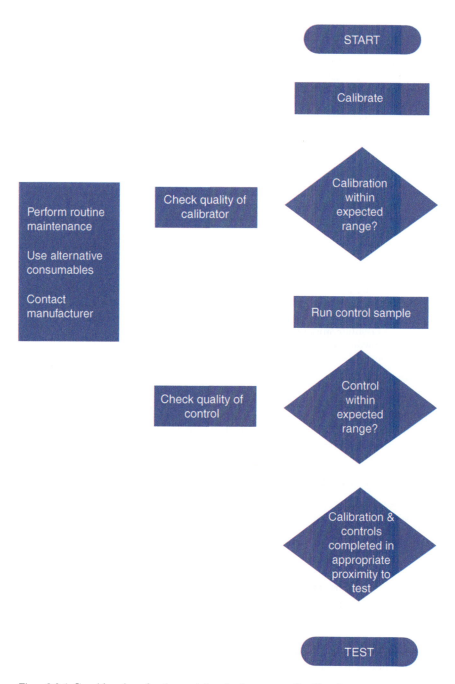

Figure 3.2.1 Considerations for determining the frequency of calibration.

- A change in the environment or equipment has occurred that might affect the method of measurement;
- When using after a period of non-use.

Maintenance of equipment

Good preventative maintenance will reduce malfunctions, promote early problem identification and maintain the validity and reliability of equipment and results. Users should tailor equipment maintenance plans according to the environment and consideration of how a piece of equipment is used. An effective maintenance plan should include a list of preventative maintenance tasks, the required frequency and documentation/training to promote competent equipment use. The initial creation of a maintenance plan should start with the manufacturer's recommendations, after which users can add components according to the specific, local laboratory environment.

Documentation and user training

Comprehensive operating procedures, risk assessments and user training are essential in preventing avoidable damage to equipment. One should not assume that a user is sufficiently competent to operate equipment because of their experience with 'similar systems'; confidence does not equal competence. Indeed, user training is the first step in ensuring correct usage and should be supplemented with a detailed, step-by-step operating procedure for ongoing reference. Although establishing protocols and procedures takes time to develop, they tend not to change a great deal over time. Importantly, documents of this nature allow for good knowledge transfer and are excellent practice in mitigating risk (loss of knowledge, for example), disaster recovery and business continuity.

Maintenance tasks

Many factors determine the appropriate type and frequency of maintenance tasks for any given piece of equipment. The following list is not exhaustive, but highlights some common considerations when constructing a maintenance plan:

- What spare parts are required, and what is the delivery time on them?
- Do certain parts/consumables have a finite life span?
- Historically, what problems have occurred?
- Can users test constituent parts individually?
- How often should a user evaluate functionality?
- Document typical calibration and control values to help with early identification of problems;
- Track usage to guide maintenance frequency.

Summary

Many professionals in the sport and exercise industry make assumptions that all laboratory environments are the same – this is not true; vast differences will be present between a well-run laboratory and a poorly run laboratory. Accuracy of equipment, safety of the environment, efficacy of exercise testing protocols, quality of analysis and interpretation and competence of staff are critical to ensure good operations. BASES laboratory accreditation provides a schema and level of quality assurance that a laboratory can follow to adhere to industry-based, good practice. As technology improves, new, more affordable equipment becomes available, and so it is critically important that laboratories can support their activities with good practice and provide an evidence base for the data produced, both in research and applied practice.

3.3 Lung and respiratory muscle function

John Dickinson and Karl Sylvester

This chapter will consider why the assessment of lung and respiratory muscle function is relevant to sport and exercise science. We will describe the theory behind assessments of lung function, upper airway flow, airway inflammation and respiratory muscle assessments and will signpost to further reading should more detail on standardisation of performance be required. The online version of the chapter also provides an introduction to breathing.

Individuals will rarely reach their maximal voluntary ventilation limits during most forms of physical activity and exercise; therefore, in many cases it has been assumed that the respiratory system is not a limiting factor to performance. Thus, routine testing and monitoring of respiratory health have taken a back seat to cardiovascular and musculoskeletal issues related to physical activity and exercise. However, times are changing, and there is more acceptance from medical, sports science and clinical physiologist teams of the importance of assessing an individual's respiratory health. There is more understanding of the best ways to manage and care for respiratory health, and full texts are now available on the subject (Dickinson and Hull, 2020). Even in moderate physical activity the respiratory system may not perform appropriately and can impact health and performance either directly during exercise or following exercise (e.g., bronchospasm post-race). We are therefore able to use assessments of upper and lower airway function at rest and following exercise to assess and monitor the individual's airway performance and health.

Assessments of upper and lower airway function are necessary, as exercise respiratory symptoms are non-specific. For example, 50% of athletes who report respiratory symptoms are inappropriately diagnosed with an asthma-related condition when symptoms are used in isolation without an objective assessment of airway function (Rundell et al., 2001). Other issues such as unexplained underperformance, regular early termination of exercise and chronic fatigue can all be linked to underlying respiratory conditions. Many individuals may experience abnormal functioning of the respiratory system that can impact on their ability to exercise optimally (see Table 3.3.1).

DOI: 10.4324/9781003045281-14

Table 3.3.1 Abnormal respiratory function

Condition	Pathology	Physiological Impact
Asthma-related conditions	Airway inflammation Airway smooth muscle constriction	Reduction in ability to expire air Compromised gas exchange (usually in moderate to severe forms) Reduction in aerobic exercise capacity (usually in moderate to severe forms) Difficulty in breathing Prolonged time to recover from exercise Post-exercise cough
COPD	Chronic airway inflammation (bronchitis) Chronic damage to the air sacs in the lungs (emphysema) Airway smooth muscle constriction	Reduction in ability to expire air Compromised gas exchange Reduction in aerobic exercise capacity (usually in moderate to severe forms) Difficulty in breathing Prolonged time to recover from exercise Post-exercise cough
Restrictive airway disease (e.g., pulmonary fibrosis)	Lung tissue is damaged and scarred Airway walls become thickened and stiff	Reduction in airway ventilation Compromised gas exchange Limited ability to exercise at moderate and high intensities
Respiratory muscle fatigue/ increased respiratory load	Prolonged endurance exercise leads to fatigue of respiratory muscles Poor coordination of respiratory muscle activation Poor conditioning of respiratory muscles	Respiratory muscle fatigue leading to early onset of respiratory metaboreflex
Dysfunctional breathing	Poor coordination of respiratory muscles and overactivation of accessory breathing muscles	Inappropriate ventilation Increased perception of breathing effort Compromised alveolar gas exchange Early termination of exercise
Rhinitis	Inflammation and swelling of the mucous membrane of the nose	Blocked nasal passage prompts mouth breathing Greater exposure to particulates entering lower airways, which can promote bronchoconstriction in susceptible individuals Can lead some individuals to develop a dysfunctional breathing pattern Can lead to increased perception of breathing effort during exercise

Condition	Pathology	Physiological Impact
Exercise-induced laryngeal obstruction	Transient, reversible narrowing of the larynx that occurs during high-intensity exercise	Development of inspiratory wheeze during moderate- to high-intensity exercise Increased perception of breathing effort during exercise Can lead to early termination of high-intensity exercise Can develop persistent dry cough post-exercise May promote a dysfunctional breathing pattern or can be present because of a dysfunctional breathing pattern

Where practitioners have appropriate resources, it may also be beneficial to screen for respiratory conditions. Several reports (Dickinson et al., 2011) have identified large numbers of elite athletes detected with respiratory issues, such as asthma-related conditions, in the absence of a previous history. When screening for respiratory conditions, it is important to complete a thorough systematic assessment of the individual's airways. This includes assessing the airflow and volumes through the upper and lower airways at rest and following exercise (or surrogate challenge).

Following is a brief description of various assessments of respiratory function. For more detail on how to perform these assessments, please see the Suggested Further Reading section of the online content for this chapter.

Spirometry (dynamic lung function)

Spirometry is probably the most commonly utilised respiratory physiological assessment. It is used to assist with a diagnosis of many respiratory diseases, such as chronic obstructive pulmonary disease (COPD) or asthma. Spirometry is also performed at regular intervals to determine the appropriateness of initiating therapies, such as anti-fibrotic medication in interstitial lung diseases (ILDs), should there be a significant decline in spirometry results.

Spirometry is also utilised in other assessments such as bronchial challenge tests. These tests assess the responsiveness of the airways to known bronchoconstricting stimulants, such as methacholine, which acts directly on the airways. Indirect airway challenges trigger bronchoconstriction via an indirect pathway. An example of an indirect airway challenge is an exercise challenge, which is useful in confirming the presence of exercise-induced bronchospasm (EIB). Although exercise is a specific indirect airway challenge for EIB, some surrogate challenge assessments (e.g., eucapnic voluntary hyperpnoea or mannitol) have a greater sensitivity when compared to exercise (Dickinson et al., 2006; Holzer et al., 2003). There is an exaggerated response in those who are hyperresponsive or have a diagnosis of

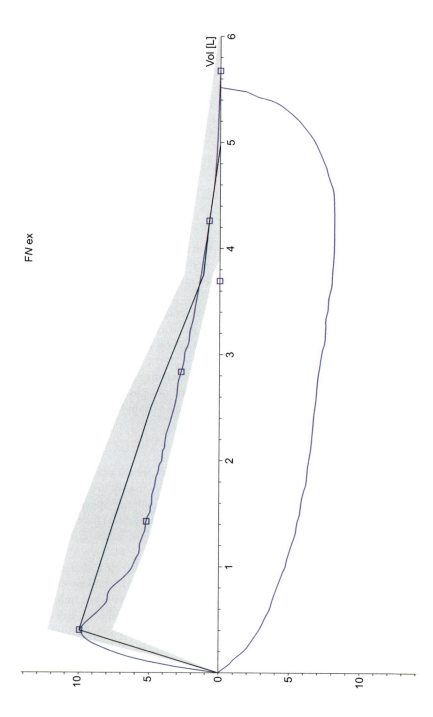

asthma that is not detected from more basic assessments. For more detail about specific challenges for asthma-related conditions, we refer you to the following American Thoracic Society2 (ATS) and European Respiratory Society (ERS) guidelines (Hallstrand et al., 2018).

Spirometry must be performed to quality-assured standards to ensure accuracy of the results. Quality assurance includes using calibrated and verified equipment, sufficient training for the professional who will be coaching the subject to perform the manoeuvre and ensuring the results obtained meet acceptability and reproducibility criteria (Sylvester et al., 2020).

Measurement of static lung volumes

In many respiratory diseases it is important to understand the extent of disease impact on overall lung volumes. Spirometry can measure some constituents of lung volume, but it is unable to measure parameters such as residual volume (RV), the volume of air left in the lungs when the subject completely exhales, or the functional residual capacity (FRC), the volume of air left in the lungs at the end of a normal tidal breath. Both these parameters are particularly important in obstructive lung diseases, as they allow the measurement of gas trapping and hyperinflation, respectively.

Being able to measure RV and FRC also allows the calculation of total lung capacity (TLC) to be made. Measuring TLC allows accurate determination of the presence of restrictive lung diseases such as ILD. Analysing all of these measurements also allows more in-depth analysis of the impact of disease and the potential origin of the disease, for example, whether it is a lung or chest wall problem or how much of an impact obesity is having on the physiology of the lungs.

Static lung volumes can be measured using several techniques that either utilise inhalation of a gas mixture, such as in the helium dilution or nitrogen washout techniques, or pressure-related measurements, such as whole-body plethysmography. Each test has its own positives and drawbacks. Gas dilutional techniques may underestimate lung volume, as the gas used may not distribute to airways that aren't being ventilated, particularly in relatively severe obstructive lung diseases, whereas the plethysmographic method may overestimate due to measurement of volumes of gas not utilised in the lungs, for example, in the buccal cavity or stomach.

Single breath gas transfer

The ability to inspire and expire the desired lung volume, as measured by the preceding techniques, is important, but only one aspect to the physiology of respiration. In order for the oxygen required for cellular respiration to reach the cells, it must first cross the alveolar-capillary membrane and enter the pulmonary circulation. The ability of the lungs to exchange gases can be altered by conditions where there is insufficient ventilation and surface area available, e.g., emphysema, or in conditions where there is thickening of the alveolar-capillary membrane, e.g., ILD.

Measurement of gas exchange is possible through the single breath gas transfer technique. The subject inspires a mix of gas in known concentrations. The gases include an inert gas, such as helium or methane. These gases do not cross the alveolar-capillary membrane and are used to estimate the volume of the lungs available for gas exchange but also the dilutional effect of other gases. The other important gas used in this technique is carbon monoxide. Carbon monoxide is used due to its similar characteristics to oxygen in terms of its molecular weight; however, it has a 250 times greater affinity for haemoglobin than oxygen. When calculating the gas exchange ability of the lungs, the important factors to consider are the thickness of the membrane across which gas diffuses, the surface area available for gas exchange, the diffusivity of the gas, the pulmonary capillary blood volume and the time factor for the gas to combine with haemoglobin. This latter can be negated when using carbon monoxide due to its rapid combination with haemoglobin. Therefore, any abnormalities detected can be attributed to either a problem with the lungs or an insufficient pulmonary capillary blood volume.

Fraction of expired nitric oxide (airway inflammation)

Fractional exhaled nitric oxide (FeNO) is recognised by the National Institute for Health and Care Excellence (NICE) as an important tool in the detection of airway inflammation, particularly in asthma. Detection of high levels of FeNO predominantly suggests the presence of eosinophilic inflammation, but FeNO levels can be high in other types of airway inflammation. NO itself is derived from the amino acid L-arginine in a process catalysed by three forms of the enzyme NO synthase (NOS). NO production can be in response to airway inflammation, but it is also released to regulate airway function. The inducible form of the enzyme (iNOS) can be induced by proinflammatory cytokines, such as tumour necrosis factor-α, interferon-γ and IL-1β. It has also been suggested that IL-13 upregulates the iNOS gene and protein expression in epithelial cells, leading to increased levels of FeNO.

FeNO measurements can be used to assess the presence of airway inflammation but can also be utilised in assessing the effectiveness of any treatment intervention provided, such as a course of oral corticosteroids. The manoeuvre required to assess levels of FeNO is relatively simple. It requires a maximal inspiration, sometimes through an NO scrubber, which captures any ambient NO, followed by a controlled expiration at a set expiration rate for approximately 10 seconds. A result is usually available between 30 and 90 seconds after the manoeuvre is completed.

Mouth pressure

The measurement of respiratory muscles can be conducted in a variety of ways during rest and exercise, as indicated by a recent ERS repot (Laveneziana et al., 2019). In most cases, the direct measurement of respiratory muscle strength is not feasible, as it requires invasive protocols, expensive equipment and skilled respiratory physiologists. Static mouth pressure is a recognised simple assessment of global respiratory muscle strength (ATS/ERS, 2002). Mouth pressure can be measured during either the inspiratory (PI_{max}) or expiratory (PE_{max}) phase. Most investigations for respiratory muscle strength are focused on the inspiratory respiratory muscles. Practitioners may choose to ask clients to carry out maximal inspiratory pressure3 assessments to investigate for weak inspiratory muscle function, inform respiratory muscle training programmes or assess the fatigue of respiratory muscles from various forms of exercise.

The measurement of mouth pressure requires the participant to be fully motivated to perform a maximal effort. The measurement is taken using a respiratory pressure meter. PI_{max} is usually measured at residual volume and PE_{max} at TLC. At these volumes participants maximally inspire or expire accordingly against an occluded opening. Efforts should be separated by at least 60 s and continue until the participant has reached a plateau in peak values. Participants should be coached between efforts to ensure their technique is good and they are attempting to provide their best effort. From experience it usually requires the participant to perform between five and ten efforts. The maximum value of the manoeuvres should be recorded if they vary by less than 10% from the second and third best efforts.

Feedback of results to practitioners, patients, coaches and athletes

The results of the assessments are in most cases available as soon as the assessment is complete. Therefore, it is possible, if required, to inform the client of the test result at the time of the assessment. In some cases where a direct referral has been made by the client, this is appropriate. However, in many cases the practitioner may report the findings to the clinical practitioner who made the referral. The advantages of reporting results to the referring clinical practitioner include:

- Consistency for the client in the messages they receive about their respiratory care;
- The results may be part of a larger clinical assessment of the client.

Regardless of whether the results are relayed immediately or via referring practitioner, it is good practice to report the following from these assessments:

- Report results from assessments that were conducted in accordance with appropriate guidelines;
- Include predicted values as well as actual values for each variable reported;
- When undertaking diagnostic assessments, report whether diagnostic thresholds have been met (e.g., has FEV_1 fallen greater than 10% from baseline following exercise challenge?).

Although as physiological practitioners we can run and interpret the respiratory assessments, we must be aware of the limits of our scope of practice and not draw conclusions on a diagnosis of respiratory disease. Physiological assessments are an excellent aid to determining a differential diagnosis, but other information is pieced together, such as a clinical history or imaging results if available, by an appropriately trained and experienced professional before a definitive diagnosis can be made. We can interpret the results of the test, but the diagnosis of any potential condition must be made by the medical practitioner who is overseeing the care of the client/patient. Building a good relationship between the physiological and medical practitioner team is therefore crucial to ensure interpretation of assessments is communicated effectively.

References

Dickinson, J. W. and Hull, J. H. (2020). *Complete Guide to Respiratory Care in Athletes*. Abingdon: Routledge.

Dickinson, J. W., McConnell, A. and Whyte, G. (2011). Diagnosis of exercise-induced bronchoconstriction: Eucapnic voluntary hyperpnoea challenges identify previously undiagnosed elite athletes with exercise-induced bronchoconstriction. *British Journal of Sports Medicine*, 45, 1126–1131.

Dickinson, J. W., Whyte, G. P., McConnell, A. K. and Harries, M. (2006). Screening elite winter athletes for exercise induced asthma: A comparison of three challenge methods. *British Journal of Sports Medicine*, 40, 179–182.

Hallstrand, T. S., Leuppi, J. D., Joos, G., Hall, G. L., Carlsen, K. H., Kaminsky, D. A., Coates, A. L., Cockcroft, D. W., Culver, B. H., Diamant, Z., Gauvreau, G. M., Horvath, I., de Jongh, F. H. C., Laube, B. L., Sterk, P. J. and Wanger, J. (2018). American Thoracic Society (ATS)/European Respiratory Society (ERS) bronchoprovocation testing task force: ERS technical standard on bronchial challenge testing: Pathophysiology and methodology of indirect airway challenge testing. *European Respiratory Journal*, 52(5), 1801033.

Holzer, K., Anderson, S. D., Chan, H. K. and Douglass, J. (2003). Mannitol as a challenge test to identify exercise-induced bronchoconstriction in elite athletes. *American Journal of Respiratory Critical Care Medicine*, 167, 534–537.

Laveneziana, P., Albuquerque, A., Aliverti, A., Babb, T., Barreiro, E., Dres, M., Dubé, B. P., Fauroux, B., Gea, J., Guenette, J. A., Hudson, A. L., Kabitz, H. J., Laghi, F., Langer, D., Luo, Y. M., Neder, J. A., O'Donnell, D., Polkey, M. I., Rabinovich, R. A., Rossi, A., Series, F., Similowski, T., Spengler, C. M., Vogiatzis, I. and Verges, S. (2019). ERS statement on respiratory muscle testing at rest and during exercise. *European Respiratory Journal*, 53(6), 1801214.

Rundell, K. W., Im, J., Mayers, L. B., Wilber, R. L., Szmedra, L. and Schmitz, H. R. (2001). Self-reported symptoms and exercise-induced asthma in the elite athlete. *Medicine and Science in Sports and Exercise*, 33, 208–213.

Sylvester, K. P., Clayton, N., Cliff, I., Hepple, M., Kendrick, A., Kirkby, J., Miller, M., Moore, A., Rafferty, G. F., O'Reilly, L., Shakespeare, J., Smith, L., Watts, T., Bucknall, M. and Butterfield, K. (2020). ARTP statement on pulmonary function testing 2020. *BMJ Open Respiratory Research*, 7(1), e000575.

3.4 Surface anthropometry

Susan C. Lennie

Anthropometry is defined as 'measurement of the human body'. Surface anthropometry may therefore be defined as the science of acquiring and utilising surface dimensional measurements which describe the human phenotype. Measurements of mass, stature, skeletal breadths, segment lengths, girths and skinfolds are used, either as raw data or derived ratios or predicted values to describe human size, proportions, shape, composition and symmetry, or to infer aspects of nutritional status or physical performance. Historically, anthropometry draws from diverse disciplines, including anatomy, physiology, nutrition and medicine, and the multiplicity of methodologies which prevail may cause some confusion for the exercise scientist in practice today and impact upon the comparability of data. The current definitive guide for all anthropometric procedures is the International Society for the Advancement of Kinanthropometry (ISAK) standards manual (Esparza-Ros et al., 2019). The purpose of this chapter is to summarise key principles and methods for measuring stature and mass and the most commonly used skinfolds and girths.

Measurement prerequisites

For all measurements, subjects require appropriate information in advance, and informed written consent should be obtained. Anthropometry requires a spacious (minimum 3 m × 3 m) well-illuminated area, affording privacy. Room temperature should ensure subject comfort. Subjects should present for measurement in suitable apparel, recovered from previous exercise, fully hydrated and voided. Clothing should conform to the natural contours of the skin and allow easy access for landmarking and measurement. For males, running shorts or swimwear is ideal, and for females, either a two-piece swimming costume or running shorts and a sports top which exposes the shoulders and abdominal area are suitable. One-piece swimwear, rowing suits or leotards are *not* suitable. Some subjects may prefer a loose-fitting shirt which can be lifted to access measurement sites. All measurements (except hip girth, which is measured over close-fitting clothing for reasons of modesty) are performed on clean, dry, unbroken skin. Cultural differences may preclude the acquisition of some or all measurements in some subjects. Measurement of females or children by male anthropometrists requires particular sensitivity and the individual's entitlement to a chaperone. It is always advisable to have another adult (preferably female) present in such circumstances (refer to Chapter 1.4).

Recommended equipment

Stadiometer – (e.g., Holtain, Crosswell, Crymych, UK, or SECA, Birmingham, UK) mounted on a wall or stand with sliding headboard and accurate to 0.1 cm.

Weighing scales – calibrated and graduated to 100 g, suggested range can be up to 150 kg (e.g., SECA, Birmingham, UK).

Skinfold callipers – Harpenden (British Indicators, c/o Assist Creative Resources, Wrexham, UK) calibrated annually to 10 g·mm^2, scale to 80 mm in new models, 40 mm in old ones, which can be read to 0.1 mm by interpolation. Holtain (Crosswell, Crymych, UK) callipers are of similar quality and can be used with equal precision.

Anthropometric tape – flexible metal tape, no wider than 7 mm, with automatic retraction to an enclosed case. A blank 'stub' extending several centimetres beyond the zero line is required. The Rosscraft anthropometric tape (Rosscraft Innovations Inc., Vancouver, Canada) is a modified version of the Lufkin W606PM (Cooper Industries, USA). Both can be read to 0.1 cm and are recommended.

Segmometer – A flexible metal tape with rigid sliding branches for identifying lengths and landmark locations, e.g., Cescorf Segmometer (Cescorf, Porto Alegre, Brazil) or UWA Segmometer (University of Western Australia, Crawley, Australia), read to 0.1 cm.

Anthropometric box – made from plywood or a strong fibre-board equivalent capable of supporting an individual who may weigh 150 kg. The box should be 30 cm × 40 cm × 50 m to facilitate ease of measuring subjects of differing size, with a cut-out at the base for the subject's feet to be positioned during some measures. Commercial anthropometric boxes are available: Anthropometric Box (Scullion Bruce, Aberdeen, UK) or Anthropobox (CartonLab, Murcia, Spain).

Procedures

Descriptions of anthropometric techniques may appear simple but require a high level of technical skill to ensure accuracy and repeatability. Care should be taken at the preparatory stage to confirm calibration of equipment, subject positioning and measurement site location. During measurement, anthropometrists should read values within their line of sight to avoid data error arising from parallax.

Stretch stature is measured to 0.1 cm without footwear and with the head in the Frankfort plane (orbitale and tragion are horizontally aligned). The heels are together, and the back should be in contact with the scale of the stadiometer. The subject inspires for measurement, and the recorder brings down the headboard to compress the hair whilst the anthropometrist applies upward traction to the head to compensate for diurnal variation.

Arm span is measured to 0.1 cm, with the heels, buttocks, upper back and dorsal aspect of the arms against a wall. The arms are stretched maximally and horizontally at 90 degrees, and the measurement is taken at maximal inspiration.

Body mass is measured to 0.1 kg. The subject wears exercise apparel or light clothing but no footwear. If nude mass is required, clothing can be weighed separately. Measurements should be taken after voiding and 12 h after food, or record the time of day to consider the impact of diurnal variation.

Skinfolds

Skeletal landmarks (bony locations defining skinfold measurement sites) are located via palpation of overlying soft tissue or measurement from a palpable site. Since some measurements vary considerably over a short distance, landmarking the correct site is essential for reproducible measurements (Hume and Marfell-Jones, 2008). Landmarks should be located generally and then released. They should then be re-located specifically before marking, as the skin can move several centimetres in relation to underlying bone. Skinfold locations are marked with a cross, with two lines intersecting at right angles or other similar symbol where there may be cultural concerns. A longer line should represent the orientation of the skinfold, and the shorter line should define the finger and thumb placement. Bony edges are commonly marked with a short (0.5-cm) line, while points (e.g., the inferior tip of the scapula) are marked with a dot, from which linear measurements are made. Measurements should be made on the *right* side of the body, unless prevented by injury; variations in protocol should be recorded. Left-handed subjects may have greater muscle mass on the left limb, in which case measurements on both sides can be recorded. Skinfold locations are described in Table 3.4.1.

Subjects are encouraged to relax their muscles before measurement to reduce discomfort and improve reproducibility. Ensure the skin is dry and unbroken and the landmark is clearly visible. The anthropometrist's left hand approaches the subject's skin surface at 90 degrees. The skinfold is raised at the marked site, with the shorter line visible at the edge of the anthropometrist's forefinger and thumb. The fold is grasped firmly in the required orientation, following natural cleavage lines of the skin and raised far enough (but no farther) so the fold has parallel sides. Palpation helps avoid incorporating underlying muscle into the grasp. The near edge of the calliper blades are applied to the raised fold 1 cm away from the thumb and forefinger, at a depth of mid-fingernail.

The callipers are held at 90 degrees to the skinfold and, with the skinfold held at all times, the spring pressure is released, allowing compression with the full force of the jaws, and the measurement value is recorded at 2 s. In the case of large skinfolds, the needle is likely to be moving at this time, but the value is recorded nonetheless. The callipers are removed before the skinfold is released. Measurements should be made in series – moving from one site to the next until the entire protocol is complete – and repeated thereafter according to the measurement proforma.

Table 3.4.1 Skinfold measurements

Skinfold	Location and Landmarking	Orientation	Body Position for Measurement
Triceps[a]	Mid-point of a straight line between the acromiale and the radiale on the posterior aspect of the arm	Vertical	Standing; shoulder slightly externally rotated
Subscapular	2 cm lateral and 2 cm inferior to the inferior angle of the scapula	Oblique – ~45-degree angle laterally	Standing
Biceps[a]	Mid-point level of a straight line between the acromiale and the radiale on the anterior aspect of the arm	Vertical	Standing; shoulder slightly externally rotated
Iliac crest	Immediately superior to the crest of the ilium, on the ilio-axilla line	Near horizontal	Standing; right arm placed across torso
Supraspinale	The intersection of a horizontal line drawn from the crest of the ilium, with a line joining the anterior superior iliac spine and the anterior axillary fold	Oblique	Standing
Abdominal	5 cm lateral of the mid-point of the umbilicus	Vertical	Standing
Thigh[a]	Mid-point of the perpendicular distance between the inguinal crease at the mid-line of the thigh and the mid-point of the posterior border of the patella when seated with the knee flexed to 90 degrees	Longitudinal	Sitting with leg extended and foot supported, the subject extends the knee and clasps hands under hamstrings and lifts gently for measurement
Medial calf	The most medial aspect of the calf, at the level of maximum girth, with subject standing and weight evenly distributed	Vertical	Standing, foot on box, with knee at 90 degrees

Note: [a] These sites ideally require a wide-spreading calliper or segmometer to locate, since curvature of the skin surface affects site location if a tape is used.

Girths

A cross-handed technique is used with the stub held in the left hand and the case in the right hand. Approaching from the side of the subject, the stub is passed around the body segment, grasped by the right hand and then passed back to the left hand, which pulls it to the appropriate tension. The middle fingers of both hands can then be used for 'pinning' the tape and moving it a short distance up or down, maintaining its orientation 90 degrees to the long axis of the segment. There should be no visible indentation of the skin at the measurement. In the case of maximal measurements, it is necessary to measure lesser measurements superior and inferior to the final measurement site. If the skin surface is concave, the tape spans the concavity in a straight line. For torso girths, limb position may influence the result, so care should be taken to follow standard protocols (Lennie et al., 2013), and measurements should be made at the end of a normal expiration (Table 3.4.2).

Measurement error

The *mean* of duplicate or the *median* of triplicate measures (when the first two measures differ by more than 5% for skinfolds and 1% for other measures) is recommended to minimise errors resulting from technical variation. Error magnitude varies with the recorder, the measurement type and site and should be reported as the *technical error of measurement (TEM)* and expressed as a percentage of the measurement value (Perini et al., 2005).

Table 3.4.2 Girth measurements

Girth	Location	Body Position	Notes
Chest	At level of mid-sternum	Arms abducted slightly	Measure at the end of a normal expiration
Waist	Narrowest circumference between thorax and pelvis	Arms folded, fingertips lightly touching shoulders	Mid-point between iliac crest and tenth rib, if no obvious narrowing
Hip	At the level of maximum posterior protuberance of buttocks	Relaxed, feet together	Measure from the side, over clothing
Upper arm	Mid acromiale-radiale	Arm abducted slightly, elbow extended	
Arm flexed and tensed	Peak of contracted biceps brachii	Arm forward at 90 degrees horizontally, elbow flexed at 90 degrees and forearm supinated	Measure at maximal contraction
Forearm	Maximum	Shoulder slightly flexed, elbow extended	
Mid-thigh	Mid trochanterion – tibiale laterale level	Weight equally distributed	
Calf	Maximum	Weight equally distributed	

TEM $[(x_2x_1)^2] \cdot 2n^1$

% TEM $100 \cdot TEM \cdot m^1$

where x_1 and x_2 are replicate pairs of measures, n is the number of pairs and m is the mean value for that measure across the sample.

The TEM is generally used to determine intra-observer error but can also be used to express inter-observer error where two anthropometrists are independently measuring the same subjects.

For serial measurements, a statistical basis for detecting real change should be included. Since the TEM equates to the standard error of a single measurement, overlapping standard errors indicate no significant change in serial measures – either at the 68% (for 1SE) or 95% (for 2SE) level. Clearly, experienced anthropometrists with low TEMs are several times more likely to detect real change than others.

Interpretation of anthropometric data

The conversion of raw data into indices may be justified in terms of fat patterning (Stewart, 2003) (skinfold ratios), corrected girths (Martin et al., 1990), proportions (the ratio of segment lengths) or anthropometric somatotype (Heath and Carter, 1967). Corrected girths involve subtracting the skinfold multiplied by pi from the limb girth and are a useful surrogate for muscularity. Predicting tissue masses of fat (López-Taylor et al., 2018) or muscle (González-Mendoza et al., 2019) has obvious appeal but is problematic (Stewart and Ackland, 2018). Numerous methodological assumptions, such as tissue density, govern the conversion of linear surface measurements into tissue mass, and sample specificity restricts the utility of many equations. If used, the same prediction formulas should be used on all occasions and should be accompanied by the standard error of the estimate or confidence limits, as well as total error of prediction equations (Stewart and Hannan, 2000). The use of raw anthropometric data, such as sum of skinfolds, is becoming more accepted as a surrogate to quantifying tissue mass (Ackland et al., 2012) and is to be encouraged. For example, Vaquero-Cristóbal et al. (2020) reported positive moderate to high correlations ($r = 0.613–0.849$) between fat mass prediction equations and the sums of six and eight skinfolds. Sex- and sport-specific anthropometric reference data are limited (Santos et al., 2014); however, smaller research studies may provide adequate comparisons in specific situations for the exercise scientist in practice.

Conclusion

Surface anthropometry plays an important role in the estimation of body composition and identifying the effect of training regimens. Its portability, together with improvements in defining procedures and control of error, maintain its relevance despite the emergence of newer imaging technologies. Selection of appropriate measures, equipment and attention to measurement procedures is essential to maximising accuracy, reliability and repeatability of results.

References

Ackland, T. R., Lohman, T. G., Sundgot-Borgen, J., Maughan, R. J., Meyer, N. L., Stewart, A. D. and Muller, W. (2012). Current status of body composition assessment in sport. *Sports Medicine*, 42, 227–240.

Esparza-Ros, R., Vaquero-Cristóbal, R. and Marfell-Jones, M. (2019). *International Standards for Anthropometric Assessment*. Spain: Catholic University San Antonio of Murcia.

González-Mendoza, R. G., Gaytán-González, A., Jiménez-Alvarado, J. A., Villegas-Balcázar, M., Jáuregui-Ulloa, E. E., Torres-Naranjo, F. and López-Taylor, J. R. (2019). Accuracy of anthropometric equations to estimate DXA-derived skeletal muscle mass in professional male soccer players. *Journal of Sports Medicine*, 2019. https://doi.org/10.1155/2019/4387636

Heath, B. H. and Carter, J. E. L. (1967). A modified somatotype method. *American Journal of Physical Anthropology*, 27, 57–74.

Hume, P. and Marfell-Jones, M. (2008). The importance of accurate site location for skinfold measurement. *Journal of Sport Sciences*, 26, 1333–1340.

Lennie, S. C., Amofa-Diatuo, T., Nevill, A. and Stewart, A. D. (2013). Protocol variations in arm position influence the magnitude of waist girth. *Journal of Sport Sciences*, 31, 1353–1358.

López-Taylor, J. R., González-Mendoza, R. G., Gaytán-González, A., Jiménez-Alvarado, J. A., Villegas-Balcázar, M., Jáuregui-Ulloa, E. E. and Torres-Naranjo, F. (2018). Accuracy of anthropometric equations for estimating body fat in professional male soccer players compared with DXA. *Journal of Sports Medicine*, 2018, 6843792. https://doi.org/10.1155/2018/6843792

Martin, A. D., Spenst, L. F., Drinkwater, D. T. and Clarys, J. P. (1990). Anthropometric estimation of muscle mass in men. *Medicine and Science in Sports and Exercise*, 22, 729–733.

Perini, R. A., de Oliveira, G. L., dos Santos Ornellas, J. and de Oliveira, F. P. (2005). Technical error of measurement in anthropometry. *Revista Brasileira de Medicina do Esporte*, 11, 86–90.

Santos, D. A., Dawson, J. A., Matias, C. N., Rocha, P. M., Minderico, C. S., Allison, D. B., Sardinha, L. B. and Silva, A. M. (2014). Reference values for body composition and anthropometric measurements in athletes. *PLoS One*, 9(5), e97846.

Stewart, A. D. (2003). Anthropometric fat patterning in male and female subjects. In T. Reilly and M. Marfell-Jones (eds.), *Kinanthropometry VIII*, pp. 195–202. London: Routledge.

Stewart, A. D. and Ackland, T. (2018). Anthropometry in physical performance and health. In H. C. Lukaski (ed.), *Body Composition: Health and Performance in Exercise and Sport*, pp. 89–108. Boca Raton: CRC Press.

Stewart, A. D. and Hannan, W. J. (2000). Prediction of fat and fat free mass in male athletes using dual x-ray absorptiometry as the reference method. *Journal of Sports Sciences*, 18, 263–274.

Vaquero-Cristóbal, R., Albaladejo-Saura, M., Luna-Badachi, A. E. and Esparza-Ros, R. (2020). Differences in fat mass estimation formulas in physically active adult population and relationship with sums of skinfolds. *International Journal of Environmental Research and Public Health*, 17, 7777.

3.5 Functional screening

Mike Duncan, Stuart Elwell, and Mark Lyons

Functional movement screening is a process that is highly debated and has become widely used within the sport and exercise sciences with both general and athletic populations (Cook et al., 2010). This chapter will provide an overview of functional screening to guide sport and exercise scientists in their selection and use of screening tools in practice. Functional movement screening is defined by the International Movement Screening and Interventions Group (IMSIG, 2016) as the quantitative or qualitative observation of a single movement and/or a composite battery of movements. Such a broad focus has resulted in numerous movement screens being developed that assess different aspects of movement, often with varying degrees of validity and reliability. It is therefore important for sport and exercise scientists to understand the main forms of functional screening tests and the key challenges when employing them with both general and athletic populations. Functional screening tests can broadly be distinguished into two types of testing: quantitative movement tests (QMTs) and movement quality tests (MQTs).

Quantitative movement tests: QMTs are more commonly considered akin to physical fitness tests and include the quantitative measurement of strength and power, often through multi-joint movements. Tests such as the Triple Hop Test, Y-Balance Test and the 6ft Timed Up and Go Test constitute QMTs where outcomes tend to be continuous, such as distance covered and repetitions completed. QMTs are sometimes referred to as physical performance or functional fitness tests.

Movement quality tests: MQTs are more commonly considered 'functional screens' and include identification and rating of movement patterns. This includes compensations, asymmetries and efficiency of movement through transitional (e.g., sit to stand) or dynamic (e.g., hopping, landing) movement tasks. Outcomes from MQTs tend to provide a classification of movement quality using some form of scoring system. These typically categorise movement as dichotomous (e.g., movement present vs. not present or pass/fail) or trichotomous (e.g., poor/fair/good) classifications. Some MQTs have more than three categories, and others such as the Functional Movement Screen use a numerical tetrachotomous classification applied to a series of different movements, which can then be summed to represent overall functional movement quality. For the majority of MQTs, specific training in administration and scoring of the different functional screens available is required.

DOI: 10.4324/9781003045281-16

Why employ functional screening?

Functional screens have been employed for a variety of reasons, and while marker-based motion capture and electromyography have become the gold standard for evaluating movement patterns and biomechanical musculoskeletal deficits in sport and exercise science (Kraus et al., 2014), functional screens tend to be used in real-world settings to provide an appraisal of movement quality. Numerous functional screens have been developed for use in athletic and general populations, with the most widely used being the Functional Movement Screen (FMS) (Cook et al., 2010) and Landing Error Scoring System (LESS) (Padua et al., 2009). These two screens will be outlined in greater depth later.

Irrespective of which functional screen is selected, they are most commonly employed for one or more reasons, including but not limited to:

- Determine movement quality;
- Identify risk (of injury);
- Guide management and prevention strategies.

Commonly used functional screening tools

Functional Movement Screen

The FMS, developed by Cook et al. (1998), was developed under the assumption that strength, movement, flexibility and stability are prerequisites for optimal athletic performance and is one of the most widely used functional screens worldwide. The FMS comprises seven movements that, combined, provide a screening tool to assess functional mobility and postural stability in different settings without locomotion. The FMS involves seven tests that examine three different levels of movement difficulty. The squat, lunge and hurdle step tests are described as higher-level patterns which are proposed to examine the three essential foot positions taken up in sport. The rotary stability and press-up tests are known as transitionary patterns and predominantly assess triplanar and sagittal stability. Finally, the primitive mobility patterns of the body are assessed by the active straight-leg raise and the shoulder mobility tests (Cook et al., 2010). The tests within the FMS can be scored individually or summed to reflect a composite functional movement score (Cook et al., 2006). Performance of each test is rated on a scale of 0 to 3 by an assessor. A score of 0 is given if pain occurs during the test, 1 if the participant cannot perform the movement, 2 if the participant can perform the movement but with some form of compensation and 3 if the movement is performed correctly by the participant (Cook et al., 2006). The maximum score attainable in the FMS is 21, although more recently, a 100-point scoring scale has been developed (Butler et al., 2012), which is suggested to be more sensitive and useful in research contexts, where the 21-point scale may be more practical in applied situations. Within the FMS, a score of 3 is taken as 'correct' movement, and anything less than this, per individual test, indicates a 'compensatory movement pattern' which leads to individuals 'sacrificing efficient movements for inefficient ones' (Cook et al., 2006).

Current research suggests performance on the FMS is related to physical activity and obesity in children (Duncan and Stanley, 2012), injury prevalence in professional athletes (Bushman et al., 2016), fitness test performance in military recruits (Lisman et al., 2013) and performance improvement in track and field athletes (Chapman et al., 2014). An arbitrary cut-off value of 14 in the FMS has been associated with greater/lower injury risk but is controversial in the literature (Monaco and Schoenfeld, 2019), and the sensitivity and specificity of the FMS in predicting injury have been questioned (Monaco and Schoenfeld, 2019). The FMS demonstrates good inter- and intra-rater reliability (Bonazza et al., 2017, inter-rater intraclass correlation coefficient [ICC] = 0.84; intra-rater ICC = 0.81), but its validity in relation to injury prediction is questionable (Monaco and Schoenfeld, 2019). This has led to recommendations that the FMS is useful and valid as a screen to assess the quality of human movement (not injury) and should be employed by practitioners as such (Monaco and Schoenfeld, 2019).

The Landing Error Scoring System

The LESS was developed to provide a standardised instrument to identify potentially high-risk movement patterns ('errors') during a jump-landing manoeuvre (Padua et al., 2009). The jump-landing task includes both vertical and horizontal movements as participants jump forward off a 30-cm-high box to a distance equal to 50% of their height away from the box. On landing, they immediately rebound for a maximal vertical jump with instruction to jump as high as they can once they land from the box. Trials are video-recorded from the frontal and sagittal plane for subsequent scoring.

The LESS score is simply a count of landing technique 'errors' on a range of readily observable items of human movement. A higher LESS score indicates poor technique in landing from a jump; a lower LESS score indicates better jump-landing technique. There are 17 scored items in the LESS (see Padua et al., 2009, for operational definitions and scoring details of each item) derived from previous research that identified specific movements that may contribute to increased risk of injury, particularly anterior cruciate ligament (ACL) injury (Padua et al., 2009). Items 1–15 are scored dichotomically as either 1 or 0. Items 16 and 17 score values 0, 1 or 2 depending on joint displacement and overall impression of technique, respectively. Scores of <5 are regarded as 'good' and assume low risk for ACL injury. A maximal score of 19 can be reached for exceptionally poor performance.

Studies to date (Padua et al., 2009; Onate et al., 2010) report good to excellent inter- and intra-rater reliability for the screen (inter-rater kappa = 0.459–0.875 [Onate et al., 2010], ICC = 0.84 [Padua et al., 2009], intra-rater ICC = 0.84–0.91 [Padua et al., 2009; Onate et al., 2010]). There is conflicting and limited evidence, however, related to the ability of the LESS to predict injury, with some studies finding no relationship between LESS scores and ACL injury risk (Smith et al.,

2013) and others reporting significantly poorer LESS scores in athletes sustaining ACL injuries over a season compared to uninjured athletes (Padua et al., 2015).

Finally, Everard et al. (2017), while examining the relationship between the FMS and LESS, found a significant moderate correlation between FMS and LESS scores but poor shared variance. Performing well in one of the screens, therefore, does not necessarily equate to performing well in the other, and both screens should not be used interchangeably.

Conclusion

Functional screening, as a process, provides effective means to assess movement quality and outcomes in general and athletic populations. There are validated and reliable tools such as the FMS and the LESS that can be used to determine movement quality and guide management of training programmes and pre-/rehabilitation. However, the evidence relating to the ability of functional screens to be a sole means of determining injury risk is less robust, and functional screens should instead be used as a collective of filters to qualify relative risk of injury with physical activity.

References

Bonazza, N. A., Smuin, D., Onks, C. A., Silvis, M. L. and Dhawan, A. (2017). Reliability, validity, and injury predictive value of the functional movement screen: A systematic review and meta-analysis. *American Journal of Sports Medicine*, 45, 725–732.

Bushman, T. T., Grier, T. L. and Canham-Chervak, M. (2016). The functional movement screen and injury risk: Association and predictive value in active men. *American Journal of Sports Medicine*, 44(2), 297–304.

Butler, R. J., Plisky, P. J. and Kiesel, K. B. (2012). Interrater reliability of videotaped performance on the functional movement screen using the 100-point scoring scale. *Athletic Training and Sports Health Care*, 4(3), 103–109.

Chapman, R. F., Laymon, A. S. and Arnold, T. (2014). Functional movement scores and longitudinal performance outcomes in elite track and field athletes. *International Journal of Sports Physiology and Performance*, 9(2), 203–211. https://doi.org/10.1123/ijspp.2012-0329

Cook, G., Burton, L., Fields, K. and Kiesel, K. (1998). *The Functional Movement Screen*. Danville, VA: Athletic Testing Services Inc.

Cook, G., Burton, L. and Hoogenboom, B. (2006). Pre-participation screening: The use of fundamental movements as an assessment of function: Part 1. *North American Journal of Sports Physical Therapy*, 1, 62.

Cook, G., Hoogenboom, B., Burton, L., Plisky, P. and Rose, G. (2010). *Movement*. Santa Cruz, CA, USA: On Target Publications.

Duncan, M. J. and Stanley, M. (2012). Functional movement is negatively associated with weight status and positively associated with physical activity in British primary school children. *Journal of Obesity*, 7244, 697563.

Everard, E. M., Harrison, A. J. and Lyons, M. (2017). Examining the relationship between the functional movement screen and the landing error scoring system in an active, male collegiate population. *Journal of Strength and Conditioning Research*, 31(5), 1265–1272.

IMSIG. (2016). *Working definitions of movement screening* [WWW document]. https://www.sportsarthritisresearchuk.org/international-movement-screening-and-interventions-group-imsig/working-definitions-of-movement-screening.aspx (accessed 25 October 2021).

Kraus, K., Schutz, E., Taylor, W. R. and Doyscher, R. (2014). Efficacy of the functional movement screen: A review. *Journal of Strength and Conditioning Research*, 28(12), 3571–3584.

Lisman, P., O'Connor, F. G., Deuster, P. A. and Knapik, J. J. (2013). Functional movement screen and aerobic fitness predict injuries in military training. *Medicine and Science in Sports and Exercise*, 45(4), 636–643.

Monaco, J.-T. and Schoenfeld, B. J. (2019). A review of the current literature on the utility of the functional movement screen as a screening tool to identify athletes' risk for injury. *Strength and Conditioning Journal*, 41, 17–23. https://doi.org/10.1519/SSC.0000000000000481

Onate, J., Cortes, N. and Welch, C. (2010). Expert versus novice inter-rater reliability and criterion validity of the landing error scoring system. *Journal of Sports Rehabilitation*, 19(1), 41–48.

Padua, D. A., DiStefano, L. J., Beutler, A. I., de la Motte, S. J., DiStefano, M. J. and Marshall, S. W. (2015). The landing error scoring system as a screening tool for an anterior cruciate ligament injury-prevention program in elite-youth soccer athletes. *Journal of Athletic Training*, 50, 589–595. https://doi.org/10.4085/1062-6050-50.1.10

Padua, D. A., Marshall, S. W., Boling, M. C., Thigpen, C. A., Garrett, W. E. and Beutler, A. I. (2009). The Landing Error Scoring System (LESS) is a valid and reliable clinical assessment tool of jump-landing biomechanics: The JUMP-ACL study. *American Journal of Sports Medicine*, 37(10), 1996–2002.

Smith, C. A., Chimera, N. J., Wright, N. J. and Warren, M. (2013). Interrater and intrarater reliability of the functional movement screen. *Journal of Strength and Conditioning Research*, 27, 982–987. https://doi.org/10.1519/JSC.0b013e3182606df2

3.6 Respiratory gas analysis

Simon Marwood and Richie P. Goulding

Respiratory gas analysis is a cornerstone of physiological testing procedures, perhaps most commonly for the determination of pulmonary gas exchange (PGE) variables, particularly oxygen uptake ($\dot{V}O_2$) and carbon dioxide production ($\dot{V}CO_2$). However, end-tidal gas tensions (PETO$_2$, PETCO$_2$), expired minute ventilation ($\dot{V}_E$) and derived variables such as the respiratory exchange ratio (RER) and ventilatory equivalents ($\dot{V}_E/\dot{V}O_2$, $\dot{V}_E/\dot{V}CO_2$) are widely applied.

Collectively, these measurements provide parameters of human function that can be used to determine metabolic rate, substrate oxidation, exercise economy/efficiency, gas exchange thresholds, gas exchange kinetics and maximal $\dot{V}O_2$. In turn, these parameters of human function can be utilised to evaluate performance, health and causes of exercise intolerance. The purpose of this chapter is to outline key aspects for ensuring the accuracy of respiratory gas data collection and describe methods of data analysis for the subsequent derivation of parameters of physiological function (see supplementary material).

Douglas bag technique

The Douglas bag technique incorporates a mouth piece (requiring a nose clip) or face mask, attached via a sample tube to a 100- to 200-L polyvinyl chloride sealed 'bag' which captures the expirate via a one-way valve operated by the practitioner. Two one-way valves at the mouth ensure flow of air from the environment to the mouth and from the mouth to the bag. The discrete and relatively prolonged duration of expired gas collections required for the Douglas bag method indicates that this method is best utilised for steady-state gas exchange measurements. Practitioners should be aware of the significant delay (exercise intensities above the gas exchange threshold [GET]) or lack of (exercise intensities above critical power [CP]) achievement of a steady state during high-intensity exercise (Whipp and Ward, 1992). However, this approach may be reasonably utilised during incremental exercise, assuming the underlying speed or power output does not continue to change during the period of expired gas collection.

The supplementary material (Section 1) details the calculations for $\dot{V}_E$, $\dot{V}O_2$ and $\dot{V}CO_2$, which provide a basis for understanding error in respiratory gas analysis using the Douglas bag technique. Accordingly, sources of error for the

DOI: 10.4324/9781003045281-17

Douglas bag method include determination of the expired gas fractions, volume and duration of gas collection. The entire apparatus should thus be checked for leaks before commencing measurements with the expirate from a whole number of breaths collected. Timing of gas collection may be improved by the installation of time switches on the Douglas bag valves. The expirate should be analysed immediately upon collection to avoid volume losses and contamination.

Error in the determination of gas fractions (FeO_2 and $FeCO_2$) is highly influential in the calculation of $\dot{V}O_2$ and $\dot{V}CO_2$. A 1% overestimation of FeO_2 leads to a ~3%–8% underestimation of $\dot{V}O_2$ for typical moderate- to severe-intensity exercise (respectively), whereas a 1% overestimation in $FeCO_2$ leads to a ~0.2%–0.3% underestimation for $\dot{V}O_2$ and a ~1% overestimation for $\dot{V}CO_2$ (Sandals, 2003). The extent of the error for $\dot{V}O_2$ is a function of using FeO_2 twice in its calculation.

Consequently, prior to undertaking measurements, the Douglas bags should be evacuated of any residual air to avoid contamination of the sample. However, air remains within the non-compressible components (i.e., neck, valve). Minimising the volume of these components is desirable; moreover, by knowing the volume of the non-compressible components and flushing them with a gas of known content (e.g., inspired air) prior to gas evacuation and subsequent collection, it is possible to correct the measured FeO_2 for this residual volume:

$$cFeO_2 = \{mFeO_2(\dot{V}_E + V_{NC}) - V_{NC} * FiO_2\} / \dot{V}_E$$

($cFeO_2$ and $mFeO_2$: corrected and measured FeO_2, respectively; V_{NC}: volume of non-compressible components; FiO_2 could be replaced by another gas of known concentration such as the O_2 span calibration [see later]).

Alternatively, the collection of a few seconds of expired gas, followed by rapid flushing of the bag and valve through the collection ports, immediately prior to collection of the sample can similarly eliminate the error due to residual air in the Douglas bag.

Errors may also be made if it is assumed that inspired gas fractions in a laboratory are equivalent to those of atmospheric gases, especially if these are standardised to 0.2093 and 0.0003 for O_2 and CO_2, respectively, when values of 0.2095 and 0.0004 better represent precise measurement of atmospheric gases (Machta and Hughes, 1970; Keeling et al., 1995). Even in a well-ventilated laboratory with one participant and two practitioners, Sandals (2003) found the mean (95% confidence limits) for FiO_2 and $FiCO_2$ to be 0.20915 (±0.00035) and 0.0007 (±0.0003), respectively. These values translated into a systematic error of 0.18% and 0.99% for $\dot{V}O_2$ and $\dot{V}CO_2$, respectively, for typical heavy-intensity exercise when atmospheric conditions were otherwise assumed in the laboratory. The only way to correct for such systematic errors is either to determine average inspired gas fractions over a series of exercise tests in normal laboratory conditions or, preferably, determine inspired gas fractions for every test.

Calibration of the gas analyser is usually through a two-point (zero and span) approach for both O_2 and CO_2, with N_2 being used as the zero setting in both cases. For the O_2 span, either a gravimetrically prepared gas of known O_2 fraction should be used (recommended to be ~0.2 O_2) or the sampling of outside air set at

0.2095 O_2 on the gas analyser. In the latter case, sampling of laboratory air is not an adequate substitute (see earlier). For CO_2, a span calibration of 0.04 to 0.08 is typical, though the higher end of the range is recommended to place typical $FeCO_2$ values approximately at the mid-point of the span.

Accurate determination of the expirate volume is subject to error at the volume measuring device, the volume of gas removed for fractional composition analysis and the determination of ambient pressure and expirate temperature. Volume is typically determined 'offline' by evacuating the expirate through a dry gas meter. The dry gas meter should be calibrated across a range of known volumes reflective of the test conditions (i.e., exercise intensity range, mode, participant characteristics) delivered to the gas meter from the Douglas bag, which itself is filled with a known volume via a gas syringe. The flow rate on the gas meter during this process should match that used during normal testing and analysis. A regression equation can then be derived to correct future meter readings to actual volume. Similarly, the sample flow rate of the fractional gas analyser can be determined by filling a Douglas bag of known volume (using a gas syringe) and timing the emptying of the bag. A barometer with a resolution of 0.05 mmHg should be utilised, with regular accuracy checks performed (WMO, 1996). Temperature probes should have a resolution of 0.1°C; errors here have a cumulative effect since temperature is used twice in the conversion of ambient temperature pressure saturated (ATPS) to standard temperature pressure dry (STPD) (see supplementary material, Section 1). Table 3.6.1 shows potential sources of error, their degree of measurement precision with best-practice approaches as indicated in this chapter and the resultant outcome on the precision in $\dot{V}O_2$ for a 45-s collection of expirate during typical heavy-intensity exercise (Sandals, 2003).

The overall effect of precision of measurement on final $\dot{V}CO_2$ values is similar to that of $\dot{V}O_2$, with precision improving for higher exercise intensities and/or longer expirate sample durations (Sandals, 2003). During typical moderate-intensity exercise, precision is ~3% for a 30-s sample duration, improving to <1% during typical severe-intensity exercise with a sample duration of 45 s and above (Sandals, 2003). The duration of gas collection should therefore be considered in the context of the exercise intensity.

Table 3.6.1 Effect of measurement precision on the determined $\dot{V}O_2$ for typical heavy-intensity exercise with 45-s expirate collection

Measurement	Precision in Measurement	Precision in $\dot{V}O_2$ (%)
Expired gas fractions	± 0.0001*	0.34
Residual volume in Douglas bag	± 0.031 l	0.05
Volume for gas fraction analysis	± 0.007 L·min^1	0.11
Volume (with dry gas meter)	± 0.057 L	0.86
Ambient pressure (via barometer)	± 0.2 mmHg	0.03
Expired gas temperature (via thermistor probe)	± 0.2°C	0.10

*BOC Gases, New Jersey, USA

Breath-by-breath method

Commercial metabolic carts for respiratory gas analysis on a breath-by-breath basis typically incorporate a measurement of ventilatory flow (either via turbine, pitot tube, ultrasonic or variable orifice flowmeter) with simultaneous, continuous sampling of gas fractions by directing samples of expirate to gas analysers. The equipment for flow measurement, with attached sample tubes for gas fractions, is normally held in place using a full-face mask or other apparatus that prevents the mass being held by force applied by the participant at the mouth. Breath-by-breath respiratory gas analysis enables the determination of physiological parameters requiring a more rapid sampling rate than can be accurately achieved using the Douglas bag technique (e.g., $\dot{V}O_2$ kinetics, gas exchange and ventilatory thresholds; see supplementary material). However, the principles outlined earlier to ensure precision for the Douglas bag technique also hold for breath-by-breath measures.

Most metabolic carts utilise chemical and non-dispersive infrared cells for the determination of fractional O_2 and CO_2, respectively. The CO_2 cell is generally very stable unless it accumulates dust; the pump on the metabolic carts should therefore only be on when a suitable particle filter is connected to the sample port. Chemical O_2 cells degrade with time such that 'drift' following calibration is increasingly rapid. Given the small amount of gas required for calibration, it is therefore advised to calibrate for gas fractions prior to every test. Moreover, in light of the issue of FiO_2 in laboratory conditions (see earlier), careful attention should be paid to the manner in which the metabolic cart determines this variable. Measurement of gas fractions must be time aligned with flow, since gas fraction analysis will be delayed relative to the measurement of flow. Depending on the system, time alignment may be undertaken during the calibration procedures (which are normally semi-automated) or in a period pre-test with the participant breathing through the system, possibly with additional delay optimization in-test. In the former case, if following calibration, the sample tubes need to be changed and then the calibration process should be restarted. When utilising hypoxic or hyperoxic gas as the inspirate, the linearity of the O_2 cell should be checked with the manufacturer to see if an alternative span is required for the O_2 calibration. In such cases the viscosity of inspirate is altered, thus impacting time alignment. Ideally, the gas utilised during the time alignment procedure will therefore match the inspirate.

Calibration of flow should be undertaken across a wide range of flow rates, and ideally the calibration should be linear across this range to avoid the use of correction factors in-test. It is advised to check the linearity of the flow calibration with the manufacturer. Common errors arise during this process due to incomplete use of the gas syringe volume, which the user should be careful to avoid.

The validity of PGE measurements with metabolic carts is ideally checked every few weeks by simultaneous measurement of PGE using the Douglas bag technique (assuming that error in the latter is both known and minimised; see earlier). These measurements should be undertaken over a wide range of exercise intensities (moderate, heavy and severe) in a range of participants. A difference <5% in measurements of PGE and $\dot{V}_E$ is generally considered acceptable in such comparisons (Lamarra et al., 1987). There is considerable breath-to-breath variability in measures of PGE even in the steady-state. An effective solution in many situations is to average the PGE values over 10- to 15-s periods, though this may be inappropriate when determining parameters of PGE kinetics (see supplementary material, Section 5). The user should also discuss with the metabolic cart manufacturer the manner in which lung gas stores are corrected for, since changes here will dissociate measured respiratory variables from those at the alveoli (Whipp et al., 2005).

References

Keeling, C. D., Whorf, T. P., Wahlen, M. and van der Plichtt, J. (1995). Interannual extremes in the rate of rise of atmospheric carbon dioxide since 1980. *Nature*, 375(6533), 666–670. https://doi.org/10.1038/375666a0

Lamarra, N., Whipp, B. J., Ward, S. A. and Wasserman, K. (1987). Effect of interbreath fluctuations on characterizing exercise gas exchange kinetics. *Journal of Applied Physiology*, 62(5), 2003–2012.

Machta, L. and Hughes, E. (1970). Atmospheric oxygen in 1967 to 1970. *Science (New York, N.Y.)*, 168(3939), 1582–1584. https://doi.org/10.1126/science.168.3939.1582

Sandals, L. E. (2003). *Oxygen Uptake during Middle Distance Running*. http://eprints.glos.ac.uk/3085/

Whipp, B. J. and Ward, S. A. (1992). Pulmonary gas exchange dynamics and the tolerance to muscular exercise: Effects of fitness and training. *The Annals of Physiological Anthropology*, 11(3), 207–214. https://doi.org/10.2114/ahs1983.11.207

Whipp, B. J., Ward, S. A. and Rossiter, H. B. (2005). Pulmonary O_2 uptake during exercise: Conflating muscular and cardiovascular responses. *Medicine and Science in Sports and Exercise*, 37(9), 1574–1585. https://doi.org/10.1249/01.mss.0000177476.63356.22

WMO: World Meteorological Organization. (1996). Guide to meteorological instruments. *WMO Publication*, 8, 1–21.

3.7 Metabolic threshold testing, interpretation and its prognostic prescriptive value

Mark Burnley and Matthew I. Black

The exercise intensity spectrum is composed of identifiable 'exercise intensity domains', within which predictable physiological and perceptual responses can be observed. These domains, in turn, are separated by specific metabolic thresholds, namely the lactate threshold (LT) and the maximal steady state (MSS) or critical power (CP). Appreciation of these domains, and the metabolic thresholds that separate them, is therefore of great importance for exercise and training prescription and the prediction of functional capacity or athletic performance. Accordingly, the determination of metabolic thresholds has become routine in exercise physiology laboratories worldwide. The aim of this chapter is to outline the physiological basis of these thresholds and to broadly describe how exercise testing should be constructed to identify them.

Exercise intensity domains

Four domains of exercise intensity have been identified: moderate (below the LT), heavy (above LT but below the MSS/CP), severe (above the MSS/CP) and extreme (wherein exercise duration is too short to achieve maximal oxygen uptake ($\dot{V}O_2$max before task failure; for a review see Burnley and Jones, 2018). The metabolic thresholds of interest, therefore, are the LT and its ventilatory and gas exchange equivalents (separating the moderate and heavy domains) and the MSS or CP (separating the heavy and severe domains). It is important to note that numerous methods, and associated nomenclature, have been proposed to determine the boundaries between moderate-, heavy- and severe-intensity exercise, and the appropriate methodology remains a topic of heated debate (Jones et al., 2019; Table 3.7.1). Whichever method of threshold determination is selected, its validity should be based on whether it can, to a reasonable and quantifiable degree of confidence, establish the intended exercise intensity domain boundary.

The moderate/heavy boundary: lactate threshold

The moderate-intensity domain is characterised by a steady-state physiological response profile after an initial transient response (the 'on-transient' kinetics of

DOI: 10.4324/9781003045281-18

oxygen uptake $\dot{V}O_2$). Thus, in this domain, steady states in gas exchange, ventilation and heart rate can be achieved within 2 to 3 min in healthy participants, and blood [lactate] (brackets denote concentration) may rise transiently, if at all, before returning to resting concentrations. In contrast, in the heavy-intensity domain, a steady state is achieved following a delay of 10–15 min, in which $\dot{V}O_2$ rises to a greater value than expected based on the relationship of $\dot{V}O_2$ and work rate below LT, and blood [lactate] is elevated above resting concentrations. This rise in blood [lactate] results in bicarbonate buffering of its associated proton, and thus CO_2 production increases. This increases respiratory drive and therefore minute ventilation ($\dot{V}_E$). The contrasting responses between moderate and heavy exercise are the basis for the determination of the LT and its gas exchange and ventilatory equivalents.

To identify the moderate-heavy domain boundary, practitioners have two options: first, to detect the LT by direct measurement of the blood lactate response to incremental exercise (using an incremental test with stage durations ≥3 min); or second, to detect the gas exchange and ventilatory consequences of exceeding the LT, which does not require blood sampling (using a ramp or incremental test with stage durations of not more than 1 min, see later). The method of choice will depend on the purpose of testing, the testing environment and the equipment available.

The protocol used to determine the LT should ensure that each stage is long enough for the participant to achieve a steady state, if possible, and provide a sufficiently small resolution of the threshold itself. In this respect, 3- to 5-min stages usually allow a steady state to be achieved and for blood [lactate] to reflect the intensity of exercise. The blood sample (usually obtained from a fingertip or venous catheter) should be collected at the end of each stage. The incrementation rate will depend on the participant, but 0.5–1.0 km·h^{-1} or 15–30 W for running and cycling, respectively, are common in healthy adults. Lastly, the choice of starting speed or power is, again, selected based on the participant's anticipated fitness. It is best to err on the side of caution, since at least three stages in the moderate domain are required to establish a baseline from which a sudden and sustained increase in blood [lactate] can be observed, and 15–20 min of exercise in the moderate domain does not cause discomfort in well-conditioned participants. Beginning at the walk-run transition (treadmill) or at 50–75 W (cycle ergometer) are reasonable starting points if the fitness of a healthy participant is unknown.

The increase in blood [lactate] at LT has been detected in a number of ways, as shown in Table 3.7.1 and Figure 3.7.1. We would caution against the use of fixed blood [lactate] measures (of 2 or 4 mM) to estimate LT, since individual lactate responses vary markedly in concentration, both at baseline and during exercise. In addition, quantification of plasma [lactate] versus whole blood [lactate] renders fixed blood [lactate] as threshold measures meaningless. Instead, detection of the increase in [lactate], either as a visually determined sudden and sustained increase (Jones and Doust, 1998) or a 1-mM increase above baseline (Coyle, 1995), usually provides a clear LT determination.

Table 3.7.1 The validity, reliability and sensitivity of the metabolic thresholds used to demarcate the exercise intensity domains (EIDs) and the abbreviations commonly used to describe these in the scientific literature

	Common Abbreviation(s)	Strong Evidence for Validity, Reliability and Sensitivity?	Determined From an Incremental Exercise Test?	Easily Assessed in the field?
Moderate-heavy EID				
Lactate threshold	LT; LT1; Tlac	✓	✓	✓
Ventilatory threshold or gas exchange threshold	VT; VT1; Tvent; GET	✓	✓	✗
Heavy-severe EID				
Lactate threshold or lactate turnpoint	LT; LT2; LTP	✗	✓	✓
Ventilatory threshold or respiratory compensation point	VT; VT2; RCP	✗	✓	✗
Onset of blood lactate accumulation	OBLA	✗	✗	✓
Maximal lactate steady state	MLSS	✓	✗	✓
Individual anaerobic threshold	IAT	✗	✗	✗
Lactate minimum speed	LMS	✗	✗	✓
Critical power/speed	CP; CS; P_{crit}	✓	✗	✓
Functional threshold power	FTP	✗	✗	✓

To determine the LT indirectly using gas exchange variables (the gas exchange threshold [GET]), a ramp or rapid incremental test is preferred, since the evolution of CO_2 from the bicarbonate buffering of lactate is most clearly identified with relatively rapid incrementation and breath-by-breath gas exchange measurement. To detect the GET, a cluster of variables is usually used, including an increase in $\dot{V}_E/\dot{V}O_2$ without a corresponding increase in $\dot{V}_E/\dot{V}CO_2$, a breakpoint in the $\dot{V}O_2/\dot{V}CO_2$ x-y plot identified using the V-slope method (Beaver et al., 1986) and the corresponding increase in partial end tension (PET)O_2 without a change in PETCO$_2$. All of these are easily identified from data acquired using standard online gas analysis systems and require only linear regression to establish the V-slope. Minute ventilation can also be interrogated to detect the LT (that is, the ventilatory threshold [VT]), but practitioners should be wary of using $\dot{V}_E$ exclusively due to low signal-to-noise ratio and idiosyncratic breathing patterns that can distort the identification of the VT.

Given that the GET (or VT) is detected under non–steady-state conditions and is the consequence of lactate efflux and buffering, the relationship between the

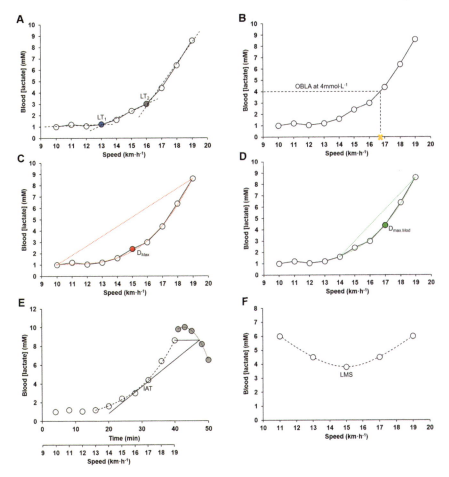

Figure 3.7.1 Schematic representation of the blood [lactate] response during incremental exercise and the methods subsequently applied to determine the metabolic thresholds. Panel A highlights two disproportionate increases in the blood [lactate]-speed relationship (i.e., LT_1 and LT_2). Panel B shows the speed corresponding to the onset of blood [lactate] accumulation at an arbitrarily defined blood [lactate]. Panel C illustrates the D_{max} method, where the speed corresponding to D_{max} is derived from the greatest perpendicular distance between the straight line drawn between blood [lactate] at exercise onset and time to task failure, and the third-order polynomial applied to the lactate-speed relationship. Panel D shows the modified D_{max} method ($D_{max.mod}$) where the polynomial and the straight line are drawn from the first increase in blood [lactate] greater than 0.4 mM above baseline. Panel E shows the individual anaerobic threshold (IAT). A third-order polynomial (dotted line) is applied to blood [lactate] measured in recovery (grey markers), and an exponential is fitted to the exercise data (dashed line). The IAT is the point at which the tangential line drawn from the recovery data at a point equivalent to peak exercise blood [lactate] transects the exercise [lactate] curve. Panel F shows the U-shaped blood [lactate] speed relationship during incremental exercise following two supramaximal bouts of exercise (at ~120% $\dot{V}O_2max$ for 60 s and 45 s, separated by 60 s recovery) and an 8-min walk. The speed or power corresponding to the nadir of this relationship is indicative of the lactate minimum speed (LMS).

metabolic rate at which GET (or VT) occurs and its corresponding running speed or power output is dissociated by approximately 40 to 50 s. For this reason, correction by subtracting approximately two-thirds of the ramp rate is necessary to provide the appropriate external measure of speed or power output (e.g., for a 30 W·min^{-1} ramp rate, ~20 W should be subtracted from the power output at which the threshold was observed).

Heavy-severe boundary: maximal steady state/critical power

The defining feature of severe-intensity exercise is that it is non–steady state. In this domain, blood [lactate] cannot be stabilised and $\dot{V}O_2$ will rise until $\dot{V}O_2$max is attained (Gaesser and Poole, 1996). Consequently, in this domain, exercise at any fixed speed or power output will result in task failure within minutes, and the precise duration is a predictable function of the speed or power output above the heavy-severe boundary. There are thus two methods of determining this boundary. The first is a 'bottom-up' approach in which the MSS is determined, usually from serial measurements of blood [lactate] (the maximal lactate steady state [MLSS]) during a series of 30-min constant speed (or power) exercise bouts. When a non–steady-state profile is identified, the previous bout is defined as the MLSS (see Figure 3.7.2). The second method is a 'top-down' approach, in which a series of constant speed or power tests in the severe-intensity domain are performed and a mathematical function is applied to the resulting power vs. time to task failure data, with the asymptote being the estimated heavy-severe domain boundary (CP; Figure 3.7.2). Both methods have their advantages and disadvantages, but the requirement for repeated and strenuous testing is a disadvantage common to both. Efforts have been made, therefore, to associate parameters derived from incremental or ramp testing with the MLSS or CP, including the lactate turnpoint, the D_{max} and modified D_{max} method, the 4 mM 'onset of blood lactate accumulation' (OBLA) and the respiratory compensation point (RCP). Unfortunately, these parameters do not appear to provide valid and reliable estimates of the heavy-severe domain boundary (e.g., Dekerle et al., 2003; Broxterman et al., 2015).

The heavy-severe domain boundary typically occurs halfway between the LT and $\dot{V}O_2$max. Thus, to conduct an MLSS determination, several 30-min efforts bracketing this intensity should be performed. Blood sampling should be performed at rest and at every fifth minute of exercise. Typically, a difference in blood [lactate] of <1 mM between minutes 10 and 30 is considered representative of a steady state (but see Jones et al. [2019]). The choice of intensities used, and the difference between them (e.g., 1 km·h^{-1} or 25 W), requires judgement, with the goal to establish MLSS with the highest possible precision in the fewest number of tests. Usually, no more than four to five tests should be required to identify the MLSS.

Two advantages of using CP in establishing the heavy-severe domain boundary are that the number of trials required can be decided before the testing begins, and the testing itself also characterises exercise tolerance in the severe-intensity domain. The only reason to increase the number of tests is if the CP estimate

Metabolic threshold testing 91

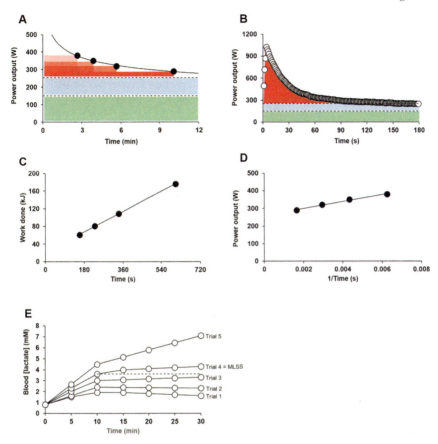

Figure 3.7.2 Schematic representation of methods used to determine the heavy-severe boundary during non-incremental exercise tests. Panels A–D illustrate the determination of CP and W' via a series of severe-intensity exercise trials performed to task failure (black markers; Panels A, C–D) or via the 3-min all-out test (Panel B). In panels A–B, the work performed above CP (red) indicative of W' and the severe intensity domain and the moderate (green) and heavy (blue) intensity domains are provided. Panel E shows the blood [lactate] response, measured every 5 min (white markers) to a series of constant speed (or power) trials, where each trial (1–5) is indicative of an increment in speed (or power). Blood [lactate] did not increase by more than 1 mM between 10 and 30 minutes during trial 4 (Δ 0.7 mM) and is therefore defined as MLSS. The dashed line is indicative of the blood [lactate] attained at 10 min during trial 4, and is projected to the end of the exercise trial.

is associated with a high standard error, and usually only one extra test is then required. The tests themselves have the disadvantage of needing to be performed to the limit of tolerance, but since the duration of each test should be between 2 and 15 min (Hill, 1993), this is not particularly arduous for well-trained participants. Curve fitting of the resulting speed- or power-duration relationship can then provide the CP and curvature constant (distance, D′, or work, W′) parameters. The simplest way of representing this relationship is to plot the linear distance or external work vs. time to task failure, wherein the slope of the relationship is the critical speed or power and the intercept is the D′ or W′. Alternatively, non-linear regression of the speed/power and time to task failure can be performed, fitting a rectangular hyperbola to the data (for cycle ergometry):

$$T_{lim} = W'/(P - CP) \qquad [1]$$

where T_{lim} is the time to task failure and P is power output. CP will then be represented by the asymptote of the power-duration relationship. Finally, the inverse time model can be used to provide a linear fit to the data, with the intercept being CP and the slope being W′. It is common to establish all three relationships and then rely on the fitting with the smallest standard error. This procedure also guards against inadvertent errors in data entry that would result in the models producing wildly different parameter estimates. It should also be noted that the estimates are only estimates; the confidence limits associated with them are also important. In this respect, practitioners should seek to maximise the degrees of freedom in the model used. For a two-parameter model, we suggest at least four predicting trials are performed, since 95% confidence limits of ±60 W are not uncommon using only three predicting trials.

The MLSS and CP do not typically agree in the literature, and this highlights a major source of controversy in the field. MLSS is, by definition, a measure of the upper limit of the heavy domain, whereas the CP is a parameter estimate of the lower limit of the severe domain (Jones et al., 2019). Both are subject to experimental error and biological variation, but the CP tends to return a higher estimate for the boundary than does the MLSS. Space does not permit us to explore these issues, but we refer readers to Jones et al. (2019). Whichever method is chosen, practitioners should seek to minimise the associated measurement errors. As a rule of thumb, however, exercise above CP is almost certainly in the severe domain, and exercise at or below MLSS is, by definition, in the heavy domain.

In recent years alternative approaches have been developed to characterise the heavy-severe domain boundary, including the 3-min all-out test (Vanhatalo et al., 2007). The 3-min all-out test, whilst extremely strenuous, has the advantage of determining CP, in principle, in a single test. Its validity has been extensively explored in the last decade, using a range of different exercise modalities.

Prognostic prescriptive value of metabolic threshold testing

Reports from highly trained endurance athletes highlight that improvements in the speed/power at a metabolic threshold and performance can occur with little change, or even a reduction, in $\dot{V}O_2max$ (Pierce et al., 1990; Coyle, 2005; Jones, 2006). Appreciation of the metabolic thresholds therefore provides the capacity to differentiate endurance capability amongst athletes.

The predictive strength of the metabolic thresholds is dependent on the intensity/duration of the exercise (e.g., Bentley et al., 2001; Coyle et al., 1988). The boundary for the moderate-heavy intensity domain is typically found at 60%–80% $\dot{V}O_2$max, and is a strong predictor of endurance exercise lasting >2 h, such as the marathon (Farrell et al., 1979; Joyner et al., 1991; Bassett and Howley, 2000; Jones, 2006), triathlon (De Vito et al., 1995; Kohrt et al., 1989; Sleivert and Wenger, 1993) and road-cycling events (Mujika and Padilla, 2001; Vogt et al., 2006). The predictive ability of this threshold is diminished during exercise at a higher intensity, and also during ultra-endurance events, where factors such as energy and fluid balance, as well as inexperience of the event distance and route, may impact performance (Laursen and Rhodes, 2001). During shorter endurance-based events (<1 h), the upper boundary for the heavy-intensity domain is a superior predictor of performance (Black et al., 2014). There is, however, some overlap in the predictive utility of the metabolic thresholds, with recent estimates highlighting that elite male athletes complete the marathon at ~96% of critical speed (CS) (Jones and Vanhatalo, 2017). Careful consideration should therefore be given to the appropriateness of the metabolic threshold to predict exercise performance, depending on the event demands and training status of the individual.

In addition to marking the boundary between the heavy-severe exercise intensity domains, determination of CP provides an estimate for the amount of work that can be performed above CP. Appreciation of CP and W′ (or CS and D′) may (or should) also be used to inform race tactics. For example, an athlete with a superior CS may optimise their chances for success by enforcing a fast pace, encouraging competitors to expend their D′, whilst an athlete with a greater D′ but lower CS may favour a slower race pace to preserve their superior D′ for a sprint finish (Fukuba and Whipp, 1999; Jones and Whipp, 2002). Hoogkamer et al., 2018).

Summary

Metabolic thresholds are of pivotal importance to any exercise testing battery for sports involving sustained or intermittent activity lasting more than a few minutes. Their establishment requires an understanding of the threshold in the exercise intensity spectrum, as well as attention to both protocol and appropriate data analysis and interpretation. This chapter has provided the basic principles from which to identify them.

References

Bassett, D. R. and Howley, E. T. (2000). Limiting factors for maximum oxygen uptake and determinants of endurance performance. *Medicine and Science in Sports and Exercise*, 32, 70–84.

Beaver, W. L., Wasserman, K. and Whipp, B. J. (1986). A new method for detecting anaerobic threshold by gas exchange. *Journal of Applied Physiology*, 60(6), 2020–2027.

Bentley, D. J., McNaughton, L. R., Thompson, D., Vleck, V. E. and Batterham, A. M. (2001). Peak power output, the lactate threshold, and time trial performance in cyclists. *Medicine and Science in Sports and Exercise*, 33, 2077–2081.

Black, M. I., Durant, J., Jones, A. M. and Vanhatalo, A. (2014). Critical power derived from a 3-min all-out test predicts 16.1-km road time-trial performance. *European Journal of Sport Science*, 14, 217–223.

Broxterman, R. M., Ade, C. J., Craig, J. C., Wilcox, S. L., Schlup, S. J. and Barstow, T. J. (2015). The relationship between critical speed and the respiratory compensation point: Coincidence or equivalence. *European Journal of Sport Science*, 15, 631–639.

Burnley, M. and Jones, A. M. (2018). Power-duration relationship: Physiology, fatigue, and the limits of human performance. *European Journal of Sport Science*, 18, 1–12.

Coyle, E. F. (1995). Integration of the physiological factors determining endurance performance ability. *Exercise and Sport Sciences Reviews*, 23, 25–64.

Coyle, E. F. (2005). Improved muscular efficiency displayed as Tour de France champion matures. *Journal of Applied Physiology*, 98, 2191–2196.

Coyle, E. F., Coggan, A. R., Hopper, M. K. and Walters, T. J. (1988). Determinants of endurance in well trained cyclists. *Journal of Applied Physiology*, 64, 2622–2630.

Dekerle, J., Baron, B., Dupont, L., Vanvelcenaher, J. and Pelayo, P. (2003). Maximal lactate steady state, respiratory compensation threshold and critical power. *European Journal Applied Physiology*, 89, 281–288.

De Vito, G., Bernardi, M., Sproviero, E. and Figura, F. (1995). Decrease of endurance performance during Olympic triathlon. *International Journal of Sports Medicine*, 16, 24–28.

Farrell, P. A., Wilmore, J. H., Coyle, E. F., Billing, J. E. and Costill, D. L. (1979). Plasma lactate acconnotation and distance running performance. *Medicine and Science in Sports and Exercise*, 11, 338–344.

Fukuba, Y. and Whipp, B. J. (1999). A metabolic limit on the ability to make up for lost time in endurance events. *Journal of Applied Physiology (1985)*, 87, 853–861.

Gaesser, G. A. and Poole, D. C. (1996). The slow component of oxygen uptake kinetics in humans. *Exercise and Sport Sciences Reviews*, 24, 35–70.

Hill, D. W. (1993). The critical power concept: A review. *Sports Medicine*, 16, 237–254.

Hoogkamer, W., Snyder, K. L. and Arellano, C. J. (2018). Modeling the benefits of cooperative drafting: Is there an optimal strategy to facilitate a sub-2-hour marathon performance? *Sports Medicine*, 48, 2859–2867.

Jones, A. M. (2006). The physiology of the world record holder of the women's marathon. *International Journal of Sports Science and Coaching*. doi: 10.1260/174795406777641258

Jones, A. M., Burnley, M., Black, M. I., Poole, D. C. and Vanhatalo, A. (2019). The maximal metabolic steady state: Redefining the 'gold standard'. *Physiological Reports*, 7, e14098.

Jones, A. M. and Doust, J. H. (1998). Validity of the lactate minimum test for the determination of the maximal lactate steady state. *Medicine and Science in Sports and Exercise*, 30, 1304–1313.

Jones, A. M. and Vanhatalo, A. (2017). The 'Critical Power' concept: Applications to sports performance with a focus on intermittent high-intensity exercise. *Sports Medicine*, 47(1), 65–78.

Jones, A. M. and Whipp, B. J. (2002). Bioenergetic constraints on tactical decision making in middle distance running. *British Journal of Sports Medicine*, 36, 102–104.

Joyner, M. J. (1991). Modeling: Optimal marathon performance on the basis of physiological factors. *Journal of Applied Physiology (1985)*, 70, 683–687.

Kirby, B. S., Winn, B. J., Wilkins, B. W. and Jones, A. M. (2021). Interaction of exercise bioenergetics with pacing behavior predicts track distance running performance. *Journal of Applied Physiology (1985)*. doi: 10.1152/japplphysiol.00223.2021

Kohrt, W. M., O'Conner, J. S. and Skinner, J. S. (1989). Longitudinal assessment of responses by triathletes to swimming, cycling and running. *Medicine and Science in Sports and Exercise*, 21, 569–575.

Laursen, P. B. and Rhodes, E. C. (2001). Factors affecting performance in an ultraendurance triathlon. *Sports Medicine*, 31, 195–209.

Mujika, I. and Padilla, S. (2001). Physiological and performance characteristics of male professional road cyclists. *Sports Medicine*, 31, 479–487.

Pierce, E. F., Weltman, A., Seip, R. L. and Snead, D. (1990). Effects of training specificity on the lactate threshold and $\dot{V}O_2$peak. *International Journal of Sports Medicine*, 11, 267–272.

Sleivert, G. G. and Wenger, H. A. (1993). Physiological predictors of short-course triathlon performance. *Medicine and Science in Sports and Exercise*, 25, 871–876.

Vanhatalo, A., Doust, J. H. and Burnley, M. (2007). Determination of critical power using a 3-min all-out cycling test. *Medicine and Science in Sports and Exercise*, 39, 548–555.

Vogt, S., Heinrich, L., Schumacher, Y. O., Blum, A., Roecker, K., Dickhuth, H.-H. and Schmid, A. (2006). Power output during stage racing in professional road cycling. *Medicine and Science in Sports and Exercise*, 38, 147–151.

3.8 Ratings of perceived exertion

John Buckley and Roger Eston

Following two decades of research, Gunnar Borg's original rating of perceived exertion (RPE) 6–20 scale was accepted in 1973 as a valid tool within the field of exercise science and sports medicine (Noble and Robertson, 1996). His seminal research provided the basic tool for numerous studies in which an individual's effort perception was of interest. It also provided the basis and incentive for the development of other scales, particularly those used with children. Borg's initial research validated the scale against heart rate and oxygen uptake. Later research focused on the curvilinear growth of perceived exertion with lactate, ventilation and muscle pain responses and led to the development of the category-ratio (CR-10) scale. The RPE 6–20 and CR-10 scales and their accompanying instructions can be found in the BACPR Reference Tables Booklet via this link: www.bacpr.com/pages/page_box_contents.asp?PageID=787.

The general aim of using RPE is to quantify an individual's perception of exertion as a means of determining or regulating exercise intensity (Borg, 1998). In this way it acts as a surrogate or concurrent marker to key relative physiological responses, including percentage of maximal heart rate (%HRmax), percentage of maximal aerobic power (%$\dot{V}O_2$max) and blood lactate. The strongest stimuli influencing an individual's RPE are breathing/ventilatory work and sensations of strain from the muscles (Chen et al., 2002).

Modes of using the RPE

Traditionally, RPE was developed as a dependent response variable to a given exercise intensity known as *estimation mode* (Noble and Robertson, 1996). Smutok et al. (1980) were among the first to evaluate RPE as an independent exercise intensity regulator (i.e., *production mode*), where participants exercise to a target effort perception and other measures become dependent response variables.

RPE and relative measures of exercise intensity

The RPE is commonly used to complement physiological measures of exercise during graded exercise testing (GXT) and prescribe intensity levels in healthy and clinical populations (ACSM, 2021; Eston and Connolly, 1996; Parfitt et al., 2012;

DOI: 10.4324/9781003045281-19

Kang et al., 2003; Scherer et al., 1999; Williams and Eston, 1989). The strong relationship between RPE and exercise intensity during GXT was demonstrated in a study involving 2560 men and women (Scherr et al., 2013), 'independent of age, gender, medical history (with respect to coronary artery disease), level of physical activity and exercise modality'. They concluded that RPE can be used to monitor and regulate exercise intensity for primary and secondary disease prevention. They recommended RPE 11–13 for less-trained individuals and RPE 13–15 when more intense aerobic training is desired. In cardiac rehabilitation patients, the recommended range of RPE 11 (for low-fit, low-active patients) to 14 (for higher-fit, more active patients) was shown to represent exercise at the anaerobic/ventilatory threshold (Nichols et al., 2020).

Several studies have shown that RPE is a useful tool for guiding exercise intensity in healthy and clinical populations. For example, Parfitt et al. (2012) observed a 17% increase in $\dot{V}O_2$max from a self-paced, 8-wk treadmill training programme (3 × 30 min/wk) clamped at RPE 13 in previously sedentary participants. During training at RPE-13, the average $\dot{V}O_2$ increased from 61% of the baseline $\dot{V}O_2$ max to 64% of the higher $\dot{V}O_2$max in week 8. As participants were blinded to speed, HR and other intensity feedback, the data provide strong evidence and proof of principle for the efficacy of RPE-13 (particularly as it was also perceived to be *pleasant*) to self-regulate training over a long period. Illarraza et al. (2004) reported similar results in post-operative cardiac patients whose exercise intensity was solely regulated by RPE-13 with similar gains in fitness and ventricular ejection fraction compared to a similar group exercising at a target intensity of 70% heart rate reserve. Table 3.8.1 summarises the relationship between RPE and related physiological markers. For example, once an individual has given an RPE of 13–14 on the RPE Scale or 3–4 on the CR-10 scale, it is highly probable that the participant is exercising at or around the ventilatory threshold.

Use of RPE to predict and assess $\dot{V}O_2$max

The RPE elicited from submaximal increments in a GXT can be used to provide estimations of $\dot{V}O_2$max that are as good as, or better than, heart rate. Morgan and Borg (1976) first observed that the linear relationship of RPE and work rate during a GXT in physically active and sedentary men permits extrapolation to a

Table 3.8.1 Summary of the relationship between the percentages of maximal aerobic power (%$\dot{V}O_2$max), maximal heart rate reserve (%HRRmax), maximal heart rate (%HRmax) and Borg's RPE (6–20) and CR-10 scales

%$\dot{V}O_2$max	<37	37–45	46–63	64–90	>91	100
%HRRmax	<30	30–39	40–59	60–89	>90	100
%HRmax	<57	57–63	64–76	77–95	>96	100
RPE (6–20)	<9	9–11	12–13	14–17	18+	20
CR-10	<1	1–1.5	2.5–3	4–6	7–9	10+

Source: Adapted from ACSM (2021) and Borg (1998).

theoretical end point, enabling prediction of maximal work capacity with better accuracy than heart rate. Many studies have since confirmed the efficacy of submaximal RPE to estimate $\dot{V}O_2max$ or maximal work rate (Coquart et al., 2014; Evans et al., 2015).

On the basis that RPE alone may be used to regulate exercise intensity, perceptually regulated exercise testing (PRET) was proposed as an alternative method of estimating maximal exercise capacity and training status (Eston et al., 2005). This method has the advantage of allowing individual autonomy to set exercise intensity at a given RPE through changes in pace, work rate or gradient. It is also a closed-loop task in which the number of bouts and time at each RPE-regulated intensity are known, allowing the subject to set a pace accordingly. The procedure was first conceived by Eston et al. (1987) and later applied in cardiac patients (Eston and Thompson, 1997). Their research provided an initial proof of concept and rationale for a series of studies on the efficacy of PRET, with a known end-point RPE, involving different exercise modalities and population groups as a valid means of predicting $\dot{V}O_2peak$. The validity of submaximal PRET has been confirmed across a broad range of age, ability, fitness levels and chronic health conditions (Eston et al., 2012; Coquart et al., 2014).

There has been considerable interest in extending Eston and colleagues' original concept of the PRET, to include a maximal stage at RPE-20 ($PRET_{max}$), also interchangeably referred to as a self-paced $\dot{V}O_2peak$ test (SPV), to measure $\dot{V}O_2peak$. The initial $PRET_{max}$ (Mauger and Sculthorpe, 2012) consisted of the same 2-min, verbally anchored RPE stages (11, 13, 15, 17) as those applied by Eston et al. (2006) with the addition of RPE-20 to produce a maximal effort and freedom to change power output or speed on a moment-to-moment basis during each of the perceptually regulated bouts. Others have used protocols with seven stages at RPE-8, -10, -12, -14, -16, -18 and -20 (Chidnok et al., 2013) and six 3-min stages at RPE-9, -11, -13, -15, -17 and -20 (Evans et al., 2014). These closed-loop protocols have the advantages of known duration and autonomy to control exercise intensity within a fixed RPE (see Eston and Parfitt, 2019, for critical review).

Factors influencing RPE

During exercise testing, the inter-trial agreement of either RPE or a concurrent physiological response at a given RPE increases with each use of the RPE scale (Buckley et al., 2000, 2004; Eston et al., 2000, 2005). Typically, the agreement is shown to be acceptable within three trials when the participant is exposed to a variety of exercise intensities.

Psychosocial factors can influence up to 30% of the variability in an RPE score (Dishman and Landy, 1988; Williams and Eston, 1989). Furthermore, the literature has identified numerous modulators of RPE, including the mode of exercise, age, audio-visual distractions, circadian rhythms, gender, haematological and nutritional status, medication, muscle mechanics and biochemical status, the physical environment and the psycho-social status or competitive milieu of the testing and training environment. These factors are exemplified in Borg's effort continua proposed in 1973 (Borg, 1998). Beta-blocking medication exerts an influence during extended periods of exercise and at intensities greater than 65% $\dot{V}O_2$ max (Eston and Connolly, 1996; Head et al., 1997).

In healthy or clinical populations that may be fearful of the exercise testing environment (e.g., cardiac patients), it is likely that they will inflate RPE (Morgan, 1973, 1994; Rejeski, 1981; Kohl and Shea, 1988; Biddle and Mutrie, 2001; Buckley et al., 2009). Such inflation of RPE relates to individuals who either lack self-efficacy or who are unfamiliar with or inhibited by the social situation of the exercise training or testing environment.

Throughout this guidance, most of the focus is on using RPE as an intensity monitor. However, like heart rate, it responds to more than just intensity stimuli. This is similar to cardiovascular drift, where during a fixed submaximal intensity and constant or steady-state $\dot{V}O_2$, RPE will grow *linearly* as a function of time as linked to the onset of sensations of 'fatigue' (Utter et al., 2002; Fontes et al., 2010; Buckley and Borg, 2011; Borg, 1998), which may be disrupted by a change in the anticipated duration of the task (Eston et al., 2012). Furthermore, any underlying perception of fatigue could be present as function of the time of day (Micklewright et al., 2017). From the evidence noted earlier, the slope or rate of RPE growth as a function of time is proportional to the intensity and becomes especially pronounced when exercise is performed above the ventilatory/anaerobic threshold. Faulkner et al. (2008) showed the same pattern for long-distance competitive running where the rate of increase in RPE was greater for a faster-paced shorter distance (7 cf. 13 mile). During marathon running, the growth of RPE is more gradual, where it takes several hours to see a similar amount of growth in RPE when compared with strength training (Buckley and Borg, 2011). In health-promoting or rehabilitative exercise, where aerobic activities typically last for 30 min, RPE for the same work rate or metabolic equivalent (MET) could increase by 2 points on the RPE scale (Joseph et al., 2008). Similarly for a given RPE (e.g., used in RPE production mode), the work rate ($\dot{V}O_2$ or METs) over this time is likely to decrease (Cochrane et al., 2015).

RPE and strength/power testing and training

Up until the late 1990s, most of the evidence in RPE focused on application and research with aerobic-type exercise. There is now a growing body of evidence in the use of monitoring somatic responses to local muscle sensations during resistive or strength training exercise (Borg, 1998; Gearhart et al., 2002; Pincivero et al., 2003; Lagally and Costigan, 2004). The important aspect to consider is that during short-term, high-intensity exercise for a localised muscle group, where 8 to 15 repetitions are performed, RPE will typically grow by 1 point on the RPE or CR-10 for every 3 to 4 repetitions (Buckley and Borg, 2011). For example, if after 12 repetitions, one wishes to end his or her last repetition at an RPE of 15 or a CR-10 scale rating of 5 (hard, heavy), then the first or second repetition should elicit an RPE of 12 or a CR-10 rating of 2 (between light and somewhat hard). Ultimately, during strength training, the rate of growth is rapid, where, for example, at the beginning of work at 70% of a one-repetition maximum, the perception of intensity is moderate/somewhat hard but rapidly grows to extremely hard/maximum in less than 30 s.

Which scale should I use?

In both Borg's RPE and CR-10 scale, semantic verbal anchors and their corresponding numbers have been aligned to accommodate for the curvilinear nature (a power function between 1.6 and 2.0) of human physiological responses (Borg, 1998). The CR-10 scale, with its ratio or semi-ratio properties, was specifically designed with this in mind. The RPE 6–20 scale was originally designed for whole-body, aerobic-type activity where perceived responses are pooled to concur with the linear increments in heart rate and oxygen uptake as exercise intensity is increased. The CR-10 scale is best suited when there is an overriding sensation arising either from a specific area of the body, for example, muscle pain, ache or fatigue in the quadriceps, or from pulmonary responses. Examples of this individualised or differentiated response have been applied in patients with McArdle disease (Buckley et al., 2014) and chronic obstructive pulmonary disease (O'Donnell et al., 2004).

Perceived exertion in children

There have been important advances in the study of effort perception in children (Kasai et al., 2020; Eston and Parfitt, 2019; Lamb et al., 2017 for reviews). In summary, a developmentally appropriate 1–10 Children's Effort Rating Table (CERT,

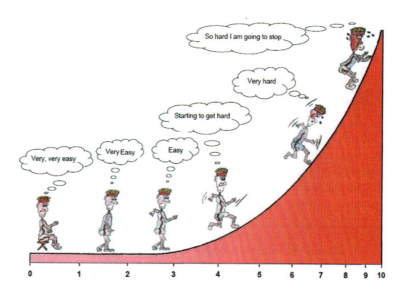

Figure 3.8.1 Eston-Parfitt (E-P) scale.

Williams et al., 1994; Eston et al., 1994) laid the foundation for several linearly sloped pictorial scales (OMNI, Robertson, 1997; Robertson et al., 2000; PCERT, Yelling et al., 2002; Cart and Load Effort Rating Scale, CALER, Eston et al., 2000). More recently, the E-P scale (Figure 3.8.1; Eston and Parfitt, 2007) depicts a character at various stages of exertion on a concave slope. The scale is intuitive, is valid and has been applied in several studies (Eston et al., 2009; Lambrick et al., 2011, 2016). Steeper slopes are harder to ascend, and the area under the curve is shaded progressively from light to dark red to further reflect increasing intensity. The horizontal distance between increments (0 to 10) is successively reduced to create equidistant intervals on the vertical axis, which allows for linear analyses and interpretation of RPE and other data.

Key points for the effective use of RPE

The following points for instructing participants are recommended (adapted from Maresh and Noble, 1984; Borg, 1998, 2004):

1. Before using the RPE scale, it is important that the participant understands the concept of sensing the exercise responses (breathing, muscle movement/strain, joint movement/speed).
2. Anchoring the perceptual range, which includes relating to the fact that no exertion at all is sitting still and maximal exertion is a theoretical concept of pushing the body to its absolute physical limits. Participants should then be exposed to several levels of exercise intensity to understand what various levels on the scale feel like.
3. The participant should first concentrate on the sensations arising from the activity, look at the scale to see which verbal descriptor relates to the effort he or she is experiencing and then link this to the corresponding numerical value.
4. Unless specifically directed, ensure that the participant focuses on all the different sensations arising from the exercise being performed. For aerobic exercise, the participant should pool all sensations to give one rating. If there is an overriding sensation, then additionally make note of this differentiated rating. Differentiated ratings can be used during muscular strength activity or where exercise is limited more by breathlessness or leg pain, as in the case of pulmonary or peripheral vascular disease, respectively.
5. Confirm that there is no right or wrong answer and it is what the participant perceives. There are three important cases where the participant may give an incorrect rating:

    (a) When there is a preconceived idea about what exertion level is elicited by a specific activity (Borg, 1998).
    (b) When participants are asked to recall the exercise and give a rating. As with heart rate, RPEs should be taken while the participant is actually engaged in the movements, not after they have finished an activity.
    (c) When participants attempt to please the practitioner by stating what should be the appropriate level of RPE. This is typically the case when

participants are advised ahead of time of the target RPE (e.g., in education sessions or during the warm-up). In the early stages of using RPE, the participant's exercise intensity should be set by heart rate or work rate (e.g., in METs), and participants need to reliably learn to match their RPE to this level in estimation mode. Once it has been established that the participant's rating concurs with the target heart rate or MET level reliably, then moving them on to production mode can be considered.

6 Keep RPE scales in full view at all times (e.g., on each machine or station or in fixed view in the exercise testing room), and keep reminding participants throughout their exercise session or test to think about what sort of sensations they have while making their judgement rating. Elite endurance athletes are known to be good perceivers, as they are well used to associating sensations to regulate an optimal pace (Morgan, 2000).

References

ACSM. (2021). *ACSM's Guidelines for Exercise Testing and Prescription* (11th ed.). Baltimore: Lippincott, Williams and Wilkins.

Biddle, S. J. H. and Mutrie, N. (2001). *Psychology of Physical Activity: Determinants, Well-Being and Interventions.* London: Routledge.

Borg, G. (1998). *Borg's Perceived Exertion and Pain Scales.* Champaign, IL: Human Kinetics.

Borg, G. (2004). *The Borg CR10 Folder: A Method for Measuring Intensity of Experience.* Stockholm, Sweden: Borg Perception.

Buckley, J. P. and Borg, G. A. (2011). Borg's scales in strength training: From theory to practice in young and older adults. *Applied Physiology, Nutrition, and Metabolism*, 36, 682–692.

Buckley, J. P., Eston, R. G. and Sim, J. (2000). Ratings of perceived exertion in Braille: Validity and reliability in production mode. *British Journal of Sports Medicine*, 34, 297–302.

Buckley, J. P., Quinlivan, R. C. M., Sim, J., Eston, R. G. and Short, D. S. (2014). Heart rate and perceived muscle pain response to a functional walking test in McArdle disease. *Journal of Sports Sciences*, 32, 1561–1569.

Buckley, J., Sim, J. and Eston, R. G. (2009). Reproducibility of ratings of perceived exertion soon after myocardial infarction: Responses in the stress-testing clinic and the rehabilitation gymnasium. *Ergonomics*, 52, 421–442.

Buckley, J. P., Sim, J., Eston, R. G., Hession, R. and Fox, R. (2004). Reliability and validity of measures taken during the Chester step test to predict aerobic power and to prescribe aerobic exercise. *British Journal of Sports Medicine*, 38, 197–205.

Chen, M. J., Fan, X. and Moe, S. T. (2002). Criterion-related validity of the Borg ratings of perceived exertion scale in healthy individuals: A meta-analysis. *Journal of Sports Sciences*, 20, 873–899.

Chidnok, W., DiMenna, F. J., Bailey, S. J., Burnley, M., Wilkerson, D. P., Vanhatalo, A., et al. (2013). $\dot{V}O_2$max is not altered by self-pacing during incremental exercise. *European Journal of Applied Physiology*, 113, 529–539.

Cochrane, K. C., Housh, T. J., Bergstrom, H. C., et al. (2015). Physiological responses during cycle ergometry at a constant perception of effort. *International Journal of Sports Medicine*, 36, 466–473.

Coquart, J. B., Garcin, M., Parfitt, G., et al. (2014). Prediction of maximal or peak oxygen uptake from ratings of perceived exertion. *Sports Medicine*, 44, 563–578.

Dishman, R. K. and Landy, F. J. (1988). Psychological factors and prolonged exercise. In D. R. Lamb and R. Murray (eds.), *Perspectives in Exercise Science and Sports Medicine*, pp. 281–355. Indianapolis, IN: Benchmark Press.

Eston, R. G. and Connolly, D. (1996). The use of ratings of perceived exertion for exercise prescription in patients receiving ß-blocker therapy. *Sports Medicine*, 21, 176–190.

Eston, R. G., Davies, B. and Williams, J. G. (1987). Use of perceived effort ratings to control exercise intensity in young, healthy adults. *European Journal of Applied Physiology*, 56, 222.

Eston, R. G., Faulkner, J. A., Parfitt, C. G. and Mason, E. (2006). The validity of predicting maximal oxygen uptake from a perceptually regulated graded exercise tests of different durations. *European Journal of Applied Physiology*, 97, 535–541.

Eston, R. G., Lamb, K. L., Bain, A., Williams, M. and Williams, J. G. (1994). Validity of a perceived exertion scale for children: A pilot study. *Perceptual and Motor Skills*, 78, 691–697.

Eston, R. G., Lamb, K. L., Parfitt, C. G. and King, N. (2005). The validity of predicting maximal oxygen uptake from a perceptually regulated graded exercise test. *European Journal of Applied Physiology*, 94, 221–227.

Eston, R. G., Lambrick, D. and Rowlands, A. V. (2009). The perceptual response to exercise of progressively increasing intensity in children aged 7–8 years: Validation of a pictorial curvilinear ratings of perceived exertion scale. *Psychophysiology*, 46, 843–851.

Eston, R. G. and Parfitt, G. (2007). Perceived exertion. In N. Armstrong (ed.), *Paediatric Exercise Physiology*, pp. 275–298. London: Elsevier.

Eston, R. G. and Parfitt, G. (2019). Perceived exertion, heart rate and other non-invasive methods for exercise testing and intensity control. In K. Norton and R. Eston (eds.), *Kinanthropometry and Exercise Physiology*, pp. 464–499. New York: Routledge.

Eston, R. G., Parfitt, G., Campbell, L. and Lamb, K. L. (2000). Reliability of effort perception for regulating exercise intensity in children using a Cart and Load Effort Rating (CALER) Scale. *Pediatric Exercise Science*, 12, 388–397.

Eston, R. G., Stansfield, R., Westoby, P. and Parfitt, G. (2012). Effect of deception and expected exercise duration on psychological and physiological variables during treadmill running and cycling. *Psychophysiology*, 49, 462–469.

Eston, R. G. and Thompson, M. (1997). Use of ratings of perceived exertion for prediction of maximal exercise levels and exercise prescription in patients receiving atenolol. *British Journal of Sports Medicine*, 31, 114–119.

Evans, H., Ferrar, K., Smith, A., et al. (2015). A systematic review of methods to predict maximal oxygen uptake from submaximal, open circuit spirometry in healthy adults. *Journal of Science and Medicine in Sport*, 18, 183–188.

Evans, H., Parfitt, G. and Eston, R. (2014). Use of a perceptually-regulated test to measure maximal oxygen uptake is valid and feels better. *European Journal of Sport Science*, 14, 452–458.

Faulkner, J. A., Parfitt, C. G. and Eston, R. G. (2008). The rating of perceived exertion during competitive running scales with time. *Psychophysiology*, 45, 977–985.

Fontes, E. B., Smirmaul, B. P., Nakamura, F. Y., et al. (2010). The relationship between rating of perceived exertion and muscle activity during exhaustive constant-load cycling. *International Journal of Sports Medicine*, 31, 683–688.

Gearhart, R. F., Jr., Goss, F. L., Lagally, K. M., Jakicic, J. M., Gallagher, J., Gallagher, K. I. and Robertson, R. (2002). Ratings of perceived exertion in active muscle during high-intensity and low-intensity resistance exercise. *Strength and Conditioning Research*, 16(1), 87–91.

Head, A., Maxwell, S. and Kendall, M. J. (1997). Exercise metabolism in healthy volunteers taking celiprolol, atenolol, and placebo. *British Journal of Sports Medicine*, 31, 120–125.

Illarraza, H., Myers, J., Kottman, W., et al. (2004). An evaluation of training responses using self-regulation in a residential rehabilitation program. *Journal of Cardiopulmonary Rehabilitation*, 24, 27–33.

Joseph, T., Johnson, B., Battista, R. A., et al. (2008). Perception of fatigue during simulated competition. *Medicine and Science in Sports and Exercise*, 40, 381–386.

Kang, J., Hoffman, J. R., Walker, H., et al. (2003). Regulating intensity using perceived exertion during extended exercise periods. *European Journal of Applied Physiology*, 89, 475–482.

Kasai, D., Parfitt, G., Eston, R. and Tsiros, M. (2020). The use of ratings of perceived exertion in children and adolescents a scoping review. *Sports Medicine*, 51, 33–50.

Kohl, R. M. and Shea, C. H. (1988). Perceived exertion: Influences of locus of control and expected work intensity and duration. *Journal of Human Movement Studies*, 15, 225–272.

Lagally, K. M. and Costigan, E. M. (2004). Anchoring procedures in reliability of ratings of perceived exertion during resistance exercise. *Perceptual and Motor Skills*, 98(3 Pt 2), 1285–1295.

Lamb, K. L., Parfitt, G. and Eston, R. G. (2017). Effort perception. In N. Armstrong and W. Van-Mechelen (eds.), *The Oxford Textbook of Children's Sport and Exercise Medicine* (3rd ed.), pp. 213–224. Oxford: Oxford University Press.

Lambrick, D., Bertelsen, H., Eston, R., et al. (2016). Prediction of peak oxygen uptake in children using submaximal ratings of perceived exertion during treadmill exercise. *European Journal of Applied Physiology*, 116, 1189–1195.

Lambrick, D., Rowlands, A. V. and Eston, R. G. (2011). The perceptual response to treadmill exercise using the Eston-Parfitt scale and a marble dropping task, in children aged 7–8 years. *Pediatric Exercise Science*, 23, 36–48.

Maresh, C. and Noble, B. J. (1984). Utilization of perceived exertion ratings during exercise testing and training. In L. K. Hall, G. C. Meyer and H. K. Hellerstein (eds.), *Cardiac Rehabilitation: Exercise Testing and Prescription*, pp. 155–173. Great Neck, NY: Spectrum.

Mauger, A. R. and Sculthorpe, N. (2012). A new $\dot{V}O_2$max protocol allowing self-pacing in maximal incremental exercise. *British Journal of Sports Medicine*, 46, 59–63.

Micklewright, D., St Clair Gibson, A., Gladwell, V., et al. (2017). Development and validity of the rating of-fatigue scale. *Sports Medicine*, 47, 2375–2393.

Morgan, W. P. (1973). Psychological factors influencing perceived exertion. *Medicine and Science in Sports and Exercise*, 5, 97–103.

Morgan, W. P. (1994). Psychological components of effort sense. *Medicine and Science in Sports and Exercise*, 26, 1071–1077.

Morgan, W. P. (2000). Psychological factors associated with distance running and the marathon. In D. Tunstall-Pedoe (ed.), *Marathon Medicine*. London: Royal Society of Medicine Press.

Morgan, W. P. and Borg, G. A. V. (1976). Perception of effort in the prescription of physical activity. In T. Craig (ed.), *The Humanistic Aspects of Sports, Exercise and Recreation*, pp. 126–129. Chicago, IL: American Medical Association.

Nichols, S., Engin, B., Carroll, S., et al. (2020). Ratings of perceived exertion at the ventilatory anaerobic threshold in people with coronary heart disease: A CARE CR study. *Annals of Physical and Rehabilitation Medicine*, 101462.

Noble, B. and Robertson, R. (1996). *Perceived Exertion*. Champaign, IL: Human Kinetics.

O'Donnell, D. E., Fluge, T., Gerken, F., Hamilton, A., Webb, K., Make, B. and Magnussen, H. (2004). Effects of tiotropium on lung hyperinflation, dyspnoea and exercise tolerance in COPD. *European Respiratory Journal*, 23(Payne), 832–840.

Parfitt, G., Evans, H. and Eston, R. G. (2012). Perceptually-regulated training at RPE 13 is pleasant and improves physical health. *Medicine and Science in Sports and Exercise*, 44, 1613–1618.

Pincivero, D. M., Campy, R. M. and Coelho, A. J. (2003). Knee flexor torque and perceived exertion: A gender and reliability analysis. *Medicine and Science in Sports and Exercise*, 35(NICE), 1720–1726.

Rejeski, W. J. (1981). The perception of exertion: A social psychophysiological integration. *Journal of Sport Psychology*, 4, 305–320.

Robertson, R. J. (1997). Perceived exertion in young people: Future directions of enquiry. In J. Weisman, N. Armstrong and B. Kirby (eds.), *Children and Exercise XIX*, Vol. 2, pp. 33–39. Exeter and Washington: Singer Press.

Robertson, R. J., Goss, F. L., Boer, N. F., Peoples, J. A., Foreman, A. J., Dabayebeh, L. M., Millich, N. B., Balasekaran, G., Riechman, S. E., Gallagher, J. D. and Thompkins, T. (2000). Children's OMNI Scale of perceived exertion: Mixed gender and race validation. *Medicine and Science in Sports and Exercise*, 32, 452–458.

Scherer, S. and Cassady, S. L. (1999). Rating of perceived exertion: Development and clinical applications for physical therapy exercise testing and prescription. *Cardiopulmonary Physical Therapy*, 10, 143–147.

Scherr, J., Wolfarth, B., Christle, J. W., et al. (2013). Associations between Borg's rating of perceived exertion and physiological measures of exercise intensity. *European Journal of Applied Physiology*, 113, 147–155.

Smutok, M. A., Skrinar, G. S. and Pandolf, K. B. (1980). Exercise intensity: Subjective regulation by perceived exertion. *Archives of Physical Medicine and Rehabilitation*, 61, 569–574.

Utter, A. C., Kang, J., Robertson, R. J., et al. (2002). Effect of carbohydrate ingestion on ratings of perceived exertion during a marathon. *Medicine and Science in Sports and Exercise*, 34, 1779–1784.

Williams, J. G. and Eston, R. G. (1989). Determination of the intensity dimension in vigorous exercise programmes with particular reference to the use of the rating of perceived exertion. *Sports Medicine*, 8, 177–189.

Williams, J. G., Eston, R. G. and Furlong, B. (1994). CERT: A perceived exertion scale for young children. *Perceptual and Motor Skills*, 79, 1451–1458.

Yelling, M., Lamb, K. and Swaine, L. L. (2002). Validity of a pictorial perceived exertion scale for effort estimation and effort production during stepping exercise in adolescent children. *European Physical Review*, 8, 157–175.

3.9 Strength testing

Dale Cannavan and Katie Thralls Butte

Maintenance of muscular strength is necessary and beneficial for sports performance and overall health (Androulakis-Korakakis et al., 2020). Maximum strength is the ability of a muscle or muscle group to generate force against an external resistance at a given velocity. The literature describes three modalities of strength testing; however, given the complex interaction of neuromuscular and tendinous factors, these modalities should not be interchanged. *Isotonic (isoinertial)* tests are easy and feasible to administer and implement in field and laboratory settings. *Isometric* tests are applicable in the field setting, but some techniques are limited to laboratory or clinical settings (i.e., manual muscle assessment). *Isokinetic* testing is considered to be the 'gold standard' for measuring strength; however, advanced technology and expertise typically dictate this approach is limited to laboratory and/or clinical settings.

Isotonic (isoinertial) testing

Isotonic contractions have traditionally been defined as moving a fixed resistance through a range of motion (ROM). However, *isoinertial* may be more appropriate terminology, as '*isotonic*' is misleading because constant muscle force is rare in human movement (Abernathy and Jürimäe, 1996). Nevertheless, this mode of strength testing is commonplace, with practitioners employing free weights, fixed machines, force plates and load cells; outcome measures include peak force/torque, rate of force development (RFD) and work/power. Tests include but are not limited to maximal concentric/eccentric strength, static and countermovement vertical or horizontal jumps and throwing assessments. The most commonly applied test involves the determination of the one-repetition maximum (1-RM: the maximum load that a person can lift for one repetition).

Choosing the type of test is based on the individual's characteristics (training background/status) and goals. The 1-RM is considered the 'gold standard' for strength assessment beyond a laboratory setting (Levinger et al., 2009). Typically 1-RM targets large muscle groups (e.g., barbell bench press or squat), demonstrating excellent reliability ($r = 0.92$ to 0.98) in experienced lifters. Less experienced lifters require four familiarisation sessions for acceptable reliability (Ritti-Dias et al.,

DOI: 10.4324/9781003045281-20

2011). Regardless of training experience and status, suitable familiarisation should always be implemented for optimal results and injury mitigation.

Suggested protocol for 1RM isotonic testing

1. Warm-up with full ROM using a load that permits five to ten repetitions, allowing familiarity of the test without fatigue.
2. Rest 1 min, then use a load approximating 80%–90% of the perceived maximum and perform three to five repetitions (various tables are available for this).
3. Rest 2–3 min and increase the load by 5%–10% for upper body and 10%–20% for lower body. Complete two to three repetitions.
4. Rest 3–4 min and increase the load as in step 3 and attempt a 1-RM.
5. If successful, repeat step 4 until a 1-RM is achieved. Perfect technique is required for this.
6. If unsuccessful, decrease the load by up to 5% for upper body and up to 10% for lower body and reattempt the 1-RM.
7. The 1-RM should be estimated within five work sets (steps 3 and 4); otherwise, fatigue would influence the result.

Submaximal tests

When 1-RM tests are unsuitable (i.e., untrained, inappropriate for training goals/time of season), a predicted 1-RM through regression equations is appropriate. Early predictive equations were developed with, and predominantly for, large muscle groups in athletic male populations (Brzycki, 1993). More recent studies have evidence of validity and reliability (less than 4 kg variation between predicted and actual 1-RM) in various populations (Macht et al., 2016). Different sport-specific equations exist (Table 3.9.1), and most prediction equations are not gender biased (for a review see Mayhew et al., 2008). Importantly, some equations exist for motor disabilities and spinal cord injury (Neto et al., 2017; Schwingel et al., 2009). Most studies report good predictive validity of 1-RM for multiple repetitions up to 10-RM, although fewer repetitions are more precise (Reynolds et al., 2006).

Important considerations for testing

1. Perform an incremental warm-up for the test procedure.
2. Minimal duration of static stretching to prevent stretch-induced strength deficits (Kay and Blazevich, 2012); dynamic stretching/mobility may be preferred.
3. Repeated testing at the same time of day in the same environmental conditions (see later) and same warm-up procedure. Nutrition, stimulants (caffeine) and sleep should be considered and noted.
4. Ensure a reproducible environment to assure representation of the individual's strength, rather than another factor (e.g., temperature, weight machine/technique used, motivational factors). For females, time of menstruation is an

Table 3.9.1 Estimated 1-RM formulas from multiple repetition tests

Test	Estimated 1-RM	Adjusted r2	SEE
Athletic population male[a]	100 × repetition mass/ (36.1115 × exp[−0.1240 × reps] + 67.9776)	0.96	1.67
Strength trained male[a]	100 × repetition mass/ (36.1133 × exp[−0.1352 × reps] + 68.2982)	0.96	2.06
Endurance trained male[a]	100 × repetition mass/ (37.4720 × exp[−0.1056 × reps] + 66.2090)	0.97	1.97
Moderately trained male[b]	(1.17 × repWt(kg)+[2.15 × reps]−12.31)	0.98	3.7
Female[c]	100 × repetition mass/ (41.9 × exp[−0.055 × reps] + 52.2)	0.98	Unavailable

Note: reps = repetitions to fatigue, exp = exponent

[a] Formula from Desgorces et al. (2010) with experienced male athletes
[b] Formula from Macht et al. (2016) with moderately trained men
[c] Formula from Mayhew et al. (1992) with untrained to moderately trained men and women

important consideration, with strength variation between the late luteal phase and the early follicular phase (Blagrove et al., 2020). Practitioners should aim to conduct subsequent tests at the same menstrual phase.
5   Sport/movement-specific tests are preferred to provide appropriate information.
6   Participants must be highly motivated.

Isometric testing

Isometric strength testing requires participants to exert a maximal force (at a specified joint angle) against an immovable object. Typical systems include dynamometers, force platforms and strain gauges recording maximal force/torque or RFD. The simplicity of these movements requires little familiarisation, with moderate-to-strong correlations ($r = 0.76$–0.97) between isoinertial force and isometric force, although this is highly dependent on the joint position (McMaster et al., 2014). As such, sports specificity is questionable.

RFD is an important athletic discriminator with early (<100 ms; intrinsic neuromuscular properties) and late (>200 ms; maximal strength) phases noted (Andersen and Aagaard, 2006). Despite its importance, RFD correlation with jumping is poor ($r < 0.4$; Nuzzo et al., 2008).

Despite non-specificity, isometric testing is useful in laboratory and clinical settings where important characteristics can be measured and monitored (see Davison et al., 2022).

Suggested protocol for isometric testing

1. Several practice contractions should be performed for tissue adaptations.
2. Careful consideration should be given to changes in tissue stiffness with excessive stretching and maximal isometric contractions during measures of RFD.

Isokinetic testing

Isokinetic testing requires the use of specialised equipment (isokinetic dynamometers), where velocity of movement is constant during a muscle contraction. Measures of concentric and eccentric muscle torques are performed at a wide range of velocities demonstrating different strength expressions over slow to fast movements. Testing is typically used for force-velocity or torque-angle relationships of a muscle group or limb, muscle fatigability and recovery and joint excursion. Measures of antagonistic muscles can be assessed with the following contractions: concentric-concentric, concentric-eccentric and eccentric-eccentric. Isokinetic dynamometers have shown very good to excellent reliability (although joint dependent) and validity up to $300^{\circ} \cdot s^{-1}$ (for a review see Caruso et al., 2012). However, a strict testing protocol must be used with at least one familiarisation session. Indeed, construct validity may decrease as a test movement pattern becomes less similar to an associated task movement pattern (e.g., stretch-shortening cycle movements). As such, the application to sports performance requires validation. Isokinetic dynamometers also measure isotonic, isometric, reactive eccentric and passive torques. Many of these measurements are more suitable in rehabilitation and laboratory settings.

Suggested protocol for isokinetic testing

1. Participant secured with joint and dynamometer axes aligned.
2. Gravity corrections performed as per manufacturer's guidelines.
3. Careful selection of ROM and velocities required to prevent joint hyperextension.
4. Three trials performed, although more are necessary as velocity increases (e.g., for knee extension, four and five trials should be given at 180° and $300^{\circ} \cdot s^{-1}$, respectively).
5. Ensure adequate rest intervals (>30 s); up to 4 min are warranted with slower velocities where perceived exertion and contraction time are greater.
6. Test order generally progresses from slower to faster velocities, being identical for subsequent testing sessions.

Conclusion

Muscular strength is an important component in a testing compendium. It is important to choose an appropriate protocol with attention to validity and reliability in the population of interest. Also, careful analysis and considerations related to the client characteristics, as well as their goals, must be considered when choosing the most appropriate test(s). These assessments must be carefully and intentionally imbedded into the periodised training/competing cycles of the individual.

References

Abernathy, P. J. and Jürimäe, J. (1996). Cross-sectional and longitudinal uses of isoinertial, isometric, and isokinetic dynamometry. *Medicine and Science in Sports and Exercise*, 28(9), 1180–1187.

Andersen, L. L. and Aagaard, P. (2006). Influence of maximal muscle strength and intrinsic muscle contractile properties on contractile rate of force development. *European Journal of Applied Physiology*, 96, 46–52.

Androulakis-Korakakis, P., Fisher, J. P. and Steele, J. (2020). The minimum effective training dose required to increase 1RM strength in resistance-trained men: A systematic review and meta-analysis. *Sports Medicine*, 50, 751–765.

Blagrove, R. C., Bruinvels, G. and Pedlar, C. R. (2020). Variations in strength-related measures during the menstrual cycle in eumenorrheic women: A systematic review and meta-analysis. *Journal of Science and Medicine in Sport*, 1, 1–11.

Brzycki, M. (1993). Strength testing-predicting a one-rep max from reps-to-fatigue. *Journal of Physical Education, Recreation, and Dance*, 64, 88–88.

Caruso, J. F., Brown, L. E. and Tufano, J. J. (2012). The reproducibility of isokinetic dynamometry data. *Isokinetics and Exercise Science*, 20, 239–253.

Desgorces, F. D., Berthelot, G., Dietrich, G. and Testa, M. S. A. (2010). Local muscular endurance and prediction of 1 repetition maximum for bench in 4 athletic populations. *Journal of Strength and Conditioning Research*, 24(2), 394–400.

Kay, A. D. and Blazevich, A. J. (2012). Effect of acute static stretch on maximal muscle performance: A systematic review. *Medicine and Science in Sports and Exercise*, 44(1), 154–164.

Levinger, I., Goodman, C., Hare, D. L., Jerums, G., Toia, D. and Selig, S. (2009). The reliability of the 1RM strength test for untrained middle-aged individuals. *Journal of Science and Medicine in Sport*, 12(3), 310–316.

Macht, J. W., Abel, M. G., Mullineaux, D. R. and Yates, J. W. (2016). Development of 1RM prediction equations for bench press in moderately trained men. *Journal of Strength and Conditioning Research*, 30(10), 2901–2906.

Mayhew, J. L., Ball, T. E., Arnold, M. D. and Bowen, J. C. (1992). Relative muscular endurance performance as a predictor of bench press strength in college men and women. *Journal of Applied Sport Science Research*, 6(4), 200–206.

Mayhew, J. L., Johnson, B. D., LaMonte, M. J., Lauber, D. and Kemmler, W. (2008). Accuracy of prediction equations for determining one repetition maximum bench press in women before and after resistance training. *Journal of Strength and Conditioning Research*, 22(5), 1570–1577.

McMaster, D. T., Gill, N., Cronin, J. and McGuigan, M. (2014). A brief review of strength and ballistic assessment methodologies in sport. *Sports Medicine*, 44, 603–623.

Neto, R., Guanais, P., Dornelas, E., Coutinho, A. C. B. and Costa, R. R. G. (2017). Validity of one-repetition maximum predictive equations in men with spinal cord injury. *Spinal Cord*, 55, 950–956.

Nuzzo, J. L., McBride, J. M., Cormie, P. and McCaulley, G. O. (2008). Relationship between countermovement jump performance and multijoint isometric and dynamic tests of strength. *Journal of Strength and Conditioning Research*, 22(3), 699–707.

Reynolds, J. M., Gordon, T. J. and Robergs, R. A. (2006). Prediction of one repetition maximum strength from multiple repetition maximum testing and anthropometry. *Journal of Strength and Conditioning Research*, 20(3), 584–592.

Ritti-Dias, R. M., Avelar, A., Salvador, E. P. and Cyrino, E. S. (2011). Influence of previous experience on resistance training on reliability of one-repetition maximum test. *Journal of Strength and Conditioning Research*, 25(5), 1418–1422.

Schwingel, P. A., Porto, Y. C., Dias, M. C. M., Moreira, M. M. and Zoppi, C. C. (2009). Predicting one repetition maximum equations accuracy in Paralympic rowers with motor disabilities. *Journal of Strength and Conditioning Research*, 23, 1045–1050.

3.10 Blood sampling

Ronald J. Maughan and Susan M. Shirreffs

The collection of blood samples from human subjects is required in many physiological, biochemical and nutritional investigations. The purpose of the sample will determine the method of collection, the volume of blood required and the way in which the specimen is handled and stored.

Blood sampling and handling

Many different methods and sites of blood sampling can be used to collect samples for analysis, and the results obtained will be affected by the procedures used in sample collection. A detailed discussion of the sampling procedures and of the consequences for the measurement of various haematological parameters is presented by Maughan et al. (2001). Standardisation of sampling conditions is crucial if meaningful results are to be obtained. Where the study design makes this impossible, it is important to appreciate the extent to which the sample is influenced by the conditions under which it is collected.

The main sampling procedures involve collection of arterial, venous, arterialised venous or capillary blood. In most routine laboratory or field investigations of interest to the sports scientist, arterial blood sampling is impractical and unnecessarily invasive and will not be considered in detail here. Where arterial blood is required, arterial puncture may be used, but in most situations, collection of arterialised venous blood as described later gives an adequate representation of arterial blood.

Pre-sampling standardisation

The composition of blood is influenced by many factors, including recent food and fluid intake and exercise. It is also influenced, however, by many less obvious factors, including posture and ambient temperature. Failure to control for these will result in an increased variability in the composition of any samples collected, but the controls that should be applied will depend in part on the variables to be measured in the sample.

Blood and plasma volumes are markedly influenced by the physical activity, hydration status and posture of the subject prior to sample collection. In many cases,

DOI: 10.4324/9781003045281-21

samples are collected after an overnight fast of at least 8 h duration and without prior exercise. Difficulties may arise in the case of athletes who are training two or three times per day. It is also known that prolonged (1–2 h) hard exercise typically results in haemoconcentration, but this is followed within a few hours by a marked haemodilution that may persist for several (at least 5) days (Robertson et al., 1990).

The sampling site and method can also affect the haemoglobin concentration, as arterial, capillary and venous samples differ in a number of respects due to fluid exchange between the vascular and extravascular spaces and to differences in the distribution of red blood cells (Harrison, 1985). The venous plasma-to-red cell ratio is higher than that of arterial blood, although the total body haemoglobin content is clearly not acutely affected by these factors. Haemodynamic changes caused by postural shifts will alter the fluid exchange across the capillary bed, leading to plasma volume changes that will cause changes in the circulating concentration. Moving from a supine position to standing, plasma volume falls by about 10% and whole blood volume by about 5% (Harrison, 1985). This corresponds to a change in the measured haemoglobin concentration of about 7 $g \cdot l^{-1}$. These changes are reversed moving from an upright to a seated or supine position. These changes make it imperative that posture is controlled in studies where haemoglobin changes are to be used as an index of changes in blood and plasma volume over the time course of an experiment. It is, however, common to see studies reported in the literature where samples were collected from subjects resting in a supine position prior to exercising in a seated (cycling or rowing) or upright (treadmill walking or running) position. The changing blood volume not only invalidates any haematological measures made in the early stages of exercise, it also confounds cardiovascular measures, as the stroke volume and heart rate will also be affected by the blood volume. Likewise, studies of running exercise often allow subjects to sit or lie down before collecting post-exercise samples.

Flow through the superficial forearm veins is very much influenced by skin blood flow, which in turn depends on ambient temperature and the thermoregulatory strain imposed on the individual. The composition of venous blood is affected by the degree of arterialisation: where sampling occurs over time, therefore, and where the degree of arterialisation of the venous blood will influence the measures to be made, this may cause major problems. In cold conditions, flow to the limbs and to the skin will be low, and venous blood will be highly desaturated. In prolonged exercise in a warm environment, a progressive increase in skin blood flow results in a corresponding increase in the degree of arterialisation of samples collected from superficial veins – the normal sampling site in such experimental conditions. For some substrates and metabolites which are routinely measured, the difference between arterial and venous concentrations is relatively small, and in many cases it may be ignored. Where a difference does occur and is of importance, the effect of a change in arterialisation of the blood at the sampling site may be critical. Pre-exercise warming of the hand on the limb from which samples are to be collected may reduce the risk of results being influenced by changes in flow.

There is some debate as to which, if any, concentration measurements should be corrected for changes in blood or plasma volume. The modern Coulter counter incorporates an autosampler and spectrophotometer, which permits automated measurement of haemoglobin concentration. While this automation has considerable attractions, including a high level of accuracy in the measures of red cell count and haemoglobin concentration, care must be taken in the interpretation of the measures of cell volume. The diluent commonly used in the preparation of samples for analysis is not isotonic with normal human blood plasma: Isoton II has an osmolality of about 340 mOsmol·kg^{-1}, compared with an osmolality of human plasma of about 285–290 mOsmol·kg^{-1}. Because the red cell membrane is freely permeable to water, a rapid equilibration will take place on mixing of blood with the diluent, leading to a change (in the case of Isoton II there will be a decrease) in the red cell volume. The measured volume is therefore different, by an amount proportional to the difference in osmolality between the plasma and the diluent, from the volume of the cells while in the circulation. In situations where the plasma osmolality changes substantially, as during intense or prolonged exercise, this will invalidate measures made using automated cell counting procedures (Watson and Maughan, 2014).

Venous blood

Venous blood sampling is probably the method of choice for most routine purposes: sampling from a superficial hand, forearm or antecubital vein is simple, painless and relatively free from risk of complications. During exercise involving the lower limbs, the composition of venous blood collected from a hand or arm vein will be very different from that of veins draining the active muscles. In exercise involving the arms, such as in many Paralympic sports, account needs to be taken of the sampling site and of the consequences of changes in flow rate that occur during exercise. Sampling may be by venous puncture or by an indwelling cannula. Where repeated sampling is necessary at short time intervals, introduction of a cannula is obviously preferred to avoid repeated venous punctures. Either a plastic cannula or a butterfly-type cannula can be used. The latter has obvious limitations if introduced into an antecubital vein, as movement of the elbow is severely restricted. However, because it is smaller and therefore less painful for the subject, it is often preferable if used in a superficial hand or forearm vein, provided that long-term (more than a few hours) access is not required. A 21-gauge cannula is adequate for most purposes, and only where large volumes of blood are required will a larger size be necessary. In most situations where vigorous movements are likely, the forearm site is preferred to the elbow. Clotting of blood in the cannula is easily avoided by flushing with sterile isotonic saline. Where intermittent sampling is performed, the cannula may be flushed with a bolus of saline to which heparin (10–50 IU·ml^{-1} of saline) is added, allowing the subject freedom to move around between samples. Alternatively, where the subject is to remain static, as in a cycle or treadmill exercise test, a continuous slow infusion (about 0.3 ml·min^{-1}) of isotonic saline may be used, avoiding the need to add heparin. Collection of samples by repeated venous puncture is not practical in most exercise situations and increases the risk that samples will be affected by venous occlusion applied during puncture.

Arterialised venous blood

Where arterial blood is required, there is no alternative to arterial puncture, but for most practical purposes, blood collected from a superficial vein on the dorsal surface of a heated hand is indistinguishable from arterial blood. This reflects both the very high flow rate and the opening of arteriovenous shunts in the hand. Sampling can conveniently be achieved by introduction of a butterfly cannula into a suitable vein. The hand is first heated, either by immersion up to the forearm for at least 10 min in hot (about 42°C) water (Forster et al., 1972) or by insertion into a hot air box (McGuire et al., 1976). If hot water immersion is used prior to exercise, arterialisation – as indicated by oxygen saturation – can be maintained for some considerable time by wearing a glove, allowing this technique to be used during exercise studies. This procedure allows large volumes of blood to be collected without problems.

Capillary blood

Where only small samples of blood are required, capillary blood samples can readily be obtained from a fingertip or ear lobe. The use of micro methods for analysis means that the limited sample volume that can be obtained should not necessarily be a problem in metabolic studies. It is possible to make duplicate measurements of the concentrations of glucose, lactate, pyruvate, alanine, glycerol, acetoacetate and 3-hydroxybutyrate, as well as several other metabolites, on a single 20 μl blood sample using routine laboratory methods (Maughan, 1982).

The sampling site should be arterialised by immersion of the whole hand in hot (42°C) water in the case of the fingertip, and by the use of a rubefacient in the case of the ear lobe. Samples can be obtained without stimulating vasodilatation, but bleeding is slower, the volumes that can be reliably collected are smaller and the composition of the sample is more variable. It is essential that a free-flowing sample is obtained. If pressure is applied, an excess of plasma over red cells will be obtained. Samples are most conveniently collected into graduated glass capillaries where only small volumes are required (typically 10–100 μl). The blood must never be expelled from these tubes by mouth because of the obvious risks involved. Volumes greater than about 0.5 ml are difficult to obtain by this method.

Blood treatment after collection

Analysis of most metabolites can be carried out using whole blood, plasma or serum, but the differential distribution of most metabolites and substrates between the plasma and the intracellular space may affect values. It is convenient to use whole blood for the measurement of most metabolites. Glucose and lactate are commonly measured on either plasma or whole blood, but glycerol and free fatty acid concentrations should be measured using plasma or serum. The differences become significant where there is a concentration difference between the intracellular and extracellular compartments.

If plasma is to be obtained by centrifugation of the sample, a suitable anticoagulant must be added. A variety of agents can be used, depending on the measurements to be made. The potassium salt of ethylenediaminetetraacetic acid (EDTA) is a convenient anticoagulant, but is clearly inappropriate when plasma potassium is to be measured. Heparin is a suitable alternative in this situation. For serum collection, blood should be added to a plain tube and left for at least 1 h before centrifugation: clotting will take place more rapidly if the sample is left in a warm place. If there is a need to stop glycolysis in serum or plasma samples (for example, where the concentration of glucose, lactate or other glycolytic intermediates is to be measured), fluoride should be added: failure to do this will result in measurable decreases in glucose concentration and increases in lactate concentration. Where metabolites of glucose are to be measured on whole blood, the most convenient method is immediate deproteinisation of the sample to inactivate the enzymes which would otherwise alter the concentrations of substances of interest after the sample has been withdrawn.

Safety issues

Whatever method is used for the collection of blood samples, the safety of the subject and of the investigator is paramount. Strict safety precautions must always be followed in the sampling and handling of blood. It is wise to assume that all samples are infected and to treat them accordingly. This means wearing gloves and appropriate protective clothing and following guidelines for handling of samples and disposal of waste material. Appropriate antiseptic procedures must always be followed, including ensuring cleanliness of the sampling environment, cleaning of the puncture site and use of clean materials to staunch bleeding after sampling. Blood sampling should be undertaken only by those with appropriate training and insurance coverage, and a qualified first-aider should be available at all times. All contaminated materials must be disposed of using appropriate and clearly identified waste containers. Used needles, cannulae and lancets must be disposed of immediately in a suitable sharps bin: re-sheathing of used needles must never be attempted. Sharps – whether contaminated or not – must always be disposed of in an approved container and must never be mixed with other waste. Any spillage of blood must be treated immediately.

There is clearly a need for appropriate training of all laboratory personnel involved in any aspect of blood sampling and handling. Most major hospitals run courses for the training of phlebotomists, who are often individuals with no medical background. The taking of blood samples is a simple physical skill, and medical training is not required when expert assistance is at hand. What is essential, though, is the necessary back-up if something goes wrong, and a suitable training in first aid and resuscitation should be seen as a necessary part of the training for the sports scientists who collect blood samples outside a hospital setting.

References

Forster, H. V., Dempsey, J. A., Thomson, J., Vidruk, E. and DoPico, G. A. (1972). Estimation of arterial PO_2, PCO_2, pH and lactate from arterialized venous blood. *Journal of Applied Physiology*, 32, 134–137.

Harrison, M. (1985). Effects of thermal stress and exercise on blood volume in humans. *Physiological Reviews*, 65, 149–209.

Maughan, R. J. (1982). A simple rapid method for the determination of glucose, lactate, pyruvate, alanine, 3-hydroxybutyrate and acetoacetate on a single 20μl blood sample. *Clinical Chimica Acta*, 122, 232–240.

Maughan, R. J., Leiper, J. B. and Greaves, M. (2001). Haematology. In R. G. Eston and T. P. Reilly (eds.), *Kinanthropometry and Exercise Physiology Laboratory Manual*, Vol. 2 (2nd ed.), pp. 99–115. London: Spon.

McGuire, E. A. H., Helderman, J. H., Tobin, J. D., Andres, R. and Berman, M. (1976). Effects of arterial versus venous sampling on analysis of glucose kinetics in man. *Journal of Applied Physiology*, 41, 565–573.

Robertson, J. D., Maughan, R. J., Walker, K. A. and Davidson, R. J. L. (1990). Plasma viscosity and the haemodilution following distance running. *Clinical Hemorheology and Microcirculation*, 10, 51–57.

Watson, P. and Maughan, R. J. (2014). Artifacts in plasma volume changes due to hematology analyzer derived hematocrit. *Medicine and Science in Sports and Exercise*, 46, 52–59.

3.11 Skeletal muscle biopsy

Techniques and applications

Richard A. Ferguson and Natalie F. Shur

Introduction and background

The successful use of the percutaneous needle biopsy technique has formed an integral part of human skeletal muscle research for many years. Originally described by Duchenne (Charriere and Duchenne, 1865), it was not until 1962 and the introduction of a new type of percutaneous biopsy needle by Jonas Bergström that the technique became an important tool, initially in clinical medicine but more recently for biochemical, physiological, nutritional, cellular and molecular research within the sport and exercise sciences. Indeed, Bergström and his colleague Eric Hultman, both Scandinavian physician scientists, were instrumental in performing some of the pioneering studies in human exercise metabolism using the muscle biopsy technique (Figure 3.11.1), frequently using themselves as subjects (Bergström and Hultman, 1966). Following a sabbatical at the Karolinska Institute in Sweden, Richard H. T. Edwards (1971), a British physician later famed for his research into muscular dystrophy, brought this technique to the United Kingdom.

The Bergström needle consists of two cylinders. The outer one is 3–5 mm in diameter with an aperture near the tip. The sharp inner trochar cuts the tissue and a sample enters the aperture. One subsequently removes the tissue sample by pushing it out with a metal rod. Using suction significantly increases muscle tissue yield to over 200 mg (Evans et al., 1982; Hennessey et al., 1997; Tarnopolsky et al., 2011). Sample yield and relative discomfort of the procedure relate to the sharpness of the inner trochar, which one should replace if it becomes blunt. Many studies require multiple samples to be taken in a single experimental session (e.g., pre- and post-exercise); therefore, care must be taken to ensure repeated samples on the same leg are taken from different incisions at least 2.5 cm apart. Whilst some aspects of muscle metabolism may still be influenced (impaired adenosine triphosphate [ATP] and glycogen resynthesis for several days; Constantin-Teodosiu et al., 1996), confounding changes in muscle transcription responses are not elicited (Murton et al., 2014).

Whilst the Bergström needle seems to be the most common method used, other percutaneous needles are available. The micro-biopsy device is a variant of a spring-loaded, one-handed automated biopsy and utilises a disposable core biopsy needle (e.g., Bard Magnum, TSK Acecut). The advantage of the micro-biopsy

DOI: 10.4324/9781003045281-22

Skeletal muscle biopsy 119

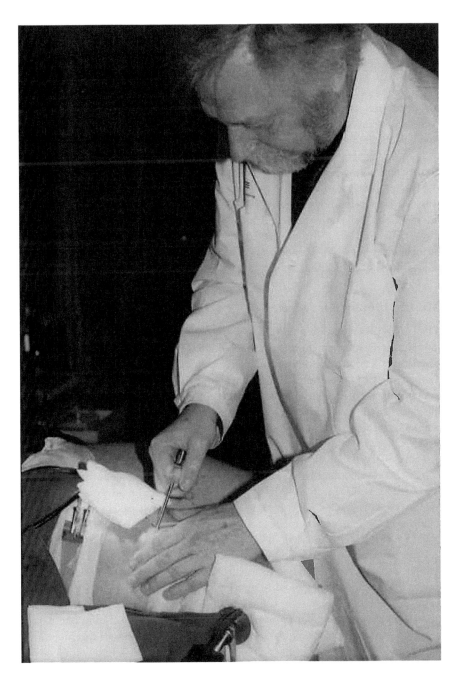

Figure 3.11.1 Professor Eric Hultman performing a muscle biopsy of the vastus lateralis using a Bergström needle.

technique is that a smaller incision (2–3 mm) is required. Alternatively, an insertion cannula can be used for biopsy needle placement, rather than making an incision. This method has been described as 'less invasive' and results in lower levels of discomfort (Hayot et al., 2005); therefore, in certain patient populations such as the frail, comorbid or sarcopenic, it may be better tolerated. A disadvantage of the micro-biopsy technique, however, is that it has a reduced yield (~20 mg) compared to Bergström, necessitating multiple passes depending on outcome measures. Smaller yields may make subsequent analyses more difficult, although previous studies have demonstrated that if the yield is sufficient, the micro-biopsy technique is equivalent to Bergström for laboratory analyses, including enzymatic activity and fibre-type distribution (Hayot et al., 2005).

Muscle biopsies can also be obtained using a conchotome forceps, which open with a scissor grip and were originally designed for ear, nose and throat (ENT) interventions. Advantages of the conchotome is a more exact placement of the instrument and less disruption of the biopsy sample, important for histology/histochemical analyses. Disadvantages include increased trauma to surrounding tissues and higher bleeding rates.

Muscle biopsy procedure

The biopsy procedure itself is relatively simple. One should check the participant for contraindications, including bleeding diatheses, current anticoagulant or antiplatelet medication, immunosuppression, active infection, musculoskeletal abnormalities such as local trauma and allergy to local anaesthetic: one must obtain written informed consent. The most common site for human muscle biopsies is the vastus lateralis, as it is generally the largest muscle of the quadriceps femoris, it is a major locomotory muscle and it is easily accessed. The optimal site for vastus lateralis biopsy is the distal portion of the muscle, between one-half and three-quarters of the length from the greater trochanter to the lateral epicondyle, just anterior to the iliotibial band, where the risk of hitting a major nerve or blood vessel is lowest (Chen et al., 2019). Other sites include the gastrocnemius (e.g., Morton et al., 2009), soleus (e.g., Harridge et al., 1996), biceps femoris (e.g., Evangelidis et al., 2017), biceps brachii (e.g., Venturelli et al., 2015), triceps brachii (e.g., Harridge et al., 1996) and deltoid (e.g., Costill et al., 1985).

Under sterile conditions, one injects local anaesthetic (typically 1% lidocaine without adrenaline) subcutaneously, which infiltrates over the superficial muscle fascia. Ideally, one should avoid infiltration of local anaesthetic into the muscle, as this can potentially interfere with outcome measures: in practice, however, infiltration might occur without ultrasound guidance. After about 2 min, one makes a 4- to 5-mm incision through the skin, which continues through the superficial muscle fascia. One then advances a biopsy needle gently through the skin incision and uses it to locate the incision in the fascia. Once located, the needle is gently but firmly advanced into the muscle 1–2 cm beyond the fascia (some resistance is usually felt). The participant is likely to feel a pressure sensation ('discomfort' rather than a 'sharp pain') and the muscle will occasionally twitch. At this point, the inner trochar is pulled back enough to open the cutting aperture, and an assistant applies suction. The needle is firmly closed and with suction maintained, one obtains two or three further samples: rotation of the needle may occur between each sample. For micro-biopsies, follow the same preparatory steps as with the Bergström needle, although it is not necessary to continue the incision through the superficial muscle fascia. With a micro-biopsy sample, one inserts a needle through the incision and advances it through the muscle fascia into the belly of the muscle. The device is then triggered and a sample taken. Multiple passes would occur, whereby the needle angle changes to ensure one samples fresh muscle. For biopsies using a conchotome, after local anaesthetic infiltration, a 5-mm skin incision is made, which continues through the superficial muscle fascia. Closed jaws of the conchotome are then inserted into the muscle, with the long axis of the jaws parallel to the muscle fibres. Subsequently, the jaws are opened, advanced and closed over the muscle and then rotated 180 degrees and withdrawn (Dietrichson et al., 1987).

In all cases, once one removes a biopsy needle, apply firm and direct pressure to the biopsy site; ice may also be applied. This pressure is maintained for a minimum of 5 min, or longer if there is persistent bleeding or oozing. The incision can be closed using sterile Steri-strips, ensuring opposition of the two wound edges. One then applies a sterile gauze over the top of the site of an incision for further protection and a compression bandage is used thereafter to maintain pressure for 12 h. Written aftercare advice is given to the participant, including details of wound care (ensuring the incision is kept clean and dry), information about performing exercise and to take simple painkillers such as paracetamol if discomfort is excessive.

Muscle tissue treatment after collection

Muscle tissue can be prepared in several ways depending on the subsequent analysis. For measurement of muscle metabolites, gene expression, mRNA/protein content and enzyme activity, the tissue is quickly snap-frozen in liquid nitrogen and subsequently stored at −80°C until analysis. In the case of analysis of high-energy phosphates, the time taken between the muscle sampling and snap freezing should be rapid (and can be as quick as 3 sec; Hultman and Sjöholm, 1983). One may perform subsequent assays on homogenised samples. One may also conduct fibre-type specific analysis on single fibres micro-dissected from freeze-dried samples. Despite being very time consuming, one section of the dissected fibre is analysed for fibre type using acid-labile myofibrillar ATPase histochemistry (Essen et al., 1975), SDS-PAGE for myosin heavy-chain isoform determination (Sant'Aana Pereirra et al., 1995) or, more recently, a dot blotting method based on Western blotting techniques (Christiansen et al., 2019). The remaining fibre fragment, or pooled samples of the same fibre type, are then analysed for the metabolites, gene transcripts or proteins of interest.

The preparation of tissue for histology/histochemical analysis requires preservation of tissue architecture and cell morphology; therefore, prompt and adequate embedding and/or fixation is essential. The three main methods of embedding tissue for sectioning are paraffin wax, optimal cutting temperature (OCT) compound (e.g., Tissue-Tek) and resin, each with their own benefits and weaknesses. One removes excess blood, fat and connective tissue prior to mounting, in most cases with OCT, on either cork or an appropriate mould. This is carefully but rapidly frozen in liquid nitrogen–cooled isopentane, which prevents the formation of ice crystals, and subsequently stored at $-80°C$ until analysis.

If fresh tissue is required, the sample is simply placed into the appropriate buffer/medium (Dulbecco's Modified Eagle's Medium [DMEM] for cell culture or 'BIOPS' for mitochondrial respiration) prior to further processing. Examination of the contractile properties of single fibres is also possible (Bottinelli et al., 1996) whereby the sample is immediately placed in skinning solution prior to micro-dissection of single fibres and subsequent analysis of force-velocity and energetic characteristics.

Risks and safety aspects

The muscle biopsy method is a safe procedure. Overall, the complication rate for biopsies is generally reported to be in the range of 0.1%–4% (for summary table see Chen et al., 2019). Normally, after a biopsy, participants experience a day or two of localised stiffness, but mobility is not affected. Indeed, for athletic populations training should not be impaired, and it may be recommended to perform light physical exercise the day after the procedure. The incision should be kept dry and any potential sources of infection should be avoided. The incision heals after about 10 days, and a small scar is visible that fades over time. On occasions, a small lump of scar tissue may form under the site of the incision, but this normally disappears within 2–3 mo. The risks of local skin infection or a deeper wound infection are extremely rare, and ensuring good clinical practice in maintaining sterility throughout the procedure minimises this risk. There is a risk of bleeding within the muscle or beneath the fatty layer of the skin next to the muscle, evident from swelling or extensive bruising. Rarely, haematomas may form, limiting the range of motion of the muscles for a few weeks. Altered sensation or numbness of an area of skin (paraesthesia) adjacent to the biopsy scar may occur, which is caused by injury to a small sensory nerve branch. There is a very low risk of damage to a small motor nerve branch to the muscle, which may result in partial atrophy and subsequent weakness of the muscle. This will not be initially obvious, but will become apparent after several months. Although this may be cosmetically visible, this complication will not influence day-to-day activities.

As muscle biopsies are an invasive clinical procedure, only trained and experienced practitioners should perform the technique: individuals performing such a procedure should be indemnified. Best practice should include appropriate clinical supervision and/or oversight with an established pathway for medical follow-up should any complications arise.

Acknowledgements

We would like to thank Professor Paul L. Greenhaff and Professor Kenny Smith for supplying some of the images.

References

Bergström, J. (1962). Muscle electrolytes in man: Determined by neutron activation analysis on needle biopsy specimens: A study on normal subjects, kidney patients, and patients with chronic diarrhaea. *Scandinavian Journal of Clinical Laboratory Investigation*, 14(Suppl. 68), 110.

Bergström, J. and Hultman, E. (1966). Muscle glycogen synthesis after exercise: An enhancing factor localized to the muscle cells in man. *Nature*, 210(5033), 309–310.

Bottinelli, R., Canepari, M., Pellegrino, M. A. and Reggiani, C. (1996). Force-velocity properties of human skeletal muscle fibres: Myosin heavy chain isoform and temperature dependence. *Journal of Physiology*, 495(2), 573–586.

Charriere, M. and Duchenne, G. B. (1865). Emporte piece histologique. *Bulletin of the Academy of Medicine*, 30, 1050–1051.

Chen, X. S., Abbey, A., Bharmal, S., Harris, E., Hudson, L., Krinner, E., Langan, A., Maling, J., Nijran, H., Street, C. and Wooley, B. R. (2019). Neurovascular structures in human vastus lateralis muscle and the ideal biopsy site. *Scandinavian Journal of Medicine and Science in Sports*, 29(4), 504–514.

Christiansen, D., MacInnis, M. J., Zacharewicz, E., Xu, H., Frankish, B. P. and Murphy, R. M. (2019). A fast, reliable, and sample-sparing method to identify fibre types of single muscle fibres. *Scientific Reports*, 9, 6473.

Constantin-Teodosiu, D., Casey, A., Short, A. H., Hultman, E. and Greenhaff, P. L. (1996). The effect of repeated muscle biopsy sampling on ATP and glycogen resynthesis following exercise in man. *European Journal of Applied Physiology*, 73(1–2), 186–190.

Costill, D. L., Fink, W. J., Hargreaves, M., King, D. S., Thomas, R. and Fielding, R. (1985). Metabolic characteristics of skeletal muscle during detraining from competitive swimming. *Medicine and Science in Sports and Exercise*, 17(3), 339–343.

Dietrichson, P., Coakley, J., Smith, P. E., Griffiths, R. D., Helliwell, T. R. and Edwards, R. H. (1987). Conchotome and needle percutaneous biopsy of skeletal muscle. *Journal of Neurology, Neurosurgery and Psychiatry*, 50(11), 1461–1467.

Edwards, R. H. (1971). Percutaneous needle-biopsy of skeletal muscle in diagnosis and research. *The Lancet*, 298(7724), 593–595.

Essen, B., Jansson, E., Henriksson, J., Taylor, A. W. and Saltin, B. (1975). Metabolic characteristics of fibre types in human skeletal muscle. *Acta Physiologia Scandinavica*, 95, 153–165.

Evangelidis, P. E., Massey, G. J., Ferguson, R. A., Wheeler, P. C., Pain, M. T. and Folland, J. P. (2017). The functional significance of hamstrings composition: Is it really a 'fast' muscle group? *Scandinavian Journal of Medicine and Science in Sports*, 27, 1181–1189.

Evans, W. J., Phinney, S. D. and Young, V. R. (1982). Suction applied to a muscle biopsy maximizes sample size. *Medicine and Science in Sports and Exercise*, 14, 101–102.

Harridge, S. D., Bottinelli, R., Canepari, M., Pellegrino, M. A., Reggiani, C., Esbjörnsson, M. and Saltin, B. (1996). Whole-muscle and single-fibre contractile properties and myosin heavy chain isoforms in humans. *Pflügers Archiv*, 432(5), 913–920.

Hayot, M., Michaud, A., Koechlin, C., Caron, M. A., Leblanc, P., Préfaut, C. and Maltais, F. (2005). Skeletal muscle microbiopsy: A validation study of a minimally invasive technique. *European Respiratory Journal*, 25(3), 431–440.

Hennessey, J. V., Chromiak, J. A., Della Ventura, S., Guertin, J. and MacLean, D. B. (1997). Increase in percutaneous muscle biopsy yield with a suction enhancement technique. *Journal of Applied Physiology*, 82, 1739–1742.

Hultman, E. and Sjöholm, H. (1983). Energy metabolism and contraction force of human skeletal muscle in situ during electrical stimulation. *Journal of Physiology*, 345, 525–532.

Morton, J. P., Croft, L., Bartlett, J. D., Maclaren, D. P., Reilly, T., Evans, L., McArdle, A. and Drust, B. (2009). Reduced carbohydrate availability does not modulate training-induced heat shock protein adaptations but does upregulate oxidative enzyme activity in human skeletal muscle. *Journal of Applied Physiology*, 106(5), 1513–1521.

Murton, A. J., Billeter, R., Stephens, F. B., Des Etages, S. G., Graber, F., Hill, R. J., Marimuthu, K. and Greenhaff, P. L. (2014). Transient transcriptional events in human skeletal muscle at the outset of concentric resistance exercise training. *Journal of Applied Physiology*, 116(1), 113–125.

Sant'Aana Pereira, J. A., Wessels, A., Nijtmans, L., Moorman, A. F. and Sargeant, A. J. (1995). New method for the accurate characterization of single human skeletal muscle fibres demonstrates a relation between mATPase and MyHC expression in pure and hybrid fibre types. *Journal of Muscle Research and Cell Motility*, 16(1), 21–34.

Tarnopolsky, M. A., Pearce, E., Smith, K. and Lach, B. (2011). Suction-modified Bergström muscle biopsy technique: Experience with 13,500 procedures. *Muscle and Nerve*, 43, 717–725.

Venturelli, M., Saggin, P., Muti, E., Naro, F., Cancellara, L., Toniolo, L., Tarperi, C., Calabria, E., Richardson, R. S., Reggiani, C. and Schena, F. (2015). In vivo and in vitro evidence that intrinsic upper- and lower-limb skeletal muscle function is unaffected by ageing and disuse in oldest-old humans. *Acta Physiologica*, 215(1), 58–71.

3.12 Non-invasive assessment of the neuromuscular system

Glyn Howatson, Kevin Thomas, Paul Ansdell, and Stuart Goodall

Understanding how the neuromuscular system responds to exercise can help us comprehend the underpinning factors contributing to fatigue, recovery and adaptation in groups ranging from elite sports performers to clinical populations. Specifically, measuring outcomes along the brain-to-muscle pathway can help provide valuable information on the immediate, short- and longer-term responses following an exercise stimulus, in turn, providing important knowledge on behaviour and limitations of the neuromuscular system during exercise, how we might recover over time and how we can optimise longer-term adaptation. This chapter will provide an overview of the common paradigms in which neuromuscular function is assessed and subsequently describe the common functional and myoelectric outcomes that can be measured to non-invasively study neuromuscular function in response to exercise.

Applications of neuromuscular assessment

Exercise-induced and pathological fatigue

Neuromuscular function is commonly used to assess factors contributing to fatigue, here defined as a symptom or feeling of tiredness, weariness or exhaustion (Thomas et al., 2018). Neuromuscular assessment can be used to provide important insights into the limits of human performance and disease progression and help to understand the magnitude and locus of impairment in the neuromuscular system that contribute to the symptom of fatigue.

Recovery and adaptation

It is well established that strenuous exercise can elicit decrements in performance, and in some circumstances these performance declines can persist for several days. By understanding the time course of recovery and the neuromuscular adjustments underpinning the performance decline, it is possible to make informed decisions on recovery strategies and the timeline required for the resolution of function. Neuromuscular assessment techniques allow researchers and practitioners to quantify the efficacy of an intervention(s) that underpins behavioural changes,

DOI: 10.4324/9781003045281-23

such as strength, rate of force development and fatigue resistance. Collectively, if there is an expectation for an intervention to modulate the brain-to-muscle pathway, neuromuscular assessment has the potential to provide a mechanistic insight into central and peripheral nervous system adaptation.

Methods to assess neuromuscular function

Adjustments in neuromuscular function can be studied through acquisition of force and electromyographic signals, during voluntary contraction and in response to external stimulation at various sites of the brain-to-muscle pathway (Figure 3.12.1). Changes in force-producing capacity (i.e., maximal voluntary contraction [MVC]), or the involuntary twitch response to stimulation, provide insight into the locus of adjustment in neuromuscular function and are typically divided into 'central' and 'peripheral' components. Central adjustments are usually quantified by changes in voluntary activation (VA), which reflects an inability to maximally activate muscle (Gandevia et al., 1995).

Peripheral adjustments are the result of changes at, or distal to, the neuromuscular junction that impact the excitation-coupling process and cross-bridge formation (Fitts, 2008), and can be quantified through studying changes in the potentiated twitch response to external stimulation. Myoelectric signals can also be acquired to provide indices of neuromuscular function. These include measurement of surface electromyography (EMG) signals during voluntary muscle actions and in response to external stimulation of the brain (motor evoked potentials [MEPs]), cervicomedullary junctions (CMEPs), spine (lumbar evoked potentials [LEPs]) or the motor nerve or muscle (maximal compound muscle action potential, M_{max}) at rest and during voluntary muscle actions (Figure 3.12.2 illustrates these techniques combined in a single applied scenario). Several stimulation paradigms to measure a multitude of variables along the brain-to-muscle pathway are possible, but how these modulate with exercise and disease is a topic of debate (a summary of these techniques is presented in Table 3.12.1).

Expression of force

A participant's MVC can be recorded from almost any muscle using an appropriate dynamometer or calibrated strain gauge. Most research has used an isometric MVC, but it is also possible to measure isotonic and isokinetic MVCs with the appropriate instruments. Prior to the performance of an MVC, participants should be taken through a warm-up, including a range of brief, submaximal maneuverers. When measuring isometric MVCs, three contractions are usually performed, each lasting ~3–5 s, separated by at least 30 s. Such a configuration also elicits full potentiation of the contractile apparatus; if resting, evoked twitches can also be studied (see later). It is important to note that participants should not perform too many contractions for assessment purposes, as these in themselves can cause functional declines.

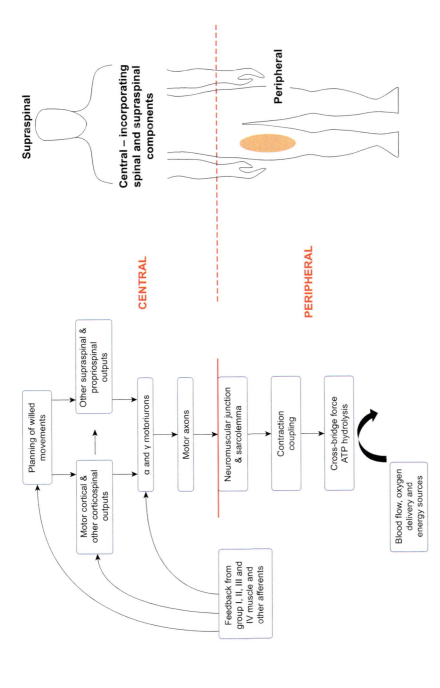

Figure 3.12.1 Neuromuscular function studied through acquisition of force and electromyographic signals.

Methodological considerations when measuring force

Force is typically the primary variable in the assessment of neuromuscular function, and thus the choice of device is very important. Traditional strain gauges attached to bespoke instruments are commonly used, but it is critical there is no compliance in the system, insofar as there is no slack between the device and the attachment to the limb expressing force. If the strain gauge needs attaching to a limb, ensure the attachment is non-compliant – a leather or Velcro strap is a good option. Traditional isokinetic dynamometers are often fitted with padded cuffs, which adds compliance to the system and can compromise sensitivity, especially for evoked responses. Dynamometers can be used; however, some modification to the 'off the counter' attachments might be required. Regardless of the instrument, the muscle of interest must be isolated, and it might be necessary to restrain other body parts to reduce movement in other muscle groups. For example, if knee extensors are being examined, a restraint across the waist to avoid extraneous movement from hip flexors and extensors prevents participants from rising out of the seat and is necessary to reduce the possibility of altering the muscle length of the rectus femoris. Lastly, it is of vital importance to regularly calibrate the strain gauge, dynamometer or other manipulandum.

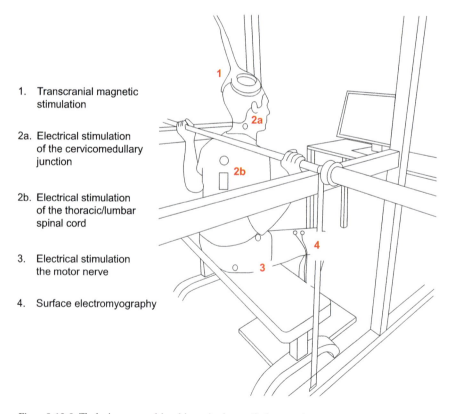

1. Transcranial magnetic stimulation

2a. Electrical stimulation of the cervicomedullary junction

2b. Electrical stimulation of the thoracic/lumbar spinal cord

3. Electrical stimulation the motor nerve

4. Surface electromyography

Figure 3.12.2 Techniques combined in a single applied scenario.

Table 3.12.1 Non-invasive techniques available for the assessment of neuromuscular function, a brief description of outcome variables and recommended reading for introductory texts and training

Technique	Physiological Variables Assessed	Recommended Reading and Training
Transcranial magnetic stimulation	Single-pulse TMS • Corticospinal excitability • TMS silent period • Voluntary activation Paired-pulse TMS • Intracortical inhibition • Intracortical facilitation	Goodall et al. (2014) Todd et al. (2016) Rossi et al. (2021)
Electrical stimulation of the spinal cord	Single stimuli • Spinal excitability	Taylor et al. (2016) McNeil et al. (2013) Škarabot et al. (2020)
Electrical stimulation of the motor nerve	Potentiated twitch • Amplitude • Rate of force development • Rate of relaxation • Low- and high-frequency fatigue Interpolated twitch technique • Voluntary activation Muscle excitability • M-wave Spinal loop excitability • H reflex Motoneuron excitability • F wave Supraspinal drive • V wave	Knikou (2008) Millet et al. (2011) McNeil et al. (2013) Rodriguez-Falces and Place (2018)
Electromyography	Uni/bipolar surface electromyography • Muscle activation High-density surface electromyography • Motor unit recruitment/derecruitment • Motor unit firing rate • Neural drive • Neuromodulation of motoneurons	Vigotsky et al. (2017) Del Vecchio et al. (2020)

Traditionally, most protocols will record force at a joint angle that approximates peak force (broadly determined by the length-tension relationship); for example, knee extensor force is usually determined at a joint angle between 70 and 90 degrees from full extension. However, it is important that the assessment task is reflective of the intervention. For example, if a fatiguing task is performed at a joint angle of 90 degrees, then the assessment task should also be conducted at the same joint angle. This is a particular issue when examining the efficacy of training interventions, so thought must be applied to ensure a good level of task specificity (Brownstein et al., 2018). Lastly, the participant needs to be thoroughly familiarised with the task and methods of stimulation. There can be substantial learning effects with MVCs, despite the seemingly simplistic execution, and thus it is prudent to have, at an absolute minimum, one familiarisation session (Nuzzo et al., 2019).

When assessing neuromuscular function, the accurate measurement of force expression is imperative. However, without the use of additional methods, it is not possible to elucidate whether changes in muscle force are attributable to alterations in voluntary activation or contractile function (Gandevia, 2001).

Evoked twitch parameters

The measurement of voluntary force for the assessment of neuromuscular function is usually accompanied by the study of evoked parameters. A resting, potentiated twitch ($Tw_{,pot}$), evoked by a single supramaximal stimulation over a motor nerve or motor point with electrical or magnetic stimulation, can be studied to monitor muscle contractility and excitability. A decrease in resting potentiated twitch force is a common method used to demonstrate peripheral adjustments following exercise (Goodall et al., 2015). In addition to changes in the maximum twitch force, within-twitch characteristics such as contraction time (CT), maximal rate of force development (MRFD), maximal rate of relaxation (MRR) and one-half relaxation time ($RT_{0.5}$) can all be modulated as a consequence of exercise. The CT and MRFD denote muscular shortening velocity, while MRR and $RT_{0.5}$ are measures of muscular relaxation (Paasuke et al., 2000). A prolonged CT is thought to reflect a decreased efficiency in the function of the sarcoplasmic reticulum to release calcium (Klitgaard et al., 1989), and a reduced MRFD indicates a decrease in the rate of cross-bridge formation (Stein and Parmiggiani, 1981). Reductions in MRR and a prolonged $RT_{0.5}$ reflect decreases in the maximal rate of weak-to-strong cross-bridge binding and decreases in the maximal rate of cross-bridge detachment (Westerblad et al., 1997; Jones, 2010). Double and tetanic trains of stimulation can provide additional information on peripheral function – specifically, such methods can demonstrate high- and low-frequency fatigue (Martin et al., 2004) and help to inform neuromuscular recovery in clinical populations.

Muscle compound action potential (M-wave)

In conjunction with measurement of force in response to the stimulation, surface EMG can be measured from the muscle. The supramaximal stimulation of the motor nerve elicits a muscle compound action potential (M-wave) detectable with EMG that is used as a robust normalisation tool for understanding changes in most muscle-related wave forms. Changes in M-wave characteristics can occur after prolonged or arduous physiological stressors and are indicative of changes in membrane excitability. However, it should be noted that phases of the

Voluntary activation

In addition to the force responses evoked by stimulation at rest, responses to motor nerve and motor point stimuli can be superimposed during maximal voluntary contractions to measure voluntary activation (Merton, 1954; Strojnik and Komi, 2000). Voluntary activation, defined as 'the level of neural drive to a muscle during exercise' (Taylor et al., 2016), is typically measured using a single or double stimulus delivered to a motor nerve or muscle during an MVC to evoke a twitch-like increment in force. The amplitude of the 'superimposed twitch' (SIT) evoked by the stimulus is compared with the amplitude of the resting potentiated twitch delivered after the MVC, and voluntary activation is determined using the following equation:

$$\text{Voluntary activation (\%)} = (1 - SIT/Tw_{,pot}) \times 100$$

where SIT is the amplitude of the superimposed twitch force evoked during an MVC, determined as the onset force minus the peak force, and $Tw_{,pot}$ is the potentiated twitch force obtained immediately after the maximal contraction (Figure 3.12.3). For example, after strenuous exercise, a larger twitch is evoked during an MVC and VA is incomplete; that is, some motor units are not voluntarily recruited or are not firing fast enough to generate fused contractions. Reductions in VA are thought to be attributable to adjustments in the central nervous system.

Motor and lumbar evoked potentials

Stimulation of the motor cortex through transcranial magnetic stimulation (TMS) and electrical stimulation of the spine have been used to further localise the site of neural change. EMG recordings in response to cortical and lumbar stimuli can be monitored and normalised to the M_{max} to reveal changes in corticospinal and spinal excitability, respectively. Descending volleys evoked from cortical stimulation depend on the stimulus intensity and excitability of cortical cells, whereas responses in the muscle depend on transmission through relevant excitatory and inhibitory interneurons and on the excitability of the motoneuron pool (Taylor and Gandevia, 2001).

Furthermore, MEPs elicited by TMS can be recorded from a relaxed or contracting muscle. During a voluntary contraction, both corticospinal neurons and motoneurons become more excitable such that the same cortical or lumbar stimulus produces a much larger response in the contracting muscle than during rest (Rothwell et al., 1991). The MEP evoked during contractions is followed by a period of EMG silence, which is attributed to increased spinal and cortical inhibition (Taylor and Gandevia, 2001; Goodall et al., 2014). For example, during

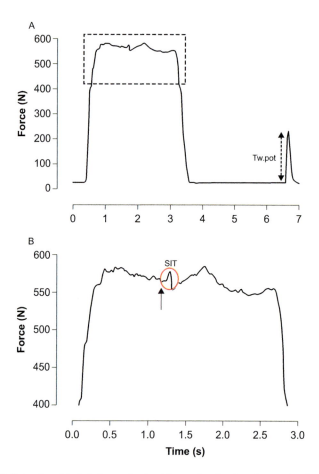

Figure 3.12.3 Potentiated twitch force obtained immediately after the maximal contraction.

sustained muscle contraction, MEP amplitude increases and corticospinal silent period duration lengthens, demonstrating increased cortical excitability and spinal inhibition, respectively (Taylor et al., 1996).

Surface EMG during voluntary muscle actions

Despite its substantial limitations (Farina et al., 2014), EMG from voluntary actions has been recorded throughout exercise as a surrogate measure of central drive to demonstrate changes in neuromuscular function. It is common to measure root mean squared EMG (rmsEMG) and its changes during voluntary contractions. For example, as voluntary force declines during brief or sustained maximal contractions, the amplitude of rmsEMG also decreases. Further, a reduced rmsEMG amplitude during maximal contractions suggests a reduced motor unit recruitment and/or a change in muscle fibre–type recruitment (Sogaard et al., 2006). During submaximal contractions, as neuromuscular changes ensue and voluntary force begins to decline, a compensatory rise in rmsEMG is commonly observed due to increases in motor unit recruitment and/or firing rate (Enoka and Stuart, 1992; Taylor and Gandevia, 2008). Such motor unit changes can only be 'globally' estimated when using bipolar EMG configuration; however, intrinsic alterations in the firing of high- and low-threshold motor units can be quantified under certain conditions by using high-density EMG (Felici and Del Vecchio, 2020).

Data acquisition

To ensure high-quality data signals are captured, it is important that the acquisition device is capable of sampling at sufficiently high frequencies. Normally, a sampling frequency of 1000 Hz is sufficient, and to conform with the Nyquist theory, the sampling rate should be at least double that of the low-pass EMG filter. The synchronisation of signals is an important and necessary element of these techniques, particularly when collecting force, stimulation and EMG data concurrently (Figure 3.12.2).

Summary

The assessment of the neuromuscular system can provide a powerful array of tools to understand the brain-to-muscle responses to an acute bout of exercise, the time course and resolution of these responses and, importantly, the longer-term adaptive responses in both healthy and clinical populations. Whilst insightful, care must be applied to consider what variables need to be assessed, the instruments and control needed to measure these variables and, importantly, experience and expertise to 1) competently operate the instruments and 2) appropriately analyse and interpret data.

References

Brownstein, C. G., Ansdell, P., Skarabot, J., Frazer, A., Kidgell, D., Howatson, G., et al. (2018). Motor cortical and corticospinal function differ during an isometric squat compared with isometric knee extension. *Experimental Physiology*, 103(9), 1251–1263.

Del Vecchio, A., Holobar, A., Falla, D., Felici, F., Enoka, R. M. and Farina, D. (2020). Tutorial: Analysis of motor unit discharge characteristics from high-density surface EMG signals. *Journal of Electromyography and Kinesiology*, 53, 102426. https://doi.org/10.1016/j.jelekin.2020.102426

Enoka, R. M. and Stuart, D. G. (1992). Neurobiology of muscle fatigue. *Journal of Applied Physiology*, 72(5), 1631–1648.

Farina, D., Merletti, R. and Enoka, R. M. (2014). The extraction of neural strategies from the surface EMG: An update. *Journal of Applied Physiology l (1985)*, 117(11), 1215–1230.

Felici, F. and Del Vecchio, A. (2020). Surface electromyography: What limits its use in exercise and sport physiology? *Frontiers in Neurology*, 11, 578504.

Fitts, R. H. (2008). The cross-bridge cycle and skeletal muscle fatigue. *Journal of Applied Physiology*, 104(2), 551–558.

Gandevia, S. C. (2001). Spinal and supraspinal factors in human muscle fatigue. *Physiological Reviews*, 81(4), 1725–1789.

Gandevia, S. C., Allen, G. M. and McKenzie, D. K. (1995). Central fatigue: Critical issues, quantification and practical implications. *Advances in Experimental Medicine and Biology*, 384, 281–294.

Goodall, S., Charlton, K., Howatson, G. and Thomas, K. (2015). Neuromuscular fatigability during repeated-sprint exercise in male athletes. *Medicine and Science in Sports and Exercise*, 47(3), 528–536.

Goodall, S., Howatson, G., Romer, L. and Ross, E. (2014). Transcranial magnetic stimulation in sport science: A commentary. *European Journal of Sports Sciences*, 14(Suppl 1), S332–S340.

Jones, D. A. (2010). Changes in the force-velocity relationship of fatigued muscle: Implications for power production and possible causes. *Journal of Physiology*, 588(Pt 16), 2977–2986.

Klitgaard, H., Ausoni, S. and Damiani, E. (1989). Sarcoplasmic reticulum of human skeletal muscle: Age-related changes and effect of training. *Acta Physiologica Scandinavia*, 137(1), 23–31.

Knikou, M. (2008). The H-reflex as a probe: Pathways and pitfalls. *Journal of Neuroscience Methods*, 171, 1–12. https://doi.org/10.1016/j.jneumeth.2008.02.012

Martin, V., Millet, G. Y., Martin, A., Deley, G. and Lattier, G. (2004). Assessment of low-frequency fatigue with two methods of electrical stimulation. *Journal of Applied Physiology*, 97(5), 1923–1929.

McNeil, C. J., Butler, J. E., Taylor, J. L. and Gandevia, S. C. (2013). Testing the excitability of human motoneurons. *Frontiers in Human Neuroscience*, 7, 152. https://doi.org/10.3389/fnhum.2013.00152

Merton, P. A. (1954). Voluntary strength and fatigue. *The Journal of Physiology*, 123(3), 553–564.

Millet, G. Y., Tomazin, K., Verges, S., Vincent, C., Bonnefoy, R., Boisson, R. C., Gergelé, L., Féasson, L. and Martin, V. (2011). Neuromuscular consequences of an extreme mountain ultra-marathon. *PloS One*, 6(2), e17059. https://doi.org/10.1371/journal.pone.0017059

Nuzzo, J. L., Taylor, J. L. and Gandevia, S. C. (2019). CORP: Measurement of upper and lower limb muscle strength and voluntary activation. *Journal of Applied Physiology*, 126(3), 513–543.

Paasuke, M., Ereline, J., Gapeyeva, H., Sirkel, S. and Sander, P. (2000). Age-related differences in twitch contractile properties of plantarflexor muscles in women. *Acta Physiologica Scandinavia*, 170(1), 51–57.

Rodriguez-Falces, J. and Place, N. (2018). Determinants, analysis and interpretation of the muscle compound action potential (M wave) in humans: Implications for the study of muscle fatigue. *European Journal of Applied Physiology*, 118(3), 501–521.

Rothwell, J. C., Thompson, P. D., Day, B. L., Boyd, S. and Marsden, C. D. (1991). Stimulation of the human motor cortex through the scalp. *Experimental Physiology*, 76(2), 159–200.

Škarabot, J., Ansdell, P., Howatson, G., Goodall, S. and Durbaba, R. (2020). Corticospinal responses during passive shortening and lengthening of tibialis anterior and soleus in older compared to younger adults. *Experimental Physiology*, 105, 419–426. https://doi.org/10.1113/EP088204

Sogaard, K., Gandevia, S. C., Todd, G., Petersen, N. T. and Taylor, J. L. (2006). The effect of sustained low-intensity contractions on supraspinal fatigue in human elbow flexor muscles. *Journal of Physiology*, 573(Pt 2), 511–523.

Stein, R. B. and Parmiggiani, F. (1981). Nonlinear summation of contractions in cat muscles. I. Early depression. *Journal of General Physiology*, 78(3), 277–293.

Strojnik, V. and Komi, P. V. (2000). Fatigue after submaximal intensive stretch-shortening cycle exercise. *Medicine and Science in Sports and Exercise*, 32(7), 1314–1319.

Taylor, J. L., Amann, M., Duchateau, J., Meeusen, R. and Rice, C. L. (2016). Neural contributions to muscle fatigue: From the brain to the muscle and back again. *Medicine and Science in Sports and Exercise*, 48(11), 2294–2306.

Taylor, J. L., Butler, J. E., Allen, G. M. and Gandevia, S. C. (1996). Changes in motor cortical excitability during human muscle fatigue. *The Journal of Physiology*, 490(Pt 2), 519–528.

Taylor, J. L. and Gandevia, S. C. (2001). Transcranial magnetic stimulation and human muscle fatigue. *Muscle and Nerve*, 24(1), 18–29.

Taylor, J. L. and Gandevia, S. C. (2008). A comparison of central aspects of fatigue in submaximal and maximal voluntary contractions. *Journal of Applied Physiology*, 104(2), 542–550.

Thomas, K., Goodall, S. and Howatson, G. (2018). Performance fatigability is not regulated to a peripheral critical threshold. *Exercise and Sport Science Reviews*, 46(4), 240–246.

Todd, G., Taylor, J. L. and Gandevia, S. C. (2016). Measurement of voluntary activation based on transcranial magnetic stimulation over the motor cortex. *Journal of Applied Physiology (Bethesda, MD: 1985)*, 121(3), 678–686. https://doi.org/10.1152/japplphysiol.00293.2016

Vigotsky, A. D., Beardsley, C., Contreras, B., Steele, J., Ogborn, D. and Phillips, S. M. (2017). Greater electromyographic responses do not imply greater motor unit recruitment and 'Hypertrophic Potential' cannot be inferred. *Journal of Strength and Conditioning Research*, 31(1) e1–e4. doi: 10.1519/JSC.0000000000001249

Westerblad, H., Lannergren, J. and Allen, D. G. (1997). Slowed relaxation in fatigued skeletal muscle fibers of Xenopus and Mouse. Contribution of [Ca2+]i and cross-bridges. *Journal of General Physiology*, 109(3), 385–399.

3.13 Field-based testing

Barry Drust and Mark Noon

This chapter presents the considerations around the processes underpinning the development of field-based testing protocols. Although generic in its application, the information presented has particular relevance for team sports. An outline of the important factors, and associated processes, should enable those interested in developing field-based tests to create practical frameworks that support the development of effective field-based assessment strategies for both individual athletes and team sports. While such approaches to athlete assessment may be considered less reliable than traditional laboratory tests, they do have the potential to provide assessments that are ecologically valid. The approach presented here is based on six developmental steps (Figure 3.13.1).

Step 1: evaluating the demands of the sport

Comprehensive insights into the demands of the sport are an important first step in the development of any field-based testing protocol. Such knowledge forms the basis for understanding key physiological characteristics and movement requirements that underpin performance in that sport. They also provide a basis by which any variability in these demands amongst the players, or between different groups of players, are identified. Observation of the activity/activities (using video analysis or optical tracking) or more direct assessments of the players' actions (with micro-electrical mechanical devices) are the most common methods utilised for data collection (Bariss and Button, 2008; Malone et al., 2017). Key information includes the volume, intensity, frequency and type of movements completed. Collecting facts that relate to the context in which these movements occur within the broader purpose of the game (i.e., attacking or defensive actions, successful or unsuccessful outcomes) may help create perspective for the purpose of the movements within the sport. Such approaches provide more objective data than simple subjective observations that are done in real time. The addition of physiological measurements (e.g., heart rate, blood samples) can add important detail to information on external load by providing data that quantify the internal response to the identified activity (Impellizzeri et al., 2018). Furthermore, these data help in confirming the relevant physiological systems used to support the actions seen to occur in the sport. If possible, evaluations of performances

Field-based testing 137

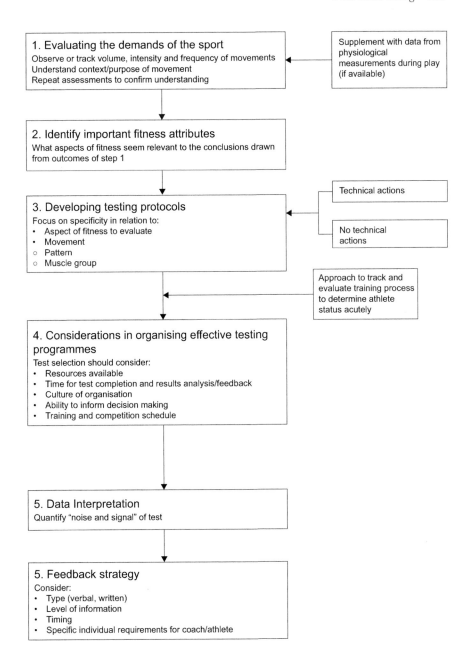

Figure 3.13.1 Six-step process underpinning the development of field-testing protocols.

should be completed in a number of different players and repeated on more than one occasion for each individual, as research indicates that the movement profile observed is highly variable and influenced by a number of contextual factors (e.g., opposition, venue, score line, etc.) (Paul et al., 2015). While such procedures may be time consuming, they will undoubtedly improve the quality of information collected and provide a more suitable basis on which to evaluate the demands of the sport.

Step 2: identifying important fitness attributes

Careful interpretation of the information collected from the performance can provide the platform for the next step in field test development. The type, duration, pattern and frequency of movements provide a basis for the identification of the fundamental fitness attributes supporting performance in the sport. It is these fitness traits which should be the focus of the field-testing programmes used with the athletes in question. Physiological data that may be available add more quantitative information to these considerations. For example, a dominance of low-intensity activities (i.e., walking and jogging) combined with a low to moderate heart rate response indicates the importance of the aerobic energy system. Technical actions (i.e., jumps and between-player contacts to obtain possession of the ball) may be partly reliant on the muscles' ability to generate force, indicating a need to consider the importance of assessing the strength and power capabilities of athletes. These foundational principles provide an important basis on which decisions on more detailed aspects of the protocols can be made.

Step 3: developing testing protocols

Creating testing protocols that are highly specific and therefore possess good ecological validity is a key consideration in the development of field-testing protocols. Specificity in this context should be operationalised on several levels. Firstly, the test protocol needs to be specific to the fitness attribute(s) that have been identified as being important to be evaluated (e.g., aerobic, anaerobic). Specificity is also needed at a movement level, where the movements included in the test replicate those seen in the sport and consequently involve identical or similar musculature. It is also important to try and re-create the pattern of activity observed (i.e., start/stop intermittent-type patterns as opposed to continuous exercise). The inclusion of other aspects of specificity, such as technical actions within physiological testing protocols (e.g., ball dribbling) are less of a concern, as this introduces factors that are not physiological in origin and likely to impact the test outcome. This may also be the case for protocols that attempt to assess multiple components of fitness concurrently. This approach makes the implementation of interventions aimed at improving performance more difficult, as the exact aspect of performance requiring development can become less clear. Complex testing protocols that involve a large number of test elements (movement types, technical skill inclusion, etc.) are also likely to require large amounts of familiarisation for participants and produce outcomes that are less reliable. The trade-off between specificity and ease of interpretation of the test outcome is therefore an important consideration at this stage of the design of all field tests.

Step 4: considerations for organising effective testing programmes

Physiological testing is used for a variety of purposes, including talent identification, talent de/selection, player/athlete development and team de/selection (Dodd and Newans, 2018). Most field testing is carried out as a part of the usual activities included in training to provide data for monitoring and development purposes. Thus, it is helpful to consider protocols, procedures and time courses that facilitate tracking and evaluating the training process (Thorpe et al., 2017). Developing an understanding of this process enables the effectiveness of the training stimulus to be monitored, assisting coaches and practitioners to make short-term decisions in manipulating the training load. Such information provides feedback to support both progression and the identification of any potential negative effects associated with training of a high load and competition schedules. A range of monitoring strategies are often employed to determine the current 'status' of the athlete. Selected tests should be indicative of the internal response to the externally delivered load. In addition, the assessments need to be sensitive to a given training stress and provide information on the physiological systems, organs and tissues stressed by training.

The range of tests undertaken may include maximal and submaximal performance tests (e.g., countermovement jump, submaximal heart rate assessments), biochemical measures (e.g., creatine kinase), markers of immune function (e.g., s-IgA) and psychological indicators (e.g., self-report questionnaires) (Halson, 2014). The physiological tests selected, where possible, should also complement the technical, tactical, physical and psychological training considerations. Therefore, some assessments may only need to be incorporated into the training plan at less regular intervals. For example, the maximal nature of some physiological tests (e.g., endurance assessments) cannot be implemented on a weekly basis and, at best, may often only be carried out at 6- to 8-wk intervals or longer. This is due to the need to meet the regular requirements of the competition schedule and ensure adequate recovery. Hence, a range of tests that can be completed on a more frequent basis (e.g., daily or weekly) which complement training and competition considerations are required to give an indication of the athlete's current training status and inform training periodisation. In practice, the selection and frequency of assessments need to be considered in relation to factors such as the resources available, time constraints, competitive fixtures, training schedule and the culture within the environment. In addition, the choice of potential tests should be dependent on whether or not the test outcome can assist in making informed decisions regarding issues such as player selection or changes to the training load.

Step 5: key considerations in data interpretation

Team sports performance is complex, multifactorial and a composite of several inter-related factors (i.e., technical, tactical, psychological and physical) (Reilly et al., 2009). Hence, the relative contribution of these factors influencing successful performance may differ across individuals. Each individual's success will be dependent on contributions from different areas, with strengths in one area compensating for weaknesses in others (Sarmento et al., 2018). Given the complexity of performance, it would be impossible to test holistically in an ecologically valid way. Hence, any physiological test is therefore a function of a reductive process. Yet this reductive process may give some valid and reliable indication of the physical capabilities of each athlete, which must then be interpreted within the holistic context of the sport (e.g., demands, context, position). The reductive process inherently alters the context of the performance variable in question and, as such, no tangible physiological evaluation is in itself completed that incorporates technical or tactical aspects. While this could be considered a limitation, it cannot be avoided, as the physical and technical aspects cannot be dichotomised in the interpretation stage. This is not to say that tests with technical and tactical elements cannot be considered in field-testing programmes – merely that it is important that such tests (if included) are interpreted in an appropriate context.

In an applied setting, quantifying whether an observed change is meaningful is important in ensuring accurate decision making. Gaining an understanding of the 'noise' within each test and determining meaningful change is a key consideration in the interpretation and feedback of the data. In practice, two methods can be employed to identify a meaningful change: 1) a direct performance observation (e.g., for a player to arrive 20–50 cm ahead of their opponent in a 20-m sprint, they would need to improve their sprint time by 0.03–0.06 s) or 2) statistical interference (e.g., 0.2 s between-subject standard deviation, in which the homogeneity or heterogeneity of the group or team determines the magnitude of the smallest worthwhile change [SWC]). For a review of the application and limitations of these methodologies, see Haugen and Buchheit (2016). If the observed change is greater than the noise and the SWC, we can be confident that the change is meaningful to performance (Hopkins, 2004). Therefore, selecting tests that are reliable, have low 'noise' and are sensitive to changes in training load, as well as developing an understanding of what constitutes a meaningful change, are important.

Step 6: feedback strategies

Several strategies, such as meetings, written reports, tables, graphs and infographics, can be employed to provide feedback from physiological testing to a range of stakeholders (e.g., athlete, coach). The most important consideration is how the data/or information is used to inform decision making (Buchheit, 2017). A key challenge is ensuring the key messages are not lost in the chosen method of communication. Often sport scientists present coaches and athletes with frequent reports from daily testing programmes (e.g., to identify each athlete's training status). If the reports are too complex or contain too much information, the most important messages conveyed may be diluted or not fully understood. In addition, each member within each team (e.g., coach, medical, support staff players) will have a different philosophy and differing levels of knowledge and experience in the interpretation of these data (Bartlett and Drust, 2020). Therefore, the communication strategy should consider the idiosyncrasies of everyone involved in the process. Hence, it is important to fully consider and understand effective methods that relate to how the data should be communicated to all important individuals in the multidisciplinary team in a way that prioritises the key aspects influencing performance.

References

Bartlett, J. D. and Drust, B. (2020). A framework for effective knowledge translation and performance delivery of Sport Scientists in professional sport. *Eur J Sport Sci*, 29, 1–9.

Barris, S. and Button, C. (2008). A review of vision-based motion analysis in sport. *Sports Medicine*, 38(12), 1025–1043.

Buchheit, M. (2017). *Aspetar Sports Medicine Journal: Want to See My Report, Coach?* www.aspetar.com/journal/viewarticle.aspx?id=350 (accessed 25 May 2021).

Dodd, K. D. and Newans, T. J. (2018). Talent identification for soccer: Physiological aspects. *Journal of Science and Medicine in Sport*, 21(10), 1073–1078.

Halson, S. L. (2014). Monitoring training load to understand fatigue in athletes. *Sports Medicine*, 44(Suppl 2), S139–S147.

Haugen, T. and Buchheit, M. (2016). Sprint running performance monitoring: Methodological and practical considerations. *Sports Medicine*, 46(5), 641–656.

Hopkins, W. G. (2004). How to interpret changes in an athletic performance test. *Sportscience*, 8, 1–7.

Impellizzeri, F. M., Marcora, S. M. and Coutts, A. J. (2018). Internal and external training load: 15 years on. *International Journal of Sports Physiology and Performance*, 14(2), 270–273.

Malone, J. J., Lovell, R., Varley, M. C. and Coutts, A. J. (2017). Unpacking the black box: Applications and considerations for using GPS devices in sport. *International Journal of Sports Physiology and Performance*, 12(Suppl 2), S218–S226.

Paul, D. J., Bradley, P. S. and Nassis, G. P. (2015). Factors affecting match running performance of elite soccer players: Shedding some light on the complexity. *International Journal of Sports Physiology and Performance*, 10(4), 516–519.

Reilly, T., Morris, T. and Whyte, G. (2009). The specificity of training prescription and physiological assessment: A review. *Journal of Sports Science*, 27(6), 575–589.

Sarmento, H., Anguera, M. T., Pereira, A. and Araújo, D. (2018). Talent identification and development in male football: A systematic review. *Sports Medicine*, 48(4), 907–931.

Thorpe, R. T., Atkinson, G., Drust, B. and Gregson, W. (2017). Monitoring fatigue status in elite team-sport athletes: Implications for practice. *International Journal of Sports Physiology and Performance*, 12(Suppl 2), S227–S234.

3.14 Application of dual energy x-ray absorptiometry

Karen Hind

Dual energy x-ray absorptiometry (DXA) is a quantitative imaging procedure for the measurement of bone mineral density (BMD) and the diagnosis of osteopenia and osteoporosis. Given the ability of DXA to concurrently measure whole-body and regional bone, lean and fat mass, DXA has become the method of choice for bone and body composition assessment in athletes. In applied science research and practice linked to both sporting and clinical groups, DXA is valuable for evaluating and monitoring athlete bone health, recovery from injury and the effects of interventions. In a sporting context, DXA is particularly useful for the evaluation of athletes at risk of relative energy deficiency in sports (RED-S), a condition associated with overtraining and/or undernutrition. However, poor-quality DXA acquisition, analysis or reporting may lead to inappropriate scan interpretation and drawing inaccurate conclusions and providing uninformed advice to athletes, patients and other colleagues who form part of a multidisciplinary support team. One must also consider the frequency of DXA scanning exposure: although the ionising radiation exposure from DXA is low, scans must always be justified.

This chapter informs on the safe and effective practice of DXA scanning and provides informed guidelines to promote high-quality standards in DXA scan acquisition and interpretation in sport and exercise sciences research and practice. These guidelines have been prepared in conjunction with the International Society for Clinical Densitometry (ISCD) position statements, but one must also consider local ionising radiation regulations. Within this chapter, reference is made to 'an athlete', but principles covered apply to any active person presenting for a DXA scan or a participant in sport, exercise and/or health-related research.

DXA technology

DXA uses two x-ray beams of different energies that are diversely attenuated by bone and soft tissue. The x-ray source (which in most models of DXA is usually below the scanner table) generates the x-ray beams containing photons, which are transmitted through electromagnetic energy. As the photons pass through the body, there is differential attenuation depending on the density of the tissues. The level of attenuation also depends on the energy of the photons and the tissue thickness. The measurement of bone is based on the assumption that the body is

DOI: 10.4324/9781003045281-25

made up of two compartments: bone and soft tissue. Bone has a higher density than soft tissue, and therefore the photon energies are attenuated less. In order to image either tissue, the two energy beams are subtracted from one to another, to either subtract the soft tissue and image the bone or subtract the bone and image the soft tissue. In distinguishing what is lean and what is fat tissue, the bone is subtracted and the ratio of the two photon energies is linearly related to the proportion of fat in the soft tissue (Laskey, 1996). The resulting outcomes are bone mineral, lean tissue mass and fat mass.

Since the introduction of DXA in the 1980s, there have been numerous advancements in the technology, including a move from pencil beam to narrow fan beam densitometers and an increased number of detectors, which improve resolution. Such advancements have led to superior image quality and reduced scan times, with the average bone density scan taking less than 2 min and the total body scan taking around 7–14 min (depending on manufacturer, model and scan mode). The most common DXA systems used in the UK are GE Lunar (Madison, WI, USA) and Hologic, Inc. (Waltham, MA, USA). Both provide bone density and body composition measurements and additional features such as visceral fat assessment, advanced hip structural analysis and paediatric applications.

Radiation dose

DXA involves a small amount of ionising radiation. The effective dose to an adult from a typical bone density scan is around 7 μSv depending on the manufacturer, model and scan mode used. The total body scan brings a lower effective dose of around 3.0 μSv. It is useful to compare these values to the natural background radiation dose in the UK, which is approximately 7.3 μSv daily (2.7 mSv annually) (Public Health England, 2011). For example, a standard-mode total body scan would give an exposure that is less than 1 day of natural background radiation. Although the dose of radiation from DXA is small, all laboratories or centres performing DXA scans must follow the regulations set out in the Ionising Radiation Regulations 2017 (IRR17) (Health and Safety Executive, 2018) and the Ionising Radiation for Medical Exposure Regulations (IRMER) (Department of Health and Social Care, 2018), and all operators must have received IRMER-specific training. DXA scans performed for human participant research must have accompanying ethical approval from a National Health Research (NHS) Research Ethics Committee, where the input from a medical imaging expert and a clinical radiation expert is required.

Indications and contraindications

DXA has an integral place in sport and exercise sciences, given its unique ability to measure bone, lean and fat mass status concurrently with a high degree of precision. Table 3.14.1 provides information relating to indications for DXA scans. DXA bone density scans have primarily been used for the assessment of BMD and diagnosis of osteoporosis. These scans require a medical referral unless part of an ethically approved research study. Information is particularly useful for bone health investigations in athletes with bone injuries, such as stress fracture, and in athletes suspected to have chronic low energy availability (LEA) and at risk of RED-S (Hind et al., 2006; Mountjoy et al., 2014; Barrack et al., 2017; Keay et al., 2019). RED-S is a condition that arises from undernutrition and/or overexercise, increasing the risk of low BMD in athletes of both sexes (Mountjoy et al., 2014). In female athletes, amenorrhea (which can develop as a result of chronic LEA) is an overt sign there is a risk to bone health. In male athletes, the signs are less clear, but a screening tool can be helpful to identify those at risk and who might benefit from DXA evaluation (Keay et al., 2018, 2019). In clinical practice, bone density scans are not usually repeated more than once annually, but in research studies, scans may need to be repeated more frequently, for example, when investigating the effects of a specific intervention on bone density.

Body composition scans provide invaluable data to inform health and injury management plans for athletes and clinical patients. For example, if an athlete is suspected to be in chronic LEA, DXA has proven useful in the body composition profiling of athletes from different sports (Bartlett et al., 2020); by ethnicity (Zemski et al., 2019); or to monitor maintenance of an optimal body composition status across an intense, competitive season (Harley et al., 2011; Lees et al., 2017). Information is also useful to evaluate risk and recovery from injury by examining any asymmetry between left and right limbs (Jordan et al., 2015). It is reasonable to include a body composition scan alongside bone density investigations, justified on the grounds of providing additional, important information on the health of the athlete, for example, very low body fat or lean mass atrophy. Although the radiation dose is very low, body composition scans must still be justified. With consideration to radiation exposure and the time required to observe a significant change in lean or fat mass, unless a change in body composition over a shorter

Table 3.14.1 Indications for DXA scans in sport and exercise sciences

Bone Density*	Body Composition
Low body mass index (<18.5 kg.m^{-2})	Chronic LEA/RED-S
Low trauma fracture	Monitor the effect of training and/or nutritional interventions
Bone stress injury, e.g., stress fracture	Monitor the effect of detraining
Chronic LEA/RED-S, eating disorder and/or frequent weight fluctuations	Investigate regional mass to understand injury risk and rehabilitation
Hypogonadism, including menstrual disturbances	Inform on body composition for weight category sports
Glucocorticoid medications	
Malabsorption conditions	

* See also NICE guidelines: www.nice.org.uk/guidance/cg146/chapter/1-guidance
LEA: low energy availability; RED-S: relative energy deficiency in sports

period is expected, one should not perform repetitive body composition scans more frequently than every 6 wk.

One should not perform a DXA scan when:

- An individual is pregnant or suspects that they may be pregnant, or is breast feeding;
- An individual is unable to provide informed consent;
- It is not possible to provide feedback;
- Where a scan will result in an annual ionising radiation exposure that is greater than 1 mSv;
- If there has been an exposure to nuclear medicine examinations or radiographic agents in the previous 48 h;
- If there is a risk that performing a body composition scan may exacerbate body image concerns or an eating disorder;
- If an individual exceeds a stipulated maximum weight capacity – most DXA models can accommodate a weight capacity range between 160 and 204 kg.

Quality densitometry

Pre-scan standardisation

Prior to any DXA scan, athletes should receive detailed information about the scans and guidance relating to how to prepare. Furthermore, as part of a consistent protocol, athletes complete a pre-DXA screening questionnaire, which covers the contraindications and gathers other important information, including the reason for the scan and any internal artefacts such as metal plates and rods that may jeopardise scan quality. For example, if an athlete reports a metal artefact in the right proximal femur, one should only perform a bone density scan on the left hip and the lumbar spine. As clothing can impact bone density and body composition outcomes (Siglinsky et al., 2018), it is recommended that athletes wear minimal clothing, avoiding heavy textile materials, reflective materials, metallic thread and metal artefacts such as zips and clasps.

Diurnal variations in biological factors can also influence information stemming from a DXA body composition scan, namely hydration and stomach and intestinal content. DXA assumes that fat-free tissue is euhydrated with a constant of 73% to enable the separation of fat tissue mass and lean tissue mass (Laskey, 1996). However, euhydration can vary significantly from 67% to 85% (Pietrobelli et al., 1998; Andreoli et al., 2009), and for athletic groups there are additional considerations for hydration based on fluid losses during exercise training and fluid replenishment post-exercise (Nana et al., 2016). Minimising potential errors arising from biological variation is especially relevant in sports science and when working with elite athletes, when the detection of the smallest change is of the highest importance. To ensure that variability is as low as practicably possible, standardised pre-scan conditions should be adopted (Table 3.14.2). To date, research indicates that morning scans following an overnight fast (rested and with normal hydration) provide the ideal condition for detecting small but true and meaningful changes (Nana et al., 2016).

Table 3.14.2 Standardising DXA body composition scans

Source	Potential Variation	Standardisation
Clothing	Technical error arising from metal artefacts on clothing presenting as bone mass.	One should undertake measurements on participants with them wearing lightweight clothing with no metal artefacts or residues such as chlorine, salt water or sweat. Jewellery and clothing that contains metal (e.g., hair clips, zips, underwire garments) should be removed.
Meal/fluid consumption	Biological variation reflected in changes to total mass and lean mass, arising from the meal consumed (Nana et al., 2012).	Participants should ideally present in an overnight fasted state (no food or fluid for 8 h). However, it is advised that athletes should be glycogen replete and euhydrated, with dietary guidance to facilitate this process. If it is not possible to perform a morning scan, advise no food or fluid for 5 h. If it is not possible to avoid consumption of food or fluids, it has been suggested that the total content should be no more than 500 g (Kerr et al., 2017).
Hydration	Biological variation reflected in decreases (dehydrated) or increases (overhydrated) in lean mass. Variable hydration of soft tissue can also result in fat estimation error (Pietrobelli et al., 1998).	Participants should be euhydrated and advised to drink one to two glasses of water with each meal/snack the day before the scan. Prior to scanning, participants should empty their bladder. One can confirm hydration status by collecting a mid-stream urine sample for the analysis of urine specific gravity (USG).
Exercise	Biological variation arising from 1) the effect of exercise on tissue hydration (loss of fluid through sweat during exercise and gain through fluid replenishment post-exercise), 2) exercise-associated fluid shifts to regional body compartments and 3) shifts in blood volume.	Participants should present in a rested state with no exercise on the morning of the scan, and participants should not have undertaken intense exercise since lunchtime the day before.

Scan acquisition and analysis

Calibration

Alterations in the accuracy and precision of DXA information can occur suddenly (calibration shift) or gradually (i.e., calibration drift; Lewiecki et al., 2006). To identify such alterations in performance and to ensure stable DXA performance over time, it is important to have a calibration and quality assurance protocol in place. This should involve the daily scanning of the calibration block and the weekly scanning of a phantom (standardised object with a known BMD content), which are provided by the DXA manufacturer. Attention should be given to shifts or drifts in calibration that exceed 1.5% (Lewiecki et al., 2006).

Bone density

One must take care to ensure a consistent approach in the interpretation of bone density assessment (see Table 3.14.3). The ISCD and the National Osteoporosis Guideline Group (NOGG) recommend bone density testing at the lumbar spine (L1–L4) and hip (including femoral neck). If either site is unsuitable for scanning, for example, due to an artefact or injury, the focus should shift to the distal radius for scanning. A manufacturer's instructions linked to scan acquisition should be followed carefully, with particular attention given to the analysis of lumbar spine scans to ensure that the region of interest (ROI) lines are placed accurately, according to the manufacturer instructions. These scans should also be carefully scrutinised for abnormalities, such as vertebral fracture and degenerative changes (Figure 3.14.1), which can be prevalent in athletes and former athletes from contact sports (Entwistle et al., 2021). An operator should manually remove any affected vertebrae from the analysis region to ensure bone density is not falsely elevated. When a lumbar spine scan is not readable, for example, two or more vertebrae are excluded, results of a hip scan can interpret bone density.

Table 3.14.3 Interpretation of DXA scans: bone density

Age <50 yr		
Z-score	*Interpretation*	*Action(s)*
>−1.0	**Normal** bone density for age	Advise on maintaining a bone-positive lifestyle (weight-bearing and resistance exercise, energy balance, calcium and vitamin D).
≤−1.0	**Low** bone density for age	Advise GP/sports doctor appointment. Advise on training and nutrition to promote bone health. Supervised plan to include RED-S screen (Mountjoy et al., 2014).

(*Continued*)

Table 3.14.3 (Continued)

Postmenopausal women and men ≥50 yr

T-score	Interpretation	Recommended action(s)
>−1.0	**Normal** bone density	Advise on maintaining a bone-positive lifestyle (weight-bearing and resistance exercise, energy balance, calcium and vitamin D).
−1.0 to −2.4	**Osteopenia**	Advise GP appointment. Advise on exercise and nutrition for bone health. Athletes – supervised plan to include RED-S screen (Mountjoy et al., 2014).
≤−2.5	**Osteoporosis**	Advise GP appointment. Advise on exercise* and nutrition for bone health. Athletes – supervised plan to include RED-S screen (Mountjoy et al., 2014).

* Refer to Royal Osteoporosis Society guidance (ROS, 2022).

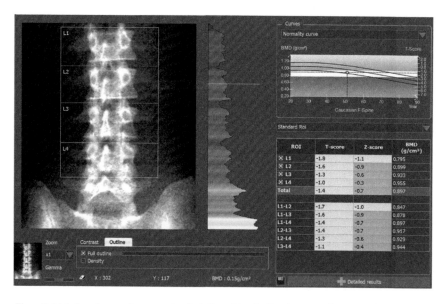

Figure 3.14.1 Lumbar spine vertebral deformities indicating requirement for vertebral exclusion.

Body composition

Each DXA centre should have standard procedures for body composition positioning that ensure consistency and accuracy. An athlete should be positioned supine with the head in the Frankfort plane position and with the whole body within the marked boundaries of the scan table. The ROI placements are summarised in Figure 3.14.2.

For tall athletes who exceed the scan boundaries, there are two options depending on the system and software. First, the latest Encore software (version 18) from GE offers a new total body–less head scan which starts at the level of the mandible. This can be adopted as a consistent protocol for all athletes, given that the composition of the head is unlikely to change, but does not provide absolute body composition. The second option is to combine two partial scans: one for the head and one for the body (Silva et al., 2013). For the head scan, the crown of the head should be ~1–3 cm below the upper scan boundary and the head placed in the Frankfort plane. Once one has captured an image of the whole head, the scan should be terminated and saved. For the body scan, the athlete should be repositioned so that the feet are fully captured within the lower scan area to allow a 1-cm gap. The ROIs should be reviewed and the head, arm, trunk and leg compartments combined.

For broad athletes who exceed the width of the scan boundaries, there are also two options. The first is the offset (mirror image) scan procedure in which the DXA software (GE – mirror mode; Hologic – reflection mode) estimates composition on the left side from the right side by assuming symmetry of the body. While this does not allow for the accurate evaluation of regional compartments or asymmetries, it is helpful for total body composition so long as care is taken to ensure the correct ROI placement (Rothney et al., 2009). The second option is to combine two partial scans. This is appropriate when there is a need for accurate evaluation of regional compartments and differences between left and right sides. The whole right side should be included in the scan window, and the scan should be performed without offsetting. Once this scan is complete, the same should be repeated for the left side and the results from the two scans combined after careful scrutiny of ROI placement.

It is recommended that the hands are placed in the mid-prone position with 1 cm air space between the hand and the upper leg (Figure 3.14.3). This position is particularly

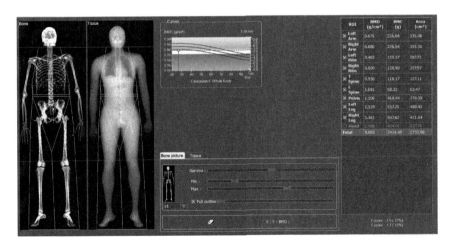

Figure 3.14.2 DXA total body scan image and region of interest placements.

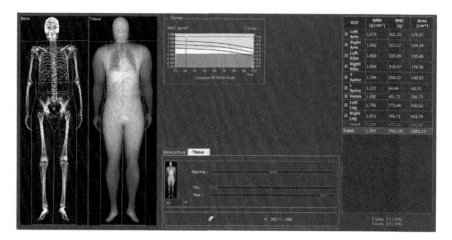

Figure 3.14.3 Mid-prone (A – recommended) and prone hand positioning (B) for DXA scans.

Source: (Thurlow et al., 2018).

useful for broad athletes, although care should be taken to ensure that the hand does not overlap the upper leg. Foam positioning aids may help consistent placement (Nana et al., 2012). The interchanging of hand position, for example hands placed prone at baseline and hands mid-prone at follow-up, is not recommended, given the impact on total BMD, arm bone and fat mass and precision (Thurlow et al., 2018).

Interpretation and reporting

DXA scans, particularly body composition scans, provide a large amount of useful information, which one must interpret accurately. Those interpreting scans must have received appropriate training, and if there are incidental health findings, one must refer an athlete to their GP or sports doctor. When preparing bone and body composition scan reports, it is important to include the model, manufacturer and software of the DXA system used. This is because there can be small differences between scans conducted on different systems (Shepherd et al., 2012; Oldroyd et al., 2018). It is also important to report scan mode (thin, standard or thick) (Hind et al., 2018). One should also record reference data used to help interpret scan results. The ISCD recommends the NHANES 1999–2004 reference data as most appropriate for bone density and body composition. However, one should recognise that reference data associated with body composition are likely to be of limited value for comparisons in highly trained athletes, given their unique physical traits (Hangartner et al., 2013; Petak et al., 2013).

Bone density

Bone density in athletes under 50 yr of age is interpreted using Z-scores (age-matched). In postmenopausal athletes or male athletes aged 50 yr or over, T-scores (young adult reference) should be used (Table 3.14.3). One can use the lowest Z-score or T-score calculated from completed scans for diagnosis.

Body composition

Total body scan reports include total and regional (arms, trunk, legs) estimates of total mass, fat mass, fat-free mass (which comprises lean mass and bone mass), lean mass, bone mineral content (BMC) and BMD. Further detailed information includes regional and tissue percent fat mass, appendicular lean mass index (appendicular lean mass/height^2) and fat mass index (fat mass/height^2). If measured, values of urine specific gravity can be included in the notes of the body composition report, as can any other relevant information. When two partial scans are used, one must collate data manually using the Excel report.

Longitudinal scans

In sport and exercise sciences, follow-up DXA scans are valuable for examining the effects of a training programme, injury rehabilitation, a competitive season or exercise or nutrition intervention on bone and body composition. To interpret change accurately, it is important to ensure the following:

- Standardised protocols are established and followed at each time point for consistency.
- Height and body mass are measured and updated at each time point.
- Consistent application of reference data.
- Careful inspection of scan images from each time point to ensure correct and consistent placement of ROIs.
- Knowledge and application of *precision* and *least significant change* (see later).
- To ensure consistency, one should always use the same densitometer. If this is not possible, one must perform a *cross-calibration* procedure (see later).

Precision and least significant change

DXA precision is the ability of the same system and the same operator to obtain the same result when measuring an individual at multiple points over a short period of time (Baim et al., 2005). All densitometrists should complete an in vivo precision study for bone and body composition outcomes in order to estimate precision error (Hangartner et al., 2013; Hind et al., 2018). In addition to operator precision, precision can vary by athlete size (Barlow et al., 2015), and it is important that the precision study sample is reflective of the usual population scanned (Hangartner et al., 2013; Hind et al., 2018).

Performing a precision study involves repeat scans, with re-positioning on either a minimum sample of n = 30 scanned twice or n = 15 scanned three times, as described by the ISCD. Published precision studies exist for a range of populations using different DXA systems (Hind et al., 2010, 2011; Hangartner et al., 2013; Bilsborough et al., 2014; Barlow et al., 2015; Farley et al., 2020). Precision error is calculated as the root-mean-square standard deviation (RMS-SD) or % coefficient of variation (www.iscd.org/learn/resources/calculators/). Once precision error is established, one can calculated least significant change (LSC) as follows:

$$RMS\text{-}SD \times 2.77 = LSC$$

The LSC represents the minimum change between two measurements that is required for 95% confidence that an actual change has occurred. For example, the LSC for DXA lean mass in high-performance rugby players might be 888 g; therefore, to confirm a meaningful change (i.e., a loss or gain of lean mass) this value would need to be exceeded (Lees et al., 2017). In sport and exercise science research, it is common to focus on the statistical analysis of change in a group mean (±SD) values. However, there is a significant limitation associated with this group-based approach, as it is not easy for one to identify important individual changes. In sport science particularly, an individualised, case study approach is recommended, whereby individual athlete changes in body composition compartments are plotted against LSC using a Bland Altman chart.

Cross calibration

One should conduct follow-up scans on the same DXA system – if this is not possible, one must perform a cross calibration between the original and subsequent DXA systems. Cross calibration is also required for multicentre studies where different DXA models are used and following a DXA system upgrade. Cross calibration can be performed in vitro with a phantom (only recommended if the two DXA systems are of the same model) or in vivo. Jankowski et al. (2019) describe an in vivo method for cross calibration. If differences exist between systems, one should create and apply a suitable regression equation (Shepherd et al., 2006; Hangartner et al., 2013).

Professional practice and communication

DXA bone and body composition assessments provide important information on athlete conditioning, injury rehabilitation and changes in response to nutrition and training interventions. However, it is important to recognise that these assessments have the potential to impact unfavourably on athletes who are sensitive about their body shape and composition and who might be recovering from or at risk for disordered eating. As such, care should be taken when communicating with athletes during scan preparation, during positioning and when discussing results. Protocols should be in place to create a safe environment for DXA assessments and to guide on appropriate communication:

- Provide an athlete with an information sheet relating to suitable clothing for DXA scans prior to the appointment. This information should advise on not wearing undergarments that contain underwire or clasps.

- Advise athletes to wear lightweight clothing, for example, shorts and a fitted t-shirt or vest. This will enable quality of data and athlete privacy.
- Provide access to a private room for the athlete to get changed in (if required) prior to and following the scan.
- Where possible, ensure that the scanning room temperature is suitable to accommodate the athlete wearing only lightweight clothing.
- Ensure that only the necessary people are in the DXA imaging room, for example, the densitometrist, the athlete and, if required, the athlete's chaperone. If an additional member of staff or a student is present for training purposes, the athlete must be consulted and provide assent.
- When measuring body weight before the scan, do not read out the weight.
- At all times, avoid comment on the physical appearance, shape, weight or stature of the athlete.
- If there is a need to physically adjust the athlete to ensure appropriate positioning within the scan boundaries, inform the athlete before doing so. When using positioning aids, inform the athlete of their purpose and location.
- Ensure DXA results remain confidential: only qualified and experienced staff (for example, densitometrists trained in DXA scan interpretation and sports dieticians) should be responsible for providing feedback on results.

Training requirements

In addition to IRMER-specific training, DXA technicians must complete practical and theoretical training on the acquisition, analysis and interpretation of DXA scans and demonstrate competency. When purchased, an equipment manufacturer will provide basic training; however, this is not sufficient to attain competency in DXA. Further (advanced) training can be achieved through completion of educational courses such as those offered by the ISCD (bone and body composition) or the Royal Osteoporosis Society (bone density). In-house, certified densitometrists can also provide training. One must keep records of training and certificates, and refresher training is necessary to keep up-to-date with regulatory and emerging technical developments.

References

Andreoli, A., Scalzo, G., Masala, S., Tarantino, U. and Guglielmi, G. (2009). Body composition assessment by dual-energy x-ray absorptiometry (DXA). *La radiologia medica*, 114(2), 286–300.

Baim, S., Wilson, C. R., Lewiecki, E. M., Luckey, M. M., Downs, Jr., R. W. and Lentle, B. C. (2005). Precision assessment and radiation safety for dual-energy x-ray absorptiometry: Position paper of the International Society for Clinical Densitometry. *Journal of Clinical Densitometry*, 8(4), 371–378.

Barlow, M. J., Oldroyd, B., Smith, D., Lees, M. J., Brightmore, A., Till, K., Jones, B. and Hind, K. (2015). Precision error in dual-energy x-ray absorptiometry body composition measurements in elite male rugby league players. *Journal of Clinical Densitometry*, 18(4), 546–550.

Barrack, M. T., Fredericson, M., Tenforde, A. S. and Nattiv, A. (2017). Evidence of a cumulative effect for risk factors predicting low bone mass among male adolescent athletes. *British Journal of Sports Medicine*, 51(3), 200–205.

Bartlett, J. D., Hatfield, M., Parker, B. B., Roberts, L. A., Minahan, C., Morton, J. P. and Thornton, H. R. (2020). DXA-derived estimates of energy balance and its relationship with changes in body composition across a season in team sport athletes. *European Journal of Sport Science*, 20(7), 859–867.

Bilsborough, J. C., Greenway, K., Opar, D., Livingstone, S., Cordy, J. and Coutts, A. J. (2014). The accuracy and precision of DXA for assessing body composition in team sport athletes. *Journal of Sports Sciences*, 32(19), 1821–1828.

Department of Health and Social Care. (2018). *Ionising Radiation (Medical Exposure) Regulations 2017: Guidance*. www.gov.uk/government/publications/ionising-radiation-medical-exposure-regulations-2017-guidance (accessed 5 April 2021).

Entwistle, I., Hume, P., Francis, P. and Hind, K. (2021). Vertebral anomalies in retired rugby players and the impact on bone density calculation of the lumbar spine. *Journal of Clinical Densitometry*, 24(2), 200–205.

Farley, A., Slater, G. J. and Hind, K. (2020). Short-term precision error of body composition assessment methods in resistance-trained male athletes. *International Journal of Sport Nutrition and Exercise Metabolism*, 31(1), 55–65.

Hangartner, T. N., Warner, S., Braillon, P., Jankowski, L. and Shepherd, J. (2013). The official positions of the International Society for Clinical Densitometry: Acquisition of dual-energy x-ray absorptiometry body composition and considerations regarding analysis and repeatability of measures. *Journal of Clinical Densitometry*, 16(4), 520–536.

Harley, J. A., Hind, K. and O'hara, J. P. (2011). Three-compartment body composition changes in elite rugby league players during a super league season, measured by dual-energy x-ray absorptiometry. *The Journal of Strength and Conditioning Research*, 25(4), 1024–1029.

Health and Safety Executive (2018). *Working with Ionising Radiation: Ionising Radiation Regulations 2017: Approved Code of Practice and Guidance*. www.hse.gov.uk/pubns/books/l121.htm (accessed 5 April 2021).

Hind, K., Oldroyd, B. and Truscott, J. G. (2010). In vivo precision of the GE Lunar iDXA densitometer for the measurement of total-body, lumbar spine, and femoral bone mineral density in adults. *Journal of Clinical Densitometry*, 13(4), 413–417.

Hind, K., Oldroyd, B. and Truscott, J. G. (2011). In vivo precision of the GE Lunar iDXA densitometer for the measurement of total body composition and fat distribution in adults. *European Journal of Clinical Nutrition*, 65(1), 140–142.

Hind, K., Slater, G., Oldroyd, B., Lees, M., Thurlow, S., Barlow, M. and Shepherd, J. (2018, July 1). Interpretation of dual-energy x-ray absorptiometry-derived body composition change in athletes: A review and recommendations for best practice. *Journal of Clinical Densitometry*, 21(3), 429–443.

Hind, K., Truscott, J. G. and Evans, J. A. (2006). Low lumbar spine bone mineral density in both male and female endurance runners. *Bone*, 39(4), 880–885.

Jankowski, L. G., Warner, S., Gaither, K., Lenchik, L., Fan, B., Lu, Y. and Shepherd, J. (2019). Cross-calibration, least significant change and quality assurance in multiple dual-energy x-ray absorptiometry scanner environments: 2019 ISCD official position. *Journal of Clinical Densitometry*, 22(4), 472–483.

Jordan, M. J., Aagaard, P. and Herzog, W. (2015). Lower limb asymmetry in mechanical muscle function: A comparison between ski racers with and without ACL reconstruction. *Scandinavian Journal of Medicine and Science in Sports*, 25(3), e301–e309.

Keay, N., Francis, G., Entwistle, I. and Hind, K. (2019). Clinical evaluation of education relating to nutrition and skeletal loading in competitive male road cyclists at risk of relative energy deficiency in sports (RED-S): 6-month randomised controlled trial. *BMJ Open Sport and Exercise Medicine*, 5(1), e000523.

Keay, N., Francis, G. and Hind, K. (2018). Low energy availability assessed by a sport-specific questionnaire and clinical interview indicative of bone health, endocrine profile and cycling performance in competitive male cyclists. *BMJ Open Sport and Exercise Medicine*, 4(1).

Kerr, A., Slater, G. J. and Byrne, N. (2017). Impact of food and fluid intake on technical and biological measurement error in body composition assessment methods in athletes. *British Journal of Nutrition*, 117(4), 591–601.

Laskey, M. A. (1996). Dual-energy x-ray absorptiometry and body composition. *Nutrition*, 12(1), 45–51.

Lees, M. J., Oldroyd, B., Jones, B., Brightmore, A., O'Hara, J. P., Barlow, M. J., Till, K. and Hind, K. (2017). Three-compartment body composition changes in professional rugby union players over one competitive season: A team and individualized approach. *Journal of Clinical Densitometry*, 20(1), 50–57.

Lewiecki, E. M., Binkley, N. and Petak, S. M. (2006). DXA quality matters. *Journal of Clinical Densitometry*, 9(4), 388–392.

Mountjoy, M., Sundgot-Borgen, J., Burke, L., Carter, S., Constantini, N., Lebrun, C., Meyer, N., Sherman, R., Steffen, K., Budgett, R. and Ljungqvist, A. (2014). The IOC consensus statement: Beyond the female athlete triad-relative energy deficiency in sport (RED-S). *British Journal of Sports Medicine*, 48(7), 491–497.

Nana, A., Slater, G. J., Hopkins, W. G. and Burke, L. M. (2012). Effects of daily activities on dual-energy x-ray absorptiometry measurements of body composition in active people. *Medicine and Science in Sports and Exercise*, 44(1), 180–189.

Nana, A., Slater, G. J., Hopkins, W. G., Halson, S. L., Martin, D. T., West, N. P. and Burke, L. M. (2016). Importance of standardized DXA protocol for assessing physique changes in athletes. *International Journal of Sport Nutrition and Exercise Metabolism*, 26(3), 259–267.

Oldroyd, B., Treadgold, L. and Hind, K. (2018). Cross calibration of the GE prodigy and iDXA for the measurement of total and regional body composition in adults. *Journal of Clinical Densitometry*, 21(3), 383–393.

Petak, S., Barbu, C. G., Elaine, W. Y., Fielding, R., Mulligan, K., Sabowitz, B., Wu, C. H. and Shepherd, J. A. (2013). The official positions of the International Society for Clinical Densitometry: Body composition analysis reporting. *Journal of Clinical Densitometry*, 16(4), 508–519.

Pietrobelli, A., Gallagher, D., Baumgartner, R., Ross, R. and Heymsfield, S. B. (1998). Lean R value for DXA two-component soft-tissue model: Influence of age and tissue or organ type. *Applied Radiation and Isotopes*, 49(5–6), 743–744.

Public Health England. (2011). *Ionising Radiation Dose Comparisons*. www.gov.uk/government/publications/ionising-radiation-dose-comparisons/ionising-radiation-dose-comparisons (accessed 5 April 2021).

Rothney, M. P., Brychta, R. J., Schaefer, E. V., Chen, K. Y. and Skarulis, M. C. (2009). Body composition measured by dual-energy x-ray absorptiometry half-body scans in obese adults. *Obesity*, 17(6), 1281–1286.

Shepherd, J. A., Fan, B., Lu, Y., Wu, X. P., Wacker, W. K., Ergun, D. L. and Levine, M. A. (2012). A multinational study to develop universal standardization of whole-body bone density and composition using GE Healthcare Lunar and Hologic DXA systems. *Journal of Bone and Mineral Research*, 27(10), 2208–2216.

Shepherd, J. A., Lu, Y., Wilson, K., Fuerst, T., Genant, H., Hangartner, T. N., Wilson, C., Hans, D. and Leib, E. S. (2006). Cross-calibration and minimum precision standards for dual-energy x-ray absorptiometry: The 2005 ISCD Official Positions. *Journal of Clinical Densitometry*, 9(1), 31–36.

Siglinsky, E., Binkley, N. and Krueger, D. (2018). Do textiles impact DXA bone density or body composition results? *Journal of Clinical Densitometry*, 21(2), 303–307.

Silva, A. M., Heymsfield, S. B. and Sardinha, L. B. (2013). Assessing body composition in taller or broader individuals using dual-energy x-ray absorptiometry: A systematic review. *European Journal of Clinical Nutrition*, 67(10), 1012–1021.

Thurlow, S., Oldroyd, B. and Hind, K. (2018). Effect of hand positioning on DXA total and regional bone and body composition parameters, precision error, and least significant change. *Journal of Clinical Densitometry*, 21(3), 375–382.

Zemski, A. J., Keating, S. E., Broad, E. M., Marsh, D. J., Hind, K. and Slater, G. J. (2019). Preseason body composition adaptations in elite white and Polynesian rugby union athletes. *International Journal of Sport Nutrition and Exercise Metabolism*, 29(1), 9–17.

Part IV
Racing sports (endurance, middle-distance and sprint)

4.1 Middle- and long-distance running

Brian Hanley and Andy Shaw

The middle- and long-distance running events comprise the 800 m, 1500 m, 3000 m steeplechase, 5000 m, 10,000 m and marathon. Although these events are described as race distances, it is useful for the physiologist to consider running duration, which will differ between athletes dependent on ability, age and sex (March et al., 2011), as highlighted in Figure 4.1.1. For both middle- and long-distance running, the aerobic system is the predominant contributor to energy turnover, with the proportion of energy from anaerobic sources decreasing as distance run increases (Spencer and Gastin, 2001). However, the absolute contribution of anaerobic energy might not differ greatly in well-trained athletes, especially over the shorter distances (Gastin, 2001).

Physiological testing is used to measure and monitor an athlete's adaptation to training across a season or their career, notwithstanding that the best test of progression is still performance in their event itself. However, the tactical nature of racing means that there is often a disconnect between an athlete's physiological capacity and their race performances; indeed, athletes do not need to even run their season's best time to win at major championships (Hanley and Hettinga, 2018). Further, as a given athlete is not always able to control the pace of a race, it is important they develop a range of physical qualities to maximise their competitive advantage in any given situation. It is clear athletes do not prepare for competition by repeatedly running the race distance; instead, training focuses on adapting to different demands of the event, including aerobic and anaerobic metabolism. Therefore, any physiological testing should take into consideration the measurement of the important contributors to fast running within the context of the race demands.

The following tests can be used to profile different physiological metrics across a distance runner's profile, shown in Figure 4.1.2, with normative data provided to facilitate the interpretation of results in Table 4.1.1. These include physiological assessments made in a laboratory and field-based assessments of performance metrics that can be used effectively when laboratory access is limited. For inexperienced athletes, general benchmarking of all factors can be effective in identifying the potential strengths and opportunities, which can in turn inform training. For more experienced or elite athletes with a greater history of testing, the testing battery should be refined, with appropriate metrics assessed to inform key performance questions in different phases of the season.

DOI: 10.4324/9781003045281-27

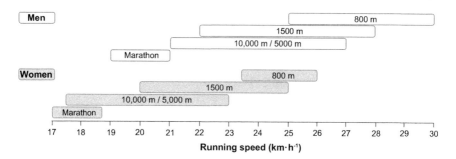

Figure 4.1.1 The range of running speeds found in men's and women's middle- and long-distance championship racing.

Source: Based on data from Hettinga et al. (2019).

Laboratory assessments

Laboratory assessments are used to profile the aerobic physiology of a runner. A two-phase test has been formulated to assess the primary physiological determinants of endurance running, namely lactate thresholds, running economy (RE) and maximal oxygen uptake ($\dot{V}O_2$max), in one visit and with only one phase of maximal running (Jones, 2007). Separately, an assessment of $\dot{V}O_2$ on-kinetics can also be conducted.

Phase one: submaximal aerobic assessment

After a 10-min warm-up (1 km·h^{-1} lower than starting speed), a multistage, discontinuous incremental test on a treadmill is completed, with 3-min stages of running interspersed by a 30-s rest to obtain blood measures. For trained runners, stages are set to 3 min to obtain a steady-state response in the moderate and heavy exercise domains (Shaw et al., 2013), with increments moving from moderate to heavy and into severe exercise within six to nine stages (typically 0.5–1 km·h^{-1} dependent on existing knowledge of the athlete's thresholds and the sensitivity required). The treadmill gradient is set to 1% to replicate the metabolic cost of outdoor running (Jones and Doust, 1996), although practitioners who are concurrently taking biomechanical measures should note the potential effect on gait parameters. The starting speed is set so that the athlete could maintain that pace for >3 h and comfortably hold a conversation, derived by exploring the typical paces used by the athlete in training. Heart rate and pulmonary gas exchange are monitored throughout the assessment, with blood [lactate] (via capillary earlobe samples) and rating of perceived exertion (RPE) assessed during rest intervals. Tests should be terminated at the stage before the athlete would reach exhaustion, with blood [lactate] typically >5 mM and heart rates within 10 b·min^{-1} of maximum. This phase of the test can be repeated every 10–12 wk throughout the season to monitor progression and inform appropriate training paces (Figure 4.1.2) and is used to calculate the following variables.

Blood lactate thresholds and the fractional utilisation of $\dot{V}O_2max$

Lactate threshold is identified as the sustained increase in blood [lactate] above baseline values. As outlined in previous chapters, this metric represents the boundary between the moderate and heavy domain (Figure 4.1.2). The lactate turnpoint (LTP) is the second lactate threshold, defined as a distinct 'sudden and sustained' breakpoint in blood [lactate], and is typically identified as a change in blood [lactate] >1 mmol·L^{-1} between stages (Figure 4.1.2). The LTP occurs below the heavy-severe boundary, representing an intensity that can be sustained for ~60 min (see also Chapter 3.7). Consequently, LTP is used to define the transition between steady and tempo running in distance runners, an important element of world-class athletes' training (Casado et al., 2020).

Although both LT and LTP are commonly expressed as a speed threshold (km·h^{-1}), it is important to note this expression is a composite of the lactate thresholds and RE. The $\dot{V}O_2$ at LT and LTP can also be expressed relative to $\dot{V}O_2max$, providing the fractional utilisation of $\dot{V}O_2max$ and therefore a measure of sustainable energetic rate rather than running speed. As changes in the $\dot{V}O_2max$ of an experienced athlete can be small (Jones, 2006), the ability to use as much of the aerobic capacity as possible at either the LT (marathons) or LTP (half-marathons or 10,000 m) is an important target, especially for long-distance runners.

Running economy

RE is commonly expressed as the oxygen cost of running, combining the energetic cost of running and the substrate utilisation of an athlete, into one variable, calculated as the average $\dot{V}O_2$ over the four stages below LTP, and expressed as ml·kg^{-1}·km^{-1} to enable inter- and intra-individual comparisons (Shaw et al., 2014). As the expression is a cost, a lower value is better for RE (Table 4.1.1). To facilitate interpretation of RE, the underlying energetic cost should still be calculated to

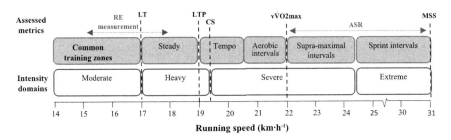

Figure 4.1.2 A schematic example of a 1500-m athlete's full physiological profile based on the testing outlined in this chapter, their relation to exercise intensity domains and commonly prescribed training zones for distance runners.

assess changes that are independent of substrate utilisation, using the following equations combining updated non-protein respiratory quotient equations (Péronnet and Massicotte, 1991) and the energy equivalents for the substrates metabolised at moderate-high intensities (Jeukendrup and Wallis, 2005):

Total energy cost (Kcal·min^{-1}) =
$(((1.695 \times \dot{V}O_2) - (1.701 \times \dot{V}CO_2)) \times 9.75) + (((4.585 \times \dot{V}CO_2) - (3.226 \times \dot{V}O_2) \times 4.07)$

Relative energy cost (Kcal·kg^{-1}·km^{-1}) = (Total energy cost/BM)/(Speed km·h^{-1}/60)

Although RE has been shown to be a key determinant in both long- and middle-distance athletes, it should be noted that the measurement of RE from pulmonary gas exchange limits is assessed at submaximal intensities and therefore is more relevant for performance in long-distance running. As RE is known to change with running speed (Shaw et al., 2014), extrapolations to the maximal/supra-maximal intensities of middle-distance events should be made with caution.

Phase two: maximal aerobic assessment

The second phase of the treadmill testing is a maximal aerobic assessment. After ~15 min of rest/active recovery after the submaximal assessment, the athlete completes a continuous ramp test. The submaximal assessment can be used to infer an appropriate starting speed, typically set 2 km·h^{-1} lower than the final increment in phase one. After 1 min to allow the athlete to settle into the pace, speed is increased by 0.5 km·h^{-1} until volitional exhaustion, demonstrated by the athlete being unable to maintain their position at the front of the treadmill despite encouragement or the athlete placing their hands on the rail and straddling the belt. Heart rate and pulmonary gas exchange are monitored throughout, with blood [lactate] assessed on completion of the test and repeated every minute until blood [lactate] begins to fall to obtain peak blood [lactate]. This phase is used to calculate the metrics discussed next.

$\dot{V}O_2max$

$\dot{V}O_2max$ remains a key physiological determinant for both middle- and long-distance runners. An athlete's $\dot{V}O_2max$ can be combined with RE to calculate the velocity at v$\dot{V}O_2max$, typically calculated by the following equation:

v$\dot{V}O_2$max = ($\dot{V}O_2$max × 60)/RE

where v$\dot{V}O_2$max is in km·h^{-1}, $\dot{V}O_2$max in ml·kg^{-1}·min^{-1} and RE in ml·kg^{-1}·km^{-1}.

Although v$\dot{V}O_2$max calculated from $\dot{V}O_2$max and RE has shown strong associations with endurance running performance, its use to demarcate the upper boundary of the severe domain is less established and appears to underestimate this threshold (Figure 4.1.2), especially in well-trained athletes with fast $\dot{V}O_2$ on-response times.

Table 4.1.1 Typical values for running economy (RE) in oxygen cost, lactate threshold (LT), lactate turnpoint (LTP), maximal oxygen uptake ($\dot{V}O_2$max) and maximal sprint speed (MSS) in endurance runners based on testing of UK athletes

	Females					Males				
	RE	LT	LTP	$\dot{V}O_2$max	MSS	RE	LT	LTP	$\dot{V}O_2$max	MSS
World Class	<185	>18	>20	>70	>9.0	<185	>19	>22	>80	>10
Good	185–204	17–18	18–20	60–69	8.2–9.0	185–204	18–19	20–22	70–79	9.2–10
Moderate	205–220	15–17	17–18	50–59	7.5–8.1	205–220	16–18	18–20	60–69	8.5–9.1
Low	>220	<15	<17	<50	<7.5	>220	<16	<18	<60	<8.5

Application to training

The results from both phases of the test can be used to inform appropriate training zones, shown in Figure 4.1.2 (Jones, 2007). In addition, results from phase 1 can be used to calculate equivalent heart rate zones for easy, steady and tempo running. As heart rate provides an index of internal load, these zones can be effective for guiding training intensity on different terrains (off road, hills, etc.) or in extreme environments (heat or altitude), accounting for the additional load an athlete might experience for a given running speed.

$\dot{V}O_2$ on-kinetics assessment

On a separate laboratory visit, the following protocol can be used to assesses the $\dot{V}O_2$ on-kinetics in both the moderate and severe exercise domains, based on procedures outlined by Carter et al. (2002). Upon arrival, a light warm-up can be conducted, but kept at a speed <80% of LT. Athletes then straddle the treadmill belt, with baseline $\dot{V}O_2$ data captured for 2 min. In this time, the belt is set to an appropriate speed, initially 90% LT. At 2 min, the athlete is instructed to drop onto the treadmill belt and begin running for 6 min, with the precise time matched with the $\dot{V}O_2$ data collection to identify this transition in the analysis. This bout provides assessment of $\dot{V}O_2$ phase II responses in the moderate domain with no priming effect on the following bout. Athletes then rest for 10 min before returning to the treadmill and repeating this procedure with the treadmill speed set to 80% of the difference (Δ) between LT and v$\dot{V}O_2$max to assess the $\dot{V}O_2$ phase II responses, in addition to the $\dot{V}O_2$ slow component, in the severe domain. It is this section that is of greatest relevance to middle/long distances, given these events occur in the severe domain. Data can then be modelled using non-linear regression techniques, as outlined in previous chapters.

This assessment can be used to monitor chronic adaptions, but also acute priming activities that are used before competitive performances (i.e., warm-ups and nutritional priming). When assessing warm-ups for events that are performed at intensities >CS, the initial moderate domain bout should be replaced with the event priming routine, with appropriate focus on the timing of the priming routine relative to the exercise bout that mimics the competition timeline.

Field-based performance testing

Critical speed (CS) and D'

As detailed in previous chapters (Chapter 3.7), maximal running trials can be used to calculate the boundary between heavy and severe domains, CS and the ability to operate above this boundary, D' (Hughson et al., 1984). Efforts are typically performed as time to complete a set distance, given an athlete's familiarity with such efforts from racing. The model requires at least three different race times, with the longest and shortest differing in duration by ~10 min (1500 m, 3000 m and 5 km from races, or 1200 m, 2400 m and 4000 m for prescribed training efforts). As this requires only a stopwatch and a track to complete, this can be an effective monitoring tool for those without laboratory access.

For a valid assessment of CS and D', performance trials must be truly maximal. Races should be included only where the goal is the shortest duration for the given distance, rather than tactical races that prioritise finishing position. Though attempts have been made to combine multiple trials into one visit to enable efficient assessment of CS and D', it has been shown that athletes do not achieve truly maximal performances when compared with exhaustive trials on separate days, leading to inaccurate D' values that do not reflect an athlete's true capacity (Galbraith et al., 2014). Finally, given that the athlete's physiology needs to be uniform through all assessments to calculate a true CS and D', efforts conducted >4 wk apart should not be combined into the same model, especially where training focus and targeted race distances have changed.

Maximal sprint speed

Maximal sprint speed (MSS) can be assessed on a straight 50 m on a running track. After a thorough warm-up and strides, athletes maximally accelerate through the first 20 m and aim to at least achieve and maintain their maximum speed for the following 30 m. Laser radars enable assessment of velocity throughout, where MSS is defined as the maximum velocity from the radar trace. Timing gates can be used where radar is not accessible, spaced at 10-m intervals from 20 m onwards, with the maximum velocity over 10 m as an index of MSS. The MSS can also be used in conjunction with $v\dot{V}O_2max$ to calculate the anaerobic speed reserve (ASR), defined as the difference between these values (Blondel et al., 2001).

Multidisciplinary considerations

Biomechanical differences between outdoor and treadmill running can occur when assessing gait spatiotemporal parameters. Because the exact differences could be exclusive to a particular model of treadmill (Sinclair et al., 2013), laboratory testing should be conducted on robust, unyielding treadmills where possible. Further, as an athlete's biomechanics can affect factors such as RE (Dutto and Smith, 2002), a pre-testing period of 8 min or more of treadmill running, which can function as a warm-up, is needed for familiarisation (Arnold et al., 2019).

In terms of psychological effects, social interaction has a strong effect on performance both in competition and within the laboratory; Halperin et al. (2015) highlighted the importance of controlling for threats to internal validity during testing, which include the number of testers, use of music and volume and frequency of verbal encouragement. For example, the use of RPE is useful when conducting laboratory-based tests but, as a subjective measure, can be influenced by social interaction as in competition.

Competition considerations

When interpreting the results of physiological testing, it is beneficial to consider the different demands of competition, such as pacing within a race and across a championship. For example, elite 800-m runners typically cover the first 200 m in a speed much faster than world record pace (Hettinga et al., 2019), which might accelerate $\dot{V}O_2$ uptake kinetics and increase the aerobic contribution to energy expenditure and sparing anaerobic capacity (Jones and Burnley, 2009). Using a treadmill makes testing easier but does not account for the changes in speed and energy cost that occur because of bend running, hills and different surfaces (Jensen et al., 1999; Mercier et al., 2021; Minetti et al., 1994). Indeed, although it is important that laboratory-based testing of distance runners is conducted in an internally valid and reliable manner, competitions rarely take place in such controlled conditions. Environmental chambers that allow for control of temperature, humidity or simulated altitude can assist the physiologist to test adaptations in conditions likely to occur in competition. Of course, not all external factors can be controlled (e.g., solar radiation and rainfall), but should nonetheless be considered when evaluating performance relative to testing results.

References

Arnold, B. J., Weeks, B. K. and Horan, S. A. (2019). An examination of treadmill running familiarisation in barefoot and shod conditions in healthy men. *Journal of Sports Sciences*, 37(1), 5–12.

Blondel, N., Berthoin, S., Billat, V. and Lensel, G. (2001). Relationship between run times to exhaustion at 90, 100, 120, and 140% of v$\dot{V}O_2$max and velocity expressed relatively to critical velocity and maximal velocity. *International Journal of Sports Medicine*, 22(1), 27–33.

Carter, H., Pringle, J. S., Jones, A. M. and Doust, J. H. (2002). Oxygen uptake kinetics during treadmill running across exercise intensity domains. *European Journal of Applied Physiology*, 86(4), 347–354.

Casado, A., Hanley, B. and Ruiz-Pérez, L. M. (2020). Deliberate practice in training differentiates the best Kenyan and Spanish long-distance runners. *European Journal of Sport Science*, 20(7), 887–895.

Dutto, D. J. and Smith, G. A. (2002). Changes in spring-mass characteristics during treadmill running to exhaustion. *Medicine and Science in Sports and Exercise*, 34(8), 1324–1331.

Galbraith, A., Hopker, J., Lelliott, S., Diddams, L. and Passfield, L. (2014). A single-visit field test of critical speed. *International Journal of Sports Physiology and Performance*, 9(6), 931–935.

Gastin, P. B. (2001). Energy system interaction and relative contribution during maximal exercise. *Sports Medicine*, 31(10), 725–741.

Halperin, I., Pyne, D. B. and Martin, D. T. (2015). Threats to internal validity in exercise science: A review of overlooked confounding variables. *International Journal of Sports Physiology and Performance*, 10(7), 823–829.

Hanley, B. and Hettinga, F. J. (2018). Champions are racers, not pacers: An analysis of qualification patterns of Olympic and IAAF World Championship middle distance runners. *Journal of Sports Sciences*, 36(22), 2614–2620.

Hettinga, F. J., Edwards, A. M. and Hanley, B. (2019). The science behind competition and winning in athletics: Using world-level competition data to explore pacing and tactics. *Frontiers in Sports and Active Living*, 1, 11.

Hughson, R. L., Orok, C. J. and Staudt, L. E. (1984). A high velocity treadmill running test to assess endurance running potential. *International Journal of Sports Medicine*, 5(1), 23–25.

Jensen, K., Johansen, L. and Kärkkäinen, O. P. (1999). Economy in track runners and orienteers during path and terrain running. *Journal of Sports Sciences*, 17(12), 945–950.

Jeukendrup, A. E. and Wallis, G. A. (2005). Measurement of substrate oxidation during exercise by means of gas exchange measurements. *International Journal of Sports Medicine*, 26(S1), S28–S37.

Jones, A. M. (2006). The physiology of the world record holder for the women's marathon. *International Journal of Sports Science and Coaching*, 1(2), 101–116.

Jones, A. M. (2007). Middle- and long-distance running. In E. M. Winter, A. M. Jones, R. C. Richard Davison, P. D. Bromley and T. H. Mercer (eds.), *Sport and Exercise Physiology Testing Guidelines: The British Association of Sport and Exercise Sciences Guide Volume I: Sport Testing* (1st ed.), pp. 147–154. Abingdon: Routledge.

Jones, A. M. and Burnley, M. (2009). Oxygen uptake kinetics: An underappreciated determinant of exercise performance. *International Journal of Sports Physiology and Performance*, 4(4), 524–532.

Jones, A. M. and Doust, J. H. (1996). A 1% treadmill grade most accurately reflects the energetic cost of outdoor running. *Journal of Sports Sciences*, 14(4), 321–327.

March, D. S., Vanderburgh, P. M., Titlebaum, P. J. and Hoops, M. L. (2011). Age, sex, and finish time as determinants of pacing in the marathon. *The Journal of Strength and Conditioning Research*, 25(2), 386–391.

Mercier, Q., Aftalion, A. and Hanley, B. (2021). A model for world-class 10,000 m running performances: Strategy and optimization. *Frontiers in Sports and Active Living*, 2, 226.

Minetti, A. E., Ardigò, L. P. and Saibene, F. (1994). Mechanical determinants of the minimum energy cost of gradient running in humans. *Journal of Experimental Biology*, 195(1), 211–225.

Péronnet, F. and Massicotte, D. (1991). Table of nonprotein respiratory quotient: An update. *Canadian Journal of Sport Sciences*, 16(1), 23–29.

Shaw, A. J., Ingham, S. A. and Folland, J. P. (2014). The valid measurement of running economy in runners. *Medicine and Science in Sports and Exercise*, 46(10), 1968–1973.

Shaw, A. J., Ingham, S. A., Fudge, B. W. and Folland, J. P. (2013). The reliability of running economy expressed as oxygen cost and energy cost in trained distance runners. *Applied Physiology, Nutrition and Metabolism*, 38(12), 1268–1272.

Sinclair, J., Richards, J. I. M., Taylor, P. J., Edmundson, C. J., Brooks, D. and Hobbs, S. J. (2013). Three-dimensional kinematic comparison of treadmill and overground running. *Sports Biomechanics*, 12(3), 272–282.

Spencer, M. R. and Gastin, P. B. (2001). Energy system contribution during 200- to 1500-m running in highly trained athletes. *Medicine and Science in Sports and Exercise*, 33(1), 157–162.

4.2 Triathlon

Laura Needham and Ben Stephenson

Triathlon, a sequential swim, bike and run, was created in the 1970s and has grown exponentially over the past half a century and internationalised (Etxebarria et al., 2019; Migliorini, 2020). Several race distances have evolved, ranging from a mixed team relay (MTR) leg (300 m swim, 7 km bike, 2 km run) to Ironman (3.8 km swim, 180 km bike, 42.2 km run), where total race duration can be <20 min to > 8 h, respectively. Olympic triathlon gained medal status in 1994 and made its debut at the Sydney Games in 2000 and has since become a staple event at the games. The Olympic triathlon distance is set at 1.5 km swim, 40 km bike and 10 km run (also known as standard distance). In addition, the Olympic distance race is a mass start and drafting is legal; athletes can shelter in the slipstream of other athletes to preserve energy. More recently, paratriathlon was added in for Rio 2016, and the Olympic MTR will debut for Tokyo 2021.

Research has demonstrated that the physiological profiles (maximal and submaximal performance measures) of elite triathletes match that of elite athletes competing in triathlon's constituent disciplines (Suriano and Bishop, 2010). Whilst triathletes may display physiological measures similar to international swimmers, cyclists and runners, their contribution to triathlon performance is not equal or independent (Etxebarria et al., 2019; Gadelha et al., 2020; Millet et al., 2002). Recent analysis confirmed the greater relative importance of the run split on athletes' overall finish time (Gadelha et al., 2020). Nonetheless, a holistic approach considering the triathlon context is advised, acknowledging the interplay and accumulation of a prior swim and stochastic bike split with regard to physiological and biomechanical measures when running (Walsh, 2019).

Physiological assessment

Lactate thresholds

A high fractional utilisation of one's aerobic capacity, i.e., lactate threshold, is a hallmark determinant of endurance performance (Joyner and Coyle, 2008). Further, evidence suggests that the maximal lactate steady state when running is a strong correlate to race performance during sprint distance triathlon races (Van Schuylenbergh et al., 2004; see also Chapter 3.7). Whilst triathlon-specific

DOI: 10.4324/9781003045281-28

research is lacking, it is logical to assume that physiological markers at a higher relative intensity, such as the second lactate threshold (LT2), will have a stronger association with standard distance races. Further, although lower than racing intensity, the first lactate threshold (LT1) represents the upper boundary of the moderate-intensity domain, where athletes will train for >75% of the time (Mujika, 2014), thus making it an important marker.

To assess both lactate thresholds in swim, bike and run, a stepwise incremental test is recommended to provide objective information on key physiological metrics around three to four times per year.

- After a thorough warm-up, the test should start at an intensity below the athlete's LT1 (if this is not known from prior testing, this intensity should be below that typical during the athlete's 'long' sessions). If in doubt, we encourage the first stage to be conservative.
- The swim distance per stage is 400 m. This should be evenly paced (consider using a swim tempo trainer). The target pace should increase by ~10 s for four stages in the swim, with the final stage being a maximal effort.
- For the bike, the power output should increase by 20 W (female) or 25 W (male) for each 5-min stage.
- For the run, the speed should increase 1 km·h^{-1} for every 5-min stage.
- A 1-min recovery period is used between all stages whereby an earlobe capillary blood sample is collected for immediate analysis of lactate concentration ([La]) and the athlete's rating of perceived exertion (RPE; Borg, 1982) is noted.
- Stroke rate is captured in each stage between 300 and 350 m for the swim.
- Gas exchange variables (O_2, CO_2 and expired volumes) and heart rate are collected throughout for bike and run, and the last 30 s is averaged for each stage.
- The test is terminated when the athlete's [La] and/or RPE exceed 4.0 mmol·l^{-1} or 17, respectively.
- LT1 is determined via the log-log transformation of [La] and the rate of oxygen uptake ($\dot{V}O_2$) for bike and run (Beaver et al., 1985) and log-log transformation of [La] for the swim.
- LT2 is determined via the log-log exponential modified Dmax method (Jamnick et al., 2018).

$\dot{V}O_2max$

Aerobic capacity is a key performance determinant in endurance sports such as triathlon and should therefore be monitored annually (Joyner and Coyle, 2008). Whilst assessment during swimming is challenging and uncommon, for a cycling or running $\dot{V}O_2max$ we recommend a ramp protocol to exhaustion, 10–20 min succeeding the submaximal testing, whereby:

- For the bike, the athletes start at 100 W (females) and 120 W (males); workload then increases by 5 W every 15 s.

- Cadence should be kept constant throughout the test and can be self-selected by the athlete.
- For the run, the athletes begin on a 1% gradient at two stages below where they finished the submaximal test. Thereafter, the gradient is increased 1% every minute.
- Gas exchange variables and heart rate are collected continuously.
- $\dot{V}O_2$max is calculated as the highest $\dot{V}O_2$ value recorded over a 30-s period.
- An athlete's maximum ramp minute power can be calculated as the average power output sustained over the final 60 s of a ramp test to exhaustion.
- An athlete's $\dot{V}O_2$max can be combined with running economy (see later) to calculate the velocity at v$\dot{V}O_2$max calculated by the following equation:

$$v\dot{V}O_2\text{max} = (\dot{V}O_2\text{max} \times 60)/RE$$
(v$\dot{V}O_2$max is in km·h^{-1}; $\dot{V}O_2$max in ml·kg^{-1}·min^{-1}; and RE in ml·kg^{-1}·km^{-1})

- Lactate is collected after 1 and 3 min post-exercise to ascertain the peak.

With the evolution of technology, cycling assessments are now performed on the athlete's own road bike fitted with a power meter and attached to a power trainer. Calibration should be performed on all equipment following manufacturer's guidelines.

Running economy

As with aerobic capacity, the efficiency of movement is another important performance determinant (Joyner and Coyle, 2008). When running, this is commonly denoted as running economy, the oxygen cost of a certain speed (ml·kg^{-1}·km^{-1}) (see Chapter 4.1 on running). This can be calculated during a step incremental test, as described earlier. It has been shown that the oxygen cost of a set speed is, on average, 2.5 ± 1.5% greater when performed after a cycling bout indicative of standard distance triathlon races compared to when fresh (du Plessis et al., 2020). Thus, practitioners may wish to determine the magnitude of this change in individual athletes as part of their testing battery for greater race specificity.

Critical power

Critical power (CP) demarcates the boundary between the heavy and severe intensity domains (Monod and Scherrer, 1965; Chapter 3.7) and thus represents a physiological measure close to triathlon race intensity. Calculation of CP, and therefore W' (Chapter 3.7), can be achieved by at least two constant work rate trials to exhaustion, or fixed-duration time trials whereby average power output is the outcome measure. In either instance, provided the trials are of adequate duration, an athlete's power-duration curve can be modelled.

We recommend

- A 3-min and 12-min time trial whereby athletes are instructed to produce the highest average power output across the trial after a thorough warm-up, including severe-intensity cycling.
- The trials should be separated by a minimum of 30 min recovery, passively or cycling in the moderate domain (Triska et al., 2021).
- CP is then calculated as the point where the linear regression line of average power output against the inverse of trial duration crosses the y-axis, whilst W' is represented by the line's slope.
- To improve the accuracy of the CP estimate, a third trial of 5 to 6 min can be included.

Short- and long-distance triathlons

With the rise in popularity of short (sprint, super-sprint, MTR) and long (Ironman, half-Ironman) distance triathlons, the triathlete population is becoming more diverse. This results in broadening physiological phenotypes dependent upon an athlete's race specialisation. It is likely, however, that this does not necessitate a new testing approach, but rather an emphasis on different outcome measures.

For short-distance athletes, it is prudent to suggest that parameters such as $\dot{V}O_2max$, CP and maximum ramp minute power take precedence over LT2 due to the higher race intensity. Opposingly, for long-distance athletes, the importance of LT1, movement efficiency and fat oxidation are heightened due to the lower-intensity, greater-duration races.

Health profiling

Alongside exercise testing, a triathlete's health should be profiled regularly. This includes the tracking of body composition, via sum of eight skinfold thickness (Chapter 3.4), and monitoring biomarkers such as iron and vitamin D status, due to their importance in bone health, oxygen delivery and systemic immunity (He et al., 2013; Petkus et al., 2017). Concurrently, in collaboration with a nutritionist, estimations of an athlete's energy balance and fuelling demands to meet the requirements of high training loads is recommended. Lastly, practitioners should consider tracking female athletes' menstrual cycle and associated symptoms to determine their relationship to training and/or competition performance.

References

Beaver, W. L., Wasserman, K. and Whipp, B. J. (1985). Improved detection of lactate threshold during exercise using a log-log transformation. *Journal of Applied Physiology*, 59, 1936–1940. https://doi.org/10.1152/jappl.1985.59.6.1936

Borg, G. A. (1982). Psychophysical bases of perceived exertion. *Medicine and Science in Sports and Exercise*, 14, 377–381.

du Plessis, C., Blazevich, A. J., Abbiss, C. and Wilkie, J. C. (2020). Running economy and effort after cycling: Effect of methodological choices. *Journal of Sports Sciences*, 38(10), 1105–1114.

Etxebarria, N., Mujika, I. and Pyne, D. B. (2019). Training and competition readiness in triathlon. *Sports*, 7(5), 101.

Gadelha, A. B., Sousa, C. V., Sales, M. M., dos Santos Rosa, T., Flothmann, M., Barbosa, L. P., da Silva Aguiar, S., Olher, R. R., Villiger, E., Nikolaidis, P. T., Rosemann, T., Hill, L. and Knechtle, B. (2020). Cut-off values in the prediction of success in Olympic distance triathlon. *International Journal of Environmental Research and Public Health*, 17, 94–91. https://doi.org/10.3390/ijerph17249491

He, C. S., Handzlik, M., Fraser, W. D., Muhamad, A., Preston, H., Richardson, A. and Gleeson, M. (2013). Influence of vitamin D status on respiratory infection incidence and immune function during 4 months of winter training in endurance sport athletes. *Exercise Immunology Review*, 19, 86–101.

Jamnick, N. A., Botella, J., Pyne, D. B. and Bishop, D. J. (2018). Manipulating graded exercise test variables affects the validity of the lactate threshold and $\dot{V}O_2$max. *PLoS One*, 13(7), e0199794.

Joyner, M. J. and Coyle, E. F. (2008). Endurance exercise performance: The physiology of champions. *The Journal of Physiology*, 586(1), 35–44.

Migliorini, S. (ed.). (2020). *Triathlon Medicine*. Cham, Switzerland: Springer.

Millet, G. P., Candau, R. B., Barbier, B., Busso, T., Rouillon, J. D. and Chatard, J. C. (2002). Modelling the transfers of training effects on performance in elite triathletes. *International Journal of Sports Medicine*, 23(1), 55–63.

Monod, H. and Scherrer, J. (1965). The work capacity of a synergistic muscle group. *Ergonomics*, 8, 329–338.

Mujika, I. (2014). Olympic preparation of a world-class female triathlete. *International Journal of Sport Physiology and Performance*, 9(4), 727–731.

Petkus, D. L., Murray-Kolb, L. E. and De Souza, M. J. (2017). The unexplored crossroads of the female athlete triad and iron deficiency: A narrative review. *Sports Medicine*, 47(9), 1721–1737.

Suriano, R. and Bishop, D. (2010). Physiological attributes of triathletes. *Journal of Science and Medicine in Sport*, 13(3), 340–347.

Triska, C., Hopker, J., Wessner, B., Reif, A., Tschan, H. and Karsten, B. (2021). A 30-min rest protocol does not affect W', critical power, and systemic response. *Medicine and Science in Sport and Exercise*, 53(2), 404–412.

Van Schuylenbergh, R., Eynde, B. V. and Hespel, P. (2004). Prediction of sprint triathlon performance from laboratory tests. *European Journal of Applied Physiology*, 91(1), 94–99.

Walsh, J. A. (2019). The rise of elite short-course triathlon re-emphasises the necessity to transition efficiently from cycling to running. *Sports*, 7(5), 99.

4.3 Swimming

Benjamin E. Scott, Adrian Campbell, and Clare Lobb

The assessment of swimmers requires an appreciation for the complex nature of the sport. Competitive swimming events require athletes to perform one of four unique strokes (butterfly, backstroke, breaststroke or butterfly), or in the case of the individual medley event, a specific combination of all four strokes. These events typically range from events from 50 to 1500 m for pool events and from 5 to 25 km for open water. Determinants of success vary between events, so testing should be scientifically robust, but also practical and appropriate for the individuals being tested. Figure 4.3.1 lists some of the key considerations for the selection of an appropriate test. Unlike some other sports, it is not advisable to carry out assessments in swimming using sport ergometers (e.g., swim benches) due to a lack of ecological validity. Established pool-based testing technologies such as tethered swimming devices can provide a more ecologically valid assessment, while developing technologies such as SmartPaddle (Trainesense Oy, Tampere, Finland) force sensors may have a future role for measuring in-water forces.

Pool-based testing

Several pool-based tests have been used by researchers to assess competitive swimmers; these include:

- 7 × 200-m step test (Pyne et al., 2001)
- 'Classic' critical speed testing (Wakayoshi et al., 1993)
- 3-min all-out test (Piatrikova et al., 2018)
- 12 × 25-m all-out test (Mitchell et al., 2018)
- 400-m time trial (Lavoie et al., 1983)
- 30-s all-out tethered swimming test (Morouço et al., 2012a)

Since physiological and biomechanical breakpoints can occur at different speeds (Zacca et al., 2018, Carvalho et al., 2020), it would be auspicious to measure stroke parameters (e.g., stroke rate) in addition to physiological parameters, regardless of the testing protocol implemented. This would also be prudent because

DOI: 10.4324/9781003045281-29

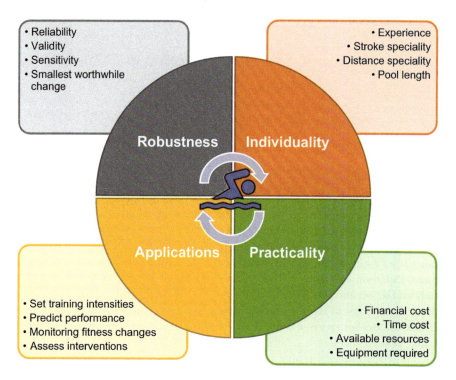

Figure 4.3.1 Some key considerations for the selection of a swimming assessment.

intra-swimmer cross-sectional and inter-swimmer longitudinal differences may be explained by both technical and physiological factors. Summary validity and reliability data relating to the listed tests are presented in Table 4.3.1.

7 × 200-m step test

The 7 × 200-m step test (Pyne et al., 2001) has been widely adopted around the world with several variations that manipulate the number and length of stages or the duration of rest recovery between stages (Lakomy and Peyrebrune, 2003; Pyne, 1994; Treffene et al., 1980). These variations allow for greater flexibility and the selection of a test protocol appropriate for the age, ability and stroke speciality of a swimmer.

By evaluating the speed-stroke rate and speed–blood lactate relationships, the 7 × 200-m test allows the characterisation of biomechanical (Carvalho et al., 2020) and physiological breakpoints (Pyne, 2001; Zacca et al., 2018) that can be used to guide pacing in training. For a successful test, the opening three to four stages should be low intensity to allow a stable heart rate and blood lactate concentrations, with the final stage close to or at maximal effort. While this final stage allows for the calculation of a complete speed-lactate profile, it is not essential for the calculation of all metrics. Standard parameters such as speed at 4-mM blood lactate can be calculated without the need for the swimmer to work at maximal paces, making the test appealing to coaches during more sensitive periods of the training cycle. Olbrecht (2000) argued that a shift in the speed–blood lactate curve is a result of the interaction of both 'aerobic' and 'anaerobic' capacities – as such, it should not be assumed that changes in the relationship are purely due to altered 'aerobic' physiology in isolation.

'Classic' critical speed testing

Critical speed (CS) testing uses evaluation of a swimmer's speed-time or distance-time relationship to estimate an 'aerobic capacity' marker in CS and an 'anaerobic capacity' marker in supra-CS distance capacity (D'). 'Classic' testing protocols require the completion of three to seven performance trials across a range of distances from 200 to 1500 m (Dekerle, 2006). To make the estimation of CS and D' more practical, Wakayoshi et al. (1993) and Dekerle (2006) suggested that completing only two performances of 200 m and 400 m may be more appropriate. Similarly, data to evaluate a swimmer's speed-time relationship could feasibly be attained from a swim meet; however, only using short-duration efforts of 50 m to 200 m would likely lead to CS being overestimated (Bishop et al., 1998).

The parameters assessed using CS protocols can be used to set individualised training intensities, to monitor the effectiveness of training blocks on short and long duration exercise tolerance, to predict competitive performances of 2- to 30-min duration and to compare the relative strengths and weaknesses of individual swimmers. Any sports scientist wishing to conduct 'classic' CS testing should first carefully evaluate the trade-off of including more and/or longer performance trials to achieve greater validity in CS estimation versus the enhanced practicality of using fewer and/or shorter trials.

3-minute all-out test

Piatrikova et al. (2018) proposed an alternative protocol to estimate CS and D', showing that a 3-min all-out test (3MT) was reliable and highly correlated to the 'classic' CS testing protocols in national swimmers swimming freestyle. The 3MT is advantageous in that it offers a one-off effort method to evaluate CS and D'; however, the successful execution of the test is reliant on the swimmer not pacing themselves and swimming as fast as possible from the start of the test. Such efforts are strongly reliant on athlete motivation to achieve valid and reliable results. Moreover, the 3MT may lead to significant fatigue that negatively alters stroke mechanics beyond what would normally be experienced in training or racing, particularly in the higher energy costing strokes of breaststroke and butterfly.

12 × 25-m all-out test

Mitchell et al. (2018) proposed a modified version of the 3MT: 12 × 25-m all-out efforts conducted in a short-course pool with 5 s rest every 25 m. These short rest periods may reduce the accumulation of fatigue and technical breakdown. The protocol has been validated against CS estimated from two competition performances of 100 m and 200 m, with strong validity demonstrated for CS but not D'. The use of these short distance competition efforts means that CS calculated using the 'classic' CS method for validation was likely itself a significant overestimation of 'true' CS. Despite this limitation, the 12 × 25-m protocol remains an attractively simple test that provides an estimate of both CS and D' with limited equipment required or time taken.

Tethered swimming

Tethered swimming assessments, conducted either fully tethered (no forward movement) or semi-tethered (enabling forward movement), allow for the calculation of propulsive forces (Amaro et al., 2017). Fully tethered swimming allows the swim duration to be manipulated as desired for flexibility of performance assessment. Semi-tethered swimming allows forward movement over a set distance, usually ~15 m, with weighted resistance applied. It has been suggested that mechanical constraints created by fully tethered swimming may alter stroke patterns; however, any changes are likely reduced in well-habituated, well-trained swimmers.

Currently there are no fully tethered swimming systems commercially available. The tethered swimming system used by British Swimming (2021) consists of

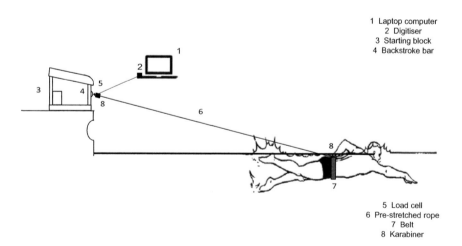

Figure 4.3.2 A schematic diagram of the fully tethered swimming system.
Source: Adapted from Taylor (2003).

Table 4.3.1 Validity and reliability of key parameters measured using a selection of pool-based swimming tests

Test	Protocol	Parameters	Validity	Reliability TE (CV)	Correlation
7 × 200-m step-test (Pyne et al., 2001)	7 × 200 m on a 5-min cycle, finishing on a maximal effort. Target times for each stage progressively getting 5 s faster, with the target time of the final stage being 5 s slower than 200-m personal best time.	Δ 1 mM (s/100 m)	N/A	1.7 (2.3%) (Turner et al., 2008)	ICC = 0.69
		4 mM (s/100 m)	Correlation with competition performance: males r = −0.21 females r = −0.31 (Anderson et al., 2006)	0.5 = male 0.6 = female (0.8%) (Anderson et al., 2006)	ICC = 0.85 (Turner et al., 2008)
		Maximal 200-m (s)	Correlation with competition performance: males r = 0.08 females r = 0.37 (Anderson et al., 2006) Correlation with 400 m speed r = 0.92 (Oliveira et al., 2012)	0.9 = male 1.0 = female (0.8%) (Anderson et al., 2006)	ICC = 0.89 (Turner et al., 2008)

(Continued)

Table 4.3.1 (Continued)

Test	Protocol	Parameters	Validity	Reliability TE (CV)	Correlation
'Classic' critical speed testing (Wakayoshi et al., 1993)	Multiple performance trials on separate days of ~2–15 min duration. Use of the distance-time relationship to calculate critical speed (CS) and supra-CS distance capacity (D'). Data presented refer to 200-m and 400-m performance trial protocol. Validity data for freestyle only.	CS (s/100m)	200/400 protocol likely overestimates 'true' CS and will be higher than MLSS (Martin and Whyte, 2000; Dekerle et al., 2005).	Butterfly: 2.0 (2.4%) Backstroke: 2.0 (2.5%) Breaststroke: 2.6 (3.0%) Front crawl: 2.3 (3.3%) (Scott et al., 2020)	ICC (95% CI) Butterfly: 0.90 (0.69–0.98) Backstroke: 0.88 (0.66–0.97) Breaststroke: 0.70 (0.31–0.93) Front crawl: 0.71 (0.39–0.91) (Scott et al., 2020)
		D' (m)	N/A	Butterfly: 4.1 (13.3%) Backstroke: 8.8 (44.7%) Breaststroke: 6.6 (35.0%) Front crawl: 8.5 (42.3%) (Scott et al., 2020)	ICC (95% CI) Butterfly: 0.76 (0.37–0.95) Backstroke: 0.40 (−0.22–0.81) Breaststroke: 0.38 (−0.30–0.82) Front crawl: −0.14 (−0.34–0.29) (Scott et al., 2020)
3-minute all-out test (Piatrikova et al., 2018)	Three minutes of all-out swimming, without any pacing of effort. Recording of distance every 15 s, using distance at 150 s and 180 s to calculate CS and D'. Freestyle data only.	CS (s/100 m)	Mean bias 0.7 s/100 m higher than CS calculated using a 'classic' CS protocol with 200-, 400-, 600- and 800-m trials. 95% LOA −3.0 to 1.9 s/100 m. r = 0.95.	0.7 (0.9%)	ICC = 0.97

	D' (m)	Mean bias −3.8 m versus D' calculated using 'classic' CS protocol. 95% LOA −11.8 to 4.2 m. r = 0.79.	1.5 (9.1%)	ICC = 0.45

12 × 25-m all-out test (Mitchell et al., 2018)			
12 × 25-m all-out efforts swum in a short-course pool, without any pacing, 5 s of rest between repetitions, two underwater kicks completed for each rep, or a single pull-out underwater phase for breaststroke swimmers. Data refer to a mixed group of freestyle, breaststroke and backstroke swimmers. CS estimated from the mean of the final three 25-m efforts.	CS (s/100 m)	Significantly overestimates CS calculated using 'classic' performance trial method with 100- and 200-m competition performance trials. Mean bias of 2.6 s/100 m. R^2 = 0.92.	0.8 (1.2%)	ICC = 0.99
	D' (m)	No significant difference from 'classic' CS protocol using 100-m and 200-m trials. Mean bias of 1.4 m. R^2 = 0.60.	1.2 (5.7%)	ICC = 0.97

400-m time trial (Lavoie et al., 1983)			
400 m swum as fast as possible, with the backwards extrapolation method of $\dot{V}O_2$ recovery applied to estimate $\dot{V}O_2$max. Data relate to freestyle only.	$\dot{V}O_2$max (l/min)	No significant difference from $\dot{V}O_2$max measured using Douglas bag method whilst swimming if test conditions are met (Lavoie et al., 1983). Correlation with 400-m speed r = 0.30 (Ribeiro et al., 1990).	N/A	N/A

(*Continued*)

Table 4.3.1 (Continued)

Test	Protocol	Parameters	Validity	Reliability TE (CV)	Correlation
All-out tethered swimming testing (Amaro et al., 2017)	All-out swimming; commonly of durations of 10 to 180 s, completed whilst attached to a tethered swimming device that measures propulsive forces. Data relate to freestyle only.	Maximum force (N)	Significantly correlated with 50-m performance time, $r = -0.75$ to -0.82 (Loturco et al., 2016; Morouço et al., 2014) and 100-m performance time $r = -0.74$ (Loturco et al., 2016).	N/A	ICC = 0.94 Cronbach's alpha = 0.97–0.99 (Amaro et al., 2014; Kjendlie and Thorsvald, 2006)
		Average force (N)	10-s average force significantly correlated with 50-m and 100-m performance time $r = -0.85$ and $r = -0.67$, respectively (Loturco et al., 2016).	N/A	ICC = 0.96 Cronbach's alpha = 0.97 (Amaro et al., 2014)
		Impulse (N/s)	10-s and 30-s impulse measures significantly correlated with 50-m performance time $r = -0.76$ to -0.80 (Loturco et al., 2016; Morouço et al., 2014).	N/A	ICC = 0.99 Cronbach's alpha = 0.99 (Amaro et al., 2014)

a laptop computer (MacBook Air, Apple, California, USA), software (DSCUSB Toolkit PC Software, Applied Measurements Ltd, Reading, UK), a starting block, a load cell (DDEN-1000N-003–000, Applied Measurements Ltd, Reading, UK), a strain gauge digitiser (DSCUSB, Applied Measurements Ltd, Reading, UK), karabiners (1000 kN, EB Viper, Bangor), 6-m pre-stretched rope (diameter 0.5 cm) and a climbing belt (Trat, Arizona, USA). Figure 4.3.2 provides a diagrammatic representation of a tethered swimming system.

Swimmers commence testing from a rolling start, taking up any slack in the rope by swimming submaximally until a whistle is blown. Standardisation of the whistle blow to hand entry of a particular stroke is advised. The swimmer then commences an all-out effort that is maintained for the duration of the test. All-out protocols using tethered swimming systems typically last 10–180 s; test duration should be selected to suit the parameters to be assessed and the individual swimmer's key performance determinants (Cortesi et al., 2010). After the select test period is complete, the whistle is blown again to signify the end of the test.

Dry-land testing for swimmers

Dry-land strength and power training may enhance the ability to produce propulsive forces in the water and therefore have a positive transfer into swimming performance (Morouço et al., 2012b). Dry-land strength and power measures correlate with swimming performance metrics of both skills and free swimming, particularly in short (i.e., 50 and 100 m) and middle (i.e., 200 and 400 m) distance events. Dry-land testing can be complementary to pool-based testing in assessing performance determinants and is easily integrated within a swimmer's strength and conditioning programme. In short-distance swimming, where the dive and underwater phases make up a large portion of the total race, 1RM squat strength, jump height, peak and relative power correlate with start time as assessed by time to 15 m (West et al., 2011, Thng et al., 2019). In 200-m swimmers, maximal upper body strength and strength endurance correlate with distance per stroke and average swim velocity (Elkins, 2018).

References

Amaro, N. M., Marinho, D. A., Batalha, N., Marques, M. C. and Morouço, P. (2014). Reliability of tethered swimming evaluation in age group swimmers. *Journal of Human Kinetics*, 41, 155–162.

Amaro, N. M., Morouço, P. G., Marques, M. C., Fernandes, R. J. and Marinho, D. A. (2017). Biomechanical and bioenergetical evaluation of swimmers using fully-tethered swimming: A qualitative review. *Journal of Human Sport and Exercise*, 12(4), 1346–1360.

Anderson, M. E., Hopkins, W. G., Roberts, A. D. and Pyne, D. B. (2006). Monitoring seasonal and long-term changes in test performance in elite swimmers. *European Journal of Sport Science*, 6(3), 145–154.

Bishop, D., Gjenkins, D. and Howard, A. (1998). The critical power function is dependent on the duration. *International Journal of Sports Medicine*, 19, 125–129.

Carvalho, D. D., Soares, S., Zacca, R., Sousa, J., Marinho, D. A., Silva, A. J., Vilas-Boas, J. P. and Fernandes, R. J. (2020). Anaerobic threshold biophysical characterisation of the four swimming techniques. *International Journal of Sport Medicine*, 41(5), 318–327.

Cortesi, M., Cesaracciu, E., Sawacha, Z. and Gatta, G. (2010). Which is the recommended duration for the tethered swimming test? In *Biomechanics and Medicine in Swimming XI*, p. 91. Oslo: Norwegian School of Sport Science.

Dekerle, J. (2006). The use of critical velocity in swimming: A place for critical stroke rate. *Portuguese Journal of Sport Sciences*, 6(S2), 201–205.

Dekerle, J., Pelayo, P., Clipet, B., Depretz, S., Lefevre, T. and Sidney, M. (2005). Critical swimming speed does not represent the speed at maximal lactate steady state. *International Journal of Sports Medicine*, 26(7), 524–530.

Elkins, A. W. (2018). *Relationship of Strength and Power on 200-m Swim Performance in National Level Swimmers*. Unpublished Master's Thesis, St Mary's University, London, UK.

Kjendlie, P. L. and Thorsvald, K. (2006). A tethered swimming power test is highly reliable. *Portuguese Journal of Sport Sciences*, 6(S2), 231–233.

Lakomy, H. K. A. and Peyrebrune, M. C. (2003). *Aerobic Fitness Assessment: 7 x 200-m Step Test*. Loughborough: British Swimming.

Lavoie, J. M., Léger, L. A., Montpetit, R. and Chabot, S. (1983). Backward extrapolation of $\dot{V}O_2$ from the O_2 recovery curve after a voluntary maximal 400m swim. *Biomechanics and Medicine in Swimming*, 222–227.

Loturco, I., Barbosa, A. C., Nocentini, R. K., Pereira, L. A., Kobal, R., Kitamura, K., Abad, C. C. C., Figueiredo, P. and Nakamura, F. Y. (2016). A correlational analysis of tethered swimming, swim sprint performance and dry-land power assessments. *International Journal of Sports Medicine*, 37(3), 211–218.

Martin, L. and Whyte, G. P. (2000). Comparison of critical swimming velocity and velocity at lactate threshold in elite triathletes. *International Journal of Sports Medicine*, 21(5), 366–368.

Mitchell, L. J., Pyne, D. B., Saunders, P. U. and Rattray, B. (2018). Reliability and validity of a modified 3-minute all-out swimming test in elite swimmers. *European Journal of Sport Science*, 18(3), 307–314.

Morouço, P. G., Marinho, D. A., Amaro, N. M., Pérez-Turpin, J. A. and Marques, M. C. (2012b). Effects of dry-land strength training on swimming performance: A brief review. *Journal of Human Sport and Exercise*, 7(2), 553–559.

Morouço, P. G., Marinho, D. A., Keskinen, K. L., Badillo, J. J. and Marques, M. C. (2014). Tethered swimming can be used to evaluate force contribution for short-distance swimming performance. *The Journal of Strength and Conditioning Research*, 28(11), 3093–3099.

Morouço, P. G., Vilas-Boas, J. P. and Fernandes, R. J. (2012a). Evaluation of adolescent swimmers through a 30-s tethered test. *Pediatric Exercise Science*, 24(2), 312–321.

Olbrecht, J. (2000). *The Science of Winning: Planning, Periodisation, Optimising Swim Training*. Antwerp: F&G Partners, Partners in Sport.

Oliveira, M. F., Caputo, F., Lucas, R. D., Denadai, B. S. and Greco, C. C. (2012). Physiological and stroke parameters to assess aerobic capacity in swimming. *International Journal of Sports Physiology and Performance*, 7(3), 218–223.

Piatrikova, E., Sousa, A. C., Gonzalez, J. T. and Williams, S. (2018). Validity and reliability of the 3-minute all-out test in national and international competitive swimmers. *International Journal of Sports Physiology and Performance*, 13(9), 1190–1198.

Pyne, D. B. (1994). *Sports Science for Age Groupers: Exercise Physiology*. Australian Swimming Coaches and Teachers Convention: ASCTA.

Pyne, D. B., Lee, H. and Swanwick, K. M. (2001). Monitoring the lactate threshold in world-ranked swimmers. *Medicine and Science in Sports and Exercise*, 33(2), 291–297.

Ribeiro, J. P., Cadavid, E., Baena, J., Monsalvete, E., Barna, A. and De Rose, E. H. (1990). Metabolic predictors of middle-distance swimming performance. *British Journal of Sports Medicine*, 24(3), 196–200.

Scott, B. E., Burden, R. and Dekerle, J. (2020). Critical speed, D' and pacing in swimming: Reliability of a popular critical speed protocol applied to all four strokes. *Research Square* [Pre-print]. www.researchsquare.com/article/rs-77508/v1 (accessed 17 May 2021).

Taylor, S. R. (2003). *The Analysis of Anaerobic Performance in Age Group Swimmers*. Unpublished PhD Thesis, Liverpool John Moores University, Liverpool, UK.

Thng, S., Pearson, S. and Keogh, J. W. (2019). Relationships between dry-land resistance training and swim start performance and effects of such training on the swim start: A systematic review. *Sports Medicine*, 49(12), 1957–1973.

Treffene, R. J., Dickson, R., Craven, C., Osborne, C., Woodhead, K. and Hobbs, K. (1980). Lactic acid accumulation during constant speed swimming at controlled relative intensities. *Journal of Sports Medicine and Physical Fitness*, 20(3), 244–254.

Turner, A. P., Smith, T. and Coleman, S. G. (2008). Use of an audio-paced incremental swimming test in young national-level swimmers. *International Journal of Sports Physiology and Performance*, 3(1), 68–79.

Wakayoshi, K., Yoshida, T., Udo, M., Harada, T., Moritani, T., Mutoh, Y. and Miyashita, M. (1993). Does critical swimming velocity represent exercise intensity at maximal lactate steady state? *European Journal of Applied Physiology and Occupational Physiology*, 66(1), 90–95.

West, D. J., Owen, N. J., Cunningham, D. J., Cook, C. J. and Kilduff, L. P. (2011). Strength and power predictors of swimming starts in international sprint swimmers. *The Journal of Strength and Conditioning Research*, 25(4), 950–955.

Zacca, R., Carvalho, D. D., Soares, S., Marinho, D. A., Silva, A. J., Vilas-Boas, J. P. and Fernades, R. J. (2018). Individual anaerobic threshold testing in elite swimmers: Comparability and interchangeability between physiological and biomechanical inflection and deflection points. In: *XIIIth International Symposium on Biomechanics and Medicine in Swimming: Japanese Society of Sciences in Swimming and Water Exercise*, p. 72.

4.4 Rowing

Richard J. Godfrey, Craig A. Williams, Sarah Gilchrist, and R. C. Richard Davison

Rowing is an Olympic sport in which athletes compete over a measured regatta course of 2000 m and there are up to 22 boat classes in an international regatta. For the elite oarsman the competitive 2000 m takes approximately 6 min. Two distinct disciplines exist within rowing; sweep rowing and sculling. In sweep rowing, boats require a crew of two ('pair'), four ('four') or eight rowers, each using a single oar, and row on either one side (e.g., bowside or starboard) or the other (e.g., strokeside or port) of the boat. A sculling boat can seat one ('single'), two ('double') or four ('quad') rowers, each using two oars.

According to British Rowing, formerly known as the Amateur Rowing Association, grassroots participation in rowing in the United Kingdom is estimated at more than 17,000 individuals. As a consequence of increasing media interest in rowing resulting from long-term and continuing Olympic and Paralympic success, there is greater awareness of the fact that elite rowers and their coaches view sport science as an essential component of their success. Therefore more sports scientists, in a university setting, are being approached by club-level rowers seeking physiology support.

Physiologically, rowing is proposed to require a good balance between strength and endurance (Hagerman and Staron, 1983; Secher, 1983), so a contribution from both aerobic and anaerobic energy metabolism is required. The determinants of performance for elite heavyweight rowers have been assessed and five important physiological parameters identified (Ingham et al., 2002). These are reported to be power at $\dot{V}O_2$peak, maximum power, maximal force ($r = 0.95$; $P < 0.001$), $\dot{V}O_2$peak ($r = 0.88$; $P < 0.001$) and oxygen consumption at the blood lactate threshold ($r = 0.87$; $P < 0.001$). All of these findings are derived from the use of a Concept IIc rowing ergometer (Concept, Nottingham, UK) with a force transducer at the handle such that force profiles and power measurements all result from the rowing action.

In prioritising which tests to implement in assessing the club-level rower, it could be argued that body composition, strength and power and aerobic endurance are key. Body composition testing is important, particularly if the competitor being tested is a lightweight rower. Dual emission x-ray absorptiometry (DEXA) is currently considered the gold standard for assessing body composition. Routinely, elite rowers continue to be tested using skinfold measurements (for further details see

DOI: 10.4324/9781003045281-30

Chapter 3.4). Rowing is often referred to as a power-endurance sport with an aerobic contribution of about 67%–88% of the energy required and, hence, being able to sustain a high power output over a prolonged period is key. Accordingly, in assessing changes in physiology, the discontinuous incremental protocol (colloquially referred to as a 'step test to max') is tried and tested.

Seven-stroke power test

This test is designed to assess peak power. The athlete carries out a warm-up on the ergometer, performs some light stretching and then a specific warm-up using hard efforts of two, three and four strokes. The athlete then carries out the test with the first two strokes not recorded to allow the rower to overcome the inertia of the flywheel and to achieve a rating of 30 strokes per minute (2 spm). From this test, work (J), mean force (N), mean power (W), stroke rate (spm) and stroke length (m) are reported from the five recorded strokes.

Step test

This is a discontinuous incremental test, consisting of five 4-min efforts, each one requiring a 25 W increase in power output and followed by a sixth and final 4-min effort at race pace. It was recently reported that stages of ≤7-min overestimated maximal lactate steady state (MLSS), but that stages ≤ 4-min more accurately measure peak values. However, by using an appropriate regression equation, both peak and MLSS levels could be accurately determined using a 4-min stage (Bourdon et al., 2018). Gas exchange, heart rate and blood lactate are monitored in the second test only. Physiological variables measured are lactate threshold (LT), oxygen cost of ergometer rowing (economy), maximum oxygen consumption ($\dot{V}O_2$max) and power associated with $\dot{V}O_2$max (W$\dot{V}O_2$max). It is possible to combine this test with a 2000-m time trial with a 15-min recovery between the trials. This enables the determination of both physiological and performance parameters in one test (Bourdon et al., 2009).

For an individual who has not been tested before, a 2000-m time trial on the Concept IIc should be performed first. This should be a maximal effort, and the time for 2000 m should be converted into a 500-m split time. For heavyweight men and women, add 15 s to this time and you have the split for the third stage of the step test. Subtract 25 W from this to get the power output (and split time) for stage 2 and subtract 50 W for stage 1. For stage 4, add 25 W and for stage 5, add 50 W. For lightweight men and women, also add 15 s to the calculated 500-m split time to find the split for the third stage. However, it may be more appropriate to use a 15–20 W increment (rather than a 25 W increment) for lightweights. The data collected and calculated from the step test include $\dot{V}O_2$peak, power at $\dot{V}O_2$peak, the percentage of maximum that can be sustained (i.e., $\dot{V}O_2$ at lactate threshold as a percentage of $\dot{V}O_2$peak), power at LT, maximum power and maximum force. The heart rate associated with LT can be used to determine a number of heart rate zones, which can be used for training.

Blood lactate

For a number of years now the EBIO plus (Eppendorf, Colone, Germany) laboratory-based analyser and the Biosen C_line (EKF Diagnostics, Germany) portable analyser have been used with elite rowers. These have superseded the long-term use of the Analox GM-7 (or portable PGM-7) (Analox Instruments Ltd, Hammersmith, UK). Generally, lab-based systems have been preferred, as their validity and reliability have been tested. Although it is possible to use new 'palm top' lactate analysers, they are currently questioned with respect to validity and reliability, but such research work is on-going. Hence, in the future, once their reliability and validity have been more fully demonstrated, they will prove to be the more practical equipment to use. With the EBIO plus and Biosen C_line, it is possible to collect the capillary sample (the earlobe is preferred, as it limits the pain of sampling and contamination of samples and is more consistent with health and safety). Blood is collected into a capillary tube, which is immediately placed in an Eppendorf tube (containing a lysing agent), which can then be kept for 24 h without the need for refrigeration.

Ergometry

The preferred ergometer used in the United Kingdom is the Concept IIc (Concept, Nottingham, UK). When lab testing takes place with elite athletes, a Concept IIc with force transducer at the handle is used: the Avicon system. This is an online system and force profiles for each stroke of the seven-stroke power test, and averages for each stage of the step-test is recorded. This provides further feedback to the coach on technique. If testing sub-elite rowers, a standard Concept IIc, without Avicon system, can be used and sufficient information provided to aid training of the individual. Despite the widespread use of the Concept II ergometer, it is recognised that the movement dynamics do not exactly replicate the on-water experience and thus potential physiological demand. In an attempt to better replicate the on-water dynamics, Concept developed the slide, which allows the ergometer to move in the opposite direction of the rower as happens on the water. The addition of the slide has been shown to impact on the physiological responses with lower $\dot{V}O_2$peak and a better correlation between on-water performance and the $\dot{V}O_2$ power relationship derived from testing using the slide. Thus this may better replicate on-water physiological responses (Mello et al., 2014).

Field testing

Coaches in many sports are increasingly demanding that field-based testing replace laboratory-based testing. Generally, physiologists do not oppose a reduction in the frequency of lab-based testing and an increase in field testing. However, it is very difficult to justify the elimination of lab-based testing altogether, as it is simply impossible to collect data more objectively. Hence, only in the lab can conditions be appropriately standardised uninfluenced by the vagaries of changing gym, weather or water conditions. Indeed, GB elite rowers are still lab-tested two to three times per year with four to five field-based (step test) sessions. In addition, the coach administers some tests such as 18-km, 30-min, 2-km and 250-m rows on the water. Regularly, blood samples are taken by a physiologist at the end of such rows, or the 18-km row can be broken into 3 × 6 km rows with a 30- to 60-s rest interval for blood samples to be taken. In the 30-min row the athlete must complete the greatest possible distance at a fixed rate of 20 spm. This provides power output, heart rate and lactate data. The standard for elite women for this test is 7000–8000 m and for men 8500–9000 m.

The competitive environment for rowing is heavily influenced by environmental conditions and thus despite its ecological validity presents significant problems in using performance times of boat speed to assess improvements in fitness. In terms of on-water performance measures in comparison to Concept II performances, the calculated standard error of measurement is relatively large and ranges from 2.6% to 7.2% (Smith and Hopkins, 2018). Recent advances in global positioning system (GPS) measurement technology do allow reasonably accurate measurement of boat speed, with standard error of estimate ~0.2%.

At field camps overseas, early morning monitoring also occurs prior to daily training. This involves the use of urine osmolality to monitor hydration status, blood urea as an index of the additional stress superimposed on training by an often extreme environment and morning body mass and supine resting heart rate. Data here are viewed in combination with a psychological inventory and, if necessary, discussion with the coach and athlete. The coach takes decisions on the necessity of modifying training with certain individuals as a consequence of all of this plus on-water and gym-based data. Further, decisions are taken 'weighing' the mass of data in the light of extensive coaching experience and the coach's personal knowledge of the individual.

References

Bourdon, P. C., David, A. Z. and Buckley, J. D. (2009). A single exercise test for assessing physiological and performance parameters in elite rowers: The 2-in-1 test. *Journal of Science and Medicine in Sport*, 12(1), 205–211.

Bourdon, P. C., Woolford, S. M. and Buckley, J. D. (2018). Effects of varying the step duration on the determination of lactate thresholds in elite rowers. *International Journal of Sports Physiology and Performance*, 13(6), 687–693.

Hagerman, F. C. and Staron, R. S. (1983). Seasonal variations among physiological variables in elite oarsman. *Canadian Journal of Applied Sports Science*, 8, 143–148.

Ingham, S. A., Whyte, G. P., Jones, K. and Nevill, A. M. (2002). Determinants of 2000 m rowing performance in elite rowers. *European Journal of Applied Physiology*, 88, 243–246.

Mello, F. D. C., et al. (2014). Rowing ergometer with the slide is more specific to rowers' physiological evaluation. *Research in Sports Medicine*, 22(2), 136–146.

Secher, N. (1983). The physiology of rowing. *Journal of Sports Science*, 1, 23–53.

Smith, T. B. and Hopkins, W. G. (2012). Measures of rowing performance. *Sports Medicine*, 42(4), 343–358. doi: 10.2165/11597230-000000000-00000.

4.5 Cycling

Len Parker Simpson, James G. Hopker, and R. C. Richard Davison

Variety of the demands of cycling events

Cycling as a sport encompasses many different events and thus a very large range of different physiological demands. Events can be as short as 30–40 s or last as long as 24 h or 21 days as a Grand Tour stage race. Initially through heart rate monitoring and, more recently, with direct measurement of power output, a substantial understanding of the physiological demands of cycling has emerged. Within cycling events there are a range of power development patterns. Individual time trials could be considered the most consistent intensity, whereas most other cycling events require a much more stochastic power production. The magnitude and frequency of these variations have a significant effect on the event-specific demands. An approach that has been used is to create a power profile (the maximum mean power for the durations of 5, 10 and 30 s and 1, 2, 5, 10, 20, 60 and 180 min, achieved within a race season), from which research has suggested achieving a top-ten result in a professional cycling road race is largely determined by shorter-duration absolute and relative maximum mean power (<5 min; van Erp and Sanders, 2020). However, this may not be appropriate for other levels of road racing. Power-to-weight ratio is an important factor in determining relative cycling power outputs, especially when working against gravity (i.e., cycling uphill). Therefore, the regular assessment of body composition is an important consideration for the cyclist (see Chapter 3.4 for methods).

Despite technological developments, not all physiological demands are easily quantifiable. For example, in both downhill and Enduro MountainBike, standard recognized terminology (MTB) racing, there are significant periods of low or zero watts interspaced by very brief high-power production. However, heart rate (HR) measured during these events suggests high sustained effort, mostly as a result of muscular activity involved in maintaining both a 'ready position' and balance through technical sections of the course.

Another approach is to characterise performance of successful cyclists across the disciplines, and unsurprisingly, it is possible to find commonality in performance determinants (e.g., track cycling disciplines of match sprint and Keirin both require strong musculature and high peak power outputs), whereas other cycling disciplines require much greater heterogeneity reflecting the varying demands of that event (e.g., cyclo-cross and criterium racing). However, it is important to

DOI: 10.4324/9781003045281-31

remember that successful cycling performance is not just related to the physiological performance of the individual rider. For a large number of cycling races, there are a number of complex interactions between the dimensions and features of each race that combine to give the final outcome.

Peak power output

Of relevance to cycling events such as BMX, F200m, Match Sprint, Team Sprint, 500 m/1 km TT, Team Pursuit, Omnium, DH MTB XCC and XC MTB, Cyclo-Cross, Circuit/Crit Racing and Road Racing.

The maximal power output the cycling musculature can produce, commonly referred to as peak power output (PPO), is of relevance to many race-winning moments across cycle sport. The assessment of PPO should be short (6–10 s) so that a rider's maximal power can be achieved in the first few seconds of accelerative effort. The inertial-load method is the most valid and reliable. The use of a high-frequency (200$^+$ Hz) torque- and angular velocity-measuring device is advised. Features of the protocol that clearly impact on maximal power are stationary ('standing') or rolling start, gear ratio and resistive load (MacIntosh et al., 2003). However, it has been suggested that providing data have been corrected for the inertia of the flywheel and a standing start is used, there is no need to individualise optimal resistance (MacIntosh et al., 2003).

Important variables from this type of test are both the maximal power and the optimal cadence for maximal power. As both variables are integrally linked by the force-velocity (or within cycling, the torque-cadence) relationship of muscle, they cannot be considered in isolation and play an important role in protocol design. The resistance chosen for the test must be large enough so that peak cadence does not limit the maximal power and not so large to limit cadence to unrealistically low values.

It is also possible to construct torque-cadence relationships in the field. In elite Track Sprint cyclists, there is no discernible differences in (predicted) peak torque, (predicted) peak cadence and (modelled) PPO between laboratory- and field-derived data, with individual variation ~±7% (Gardner et al., 2007). Interestingly the inertial load calculated for the field assessments was ~7 times larger than the inertial load of the laboratory ergometer. This should provide some confidence as to the sensitivity of the torque-cadence relationship and PPO parameters to the resistive load applied for assessments. Yet it will be important to replicate the resistive load longitudinally for a given cyclist to monitor changes.

Anaerobic power reserve

Of relevance to cycling events such as BMX, Team Sprint, 500m/1km TT, Team Pursuit, Omnium, XCC and XC MTB, Cyclo-Cross, Circuit/Crit Racing and Road Racing.

The anaerobic power reserve (APR) describes the exponential relationship between power output and duration for very short (<~200 s) performances (Weyand et al., 2006; Figure 4.5.1) and refers to the range of power outputs between 'power at $\dot{V}O_2$max' (referred to as P_{aer}; 'maximal aerobic power') and PPO.

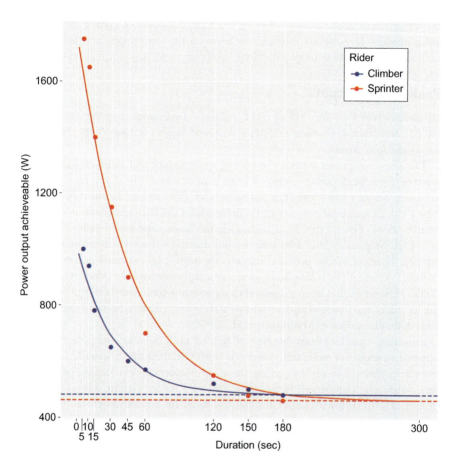

Figure 4.5.1 Example short-term power output capabilities from a 'climber' (blue circles) and a 'sprinter' (red circles) with an APR 'predicted' power capability line visible for each rider (climber = solid blue line; sprinter = solid red line). In each case, the k used in the APR model is derived individually from the data (circles) presented (climber k = 0.030; sprinter k = 0.022). P_{aer} is taken as the 180-s power output (dashed horizontal lines).

All cyclists exhibit approximately the same decay in power output between ~1 sec and ~200 sec relative to their PPO and P_{aer} (see Figure 4.5.2), characterised by the exponential decay constant (k) of 0.026 (range: 0.020–0.033; Weyand et al., 2006). To characterise a cyclist's APR, all that is required is PPO, P_{aer} and the exponential equation:

$$P(t) = P_{aer} + (PPO - P_{aer}) \cdot e^{(-k \cdot t)}$$

where P(t) is the predicted power output achievable for time t, and k is the decay constant, which, for cycling at ~100 rpm, is ~0.026.

Sanders and Heijboer (2019) have demonstrated that the predictive capability of the APR model is improved by replacing P_{aer} with 3-min 'record power' and individualising the k for each cyclist (see Figure 4.5.2). The modified k for the professional road cyclists averaged 0.0277 for a range of cadences between (mean) ~85–105 rpm.

The maximum steady state: critical power

Of relevance to cycling events such as Team and Individual Pursuit, Omnium, 10- and 25-mile TT, XCC and XC MTB, Cyclo-Cross, Circuit/Crit Racing and Road Racing.

The critical power (CP) model is a practical, empirical tool that describes the hyperbolic relationship between power output and its tolerable duration within the severe-intensity domain (Poole et al., 2016). By establishing at least three different points (power output for given durations or vice versa) on the power-duration (P-D) spectrum, it is possible to model both the CP and the fixed quantity of work achievable above CP: the W'. Combined, these parameters provide a 'fuller picture' of an athlete's physiological 'profile' and enable performance prediction within the severe-intensity domain.

Briefly, the following five factors will influence the CP and W' parameters:

The duration of the severe-intensity exercise trials used within the model

Trials used to model CP and W' should span ≥2 to ~15 min. The use of exclusively 'short' trials (e.g., ~70 to ~200 sec) will result in inflated CP and diminished W' estimates, respectively; the opposite is true of the use of exclusively 'long' trials (e.g., 500⁺ sec). In the laboratory it is commonplace to fix power output and measure time to exhaustion (T_{lim}). An alternative approach is to use fixed-duration time trials.

The performance of each trial used within the P-D model

All trials must be completed within the severe-intensity domain. 'Fixed-power' trials to T_{lim} ensure this. However, for longer-duration, self-paced trials, the 'risk' of dropping below CP (into the heavy-intensity domain) increases (Figure 4.5.3). Completing the shorter-duration trials first is both 'safer' and permits the long-duration trial(s) power output or T_{lim} to be forecast (Parker Simpson and Kordi, 2017).

The number of trials used to estimate CP and W'

It is common that four to five trials are used to model the P-D relationship. Two trials are the minimum required to compute CP and W'; however, only linear models may be employed, and no error terms are calculable. Thus, it is advisable to include at least a third trial within the P-D model or additional trials to reduce the sum of error to ≤10%. Additionally, a familiarisation effect is apparent until trials have been completed at least twice (Parker Simpson and Kordi, 2017).

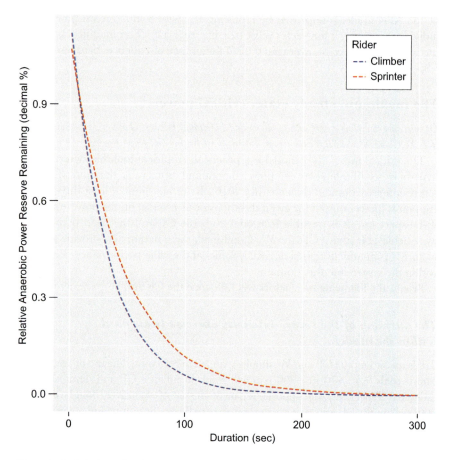

Figure 4.5.2 Relative APR for the 'climber' and the (sprinter) from Figure 4.5.1. Even with the different k values used for the vastly different riders (see Figure 4.5.1), once relativised to both PPO and P_{aer}, these two 'very different' riders exhibit a remarkably similar relative short-term power-duration relationship. For this reason, using the APR for extreme-intensity interval prescription may be of interest to the practitioner or researcher.

The particular model used to generate CP and W' parameter estimates

Of the five commonly employed P-D models, the work vs. time model consistently provides the median CP and W' estimate. However, selecting the model providing the 'best individual fit' (the lowest sum of CP and W' coefficient of variation: CV) is a sensible approach for an acute assessment. For longitudinal assessments, the same model must be employed successively. In familiarised cyclists who conduct three trials, CP can be determined with <2% CV and W' with < 7% CV (Parker Simpson and Kordi, 2017).

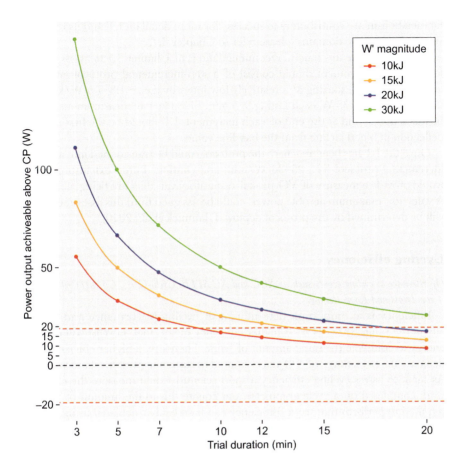

Figure 4.5.3 Theoretically achievable power output, above CP, for cyclists with W' of magnitudes 10 kJ (red), 15 kJ (orange), 20 kJ (blue) and 30 kJ (green) for different durations of trials. CP is denoted with a horizontal black dashed line. The red dashed lines represent the upper and lower 90% confidence intervals for a CP with 2% coefficient of variation (three trials; CP value of ~300 W; linear work-time model). Notice the relatively 'safe' durations, where the whole trial can be 'easily' paced well above CP (durations 3–7 min) and the relatively 'riskier' trial durations (W' magnitude dependant) where it would be increasingly more difficult to ensure the entirety of the self-paced trial was performed above CP (duration 10–20 min, especially so when the W' magnitude is <20 kJ).

Lactate threshold

Of relevance to cycling events such as XCC and XC MTB, Cyclo-Cross, Circuit/Crit Racing, Time Trials and Road Racing.

Lactate threshold (LT) is the marker that defines the transition from moderate- to heavy-intensity exercise and is important to many cyclists, but possibly more so those who take part in longer events where conservation of energy and reliance of fat metabolism are contributors to success. For more detail on LT and its relationship to the exercise domains, please refer to Chapter 3.7.

To contextualise the general recommendations of Chapter 3.7 to assess the LT for cycling, the protocol should consist of a step-incremental protocol involving at least five stages, starting at a relatively low intensity (i.e., ~1.3–1.5 W/kg) with increments of 15–35 W, each lasting 3–5 min. Blood lactate measurement should be taken at rest and at the end of each increment. LT should be the first upward deflection in blood lactate from the baseline value.

Once the LT has been reached, the protocol could be transitioned into a ramp-incremental protocol (i.e., 25–30 W/min) and continued until exhaustion. This would provide a measure of $\dot{V}O_2$peak if respiratory variables are being measured. A value for 'maximum aerobic power' could be assigned from this assessment, but will be determined by the protocol deployed (Jamnick et al., 2020).

Cycling efficiency

Of relevance to cycling events such as XCC and XC MTB, Cyclo-Cross, Circuit/Crit Racing, Time Trials and Road Racing.

Efficiency is an important determinant of cycling performance and is usually in the range 16%–24%. A higher efficiency means that a cyclist will use less energy to complete the same amount of work. Therefore, a higher efficiency will decrease the percentage of $\dot{V}O_2$max required to sustain a given mechanical work. As such, to assess cycling efficiency a sport scientist would measure the effective work completed on a cycle ergometer and equate this to the amount of energy required to perform that work. Efficiency can be reliably calculated using one of two methods (Hopker et al., 2012):

Gross efficiency, defined as the ratio of work accomplished to energy expended at a fixed work rate:

$$GE = \frac{\text{Work accomplished}}{\text{Energy expended}} \times 100\%$$

Delta efficiency, the ratio of the change in work accomplished to the change in energy expended between two different work rates. Suggested to be more reflective of muscle efficiency.

$$GE = \frac{\text{Change in work accomplished}}{\text{Change in energy expended}} \times 100\%$$

Efficiency is usually measured from a series of submaximal exercise trials undertaken at power outputs below CP. Often, three to four successive power outputs are used, with a short rest between them. Either preferred or fixed cadences can be used, but this should be kept constant throughout the test and in any subsequent tests. Similarly, it is important that cyclists either use their own bicycle during tests or have their set-up replicated on a laboratory ergometer.

During the submaximal cycling bouts, it is necessary to measure O_2 consumed, which can be performed using either online or offline gas analysis methods. However, regardless of which method is used, it is recommended that 6- to 8-min stages are used, with gas sampling occurring during the last 2–3 min. Subsequently, average $\dot{V}O_2$, average $\dot{V}CO_2$ and the energetic equivalent according to the table of nonprotein respiratory quotient (Péronnet and Massicotte, 1991) should be determined for each work stage. These data are then used to calculate energetic expenditure via multiplication of the $\dot{V}O_2$ by the energetic equivalent per L O_2. Power output recorded in parallel to expired gas collection should be converted into work accomplished. Efficiency can then be calculated using the previous formula.

Monitoring the balance between training load and recovery

Ensuring that cyclists can perform at their highest level is reliant on identifying an optimal balance between the training workload and recovery period for the training effect to be maximised. It is therefore important that changes in performance and symptoms of fatigue are closely monitored to ensure that a balance between training stress and recovery is achieved.

The Lamberts submaximal cycling test (LSCT; Lamberts et al., 2011) has been developed as a tool to monitor fatigue in high-level cyclists. The LSCT consists of three stages, with stages 1 and 2 being 6 min and stage 3 being 3 min in length. At the end of the cycling part of the test, HR recovery should be monitored for 1 min. In stage 1, 2 and 3 the goal is to achieve and maintain 60% (±1 bpm), 80% and 90% HR_{max} (respectively). During the test, practitioners should record the cyclist's stage average power output, HR and RPE after excluding the first minute of each stage due to the lag time in HR response to changes in exercise intensity. Finally, HR during the final 60 s of the recovery period should be recorded.

If simply interested in monitoring 'recovery' or athlete condition on a day-to-day basis, the same principles of the LSCT could be employed. 'Clamping' power or RPE as opposed to %HRmax may be advantageous, with the responses of the other variables being observed. An inherent challenge with 'fatigue monitoring' using only 'objective measures' is that we expect to witness similar responses (lower HR for a given power, or more power for a given HR) for *both* increased 'fitness' (so chronic change over months) and increased 'fatigue' (acute effect of recent training and 'stress').

References

Gardner, A. S., Martin, J. C., Martin, D. T., Barras, M. and Jenkins, D. G. (2007). Maximal torque- and power-pedaling rate relationships for elite sprint cyclists in laboratory and field tests. *European Journal of Applied Physiology*, 101(3), 287–292.

Hopker, J. G., Jobson, S. A., Gregson, H. C., Coleman, D. and Passfield, L. (2012). Reliability of cycling gross efficiency using the Douglas bag method. *Medicine and Science in Sports and Exercise*, 44(2), 290–296.

Jamnick, N. A., Pettitt, R. W., Granata, C., Pyne, D. B. and Bishop, D. J. (2020). An examination and critique of current methods to determine exercise intensity. *Sports Medicine (Auckland, N.Z.)*, 50(10), 1729–1756.

Lamberts, R. P., Swart, J., Noakes, T. D. and Lambert, M. I. (2011). A novel submaximal cycle test to monitor fatigue and predict cycling performance. *British Journal of Sports Medicine*, 45(10), 797–804.

MacIntosh, B. R., Rishaug, P. and Svedahl, K. (2003). Assessment of peak power and short-term work capacity. *European Journal of Applied Physiology*, 88(6), 572–579.

Parker Simpson, L. and Kordi, M. (2017). Comparison of critical power and W' derived from 2 or 3 maximal tests. *International Journal of Sports Physiology and Performance*, 12(6), 825–830.

Péronnet, F. and Massicotte, D. (1991). Table of nonprotein respiratory quotient: An update. *Canadian Journal of Sport Sciences = Journal Canadien Des Sciences Du Sport*, 16(1), 23–29.

Poole, D. C., Burnley, M., Vanhatalo, A., Rossiter, H. B. and Jones, A. M. (2016). Critical power: An important fatigue threshold in exercise physiology. *Medicine and Science in Sports and Exercise*, 48(11), 2320–2334.

Sanders, D. and Heijboer, M. (2019). The anaerobic power reserve and its applicability in professional road cycling. *Journal of Sports Sciences*, 37(6), 621–629.

van Erp, T. and Sanders, D. (2020). Demands of professional cycling races: Influence of race category and result. *European Journal of Sport Science*, 1–12.

Weyand, P. G., Lin, J. E. and Bundle, M. W. (2006). Sprint performance-duration relationships are set by the fractional duration of external force application. *American Journal of Physiology: Regulatory, Integrative and Comparative Physiology*, 290(3), R758–R765.

4.6 Canoeing and kayaking

Ciara Sinnott-O'Connor and Caroline MacManus

Canoe disciplines include canoe sprint, canoe slalom, canoe ocean racing, canoe marathon, canoe polo and canoe freestyle (Messias et al., 2014). Since 2009, paracanoeing has also been a recognised event by the International Canoe Federation (ICF) and a Paralympic Games event since 2016. Furthermore, canoeing can be categorised as Kayak (K) or Canoe (C). Kayaks are closed boats where athletes paddle from a seated position with a double-blade paddle, whereas canoes are open boats with the athlete in a kneeling position using a single-blade paddle. Canoeing is a technical, dynamic sport that involves symmetric (kayak) or asymmetric (canoe) rhythmical movements (Wietrzyński et al., 2013).

Canoe sprint is one of the canoeing Olympic events with athlete teams or individuals racing head-to-head on a flat-water course over a set distance (200 m, 500 m and 1000 m) in either a canoe (C1, C2 and C4) or kayak (K1, K2 and K4). Narrow hulls on the boat allow for speed. It requires strength and efficient technique to move as quickly as possible across the racing distance. The shortest races take approximately 30 s to complete; upper body strength and explosive power are key determinants of success, alongside technique and posture. In paracanoe, two boat types are used – kayaks, propelled by a double-blade paddle, and outrigger canoes referred to as va'as, propelled by a single-blade paddle. Both race over the same 200-m distance for males and females.

Canoe slalom, also an Olympic event, requires athletes to race (run) through rapids and pass through suspended poles (slalom gates) above the water in the correct order and direction, avoiding a touch with any part of the boat, paddle or body. Green and white striped poles must be passed in a downstream direction and red poles in an upstream direction. Each gate tests the ability of the athlete to read and work with the water flow whilst maintaining balance, trajectory and speed. Penalty seconds for any infringement on poles or passing in the wrong direction are added to finishing time for an overall score. Slalom can be raced as kayak (K1), canoe (C1) and Canadian doubles (C2). Most runs last between 90 and 120 s, and despite the large anaerobic contribution to the event of this duration, Zamparo et al. (2006) determined that approximately 50% of aerobic metabolism and 30% of anaerobic metabolism contributed to the event. Consequently, this large contribution from aerobic metabolism suggests the importance of aerobic assessment to track development along with anaerobic and alactic metabolism assessments.

DOI: 10.4324/9781003045281-32

Laboratory testing

Laboratory-based assessment should be conducted two to three times per year, based on competition and training schedule of the athlete, with data being used to set training intensities, as well as tracking positive or negative adaptations to training. Body composition should be routinely recorded across multiple time points in the season, as outlined in Chapter 3.4.

Incremental step test

Athletes should complete a short warm-up of 10 min duration, at an intensity at or just below the first stage of the step test. A lactate sample is taken at the end of the warm-up as a baseline measure and should be below 2.0 mmol·l^{-1}. Prior to commencing the test, the athlete is fitted with a face mask for the gas analysis system and asked to relax breathing for 15–30 sec to confirm data are being collected. Laboratory tests should be conducted on a canoe ergometer set up for either K1/sprint testing or with modifications for C1 testing to facilitate the kneeling athlete and the paddle moved to the preferred side. A strain gauge should be used to determine the tension in the ergometer ropes, and this should also be recorded in order to standardise the ergometer set-up for each test. The canoe ergometer should be zeroed on screen and the athlete instructed to begin the first stage of testing following the protocol outlined in Table 4.6.1.

Gas analysis continues throughout the test until volitional exhaustion. Lactate sampling continues at the end of each step, as well as post-test, 2 min and 5 min, to determine peak lactate. Blood lactate should be measured using a capillary blood sample taken from the earlobe so as not to require movement of the athlete's hands and reduce contamination of samples via sweat. At the end of the test, the maximal oxygen uptake value should be recorded, as well as corresponding carbon dioxide and respiratory exchange ratio (RER) values. Maximal HR is recorded as the highest value in the last stage of the test.

Table 4.6.1 Canoeing/kayak laboratory incremental test protocol

	K1	C1	Sprint
Starting intensity	60 W	30 W	100 W
Step 2	80 W	40 W	125 W
Step 3	100 W	45 W	150 W
Step 4 to end	10–20 W increments *	5–10 W increments *	25 W increments
Stage duration	3 min with 1 min rest interval	3 min with 1 min rest interval	3 min with 1 min rest interval
Measures for each stage	Average in last 30 s for heart rate, average power, stroke rate, metabolic data. Blood lactate and RPE taken at end of stage.		
Test completion	Last stage completed holding target power and maximal effort required.		

*Increments for steps may be lower for younger paddlers or novice athletes.

Blood lactate–power output (lactate curve) and HR–power output plots can be used to illustrate the response of the athlete during the incremental step test. Interpretation of the data is dependent on the point of the season that the athlete has reported for testing. Corresponding power and HR at lactate thresholds can be used to prescribe training zones and intensities. The data are reported to the coach, who can implement and amend training zones accordingly. The feedback to the athlete and coach should interpret the data in a way that both can understand and allow them to use the information to further enhance both the training programme and performance.

Field testing

This section intends to detail the field-based work done on the water. Field testing has two aims – to verify that data from the lab test are translating to the water and to provide a water-based testing protocol which is more sport-specific but requires careful consideration and familiarisation to be repeatable. Use of an ergometer in a controlled lab environment for lab testing provides favourable conditions for repeatability and reliability of test comparisons. However, it also removes the athlete from the natural training environment, and test data must be verified when they have returned to the water to ensure prescribed training zones are fitting. A monitoring session at the regular training venue should be completed as soon as possible following the lab test and before new training zones have been confirmed.

Indoor sprint testing

The purpose of this testing provides a controlled environment for a more sport-specific protocol. A 50-m swimming pool is required with flags and lane ropes removed. Overhead poles can be suspended 9 m apart across the pool area; this can be facilitated by tying to the ceiling or to stands around the pool area. Two test protocols are used: sprint testing and anaerobic shuttle. The athlete should perform a 15- to 20-min warm-up – a competition warm-up routine may be used here to ensure the athlete is ready to perform. Two or three short sprints should also be completed towards the end of the warm-up. A baseline lactate sample should be taken and the athlete prepared for testing, including confirmation of the testing protocol.

Defined start and end points at 35 m should be identified. This distance is calculated on the approximate time of 10 s per sprint. The athlete prepares themselves for the start behind the start line. When ready, they will sprint over the 35 m course at maximal effort. A 3-min rest interval between each sprint is given, with the athlete slowly returning to the start line during this time. Sprint time can be manually recorded using stopwatch, while speed and acceleration are recorded using a laser speed gun. Instrumented paddles can also be used to measure peak and average wattage along with other stroke mechanic markers (e.g., stroke rate, stroke duration, stroke symmetry).

Indoor anaerobic capacity testing

Six to eight circuits of a figure 8 should be completed around two overhead suspended poles, 9 m apart. Athletes should start with their body flush with the first gate. A split time should be recorded every time the athlete's head passes through the gate with the bow of the boat pointing forward. HR should be monitored continuously throughout, with blood lactate being measured immediately upon finishing, 2 min and 5 min after the test. After a 20-min recovery period to including light paddling in water or walking on poolside, the shuttle test should be repeated.

The time for both efforts is recorded, with a fatigue index determined by the difference in time between each circuit and across test repeats. Speed profiles over the course of an effort can be determined by lap times and/or video analysis post-test session. Depending on the time of season, these tests can inform the focus of training in specific condition training phases.

Sport-specific outdoor testing

An adaptation of the swimming pool anaerobic testing can also be performed outdoors in the natural training environment. This removes the controlled setting of the swimming pool but provides a more sport-specific environment for testing. A significant difference in feel on water versus ergometer for athletes is the rationale for using water-based testing over the lab. Identify a space for testing that can be used again to ensure reliability and repeatability of the testing protocol. Calm weather conditions are preferred for this session because extreme winds can influence intensity or measured data – water conditions, weather, pole positions and other relevant information that will be needed when repeating testing.

Laboratory training zone verification

The athlete should perform multiple bouts of a circuit around slalom gates on flat water. The end point of the circuit should be as close as possible to where the physiologist is positioned. Each circuit duration should be ~5 min. The athlete should be given a target HR zone for each circuit, starting at the lower aerobic zone and slowly increasing through aerobic, anaerobic threshold and high intensity. If the range is large, smaller increments of 5 bpm per circuit are recommended. If instrumented paddles are available, average wattage for each tested bout can be measured. HR should be recorded throughout, and the athlete should 'lap' for each circuit to indicate start and end points. A blood lactate sample should be taken within 20 s of completing each circuit and rate of perceived exertion (RPE) recorded. RPE can be recorded using a simplified 1–10 scale or using the 6–20 Borg scale. The data should be used to verify the training zones established in the laboratory setting and changes made where necessary following consultation with the coach and the athlete.

References

Messias, L. H. D., dos Reis, I. G. M., Ferrari, H. G. and Manchado-Gobatto, F. B. (2014). Physiological, psychological and biomechanical parameters applied in canoe slalom training: A review. *International Journal of Performance Analysis in Sport*, 14(1), 24–41.

Wietrzyński, M., Mazur-Różycka, J., Gajewski, K., Michalski, R., Różycki, S. and Buśko, K. (2013). The assessment of muscle strength symmetry in kayakers and canoeists. *Biomedical Human Kinetics*, 5(1), 65–71.

Zamparo, P., Tomadini, S., Didonè, F., Grazzina, F., Reic, E. and Capeilli, C. (2006). Bioenergetics of a slalom kayak (K1) competition. *International Journal of Sports Medicine*, 27(7), 546–552.

4.7 Speed skating (long-track and short-track)

Florentina Hettinga, Martha Brouwer Muñoz, and Andrew Hext

In speed skating, athletes aim to achieve high mechanical power outputs and lower frictional losses while skating counter-clockwise on a 400-m oval (Hettinga et al., 2011) in time-trial conditions, where the fastest time leads to a win. Events can be classified in sprint (500 and 1000 m), middle-distance (1500 m) and long-distance (3000, 5000 and 10,000 m). Short-track skating involves individual (500, 1000 and 1500 m) and relay (3000 and 5000 m) events on a 111.12-m oval, typically involving four to six skaters racing head-to-head at speeds exceeding 45 km·h^1. Skaters must advance through several heats of qualification to reach the medal contest. Advancement through competition, and medal colour, is dependent on the finishing position in that race only. Thus, in addition to high mechanical outputs, a skater's tactical decision-making process regarding 'how' and 'when' to invest their energy plays an important role in short-track speed skating (Hettinga et al., 2017; Muehlbauer and Schindler, 2011).

This chapter will discuss physiological challenges, testing, training, pacing and tactics in both long-track and short-track speed skating. Both events share similar challenges, for example, related to the technically/biomechanically favourable crouched skating technique impacting on training and testing. However, there are also differences, for example, related to asymmetry, pacing and tactics in head-to-head competition vs. time-trial formats.

Physiological challenges

The characteristic crouched position in speed skating, combined with a relatively long gliding phase and high intramuscular forces, leads to a physiological challenge: increased deoxygenation of the working muscles (Konings et al., 2015). Technical differences between the skating modes (short- vs. long-track) also impact on muscle oxygenation and affect processes related to the regulation of exercise intensity such as fatigue and recovery (Hettinga et al., 2016). For example, short-track skaters exhibit higher levels of deoxygenation in their right leg due to the tighter corner radius necessitating that they 'hang' on this leg to maintain the balance of forces between the skate and ice (Chun, 2001). Moreover, short-track skaters experience higher fatigue after training than long-track athletes, and slower recovery, when comparing training sessions with similar lactate values, heart rate

DOI: 10.4324/9781003045281-33

data and experienced fatigue (Hettinga et al., 2016). For trainers and coaches, it is important to realise that due to this increased deoxygenation, physiological load is higher in skating compared to many other sports. Therefore, training schedules based on physiological variables achieved during other non-occluded sports, such as commonly used (maximal) cycling tests, might not represent the actual physiological load of the training sessions for both skating modes (Hettinga et al., 2016).

Exercise testing

Occlusion and reduced blood flow also play a role in exercise testing, as athletes should ideally complete testing in a similar posture to which they compete and train. During the on-ice season, portable gas analysers, near-infrared spectrometers, blood lactate analysers and heart rate monitors make it possible to test exercise mode specifically on ice (Hettinga et al., 2016; Hesford et al., 2013). For example, St-Jean et al. (2017) created an on-ice, continuous, multistage test to measure short-track skaters' $\dot{V}O_2max$.

During the off-ice season, exercise testing is completed on cycle ergometers, involving the relevant muscle groups in speed skating. Hofman et al. (2017) and Orie et al. (2020) demonstrated that the cycling Wingate test, going all out for 30 s from a standing start, is a good predictor for performance up to the 1500 m. However, since no reduced blood flow occurs in cycling, $\dot{V}O_2max$ will be slightly overestimated compared to speed skating (Piucco et al., 2017).

Alternative off-ice exercise tests replicating the skating posture and occlusion elements inherent to speed skating such as slide-board skating are a feasible, inexpensive alternative eliciting similar $\dot{V}O_2$ kinetics to treadmill skating (Piucco et al., 2017). Still, two elements need to be considered: 1) the slide board technique must be well known by the athlete and (2) similar to cycling, the test does not replicate the aerodynamics or skating the curves, which accounts for a large proportion of the overall skating time, particularly in short-track skating.

Training and monitoring

The distribution of training time, intensity and volume in long-track skating has shifted towards a more polarised distribution, which has resulted in fairly increased long-track performance (Orie et al., 2014, 2020). More cycling and strength training, more low-intensity training and less medium-intensity training in the 4 years leading up to the Olympic 1500-m medal were reported as key aspects of the success of an Olympic medallist (Orie et al., 2020). Also, wireless force measuring instrumented skates for both long-track and short-track (van der Kruk et al., 2019) could be used routinely in training to monitor push-off forces and the centre of pressure on the blade to provide evidence to coaches related to technique.

Elite short-track athletes train up to 25–30 h per week, and the training volume may reach 4–6 h per day during overload periods (Méline et al., 2019). The high incidence of injury reported in short-track skating (Quinn et al., 2003) may be related to excessive training or chronic fatigue, and taper strategies should be explored (Méline et al., 2019). Training diaries and session rate of perceived exertion (RPE) provide subjective information of the athlete in addition to, or when, physiological or biomechanical measurements are not available. One thing to keep in mind is that differences have been found between the training plan as designed by coaches and executed by the athletes (Foster et al., 2001). Athletes trained less polarised, i.e., harder on coach-intended recovery days, and easier on coach-intended hard days, without the presence of the coach. Power meters and other monitoring devices, as well as awareness of this occurring, could minimise the difference.

Competition considerations: pacing and tactics

The distribution of energy over a race is essential for skating performance: a fast start strategy is optimal for the shorter distances, where for the longer distances an even-paced strategy is optimal (Konings et al., 2015). For middle distances, a fast start is only favourable if skaters can continue their pace at a reasonable level during the final laps, particularly in the 700–1100 m segment (Muehlbauer et al., 2010; Wiersma et al., 2017). Early fatigue when starting too fast results in postural changes affecting aerodynamics, coordination, push-off mechanics and thus technical ability (Stoter et al., 2016). Because of the physiological demands associated with the crouched position and the large impact of premature fatigue on technical ability, pacing is of relatively large importance in speed skating. Based on lap times of previous generations of speed skaters, benchmarking tools have been developed to support testing and monitoring of pacing and performance, particularly relevant for youth speed skating athletes (Stoter et al., 2016). Development and testing of self-regulation and pacing skills throughout adolescence are recommended as aspects of talent development (Elferink-Gemser and Hettinga, 2017; Menting et al., 2019).

In short-track speed skating, the tactical decision-making process about when to accelerate and decelerate is not only informed by physiology and technical ability; avoiding collisions, drafting possibilities and competing for the optimum line also play a role (Konings et al., 2018d; Hettinga et al., 2017; Smits et al., 2014). In the 500 m, a fast-starting strategy appears to be optimal, with winners positioning themselves in the leading positions throughout the whole race (Noorbergen et al., 2016), while overtaking at high speeds is increasingly difficult (Bullock et al., 2008). For this reason, the start of the race is crucial for success (Muehlbauer and Schindler, 2011), which requires a specific focus on quick accelerations and Wingate-type testing. In contrast, the 1000 and 1500 m are characterised by much slower, tactical starts, with low correlations between intermediate and final rankings until the sixth and tenth lap, respectively (Noorbergen et al., 2016; Konings et al., 2016), and conserving energy in the early stages for the decisive final part of the race is beneficial. Training, monitoring and testing while using avatars or virtual reality competition simulations could provide further interesting opportunities (Menting et al., 2019).

Training recommendations and performance analysis

In addition to exercise testing, and particularly relevant for short-track speed skating, online data sets of competition can provide insights in different competitive scenarios (Konings et al., 2018b), effects of preceding race efforts (Konings et al., 2018a), how to objectify tactics (Konings et al., 2018c) and the temporal structure and interrelationships between discrete events (Borrie et al., 2002). Single panning cameras (Liu et al., 2016; Wang et al., 2014), overhead multicamera networks and local positioning systems (Stelzer et al., 2004) present opportunities for higher-resolution analyses, such as using spatiotemporal data to examine the influence of the relay exchange on a team's progression (Hext et al., 2017).

Ultimately, coaches can use these insights to help construct highly representative learning environments to replicate the specific perceptual motor demands required of athletes to regulate their pace, particularly when direct opponents are involved (Menting et al., 2019). Recent advances in virtual reality offer exciting opportunities to create immersive and interactive virtual environments, potentially leading to greater decision-making transfer to competition through perception action coupling (Stone et al., 2019). Less expensive methods, such as projecting different competitive scenarios using life-size images of opponents using video or avatars on to screens, may also be advantageous in enhancing perception-action coupling (Konings and Hettinga, 2018d).

References

Borrie, A., Jonsson, G. K. and Magnusson, M. S. (2002). Temporal pattern analysis and its applicability in sport: An explanation and exemplar data. *Journal of Sports Sciences*, 20(10), 845–852.

Bullock, N., Martin, T. D. and Zhang, A. (2008). Performance analysis of world class short track speed skating: What does it take to win? *International Journal of Performance Analysis in Sport*, 8(1), 9–18.

Chun, M. K. (2001). The kinematic analysis of the cornering movements in short track speed skating. *The International Journal of Applied Sports Science*, 13(2), 63–80.

Elferink-Gemser, M. T. and Hettinga, F. J. (2017). Pacing and self-regulation: Important skills for talent development in endurance sports. *International Journal of Sports Physiology and Performance*, 12(6), 831–835.

Foster, C., Heimann, K. M., Esten, P. L., Brice, G. and Porcari, J. P. (2001). Differences in perception of training by coaches and athletes. *South African Medical Journal*, 8, 3–7.

Hesford, C., Cardinale, M., Laing, S. and Cooper, C. E. (2013). NIRS measurements with elite speed skaters: Comparison between the ice rink and the laboratory. *Advances in Experimental Medicine and Biology*, 765, 81–86.

Hettinga, F. J., De Koning, J. J., Schmidt, L. J., Wind, N. A., MacIntosh, B. R. and Foster, C. (2011). Optimal pacing strategy: From theoretical modelling to reality in 1500-m speed skating. *British Journal of Sports Medicine*, 45(1), 30–35.

Hettinga, F. J., Konings, M. J. and Cooper, C. E. (2016). Differences in muscle oxygenation, perceived fatigue and recovery between long-track and short-track speed skating. *Frontiers in Physiology*, 7, 619.

Hettinga, F. J., Konings, M. J. and Pepping, G. J. (2017). The science of racing against opponents: Affordance competition and the regulation of exercise intensity in head-to-head competition. *Frontiers in Physiology*, 8, 118.

Hext, A., Heller, B., Kelley, J. W. and Goodwill, S. R. (2017). Relay exchanges in elite short track speed skating. *European Journal of Sport Science*, 17(5), 503–510.

Hofman, N., Orie, J., Hoozemans, M. J., Foster, C. and de Koning, J. J. (2017). Wingate test as a strong predictor of 1500-m performance in elite speed skaters. *International Journal of Sports Physiology and Performance*, 12(10), 1288–1292.

Konings, M. J., Elferink-Gemser, M. T., Stoter, I. K., Van der Meer, D., Otten, E. and Hettinga, F. J. (2015). Performance characteristics of long-track speed skaters: A literature review. *Sports Medicine*, 45(4), 505–516.

Konings, M. J. and Hettinga, F. J. (2018a). The effect of preceding race efforts on pacing and short-track speed skating performance. *International Journal of Sports Physiology and Performance*, 13(8), 970–976.

Konings, M. J. and Hettinga, F. J. (2018b). The impact of different competitive environments on pacing and performance. *International Journal of Sports Physiology and Performance*, 13(6), 701–708.

Konings, M. J. and Hettinga, F. J. (2018c). Objectifying tactics: Athlete and race variability in elite short-track speed skating. *International Journal of Sports Physiology and Performance*, 13(2), 170–175.

Konings, M. J. and Hettinga, F. J. (2018d). Pacing decision making in sport and the effects of interpersonal competition: A critical review. *Sports Medicine*, 48(8), 1829–1843.

Konings, M. J., Noorbergen, O. S., Parry, D. and Hettinga, F. J. (2016). Pacing behavior and tactical positioning in 1500-m short-track speed skating. *International Journal of Sports Physiology and Performance*, 11(1), 122–129.

Liu, C., Cheng, H. D., Zhang, Y., Wang, Y. and Xian, M. (2016). Robust multiple cue fusion-based high-speed and nonrigid object tracking algorithm for short-track speed skating. *Journal of Electronic Imaging*, 25(1).

Méline, T., Mathieu, L., Borrani, F., Candau, R. and Sanchez, A. M. J. (2019). Systems model and individual simulations of training strategies in elite short-track speed skaters. *Journal of Sports Sciences*, 37(3), 347–355.

Menting, S., Hendry, D. T., Schiphof-Godart, L., Elferink-Gemser, M. T. and Hettinga, F. J. (2019). Optimal development of youth athletes towards elite athletic performance: How to coach their motivation, plan training exercise and pace the race. *Frontiers in Sports and Active Living*, 1, 14.

Menting, S. G. P., Huijgen, B. C., Konings, M. J., Hettinga, F. J. and Elferink-Gemser, M. T. (2019). Pacing behavior development of youth short-track speed skaters: A longitudinal study. *Medicine and Science in Sports and Exercise*, 52(5), 1099–1108.

Muehlbauer, T. and Schindler, C. (2011). Relationship between starting and finishing position in short track speed skating races. *European Journal of Sport Science*, 11(4), 225–230.

Muehlbauer, T., Schindler, C. and Panzer, S. (2010). Pacing and performance in competitive middle-distance speed skating. *Research Quarterly for Exercise and Sport*, 81(1), 1–6.

Noorbergen, O. S., Konings, M. J., Micklewright, D., Elferink-Gemser, M. T. and Hettinga, F. J. (2016). Pacing behavior and tactical positioning in 500- and 1000-m short-track speed skating. *International Journal of Sports Physiology and Performance*, 11(6), 742–748. https://doi.org/10.1123/ijspp.2015-0384

Orie, J., Hofman, N., Meerhoff, L. A. and Knobbe, A. (2021). Training distribution in 1500-m speed skating: A case study of an Olympic gold medalist. *International Journal of Sports Physiology and Performance*, 16(1), 149–153.

Piucco, T., Diefenthaeler, F., Soares, R., Murias, J. M. and Millet, G. Y. (2017). Validation of a maximal incremental skating test performed on a slide board: Comparison with treadmill skating. *International Journal of Sports Physiology and Performance*, 12(10), 1363–1369.

Quinn, A., Lun, V., McCall, J. and Overend, T. (2003). Injuries in short track speed skating. *American Journal of Sports Medicine*, 31(4), 507–510.

Smits, B. L. M., Pepping, G. J. and Hettinga, F. J. (2014). Pacing and decision making in sport and exercise: The roles of perception and action in the regulation of exercise intensity. *Sports Medicine*, 44(6), 763–775.

Stelzer, A., Pourvoyeur, K. and Fischer, A. (2004). Concept and application of LPM: A novel 3D local position measurement system. *IEEE Transactions on Microwave Theory and Techniques*, 52(12), 2664–2669.

St-Jean, M. F., Parent, A., Boucher, V. G. and Comtois, A. S. (2017). Validation of an on-ice continuous multistage test for short track speed skaters. *Medicine and Science in Sports and Exercise*, 49(5S), 605–606. doi: 10.1249/01.mss.0000518585.35428.e2

Stone, J. A., Strafford, B. W., North, J. S., Toner, C. and Davids, K. (2019). Effectiveness and efficiency of virtual reality designs to enhance athlete development: An ecological dynamics perspective. *Movement and Sport Sciences – Science and Motricité*, 102, 51–60.

Stoter, I. K., MacIntosh, B. R., Fletcher, J. R., Pootz, S., Zijdewind, I. and Hettinga, F. J. (2016). Pacing strategy, muscle fatigue, and technique in 1500-m speed-skating and cycling time trials. *International Journal of Sports Physiology and Performance*, 11(3), 337–343. https://doi.org/10.1123/ijspp.2014-0603

Van der Kruk, E., Reijne, M. M., de Laat, B. and Veeger, H. E. J. (2019). Push-off forces in elite short-track speed skating. *Sports Biomechanics*, 18(5), 527–538.

Wang, Y., Cheng, H. D. and Shan, J. (2014). Multiplayer tracking system for short track speed skating. *IET Computer Vision*, 8(6), 629–641.

Wiersma, R., Stoter, I. K., Visscher, C., Hettinga, F. J. and Elferink-Gemser, M. T. (2017). Development of 1500-m pacing behavior in junior speed skaters: A longitudinal study. *International Journal of Sports Physiology and Performance*, 12(9), 1224–1231. https://doi.org/10.1123/ijspp.2016-0517

4.8 Cross-country skiing and biathlon

Thomas W. Jones and Kerry McGawley

Cross-country skiing (XC) and biathlon are physically demanding winter sports that involve a variety of competition formats, race durations and distances performed over mixed terrain and in challenging environmental conditions. The obvious distinction between the two sports is the component of marksmanship in biathlon, which involves both prone and standing shooting interspersed between repeated bouts of high-intensity skiing. In addition, biathlon uses the skate (or 'freestyle') technique exclusively, while XC involves both the skate and classic techniques. Within these two skiing techniques are a number of further sub-techniques (or 'gears') (Losnegard, 2019), and the choice of sub-technique is primarily determined by skiing speed and terrain (Andersson et al., 2010) (Figure 4.8.1).

Competition formats

Traditional international XC includes sprint and distance competitions (Sandbakk and Holmberg, 2014; FIS, 2020). Sprint competitions consist of a qualification time trial (TT) and three subsequent head-to-head races (for the six most successful athletes), with each race lasting 2–4 min and separated by approximately 10–120 min. By contrast, distance competitions involve TT and mass-start races lasting approximately 25–120 min (10–50 km). International biathlon competitions last approximately 20–55 min (6–20 km) (Laaksonen et al., 2018), with the high-intensity skiing bouts each lasting 5–8 min and interspersed with two or four shooting bouts lasting 25–40 s (Laaksonen et al., 2020).

Energetic demands

In laboratory-based roller-ski race simulations lasting approximately 3 min, the distribution of aerobic/anaerobic energy supply is 75%/25% (Losnegard et al., 2012; McGawley and Holmberg, 2014; Andersson et al., 2017), which is comparable to other events of similar durations (Gastin, 2001). During simulated races of 3–4 min at a constant incline, skiers exhibit supramaximal power outputs corresponding to 110%–120% of peak oxygen uptake ($\dot{V}O_2$peak) (Losnegard et al., 2012; Losnegard et al., 2013). Furthermore, in a simulated 15-km TT lasting 30–36 min, skiers experience work rates corresponding to 89%–157% of $\dot{V}O_2$peak, depending

DOI: 10.4324/9781003045281-34

Cross-country skiing and biathlon 209

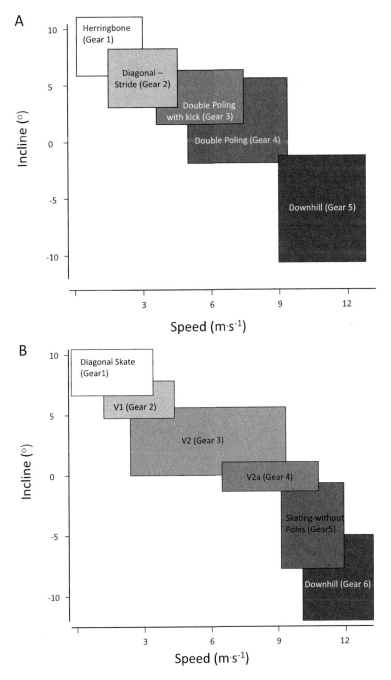

Figure 4.8.1 An illustration of the sub-techniques employed across speeds and inclines in classic and skate skiing.

Source: Replicated from Figure 2 in Losnegard (2019) with permission from the author.

on the terrain (Karlsson et al., 2018). Due to the irregular energetic demands that characterise both XC and biathlon, with intermittent competition formats, hilly course profiles and the opportunity to draft, an athlete's ability to repeatedly perform at metabolic rates well above $\dot{V}O_2$peak is important for success (Gløersen et al., 2018, 2020; Karlsson et al., 2018; Losnegard, 2019). High blood lactate concentrations (BLa) of >12 mmol·L^{-1} have also been observed following simulated sprint XC races and distance skiing (Mygind et al., 2007; Stöggl et al., 2007; Vesterinen et al., 2009), implying a substantial anaerobic contribution to energy turnover.

Terrain

The International Ski Federation rules stipulate that XC courses should consist of one-third uphill terrain, one-third undulating terrain (with short climbs and downhills) and one-third downhill terrain (FIS, 2020). As a result, approximately 50% of the time is spent skiing uphill, with the remainder of the race duration comprising flat (~35%) and downhill (~15%) skiing (Losnegard, 2019). More successful XC skiers perform better than their lower-performing counterparts on uphill sections (Andersson et al., 2010), and the same concept holds true for men versus women (Andersson et al., 2019). The latter comparison has been related to the requirement for increased upper body activity during uphill skiing, coupled with relatively superior upper body strength in men versus women (Bishop et al., 1987). Indeed, metabolic demands increase in uphill terrain to approximately 130%–160% of $\dot{V}O_2$peak (Karlsson et al., 2018; Andersson et al., 2019), and the summed O_2 deficit of all uphill sections of a 15-km race may be four times greater than the athletes' maximal accumulated oxygen deficit (MAOD) (Gløersen et al., 2020). As such, rapid recovery of anaerobic energy potential is necessary during downhill and flat sections.

Pacing

The competition formats in XC and biathlon include TTs, pursuits, mass starts and head-to-head races, all of which influence how athletes approach race tactics and pacing strategies. In addition, biathletes must consider how their pacing may influence shooting performance. Owing to the aforementioned importance of performance in uphill sections of races and the influence of drafting on skiing performance, athletes often employ terrain-specific pacing strategies (Andersson et al., 2016, 2019; Gløersen et al., 2018), and these strategies have a direct effect on the immediate metabolic demands. Regarding sex differences, women ski relatively more slowly on uphill sections compared with men, which leads to greater variations in female skiers' speed profiles and has implications for both energy requirements and performance (Andersson et al., 2019).

Techniques and sub-techniques

The relative contributions of specific muscle groups across ski techniques and sub-techniques can influence energetic demands. Irrespective of exercise modality, it has been demonstrated that whole-body $\dot{V}O_2$peak increases when the arms contribute 10%–30% of the total power output, while $\dot{V}O_2$peak decreases when the arms contribute >30% of the total power output (Bergh et al., 1976). This principle is reflected in comparisons between running and diagonal-stride skiing, with skiers exhibiting a 3% higher $\dot{V}O_2$peak when performing diagonal skiing (which involves moderate levels of arm activity) (Holmberg et al., 2006). By contrast, compared to running, $\dot{V}O_2$peak is typically 3% lower when using gear 3 in skating and 10% lower when double poling (which both involve high levels of arm activity) (Rundell, 1996; Losnegard and Hallén, 2014).

Rifle carriage

Unlike XC athletes, biathletes are required to carry a rifle weighing ≥3.5 kg throughout competition. Research has indicated that submaximal $\dot{V}O_2$, gross efficiency, speed at a BLa of 4 mmol·L^{-1}, TT performance and anaerobic metabolic rate are all negatively affected when skiing with a rifle versus without (Jonsson Kårström et al., 2019).

Testing protocols

Performance determinants

A range of laboratory-assessed qualities have been related to successful competitive performance in XC and biathlon, including lean body mass (Carlsson et al., 2014a; Carlsson et al., 2016; Østerås et al., 2016), upper and lower body strength (Østerås et al., 2016), the speed at a BLa of 4 mmol·L^{-1} (Rundell and Bacharach, 1995; Carlsson et al., 2016; Laaksonen et al., 2020), gross efficiency (Sandbakk et al., 2010, 2011; Laaksonen et al., 2020), $\dot{V}O_2$peak (Rundell and Bacharach, 1995; Losnegard et al., 2013; Carlsson et al., 2016; Carlsson et al., 2016; Østerås et al., 2016), acceleration (Hébert-Losier et al., 2017), maximal speed (Andersson et al., 2017) and roller-ski TT performance (Carlsson et al., 2014b; Luchsinger et al., 2019; Laaksonen et al., 2020). Successful performance in XC skiing is likely influenced by a combination of these factors, rather than any one in isolation (Mahood et al., 2001; Carlsson et al., 2012, 2014b; Østerås et al., 2016). In biathlon, shooting performance is an important performance determinant, with approximately 35%–58% of the variance in overall biathlon performance explained by shooting accuracy (Luchsinger et al., 2018; Luchsinger et al., 2019). While the test protocols outlined here are without rifle carriage, it is important for practitioners involved in biathlon to consider including rifle carriage when testing in order that derived parameters are sport specific.

Laboratory-based testing

While field-based testing is becoming increasingly accessible and accurate due to technological advancements (e.g., in global positioning system [GPS] and artificial intelligence [AI] methods), numerous uncontrollable factors (including weather, snow conditions and waxing) make treadmill roller-skiing and double-poling ergometry more appropriate methods of quantifying physiological qualities among XC athletes and biathletes. However, important safety and methical considerations are associated with treadmill roller-ski assessments (see Figure 4.8.2):

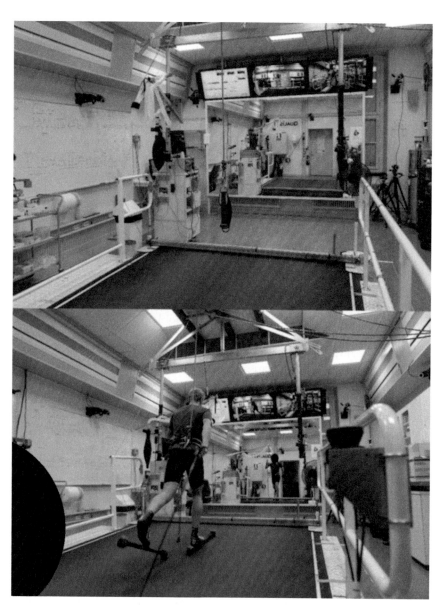

Figure 4.8.2 A laboratory set-up for roller-ski assessments in cross-country skiers and biathletes.

- Athletes should be secured using a safety harness during roller-ski assessments;
- In case of sudden adverse events, emergency break buttons should be placed strategically around the laboratory;
- A large treadmill is required to perform all necessary sub-techniques;
- A self-pacing system (Swaren et al., 2012) is required to perform TT assessments or race simulations;
- Visual feedback using appropriately placed mirrors, cameras and screens will enable good skiing technique;
- The rolling resistance coefficient of the roller-skis needs to be accurately quantified (Ainegren et al., 2008).

Incremental submaximal assessments

Submaximal roller-ski assessments consisting of fixed-duration incremental workloads provide useful information relating to $\dot{V}O_2$, BLa and heart rate profiles. The $\dot{V}O_2$-power output relationship can also be used for calculations of accumulated oxygen deficit and subsequent relative anaerobic contributions (McGawley and Holmberg, 2014). It is important that protocols are specific to athletic demands and that sub-techniques and inclines are standardised when comparing responses and for calculations of gross efficiency or accumulated oxygen deficit, since energetic costs differ as these variables change (Losnegard and Hallén, 2014; Andersson et al., 2017). Proposed submaximal protocols across sexes and ages in XC and biathlon are presented in Table 4.8.1.

Maximal assessments

Incremental ramp tests to exhaustion (RAMP) are traditionally used to obtain a measure of maximal oxygen uptake ($\dot{V}O_2$max), with workload increasing progressively until the athlete is unable to maintain the required power output (Poole and Jones, 2017). However, race-specific simulations using self-paced TTs are more ecologically valid and are able to provide $\dot{V}O_2$peak values similar to those obtained from a RAMP (Losnegard et al., 2012; McGawley and Holmberg, 2014). Unpublished observations from a national Olympic test centre have also indicated that the $\dot{V}O_2$peak obtained from 661 RAMP and 356 roller-ski TTs were not different over a 7-yr period in XC athletes and biathletes. Furthermore, self-paced TTs enable assessments of performance, pacing strategies and anaerobic energy contributions and, as such, are recommended as maximal roller-ski assessments for XC athletes and biathletes (Table 4.8.2).

Short-duration, all-out double-poling tests may be used as a sport-specific Wingate test (Katch et al., 1977) for the assessment of absolute and relative peak power output, average power output, fatigue index, cycle rate and peak BLa. The test can be performed on a double-poling ergometer (e.g., Concept2 SkiErg) with the resistance adjusted to the population being tested (e.g., drag factors of 100 and 120 kg for women and men, respectively). Technique is improved if the athletes

Table 4.8.1 Proposed submaximal roller-ski assessment protocols for experienced cross-country skiers and biathletes. All stage durations are proposed to last 4 min, with a 1-min interval between each stage for the collection of capillary blood samples.

Sex	Age Group	Starting Speed (km·h⁻¹)	Gradient (°)	Speed Ramp Rate (km·h⁻¹·stage⁻¹)	Gradient Ramp Rate (°·stage⁻¹)	Test Termination Criteria
Cross-country skiing – classic (diagonal stride)						
Female	Senior	8.0	3.0	0.5	1.0	– Athlete's request
	Junior	7.5	2.0			– RER >1.00
Male	Senior	9.0	4.0	0.5	1.0	– $\dot{V}E / \dot{V}O_2$ >30
	Junior	8.0	2.0			– HR >90% HR_{max}
						– After 7 stages
Biathlon – skate (gear 3)						
Female	Senior	7.0	3.5	1.5	-	– Athlete's request
	Junior	5.5				– RER >1.00
Male	Senior	8.0	4.5	1.5	-	– $\dot{V}E / \dot{V}O_2$ >30
	Junior	6.5				– HR >90% HR_{max}
						– After 7 stages

HR = heart rate, HR_{max} = maximum heart rate, $\dot{V}E$ = minute ventilation, RER = respiratory exchange ratio, $\dot{V}O_2$ = rate of oxygen consumption

Table 4.8.2 Proposed maximal self-paced time trial roller-ski assessment protocols for experienced cross-country skiers and biathletes. In all cases athletes are instructed to complete the fixed distance in the shortest possible time, as is characteristic of a real-world race scenario.

Sex	Age Group	Starting Speed (km·h⁻¹)	Gradient (°)	Distance (m)	Estimated Completion Time (mm:ss)	
Cross country skiing – classic (diagonal stride)						
Female	Senior	10.0	7.0	700	03:00–03:30	
	Junior				03:30–04:00	
Male	Senior	13.0	7.0	800	03:00–03:30	
	Junior				03:30–04:00	
Biathlon – skate (gear 3)					With rifle	Without rifle
Female	Senior	13.0	3.5	900	03:10–03:40	03:00–03:30
	Junior				03:40–04:10	03:30–04:00
Male	Senior	14.0	4.5	1000	03:10–03:40	03:00–03:30
	Junior				03:40–04:10	03:30–04:00

wear ski boots attached to bindings fixed to a base beneath them and use a resistance belt fixed to the rear wall, allowing the natural use of body mass when leaning forwards. An illustration of the set-up used at a national Olympic test centre is presented Figure 4.8.3.

Figure 4.8.3 An experimental set-up for the 'Wingate'-style double-poling test on the SkiErg.

Summary

As detailed in this chapter, XC and biathlon are complex endurance sports, and successful performance is influenced by numerous physiological qualities. It is essential that practitioners supporting XC athletes and biathletes employ valid and reliable testing methods to assess the effectiveness of any performance-based interventions, training or otherwise. The testing protocols proposed here serve as guidance to those performing physiological testing in experienced athlete groups. To further develop physiological testing methods, future research should seek to develop bespoke protocols for specific athlete sub-groups, the full range of skiing sub-techniques (including double-poling), race-specific simulations and measurements of anaerobic energy contributions.

References

Ainegren, M., Carlsson, P. and Tinnsten, M. (2008). Rolling resistance for treadmill roller skiing. *Sports Engineering*, 11(1), 23–29. doi: 10.1007/s12283-008-0004-1

Andersson, E., et al. (2010). Analysis of sprint cross-country skiing using a differential global navigation satellite system. *European Journal of Applied Physiology*, 110(3), 585–595. doi: 10.1007/s00421-010-1535-2

Andersson, E., et al. (2016). Metabolic responses and pacing strategies during successive sprint skiing time trials. *Medicine and Science in Sports and Exercise*, 48(12), 2544–2554. doi: 10.1249/MSS.0000000000001037

Andersson, E. P., et al. (2017). Energy system contributions and determinants of performance in sprint cross-country skiing. *Scandinavian Journal of Medicine and Science in Sports*, 27(4), 385–398. doi: 10.1111/sms.12666

Andersson, E. P., et al. (2019). Sex differences in performance and pacing strategies during sprint skiing. *Frontiers in Physiology*, 10. doi: 10.3389/fphys.2019.00295

Bergh, U., Kanstrup, I. L. and Ekblom, B. (1976). Maximal oxygen uptake during exercise with various combinations of arm and leg work. *Journal of Applied Physiology*, 41(2), 191–196. doi: 10.1152/jappl.1976.41.2.191

Bishop, P., Cureton, K. and Collins, M. (1987). Sex difference in muscular strength in equally-trained men and women. *Ergonomics*, 30(4), 675–687. doi: 10.1080/00140138708969760

Carlsson, M., et al. (2012). Validation of physiological tests in relation to competitive performances in elite male distance cross-country skiing. *Journal of Strength and Conditioning Research*, 26(6), 1496–1504. doi: 10.1519/JSC.0b013e318231a799

Carlsson, M., et al. (2014a). Prediction of race performance of elite cross-country skiers by lean mass. *International Journal of Sports Physiology and Performance*, 9(6), 1040–1045. doi: 10.1123/ijspp.2013-0509

Carlsson, M., et al. (2014b). Time trials predict the competitive performance capacity of junior cross-country skiers. *International Journal of Sports Physiology and Performance*, 9(1), 12–8. doi: 10.1123/ijspp.2012-0172

Carlsson, M., et al. (2016). Physiological demands of competitive sprint and distance performance in elite female cross-country skiing. *Journal of Strength and Conditioning Research*, 30(8), 2138–2144. doi: 10.1519/JSC.0000000000001327

Carlsson, T., Tonkonogi, M. and Carlsson, M. (2016). Aerobic power and lean mass are indicators of competitive sprint performance among elite female cross-country skiers. *Open Access Journal of Sports Medicine*, 7, 153–160. doi: 10.2147/OAJSM.S116672

FIS. (2020). *The International Ski Competition Rules (ICR)*. https://assets.fis-ski.com/image/upload/v1604421981/fis-prod/assets/ICR_CrossCountry_2020_clean.pdf

Gastin, P. B. (2001). Energy system interaction and relative contribution during maximal exercise. *Sports Medicine*, 31(10), 725–741. doi: 10.2165/00007256-200131100-00003

Gløersen, Ø., et al. (2018). Propulsive power in cross-country skiing: Application and limitations of a novel wearable sensor-based method during roller skiing. *Frontiers in Physiology*, 9. doi: 10.3389/fphys.2018.01631

Gløersen, Ø., et al. (2020). Oxygen demand, uptake, and deficits in elite cross-country skiers during a 15-km race. *Medicine and Science in Sports and Exercise*, 52(4), 983–992. doi: 10.1249/MSS.0000000000002209

Hébert-Losier, K., et al. (2017). Factors that influence the performance of elite sprint cross-country skiers. *Sports Medicine*, 47(2), 319–342. doi: 10.1007/s40279-016-0573-2

Holmberg, H.-C., Rosdahl, H. and Svedenhag, J. (2006). Lung function, arterial saturation and oxygen uptake in elite cross country skiers: Influence of exercise mode. *Scandinavian Journal of Medicine and Science in Sports*, 061120070736012-???. doi: 10.1111/j.1600-0838.2006.00592.x

Jonsson Kårström, M., McGawley, K. and Laaksonen, M. S. (2019). Physiological responses to rifle carriage during roller-skiing in elite biathletes. *Frontiers in Physiology*, 10, 1–25. doi: 10.3389/fphys.2019.01519

Karlsson, Ø., et al. (2018). Exercise intensity during cross-country skiing described by oxygen demands in flat and uphill terrain. *Frontiers in Physiology*, 9. doi: 10.3389/fphys.2018.00846

Katch, V., et al. (1977). Optimal test characteristics for maximal anaerobic work on the bicycle ergometer. *Research Quarterly*, 48(2), 319–327. www.ncbi.nlm.nih.gov/pubmed/267972

Laaksonen, M. S., et al. (2020). Laboratory-based factors predicting skiing performance in female and male biathletes. *Frontiers in Sports and Active Living*, 2. doi: 10.3389/fspor.2020.00099

Laaksonen, M. S., Jonsson, M. and Holmberg, H.-C. (2018). The Olympic biathlon: Recent advances and perspectives after pyeongchang. *Frontiers in Physiology*, 9, 796. doi: 10.3389/fphys.2018.00796

Losnegard, T. (2019). Energy system contribution during competitive cross-country skiing. *European Journal of Applied Physiology*, 119(8), 1675–1690. doi: 10.1007/s00421-019-04158-x

Losnegard, T., et al. (2013). Seasonal variations in $\dot{V}O_2$max, O2-cost, O2-deficit, and performance in elite cross-country skiers. *Journal of Strength and Conditioning Research*, 27(7), 1780–1790. doi: 10.1519/JSC.0b013e31827368f6

Losnegard, T. and Hallén, J. (2014). Elite cross-country skiers do not reach their running $\dot{V}O_2$max during roller ski skating. *The Journal of Sports Medicine and Physical Fitness*, 54(4), 389–393. www.ncbi.nlm.nih.gov/pubmed/25034543

Losnegard, T., Myklebust, H. and Hallén, J. (2012). Anaerobic capacity as a determinant of performance in sprint skiing. *Medicine and Science in Sports and Exercise*, 44(4), 673–681. doi: 10.1249/MSS.0b013e3182388684

Luchsinger, H., et al. (2018). Comparison of the effects of performance level and sex on sprint performance in the biathlon world cup. *International Journal of Sports Physiology and Performance*, 13(3), 360–366. doi: 10.1123/ijspp.2017-0112

Luchsinger, H., Kocbach, J., et al. (2019). The contribution from cross-country skiing and shooting variables on performance-level and sex differences in biathlon world cup individual races. *International Journal of Sports Physiology and Performance*, 14(2), 190–195. doi: 10.1123/ijspp.2018-0134

Luchsinger, H., Talsnes, R. K., et al. (2019). Analysis of a biathlon sprint competition and associated laboratory determinants of performance. *Frontiers in Sports and Active Living*, 1. doi: 10.3389/fspor.2019.00060

Mahood, N. V., et al. (2001). Physiological determinants of cross-country ski racing performance. *Medicine and Science in Sports and Exercise*, 33(8), 1379–1384. doi: 10.1097/00005768-200108000-00020

McGawley, K. and Holmberg, H.-C. (2014). Aerobic and anaerobic contributions to energy production among junior male and female cross-country skiers during diagonal skiing. *International Journal of Sports Physiology and Performance*, 9(1), 32–40. doi: 10.1123/ijspp.2013-0239

Mygind, E., Andersen, L. B. and Rasmussen, B. (2007). Blood lactate and respiratory variables in elite cross-country skiing at racing speeds. *Scandinavian Journal of Medicine and Science in Sports*, 4(4), 243–251. doi: 10.1111/j.1600-0838.1994.tb00435.x

Østerås, S., et al. (2016). Contribution of upper-body strength, body composition, and maximal oxygen uptake to predict double poling power and overall performance in female cross-country skiers. *Journal of Strength and Conditioning Research*, 30(9), 2557–2564. doi: 10.1519/JSC.0000000000001345

Poole, D. C. and Jones, A. M. (2017). Measurement of the maximum oxygen uptake $\dot{V}O_2$max: $\dot{V}O_2$peak is no longer acceptable. *Journal of Applied Physiology*, 122(4), 997–1002. doi: 10.1152/japplphysiol.01063.2016

Rundell, K. W. (1996). Differences between treadmill running and treadmill roller skiing. *The Journal of Strength and Conditioning Research*, 10(3), 167. doi: 10.1519/1533-4287(1996)010<0167:DBTRAT>2.3.CO;2

Rundell, K. W. and Bacharach, D. W. (1995). Physiological characteristics and performance of top U.S. biathletes. *Medicine and Science in Sports and Exercise*, 27(9), 1302–1310. www.ncbi.nlm.nih.gov/pubmed/8531629

Sandbakk, Ø., et al. (2010). Metabolic rate and gross efficiency at high work rates in world class and national level sprint skiers. *European Journal of Applied Physiology*, 109(3), 473–481. doi: 10.1007/s00421-010-1372-3

Sandbakk, Ø., et al. (2011). The physiology of world-class sprint skiers. *Scandinavian Journal of Medicine and Science in Sports*, 21(6), e9–e16. doi: 10.1111/j.1600-0838.2010.01117.x

Sandbakk, Ø. and Holmberg, H.-C. (2014). A reappraisal of success factors for Olympic cross-country skiing. *International Journal of Sports Physiology and Performance*, 9(1), 117–121. doi: 10.1123/ijspp.2013-0373

Stöggl, T., Lindinger, S. and Müller, E. (2007). Analysis of a simulated sprint competition in classical cross country skiing. *Scandinavian Journal of Medicine and Science in Sports*, 17(4), 362–372. doi: 10.1111/j.1600-0838.2006.00589.x

Swaren, M., et al. (2012). Treadmill simulation of Olympic cross-country ski tracks. In A. Hakkarainen (ed.), *International Congress on Science and Nordic Skiing*, pp. 237–242. Jyväskylä, Finland: Meyer and Meyer Verlag.

Vesterinen, V., et al. (2009). Fatigue in a simulated cross-country skiing sprint competition. *Journal of Sports Sciences*, 27(10), 1069–1077. doi: 10.1080/02640410903081860

Part V
Invasion games

5.1 Soccer

Liam Anderson, Chris Barnes, and Barry Drust

Association football (soccer) is an intermittent team sport in which bouts of high-intensity activity are superimposed on longer periods of lower-intensity activity (Svensson and Drust, 2005). This intermittent pattern is somewhat random and varies according to numerous individual and situational variables. During training and match play, physical reserves of players are utilised to different extents, depending on the nature of the training drills/session or on the situational factors inherent in any match play scenario, but players are rarely required to perform to the peak of their physical capacity. Therefore, soccer requires high levels of physical fitness across multiple different components, which makes testing and monitoring of soccer players somewhat complex.

In applied practice, it is important that terminology is used appropriately and consistently. We often hear the terms 'fitness' and 'physical performance' used somewhat interchangeably, as we sometimes do with reference to 'testing' and 'monitoring'. Fitness testing of soccer players is normally conducted via a series of protocols, each designed to profile individual performance capacity in one of a number of domains (e.g., endurance, speed, repeated high-intensity actions). These tests are usually performed on a limited number (usually fewer than four) of occasions each season due to limited time between competitive fixtures and so as not to interfere with the training process. Such tests generally induce low levels of systematic 'noise' in the measurement due to high methodological repeatability. The steps taken to impart this control do, however, often reduce the ecological validity of tests. The results from tests of the physical characteristics of soccer players allow practitioners to establish physical and physiological boundaries and thresholds and to identify individual player strengths and weaknesses.

More recently, the advent of wearable technologies has allowed practitioners to regularly monitor physical performance of football players in training and in matches. This type of monitoring allows practitioners to understand both the external (locomotive and mechanical) stresses imposed on players in training and match play and the internal responses to those stresses. The complex nature of soccer means that training sessions are rarely used to enhance fitness of players in isolation of technical and tactical components of the game, making an understanding of the training stimulus difficult. Monitoring of physical performance and physiological status thus has huge importance in evaluating whether

DOI: 10.4324/9781003045281-36

internal and external load is adequate and appropriate to maintain or enhance fitness and to optimise match physical performance.

Fitness testing in soccer

Energy system contribution during soccer match play is extremely difficult to directly measure. However, heart rate responses recorded during matches suggest mean work rates corresponding to 70% of individual maximal oxygen uptake ($\dot{V}O_2$max), something which is clearly reflective of a large contribution from aerobic metabolism (Bangsbo et al., 2006). Whilst these data identify that the contribution of aerobic metabolism during soccer match play is high, it is recognised that key moments in matches are often characterised by explosive actions (e.g., accelerations, decelerations, changes of direction), which can be multidirectional and highly anaerobic in nature (Faude et al., 2012). Therefore, it is important to utilise soccer-specific protocols to test the fitness capacities of players.

As opposed to traditional laboratory-based methods to directly assess aerobic capacity of soccer players, practitioners have a preference for employment of indirect field-based tests, which innately possess greater ecological validity. This is largely due to the intermittent nature of these tests and the fact that they involve change of direction, acceleration and deceleration movements. Indeed, since the early 1990s practitioners have utilised both continuous and intermittent versions of multistage fitness tests, which were designed to measure the ability to perform bouts of both continuous and intermittent exercise and also to evaluate the capacity of players to recover from intense exercise (Bangsbo, 1994). Results from such tests positively correlate with direct measures of aerobic capacity and with players running performances within match play. These findings are consistent at varying levels of soccer and have also been shown to be sensitive to training (Bradley et al., 2013; Bangsbo et al., 2008). More recently, the 30–15 intermittent fitness test, developed by Martin Buchheit and colleagues (2008), has been widely used and also demonstrates strong repeatability and ecological validity. Furthermore, results from this test can be used to provide individualised training prescriptions for soccer players (Buchheit, 2008). Typical data from a range of field-based tests of soccer-specific endurance can be found in Table 5.1.1.

The increasing constraints of fixture congestion and tight training schedules limit the frequency with which soccer players can be tested maximally throughout a season, especially in an exhaustive capacity. In response, a number of submaximal versions of the intermittent running tests have been developed. Such tests have little impact on daily routines and can be scheduled as part of a standardised warm-up. Practitioners conducting these tests typically seek to contrast absolute (bpm) or relative (%max) heart rate at various time points and thus map internal responses to standardised bouts of external work. Such an approach allows inferences to be drawn relating to player recovery/readiness and fitness levels. Data derived from a submaximal 6-min yo-yo intermittent endurance (level 2) test have been shown to possess robust levels of reproducibility (CV = 1.4%) and correlate well with maximal yo-yo test performance (Bradley et al., 2010).

As referred to previously, critical periods within soccer match play are characterised by high-intensity (anaerobic) activity, which can be linear or multidirectional in nature. Assessment of anaerobic qualities in soccer players through linear and multidirectional field tests are standard practice in most professional clubs (Turner et al., 2011). Match analysis has reported typical sprint distance in soccer match play to range between 10 and 30 m. To reflect this, linear sprinting tests are typically conducted over 30 m, with several split times (e.g., 5 m, 10 m, 20 m) also recorded (Altmann et al., 2019) as part of standard practice in professional clubs. Such an approach allows acceleration and linear speed qualities to be tested within the same protocol.

In addition to linear sprinting, soccer players are required to produce rapid whole-body movements with a change of speed or direction in response to a stimulus, commonly referred to as agility (Sheppard and Young, 2006). The fast pace and increasing intensity of elite competitive soccer require players to possess high levels of agility. There is no single 'gold standard' test for assessing agility, and it is therefore the practitioner's responsibility to determine which test(s) are more applicable to them. For example, the practitioner may break down performance positionally or in relation to the team playing style to identify the most suitable test (e.g., players who play in central midfield are often required to change direction the most at multiple different angles; therefore, a T-test may be more suitable for this playing position). It is recommended that practitioners perform either the T-test or 505 agility tests to assess for 90- and 180-degree changes of direction and a zig-zag movement-based test to account for cutting and linear changes of direction. Results from these tests have been frequently reported within the literature (Altmann et al., 2019). Reference data from tests of linear and multidirectional speed are provided in Table 5.1.1.

An array of validated tests for soccer players is available to practitioners. In choosing which to use, consideration should be given to a number of factors, including available physical and financial resources and the profile of the players being tested. We have provided the coefficient of variation (CV%) of the tests in Table 5.1.1 for reference purposes. However, whichever protocols are employed, practitioners are strongly encouraged to perform their own checks on test reliability and to establish boundaries of 'noise' in their own environment using appropriate statistical procedures. Only then can they truly establish whether changes in performance are meaningful or merely an artefact of the test itself (Hopkins, 2000).

Monitoring in soccer

In recent years the efforts of applied scientists working in soccer have moved towards regular monitoring of players' physical performance and training status and away from the testing of fitness. The reasons for this are due to the non-invasive nature of most monitoring protocols, the limited disruption to routine training schedules and the fact that resultant data can have a significant role in player and squad load management.

Monitoring can be viewed in terms of that performed 'off-field' and that performed 'on-field'. Off-field monitoring tends to focus on assessment of readiness to train or recovery status of players and can involve, for example, the use of simple questionnaires, analysis of body fluids (e.g., urine, saliva, blood) and monitoring of physiological status (e.g., through collection of heart rate variability data). Useful information can also be obtained by collecting performance measures that can serve as an indicator of functional status. Such measurements may include the use of multijoint movements (e.g., unilateral and bilateral vertical and horizontal jumps) or assessment of isolated isometric or eccentric muscular performance with data from force plates or inertial sensors. A multitude of factors (e.g., recent training history, travel, sleep patterns) can impact on the aforementioned points; thus, collection of information related to these elements will provide insight into player 'performance status' and can be used to inform decisions related to scheduled training and match programmes if necessary. While these approaches are cheap to use and are relatively simple to administer, they do require robust and consistent implementation to ensure the data collected are truly representative of player status and not contaminated by methodological or environmental noise.

Direct monitoring during training and match play of external load (via global positioning system [GPS] and inertial sensors) and internal load (via heart rate monitors) is routine in contemporary professional soccer. Such information can be accessed live or post-event, with live data clearly having an important role in mapping workload and intensity of activities and potentially making strategic decisions within the session. The relationship between the intensity and volume of internal and external load is highly individual and sits at the heart of contemporary soccer monitoring practice (Morgans et al., 2014). Although soccer-specific activity impacts on the function of many physiological systems (e.g., neuromuscular, endocrine, cardiovascular and/or metabolic), the practicalities of monitoring players usually mean there is a heavy reliance on the use of heart rate monitoring to give an indication of overall physiological deviation from resting equilibrium.

The choice of approach to testing and monitoring in any environment often comes down to pragmatic decisions, which might be purely driven by available resources (human or physical) or more practical in nature (e.g., limited time in daily schedules, access to players) rather than the underpinning scientific validity of the approach. Situational variables will also impact on decisions taken regarding routine monitoring of players (e.g., if a player has been identified as being at elevated risk of injury, then a more forensic approach to monitoring that particular player may be implemented). That having been said, monitoring of player performance status is a key function of all sport science departments in modern professional soccer, with strategies employed being a function of the expertise and resources available to individuals. Monitoring should not be viewed and conducted in isolation of the football curriculum in clubs, and the success of monitoring strategies is dependent on collective understanding and an integrated approach between departments.

Table 5.1.1 Selected reference values for a battery of fitness tests

Test	Reference Value Mean ± SD	Range	Population	Reference	CV (%)
YYIE1 (m)	1890 ± 457	Non-available	Elite professional	Schmitz et al. (2018)	10.2
YYIE2 (m)	2364 ± 478	Non-available	EPL	Bradley et al. (2013)	3.9
YYIR1 (m)	2738 ± 377	2000–3320	EFL Championship	Unpublished Data	4.9
YYIR2 (m)	1260 ± 62	Non-available	Elite professional	Bangsbo et al. (2008)	9.6
30–15 IFT (V)	21.5 ± 1.14	18.5–23.5	SPL		4.8
5-m Sprint (s)	0.96 ± 0.07	0.87–1.20	EFL championship	Unpublished data	
10-m sprint (s)	1.65 ± 0.06	1.56–1.72	EFL championship	Unpublished data	3.1
20-m sprint (s)	2.82 ± 0.07	2.67–2.97	EFL championship	Unpublished data	1.8
30-m sprint (s)	4.04 ± 0.07	3.75–4.41	EFL championship	Unpublished data	2.0
40-m sprint (s)	5.22 ± 0.17	4.87–5.61	EFL championship	Unpublished data	1.3
505 (s)	2.29 ± 0.09	2.14–2.48	EFL championship	Unpublished data	2.8
T-test	7.79 ± 0.29	7.10–8.18	EFL championship	Unpublished data	3.3

YYIE = Yo-yo intermittent endurance, YYIR = Yo-yo intermittent recovery, IFT = Intermittent fitness test, EPL = English Premier League, SPL = Scottish Premier League, EFL = English Football League

References

Altmann, S., Ringhof, S., Neumann, R., Woll, A. and Rumpf, M. C. (2019). Validity and reliability of speed tests used in soccer: A systematic review. *PLoS One*, 14, e0220982.

Bangsbo, J. (1994). Physiology of soccer: With special reference to fatigue. *Acta Physiologica Scandinavica*, 151, 1–155.

Bangsbo, J., Iaia, F. M. and Krustrup, P. (2008). The yo-yo intermittent recovery test: A useful too for evaluation of physical performance in intermittent sports. *Sports Medicine*, 38, 37–51.

Bangsbo, J., Mohr, M. and Krustrup, P. (2006). Physical and metabolic demands of training and match-play in the elite football player. *Journal of Sports Sciences*, 24, 665–674.

Bradley, P. S., Carling, C., Gomez Diaz, A., Hood, P., Barnes, C., Ade, J., Boddy, M., Krustrup, P. and Mohr, M. (2013). Match performance and physical capacity of players in the top three competitive standards of English professional soccer. *Human Movement Science*, 32, 808–821.

Bradley, P. S., Mohr, M., Bendiksen, M., Randers, M. B., Flindt, M., Barnes, C., Hood, P., Gomez, A., Andersen, J. L., Di Mascio, M., Bangsbo, J. and Krustrup, P. (2010).

Sub-maximal and maximal yo-yo intermittent endurance test level 2: Heart rate response, reproducibility and application to elite soccer. *European Journal of Applied Physiology*, 111, 969–978.

Buchheit, M. (2008). The 30–15 intermittent fitness test: Accuracy for individualizing interval training of young intermittent sport players. *Journal of Strength and Conditioning Research*, 22, 365–374.

Faude, O., Koch, T. and Meyer, T. (2012). Straight sprinting is the most frequent action in goal situations in professional football. *Journal of Sports Sciences*, 30, 625–631.

Hopkins, W. (2000). Measures of reliability in sports medicine and science. *Sports Medicine*, 30(1), 1–15.

Morgans, R., Orme, P., Anderson, L. and Drust, B. (2014a). Principles and practices of training in soccer. *Journal of Sport and Health Science*, 3, 251–257.

Schmitz, B., Pfeifer, C., Kreitz, K., Borowski, M., Faldum, A. and Brand, S. M. (2018). The yo-yo intermittent tests: A systematic review and structured compendium of test results. *Frontiers in Physiology*, 9, 870.

Sheppard, J. M. and Young, W. B. (2006). Agility literature review: Classifications, training and testing. *Journal of Sports Sciences*, 24, 919–932.

Svensson, M. and Drust, B. (2005). Testing soccer players. *Journal of Sports Sciences*, 23, 601–618.

Turner, A., Walker, S., Stembridge, M., Coneyworth, P., Reed, G., Birdsey, L., Barter, P. and Moody, J. (2011). A testing battery for the assessment of fitness in soccer players. *Strength and Conditioning Journal*, 33, 29–39.

5.2 Field hockey

Caroline Sunderland and Hannah MacLeod

Field hockey is a high-intensity intermittent sport that incorporates periods of high-speed running, sprinting and repeated sprinting interspersed with lower-speed running and passive recovery during periods of substitution. Senior female international players have been shown to cover ~5500 m during matches, with ~850 m at high speed (>15.1 km·h^{-1}) (Macutkiewicz and Sunderland, 2011), and senior male international players cover ~6000 m, with ~900–1400 m at high speed (>15 km·h^{-1}; unpublished observations). Regular physiological testing is essential for the purposes of tailoring and monitoring training, talent identification, player development and rehabilitation and recovery monitoring. Due to the high-intensity intermittent nature of field hockey and the ability to use unlimited substitutions, it is important to complete a battery of field tests that incorporate endurance, speed, agility and repeated sprint ability. Tests of strength and power should also be included at the elite level.

Laboratory-based testing is uncommon, even at the elite level, due to the time-consuming nature of the tests. Field tests have the benefit of providing valid results with minimal equipment in a convenient and time-efficient manner. Field tests that provide results specific to field hockey match performance include the multistage shuttle run test, yo-yo intermittent recovery test level 1 and interval shuttle run test (Harry and Booysen, 2020; Leslie, 2012). Tests of endurance, speed, agility and skill have also been shown to be able to discriminate between playing standards (Aumack et al., 2019; Leslie, 2012), though slalom and dribbling performance did not discriminate between Division 1 and 2 male Italian players (Bartolomei et al., 2019).

Obtaining valid and reliable physiological testing data requires players to be habituated with all tests that they complete prior to testing sessions; complete standardised warm-ups and testing should be at the same time of day with similar environmental conditions whenever possible. It is also worth considering whether players carry their field hockey stick during the tests that they complete. Finally, testing should be a positive experience for all. Therefore, complete testing regularly and make sure players know when testing will occur and that players feel supported throughout, with a focus on player development rather than selection. Tables 5.2.1 and 5.2.2 provide data from elite and sub-elite hockey players from many of the tests recommended later. A suggested testing battery would be completed over two separate days: day 1 undertaking endurance, followed by 30-min recovery and linear speed and day 2 undertaking repeated sprint ability followed by 30-min recovery and slalom sprint and dribble.

DOI: 10.4324/9781003045281-37

Table 5.2.1 Selected performance data from field hockey field tests for elite senior and youth players (mean ±SD)

Parameter	Test	Senior Males	Senior Females	Youth (age) Males	Youth (age) Females	Source
Endurance	Multistage fitness test (m)	2484 ± 306		2556 ± 157 (U21)		(Leslie, 2012)
	Multistage fitness test (m)			2162 ± 227 (U18)		(Leslie, 2012)
	Multistage fitness test (m)			1931 ± 204 (U16)		(Leslie, 2012)
	Multistage fitness test (m)		1255 ± 344			(Schmitz et al., 2018)
	Yo-yo IR1 (m)		20 ± 0.6			Unpublished observations
	30:15 (km·h^{-1})	22 ± 0.7				
	Interval shuttle run test (runs of 20 m)			91.46 ± 21.55 (16.1 ± 0.3 yr)	59.8 ± 18.16 (16.1 ± 0.3 yr)	(Elferink-Gemser et al., 2006)
	Interval shuttle run test (runs of 20 m)			58.82 ± 18.64 (12.9 ± 0.6 yr)	48.50 ± 12.56 (13.0 ± 0.3 yr)	(Elferink-Gemser et al., 2006)
Linear speed	10-m sprint (s)	1.69 ± 0.07	1.82 ± 0.09			Unpublished observations
	40-m sprint (s)	5.23 ± 0.14	5.76 ± 0.19			Unpublished observations
	5-m sprint (s)	1.06 ± 0.05		0.95 ± 0.05 (U21)		(Leslie, 2012)
	10-m sprint (s)	1.77 ± 0.07		1.66 ± 0.06 (U21)		(Leslie, 2012)
	5-m sprint (s)			1.02 ± 0.07 (U18)		(Leslie, 2012)
	10-m sprint (s)			1.78 ± 0.06 (U18)		(Leslie, 2012)
	5-m sprint (s)			1.11 ± 0.06 (U16)		(Leslie, 2012)
	10-m sprint (s)			1.88 ± 0.08 (U16)		(Leslie, 2012)
Repeated sprint ability	8 × 20m shuttle, 30 s per repetition	6.64 ± 0.14 (fastest shuttle)	7.10 ± 0.16 (fastest shuttle)			Unpublished observations
	8 × 20m shuttle, 30 s per repetition	6.95 ± 0.19 (mean of 8)	7.45 ± 0.18 (mean of 8)			Unpublished observations

Table 5.2.2 Selected performance data from field hockey field tests for sub-elite senior and youth players (mean ±SD)

Parameter	Test	Senior Males	Senior Females	Youth (age) Males	Youth (age) Females	Source
Endurance	Multistage fitness test		1140 ± 405			(Schmitz et al., 2018)
	Yo-yo IR1 (m)		929			(Harry and Booysen, 2020)
	Yo-yo IR1 (m)		(811–1048*)			Unpublished observations
	30:15 (km·h^{-1})	20.5 ± 0.9	19.1 ± 0.8			
	Interval shuttle run test (runs of 20 m)			84.59 ± 20.48 (16.0 ± 0.3 yr)	48.88 ± 15.92 (15.9 ± 0.3 yr)	(Elferink-Gemser et al., 2006)
	Interval shuttle run test (runs of 20 m)			54.67 ± 23.77 (13.0 ± 0.4 yr)	47.79 ± 16.70 (12.9 ± 0.5 yr)	(Elferink-Gemser et al., 2006)
Agility	Shuttle sprint test				7.40 ± 0.33 s (19.5 ± 0.8 yr)	(Aumack et al., 2019)
	Slalom sprint test				10.49 ± 0.72 s (19.5 ± 0.8 yr)	(Aumack et al., 2019)
Linear speed	40-m sprint (s)	5.52 ± 0.27				Unpublished observations
	5-m sprint (s)		1.09 ± 0.06			Unpublished observations
	10-m sprint (s)		1.91 ± 0.09			Unpublished observations
	20-m sprint (s)		3.37 ± 0.14			Unpublished observations
Repeated sprint ability	6 repetitions of 2 × 15 m, 20 s per repetition		Mean = 6.72 s (6.60–6.83)*			(Harry and Booysen, 2020)
	6 × 30 m, 25 s per repetition (s)	26.79 ± 0.76 (total time)				(Spencer et al., 2006)
	6 repetitions of 2 × 20m, 30 s per repetition (s)	59.00 ± 1.66 (total time)				Unpublished observations
Skill/dribble	Shuttle dribble test				8.38 ± 0.29 s (19.5 ± 0.8 yr)	(Aumack et al., 2019)
	Slalom dribble test				11.37 ± 1.09 s (19.5 ± 0.8 yr)	(Aumack et al., 2019)

* 95% Confidence interval.

Endurance tests

Continuous endurance tests include the 20-m multistage shuttle run test (Ramsbottom et al., 1988) and the 1000-yd (914.4 m) or 10 × pitch length run. Performance for the multistage fitness test can be recorded as the level and shuttle number achieved and/or estimated maximal oxygen uptake (cardiorespiratory fitness) from published equations, which have recently been updated for both youth and adults (Nevill et al., 2020). Total time for the 10 × pitch length run provides a simple measure of endurance performance and is used by senior international squads to measure training status.

Intermittent tests of endurance include the 30:15 intermittent fitness test (Buchheit, 2008), the interval shuttle run test (Elferink-Gemser et al., 2006), the yo-yo intermittent recovery test (Bangsbo et al., 2008) and the 5-m multiple shuttle run test (Boddington et al., 2004). The interval shuttle run test and 30:15 are similar in nature and incorporate work to rest periods of 30 s running, interspersed with 15 s walking. The interval shuttle run test requires 20-m shuttles to be completed, whereas 40-m shuttles are used in the 30:15 test. Speed increases over time until the player can no longer complete the required distance, with the number of completed 20-m runs recorded for the interval shuttle test and the speed for the last completed stage recorded for the 30:15 test. The interval shuttle run test was shown to be sensitive to changes in training and able to discriminate between elite and sub-elite youth field hockey players (Elferink-Gemser et al., 2006). The maximal running speed attained from the 30:15 test can be used to prescribe speeds for high-intensity interval training sessions. The yo-yo intermittent recovery test requires players to complete 2 × 20 m shuttle runs, interspersed with 10 s of activity recovery, at increasing speeds.

When selecting the most appropriate battery of tests, it is important to consider the continuous or intermittent nature of the endurance test and therefore the equipment required to conduct the test. Regular testing throughout the season can be used for monitoring changes in players' fitness and for guiding their training prescription.

Speed and agility

Linear speed should be completed over a distance up to 40 m, with intermediate distances of 5, 10, 20 and 30 m. Timing gates should be used, with players starting at 1 m behind the 0 m gate with a minimum of 2 min recovery between each sprint and the fastest sprint recorded.

Multidirectional speed or agility can be determined by completing the field hockey-specific shuttle sprint and slalom sprint test (Lemmink et al., 2004). The shuttle sprint requires the player to sprint 32 m by completing a 6-m shuttle, followed by a 10-m shuttle, with timing for 30 m recorded (Figure 5.2.1A). Players complete this three times, starting every 20 s, with the individual sprint times, peak sprint time and total sprint time recorded. The slalom sprint test also requires players to cover 30 m (Figure 5.2.1B), with the time to complete the sprint recorded. It is recommended that players carry their hockey stick during these tests.

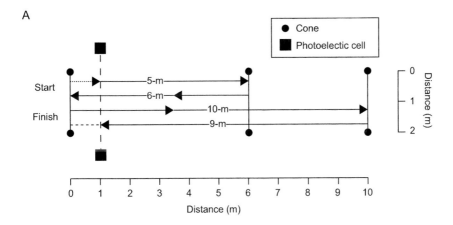

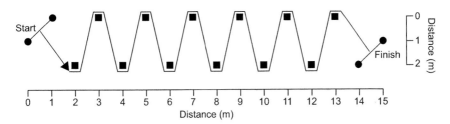

Figure 5.2.1 The shuttle sprint and dribble test course (A) and the slalom sprint and dribble test course (B). Solid circles represent cones 8 cm high, and solid squares represent cones 35 cm high.

Source: Both redrawn from Lemmink et al. (2004).

Repeated sprint ability

Tests of repeated sprint ability for field hockey are easy to complete and provide information relating to maximal sprint time and fatigue. Record each sprint time and report the fastest sprint, mean sprint time, total sprint time and fatigue index (%) (((slowest time-fastest time)/fastest time) × 100). Timing gates should be used where possible, with players starting 1 m back from the timing gate.

Repeated sprint tests include 6 × 30 m, with a sprint starting every 25 s with a jog recovery (Spencer et al., 2006), six repetitions of a 2 × 15 m shuttle (30 m total per sprint) every 20 s (Harry and Booysen, 2020) and a 8 × 20 m shuttle (40 m total per sprint), with a sprint shuttle starting every 30 s. A field hockey–specific repeated sprint ability test that simulates activities during a match, which is completed both with and without dribbling a hockey ball, can also be used for research (Lemos et al., 2017).

Skill

The shuttle dribble test is identical to the shuttle sprint test (Figure 5.2.1A), but is completed whilst dribbling a hockey ball (Lemmink et al., 2004). This should be completed following 5 min of walking recovery after the shuttle sprint test. From three repetitions, individual dribble times, peak dribble time and total dribble time are recorded, as well as delta shuttle time (difference between the total dribble time and the total sprint time). Similarly, the slalom dribble test (Figure 5.2.1B) should be completed after 5 min of walking recovery after the slalom sprint test (Lemmink et al., 2004). Record the slalom dribble time and the difference between the slalom dribble and slalom sprint times.

A more complex skill test that incorporates dribbling, passing, shooting and decision making has also been developed for field hockey, but would be recommended for use primarily in research (Sunderland et al., 2006).

References

Aumack, P., Larson, A. and DeBeliso, M. (2019). The validity and reliability of two novel field hockey specific tests among female collegiate field hockey athletes. *International Journal of Sports Science*, 9(5), 108–113.

Bangsbo, J., Iaia, F. M. and Krustrup, P. (2008). The yo-yo intermittent recovery test: A useful tool for evaluation of physical performance in intermittent sports. *Sports Medicine*, 38(1), 37–51.

Bartolomei, S., Nigro, F., Gubellini, L., Ciacci, S., Merni, F., Treno, F., Cortesi, M. and Semprini, G. (2019). Physiological and sport-specific comparison between division I and division II Italian male field hockey players. *Journal of Strength and Conditioning Research*, 33(11), 3123–3128. doi: 10.1519/JSC.0000000000002503

Boddington, M. K., Lambert, M. I. and Waldeck, M. R. (2004). Validity of a 5-meter multiple shuttle run test for assessing fitness of women field hockey players. *Journal of Strength and Conditioning Research*, 18(1), 97–100.

Buchheit, M. (2008). The 30–15 intermittent fitness test: Accuracy for individualizing interval training of young intermittent sport players. *Journal of Strength and Conditioning Research*, 22(2), 365–374. doi: 10.1519/JSC.0b013e3181635b2e

Elferink-Gemser, M. T., Visscher, C., van Duijn, M. A. and Lemmink, K. A. (2006). Development of the interval endurance capacity in elite and sub-elite youth field hockey players. *British Journal of Sports Medicine*, 40(4), 340–345. doi: 10.1136/bjsm.2005.023044

Harry, K. and Booysen, M. J. (2020). Faster heart rate recovery correlates with high-intensity match activity in female field hockey players-training implications. *Journal of Strength and Conditioning Research*, 34(4), 1150–1157. doi: 10.1519/JSC.0000000000003073

Lemmink, K. A., Elferink-Gemser, M. T. and Visscher, C. (2004). Evaluation of the reliability of two field hockey specific sprint and dribble tests in young field hockey players. *British Journal of Sports Medicine*, 38, 138–142.

Lemos, R. S., Paz, G. A., Maia, M. D. F., Silva, J. B. D., Lima, V. P., Castro, J. B. P. D. and Miranda, H. (2017). Anthropometric and physical fitness parameters versus specific performance tests in Brazilian field hockey athletes: A pilot study. *Biomedical Human Kinetics*, 9, 57–63. doi: 10.1515/bhk-2017-0009

Leslie, V. (2012). *Physiological and Match Performance Characteristics of Field Hockey Players*. Loughborough University.

Macutkiewicz, D. and Sunderland, C. (2011). The use of GPS to evaluate activity profiles of elite women hockey players during match-play. *Journal of Sports Science*, 29(9), 967–973. doi: 10.1080/02640414.2011.570774

Nevill, A. M., Ramsbottom, R., Sandercock, G., Bocachica-Gonzalez, C. E., Ramirez-Velez, R. and Tomkinson, G. (2020). Developing a new curvilinear allometric model to improve the fit and validity of the 20-m shuttle run test as a predictor of cardiorespiratory fitness in adults and youth. *Sports Medicine*. doi: 10.1007/s40279-020-01346-0

Ramsbottom, R., Brewer, J. and Williams, C. (1988). A progressive shuttle run test to estimate maximal oxygen uptake. *British Journal of Sports Medicine*, 22(4), 141–144.

Schmitz, B., Pfeifer, C., Kreitz, K., Borowski, M., Faldum, A. and Brand, S. M. (2018). The yo-yo intermittent tests: A systematic review and structured compendium of test results. *Frontiers in Physiology*, 9, 870. doi: 10.3389/fphys.2018.00870

Spencer, M., Fitzsimons, M., Dawson, B., Bishop, D. and Goodman, C. (2006). Reliability of a repeated-sprint test for field-hockey. *Journal of Science and Medicine in Sport*, 9(1–2), 181–184. doi: 10.1016/j.jsams.2005.05.001

Sunderland, C., Cooke, K., Milne, H. and Nevill, M. E. (2006). The reliability and validity of a field hockey skill test. *International Journal of Sports Medicine*, 27(5), 395–400.

5.3 Rugby

Craig Twist and Jamie Highton

Physical qualities differentiate between playing standards for both rugby codes (Argus et al., 2012; Dobbin et al., 2019), positively influence a player's match performance (Smart et al., 2014; Delaney et al., 2016) and are associated with a lower risk of injury (Hulin et al., 2019). The physical qualities of rugby players might be classified broadly as body composition, maximal upper and lower body strength, upper and lower body power output, acceleration (including sprint momentum), maximal running speed and intermittent running capacity (see Table 5.3.1 and Table 5.3.2 in the supplementary material).

Body composition

Higher standard players generally have a higher body mass (Dobbin et al., 2019), with lower body fat and greater lean mass than lower standard players (Geeson-Brown et al., 2020). Whilst skinfold measurements do not accurately predict body composition in rugby players, *changes* in Σ7 skinfold thickness and lean mass index (i.e., body mass relative to skinfold thickness) over time do indicate whether body composition has changed (Zemski et al., 2019). Skinfolds can therefore be used to track a player's body composition within and between seasons.

Skinfolds: Skinfold thickness should be measured and summed in accordance with Chapter 3.4 using the following sites:

- Triceps*;
- Biceps*;
- Subscapular*;
- Supraspinale*;
- Abdominal;
- Mid-thigh;
- Medial calf.

* Can be taken to provide a Σ4 skinfold.

Lean mass index: The lean mass index can be used to estimate changes in lean mass in rugby players, using the following equation:

DOI: 10.4324/9781003045281-38

Lean Mass Index = Body Mass (kg)/$\Sigma 7$ Skinfolds^x (mm)

where ^{x} is an exponent and = 0.14 for forwards and 0.13 for backs.

Upper and lower body strength and power

Maximal strength and power are physical qualities that differentiate between rugby playing standards (Argus et al., 2012) and enable the prescription of resistance training loads.

Strength assessment: After a warm-up, the load is gradually increased until the pre-determined repetition maximum (RM) is achieved. The bench press requires holding the bar with a prone grip and lowering it to the chest, before maximally pushing until full elbow extension. The back squat has the bar across the athlete's shoulders, descending until the hips are below the knee joint and then ascending until knees are at full extension. Upper body maximum strength can be determined using 1–3 RM, whereas squatting exercise should use lifts of 3–5 RM.

Power assessment: Jump squat and bench throws performed against varying external loads can be used to determine lower and upper body force-velocity-power profiles, respectively. For jump squats, players warm up and then randomly perform maximal squat jumps against loads of 0% (no bar, body weight only), 20%, 40%, 60% and 80% of body mass, loaded to the nearest 0.5 kg. With the bar positioned across the shoulders, or arms across the chest for unloaded jumps, players perform a squat jump maximal vertical height from a 90-degree knee angle, landing in the same position as take-off. For the bench throw, a warm-up is followed by randomised throws against loads corresponding to 20%, 40%, 60% or 80% body mass, loaded to the nearest 0.5 kg. With shoulder-width pronated grip, the bar is lowered to a ~90-degree angle at the elbow, then thrown vertically and explosively for maximum height. On the downward phase, the bar should be caught by two spotters and lowered to the player's hands. For both exercises, players perform two successful repetitions under each load with ~2 min between trials; the best performance for each load is taken for analysis. Exercises are performed using a free or fixed-bar (Smith machine) connected to an optical encoder (e.g., Gymaware, Kinetic Performance Technology, Australia) to calculate bar displacement and power output (W). Maximised mechanical power output can be estimated by fitting a quadratic to players' power output and load data (see Argus et al., 2011).

Sprint speed and sprint momentum

Sprint running over distances <30 m are a key feature of training and match play for rugby players (Waldron et al., 2011). Assessing sprint distances between 2–10 m and 30–40 m allows assessment of acceleration and maximal running speed, respectively. Combining the product of body mass and sprint speed also enables calculation of players' momentum ($P = m \times \bar{v}$), a measure known to differentiate between playing standards (Dobbin et al., 2019), and has positive associations with ball-carrying ability during match play (Waldron et al., 2014).

Sprint assessment: Sprint performance is measured using electronic timing gates positioned at 0 m, 10 m and 40 m. Trials should be completed outdoors on a suitable surface (e.g., artificial 4G turf), with players in studded footwear. Players start each sprint positioned 30 cm behind the start line (zero) and timing gates positioned at 90 cm from the floor. After a warm-up, three maximal effort sprints should be recorded to the nearest 0.01 s, with the best 10 m and 40 m times reported.

High-intensity intermittent running capacity

High-intensity intermittent running capacity is influenced by a combination of an individual's maximal aerobic (i.e., $\dot{V}O_2$max) and anaerobic capacities and influences rugby performance (see earlier). The 30–15 intermittent fitness test (*the 30–15$_{IFT}$*; Buchheit, 2008) offers a sensitive and reliable measure of intermittent running capacity, can be used to prescribe training intensities, enables the testing of multiple players simultaneously and requires minimal time (<30 min).

The 30–15$_{IFT}$: The test comprises 30-s shuttle runs interspersed with 15-s periods, starting at 8 km·h^{-1} for the first 30-s run and increasing by 0.5 km·h^{-1} for every subsequent 45-s stage. Players run between two lines positioned 40 m apart controlled by an audio signal. To control pacing, a short beep indicates when players must be in the 3-m zones either at each end of the running area or the midline (20-m line). During the 15-s recovery, players walk forward to the closest of the three lines (Line A [0 m], Line B [20 m] or Line C [40 m], depending on where the previous stage was completed) to start the next stage. The test ends when the player cannot maintain the required running speed or when they are unable to reach a 3-m zone around each line at the moment of the audio signal on three consecutive occasions. The last running speed completed successfully is the player's maximal running speed.

Data analysis and interpretation

The precision and magnitude of measurements should be considered when interpreting the physical qualities described in this chapter. This makes it necessary to quantify 1) the reliability of the measurement and 2) the smallest meaningful change in a physical quality (see Chapter 2.2). Practitioners should determine their own 'in-house' reliability by performing repeated measurements in closely matched conditions (e.g., 40-m sprints performed a week apart at the start of pre-season). Where this is not possible, we have provided published typical error and/or coefficient of variation values for rugby players in Table 5.3.2. Procedures for calculating and interpreting the smallest meaningful change can also be found in the online supplementary material (5.3.1).

References

Argus, C. K., Gill, N. D., Keogh, J. W., et al. (2011). Assessing lower body peak power in elite rugby-union players. *Journal of Strength and Conditioning Research*, 25, 1616–1621.

Argus, C. K., Gill, N. D. and Keogh, J. W. (2012). Characterization of the differences in strength and power between different levels of competition in rugby union athletes. *The Journal of Strength and Conditioning Research*, 26(10), 2698–2704.

Buchheit, M. (2008). The 30–15 intermittent fitness test: Accuracy for individualizing interval training of young intermittent sport players. *The Journal of Strength and Conditioning Research*, 22(2), 365–374.

Delaney, J. A., Thornton, H. R., Duthie, G. M. and Dascombe, B. J. (2016). Factors that influence running intensity in interchange players in professional rugby league. *International Journal of Sports Physiology and Performance*, 11(8), 1047–1052.

Dobbin, N., Moss, S. L., Highton, J. and Twist, C. (2019). The discriminant validity of standardised testing battery and its ability to differentiate anthropometric and physical characteristics between youth, academy and senior professional rugby league players. *International Journal of Sports Physiology and Performance*, 14, 1110–1116.

Geeson-Brown, T., Jones, B., Till, K., Chantler, S. and Deighton, K. (2020). Body composition differences by age and playing standard in male rugby union and rugby league: A systematic review and meta-analysis. *Journal of Sports Sciences*, Epub ahead of print. doi: 10.1080/02640414.2020.1775990

Hulin, B. T., Gabbett, T. J., Pickworth, N. J., Johnston, R. D. and Jenkins, D. G. (2019). Relationships among PlayerLoad, high-intensity intermittent running ability, and injury risk in professional rugby league players. *International Journal of Sports Physiology and Performance*, 1(aop), 1–7.

Smart, D., Hopkins, W. G., Quarrie, K. L. and Gill, N. (2014). The relationship between physical fitness and game behaviours in rugby union players. *European Journal of Sport Science*, 14(sup1), S8–S17.

Waldron, M., Twist, C., Highton, J., Worsfold, P. and Daniels, M. (2011). Movement and physiological match demands of elite rugby league using portable global positioning systems. *Journal of Sports Sciences*, 29(11), 1223–1230.

Waldron, M., Worsfold, P. R., Twist, C. and Lamb, K. (2014). The relationship between physical abilities, ball-carrying and tackling among elite youth rugby league players. *Journal of Sports Sciences*, 32(6), 542–549.

Zemski, A. J., Keating, S. E., Broad, E. M. and Slater, G. J. (2019). Longitudinal changes in body composition assessed using DXA and surface anthropometry show good agreement in elite rugby union athletes. *International Journal of Sport Nutrition and Exercise Metabolism*, 29(1), 24–31.

5.4 Netball

Sarah Whitehead and Cameron Owen

Netball is a dynamic, high-intensity intermittent, court-based team sport. It has unique physical requirements due to its rules, with players restricted to moving only one step when in possession of the ball and releasing the ball within 3 s of receiving it. During match play, netballers have been reported to cover between ~2100 and 5500 m, complete up to 81 high-intensity sprints, 83 jumps, a range of landing patterns and agility manoeuvres (Brooks et al., 2020).

The physical demands of netball are greatly influenced by playing position (Young et al., 2016), with different roles and large discrepancies in the space available for each position on court. However, all netballers require a certain level of physical qualities to meet the demands of the sport. High levels of strength, speed, agility, lower limb stability and power are required to perform the high-intensity movement patterns (Simpson et al., 2019), with good aerobic fitness required to be able to maintain the repeated high-intensity activity over a match. Therefore, a testing battery must evaluate these physical qualities.

Testing battery and rationale

Testing should be completed at regular intervals throughout the season (e.g., start of pre-season, end of pre-season, mid-season and end of season) to support player evaluation and training prescription. Performing the testing battery in the order outlined will maintain reliability and limit the effect of fatigue from the preceding tests. Testing should ideally be completed over 2 days split into 1) jump and strength testing and 2) running assessments. It is possible to complete the tests in one session if more practically feasible; however, there will be a greater fatiguing effect, and therefore the format should be maintained for each testing period.

Single-leg hop

As a result of the high-intensity landing and pivoting that occur during match play, the ability to produce and absorb force effectively on one leg is important for performance and reducing injury risk in netballers (Otago, 2004). Therefore, the single-leg hop is important for assessing landing mechanics. This test is included within the England Netball testing battery.

DOI: 10.4324/9781003045281-39

A tape measure is placed on the floor with a start line marked at 0. Players, standing on one leg, position their toes behind the start line. They are then told to complete a horizontal jump with no constraints placed on the countermovement depth or arm swing. For the trial to be recorded, players must stick the landing on one leg (same as take-off leg), and the hop distance is marked at the most posterior aspect of the foot and measured to the nearest 0.01 cm on the tape measure. If the participant does not stick the landing (i.e., maintain balance for 3 s), another trial is attempted until three trials are acquired on each leg. Qualitative assessment of landing can be performed at the same time, assessing factors which may contribute to injury risk, such as poor hip stability and knee valgus.

Countermovement jump

Netball match play requires dynamic movements of the lower body, including multiple jumps, with jump height being key to contest for a high ball. Therefore, vertical jump testing is ideal as an indirect measure of lower body power and a sport-specific action assessment. England Netball also employs this test within their testing battery.

Using a jump mat, the player steps on the mat and with their hands placed on hips. Following a count of '3, 2, 1, jump' the player performs a countermovement prior to jumping as high as possible. Players are told to jump 'as high as possible', with no specific instruction on the depth or speed of the countermovement. While in the air hands should remain on hips and legs kept straight. Three trials are performed, with the highest jump used for analysis. If comparing these results to the criterion method of jump assessment (force plate), the following correction equation should be used: criterion jump height = (0.8747 × alternative jump height) − 0.0666.

In the instance where practitioners cannot access a jump mat, advances in phone apps provide an accessible opportunity for the valid and reliable assessment of countermovement jump height using only a mobile phone camera (Balsalobre-Fernández et al., 2015).

Isometric mid-thigh pull

Strength underpins the performance of many physical qualities such as power and speed and reduces the risk of injury. The isometric mid-thigh pull provides a safe and quick assessment of full body strength to be carried out on court.

Using a dynamometer attached to a wooden platform, the isometric mid-thigh pull can be performed on court. With the dynamometer positioned between the legs, the player holds a latissimus dorsi pull-down bar attached to the dynamometer via a chain and positioned at the mid-thigh (see Figure 5.4.1). Shoulders should be positioned over the bar with knees flexed to ~140 degrees, similar to the second pull position of the clean. Prior to the pull, slack is removed from the chain, and then the player pulls as hard and fast as possible for 5 s. Three attempts should be performed, with the largest used for analysis. Results can be compared to the criterion method (force plates) using the following correction equation: criterion peak force = (1.300 * peak force) + 448.7. It should be noted that the current correction equation was identified for youth athletes, and future research is required for a netball-specific correction equation.

10-m speed

Due to the court size, superior acceleration qualities are desirable for players to create separation from defenders and close attacking space. A 10-m speed assessment is an appropriate test to evaluate such qualities.

A timing gate system should be used, forming a start and finish line 10 m apart (measured using a tape measure). Gates should be placed at approximately hip height to reduce the chance of beams being broken by limbs. Players are instructed to start in their own time on a line marked 0.5 m behind the starting gates and not to slow down until past the final gates. Three trials should be performed, with the fastest trial used for analysis.

If unable to use timing gates, a video camera (e.g., phone) can be used as a valid alternative (Haugen and Buchheit, 2016).

5–0–5 agility test

Netballers are required to change direction quickly to receive and prevent passes, especially 'circle' players, who have limited space to work in. The 5–0–5 agility test provides a reliable assessment of change of direction performance in netball players (Barber et al., 2016).

Figure 5.4.1 Isometric mid-thigh pull performed using a dynamometer.

Table 5.4.1 Netball testing standards

Test	Elite GS/GK	Elite GA/GD	Elite WA/C/WD	Emerging GS/GK	Emerging GA/GD	Emerging WA/C/WD	Talent GS/GK	Talent GA/GD	Talent WA/C/WD
CMJ (cm)	42	46	46	36	40	40	30	32	32
IMTP (N)	2750	2750	2750	2375	2375	2375	2000	2000	2000
10 m speed (s)	1.95	1.90	1.85	2.0	1.95	1.90	2.05	2.0	1.95
5–0–5 agility (s)	2.33	2.30	2.27	2.44	2.41	2.38	2.55	2.52	2.49
30–15IFT (km·h^{-1})	20	21	21	19.5	20.5	20.5	19	20	20

CMJ = countermovement jump, IMTP = isometric mid-thigh pull, 30–15IFT = 30–15 Intermittent Fitness Test
GS = Goal Shooter, GK = Goalkeeper, WA = Wing Attack, WD = Wing Defence, GA = Goal Attack, GD = Goal Defence
Note: Due to the limited assessment of physical qualities in netballers, standards are based on a mixture of research and data provided from national governing bodies.

30–15 intermittent fitness test (28 m)

Netball is an intermittent sport, where a high aerobic capacity is required to recover in the periods of rest between high-intensity actions. The shorter 28-m 30–15 intermittent fitness test (30–15IFT) is a reliable assessment of inter-effort recovery (Haydar et al., 2011) and should be used in accordance with the England Netball testing battery. The shorter 28-m shuttles are separated by line B at 14 m, with the 3-m safe zone at lines A and C.

Testing feedback and monitoring

The data derived from this testing battery can be used to identify strengths and weaknesses of the physical qualities of netballers to help inform training practices, specific to the sport and positions. Given the high injury incidence rate in netball, further analysis of the data derived from the hop test can be carried out, such as limb asymmetry with players aiming to have <10% asymmetry. The position-specific interpretation is particularly important for certain tests, such as the 30–15IFT. During match play centre court positions accumulate higher workloads compared to shooters and defenders (Brooks et al., 2020) and require a higher aerobic capacity to meet these demands. As such, the final velocity achieved in the 30–15IFT should be interpreted and feedback to coaches provided and monitored specific to the netballers' playing position.

Practitioners should use comparative data to identify strengths and weaknesses to provide feedback to the coach and athletes for their respective playing position and target playing standard. In addition to positional considerations, further between-athlete differences such as body mass, maturation, training age and injury history should be considered when comparing data to testing standards. The identified development areas of the players can be targeted on court using periodised approaches, such as tactical periodisation.

Comparative data for netballers of various playing standards and positions are provided for practitioners in Table 5.4.1 to support the feedback and monitoring of the data derived from this testing battery.

References

Balsalobre-Fernández, C., Glaister, M. and Lockey, R. A. (2015). The validity and reliability of an IPhone app for measuring vertical jump performance. *Journal of Sports Sciences*, 33(15), 1574–1579.

Barber, O., Thomas, P., Jones, P. A., McMahon, J. and Comfort, P. (2016). Reliability of the 505 change-of-direction test in netball players. *International Journal of Sports Physiology and Performance*, 11(3), 377–380.

Brooks, E. R., Benson, A. C., Fox, A. S. and Bruce, L. M. (2020). Physical movement demands of training and matches across a full competition cycle in elite netball. *Applied Sciences*, 10(21), 7689.

Haugen, T. and Buchheit, M. (2016). Sprint running performance monitoring: Methodological and practical considerations. *Sports Medicine*, 46(5), 641–656.

Haydar, B., Al Haddad, H., Ahmaidi, S. and Buchheit, M. (2011). Assessing inter-effort recovery and change of direction ability with the 30–15 intermittent fitness test. *Journal of Sports Science and Medicine*, 10(2), 346–354.

Otago, L. (2004). Kinetic analysis of landings in netball: Is a footwork rule change required to decrease ACL injuries? *Journal of Science and Medicine in Sport*, 7(1), 85–95.

Simpson, M. J., Jenkins, D. G., Leveritt, M. D. and Kelly, V. G. (2019). Physical profiles of elite, sub-elite, regional and age-group netballers. *Journal of Sports Sciences*, 37(11), 1212–1219.

Young, C. M., Gastin, P. B., Sanders, N., Mackey, L. and Dwyer, D. B. (2016). Player load in elite netball: Match, training, and positional comparisons. *International Journal of Sports Physiology and Performance*, 11(8), 1074–1079.

5.5 Basketball

Anne Delextrat, Mark Williams, and Andy Howse

Physiological demands and movement patterns of the sport

Basketball is an intermittent team sport characterised by short high-intensity actions separated by recovery periods of low to moderate intensity, with a work:rest ratio of about 1:4. The highly intermittent nature of basketball is illustrated by a change in activity type every 1.1–2.8 s during matches (Stojanović et al., 2018). Basketball players perform a variety of movements on court in all directions, such as forward running, side-shuffling and backwards running, and the use of the vertical dimension is a crucial aspect of this sport, as shown by the high number of jumps occurring in a match. Therefore, physical conditioning and fitness testing should consider all these aspects. In addition, while these high-intensity movements are essential factors of success in basketball (fast breaks, jump shots, defensive blocks or fast shuffles), players need a good aerobic capacity to be able to repeat the actions and cover 7–8 km during matches (Stojanović et al., 2018). All these observations highlight that both aerobic and anaerobic conditioning are essential aspects of the physical fitness of basketball players.

Rationale and description of testing battery

Neuromuscular assessment

The battery of tests listed here will enable practitioners to see consistent changes over time with their athletes that may guide ability to load. Wellness scores and strong personal relationships help to cement this. Testing based on medical or injury history will also aid decisions on more formal testing. Previous lumbar dysfunction, hamstring or adductor strains and ankle sprains are usually prominent amongst basketball players; therefore, targeted testing for these areas is advised. Most of these tests were described in previous chapters:

- Knee to wall test (weight-bearing lunge test): measurement of ankle dorsiflexion.
- Passive or Active Straight Leg Raise: measurement of tension through the posterior chain.

DOI: 10.4324/9781003045281-40

- Adductor Squeeze test (hip flexed at 45°, with a handheld dynamometer or sphygmomanometer.

(Dallinga et al., 2012)

- Qualitative Analysis of Single Leg Loading.
- Y-Balance Test.

(Dallinga et al., 2012)

Vertical jump test

Rationale

Jumping is a key motor ability in basketball and underpins many specific actions (lay-ups, jump shots, rebounding, blocking). A jump occurs approximately every minute during a match. While each jump is constrained by conditions imposed by the game, the ability to produce propulsive force is important, as well as the attenuation of landing ground reaction force (linked to injuries). This array of data can be captured using portable dual-force platforms, enabling bilateral data collection and calculation of inter-limb asymmetry. This is especially useful when testing larger players (forwards) who do not usually perform single-leg jumps. In the absence of a force platform, jump height can be measured by jump mats.

Test procedure for bilateral countermovement jump (CMJ) without arm swing

- Players step onto the force platforms (or jump mat).
- Players stand upright and keep hands on the hips throughout the jump.
- After 3 sec of *quiet* standing counted down by the tester, players are instructed to continuously flex their knees to an approximate 90-degree angle and, without pause, jump as high as possible before landing back on the force platforms.
- The average of three attempts is calculated, with 30 s of rest between.

Test procedure for single-leg CMJ without arm swing

The same procedures are followed as per the bilateral jump. Players are instructed to stabilise upon landing before placing their non-jumping limb down.

Reliability

High inter- and intra-test reliability (intraclass correlation coefficients [ICC] <0.900) were reported for CMJ without arm swings for jump height and kinetic variables measured by the ForceDecks software (Heishman et al., 2020).

The 30–15 intermittent fitness test (IFT)

Rationale

The importance of aerobic fitness in basketball is illustrated by mean match heart rate (HR) during live time (i.e., excluding stoppage time) of 81.8%–94.6% of peak HR (HR_{peak}, Stojanović et al., 2018). The amount of runs at maximal and high speed during a match has been significantly correlated to players' endurance performance ($r = 0.52$ and $r = 0.49$, respectively, ben Abdelkrim et al., 2010). While several field-based tests exist for assessment of this fitness quality, the 28-m version of the 30–15 IFT is a highly practical test because of its frequent changes in direction (COD) and strong relationship with measures of anaerobic capacity.

The test procedure for the 28-m 30–15 IFT can be found in Chapter 5.3.

Speed and acceleration

Rationale

Basketball players perform between 45 and 85 sprints per match (Stojanović et al., 2018), with an average sprint duration of 1.7–2.43 s (Ben Abdelkrim et al., 2010; Delextrat et al., 2015). These durations are too short to allow the development of maximal velocity; therefore, acceleration is more important in basketball.

Test procedures for the 10-m sprint

- Players adopt a two-point stance with feet staggered 0.50 m back from the first timing gate;
- When ready, they self-govern the initiation of the test (no rearward preparatory action permitted);
- They sprint through the second timing gates;
- The best of three attempts is recorded (60 s rest in between);
- An additional light gate could be used for the 5-m split time.

Pre-planned and reactive agility

The frequent change in activity type during basketball matches suggests the importance of assessing players' agility. Agility performance has been correlated to high-intensity shuffling distance during basketball matches ($r = -0.68$; ben Abdelkrim et al., 2010). Agility tests are commonly separated into two categories: pre-planned agility (i.e., no reliance on external stimulus) and reactive agility (i.e., in response to an external stimulus). The type of stimulus used must be representative of those experienced within a game-based environment.

Test procedure for the 505 planned agility test

- Players adopt a two-point stance at the start line;
- They accelerate 10 m through the timing gates and then continue sprinting for a further 5 m before touching the line with their foot, turning 180 degrees, and sprinting back through the timing gates;

- Three trials are completed with a left foot turn and three trials with a right foot turn (2-min rest in between);
- The times for each limb are averaged for comparison;
- High-speed video capture can help analyse the kinematics of the player's COD ability (lower limb joint angles, trunk positioning);
- A COD speed deficit is calculated as the difference between the 505 and 10-m times (Nimphius et al., 2016);
- Good reliability is reported for this test (CV: 5.5%, Stojanović et al., 2019).

Procedure for the Y-shaped reactive agility test
- Players adopt a two-point stance at the start line;
- They accelerate for 5 m through the first set of timing gates;
- Then they perform a 45-degree COD in response to a visual signal coming from either finish line and sprint another 5 m to go through the timing gates at the finish line;
- The visual signal can be either automatically triggered by some reactive light gates when the player reaches the first 5 m, or it could be manually managed by coaches standing behind the two finish lines.

Reliability

Very good reliability data are published for the automatic version of this test (CV: 2.7%–3.3%, Oliver et al., 2009).

Upper body strength

Rationale

Basketball players require good upper body strength because of the numerous contacts between players in the key area (in particular, forwards) to perform screens and large passes across the court (guards). Match analyses show up to 200 upper body actions that can take up to 7.1% of match live time (Delextrat et al., 2015; Stojanović et al., 2019). The use of the multijoint measures described here for pushing and pulling actions provides a practical means for assessing upper limb strength capabilities. Further details can be found in Chapter 3.9.

Feedback and monitoring

Table 5.5.1 shows comparative data for the national squad standard in most of the tests described earlier to provide practitioners with support for feedback and monitoring. There are differing constraints in international windows compared to that of domestic league clubs which influence the battery of tests administered. The limited time allocated to assess players upon arrival to an international training camp dictates a prudent approach to test selection. For example, in elite female basketball players, change of direction ability has been found to be significantly correlated with eccentric strength, highlighting that in a camp setting, the use of

Table 5.5.1 Basketball testing standards

	Women	Men
Body mass (kg)	79.7 ±11.3	98.6 ± 11.4
Jump		
Concentric mean force (N)		
Guard	1280 ± 106	1842 ± 47
Forward	1587 ± 143	1924 ± 216
Squad mean	1410 ± 199	1930 ± 170
Concentric peak velocity (m·s^{-1})		
Guard	2.49 ± 0.06	2.68 ± 0.07
Forward	2.29 ± 0.15	2.86 ± 0.38
Squad mean	2.42 ± 0.17	2.87 ± 0.31
Landing impulse (N·s)		
Guard	90.7 ± 20.9	145.6 ± 38.4
Forward	137.3 ± 30.2	141 ± 28.3
Squad mean	114.4 ± 34.4	137.5 ± 30.8
Jump height relative peak landing force (N·cm^{-1})		
Guard	84.52 ± 16.05	100.08 ± 26.72
Forward	142.91 ± 23.21	107.12 ± 33.46
Squad mean	113.71 ± 35.36	104.77 ± 31.55
30–15		
Squad mean	18.2 ± 1.1	20.6 ± 0.7
Guards	19 (range 18–20)	21 (range 19–21)
Forwards	18 (range 17–18.5)	20 (range 20–21.5)
505 agility		
Elite male U18	-	2.42 (range 2.11–2.67)
Upper body atrength		
Bench press 1RM (per kg of body mass)	0.77 [range: 0.6–1.0]	0.94 (range 0.51–1.43)
Bench pull 1RM (per kg of body mass)	0.62 [range 0.5–0.7]	0.98 (range 0.71–1.36)

portable force platforms to capture eccentric force data might provide a time-efficient means to measure related qualities. In contrast, with the longer preparatory time available, within club environments, scheduling of physical performance testing and screening can be more elaborate and measure physical qualities more specifically.

Further, within international windows, data capture must be time-efficient, with results analysed and actionable within a 24-h period. The emphasis is on maintaining player health and availability for the squad practices in contrast to the club environment, where time available in the preparatory phases may provide opportunities for performance enhancement of physical outputs. Similarly, the physical preparation of players in international camps will likely adopt a *microdosing* strategy compared to the club-based training configuration, with the former being programmed from the data captured from the players upon arrival to the training camp.

References

Ben Abdelkrim, N. B., Castagna, C., El Fazaa, S. and El Ati, J. (2010). The effect of players' standard and tactical strategy on game demands in men's basketball. *Journal of Strength and Conditioning Research*, 24(10), 2652–2662.

Dallinga, J. M., Benjaminse, A. and Lemmink, K. A. (2012). Which screening tools can predict injury to the lower extremities in team sports?: A systematic review. *Sports Medicine*, 42(9), 791–815.

Delextrat, A., Badiella, A., Saavedra, V., Matthew, D., Schelling, X. and Torres-Ronda, L. (2015). Match activity demands of elite Spanish female basketball players by playing position. *International Journal of Performance Analysis in Sport*, 15(2), 687–703.

Heishman, A. D., Daub, B. D., Miller, R. M., Freitas, E. D. S., Frantz, B. A. and Bemben, M. G. (2020). Countermovement jump reliability performed with and without an arm swing in NCAA division 1 intercollegiate basketball players. *Journal of Strength and Conditioning Research*, 34(2), 546–558.

Nimphius, S., Callaghan, S. J., Spiteri, T. and Lockie, R. G. (2016). Change of direction deficit: A more isolated measure of change of direction performance than total 505 time. *Journal of Strength and Conditioning Research*, 30(11), 3024–3032.

Oliver, J. L. and Meyers, R. W. (2009). Reliability and generality of measures of acceleration, planned agility, and reactive agility. *International Journal of Sports Physiology and Performance*, 4(3), 345–354.

Stojanović, E., Aksović, N., Stojiljković, N., Stanković, R., Scanlan, A. T. and Milanović, Z. (2019). Reliability, usefulness, and factorial validity of change-of-direction speed tests in adolescent basketball players. *Journal of Strength and Conditioning Research*, 33(11), 3162–3173.

Stojanović, E., Stojiljković, N., Scanlan, A. T., Dalbo, V. J., Berkelmans, D. M. and Milanović, Z. (2018). The activity demands and physiological responses encountered during basketball match-play: A systematic review. *Sports Medicine*, 48(1), 111–135.

Part VI
Racket sports

6.1 Squash

Carl James, Timothy Jones, and Olivier Girard

Physical demands

Squash is a skill sport that challenges upper and lower body musculature as players perform repeated high-intensity movements and powerful shots. Matches are played over the best of five games, which commonly last ~10 min, separated by 2 min. Therefore, typical match duration is ~45 min, but can extend to 2 h. Rally duration is highly variable, with the mean around ~15–20 s. Time between points is short, providing an effective playing time of 50%–70% (work:rest ~1:1). During matches players perform hundreds of multidirectional accelerations, decelerations and changes of direction across short distances (3–6 m). As neuromuscular fatigue (strength loss) develops, impairments to performance manifest through altered on-court movements (i.e., reduced speed, incorrect positioning to the ball) and mistimed shots (i.e., power and precision). The concurrent locomotive and shot-playing demands elicit a mean exercise intensity of 86% of maximum oxygen uptake ($\dot{V}O_2$max) and 80%–90% of maximum heart rate (HR) (Girard et al., 2007; James et al., 2021), demonstrating considerable aerobic energy provision. However, as 25% of match duration may exceed 90% of $\dot{V}O_2$max and mean blood lactate concentration ranges between 6 and 10 mM·L^{-1} (Girard et al., 2007), matches also require significant anaerobic energy contribution.

Physical characteristics

Elite players demonstrate a range of well-developed physical attributes. Higher and lower performing players may be differentiated by both performance and submaximal physiology (e.g., lap at 4 mM·L^{-1}) on a squash-specific fitness test (author's unpublished observations). While $\dot{V}O_2$max does not differentiate between the standard of players, those possessing higher values (typically >50 and 60 ml·kg^{-1}·min^{-1} in females and males, respectively) will recover faster between rallies. Positive associations between playing standard and both repeated sprint ability (RSA) and change of direction (COD) speed reinforce the importance of integrated anaerobic energy provision and strength qualities (e.g., stretch-shortening cycle ability) (Wilkinson et al., 2012). Body composition (i.e., reduced

DOI: 10.4324/9781003045281-42

fat mass and elevated lean mass), measures of cardiovascular fitness, RSA and COD all demonstrate strong associations with player ranking and may be considered *gold* qualities for testing and training (Figure 6.1.1). Lower body strength qualities, including reactive strength index (RSI) and countermovement jump height (CMJ), demonstrate some discriminant ability across playing standards in squash and thus complement the *gold* qualities. However, the range of values currently reported for these assessments is large, hindering specific inferences of their

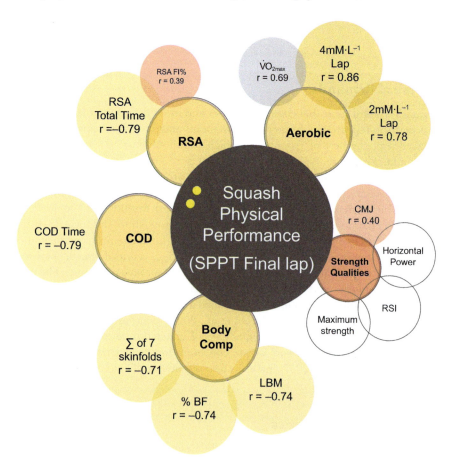

Figure 6.1.1 Gold, silver and bronze physical qualities for squash performance profiling. Correlations (Pearson's r) are shown between physical attributes and performance on the squash-specific physical performance test (SPPT) (James et al., 2019). Correlations are derived from author's unpublished data from elite squash players. Colours indicate strength of correlation: gold = 'Very-large' (r = 0.70–0.89), silver = 'large' (r = 0.50–0.69), bronze = 'moderate' (r = 0.30–0.49) and no colour = 'unknown'.

Note: SPPT = squash-specific physical performance test, RSA = repeated sprint ability, FI% = fatigue index percent reduction, COD = change of direction speed, Body Comp = body composition, % BF = percent body fat, LBM = lean body mass, CMJ = countermovement jump, RSI = reactive strength index.

relative importance. Other strength qualities, including maximum strength, have not been investigated in elite squash players, but may be considered determinants of RSA and COD performances.

Specificity of testing

Given the specific movement patterns in squash, generic fitness tests provide limited information for assessing fitness and prescribing on-court training. Assessments of aerobic fitness, including graded exercise tests or field tests (e.g., 30–15/yo-yo test[s]), therefore predominantly inform off-court training prescription. Similarly, generic anaerobic assessments (e.g., Illinois agility test or 5–10 m sprints) do not discriminate across playing ability and hence lack construct validity. Changes in performance using generic tests provide less confidence that a player is 'fitter' for squash but may help to isolate specific physical qualities (e.g., linear acceleration). Consequently, squash-specific assessments are broadly recommended.

Several on-court aerobic tests have been developed, sharing common characteristics of an incremental, intermittent activity profile and repeated COD. Some tests offer greater squash specificity by including technical requirements, such as specific footwork patterns, reactive cues and/or shot-playing actions. Despite higher construct validity, tests with technical requirements hinder the isolation of specific physiological qualities. Tests without technical requirements but containing an intermittent activity profile and repeated on-court COD therefore allow greater interpretation of specific physiological qualities. Tests containing racquet strokes, reactive movements and squash footwork requirements appear useful for practitioners when only a performance assessment is wanted. When both performance and physiological monitoring are required, a less specific on-court test that enables the measurement of both submaximal and maximal physiology is more suitable. Moreover, test structures permitting blood lactate sampling (i.e., longer stages and rest durations) provide a practical alternative to cardiorespiratory gas analysis for *in-season* submaximal monitoring. The ability to assess both submaximal and maximal physiological markers also helps with test interpretation and facilitates individualised training prescription. This reflects that changes in test performance may arise due to different physiological adaptations, such as changes in the lactate turnpoint, movement economy or $\dot{V}O_2$max. Practitioners should identify fitness testing objectives, as different tests may be more advantageous at different times of the year. Therefore, the variety of available tests is considered complementary, rather than dichotomous.

Procedures

Gold: squash-specific physical performance test

The SPPT involves repeated incremental shuttle runs with accompanying audio beeps until volitional exhaustion, providing a standalone test score (finishing lap). Lap numbers corresponding to 2 and 4 mM·L^{-1} are identified from the polynomial regression equation for blood lactate versus lap number. A portable metabolic cart is used for $\dot{V}O_2$max and submaximal oxygen consumption measurements (average across the first four stages). The finishing lap is therefore supplemented by the following aerobic fitness markers:

- 2 and 4 mM·L^{-1} laps;
- $\dot{V}O_2$max;
- Submaximal oxygen consumption;
- Maximum HR;
- On-court HR training zones.

Gold: squash-specific change of direction speed and repeated sprint ability

For COD, players undertake three attempts of the course in Figure 6.1.2 (Panel B), each separated by 3-min rest (Wilkinson et al., 2012). RSA is assessed using the same layout, but requires two laps for each repetition, across ten repetitions, with 20 s rest between (Willkinson et al., 2010). Total time to complete ten repetitions is recorded and a fatigue index (percentage reduction) calculated by dividing the total time by 'ideal time' (total number of sprints × fastest repetition).

Gold: body composition

A seven-site skinfold assessment is undertaken by a trained practitioner (i.e., International Society for the Advancement of Kinanthropometry [ISAK] certified) across the biceps, triceps, sub-scapular, suprailiac, mid-thigh, proximal calf and medial calf. Derivative calculations are made for the sum of seven skinfolds, body fat percentage and lean body mass. For more details refer to Chapter 3.4.

Maximum leg strength (back squat)

Maximum strength is assessed using a 1-repetition maximum (1RM) test (McGuigan, 2016). Where lifting maximal loads is inappropriate, 3RM or 5RM can predict the 1RM, corresponding to 90% and 85% of 1RM, respectively. Scores are expressed relative to body mass, reflecting the weight-bearing nature of squash and enabling comparisons between players.

Countermovement jump

Force production is assessed via a CMJ using a force platform or jump mat. Jumps are executed with hands on hips. Players squat to approximately 90 degrees before jumping vertically and landing in the same place. Jump height is calculated as:

$$\text{Height (cm)} = [(\text{flight time})^2 \times \text{acceleration due to gravity}/8] \times 100$$

Practitioners may also consider assessments of horizontal force production for squash players, such as the standing broad jump, although no empirical evidence is currently available on this quality within squash.

Reactive strength index

The highest jump height is identified through single reactive jumps using boxes of progressively greater heights, starting from 30 cm, in 15-cm increments. Players step off the box and upon landing, immediately jump as high and fast as possible. The test ends when ground contact time is >0.25 s or jump height decreases, with RSI calculated as:

$$RSI = jump\ height\ (cm)/ground\ contact\ time\ (s)$$

Interpretation of data

The assessments described enable individual squash-specific physical profiles to be developed. This creates a greater understanding of how a player's physical attributes relate to the physical demands of squash. An example is shown in Figure 6.1.3, where a player displays a low SPPT score. The SPPT score is a global indicator of squash physical performance, with the final lap representing a composite speed of metabolic conditioning, movement qualities and neuromuscular

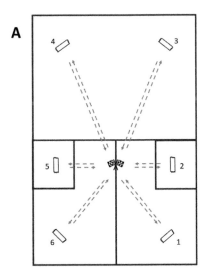
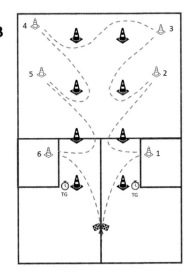

Figure 6.1.2 Overview of the squash-specific aerobic fitness test (SPPT – Panel A) and squash-specific repeated sprint ability (RSA) and change of direction speed (COD) tests (both Panel B). Numbers and arrows indicate running direction.

Source: Panel A (James et al., 2019) and Panel B (Wilkinson et al., 2009 and 2010).

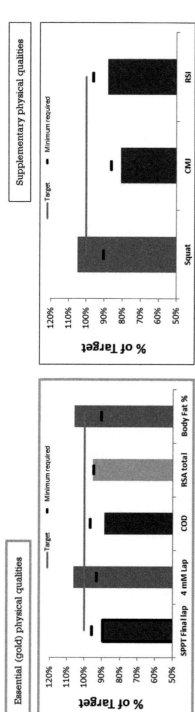

Figure 6.1.3 Example of squash-specific physical profile. Test performances are displayed as percentages of an ideal performance (target) and minimum required level for respective player categories (senior and junior, male and female). Traffic light colour-coding indicates performance relative to targets and minimum required levels. Example normative data are provided for each test, although practitioners are encouraged to establish their own norms and reliability of testing protocols to identify appropriate targets for their own cohort.

properties. In Figure 6.1.3, cardiovascular fitness (i.e., 4 mM·L^{-1} lap) exceeds the target level, but COD, CMJ and RSI are below the minimum required level. Interventions targeting strength qualities, including plyometrics, combined with speed and agility training are therefore relevant for improving the SPPT score. On-court 'feeding' sessions will complement COD development due to the considerable number of specific high-intensity accelerations and decelerations. In Figure 6.1.3, players who meet COD and RSA targets but not 4 mM·L^{-1} lap may utilise generic off-court training interventions (i.e., interval training) but may also benefit from on-court 'group' or 'ghosting' sessions prescribed from the STTP to achieve specific cardiovascular stimuli.

Summary

Squash elicits unique physical demands, such that sport-specific assessments are recommended. Practitioners should identify the purpose of fitness testing to select the most relevant test. A proposed framework is presented in this chapter, which supports individualised training of relevant physical attributes.

References

Girard, O., Chevalier, R., Habrard, M., Sciberras, P., Hot, P. and Millet, G. P. (2007). Game analysis and energy requirements of elite squash. *Journal of Strength and Conditioning Research*, 21(3), 909–914. https://doi.org/10.1519/R-20306.1

James, C., Dhawan, A., Jones, T. and Girard, O. (2021). Quantifying training demands of a 2-wk in-season squash microcycle. *Int J Sports Physiol Perform*, in press.

James, C., Tenllado-Vallejo, F., Kantebeen, M. and Farra, S. (2019). Validity and reliability of an on-court fitness test for assessing and monitoring aerobic fitness in squash. *Journal of Strength and Conditioning Research*, 33(5), 1400–1407. https://doi.org/10.1519/JSC.0000000000002465

McGuigan, M. R. (2016). Administration, scoring, and interpretation of selected tests. In G. G. Haff and N. T. Triplett (eds.), *Essentials of Strength Training and Conditioning* (4th ed.). Champaign, IL: Human Kinetics.

Wilkinson, M., Cooke, M., Murray, S., Thompson, K. G., St Clair Gibson, A. and Winter, E. M. (2012). Physiological correlates of multiple-sprint ability and performance in international-standard squash players. *Journal of Strength and Conditioning Research/National Strength and Conditioning Association*, 26(2), 540–547. https://doi.org/10.1519/JSC.0b013e318220ddbb

Wilkinson, M., Leedale-Brown, D. and Winter, E. M. (2009). Validity of a squash-specific test of change-of-direction speed. *International Journal of Sports Physiology and Performance*, (4), 176–185.

Willkinson, M., McCord, A. and Winter, E. M. (2010). Validity of a squash-specific test of multiple sprint ability. *Journal of Strength and Conditioning Research*, 24(12), 3381–3386.

6.2 Table tennis

Terun Desai, Goran Munivrana, and Irene R. Faber

Characteristics and physiological demands of table tennis

Table tennis is one of the fastest ball sports, requiring athletes to possess multidimensional fitness components. International competitions can last up to 7 days, with athletes competing in various formats (group stage followed by knockout rounds or straight knockout), in singles and/or doubles events. Athletes may be required to compete in numerous matches in a day, throughout successive days of competition. Recovery time between competitions is limited; therefore, athletes are required to be highly conditioned aerobically to facilitate recovery, minimise injury risk and crucially maintain high performance levels (Zagatto et al., 2018).

Table tennis is an intermittent sport requiring explosive high-intensity efforts involving the upper and lower body, interspersed with short rest periods (Zagatto et al., 2018). The temporal characteristics of the sport, particularly the low effort to rest ratio (Table 6.2.1), influence metabolic demands whereby the anaerobic alactic system (2.5%) is mainly utilised during repeated high-intensity efforts (anaerobic system contributes 1%), and the aerobic system (96.5%) is used during rest periods to restore phosphocreatine levels (Zagatto et al., 2018). Hence, athletes will benefit from conditioning aerobic and anaerobic alactic energy systems. The decisive moments in matches are determined by actions during rallies which can be played at higher intensities by training the anaerobic energy systems, conferring performance advantages. Since the aerobic and alactic anaerobic systems are mainly utilised, lactate levels remain low (1.8–2.2 mmol·L^{-1}) despite heart rates (162–172 beats·min^{-1}) reaching ~81% of HR$_{max}$ during matches (Zagatto et al., 2018) in elite men's competitions. Further data are required for female athletes.

In addition to conditioning energy systems, other physiological/fitness components are important in table tennis, including intermittent endurance capacity, speed and agility, explosive power, quickness of actions and functional mobility and stability. These characteristics are considered essential to optimise competitive performance and perseverance with training programmes.

DOI: 10.4324/9781003045281-43

Table 6.2.1 Average temporal characteristics of table tennis matches (men's singles, best of seven games)

Characteristic	Average
Total match duration (min)	24
Rally duration(s)	3.5
Total playing time (min)	6
Rest time between rallies (s)	8.2
Effort to rest ratio	0.43
Effective playing time (%)	23.5
Number of shots per rally	4
Rate of shots (shots/s)	1.12

Source: (Zagatto et al., 2016).

Lab-based tests

General assessment

Anthropometry and body composition (stature, body mass and sum of eight skinfolds, see Chapter 3.4), lung function (see Chapter 3.3) and flexibility (see Chapter 3.5) should be assessed according to relevant BASES guidelines.

Aerobic capacity

Normative maximal oxygen uptake values are provided in Table 6.2.2. Average oxygen uptake during men's singles match play ranges between 26 and 33 ml·kg·min^{-1} (58%–74% $\dot{V}O_2$max) (Zagatto et al., 2016). Aerobic capacity can be determined on a treadmill according to guidelines outlined in Chapter 11.3, which increases both speed and gradient. To better simulate sporting demands, a table tennis–specific graded exercise test may be used if required equipment is available (Zagatto et al., 2016). Athletes perform only forehand offensive strokes against a ball throwing machine used as an ergometer. Ball speed (~35 km·h^{-1}) and lateral ball oscillation are kept constant. The machine alternately shoots balls to two points on the table (30–40 cm either side of the table centre line, so that the ball contacts the table 50–60 cm from the net) simulating an opponent's shot. The frequency of ball deliveries by the machine (ball/min) determines exercise intensity. Typically, initial intensity is 30 balls·min^{-1} with increments of 3–4 balls·min^{-1} every 2 min until volitional exhaustion.

Alactic anaerobic performance

This repeated sprint test has been adapted from the original Wingate test to simulate the effort:rest ratio and intermittent nature of table tennis. Athletes should warm up for 5 min on a cycle ergometer against a resistance equivalent to 1%

body weight. Athletes should cycle maximally for 7 s followed by 16 s rest repeated ten times to reflect the duration of one game. Recommended resistances are 8% (males) and 6% (females) body weight. Peak power (W, W·kg^{-1}) and percentage decrement (%) across ten sprints can be calculated:

$$Decrement\% = \left(1 - \frac{(\Sigma Peak\ Power\ of\ all\ Sprints)}{Best\ Sprint\ Peak\ Power \times No.\ of\ Sprints}\right) \times 100$$

Field-based tests

These tests are based on physiological/fitness components that determine performance in elite table tennis. Only reliable tests with high practical feasibility are selected. Athletes need to warm up before tests are administered.

Intermittent endurance capacity

The *interval shuttle run test* measures intermittent endurance capacity of athletes and can be administered to groups of athletes in ~20 min. Athletes are instructed to run back and forth as many times as possible on a 20-m course with pylons set 3 m before the turning lines (Figure 6.2.1). Running speed is indicated by pre-recorded sound signals ('beep'), starting at 10 km·h^{-1} and increasing 1 km·h^{-1} every 90 s or starting at 13 km·h^{-1} and increasing 0.5 km·h^{-1}. Each 90-s period is divided into two 45-s periods in which athletes run for 30 s and walk 15 s. Different sound signals indicate running and walking periods. During walking, athletes need to walk back and forth to the 8-m line. The number of fully completed 20-m runs is recorded as the final score (Lemmink et al., 2004).

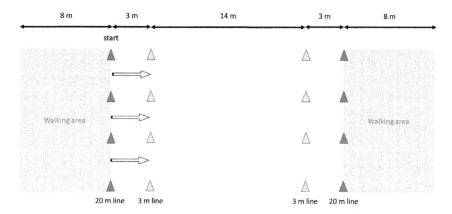

Figure 6.2.1 Interval shuttle run test course.

Speed and agility

The repeated sprint ability test can also be performed in the field (Chapman and Sheppard, 2011). Light gates should be set up 20 m apart. Athletes sprint between the light gates ten times with 20 s recovery between each sprint. Each sprint is timed to determine the percentage decrement; lower scores (<6%) indicate better anaerobic function.

$$Decrement\% = \left(1 - \frac{(\Sigma Sprints\ Times)}{Best\ Sprint\ Times \times No.\ of\ Sprints}\right) \times 100$$

The modified *Edgren side-step test* (Raya et al., 2013) measures lateral (left to right) movement ability, which is the most common table tennis footwork technique. The test assesses lateral speed, agility and body control. On a course of 4 m in length with four 10-m increments (Figure 6.2.2), athletes start on the far left cone and side-step to the right until their right foot crosses the outside cone/mark, then side-step to the left until their left foot crosses the left outside cone/mark, back and forth as rapidly as possible for 10 s. Athletes score 1 point per completion of each 1-m increment indicated by a cone/mark. Athletes score 0 if they always fail to keep their trunk and feet pointed forwards or cross their legs when side-stepping. The total score is calculated, and higher scores indicate improved performance.

Explosive power

Lower extremity power is assessed by the *standing broad jump*. Standing behind a line with the feet shoulder-width apart, the athlete jumps with both feet together as far forward as possible. Distance is measured (cm), and the best of two jumps taken as the final score. Upper extremity power is measured by throwing a table tennis ball as far as possible with their playing hand. Distance is measured (m) to where the ball first bounces. The best of three attempts is used as the final score (Faber et al., 2016).

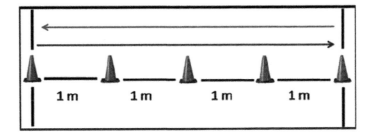

Figure 6.2.2 Modified Edgren side-step test set-up.
Source: From Raya et al. (2013)

Quickness of actions

Quickness of actions (QoA) refers to an athlete's speed of handling during games. Players need to quickly read and react to changes in play, and lateral footwork is critical for success; hence QoA is measured with sideways jumping. Athletes jump sideways over a wooden bench (60 × 4 × 2 cm) as many times as possible within 15 s. The number of correct jumps of two trials is summed for a final score (Kiphard and Schilling, 2007). Upper extremity QoA is measured by Faber's eye-hand coordination test. Athletes throw a ball to a vertically positioned table tennis table (1 m distance) with one hand and catch the ball with the other hand as frequently as possible in 30 s. The number of catches is counted, and the best of two attempts is used as a final score (Faber et al., 2016).

Functional mobility and stability

The Functional Movement Screen (FMS) assesses functional mobility and stability through seven movement patterns: deep squat, hurdle step, inline lunge, shoulder mobility, active straight-leg raise, trunk stability push-up and rotary stability (Teyhen et al., 2012). All movements are scored 0–3; higher scores indicate better performance. FMS can be used to screen for asymmetries and deficits and to monitor training programme effectiveness (Kraus et al., 2014). Also see Chapter 3.5.

Summary

The physiological and fitness components noted in this chapter should be trained throughout the season and tested at regular intervals (pre-season, mid-season and post-season) by coaches and scientists using either lab or field-based tests as described earlier, factoring the feasibility and practicality of performing each test.

Table 6.2.2 Normative values for elite table tennis athletes collated from published and unpublished data

	Male	Female
Body fat (%)	14.5	21.9
$\dot{V}O_2$max – treadmill (ml·kg·min^{-1})	43–48	
$\dot{V}O_2$max – table tennis protocol (ml·kg·min^{-1})	40–46	
Peak heart rate during treadmill GXT (beats·min^{-1})	192	
30-s Wingate – peak power (W·kg^{-1})	10.6	8.03
30-s Wingate – mean power (W·kg^{-1})	8.5	6.55
Intermittent shuttle run test (runs)	>116	
Edgren side-step test (score)	46–49	41–45
Standing broad jump (cm)	228	178
Jumping sideways (total jumps per 2 sets of 15 s)	98–114	
Faber's eye-hand coordination test (catches/30 s)	34–42	28–36
Functional Movement Screen (points)	>14*	>14*

* Score ≤14 indicates a higher risk for injuries.

References

Chapman, D. and Sheppard, J. (2011). Relibility and interpretation of a tennis specific repeated sprint protocol in elite athletes. *The Journal of Strength and Conditioning Research*, 25, S17–S18.

Faber, I. R., Elferink-Gemser, M. T., Faber, N. R., Oosterveld, F. G. and Nijhuis-Van der Sanden, M. W. (2016). Can perceptuo-motor skills assessment outcomes in young table tennis players (7–11 years) predict future competition participation and performance? An observational prospective study. *PLoS One*, 11(2), e0149037.

Kiphard, E. J. and Schilling, F. (2007). *Körperkoordinationstest für kinder: KTK*. Gottingen, Germany: Beltz-Test.

Kraus, K., Schütz, E., Taylor, W. R. and Doyscher, R. (2014). Efficacy of the functional movement screen: A review. *The Journal of Strength and Conditioning Research*, 28(12), 3571–3584.

Lemmink, K., Visscher, C., Lambert, M. I. and Lamberts, R. P. (2004). The interval shuttle run test for intermittent sport players: Evaluation of reliability. *Journal of Strength and Conditioning Research*, 18, 821–827.

Raya, M. A., Gailey, R. S., Gaunaurd, I. A., Jayne, D. M., Campbell, S. M., Gagne, E., Manrique, P. G., Muller, D. G. and Tucker, C. (2013). Comparison of three agility tests with male servicemembers: Edgren side step test, T-test, and Illinois agility test. *Journal of Rehabilitation Research and Development*, 50(7), 951–960.

Teyhen, D. S., Shaffer, S. W., Lorenson, C. L., Halfpap, J. P., Donofry, D. F., Walker, M. J., Dugan, J. L. and Childs, J. D. (2012). The functional movement screen: A reliability study. *Journal of Orthopaedic and Sports Physical Therapy*, 42(6), 530–540.

Zagatto, A. M., de Mello Leite, J. V., Papoti, M. and Beneke, R. (2016). Energetics of table tennis and table tennis: Specific exercise testing. *International Journal of Sports Physiology and Performance*, 11(8), 1012–1017.

Zagatto, A. M., Kondric, M., Knechtle, B., Nikolaidis, P. T. and Sperlich, B. (2018). Energetic demand and physical conditioning of table tennis players: A study review. *Journal of Sports Sciences*, 36(7), 724–731.

Part VII
Bat and ball sports

7.1 Cricket

Will Vickery and Jamie Tallent

The domestic and global cricket landscape has evolved rapidly over the last decade. During this time there has been a considerable growth in playing schedules due mostly to the increase in the number of limited overs matches. The more congested playing schedules have considerably modified the physical and physiological demands of cricket play (Scanlan et al., 2016; Vickery et al., 2018) and the incidence of injuries (Orchard et al., 2010). This increased playing schedule has coincided with an improvement in the economic fortunes of players, leading to a higher level of professionalism and allowing players to devote more time to improving all facets of their game, including physiological aspects.

To combat the evolving nature of cricket, there has been a significant increase in the knowledge available for practitioners regarding the demands of elite cricket, allowing for more format- and position-specific programming. Cricket-specific physical and physiological assessments have been created (or adapted from other sports) in recent times, with the intention of providing practitioners with information which can be used to inform physical preparation programmes, as well as highlight potential acute or chronic injury. The assessments detailed in this chapter are those which are commonly used by clubs from the English cricket county system. Table 7.1.1 provides the recommended standards for male and female elite cricketers for each test.

Table 7.1.1 Recommended standards for male and female elite cricketers

Test	Men	Women
Sum of 8 skinfolds	60 mm	75 mm
Isometric holds (prone, supine and lateral)	120 min (capped)	120 min (capped)
Isometric mid-thigh pull (including body weight)	4.5 (N/N)	3.7 (N/N)
Countermovement jump	45 cm	40 cm
10-m sprint	1.70 s	1.86 s
20-m sprint	2.90 s	3.20 s
40-m sprint	5.10 s	5.70 s
Run-2	5.85 s	6.40 s
2-km time trial	435 s	495 s

DOI: 10.4324/9781003045281-45

Skinfolds

Rationale

Cricketers spend large amounts of time on their feet during competition and practice. Consequently, optimal levels of body fat are essential for efficiency of movement and optimising performance.

Test procedure

For details see Chapter 3.4. The sum of eight sites (triceps, subscapular, biceps, iliac crest, supraspinale, abdominal, front thigh and medial calf) should be recorded.

Isometric holds (prone, supine and lateral)

Rationale

With the large amounts of torso rotational and bracing movements in bowling and batting, it is vital that cricketers have a strong trunk. There is evidence that stronger lower torso muscles are associated with a reduction in injury (Crewe et al., 2013).

Procedure

The isometric holds can be performed on a glute hamstring developer or adapted for a bench with another person holding the athlete's lower body to the bench. Athletes should start prone, supine or lateral with the waist on the end of the glute hamstring developer or bench. The objective for the athlete is to remain straight from the feet to head. The test ceases if the athlete fails to hold this position or reaches the 2-min time cap. One attempt should be performed when supine and prone followed by one each side.

Isometric mid-thigh pull

Rationale

As fast bowlers are exposed to seven times their body weight during the delivery stride of bowling (Worthington et al., 2013), it is essential that they can generate high amounts of force. Strength is also a key physical attribute in sprinting, which is important for both fast bowlers and batters.

Procedure

The isometric mid-thigh pull assesses an athlete's maximal strength. The test should be performed on a force platform that samples at >1000 Hz. The bar is fixed in the second pull clean position, with the knee and hip angles set between

125–145 degrees and 140–150 degrees, respectively. Athletes should use handwraps to ensure the test is not limited by grip strength. The warm-up should consist of multiple submaximal trials before the highest peak force of three maximal effort trials is taken. During the maximal trials, participants should pull as hard as they can until there is a drop in force (Joffe and Tallent, 2020).

Countermovement jump

Rationale

Cricketers are required to perform numerous explosive actions when fielding and batting. Jump height provides a good indication of the lower body explosive power of an athlete without needing access to a force plate.

Procedure

The countermovement jump can be performed on a force platform or a jump mat. Athletes should be instructed to jump as high as they can using a self-selected depth. The highest of three jumps should be recorded.

Sprints

Rationale

Cricket requires players to perform numerous sprints and have been recorded to reach speeds approaching 10 $m·s^{-1}$ during matches (Bliss et al., 2021). Consequently, it is vital that athletes are assessed for both shorter (10 m) and longer sprints (40 m).

Procedure

Sprints should be performed on a hard surface, such as an indoor track or cricket hall. Athletes will need to perform a dynamic warm-up consisting of progressive submaximal sprinting over 40 m. Athletes should rest for 3–5 min between sprints. A line 0.5 m behind the start line should be marked where athletes begin from a split-stance position. Timing gates should be set at 0, 10, 20, and 40 m, with the first gate placed 1 m above the ground and subsequent gates at 1.3 m. Three maximal 40-m sprints should be performed with the fastest time recorded.

Run-2 test

Rationale

It is vital that cricket players are agile and can perform 180-degree turns, particularly when running between the wickets whilst batting. In scoring a century, a

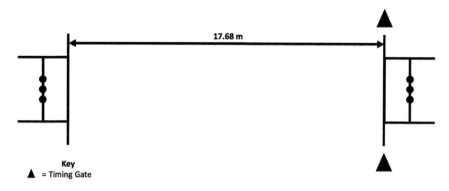

Figure 7.1.1 Set-up for the run-2 test.

batter will perform around 39 turns (Duffield and Drinkwater, 2008), making it essential that the athlete's speed and agility between the wickets are assessed.

Procedure

Figure 7.1.1 outlines the set-up for the run-2 test. The test should be preceded by a dynamic warm-up consisting of 180-degree turns to ensure the athletes are physically prepared. The test should ideally be performed in an indoor cricket hall where the dimensions of the wicket are already marked out. If an indoor cricket hall is unavailable, then two lines 17.68 m apart should be marked. Athletes should perform the run-2 with a cricket bat but without pads. The timing gate should be placed over the crease and set at 0.6 m above the ground. As per the sprint protocol set-up, a line 0.5 m behind the start line should be marked where athletes begin from a split-stance position. Athletes finish by running their bat through the original timing gates as they normally would for a run between the wickets. The fastest of three trials should be recorded.

2-km time trial

Rationale

Given the long duration of professional cricket matches and the need to quickly recover from high-intensity efforts that are interspersed throughout each inning, the 2-km time trial is commonly used as a measure of speed endurance. Additionally, this test can assist with the prescription of training intensity based on maximal aerobic speed (Bellenger et al., 2015).

Procedure

Players have one attempt to run 2 km in the fastest time possible, which can be timed using a stopwatch. It is not necessary for this to take place on an athletic running track, but all attempts should be made on the same track (e.g., exterior of the cricket field) if assessing several times during a season. If calculating maximal aerobic speed from the 2-km time trial results, the following formula can be used:

MAS = distance/time (sec)

Summary

As addressed earlier, these tests are commonly used by support staff (i.e., sport scientists) within the English county cricket system, alongside other training and development activities. It is important that all stakeholders (players, coaches and support staff) understand the relevance of these tests and their role in shaping a player's physical development programme. Not all players and coaches are familiar with this information, though, suggesting that support staff must consider the most appropriate strategies in which to communicate this information.

References

Bellenger, C. R., Fuller, J. T., Nelson, M. J., Hartland, M., Buckley, J. D. and Debenedictis, T. A. (2015). Predicting maximal aerobic speed through set distance time-trials. *European Journal of Applied Physiology*, 115(12), 2593–2598.

Bliss, A., Ahmun, R., Jowitt, H., Scott, P., Jones, T. W. and Tallent, J. (2021). Variability and physical demands of international seam bowlers in one-day and Twenty20 international matches across five years. *Journal of Science and Medicine in Sport*, 24(5), 505–510.

Crewe, H., Campbell, A., Elliott, B. and Alderson, J. (2013). Lumbo-pelvic biomechanics and quadratus lumborum asymmetry in cricket fast bowlers. *Medicine and Science in Sports and Exercise*, 45(4), 778–783.

Duffield, R. and Drinkwater, E. J. (2008). Time-motion analysis of test and one-day international cricket centuries. *Journal of Sports Sciences*, 26(5), 457–464.

Joffe, S. A. and Tallent, J. (2020). Neuromuscular predictors of competition performance in advanced international female weightlifters: A cross-sectional and longitudinal analysis. *Journal of Sports Sciences*, 38(9), 985–993.

Orchard, J., James, T., Kountouris, A. and Portus, M. (2010). Changes to injury profile (and recommended cricket injury definitions) based on the increased frequency of Twenty20 cricket matches. *Open Access Journal of Sports Medicine*, 1, 63–76.

Scanlan, A. T., Berkelmans, D. M., Vickery, W. M. and Kean, C. O. (2016). A review of the internal and external physiological demands associated with batting in cricket. *International Journal of Sports Physiology and Performance*, 11(8), 987–997.

Vickery, W., Dascombe, B. J. and Scanlan, A. T. (2018). A review of the physical and physiological demands associated with cricket fast and spin bowlers. *International Journal of Sports Science and Coaching*, 13(2), 290–301.

Worthington, P., King, M. and Ranson, C. (2013). The influence of cricket fast bowlers' front leg technique on peak ground reaction forces. *Journal of Sports Sciences*, 31(4), 434–441.

Part VIII
Target sports

8.1 Golf

Mark F. Smith

Golf, both as a recreational activity and high-performance sport, has received a growing level of scientific interest over the past decade (Elhert, 2020a; Murray et al., 2017; Smith, 2018, Toms, 2017). This came at a time when the concept of the athlete golfer gained momentum. Elite players looked to take advantage as both technology and course changes placed a heightened emphasis on a player's functional physical capabilities. With the scientific and coaching community seeing the inquiry into golf performance as a means of examining player movement dynamics (Sheehan et al., 2019), player screening (Wells and Langdown, 2020), enhancement strategies (Elhert, 2020a) and reducing injury incidences (Edwards et al., 2020), efficacious ways of transferring empirical research findings directly into lower on-course score still remain an elusive panacea.

Athlete golfer attributes

The focus on performance screening (assessment) and subsequent player development strategies has largely centred upon dynamic functional swing-related movements (Sheehan et al., 2019) and how these alter (impact) measurable performance outcomes (e.g., clubhead speed, ball displacement, injury reduction, movement [in]variability). The premise that optimised golf performance could be compromised by player physicality, affecting the attainment of required swing mechanics, has led to varying physical development strategies (Elhert, 2020a; Langdown et al., 2019). Genotypic attributes, such as maturational status (Coughlan et al., 2020), anatomical characteristics (e.g., limb length and limb symmetry) and stature (Keogh et al., 2012; Cole et al., 2016), in combination with physiological indices such as muscular activation patterns, muscle balance and symmetry, muscle fibre type, strength, flexibility, mobility, coordination, proprioception and somatotype (Elhert, 2020b; Horan, 2017; Smith, 2010, 2018), have all led to on-course performance assumptions and subsequent assessment screening practices.

Performance demands

Viewed holistically as a global activity of connected discrete kinetic-chain movements interspersed with low-intensity locomotive movements, the interrelationship

DOI: 10.4324/9781003045281-47

between energy system utilisation, thermoregulatory control and fluid balance management will further impact on the player's condition when performing movements throughout the course of play (Smith, 2018). Performing in a varied range of conditions will also contribute to altered physical status and further compromise swing dynamics. Environmental factors will have considerable impact on the golfer's status. Temperature, altitude and course topography will alter internal physical conditions, and the player must have the appropriate physical conditioning and on-course management strategies to ensure that any potential physical change is minimised and does not manifest in detrimental swing performance (Smith, 2010, 2018; Toms, 2017).

Application of assessment

By determining physical attributes of the athlete golfer, requirements of the activity and associated on-course physiological demands, a spectrum of primitive through to sophisticated self-assessment and practitioner-assisted tools have been developed, validated and used both in research and practice settings (Elhert, 2020a; Peng et al., 2021; Smith, 2010). The application of self-assessment tools, normally focused upon basic functional movement screening, provides a starting point for any player, in which basic screening procedures and techniques can be integrated into any development plan (Speariet and Armstrong, 2019; Smith, 2010; Wells and Langdown, 2020). Allowing for regular self-monitoring ensures continuous reflection and micro changes to any improvement plan. With comprehensive activities and resources available to player and coach (e.g., Titleist Performance Institute, PGA Coaching Performance manuals), self-evaluation packages provide the tools that allow the player to feel in control of their own development. However, the need for more scientifically rigorous and reliable screening practices across a wider range of physiological indices will provide both player and coach with more specific diagnostic performance tools.

As advocated within the applied literature, physical screening should be a player and practitioner's first strategy in developing any effective conditioning and improvement programme. Elite performers approach performance development from a multidisciplinary team perspective, assembling swing coaches, strengthening and conditioning specialists, physiotherapists and 'mind' coaches to assist the formation of a tailored plan. The amateur club player, however, relies solely on the club or local coach, with sport science knowledge acquired through their formal professional training programmes. Dependent on local expertise and facility, strength and conditioning coaches may also provide a level of service and support to complement coaching insight at elite amateur levels (Wells and Langdown, 2020). As outlined by Russell and Owies (2000) and Smith et al. (2011), a range of assessment approaches should be applied to effectively evaluate the player's strengths and weaknesses, establish baseline movement capabilities and provide the educational impetus for player improvement on- or off-course.

Practitioners and researchers alike have applied a wide range of testing protocols (Elhert, 2020a; Horan, 2017; Smith, 2010) to examine a broad range of physical performance domains among athletic golfers. Notwithstanding the importance of reliable and valid protocol use, most significant are their relevance to on-course performance. The range of physical assessments typically used is described in Table 8.1.1 and accounts for the major assessment types located with the literature and covered within these guidelines. Although not limited to these assessment approaches, the diversity of commonly selected methods is a consequence of resource availability, their global measure of physical function and wide accessibility to normal reference values (Elhert, 2020a; Horan, 2017; Smith, 2010). Given this, standard protocol administration should be followed by the physiologist or sport science practitioner working closely with the coach and player to determine the relevance of findings to on-course golf performance.

Table 8.1.1 Physiological assessments for golf

Physical Attribute	Assessment Method
Cardiorespiratory fitness	
Maximal oxygen uptake	Incremental exercise assessment (bicycle/treadmill)
	2-min step test
	One-mile walking test
Lung function (FVC, FEV, PEF)	Spirometry
Resting heart rate	Seated rest
Maximal heart rate	Incremental exercise assessment (bicycle/treadmill)
Anaerobic functioning	
Peak power output	Wingate 30-s sprint test
Functional strength	
Isolated single/multijoint strength	Isokinetic dynamometer
	Maximal repetition on static machines/free weights
Grip strength	Handgrip dynamometer
Functional power	
Upper limb dynamic power	Medicine ball throw
Lower limb dynamic power	Vertical jump/standing broad jump
	Countermovement jump
Flexibility/range of motion	
Functional range of motion	Flexibility machine (i.e., torso rotator)
	Goniometry assessment
Global flexibility (lower back/hamstrings)	Sit-and-reach test
Balance	Star excursion test
Postural stability	Stork test (bilateral balance with open/closed eye)
Neuromuscular movement control	3D motion analysis
	Electromyography
Anthropometry	
Physical dimensions	Length, breadth and girth measures
Body fat	Skinfold assessment (3/4/7 sites)
	Bioelectrical impedance
Somatotype	Heath-Carter assessment instrument

Holistic screening approach

Such consideration of physical screening type by both practitioner and player must be tightly coupled with on-course performance statistics. Data collection during play, whether practice or competition, offers a more holistic and evidence-based approach to any diagnostic assessment and follow-up screening activity (Brodie, 2014; Drappi and Co Ting Keh, 2019; Smith, 2018). By capturing shot patterns (i.e., shot distribution across a range of golf clubs and shot types) over a number of rounds, performance data provide an early insight into possible movement patterns and restrictions. Furthermore, such rich data can provide tangible illustrations demonstrating the effectiveness of any intervention that may precede screening practices. It has now become a rarity for elite players not to record and monitor their on-course performance, and with professional tournaments now measuring every shot as a matter of course, players have instant access to performance data (e.g., www.pgatour.com/stats.html). Such information is commonplace in the coaches' armoury too, and with the mainstream use of ball flight monitoring devices (e.g., Trackman Launch Monitor) found at most golf clubs and fitting centres, the application of player assessment is now becoming a mainstay of performance analysis. The inter-disciplinary nature of athlete golf assessment offers the performer access to practitioners who understand the connection between biomechanic principles of the golf swing through to the application on-course.

Practical considerations

An increasing body of evidence supports the role of assessment screening within golf, offering an understanding and means to determine dynamic activation patterns during the swing through to on-course performance (Elhert, 2020a; Horan, 2017). The impact of this has advanced our approaches to measurement, analysis and evaluation of the athlete golfer. Performance assessment and analysis now feature highly in any coach's, player's or sport scientist's armoury, and it is uncommon to see a practitioner not including screening and physical assessment into their performance development programmes. Player profiling through comprehensive on-course and off-course screening allows for specific conditioning programmes to be developed. Monitoring player development through continual assessment of training and associated adaptive response provides an indication of key physical factors that may impact most on performance success (Smith, 2010, 2018). To establish an inter-disciplinary physiological support system that truly pushes the limits of performance, a formal systematic process of data gathering, player screening, player profiling, training implementation and long-term development planning must occur.

Further considerations

It must be recognised that the majority of evidence pertaining to the demands, requirements and assessment profiling of the athlete golfer is gained from homogenous subsets (i.e., typically low-handicap males). Further applied evidence is required on the physical and performance outcomes of women, junior, the ageing golfer and disability groups. It should not be assumed that research findings, associated performance models and practical applications apply to all, and therefore caution must be taken when translating and applying evidence to specific performance groups.

References

Brodie, M. (2014). *Every Shot Counts: Using Revolutionary Strokes Gained Approach to Improve Your Golf*. New York, NY, USA: Penguin Random House; Illustrated edition.

Cole, M. H. and Grimshaw, P. N. (2016). The biomechanics of the modern golf swing: Implications for lower back injuries. *Sports Medicine*, 46(3), 339–351.

Coughlan, D., Taylor, M. J., Wayland, W., Brooks, D. and Jackson, J. (2020). The effect of a 12-week strength and conditioning programme on youth golf performance. *International Journal of Golf Science*, 8(1).

Drappi, C. and Co Ting Keh, L. (2019). Predicting golf scores at the shot level. *Journal of Sports Analytics*, 5(2), 65–73.

Edwards, N., Dickin, C. and Wang, H. (2020). Low back pain and golf: A review of biomechanical risk factors. *Sports Medicine and Health Science*, 2(1), 10–18.

Ehlert, A. (2020a). The effects of strength and conditioning interventions on golf performance: A systematic review. *Journal of Sports Sciences*, 38(23), 2720–2731.

Ehlert, A. (2020b). The correlations between physical attributes and golf clubhead speed: A systematic review with quantitative analyses. *European Journal of Sport Science*, 1–13.

Horan, S. A. (2017). Physiological and musculoskeletal characteristics of the modern golfer. In *Routledge International Handbook of Golf Science*. London: Routledge.

Keogh, J. W. and Hume, P. A. (2012). Evidence for biomechanics and motor learning research improving golf performance. *Sports Biomechanics*, 11(2), 288–309.

Langdown, B. L., Wells, J. E., Graham, S. and Bridge, M. W. (2019). Acute effects of different warm-up protocols on highly skilled golfers' drive performance. *Journal of Sports Sciences*, 37(6), 656–664.

Murray, A. D., Daines, L., Archibald, D., Hawkes, R. A., Schiphorst, C., Kelly, P., Grant, L. and Mutrie, N. (2017). The relationships between golf and health: A scoping review. *British Journal of Sports Medicine*, 51(1), 12–19.

Peng, Y. C., Hsu, C. Y. and Tang, W. T. (2021). Deficits in the star excursion balance test and golf performance in elite golfers with chronic low back pain. *Journal of Sports Science and Medicine*, 20(2), 229–236.

Russell, A. and Owies, D. (2000). Protocols for the physiological assessment of golfers. In C. J. Gore (ed.), *Physiological Tests for Elite Athletes: Australian Sports Commission*, pp. 278–285. Champaign, IL: Human Kinetics.

Sheehan, W. B., Watsford, M. L. and Pickering Rodriguez, E. C. (2019). Examination of the neuromechanical factors contributing to golf swing performance. *Journal of Sports Sciences*, 37(4), 458–466.

Smith, C. J., Callister, R. and Lubans, D. R. (2011). A systematic review of strength and conditioning programmes designed to improve fitness characteristics in golfers. *Journal of Sports Sciences*, 29(9), 933–943.

Smith, M. F. (2010). The role of physiology in the development of golf performance. *Sports Medicine*, 40(8), 635–655.

Smith, M. F. (2018). *Golf Science: Optimum Performance from Tee to Green*. Brighton, UK: Ivy Press.

Speariett, S. and Armstrong, R. (2019). The relationship between the golf-specific movement screen and golf performance. *Journal of Sport Rehabilitation*, 29(4), 425–435.

Toms, M. (ed.). (2017). *Routledge International Handbook of Golf Science*. Abingdon, UK: Routledge.

Wells, J. E. and Langdown, B. L. (2020). Sports science for golf: A survey of high-skilled golfers' 'perceptions' and 'practices'. *Journal of Sports Sciences*, 38(8), 918–927.

8.2 Curling

David Leith, Helen M. Collins, and Audrey Duncan

Curling is a winter sport traditionally played by two teams of four players on an ice sheet ~42 m long (Olympic men's and women's format). Players take it in turn to deliver two granite stones, weighing ~18.6 kg, towards the target 'house' area of four concentric circles. The curl and distance the stone travels can be influenced by sweeping the ice in front of the stone, changing the stone-ice friction and thereby the path of the stone. Points are scored for the stones lying closest to the house centre at the conclusion of each end (16 stones). The team with the most points at the end of the game, usually ten ends, wins. Games can last up to 3 h, and at the Olympic/World level it can take up to 15 games (2 games/day) to conclude. This makes curling one of the longest-duration Olympic events.

Reflecting this long duration of competitive matches, endurance is required to minimise the effects of fatigue on performance. Strength, balance and flexibility are also fundamental to the key movement patterns involved in sweeping and stone delivery, as well as for injury prevention. An appropriate test battery should be designed with these factors in mind.

Anthropometry

Standard tests of anthropometry (stature, body mass, sum of skinfolds) are recommended to be undertaken in accordance with BASES guidelines (see Chapter 3.4), with target values developed to reflect the performance and health needs of the individual.

Energy systems

While sweep durations are typically short (6 s average, 24 s maximum), they are repeated (averaging 32 per game) and game duration is long (2–3 h) (British Curling, internal data). As such, a high aerobic capacity is recommended to enhance the ability to recover between maximal and submaximal efforts to offset fatigue and to sustain consistent performance across consecutive games.

An on-ice curling-specific repeated sweep test has been developed (8 × 20 s, 40 s recovery), but due to the requirement for a specialist sweep ergometer to undertake this, a standard laboratory-based $\dot{V}O_2$max test and/or field test of aerobic fitness is recommended and demonstrates strong correlation with the sweep

DOI: 10.4324/9781003045281-48

performance fatigue index (r = −0.98, British Curling, internal data). For practical reasons, British Curling currently utilise a Cooper 12-min walk-run test and/or 2-km timed row. Reference values for all tests are shown in Table 8.2.1.

Flexibility

To maximise accuracy and speed of stone delivery, a low extended lunge position is employed. Stable range of motion (ROM) at the hip is therefore key. While a rounded physiotherapist-led assessment of static and dynamic flexibility would be recommended, the following tests are advised for performance purposes (see Table 8.2.2 for scoring).

Modified Thomas test (Figure 8.2.1A), which assesses flexibility of the hip flexors:

- The athlete sits on the end of a plinth before rolling back to supine, pulling both knees into the chest, ensuring a flat lumbar spine and posteriorly rotated pelvis;
- Holding the contralateral hip in maximal flexion, the test limb is lowered towards the floor;
- Hip flexion, knee flexion and hip abduction angles are measured reflecting iliopsoas, quadriceps and tensor fascia lata/iliotibial band length, respectively.

Table 8.2.1 Normative test data provided courtesy of British Curling. For single-leg squat scoring, refer to McKeown et al. (2014).

	Podium Performance		High Performing		Development Level		Foundation Level	
	Male	Female	Male	Female	Male	Female	Male	Female
2-km row (min)	< 7:05	< 7:50	7:05–7:19	7:50–8:09	7:20–7:40	8:10–8:30	>7:40	> 8:30
Cooper 12-min (km)	>3.0	>2.7	2.7–3.0	2.5–2.7	2.3–2.6	2.1–2.4	<2.3	<2.1
Relative strength: back squat (× body weight)	>1.8	>1.6	1.7–1.8	1.5–1.6	1.5–1.6	1.2–1.4	<1.5	<1.2
Relative strength: bench press (× body weight)	>1.5	>1	1.4–1.5	0.9–1.0	1.2–1.3	0.8–0.9	<1.2	<0.8
Single-leg squat (score)	18		15–17		12–14		<12	
Prone hold (min)	>3:00		2:30–3:00		2:00–2:29		<2:00	
Broad jump (cm)	>270	>220	260–270	205–220	240–255	180–200	<240	<180

Table 8.2.2 Scoring data provided courtesy of British Curling

	Green	Amber	Red
Modified Thomas test			
Hip flexion (degrees)	>10	0–10	<0
Knee flexion (degrees)	>95	90–95	<90
Hip abduction (lateral deviation)	No deviation from midline	Deviation from midline can be corrected	Deviation from midline restricted
FABER test	<23 cm and minimal difference between left and right	23–26 cm and/or >4 cm difference between left and right	>27 cm and/or >6 cm difference between left and right

FABER Test (Figure 8.2.1B), which assesses multidirectional hip ROM:

- With the athlete supine, the lateral ankle is rested on the contralateral thigh, proximal to the knee, in a figure-4 position;
- Stabilising the contralateral anterior superior iliac spine, light overpressure is applied to the ipsilateral medial knee until end ROM is met;
- The perpendicular distance from the lateral femoral epicondyle to the table is measured.

Strength and power

A curler with higher levels of strength (and ability to apply this strength) will generally experience less fatigue, be able to maintain greater technical control and accuracy during sweeping and stone delivery and reduce injury risk resulting from the cumulative impact of repetitive submaximal work (see also Chapter 3.9). The following tests are recommended to provide a broad assessment of curling-specific strength and power.

One repetition maximum (1RM): back squat and bench press

Athletes should be familiar with these exercises prior to testing, with appropriate safety measures employed (see Chapter 3.9).

- A warm-up of two to three sets, using a light weight, is completed;
- The test commences with one repetition at ~50% of estimated maximum weight, gradually increasing to reach 1RM within five attempts (2–5 min rest between repetitions);
- The final weight lifted is expressed relative to body mass.

Force-velocity profiles provide a useful complement to this test, equipment permitting.

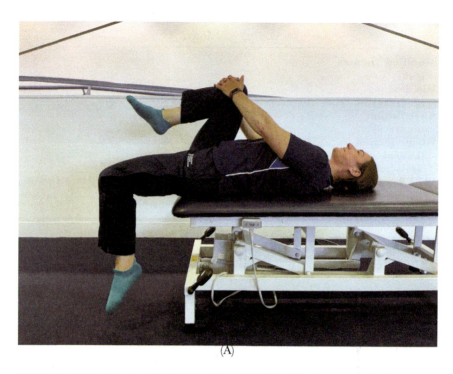

(A)

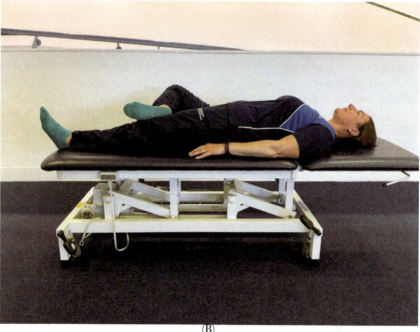

(B)

Figure 8.2.1 A. Modified Thomas test position. B. FABER test position.

Single-leg aquat: Unilateral knee extensor strength is critical when pushing out of the hack (the on-ice footholds). Increased strength of external rotators of the hip also prevents knee valgus/collapse when sliding and offers stability around the lumbo-pelvic region for sweeping.

- The athlete stands on one leg on a box edge, contralateral leg extended in front;
- Pushing the hips back, bending the knee of the standing leg and keeping torso straight, the hips are lowered towards the box, aiming for maximum depth, before pushing through the standing leg to return to the start position;
- Five repetitions are completed on each leg and scored.

(as McKeown et al., 2014)

Prone hold: Structural integrity, especially of the trunk, affords increased force contribution and enhanced maintenance of the sweeping and delivery technique.

- The athlete assumes a prone position, toes and hands in contact with the floor;
- Head, neck, back and hips are held in neutral alignment;
- Time to failure is recorded.

Broad jump: Coordinated horizontal triple extension of the hip, knee and ankle is integral to optimal stone delivery.

- Heels are positioned on a start line, feet parallel.
- The athlete jumps maximally in a horizontal direction, landing stable.
- Distance is measured between the start line and closest heel. The best of three trials (5 min rest) is recorded.

Using a force plate, where available, to monitor time-to-peak force would also be recommended.

Balance

Static and dynamic balance are considered essential physical qualities in curling to ensure effective stone delivery and sweeping on ice. A curling-specific balance test has been developed and validated (Pojskic et al., 2020) to assess balance in the delivery position. In the absence of this specialist test equipment (MFT Challenge Disc, MFT, Austria), a single-leg straight-leg deadlift balance test could be employed.

- The athlete places their bare front foot centrally on the MFT plate and the rear foot on a platform of equivalent elevation. The distance between the feet is individualised to replicate delivery position, with the hands simulating stone and broom holds.

- Three trials (3 × 20 s, 10 s rest) are completed with 3-min rest intervals. During attempts, the athlete is not permitted to touch the floor.
- A stability index is generated, with results averaged for dominant/non-dominant legs. See Pojskic et al. (2020) for reference data.

Other considerations

It is recommended that a physiological test battery be undertaken as part of a multidisciplinary approach to athlete support. At the elite level, additional considerations for competition environment and international travel would be recommended.

References

McKeown, I., Taylor-McKeown, K., Woods, C. and Ball, N. (2014). Athletic ability assessment: A movement assessment protocol for athletes. *International Journal of Sports Physical Therapy*, 9(7), 863–873.

Pojskic, H., McGawley, K., Gustafsson, A. and Behm, D. G. (2020). The reliability and validity of a novel sport-specific balance test to differentiate performance levels in elite curling players. *Journal of Sports Science and Medicine*, 19(2), 337–346.

Part IX
High-intensity skill sports

9.1 Motorsports

Pete McKnight and John Noonan

Automobile racing is a sport with worldwide popularity and appeal, having viewing numbers on a comparable level to football (soccer). There are many categories of racing, using different types of cars (open cockpit or closed cockpit), on different circuits or surfaces, on-road or off-road. As a consequence, the demands on racing drivers are varied depending upon a variety of factors, including the performance capacity of the cars, circuit layout, duration of racing, geographical location of the circuit and climate. This chapter will first review the physiological demands on elite race car drivers before outlining some of the more commonly used methods of physiological assessment.

Physiological demands and profile of elite race car drivers

The demands of the sport are based on the following six areas.

Cardiovascular demands

Demands on race car drivers are dependent on the intensity and duration of the race; for example, a Formula 1 race typically lasts between 90 min and 2 h with g-forces which average 2–3 g's and go up to 6.5 g's in cornering. This impact on the driver causes an elevated heart rate response. Heart rate levels are usually between 70% and 80% of maximum, and a driver will burn between 1000 and 1500 calories during the duration of a race. McKnight et al. (2019) showed that Formula 1 drivers have an average $\dot{V}O_2$max of 62.0 ml·kg^{-1}·ml^{-1}, which was higher than drivers from IndyCar, NASCAR and IMSA GTD. Endurance racing is less intense (lower heart rates) than Formula racing but longer in duration and can last up to 24 h. As a result, the total calorie expenditure is higher.

Heat

Motor racing is often contested in hot and humid environments, so drivers have to deal with cockpit temperatures of 50°–60°C. Furthermore, their fireproof undergarments and race suits make skin temperatures extremely high, with water and

DOI: 10.4324/9781003045281-50

electrolyte loss from sweat being as high as 2–3 kg for a driver with a body weight of under 70 kg, which makes it an important factor to consider.

Strength demands

Shoulder and forearm strength are required in steering and gripping the steering wheel. In IndyCar, the forces applied to the steering wheel (which lack power assist) while cornering on a road course averaged 157 N per turn (Reid and Lightfoot, 2019). The violent vibrations in racing cars require a strong trunk and lower back musculature to maintain a stable position. Leg strength is an important factor in braking. During an IndyCar road race, drivers negotiated 13 turns during each of 85 laps, resulting in a cumulative steering demand of 157 N × 1105 repetitions during a 2-h race (Reid and Lightfoot, 2019).

Neck strength is fundamental in maintaining a neutral head position in working against the g-forces. Studies report that Formula One drivers' average necks could withstand 48.7 newtons in extension, 39.4 in lateral flexion left and 38.8 in lateral flexion right. If the neck is not able to withstand these forces, it may impede vision and negatively affect performance, or even be dangerous (McKnight et al., 2019).

Body composition

Data from 2018 showed that male Formula 1 drivers had a mean body mass of 68.6 ± 1.5 kg and a body fat percentage of 8.1 ± 1.7% (McKnight et al., 2019). This body fat percentage was lower than drivers from IndyCar, NASCAR and IMSA GTD. In 2019 the regulations changed, and the Federation Internationale de l'Automobile (FIA) set a minimum weight of 80 kg for the driver and the seat, meaning that a 70-kg driver would need 10 kg of ballast (FIA, 2020). This change allows drivers to be heavier.

The small size of the cockpit in closed-cockpit cars means that shorter drivers are generally more comfortable in the confined space, and as a result most elite-level drivers are not over 1.80 m in height.

Intercontinental travel

Sleep, jet lag management and recovery are key factors in performance due to the number of races across five continents during the course of the season. Tracking and monitoring of these variables can help the driver optimise recovery and be ready for each competition.

Cognitive demands

Unlike the extensive body of knowledge on the technological aspects of motor racing, comparatively little is known about the motor, perceptual and cognitive skills of athlete performance in motorsports (Reid and Lightfoot, 2019). The cognitive element of motor racing can be categorised into three areas: perception (input), cognition (processing) and motor skill (output). All areas of focus, attention, task switching, memory, decision making, reaction, hand-eye coordination and precision come under these categories.

Protocols to assess and monitor performance

During the pre-season, physiological testing is undertaken to establish baseline fitness and strength levels, body composition, blood profiles and sweat profiles of the individual. The fitness testing and body composition results enable the performance coach to create training and recovery programmes for the drivers, whilst the blood and sweat profiles inform the doctor and nutritionist to establish an individualised diet and hydration plan.

The battery of tests used to assess drivers includes the following

Body mass and body composition

Elite drivers typically look to maintain a low body mass index year-round to meet FIA regulations (FIA, 2020). Body composition assessments are assessed via dual-energy x-ray absorptiometry (DXA) to characterise fat mass, fat-free mass and bone mineral density. Skinfold measurements (eight-site protocol) are also conducted approximately once per month throughout the year as a practical means to track body composition, with data used to inform nutrition and training interventions (see Chapter 3.4 for methods of assessing body composition).

Movement screening

A thorough movement screen using the Functional Movement Screen (FMS; Cook et al., 2014) as well as joint active range of motion (ROM) tests with a goniometer are conducted to determine general mobility and joint health of the driver. Recommended ROM measures include shoulder flexion, shoulder internal and external rotation, 90/90 hip internal and external rotation, and ankle dorsiflexion (knee to wall). More specifically, these tests provide crucial information for issues which may arise from postural and anatomical asymmetries that are related to seat fit and comfort in the cockpit.

Cardiovascular testing

The cardiovascular fitness of the drivers is determined through an incremental running or cycling $\dot{V}O_2$max test. Additional metabolic threshold testing (see Chapter 3.7) can be undertaken to establish the ventilatory threshold, heart rate training zones and optimal fat burning zones.

Indirect calorimetry also is used to determine the driver's resting metabolic rate (RMR) and efficiency at rest. Having fasted for 4 h, the driver lies down and rests for 30 min whilst the amount of oxygen consumed and carbon dioxide produced are measured. These data are used to determine their caloric energy requirements and efficiency at rest. The results of this analysis can then be used to create a bespoke nutrition strategy tailored to the driver's metabolism, providing vital information to manipulate the diet of the driver when targeting a new racing weight.

Sweat testing

The amount of sodium a driver loses in their sweat is measured by artificially stimulating the sweat gland with electrical stimulation under the skin for 5 min. The sweat is then analysed for its sodium content. The sodium content is crucial, as it can vary greatly between seemingly similar individuals. Sodium is important for muscle contraction, sending nerve impulses and also electrolyte and fluid balance in the body. This process helps the practitioner understand the composition of sweat so that they can prepare suitable sports drinks with the appropriate levels of minerals, salts and carbohydrates when training and competing in hot environments.

Strength testing

Full-body strength testing and diagnostics allow the practitioner to understand areas of strength, weakness or imbalance of the driver and address these accordingly, as well as build a base of general strength before preparing the body for the strength demands of driving in a sport-specific way (see also Chapter 3.9). Common practical strength assessments include 1RM pull-up, 3RM deadlift and 1RM isometric neck extension (see Neck strength testing). Combined, these tests provide an indication of grip, arm, shoulder girdle and upper back strength, as well as lower limb and neck strength. Submaximal time to fatigue tests such as the plank, prone extension and side plank are also useful to establish fatigue resistance abilities of the trunk. Dynamic assessments including the countermovement jump (CMJ) and drop jump (RSI) are also useful to understand the dynamic capabilities of drivers and to monitor the fatigue status of drivers utilising reactive strength index (RSI) data.

Neck strength testing

Isometric strength testing is important to identify maximal and submaximal capacities of the neck in extension, flexion, side flexion left and side flexion right. Subjects should be seated with hips, knees and ankles positioned at 90 degrees, with the head and neck positioned in a neutral anatomical position at all times. Maximal testing should be preceded by a sufficient warm-up involving low to moderate isometric resistance applied briefly in the directions of testing. The maximal isometric strength test (1RM) is conducted using a load cell measuring peak force (PF) (newtons), requiring the subject to voluntarily resist an incremental, maximal load to the point of test position failure, typically achieved over 1.5–3.5 s. An average of three tests should be performed McKnight et al. (2019). The submaximal isometric strength test requires subjects to resist 50% of their 1RM force until 80% of the target load is no longer maintained (Barrett et al., 2015). At least 5 min rest should be provided between tests. Results of PF and time to fatigue should be used to inform the design of strength development training programmes by physical preparation practitioners, with testing repeated periodically throughout the season to monitor and augment improvements where necessary.

Sleep tracking and management

Elite racing drivers and performance staff look to reduce the impact of regular international travel on cognitive and biological systems through optimising sleep patterns via regular sleep tracking. Sleep tracking wearables, such as the OURA ring and the Whoop band, offer a non-invasive approach to evaluate the sleep activity and the effectiveness of driver sleep routines. Said technologies offer objective data to support and inform coach-driver conversations around optimising pre-bed sleep routines, considering the following: food and caffeine use, minimising light exposure, use of mental practices, optimal sleep environment (comfort, timing and temperature) and physical activity. It's also useful to evaluate the effectiveness of sleep routines/behaviours by assessing the relationship with other markers such as resting heart rate, heart rate variability (HRV) and reporting subjective wellness and recovery. In combination these methods are useful to understand how sleep interacts and supports the wider wellness and performance needs of the driver athlete.

Feedback of results

Feedback should be provided to the driver and the team and presented as a report, with their results and targets for each area that has been assessed.

Field assessment

Biometric devices are currently not allowed to be worn by drivers in testing and racing; however, work has been done with the FIA (the governing body) to design an in-ear device to monitor heart rate through photoplethysmography (PPG) using the radio piece.

References

Barrett, M. D., et al. (2015). Effectiveness of a tailored neck training program on neck strength, movement, and fatigue in under-19 male rugby players: A randomized controlled pilot study. *Open Access Journal of Sports Medicine*, 6, 137–147.
Cook, C., Burton, L., Hoogenboom, B. J. and Voight, M. (2014). Functional movement screening: The use of fundamental movements as an assessment of function – part 1. *International Journal of Sports Physical Therapy*, 9(3), 396–409.

FIA. (2020). *2021 Formula 1 Technical Regulations*.

McKnight, P. J., Bennett, L. A., Malvern, J. J. and Ferguson, D. P. (2019). $\dot{V}O_2$peak, body composition, and neck strength of elite motor racing drivers. *Medicine and Science in Sports and Exercise*, 51(12), 2563–2569.

Reid, M. B. and Lightfoot, J. T. (2019). The physiology of auto racing. *Medicine and Science in Sports and Exerccise*, 51(12), 2548–2562.

9.2 Sport climbing

Edward Gibson-Smith, David Giles, Simon Fryer, and Mayur Ranchordas

Rock climbing encompasses a range of disciplines which can be performed in multiple environments, both recreationally and competitively. Of these, the most common are lead climbing and bouldering conducted indoors on artificial holds or outdoors on natural rock. Typically, a lead climbing ascent lasts 3–6 min, whereas a bouldering problem consists of four to eight powerful moves close to the ground. Whilst determining what makes a successful performance in this sport is important, only within the last two decades has research focused on understanding the anthropometric, physiological, biomechanical and psychological characteristics of climbing. Defining these characteristics is complex, due to the large variations in the physiological and technical demands of each climbing task and the lack of homogeneity in the profile of elite performers. Moreover, psychological factors such as anxiety may alter an individual's physiological response depending on the context, task demands, climber's perceptions of a route and the level of physical exposure perceived by the climber.

Assessments

Defining the physical characteristics of a successful climber has required sport scientists to develop novel testing procedures which are reliable and sensitive in ecologically valid settings. The following comprises a brief overview of a battery of physical tests suitable for the assessment of experienced climbers of intermediate- to elite-level ability, classified according to ability position statement of Draper et al. (2015), who are familiar with maximal testing and training. Where possible, field tests are presented (equipment typically found in gyms or climbing walls). Typical data ranges are given for most tests, and data are always male unless stated otherwise.

Anthropometric and descriptive characteristics

Anthropometric data for climbers are similar to other weight-sensitive sports (Gibson-Smith et al., 2020). The importance of strength-to-weight ratio in the finger flexors and the key musculature involved in climbing are widely acknowledged as key determinants. However, there is currently no consensus on the optimal

DOI: 10.4324/9781003045281-51

anthropometric profile (Mermier et al., 2000; Giles et al., 2020a). Nevertheless, key anthropometric characteristics, including height, body mass, ape index, body fat and fat-free mass, should still be routinely assessed. The four-site Durnin and Womersley (1974) equation has been validated against dual-energy x-ray absorptiometry (DEXA) in elite sport climbers and is an acceptable method for the assessment of body composition (see Chapter 3.4) when more robust methods (e.g., DEXA) are not viable (España-Romero et al., 2009a).

Whole-body exhaustive climbing

Exhaustive climbing tasks provide a systemic assessment of climbing performance and are particularly relevant for lead climbers. Fatigue is localised to the finger flexors and, to a lesser extent, the shoulder girdle. Consequently, there is little benefit in the assessment of oxygen uptake breakpoints, and when performing assessments of maximum oxygen uptake, the term $\dot{V}O_2$peak is preferred. Furthermore, heart rate (HR) does not provide a valid means of monitoring climbing intensity due to its non-linear relationship with $\dot{V}O_2$.

Stepped-angle treadwall test

This is an exhaustive test performed on a rotating climbing treadwall with adjustable speed and angle. Starting difficulty (climbing angle and/or handhold choice) should be chosen based on the climber's ability to elicit failure in 6–12 min of climbing; a familiarisation session is crucial to enhance validity and reliability of the test. The test begins at 86–90 degrees, depending on the climber's ability (see España-Romero et al., 2009b). The climbing angle increases 4 degrees every 2 min. Climbing speed is maintained at 6–10 m/min until volitional exhaustion. Climbing time to exhaustion (sec), rate of perceived exertion (see Chapter 3.8), peak oxygen uptake (ml·kg·min^{-1}), maximal desaturation of the flexor digitorum profundus (FDP; using near-infrared spectroscopy [NIRS]) and Δ Tissue Saturation Index (TSI%) have all been shown to be able to differentiate ability groups or explain significant variances in performance and should be recorded (España-Romero et al., 2009b; Fryer et al., 2018). Comparisons of time to exhaustion between climbers are valid only on identical routes. A simpler test to assess time to exhaustion is possible on a fixed circuit at a constant angle.

Forearm strength, endurance and rate of force development

The ability to generate a high level of force (and a large rate of force development) through the fingers is a key performance characteristic to support the climber's body mass during an ascent (Levernier et al., 2019; Torr et al., 2020). In addition, the contraction of the finger flexors causes regular periods of ischemia in the forearm muscles, and their fatigue resistance is considered one of the most important factors in climbing performance (Giles et al., 2019).

Testing equipment, body and hand positions

Although widely available, handgrip dynamometry is not a valid assessment of climbing strength (Watts et al., 2008). Tests should be performed using a climbing-specific fingerboard, either unilateral or bilateral (single arm is more suitable for higher-level climbers). When using a fingerboard, the climber's mass can be removed for sub-body mass loads using a 1:1 pulley system, and for supra-body mass loads, weight can be added using a climbing harness or a commercially available 'dipping' belt.

Edge depth: In all climbing abilities, edge depths of ~20–25 mm allow for maximum strength to be measured. As hold sizes vary, the advanced and elite climbers may test at smaller edge depths (<10 mm) depending on the desired assessment outcome.

Body position: All tests should be completed hanging (or in a hanging position) with arms extended above the head (~170–180 degrees shoulder flexion), maintaining a slight bend in the elbow with shoulder(s) engaged.

Hand position and arms: Allow the climber to choose an open or half-crimp position based on their preference, unless the objective is to understand positional differences (Figure 9.2.1). Full-crimp should be avoided due to very high loading of the finger flexor pulleys.

Finger strength

This is the amount of force that the finger flexors can produce in a single maximal effort, and this is performed as an incremental test, with either one or two arms (alternate single arm). The aim is to reach maximum strength within five attempts, each separated by a 3-min recovery period (90 s if alternating arms). A successful attempt in either method is defined as being able to maintain the chosen hand position with the shoulders remaining engaged for the entire test duration (see Table 9.2.1 for normative data).

Figure 9.2.1 Illustration of recommended four-finger open and half-crimp hand positions.

Rate of force development

This is the speed at which the contractile elements of the finger flexors can develop force. A climbing-specific finger dynamometer is required for this test, with a minimum sample rate of 1000 Hz being recommended. During the test, the climber's feet must remain on the ground throughout; when a climber can lift their body mass, weight can be added to a climbing harness.

To assess rate of force development (RFD), the climbers should attempt to produce maximal force as quickly as possible on a fingerboard dynamometer. Use five attempts per arm separated by 30 s recovery (alternating). Each attempt should last a maximum of 3 s, but may stop as soon as a peak is observed. A successful attempt is defined as maintaining the chosen hand position with the shoulders remaining engaged throughout. See Table 9.2.1 for normative data.

Critical force and W'

Critical force is the greatest metabolic rate that results in wholly oxidative energy provision during intermittent contractions of the finger flexors and extensors. W' is the 'buffer' available to resist exercise intolerance during exercise above critical force, where the source of the buffer will vary depending on the conditions.

Using both arms, a valid assessment should consist of at least three intermittent exhaustive yet submaximal trials above critical force (e.g., 50%, 65% and 80% two-arm maximal voluntary contraction (MVC), as described previously). These should be separated by at least 20 min of active recovery (provides valid assessment of critical force but not W'), but ideally on separate days. Intermittent contractions should be 7 s on, 3 s off, with no arm or hand shaking between contractions. The climber should maintain the chosen hand position, and the shoulders must remain engaged for the duration of the test. The test ends when the climber is unable to maintain the chosen hand/shoulder position or they are unable to sustain the contraction despite encouragement.

Critical force is calculated as the slope and W' of the intercept of linear fit of the force multiplied by time (y axis) plotted against time (x axis) (see Figure 9.2.2). An all-out critical force test using a fingerboard dynamometer has also recently been found to be valid and reliable (Giles et al., 2020b). See Table 9.2.1 for representative data for two-arm critical force data.

Upper body strength, endurance and power

A climber's ability to displace body mass is dependent on the action of both the lower and upper body; however, performance is limited to a much greater extent by the upper body. The strength (authors' unpublished data) and power (Draper et al., 2011) of the upper arm and shoulder girdle, along with muscular endurance (Baláš et al., 2012), are considered important physical performance characteristics.

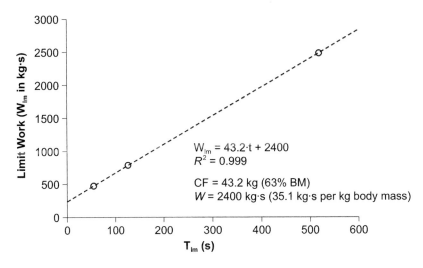

Figure 9.2.2 Exemplar of the calculation of critical force for an elite climber calculated as the slope and W' of the intercept of linear fit of the force multiplied by time (Limit work, y axis) plotted against time (T_{lim}, x axis).

Table 9.2.1 Normative data for forearm strength, rate of force development and critical force. Lead climbers will typically score toward the higher end of the provided ranges for finger strength and critical force and lower on RFD and W', while the opposite is true for boulders.

	Ability Category			
	Intermediate	Advanced	Elite	Higher Elite
Strength – female				
Single-arm average (% body mass)	ND	71–88	77–93	ND
Two-arm average (% body mass)	ND	111–152	131–174	N/A
Strength – male				
Single-arm average (% body mass)	74–93	76–96	86–108	ND
Two-arm average (% body mass)	110–157	127–190	139–198	N/A
Rate of force development				
RFD 200 ms ($kg \cdot s^{-1}$) open	68–77	89–101	115–134	152–168
RFD 200 ms ($kg \cdot s^{-1}$) half	62–71	111–122	121–144	138–167
RFD 95% ($kg \cdot s^{-1}$) open	21–27	29–35	48–53	56–70
RFD 95% ($kg \cdot s^{-1}$) half	22–26	32–38	55–61	51–73

(*Continued*)

Table 9.2.1 (Continued)

	Ability Category			
	Intermediate	Advanced	Elite	Higher Elite
Critical force – female				
Critical force (% body mass)	ND	18–44	21–54	ND
W' (kg·s per kg body mass)	ND	523–1829	844–5351	ND
Critical force – male				
Critical force (% body mass)	17–32	18–50	20–63	ND
W' (kg·s per kg body mass)	539–1445	617–3473	694–4868	ND

Notes:

1. Ability groupings classified as follows: **Intermediate** Male: f5+ – f7a | V0 – V3, Female: f5+ – f6b | V0 – V1; **Advanced** Male: f7a+ – f8a | V4 – V8, Female: f6c – f7b+ | V2 – V6; **Elite** Male: f8a+ – f8c | V9 – V12, Female: f7c – f8b+ | V7 – V11; **Higher elite** Male: >f8c | >V12, Female: >f8b+ | >V11 (Draper et al., 2015).
2. Abbreviations: RFD = rate of force development; N/A = not applicable to this population; ND = no or limited data at the time of writing.

Testing equipment and hand positions

Mass can be removed for sub-body mass load using a 1:1 pulley system, and for supra-body mass, load can be added using a waist harness. All tests should begin in an engaged but extended (other than bent-arm hang) hanging position, with the hands pronated. The distance between the hands on the pull-up bar is self-selected and recorded for each attempt.

Two-repetition max pull-up

This is the amount of force that the upper arm and shoulder girdle can produce in a two-repetition maximal effort. Beginning at a submaximal load in an engaged hanging position on a pull-up bar, climbers must pull themselves to a height at which the chin is level with the bar (while keeping the head level) for two repetitions without using the lower body to generate momentum. Load can then be added over the course of five attempts (maximum eight), recording body mass and change in load for each attempt. See Table 9.2.2 for normative data.

Upper body powerslap

This is the ability of the upper body to produce external force during dynamic contraction and produce maximum displacement of the hand; a familiarisation session is crucial. Begin in a two-armed hanging position on a deep rung at the

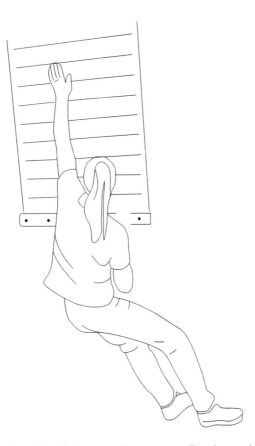

Figure 9.2.3 The end position of the powerslap test, recording the maximal slap height to the nearest centimetre.

Table 9.2.2 Representative data for two-repetition max pull-up, power-slap and bent-arm hangs. Lead climbers will typically score toward the lower end of the provided ranges for all of these tests, while the opposite is true for boulders.

	Ability Category			
	Intermediate	Advanced	Elite	Higher Elite
Pull-up – female Two-rep max (% body mass)	ND	126–155	ND	ND
Strength – male Two-rep max (% body mass)	142–162	133–167	139–170	ND

(*Continued*)

Table 9.2.2 (Continued)

	Ability Category			
	Intermediate	Advanced	Elite	Higher Elite
Powerslap – female Distance (cm)	25–53	56–63	72–80	ND
Powerslap – male Distance (cm)	61–80	88–91	96–102	ND
Bent-arm hang – female Hang time (s)	11–17	31–41	54–65	64–74
Bent-arm hang – male Hang time (s)	24–35	43–48	60–69	74–95

Notes:

1. Ability groupings classified as follows: **Intermediate** *Male: f5+ – f7a | V0 – V3, Female: f5+ – f6b | V0 – V1;* **Advanced** *Male: f7a+ – f8a | V4 – V8, Female: f6c – f7b+ | V2 – V6;* **Elite** *Male: f8a+ – f8c | V9 – V12, Female: f7c – f8b+ | V7 – V11;* **Higher elite** *Male: >f8c | >V12, Female: >f8b+ | >V11* (Draper et al., 2015).
2. Abbreviations: n/a = not applicable to this population; ND = no or limited data at the time of writing.

base of the powerslap board, as shown in Figure 9.2.3. The climber will perform an explosive pull-up movement initiated through the shoulder girdle (no lower body momentum), releasing one hand to slap the scaled board above as high as possible. The test must be repeated twice per arm, alternating between left and right sides, with each test separated by 2 min. Distance should be averaged between the two attempts and recorded to the nearest whole centimetre. See Table 9.2.2 for normative data.

Upper body muscular endurance

This is muscular endurance of the upper arm and shoulder girdle. Begin in a two-armed hanging position with the arms bent at 90 degrees. The climber hangs in this position, maintaining engaged shoulders and both hands on the bar. The time to exhaustion is recorded as the point at which the climber is no longer able to maintain the 90-degree bent-arm position and shoulder engagement.

References

Baláš, J., Pecha, O., Martin, A. J. and Cochrane, D. (2012). Hand: Arm strength and endurance as predictors of climbing performance. *European Journal of Sport Science*, 12(1), 16–25.

Draper, N., Dickson, T., Blackwell, G., Priestley, S., Fryer, S., Marshall, H., Shearman, J., Hamlin, M., Winter, D. and Ellis, G. (2011). Sport-specific power assessment for rock climbing. *Journal of Sports Medicine and Physical Fitness*, 51(3), 417.

Draper, N., Giles, D., Schöffl, V., Konstantin Fuss, F., Watts, P., Wolf, P., Baláš, J., Espana-Romero, V., Blunt Gonzalez, G., Fryer, S., Fanchini, M., Vigouroux, L., Seifert, L.,

Donath, L., Spoerri, M., Bonetti, K., Phillips, K., Stöcker, U., Bourassa-Moreau, F., Garrido, I., Drum, S., Beekmeyer, S., Ziltener, J.-L., Taylor, N., Beeretz, I., Mally, F., Mithat Amca, A., Linhart, C. and Abreu, E. (2015). Comparative grading scales, statistical analyses, climber descriptors and ability grouping: International Rock Climbing Research Association position statement. *Sports Technology*, 8(3–4), 88–94.

Durnin, J. V. and Womersley, J. (1974). Body fat assessed from total body density and its estimation from skinfold thickness: Measurements on 481 men and women aged from 16 to 72 years. *The British Journal of Nutrition*, 32(1), 77–97.

España-Romero, V., Porcel, F. B. O., Artero, E. G., Jiménez-Pavón, D., Sainz, A. G., Garzón, M. J. C. and Ruiz, J. R. (2009b). Climbing time to exhaustion is a determinant of climbing performance in high-level sport climbers. *European Journal of Applied Physiology*, 107(5), 517.

España-Romero, V., Ruiz, J. R., Ortega, F. B., Artero, E. G., Vicente-Rodríguez, G., Moreno, L. A., Castillo, M. J. and Gutierrez, A. (2009a). Body fat measurement in elite sport climbers: Comparison of skinfold thickness equations with dual energy x-ray absorptiometry. *Journal of Sports Sciences*, 27(5), 469–477.

Fryer, S. M., Giles, D., Palomino, I. G., de la O Puerta, A. and España-Romero, V. (2018). Hemodynamic and cardiorespiratory predictors of sport rock climbing performance. *The Journal of Strength and Conditioning Research*, 32(12), 3534–3541.

Gibson-Smith, E., Storey, R. and Ranchordas, M. (2020). Dietary intake, body composition and iron status in experienced and elite climbers. *Frontiers in Nutrition*, 7, 122.

Giles, D., Barnes, K., Taylor, N., Chidley, C., Chidley, J., Mitchell, J., Torr, O., Gibson-Smith, E. and España-Romero, V. (2020a). Anthropometry and performance characteristics of recreational advanced to elite female rock climbers. *Journal of Sports Sciences*, 39(1), 48–56.

Giles, D., Chidley, J. B., Taylor, N., Torr, O., Hadley, J., Randall, T. and Fryer, S. (2019). The determination of finger-flexor critical force in rock climbers. *International Journal of Sports Physiology and Performance*, 14(7), 972–979.

Giles, D., Hartley, C., Maslen, H., Hadley, J., Taylor, N., Torr, O., Chidley, J., Randall, T. and Fryer, S. (2020b). An all-out test to determine finger flexor critical force in rock climbers. *International Journal of Sports Physiology and Performance*, 14(7), 972–979.

Levernier, G. and Laffaye, G. (2019). Rate of force development and maximal force: Reliability and difference between non-climbers, skilled and international climbers. *Sports Biomechanics*. doi: 10.1080/14763141.2019.1584236

Mermier, C. M., Janot, J. M., Parker, D. L. and Swan, J. G. (2000). Physiological and anthropometric determinants of sport climbing performance. *British Journal of Sports Medicine*, 34(5), 359–365.

Torr, O., Randall, T., Knowles, R., Giles, D. and Atkins, S. (2020). Reliability and validity of a method for the assessment of sport rock climbers' isometric finger strength. *The Journal of Strength and Conditioning Research*, 89(2), 246–254.

Watts, P. B., Jensen, R. L., Gannon, E., Kobeinia, R., Maynard, J. and Sansom, J. (2008). Forearm EMG during rock climbing differs from EMG during handgrip dynamometry. *International Journal of Exercise Science*, 1(2), 62–70.

Part X

Aesthetic physical sports

10.1 Artistic gymnastics

Monèm Jemni

Male and female artistic gymnastics (AG) is one of the sports that has witnessed significant and rapid expansion in the last four decades, with performers reaching top levels at younger ages (Jemni et al., 2001). AG is, in short, many sports all in one, with slight differences between males and females. Females compete in four events: vault, uneven bars, balance beam and floor exercises. Males compete in six events, with the floor exercises and the vault similar to the females, but the pommel horse, the rings, the parallel bars and the high bar are different. These differences encompass not only different rules and technical specificities but also different levels of executions that require a variety of physico-fitness prerequisites. Similar to pentathlon, the duration, the effort, the intensity, the power, the strength, the flexibility, the speed of the stretch, the coordination and the endurance, as well as the energy, required to perform each of these events differ from one to another. The International Gymnastics Federation (FIG) is the international governing body for all related gymnastics activities. The FIG reviews and updates the code of judging every 4 years (following every Olympic Games); hence, performance demands on gymnasts are continually changing to meet the new code requirements.

We generally describe gymnasts' physiological conditions as their 'fitness' and/or 'profile', which implies how prepared they are to perform. Some authors have tried to 'frame' their fitness with some theoretical models in order to help coaches to target their micro-training. Sands (2018) has put together a fitness model based on strength, speed, flexibility, skill and stamina (commonly used to mean muscular endurance). The author also emphasised that none of these physical fitness categories should be considered alone, but rather in combination with every other category. We simply do not have the unique words in English to describe the blending of physical fitness categories that often spell the qualities of sport-specific fitness. An example of a double combination between these categories could, for example, be 'strength-speed', which refers to the application of high levels of force, but rapidly. 'Speed-strength' is a similar combination, but the emphasis is on the speed component. A triple combination would, for instance, be 'speed-strength-flexibility'. Micro-training would mean the coaches target specific sessions to develop these abilities in a combined fashion. Sands (2018) acknowledged that 'while the model helps to narrow our universe of things that merit consideration, we must acknowledge that actually getting the model to work in

DOI: 10.4324/9781003045281-53

the real world with real people can be considerably more difficult'. Therefore, it is quite important to assess those physical abilities separately in order to know if they are developing.

The following paragraphs embark on a review of the most specific physical and physiological assessments of these abilities specifically for AG.

Important considerations

Apart from the previously mentioned different apparatus/events and complex technicalities, the wide range of muscular contractions and speed of the stretch in AG, assessing the physical and physiological abilities is made difficult by the lack of standardised specific laboratory tests. It is also important to know that the longest event is the balance beam (maximum 120 s) followed by the floor exercises (70 or 90 s maximum for males and females, respectively) and the shortest is the vault with an approximate 5 s. The average of all the other events is around 45 s.

The literature provides evidence that artistic gymnasts' cardiorespiratory fitness, assessed by the maximal oxygen uptake ($\dot{V}O_2$max), is very poor and has not changed for more than 6 decades (Jemni et al., 2001; Jemni, 2018). The average $\dot{V}O_2$max for elite and sub-elite gymnasts was and continues to be around 42 ml/kg/min, although training volume, intensity and technical difficulties have significantly increased. However, some scientists are still assessing gymnasts' endurance via their $\dot{V}O_2$max and estimating their routines' energetics via extrapolating the heart rate data versus their equivalent measured during the $\dot{V}O_2$max tests. Unfortunately, this estimation cannot be correct, as there are obvious differences between the nature and the length of the efforts when comparing AG to running and/or cycling (Jemni et al., 2003, 2006; Jemni, 2018). Above all, investigations revealed that gymnasts' heart rate does not reach any steady state during their routines, but rather work out at very high heart rate range that could be closer to their maximal (Jemni et al., 2000; Jemni, 2018). Nonetheless, there is also evidence that shows that muscular endurance is in fact a crucial element in modern AG.

Another factor to consider when assessing physical and physiological abilities of artistic gymnasts is the fact that they significantly use their upper body in their routines (Jemni et al., 2003, 2006). Only two events out of six involve short runs, walks and tumbling/jumping in males AG, for example; therefore, it is quite important to assess their upper body.

Laboratory and field tests

Table 10.1.1 summarises the most common lab and field-based tests for AG. There are currently no normative data for lab-based tests; however, the normative data for the field tests can be found in the supplementary material. It is important that verbal feedback be provided on the day of the test battery and written feedback within 7 days. Feedback should be provided in an appropriate format for the gymnast and coach.

Table 10.1.1 Summary of the most common lab and field-based tests for artistic gymnastics

	Power	Integrated Power – Strength and Agility	Strength	Speed	Muscular Endurance	Flexibility	Technical Tests (mostly used for talent identification and selection)
Lab	Force velocity test; Wingate test; force plate tests		Isokinetic tests (forearms, arms, shoulders, hips, ankles)		Isokinetic tests (arms, shoulders, hips)		
Field	Jump tests with and without arms (vertical and long; drop; squat; plyometric; 30-s repeated jumps)	Rope climbing test; leg lift tests; push-up tests; pull-up tests	Leg lift tests; push-up tests; pull-up tests	20-m sprint test	Bosco 60-s jumps; max leg lifts; max pull-ups; push-ups in 60 s; pull-ups in 60 s; support half lever	Passive tests (right and left forward split; hip flexion; back extension; shoulder extension) Active tests (leg lifts – front and side; shoulder flexion and extension; hip flexion; back extension)	Held handstand; handstand push-ups in 10 and 60 s; cross on rings; Maltese on rings; front and back horizontal hang; horizontal support (planche); inverted cross; front support half lever; front swing on low bar, upstart to handstand; mini routine test

References

Jemni, M. (2018). *The Science of Gymnastics: Advanced Concepts* (2nd ed.). London and New York: Routledge, Taylor & Francis Grp. ISBN: Paperback 9781138701939; Hardback 9781138701922; eBook 9781315203805. www.routledge.com/The-Science-of-Gymnastics-Advanced-Concepts/Jemni/p/book/9781138701939

Jemni, M., Friemel, F., Le Chevalier, J. M. and Origas, M. (2000). Heart rate and blood lactate concentration analysis during a high level men's gymnastics competition. *Journal of Strength and Conditioning Research*, 14(4), 389–394.

Jemni, M., Friemel, F., Sands, W. and Mikesky, A. (2001). Evolution du profil physiologique des gymnastes Durant les 40 dernières années. (Evolution of gymnasts physiological profile during the last 40 years). *Canadian Journal of Applied Physiology*, 26(5), 442–456.

Jemni, M., Sands, W., Friemel, F., Cooke, C. and Stone, M. (2006). Effect of gymnastics training on aerobic and anaerobic components in elite and sub elite men gymnasts. *Journal of Strength and Conditioning Research*, 20(4), 899–907.

Jemni, M., Sands, W., Friemel, F. and Delamarche, P. (2003). Effect of active and passive recovery on blood lactate and performance during simulated competition in high level gymnasts. *Canadian Journal of Applied Physiology*, 28(2), 240–256.

Sands, W. A. (2018). Fitness model of high level gymnasts. In M. Jemni (ed.), *The Science of Gymnastics: Advanced Concepts*, 2nd ed., pp. 45–48. London and New York: Routledge, Taylor & Francis Grp. www.routledge.com/The-Science-of-Gymnastics-Advanced-Concepts/Jemni/p/book/9781138701939

Part XI
Combat sports

11.1 Judo

Kyle Wallace and Emerson Franchini

General and laboratory testing

During a judo match, it has been estimated that ~70% of energy contribution is from the oxidative energy system (increasing from 50% to 80% for matches lasting 1–5 min), followed by ~21% from the adenosine triphosphate–phosphocreatine (ATP-PCr) pathway (decreasing from 40% to 12% for matches lasting 1–5 min) and lastly the glycolytic system contributes ~8% (with non-significant variations from 10% to 6% for matches between 1 and 5 min) (Julio et al., 2017). Moreover, judo athletes need to improve their maximal isometric and dynamic strength, muscle power, strength endurance, aerobic power and capacity and anaerobic power and capacity to cope with the physiological demands imposed by actions executed during the match, while maintaining low body fat and high muscle mass percentages to perform well during competitions (Franchini et al., 2011a).

As Olympic-level judo athletes engage in several non-specific training modalities (Franchini and Takito, 2014), such as continuous and sprint running and resistance training, the determination of maximal aerobic power, maximal speed, muscle power and maximal dynamic and isometric strength can be useful for prescribing training and/or evaluating the training effects.

Typically, aerobic power is assessed via direct oxygen consumption measurement (see Chapter 3.6) during treadmill tests. Although there are no normative data for the maximal oxygen consumption ($\dot{V}O_2$max) for judo athletes, males typically present with values between 50 and 60 ml·kg^{-1}·min^{-1}, whereas female present with values between 40 and 50 ml·kg^{-1}·min^{-1} (Franchini et al., 2011a).

Lower body muscle power is a key element for successful throwing technique execution. Indeed, lower body muscle power has been used to monitor the acute effects of judo matches (Detanico et al., 2015) and could also be implemented to monitor recovery after the weigh-in. Muscle power has been assessed using the countermovement jump (CMJ), squat jump (SJ) and standing long jump (SLJ) tests (Franchini et al., 2011a). The constant pushing and pulling actions during grip dispute and in the preparatory movements for throwing technique execution result in high physiological demand, which is provided mainly by the anaerobic pathways (Julio et al., 2017). The Wingate test is commonly used to assess anaerobic power and capacity, and the upper body version has been recommended for judo athletes' evaluation. Normative data have been calculated for the upper body Wingate test (using 0.06 kg·kg^{-1} of body mass as load), peak and mean power for male adult judo athletes and their weight categories (Franchini, 2019).

Maximal isometric handgrip strength of the dominant hand has been shown to decrease post-match compared to pre-match values, and baseline values decrease before matches 3 and 4 compared to pre-match 1, when judo athletes performed four 5-min matches with 15-min intervals. This suggests that maximal isometric strength maintenance can be a relevant aspect for successive judo matches (Bonitch-Góngora et al., 2012). Resistance training is a key element of a judo athlete's training routine (Franchini and Takito, 2014); therefore, evaluating the maximum strength in some exercises can provide coaches and strength and conditioning professionals valuable information concerning the evolution of these athletes in specific training phases (Franchini et al., 2011a).

Judo-specific tests

As the specificity principle is quite important for high-level sports performance, many investigations tried to establish judo-specific tests (Chaabene et al., 2018). Together with higher specificity, frequently judo-specific tests are more coach friendly in terms of application, training and materials needed, whereas judo athletes are likely to be more motivated to test themselves in their own training facility using sport-specific actions.

Recently, a maximal aerobic power test using hikidashi uchi-komi (basic technique repetition up to the point where the throw would be executed) has been validated (Shiroma et al., 2019). This test starts with 32 rep·min^{-1} and the speed is increased in 3 rep·min^{-1} up to voluntary exhaustion. As the oxygen consumption measurement is not easily executed, it has been recommended that coaches prescribe high-intensity interval training using the maximal aerobic speed achieved in this test (Franchini, 2020).

A special interest exists concerning strength endurance gripping the judogi due to the fact that most of the judo match time is spent in grip dispute (Franchini et al., 2011b). Dynamic and isometric strength endurance chin-up tests have been proposed to evaluate judo athletes. Briefly, these tests are completed practically the same as regular chin-up tests, but the grip is made in a judogi (rolled around the bar) instead of the bar. Therefore, the athlete's chin must pass the hand position gripping the judogi, and a full elbow extension must occur during the dynamic test to register one repetition, whereas in the isometric test the elbows must be flexed and time is registered when the athlete starts to extend them. In both tests no hip or knee flexions are allowed to help to execute a repetition or to increase the time in suspension. Normative data for each test are provided for different sexes and age groups (Table 11.1.1).

As judo is a complex sport demanding multiple physical abilities, sport-specific tests comprising some of these physical capacities were developed. Among these tests, the most used is the Special Judo Fitness Test (SJFT) (Sterkowicz-Przybycień et al., 2019). Briefly, this test is executed in three sets (A = 15 s; B and C = 30 s

Table 11.1.1 Normative data for dynamic and isometric strength endurance chin-up gripping in the judogi tests for judo athletes from different sexes and age groups

Test/Authors	Sex	Age (n)	Unit	Very Poor	Poor	Regular	Good	Excellent
Dynamic strength endurance chin-up gripping the judogi								
Branco et al. (2017)	Male	Adult (n = 138)	rep	≤1	2–6	7–16	17–19	≥20
			rep·kg	≤121	122–474	475–1190	1191–1463	≥1464
Agostinho et al. (2018)	Male	Cadet (n = 80)	rep	≤2	3–13	14–25	26–31	≥32
			rep·kg	≤226	227–784	785–1737	1738–2244	≥2245
	Male	Junior (n = 47)	rep	≤3	4–15	16–28	29–30	≥31
			rep·kg	≤411	412–1158	1159–2026	2027–2366	≥2367
	Female	Cadet (n = 60)	rep	≤1	2–5	6–16	17–22	≥23
			rep·kg	≤144	145–350	351–799	800–1142	≥1143
	Female	Junior (n = 35)	rep	0	1–3	4–20	21–23	≥24
			rep·kg	≤58	59–306	307–1056	1057–1296	≥1297
Isometric strength endurance chin-up gripping the judogi								
Branco et al. (2017)	Male	Adult (n = 138)	s	≤10	11–25	26–55	56–62	≥63
			s·kg	≤1051	1052–2041	2042–3962	3963–4008	≥4009
Agostinho et al. (2018)	Male	Cadet (n = 83)	s	≤7	8–40	41–69	70–89	≥90
			s·kg	≤626	627–2744	2,745–4506	4507–5856	≥5857
	Male	Junior (n = 43)	s	≤6	7–34	35–65	66–75	≥76
			s·kg	≤822	823–3158	3159–4732	4733–5713	≥5714
	Female	Cadet (n = 52)	s	≤12	13–26	27–55	56–74	≥75
			s·kg	≤554	555–1514	1515–2932	2933–3405	≥3406
	Female	Junior (n = 30)	s	≤2	3–17	18–57	58–71	≥72
			s·kg	≤243	244–1232	1233–3216	3217–3933	≥3934

Classification for Agostinho et al. (2018) was as follows: excellent – highest 5%; good – next 15%; regular – middle 60%; poor – next lowest 15%; very poor – lowest 5%.
Classification for Branco et al. (2017) was as follows: excellent – >90th percentile; good – 76–90th percentile; regular – 26–75th percentile; poor – 11–25th percentile; very poor – ≤10th percentile.

Table 11.1.2 Normative data for the Special Judo Fitness Test for judo athletes from different sexes and age groups

Authors	Sex	Age (n)	Variable	Very Poor	Poor	Regular	Good	Excellent
Franchini et al. (2009)	Male	16–34 yr (n = 141)	Throws (n)	≤24	25	26	27–28	≥29
			HR final (bpm)	≥196	188–195	185–187	174–184	≤173
			HR 1 min (bpm)	≥175	166–174	162–165	144–161	≤143
			Index	≥14.85	13.95–14.84	13.04–13.94	11.74–13.03	≤11.73
Sterkowicz-Przybycień and Fukuda (2014)	Female	Junior (n = 65)	Throws (n)	≤21	22	23–24	25	≥26
			HR final (bpm)	≥199	191–198	176–190	168–175	≤167
			HR 1 min (bpm)	≥172	162–171	140–161	129–139	≤128
			Index	≥17.42	16.14–17.41	13.72–16.13	12.19–13.71	≤12.18
	Female	Senior (n = 96)	Throws (n)	≤23	24–25	26–28	29	≥30
			HR final (bpm)	≥200	190–199	171–189	161–170	≤160
			HR 1 min (bpm)	≥168	159–167	139–158	130–138	≤129
			Index	≥14.53	13.49–14.52	11.32–13.48	10.22–11.31	≤10.21
Agostinho et al. (2018)	Female	Cadet (n = 64)	Throws (n)	≤20	21–22	23–26	27	≥28
			HR final (bpm)	≥203	194–202	177–193	169–176	≤168
			HR 1 min (bpm)	≥190	177–189	149–176	133–148	≤132
			Index	≥18.01	15.46–18.00	12.64–15.45	11.54–12.63	≤11.53
	Male	Cadet (n = 93)	Throws (n)	≤22	23–24	25–27	28–29	≥30
			HR final (bpm)	≥201	196–200	175–195	164–174	≤163
			HR 1 min (bpm)	≥185	176–184	149–175	133–148	≤132
			Index	≥15.93	14.33–15.92	12.39–14.32	11.16–12.38	≤11.15
Sterkowicz-Przybycień et al. (2019)	Male	Junior (n = 209)	Throws (n)	≤20	21–22	23–26	27–28	≥29
			HR final (bpm)	≥199	191–198	174–190	166–173	≤165
			HR 1 min (bpm)	≥176	165–175	141–164	130–140	≤129
			Index	≥15.93	14.74–15.92	12.24–14.73	11.05–12.23	≤11.04
	Male	Senior (n = 515)	Throws (n)	≤21	22–23	24–27	28–29	≥30
			HR final (bpm)	≥196	189–195	174–188	167–173	≤166
			HR 1 min (bpm)	≥174	164–173	142–163	131–141	≤130
			Index	≥15.44	14.23–15.43	11.69–14.22	10.48–11.68	≤10.47

Source: (Franchini et al., 2007).

Each classification represents 20% of the athletes.

Classification for Sterkowicz-Przybycień et al. (2019) was as follows: excellent – highest 5%; good – next 15%; regular – middle 60%; poor – next lowest 15%; very poor – lowest 5%.

each) with 10-s intervals between them. The executant throws two other athletes positioned 6 m from each other using the ippon-seoi-nage technique; for each set the executant starts in the middle distance between the other athletes. The total number of throws and the heart rate (HR) just after and 1 min after the last set are recorded. A special index is calculated by summing up the HRs and dividing this value by the number of throws. Therefore, the lower the index, the better the performance in the SJFT. Normative data are presented in Table 11.1.2.

References

Agostinho, M. J., Olivio, Jr., J. A. O., Stankovic, N., Escobar-Molina, R. and Franchini, E. (2018). Comparison of special judo fitness test and dynamic and isometric judo chin-up tests' performance and classificatory tables' development for cadet and junior athletes. *Journal of Exercise Rehabilitation*, 14(2), 244–252.

Aruga, S., Onda, T., Aso, K., Shirase, H., Yamashita, Y., Nakanishi, H. and Ubukata, K. (2003). Measurement of barbell lifting capacity and making strength standards in judo players. *Tokai Journal of Sports Medical Science*, 15(1), 7–17.

Bonitch-Góngora, J. G., Bonitch-Domínguez, J. G., Padial, P. and Feriche, B. (2012). The effect of lactate concentration on the handgrip strength during judo bouts. *Journal of Strength and Conditioning Research*, 26(7), 1863–1871.

Branco, B. H. M., Diniz, E., da Silva Santos, J. F., Shiroma, S. A. and Franchini, E. (2017). Normative tables for the dynamic and isometric judogi chin-up tests for judo athletes. *Sport Science for Health*, 13, 47–53.

Chaabene, H., Negra, Y., Bouguezzi, R., Capranica, L., Franchini, E., Prieske, O., Hbacha, H. and Granacher, U. (2018). Tests for the assessment of sport-specific performance in Olympic combat sports: A systematic review with practical recommendations. *Frontiers in Physiology*, 9, 386.

Detanico, D., Dal Pupo, J., Franchini, E. and Dos Santos, S. G. (2015). Effects of successive judo matches on fatigue and muscle damage markers. *Journal of Strength and Conditioning Research*, 29(4), 1010–1016.

Franchini, E. (2019). Upper-body Wingate test classificatory table for adult judo athletes. *Journal of Exercise Rehabilitation*, 15(1), 55–59.

Franchini, E. (2020). High-intensity interval training prescription for combat-sport athletes. *International Journal of Sports Physiology and Performance*, 15(6), 767–776.

Franchini, E., Del Vecchio, F. B., Matsushigue, K. A. and Artioli, G. G. (2011a). Physiological profiles of elite judo athletes. *Sports Medicine (Auckland, N.Z.)*, 41(2), 147–166.

Franchini, E., Miarka, B., Matheus, L. and Del Vecchio, F. (2011b). Endurance in judogi grip strength tests: Comparison between elite and non-elite judo players. *Archives of Budo*, 7.

Franchini, E., Nunes, A. V., Moraes, J. M. and Del Vecchio, F. B. (2007). Physical fitness and anthropometrical profile of the Brazilian male judo team. *Journal of Physiological Anthropology*, 26(2), 59–67. doi: 10.2114/jpa2.26.59. PMID: 17435345.

Franchini, E., Sterkowicz-Przybycien, K. L. and Takito, M. Y. (2014). Anthropometrical profile of judo athletes: Comparative analysis between weight categories. *International Journal of Morphology*, 32(1), 36–42.

Franchini, E. and Takito, M. Y. (2014). Olympic preparation in Brazilian judo athletes: Description and perceived relevance of training practices. *Journal of Strength and Conditioning Research*, 28(6), 1606–1612.

Julio, U. F., Panissa, V., Esteves, J. V., Cury, R. L., Agostinho, M. F. and Franchini, E. (2017). Energy-system contributions to simulated judo matches. *International Journal of Sports Physiology and Performance*, 12(5), 676–683.

Shiroma, S. A., Julio, U. F. and Franchini, E. (2019). Criterion validity, reliability and usefulness of a judo-specific maximal aerobic power test. *International Journal of Sports Physiology and Performance*, 14(7), 987–993.

Sterkowicz-Przybycień, K. L. and Fukuda, D. H. (2014). Establishing normative data for the special judo fitness test in female athletes using systematic review and meta-analysis. *Journal of Strength and Conditioning Research*, 28(12), 3585–3593.

Sterkowicz-Przybycień, K. L., Fukuda, D. H. and Franchini, E. (2019). Meta-analysis to determine normative values for the special judo fitness test in male athletes: 20+ years of sport-specific data and the lasting legacy of Stanisław Sterkowicz. *Sports (Basel, Switzerland)*, 7(8), 194.

11.2 Amateur and professional boxing

Alan Ruddock and Laura Needham

From its origins in prize-fighting almost 400 years ago, professional boxing is now a multimillion-pound international business, with four major governing bodies awarding world titles across 17 weight classes from 47.6 kg (minimum) to over 90.7 kg (heavyweight). Amateur boxing is a major Olympic sport, featured in each Summer Games over the last 100 years, with 39 medals (approximately 4% of total) awarded across eight male (flyweight 52 kg to super heavyweight >91 kg) and five female weight classes (flyweight 51 kg to middleweight 75 kg).

Physiological demands

Importantly, both professional and amateur boxing contests are weight restricted. Boxers will often undertake chronic and/or 'rapid weight-loss strategies' to make their weight classification (Reale et al., 2018; Reljic et al., 2013; Zubac et al., 2018). Consequently, the physiological demands of boxing and interpretation of physiological testing are influenced by transient decreases in body mass and should be taken into consideration in evaluating the physiological and physical demands of the sport. It should be noted that the recommendations in this chapter are based exclusively on male boxer data, as there are limited data pertaining to female boxers.

The aerobic energy system contribution to simulated amateur boxing is approximately 77%, with 19% and 4% derived from phosphocreatine and anaerobic glycolytic pathways, with accompanying oxygen uptake equivalent to 85%–90% $\dot{V}O_2$max corresponding to 90%–95% HR_{max} (Davis et al., 2014) and blood lactate concentrations greater than 12 mmol·L^{-1} (Hanon et al., 2015; Smith, 2006). A high-intensity performance strategy is therefore dependent upon a well-developed aerobic capability ($\dot{V}O_2$max > 65 ml·kg^{-1}·min^{-1} up to middleweight and greater than ml·kg^{-1}·min^{-1} up to heavyweight) (Chaabène et al., 2014) supported by a neuromuscular system capable of producing rapid high-force punches (Nakano et al., 2014; Piorkowski et al., 2011). Data regarding the physiological demands of professional boxing are not available in the scientific literature; however, experience providing scientific support to professional boxers suggests they have similar aerobic capabilities but with a greater rate and magnitude of force development, providing the foundation for better repeated high-intensity actions.

DOI: 10.4324/9781003045281-56

Protocols to assess physiological characteristics

Body mass, body composition and resting metabolic rate

Assessments of body mass and composition (seven-site skinfold, girth measurement; see Chapter 3.4) and/or multifrequency bioelectrical impedance analysis/spectroscopy) should be made at the start of the season or camp to estimate competition mass; thereafter, morning nude-body mass should be assessed weekly. Body composition assessments can be made after specific training blocks in amateur boxers, whilst professional boxers' body composition can be assessed biweekly during the first 6 weeks of a training camp and weekly in the latter weeks. Assessment of body composition is important to monitor body fat percentage and to inform strength training interventions designed to limit segmental atrophy associated with prolonged periods in a negative energy balance. These tests should be accompanied by an assessment of resting metabolic rate at the same timepoint to assist nutritional interventions designed to safely make competitive the desired weight category.

Movement assessment

A boxer's stance promotes significantly elevated international shoulder rotation, flexion of thoracic spine and flexion and external rotation of the rear leg hip – these challenging positions are compounded by thousands of high-force punches that challenge rotational function (Ruddock et al., 2018). It is common to find boxers with several movement dysfunctions related to these stance-related positions that increase the risk of overuse injury. Simple overhead squat and single-leg squat assessments can identify common movement dysfunctions and inform mobility training designed to address muscular imbalances (Ruddock et al., 2018). These can be formal assessments but also included informally in a warm-up.

Strength assessments

Punch force is related to the rate of lower body force production (Ruddock et al., 2016). A squat jump can be used to identify a boxer's ability to rapidly produce force concentrically, whilst a countermovement jump can be used to assess eccentric capabilities – the latter is important in boxing since stretch-shortening cycle ability is required for high-force punching. The landmine-punch throw profile, using a linear position transducer, can also provide insight into punch-force capability and direct strength training programmes (Ruddock et al., 2018).

Physiology assessments

When determining the choice of physiological assessment, practitioners should consider validity, reliability and sensitivity of outcome variables, as well as practical implementation of the protocol (laboratory vs. field). Table 11.2.1 (see also Chapter 3.7) provides practitioners with an overview of these considerations. In

Table 11.2.1 Target standards for physiological assessments

	Target Standards			
	Flyweight to Featherweight	Super-Featherweight to Welterweight	Super-Welterweight to Light-Heavyweight	Cruiserweight and Heavyweight
LT1 (km·h^{-1})	13 to 15	12 to 14	11 to 13	10 to 12
LT2 (km·h^{-1})	16 to 18	15 to 17	14 to 16	13 to 15
$\dot{V}O_2$max (ml·kg·min^{-1})	≥ 70	≥ 65	55 to 60	50 to 55
Yo-yo IRTL1 (m)	> 2200	2000 to 1800	1600 to 1800	1200 to 1400
1000-m time trial (mm:ss)	03:00	03:00	03:00	03:15
3000-m time trial (s)	10:45	10:50	11:00	12:15
Critical speed (m.s^{-1})	4.30	4.26	4.17	3.70
D' (m)	225	234	250	278

LT = Lactate turnpoint, Yo-yo IRTL1 (m) = yo-yo intermittent recovery test level 1.

accordance with these recommendations, standard treadmill laboratory assessments of the lactate turnpoints (LT1/lactate threshold/Tlac and LT2/LTP) are useful for benchmarking and to set training zones. These can be accompanied by quantification of heart rate, running economy (oxygen uptake, energy expenditure, carbohydrate and fat utilisation) and rating of perceived exertion. Assessment of aerobic capacity can be made using a speed-based step test (increments of 1 kph^{-1} each minute with a fixed 1% gradient). Where access to the physiology laboratories is limited, boxers can undertake field tests such as yo-yo intermittent recovery test level 1 (Krustrup et al., 2003), 30:15 intermittent running test (Buchheit, 2008) and a combination of 1000-m and 3000-m runs to estimate critical speed and D' (pronounced D-prime). Physiological assessments should be made at the start and 2 weeks before the end of a training camp, and preferably after each training block, taking care to avoid days with significant sparring volume and negative energy balance.

References

Buchheit, M. (2008). The 30–15 intermittent fitness test: Accuracy for individualizing interval training of young intermittent sport players. *Journal of Strength and Conditioning Research/National Strength and Conditioning Association*, 22(2), 365–374.

Chaabène, H., Tabben, M., Mkaouer, B., Franchini, E., Negra, Y., Hammami, M., Amara, S., Chaabène, R. B. and Hachana, Y. (2014). Amateur boxing: Physical and physiological attributes. *Sports Medicine*, 337–352.

Davis, P., Leithäuser, R. and Beneke, R. (2014). The energetics of semicontact 3 × 2-min amateur boxing. *International Journal of Sports Physiology and Performance*, 9(2), 233–239.

Hanon, C., Savarino, J. and Thomas, C. (2015). Blood lactate and acid-base balance of world-class amateur boxers after three 3-minute rounds in international competition.

Journal of Strength and Conditioning Research / National Strength and Conditioning Association, 29(4), 942–946.

Krustrup, P., Mohr, M., Amstrup, T., Rysgaard, T., Johansen, J., Steensberg, A., Pedersen, P. K. and Bangsbo, J. (2003). The yo-yo intermittent recovery test: Physiological response, reliability, and validity. *Medicine and Science in Sports and Exercise*, 35(4), 697–705.

Nakano, G., Iino, Y., Imura, A. and Kojima, T. (2014). Transfer of momentum from different arm segments to a light movable target during a straight punch thrown by expert boxers. *Journal of Sports Sciences*, 32(6), 517–523.

Piorkowski, B. A., Lees, A. and Barton, G. J. (2011). Single maximal versus combination punch kinematics. *Sports Biomechanics / International Society of Biomechanics in Sports*, 10(1), 1–11.

Reale, R., Slater, G. and Burke, L. M. (2018). Weight management practices of Australian Olympic combat sport athletes. *International Journal of Sports Physiology and Performance*, 13(4), 459–466.

Reljic, D., Hässler, E., Jost, J. and Friedmann-Bette, B. (2013). Rapid weight loss and the body fluid balance and hemoglobin mass of elite amateur boxers. *Journal of Athletic Training*, 48(1), 109–117.

Ruddock, A. D., Wilson, D. C. and Hembrough, D. (2018). Boxing. In A. Turner (ed.), *Routledge Handbook of Strength and Conditioning* (1st ed.), pp. 384–399. Abingdon, UK: Routledge.

Ruddock, A. D., Wilson, D. C., Thompson, S. W., Hembrough, D. and Winter, E. M. (2016). Strength and conditioning for professional boxing: Recommendations for physical preparation. *Journal of Strength and Conditioning Research / National Strength and Conditioning Association*, 38(2), 81–90.

Smith, M. S. (2006). Physiological profile of senior and junior england international amateur boxers. *Journal of Sports Science and Medicine*, 5(CSSI), 74–89.

Zubac, D., Karnincic, H. and Sekulic, D. (2018). Rapid weight loss is not associated with competitive success in elite youth Olympic-style boxers in Europe. *International Journal of Sports Physiology and Performance*, 13(7), 860–866.

11.3 Fencing

Lindsay Bottoms, Robert Cawdron, Steve Kemp, and Luke Oates

Fencing is an intermittent sport with three weapon categories: sabre, epée and foil. During a fight, fencers undertake multiple explosive actions (particularly lunging movements) to outscore their opponent. Typical work-to-rest ratios of 1:1.2 are observed for epée (Bottoms et al., 2013), 1:3 for foil (Roi and Bianchedi, 2008) and 1:6.5 for sabre (Aquili et al., 2013), whereby fencers will work for an average of 10, 5 and 2.5 s, respectively. Therefore, there are distinct differences between the weapons within fencing; sabre is more explosive, whereas epée has a greater submaximal component. Differences between weapons are primarily due to the specific rules of the discipline, whereby foil and sabre are played by a priority system (Roi and Bianchedi, 2008) where engaging the first attack could be vital to score points over an opponent. Epée is not played with a priority system and is therefore more tactical to outscore an opponent.

International fencing competitions last between 1 and 3 days. Although each competition day can last up to 12 h, actual fencing time has been estimated at between 5% and 15% of competition time (Roi and Bianchedi, 2008). Fencing competition runs in a similar format to a major football tournament, comprising an initial phase of pool fights in a round-robin stage (first to 5 points or maximum of 3 min), which then ranks subsequent knockout rounds of direct elimination (DE) fights (first to 15 points, timed 3 × 3 min bouts with 1-min rests). There are frequent rest periods between each DE fight, which can last from 5 min to multiple hours.

Within competitive fencing there is an emphasis on the phosphocreatine and aerobic energy systems, consequently demonstrating low concentrations of blood lactate (Oates et al., 2019). The cardiorespiratory demands during fencing competitions need to be considered as an important training component. For example, competitive fencers typically exhibit maximal oxygen uptake values within the range of ~50–60 ml·kg^{-1}·min^{-1} for men (Bottoms et al., 2013) and ~40–50 ml·kg^{-1}·min^{-1} for women (Bottoms et al., 2011). The mean estimated oxygen cost of both foil and epée competition has been found to be between 56% and 74% maximal oxygen uptake ($\dot{V}O_2$max; Iglesias i Reig and Rodríguez Guisado, 1999) with average heart rate (HR) values as high as 96% maximal heart rate (HR$_{max}$; Oates et al., 2019).

DOI: 10.4324/9781003045281-57

Laboratory testing

Aerobic capacity: treadmill test

A continuous incremental protocol is utilised to elicit volitional exhaustion within 8–12 min. This is typically an initial motorised treadmill speed of 8 km·h^{-1} at 1% gradient. An increase of 2 km·h^{-1} every 2 min for first 6 min occurs; thereafter, the gradient is increased by 2% every minute until volitional exhaustion. Expired gas analysis and HR are recorded throughout the test. Peak blood lactate concentration is determined 3 min following the cessation of exercise. Such protocols are selected, as the faster running speeds utilised in traditional treadmill protocols are too great for fencers, who do not routinely perform large volumes of running as part of their training.

Anaerobic capacity: multiple sprints

This test has been adapted from the original Wingate test (Bar-Or, 1987) to simulate the intermittent demands of fencing based on analyses of different weapons outlined earlier. Fencers undergo a 5-min warm-up on a cycle ergometer against a resistance equivalent to 1% body weight. For the main test, epée fencers pedal maximally for 10 s followed by 12 s rest, whereas foil and sabre fencers undertake a 5-s sprint followed by 15 s rest. All fencers repeat this combination eight times to reflect the duration of a pool fight. Recommended resistances are 8% and 6% body mass for males and females, respectively. Peak power (W, W·kg^{-1}) percent fatigue index for each sprint is recorded. Further indices of fatigue can be calculated over the eight sprints [((Peak power 1 – peak power 8)/Peak power 1) × 100].

Strength: isokinetic dynamometry

Strength asymmetries can be an issue for fencers (Roi and Bianchedi, 2008), with the dominant side being overdeveloped compared to the non-dominant side. Performing knee flexion and extension, shoulder flexion and extension and hip flexion and extension on both sides of the body is important to provide information for conditioning training programmes. Bilateral comparisons for each joint should be within 10% of each other. A warm-up of the flexion and extension movement to be tested at 50% perceived exertion should be performed followed by a 1-min passive recovery followed by three maximal efforts at 60 degrees·s^{-1} and 180 degrees·s^{-1}. Peak torque and mean power are recorded. Normative data for club-level fencers are shown in Table 11.3.1.

Field testing

The following field tests: 30–15 intermittent test, in-line lunge, repeated sprint ability (RSA) and the 5–0–5 agility test, are recommended for fencers by the athlete development team at British Fencing. These tests were introduced in 2021, and therefore there are little normative data for fencers available at the time of press (Table 11.3.2). However, improved performance in all these tests is relevant

Table 11.3.1 Mean ± SD isokinetic data for club-level fencers

	Mean ± SD Peak Torque: Dominant (Nm)	Mean ± SD Peak Torque: Non-dominant (Nm)
Knee flexion	87.3 ± 26.7	80.0 ± 23.1
Knee extension	155.8 ± 54.9	147.4 ± 52.6
Shoulder flexion	51.6 ± 20.1	54.2 ± 19.6
Shoulder extension	60.1 ± 23.2	59.4 ± 21.7
Hip flexion	102.5 ± 45.0	95.6 ± 44.8
Hip extension	155.8 ± 54.9	106.7 ± 29.6

Source: Unpublished data from authors.

Table 11.3.2 Mean ± SD unpublished data (from British Fencing) for male and female (16–20 yr) fencers

	Male Mean ±SD	Female Mean ±SD
Agility 5–0–5 left leg (s)	4.36 ± 1.16	4.54 ± 1.33
Agility 5–0–5 right leg (s)	4.40 ± 1.40	4.59 ± 1.40
30–15 test: final speed (km·h^{-1})	17.7 ± 3.0	15.0 ± 3.8
RSA best time (s)	3.43 ± 0.45	3.66 ± 0.45
RSA average time (s)	4.09 ± 0.65	4.41 ± 0.67

to all three weapons. Some variance might be expected between weapons, with epée fencers tending to score higher on the 30–15 intermittent test and sabre fencers higher on RSA.

The 30–15 intermittent test is a composite, incremental, intermittent running test that assesses $\dot{V}O_2$max and maximal HR in the field through frequent changes in direction and regular low-intensity recovery periods between running bouts (Buchheit, 2008). The test consists of intermittent 30-s runs on a 40-m course, interspersed by 15 s of walking recovery (Buchheit, 2008). The initial running speed starts at 10 km·h^{-1} with an increase of 0.5 km·h^{-1} per running stage (every 45 s) guided by commercially available software. Running speed at the final stage is recorded as the outcome measure. An equation to convert to estimated $\dot{V}O_2$max can be found in the supplementary material.

The in-line lunge test is taken from the functional movement screening assessment, and methods can be found elsewhere (Cook et al., 2014) and in the supplementary material. The test identifies imbalances in mobility, stability and movement patterns.

The RSA test follows the guidelines of Aziz et al. (2008) and involves ten maximal 20-m sprints separated by 20 s of recovery. The time for each sprint is recorded using light gates. The fastest time and the average time over all ten sprints are recorded. The difference in time between best and average times indicates RSA.

Finally, the 5–0–5 change of direction test can be completed as per the original protocol by Draper and Lancaster (1985). Three lines are marked out; the first is the start line, the second line is 10 m away and the third is a further 5 m from that. Timing gates should be placed at the second line. The fencer sprints from the start line to the third line as fast as they can, turns using their left leg and sprints back through the second line. Sprints are repeated three times for turning on each leg with 2 min rest between repetitions. The best time and the average time are recorded.

Further field testing includes the following assessments: single- and double-legged broad jumps, muscular endurance (using a repeated lunge test for 60 s, where the number of lunges completed is recorded), core strength (target plank duration of 90 s), flexibility (sit and reach) and power (three maximal hops for distance).

Summary

It is important that verbal feedback is provided on the day of the test battery and written feedback within 7 days. Feedback should be provided in an appropriate format for the fencer and coach. Fencers should repeat testing every 12 wk to ensure progression is monitored. The tests outlined in this chapter assess the major physiological characteristics required of an elite-level fencer. The laboratory tests give an indication of physiological variables that impact fencing performance and field-based tests, established by British Fencing, and provide an easy and inexpensive method to measure specific attributes required to be an elite fencer.

References

Aquili, A., Tancredi, V., Triossi, T., De Sanctis, D., Padua, E., D'Arcangelo, G. and Melchiorri, G. (2013). Performance analysis in saber. *Journal of Strength and Conditioning Research*, 27(3), 624–630. doi: 10.1519/JSC.0b013e318257803f

Aziz, A. R., Mukherjee, S., Chia, M. Y. H. and Teh, K. C. (2008). Validity of the running repeated sprint ability test among playing positions and level of competitiveness in trained soccer players. *International Journal of Sports Medicine*, 29(10), 833–838. doi: 10.1055/s-2008-1038410

Bar-Or, O. (1987). The Wingate anaerobic test an update on methodology, reliability and validity. *Sports Medicine: An International Journal of Applied Medicine and Science in Sport and Exercise*, 4(6), 381–394. doi: 10.2165/00007256-198704060-00001

Bottoms, L., Sinclair, J., Gabrysz, T., Gabrysz, U. and Price, M. (2011). Physiological responses and energy expenditure to simulated epée fencing in elite female fencers. *Serbian Journal of Sports Sciences*, 5(1), 17–20.

Bottoms, L., Sinclair, J., Rome, P., Gregory, K. and Price, M. (2013). Development of a lab based epée fencing protocol. *International Journal of Performance Analysis in Sport*, 13(1), 11–22. doi: 10.1080/24748668.2013.11868628

Buchheit, M. (2008). The 30–15 intermittent fitness test: Accuracy for individualizing interval training of young intermittent sport players. *Journal of Strength and Conditioning Research*, 22(2), 365–374. doi: 10.1519/JSC.0b013e3181635b2e

Cook, G., Burton, L., Hoogenboom, B. J. and Voight, M. (2014). Functional movement screening: The use of fundamental movements as an assessment of function-part 2.

International Journal of Sports Physical Therapy, 9(4), 549–563. www.ncbi.nlm.nih.gov/pubmed/25133083%0Awww.pubmedcentral.nih.gov/articlerender.fcgi?artid=PMC4127517

Draper, J. A. and Lancaster, M. G. (1985). The 505 test: A test for agility in the horizontal plane. *Australian Journal of Science and Medicine in Sport*, 15–18.

Iglesias i Reig, X. and Rodríguez Guisado, F. (1999). Consumo de oxígeno estimado y gasto energético en competiciones de esgrima. *Apunts: Educación física y deportes*, (55), 35–46.

Oates, L. W., Campbell, I. G., Iglesias, X., Price, M. J., Muniz-Pumares, D. and Bottoms, L. M. (2019). The physiological demands of elite epée fencers during competition. *International Journal of Performance Analysis in Sport*, 19(1), 76–89. doi: 10.1080/24748668.2018.1563858

Roi, G. S. and Bianchedi, D. (2008). The science of fencing. *Sports Medicine*. doi: 10.2165/00007256-200838060-00003

Part XII
Paralympic specific

12.1 Ambulant para-athletes

Ben Stephenson, Michael Hutchinson, and Vicky L. Goosey-Tolfrey

Ambulant para-athletes, i.e., those not relying on a wheelchair for mobility, are a large and heterogeneous subset of the para-athlete population. There are numerous unique or adapted sports featuring ambulant para-athletes. For example, at the 2021 Summer Paralympic Games in Tokyo, ambulant athletes will feature in 21 of the 22 sports (Tokyo, 2020, 2020). Using the ten impairment types eligible for participation in the Paralympic Games (International Paralympic Committee [IPC], 2016), whilst acknowledging this is a non-exhaustive list of potential impairments exhibited by athletes in para-sport, this chapter aims to map considerations for each impairment across testing scenarios.

Presented in this chapter are both general considerations and specific aspects exclusive to para-athletes of varying impairments. However, it must be stressed that para-athletes are an inherently diverse population where two athletes with the same impairment are likely to display different test modification requirements. Although common considerations are provided, the athlete themselves will likely provide the richest information. As such, before testing a para-athlete for the first time, it is advised that specific questions are asked in addition to the formal health screen (including medication) to better understand a specific athlete's needs. For example: What is the nature of your impairment and how does that impact on your body's function? Does your impairment necessitate any modifications to your sport (e.g., equipment)? How might your impairment impact on your ability to undertake this test (having explained the test protocols)?

General considerations

Whilst many impairment-specific testing considerations exist, there are factors common across multiple para-athlete cohorts that diverge from able-bodied guidelines; these are as follows:

1 Para-athletes are more likely to have a carer/handler/nurse present with them during testing. This accompanying person should be acknowledged in any risk assessment.
2 In most cases, performance levels will be inferior to athletes in able-bodied sports due to the impairment and typically shorter training histories. A

DOI: 10.4324/9781003045281-59

well-trained, senior para-athlete with a minor impairment is likely to display performance values closer to an able-bodied junior athlete. Consequently, starting intensities and increments for step and ramp tests should be modified from able-bodied recommendations.

3. Due to the significant heterogeneity and small population size of ambulant para-athletes, reference values (e.g., running peak rate of oxygen uptake; $\dot{V}O_2$peak) are currently unavailable for physiological parameters.
4. Formulae and assumptions for body composition estimates will be invalid in most para-athletes due to anthropometric differences (e.g., short stature or arthrogryposis) (Willems et al., 2015).
5. When assessing skinfold thickness, it may not be possible to sample each site on the same side of the body; in this instance, sampling may mix between sides but should be consistent within an athlete during subsequent tests.
6. Due to the potential for limb deficiencies and/or impairments in muscle function, relativising values (e.g., oxygen consumption [$\dot{V}O_2$] or power output) to body mass is likely inappropriate when making comparisons between athletes.
7. Because of anthropometric differences (e.g., short stature or upper limb deficiencies) or impairments to peripheral blood flow, venous or arterialised venous blood sampling may be challenging using sites on the upper limbs.
8. For athletes with impairments in muscle function, maximal rate of oxygen uptake ($\dot{V}O_2$max) is likely not attained during incremental tests to exhaustion; thus, $\dot{V}O_2$peak is more appropriate.

Upper body impairments

1. Able-bodied reference values for lung and respiratory muscle function will be invalid if the athlete displays an impairment in their thoracic cage and/or respiratory muscle activation.
2. During tests on a treadmill, athletes will likely have trouble suspending their body using the sidebars and straddling the belt. In this instance, the treadmill belt should be gradually slowed to a stop between stages to facilitate blood sampling.
3. Testing lower body power via a vertical jump may not be possible using a Vertex or similar apparatus. Whilst cognisant of their limitations, a timing mat or use of video software is a better alternative.

Lower body impairments

1. Equipment modifications may be required. For example:
    a. Wheelchair scales may be more accessible even for ambulant athletes when measuring body mass.
    b. If testing upper body strength using bench press one repetition max, a modified bench may be required for athletes who lack the ability to stabilise their abdomen from below.

2   During swimming tests (e.g., 7 × 200 m step test), athletes may have challenges when 'pushing off' the wall to start a rep or during turns. This should be acknowledged when implementing a protocol, and practitioners should seek to minimise this interference, for example using a 50-m rather than a 25-m pool.

Impairment-specific considerations

Impaired muscle power

Athletes in this group display reduced force generated by muscles as caused, for example, by incomplete spinal cord injuries, spina bifida or polio (IPC, 2016). Athletes in this group are commonly wheelchair users (see Chapter 12.2); however, a minority will be ambulant.

1   Athletes may lack the muscle function for active tests of flexibility. Passive tests may be more appropriate.
2   Athletes may be susceptible to thermoregulatory strain (Griggs et al., 2019). The test environment should be cooler (16°–18°C), with fans and/or misting sprays employed during prolonged protocols (Griggs et al., 2017).
3   Athletes with a spinal cord injury may have irregularities in cardiac function, including a reduced maximum heart rate (Krassioukov and Claydon, 2006). Consequently, production of training zones based on heart rate may be inappropriate and should use external workload and/or perceptual variables instead (Paulson et al., 2015).
4   Catheterised athletes should empty their bag before providing a fresh urine sample. These athletes will usually have a regular pattern for when they void; discuss this with them when implementing hydration monitoring.

Impaired passive range of movement

Athletes in this group have their range of movement in one or more joints reduced permanently, for example, due to arthrogryposis (IPC, 2016).

1   Caution should be applied when assessing flexibility of impaired joints, and tolerable limits should be known.
2   Tests involving a significant eccentric muscular contraction component, for example, isokinetic or isoinertial strength tests or countermovement and drop jumps for power, may be a risk to impaired joints.

Limb deficiency or leg length difference

Athletes in these groups have a total or partial absence of, or shortening of, bones or joints due to trauma, illness or congenital limb deficiency (IPC, 2016).

1. Athletes may require more preparation time to equip or change a liner and prosthetic. This should be factored into the test duration.
2. For athletes who use running blades, increments in speed may be preferable during ramp tests due to difficulties running at steep gradients.
3. Athletes with a running blade will have greater difficulty stabilising whilst running on uneven surfaces, which must be considered for any field-based testing (e.g., an athletics track is preferable to running on grass).
4. Athletes with an above-knee amputation or equivalent may require a wide treadmill due to significant lateral motion caused as they 'hitch' their leg forward.

Hypertonia, ataxia or athetosis

Athletes in these three groups show abnormal increases in muscle tension and a reduced ability of a muscle to stretch; lack of coordination of muscle movements (hypertonia); unbalanced, involuntary movements (ataxia); or difficulty in maintaining a symmetrical posture (athetosis) due to a neurological condition such as cerebral palsy, brain injury or multiple sclerosis (IPC, 2016).

1. Warm testing environments should be avoided due to the risk of heat strain caused by thermoregulatory dysfunction, manifested by extreme temperature sensitivity (Christogianni et al., 2018).
2. Cold environments and surfaces which can trigger increased spasticity should equally be avoided.
3. Caution should be applied when assessing flexibility of joints controlled by impaired hypertonic muscle groups, and tolerable limits should be known.
4. Tests involving a significant eccentric muscular contraction component, for example, isokinetic or isoinertial strength tests or countermovement and drop jumps for power, may be a risk to hypertonic muscles.
5. Athletes with ataxia have impaired intermuscular coordination.
    a. During cycling tests of peak power output, athletes may display a slower optimal cadence.
    b. During running ramp tests, gradient increases may be preferable to speed increments.
6. Due to movement inefficiencies, using fixed blood lactate concentration values (e.g., 4 $mmol \cdot L^{-1}$) may be an inappropriate parameter for comparisons between athletes.

Short stature

Athletes in this group present a reduced standing height due to abnormal dimensions of bones of the upper and lower limbs or trunk, for example, due to achondroplasia or growth hormone dysfunction (IPC, 2016).

1   The size and dimensions of ergometers or dynamometers must be accessible, acknowledging the unique differences in limb length. So, too, should the height of testing equipment such as timing gates for field-based tests of speed and agility or the equipment used for drop jumps to assess lower body power.
2   Similarly, the size of wearable equipment (e.g., heart rate monitors or harnesses) should be appropriate.

Vision impairment

For athletes in this group, vision is impacted by either an impairment of the eye structure, optical nerves or optical pathways or the visual cortex (IPC, 2016).

1   The test environment must be free from any trip hazards or protruding edges that an athlete may walk into. Athletes may require guiding around the laboratory.
2   Athletes may have difficulty sensing their position on a treadmill during running tests and should be provided with constant feedback.
3   Athletes may also struggle to run in a straight line for field-based speed tests and should be guided through, with timing gates spaced far enough apart to account for this.
4   During swimming tests, athletes should be provided with auditory or tactile feedback when they near a wall.
5   Field-based tests of agility requiring athletes to navigate their way around markers may not be feasible.
6   Athletes may not be able to see information on a screen (e.g., power output or heart rate) to regulate their intensity during time trials. Similarly, athletes may not be able to read a rating of perceived exertion (RPE) scale. In both cases, the practitioner should read out this information for the athlete.

Intellectual impairment

Those with an intellectual impairment show a limitation in intellectual functioning and adaptive behaviour as expressed in conceptual, social and practical adaptive skills, which originates before the age of 18 (IPC, 2016).

1   Additional precautions may need to be considered in a risk assessment, depending on an athlete's impairment severity, and a witness may be required when consent to testing is provided.
2   Athletes may struggle with the cognitive requirements of new test situations. It is important an athlete is fully familiar with the test demands via prior experience (e.g., familiarisation tests).
3   Athletes can display difficulties in the regulation of effort (Van Biesen et al., 2017). As such, pacing with and between time trials (e.g., 400-m sprint or 12-min cycling critical power test) may be sub-optimal. Full familiarisation

and constant feedback may ameliorate this issue. Alternatively, constant work-rate tests to exhaustion could better depict the intensity-duration curve in linear sports.

4 Athletes may not fully comprehend a typical RPE scale; thus, a pictorial scale may be better suited.

References

Christogianni, A., Bibb, R., Davis, S. L., Jay, O., Barnett, M., Evangelou, N. and Filingeri, D. (2018). Temperature sensitivity in multiple sclerosis: An overview of its impact on sensory and cognitive symptoms. *Temperature*, 5(3), 208–223.

Griggs, K. E., Havenith, G., Paulson, T., Price, M. J. and Goosey-Tolfrey, V. L. (2017). Effects of cooling before and during simulated match play on thermoregulatory responses of athletes with tetraplegia. *Journal of Science and Medicine in Sport*, 20(9), 819–824.

Griggs, K. E., Stephenson, B. T., Price, M. J. and Goosey-Tolfrey, V. L. (2019). Heat-related issues and practical applications for Paralympic athletes at Tokyo 2020. *Temperature*, 7(1), 37–57.

International Paralympic Committee. (2016). *International Standard for Eligible Impairments*. www.paralympic.org/sites/default/files/document/161004145727129_2016_10_04_International_Standard_for_Eligible_Impairments_1.pdf (accessed 31 March 2020).

Krassioukov, A. and Claydon, V. E. (2006). The clinical problems in cardiovascular control following spinal cord injury: An overview. *Progress in Brain Research*, 152, 223–229.

Paulson, T. A. W., Mason, B., Rhodes, J. and Goosey-Tolfrey, V. L. (2015). Individualized internal and external training load relationships in elite wheelchair rugby players. *Frontiers in Physiology*, 6. doi: 10.3389/fphys.2015.00388

Tokyo 2020. (2020). *Sports*. https://tokyo2020.org/en/paralympics/sports/ (accessed 19 November 2020).

Van Biesen, D., Hettinga, F. J., McCulloch, K. and Vanlandewijck, Y. C. (2017). Pacing ability in elite runners with intellectual impairment. *Medicine and Science in Sports and Exercise*, 49(3), 588–594.

Willems, A., Paulson, T. A. W., Keil, M., Brooke-Wavell, K. and Goosey-Tolfrey, V. L. (2015). Dual-energy x-ray absorptiometry, skinfold thickness, and waist circumference for assessing body composition in ambulant and non-ambulant wheelchair games players. *Frontiers in Physiology*, 27(6), 356.

12.2 Wheeled para-sport

Michael Hutchinson, Tom O'Brien, Connor Murphy, and Vicky L. Goosey-Tolfrey

Wheeled sport is a broad term that can be broken down broadly into two categories: court and non-court based. Court sports include wheelchair basketball (WB), wheelchair rugby (WRug), and wheelchair tennis (WT). The non-court sports handcycling (HC) and wheelchair racing (WRac) are elements of the road cycling and athletics schedule, respectively, with both featuring as elements of paratriathlon (PTWC class). Court sports require aerobic fitness combined with speed, power, repeated sprint ability and agility. While HC and WRac are predominantly endurance-based, there are aspects that require significant anaerobic contributions (e.g., sprint/middle distance events, changes of pace, sprint finishes). This chapter will aim to outline laboratory and field-based protocols for components of fitness that are relevant to each sport.

As athletes with a wide range of impairments are eligible for wheeled sports, it is not possible to discuss all the specific considerations for conducting a test. One pertinent consideration, though, is that athletes with a spinal cord injury (above the T6 level) are at risk of autonomic dysreflexia (AD), a sympathetic reflex resulting in hypertension and tachycardia. To reduce the likelihood of AD, athletes should fully void their bladder and have blood pressure recorded before testing (Cragg and Krassioukov, 2012). Heart rate should be monitored, and if AD is evident (raised blood pressure, bradycardia, headache, sweating above the level of injury, goosebumps below the level of injury, blurred vision), the test must be immediately terminated, blood pressure frequently monitored and medical assistance sought (Cragg and Krassioukov, 2012). For further, more specific impairment-related information, the reader is directed to Goosey-Tolfrey et al. (2013).

Laboratory assessment of aerobic capacity

Exercise modes

An important aspect of laboratory testing is to maintain a degree of ecological validity. The preference is for athletes to use their own sports chair/handcycle in conjunction with specialised equipment such as a motorised treadmill, wheelchair ergometer (WERG) or Cyclus 2 ergometer, which some laboratories may not have. That said, rollers or a turbo trainer could be used, provided the wheelchair/

DOI: 10.4324/9781003045281-60

handcycle is fitted with a speedometer/power meter and the resistance can be reproduced. In these situations, the athlete should be encouraged to incorporate any individual factors regarding their set-up, such as strapping or gloves. Before testing, it is important to check the tyre pressure of the main wheels and inflate if required.

Arm crank ergometry (ACE), though not sport-specific, is an alternative testing modality that may be more accessible. Though there are important differences compared to wheelchair propulsion in terms of technique and mechanical efficiency that influence the power outputs achieved from the tests, ACE still provides a useful measure of aerobic capacity. If using ACE, standardise the vertical position of the ergometer such that the crank axis centre is level with the athlete's shoulder and the horizontal position to allow slight flexion at the farthest point in the crank cycle (Goosey-Tolfrey and Sindall, 2007).

Step and ramp tests

As mentioned previously, athletes with a range of different impairments and health conditions are eligible for wheeled sports. However, key protocols generally reflect those undertaken for able-bodied sports.

To determine ventilatory/blood lactate thresholds for all sports, submaximal tests utilising 3-min stages are recommended. If using a treadmill, the gradient should be set to 1%. A discontinuous treadmill/WERG protocol will be necessary if measuring blood lactate, whereas HC and ACE tests can be continuous. Capillary blood will need to be sampled from an earlobe, rather than from a fingertip.

Starting speed/power output, as well as the increment, will largely depend on the athlete's level of impairment and training status. An athlete with a greater level of impairment (e.g., WRug player with tetraplegia) or lower training status will require a slower starting speed and smaller increment, with each stage compared to one with a lower level of impairment (e.g., WB player with lower limb amputation) or higher training status. Aim to complete six to eight stages and end the test when blood lactate concentration exceeds 4 mmol·L^{-1}. Athletes with tetraplegia or high-level paraplegia may have blunted blood lactate responses to exercise. Therefore, for more applicable training prescription information, collect the rating of perceived exertion (RPE) for each exercise stage, terminating the test at 17 on Borg's 6–20 scale or 8 on Borg's 0–10 category-ratio scale. Table 12.2.1 shows recommendations for starting speed ranges and stage increments per sport.

Following a submaximal test, participants should receive 10–15 min of recovery before undertaking a graded exercise test (GXT) to exhaustion. Start the GXT at the speed/power output, coinciding with the first increase in blood lactate concentration above rest (RPE of 10–12/2–4) for 1 min. Subsequent increases each minute of 0.1 m·s^{-1} (court sports), 15–20 W (HC/ACE), or 1 km·h^{-1} (WRac) are appropriate. Expected values for peak oxygen uptake can be found in Table 12.2.2.

Table 12.2.1 Sport-specific starting workload

Sport	Starting Speed or Power and Stage Increment
Wheelchair basketball	Low point (<2.0 classification): 1.4–2.0 + 0.3 m·s^{-1}
	Mid and High point (≥2.0 classification): 1.6–2.4 + 0.4 m·s^{-1}
Wheelchair rugby	Low point (≤2.0 classification): 0.8–1.8 + 0.2 m·s^{-1}
	High point (>2.0 classification): 1.4–2.4 + 0.3 m·s^{-1}
Wheelchair tennis	Quad class: 1.0–1.6 + 0.2 m·s^{-1}
	Open class: 1.4–2.0 + 0.3 m·s^{-1}
Handcycling*	15–60 W + 10–20 W
Wheelchair racing*	10–20 km·h^{-1} + 1–1.5 km·h^{-1}

* Large range of starting speeds reflects the wide range in level of impairment of athletes competing in these sports.

Table 12.2.2 Sport-average reference values for laboratory-based tests

Component of Fitness	Outcome	Sport	Sport Class	Reference Values
Aerobic capacity	Peak oxygen uptake[1]	Wheelchair basketball		2.5 ± 0.1 L·min^{-1}
		Wheelchair rugby		1.3 ± 0.1 L·min^{-1}
		Wheelchair tennis		2.2 ± 0.2 L·min^{-1}
		Handcycling		2.6 ± 0.2 L·min^{-1}
		Wheelchair racing		2.2 ± 0.2 L·min^{-1}
Anaerobic capacity	Peak power output	Handcycling[2]	H3–H4	Trained: 334 ± 18 W
				Elite: 377 ± 59 W
		Wheelchair basketball[3]	1.0–2.5	530 ± 131 W
			3.0–4.5	657 ± 104 W
		Wheelchair rugby[4]	0.5–1.5	345 ± 138 W
			2.0–3.5	867 ± 208 W
	Mean power output	Wheelchair basketball[3]	1.0–2.5	284 ± 41 W
			3.0–4.5	344 ± 75 W
		Wheelchair rugby[4]	0.5–1.5	245 ± 91 W
			2.0–3.5	546 ± 148 W
	Fatigue index	Wheelchair basketball[3]	1.0–2.5	14 ± 6%
			3.0–4.5	17 ± 5%
		Wheelchair rugby[4]	0.5–1.5	27 ± 7%
			2.0–3.5	38 ± 11%

Data presented as mean ± SD.

1 Values from Baumgart et al. (2018).
2 Values from Stone et al. (2019).
3 Values from Marszałek et al. (2019).
4 Values from unpublished testing.

Critical power/speed

An alternative to ventilatory/blood lactate thresholds for HC and WRac is to estimate the transition between heavy and severe exercise intensity domains through monitoring critical power (CP) or critical speed (CS) (see also Chapter 3.7). CP and CS denote an important fatigue threshold relating to exercise (in)tolerance and offer great potential for predicting athletic performance (Poole et al., 2020). They can be calculated by having athletes complete three to five time trials or time to exhaustion tests, lasting 2–15 min, with analysis using a combination of completion time, work done (CP) and distance covered (CS). Though there is limited work in these specific sports using CP and CS, the principles and testing parameters can be directly applied from able-bodied testing (Antunes et al., 2019).

Laboratory assessment of anaerobic capacity

As with able-bodied sports, a 30-s Wingate test (WAnT) is commonly used in the laboratory to determine anaerobic performance. Though ACE can be used, a WERG is more suitable for court sports and WRac, whilst a Cyclus 2 is preferable for HC. Main outputs include peak and mean power output and fatigue index (Table 12.2.2). Dual-roller WERGs also allow for analysis of left/right side (a)symmetry.

Discrete specifications exist related to WERG design and braking systems (see De Klerk et al., 2020). The following information pertains to conducting a WAnT using a Lode Esseda, a mechanically braked, dual-roller WERG:

1. Securely attach the wheelchair to the WERG, ensuring both wheel centres are positioned on the apex of the roller.
2. Perform an automatic calibration after inputting the athlete's body mass and chair dimensions. The calibration produces a braking load based on the combined mass to reflect overground propulsion for the individual athlete.
3. This initial braking load is likely insufficient to facilitate peak power generation, so a constant resistance coefficient should be added. Our laboratory uses 0.027. Note: Further work is required to determine the optimal braking load that is sport and classification specific.
4. A rolling start is recommended to overcome the initial inertia associated with the braking load.

If using ACE or HC, application of resistances equal to 5% of body mass is common (Stephenson et al., 2021), though unpublished observations from our laboratory suggest resistances up to 10% may be required for less impaired and more well-trained athletes.

Assessment of speed, agility and repeated sprint performance

Field-based testing is an attractive and important option for testing an athlete's physical capacity. For court sports, field-based testing is most relevant for

Table 12.2.3 Sport-average reference values for field-based tests

Component of Fitness	Outcome	Sport	Sport Class	Reference Values
Speed	5 m	Wheelchair basketball[1]	1.0–2.5 3.0–4.5	2.14 ± 0.73 s 1.87 ± 0.15 s
		Wheelchair rugby[2]	0.5–1.5 2.0–3.5	2.09–3.19 s 1.69–2.38 s
	10 m	Wheelchair basketball[1]	1.0–2.5 3.0–4.5	3.28 ± 0.27 s 3.22 ± 0.22 s
		Wheelchair rugby[2]	0.5–1.5 2.0–3.5	3.58–5.35 s 2.87–3.85 s
	20 m	Wheelchair basketball[1]	1.0–2.5 3.0–4.5	5.57 ± 0.47 s 5.40 ± 0.48 s
		Wheelchair rugby[2]	0.5–1.5 2.0–3.5	6.10–9.06 s 4.86–6.34 s
Agility	Agility test	Wheelchair rugby[2]	0.5–1.5 2.0–3.5	10.43–14.36 s 9.17–10.84 s
	Box test	Wheelchair rugby[2]	0.5–1.5 2.0–3.5	11.16–16.57 s 8.95–11.90 s
	Fan drill	Wheelchair tennis[2]	Open Quad	20–25 s 24–30 s

Data presented as mean ± SD, or typical range.

1 Values from Marszałek et al. (2019).
2 Values from unpublished testing in the author's laboratory.

investigating anaerobic components of fitness and chair manoeuvrability skills whilst also providing ecological validity by utilising the competition environment (e.g., indoor court, grass tennis court). Expected values for the various tests presented can be found in Table 12.2.3.

20-m linear sprint

Mark a starting line and place timing gates at the start, 5, 10 and 20 m. Individual pairs of timing gates should be separated by 3 m. Athletes should position their front castors 30 cm behind the starting line and begin from stationary. Each athlete performs three sprints with all splits recorded.

Agility test

This tests the ability to change direction with varying angles at high speed. A rolling start of 5 m is given before the athlete manoeuvres around the cones in the

344 *Michael Hutchinson et al.*

direction shown (Figure 12.2.1A), performing the test twice on the right side and twice on the left with the best and mean scores taken.

Box test

This tests a number of chair manoeuvrability skills. Athletes must accelerate into and stop within the left box before pulling backwards, turning outwards and

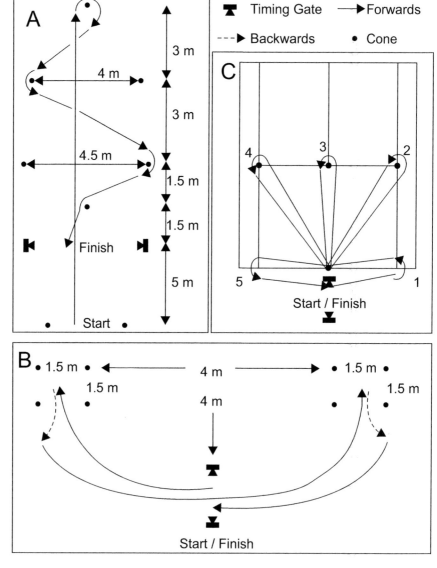

Figure 12.2.1 Schematic for (A) agility test, (B) box test and (C) fan drill. In each case the start and finish are marked with the direction of travel shown by the arrows.

accelerating forwards through the gates into the right box. The reverse manoeuvre is then performed before finishing by going back through the timing gates (Figure 12.2.1B). This is repeated four times with two attempts each starting with the left and right boxes. All split times should be recorded, with the total time being the most important.

Fan drill (wheelchair tennis specific)

This test can be performed with or without a racket. Athletes start behind the centre of the baseline and sequentially push around cones where the baseline and service line meet the singles tramline in an anti-clockwise manner, returning to the centre baseline each time (Figure 12.2.1C). Athletes generally complete this test three times, with the potential to complete more repetitions for an analysis of fatigue index (see later).

20 × 20 m repeated sprint test

Repeated sprint ability is important, given the intermittent nature of wheelchair court sports. Place pairs of timing gates 20 m apart, with at least 5 m of space beyond both sets. Athletes complete 20 repeated 20-m sprints, with the start line of each sprint being the finishing line of the previous sprint. The rest time is double that of their first sprint time (1:2 work:rest ratio). Each sprint time is recorded and can be used to assess the atigue index (Gee et al., 2018):

*Fatigue index (%) = [(worst time − best time)/best time] * 100*

Timing gates can also be placed at 5 and 10 m to allow analysis of acceleration under fatigue.

References

Antunes, D., Nascimento, E. M. F., Tremel, A., do Nascimento Salvador, P. C., Fischer, G., Dantas de Lucas, R. and Brickley, G. (2019). Different approaches to determine physiological thresholds in handcycling athletes. In *XXI Brazilian Congress of Sport Sciences*. http://congressos.cbce.org.br/index.php/conbrace2019/8conice/paper/viewFile/12274/7237

Baumgart, J. K., Brurok, B. and Sandbakk, Ø. (2018). Peak oxygen uptake in Paralympic sitting sports: A systematic literature review, meta- and pooled-data analysis. *PLoS ONE*, 13(2), e0192903. https://doi.org/10.1371/journal.pone.0192903

Cragg, J. and Krassioukov, A. (2012). Autonomic dysreflexia. *CMAJ*, 184(1), 66. https://doi.org/10.1503/cmaj.110859

De Klerk, R., Vegter, R. J. K., Goosey-Tolfrey, V. L., Mason, B. S., Lenton, J. P., Veeger, D. H. E. J. and Van Der Woude, L. H. V. (2020). Measuring handrim wheelchair propulsion in the lab: A critical analysis of stationary ergometers. *IEEE Reviews in Biomedical Engineering*, 13, 199–211. https://doi.org/10.1109/RBME.2019.2942763

Gee, C. M., Lacroix, M. A. and West, C. R. (2018). A 20×20m repeated sprint field test replicates the demands of wheelchair rugby. *Journal of Science and Medicine in Sport*, 21(7), 753–757. https://doi.org/10.1016/j.jsams.2017.12.006

Goosey-Tolfrey, V., Leicht, C., Lenton, J., Diaper, N. and Mason, B. (2013). The BASES expert statement on assessment of exercise performance in athletes with a spinal cord injury. *Sport and Exercise Scientist*, (37), 8–9.

Goosey-Tolfrey, V. L. and Sindall, P. (2007). The effects of arm crank strategy on physiological responses and mechanical efficiency during submaximal exercise. *Journal of Sports Sciences*, 25(4), 453–460. https://doi.org/10.1080/02640410600702883

Marszałek, J., Kosmol, A., Morgulec-Adamowicz, N., Mróz, A., Gryko, K., Klavina, A., Skucas, K., Navia, A. and Molik, B. (2019). Laboratory and non-laboratory assessment of anaerobic performance of elite male wheelchair basketball athletes. *Frontiers in Psychology*, 10, 514. https://doi.org/10.3389/fpsyg.2019.00514

Poole, D. C., Rossiter, H. B., Brooks, G. A. and Gladden, L. B. (2020). The anaerobic threshold: 50+ years of controversy. *The Journal of Physiology*. https://doi.org/10.1113/jp279963

Stephenson, B. T., Stone, B., Mason, B. S. and Goosey-Tolfrey, V. L. (2021). Physiology of handcycling: A current sports perspective. *Scandinavian Journal of Medicine and Science in Sports*, 31(1), 4–20. https://doi.org/10.1111/sms.13835

Stone, B., Mason, B. S., Warner, M. B. and Goosey-Tolfrey, V. L. (2019). Shoulder and thorax kinematics contribute to increased power output of competitive handcyclists. *Scandinavian Journal of Medicine and Science in Sports*, 29(6), 843–853. https://doi.org/10.1111/sms.13402

12.3 Intellectual impairment

Jan Burns, Mohammed Khudair, and Florentina J. Hettinga

Intellectual impairment is characterised by significant limitations in both intellectual functioning (low IQ score) and adaptive behaviours (difficulties in communication, problem solving, planning, abstract thinking and learning from experiences), assessed before the age of 18 (AAIDD, 2010). Consequently, cognitive functioning in individuals with intellectual impairment can be delayed and underdeveloped (Nader-Grosbois, 2014). These deficits in cognitive functioning can impact the individual's ability to understand and attend to instructions, adapt to the environment, regulate behaviour and motivation and manage emotional and physical/physiological discomforts (Nader-Grosbois, 2014; Sakalidis et al., 2021). Individuals with intellectual impairment comprise about 2% of the general population and represent a wide range of sub-populations, depending on aetiology and severity of the intellectual impairment, age, level of cognitive development and additional limitations that accompany the impairment (Wouters et al., 2017). Individuals with intellectual impairment experience a high prevalence of additional health issues, with 98.7% having multimorbidity, including additional sensory impairments, i.e., visual and auditory, and limitations in physical function, i.e., muscular, motor and cardiorespiratory functions (Frey and Chow, 2006; Hilgenkamp et al., 2010; Kinnear et al., 2018). The number of additional health issues are related to the severity of the initial impairment, with higher severity leading to increased multimorbidity (Kinnear et al., 2018).

Significant differences may be found within this population in terms of performing physical activities. Generally, lower levels of physical fitness have been found across the life span for individuals with intellectual impairment, and this problem increases the more severe the disability (Hilgenkamp et al., 2012; Wouters et al., 2019). Low physical fitness for this group is related to both a reduction in independence and an increase in mortality (Oppewal et al., 2015; Oppewal and Hilgenkamp, 2019). Significant differences have been found in the areas of balance and fine motor control (Maïano et al., 2019), muscle strength and endurance (Blomqvist et al., 2013), flexibility (Skowroński et al., 2009), cardiorespiratory factors (Oppewal et al., 2013) and cognitive factors such as reaction time (Esposito et al., 2017). Importantly, differences can be found related to specific syndromes, for example, in Down syndrome (DS) there is an increased probability

DOI: 10.4324/9781003045281-61

of atlantooccipital and atlantoaxial instabilities (Tomlinson et al., 2020), and peak heart rate during exercise can be 15% lower (Mendonca et al., 2013).

Using and adapting general and sport-specific tests for individuals with intellectual impairment

A wide range of general as well as sport-specific exercise testing methodologies have been described in this edition of the BASES Guidelines for physiological testing that are very relevant to individuals with intellectual impairment. It is important to understand how intellectual impairment impacts on sports performance so that appropriate adaptations can be made when planning exercise testing strategies. Wouters et al. (2017) performed a systematic review of field-based physical fitness tests for children and adolescents with intellectual impairment, investigating the feasibility, reliability and validity of 18 tests. The tests covered body composition, muscular strength and endurance and cardiorespiratory fitness, with body mass index (BMI), bioelectrical impedance analysis (BIA), grip strength, arm hang and the fixed distance walk/run test meeting the highest standards. However, the authors cautioned that these tests have not been studied across the range of age and severity of intellectual impairment, and more work is required to assess their psychometric properties for wider use. In a comparable review of six fitness tests for autistic children, similar results were found, and the authors recommended the choice of shorter tests as being more reliable (Bremer and Cairney, 2019).

Nevertheless, certain adaptations can be made to the testing context to increase the feasibility, reliability and validity of the tests. The American College of Sports Medicine (2017, 329–331) provides some helpful guidelines in this respect. The testing environment can be intimidating and the athlete may be unfamiliar with the tasks, leading to anxiety and reducing motivation. Therefore, allowing additional time and practice opportunities and not assuming prior knowledge or experience can reduce anxiety and increase engagement. The athlete's performance expectations may need to be adjusted, with knowledge of any additional health issues or issues associated with the syndrome, such as the physiological limitations that reduce exercise capacity in individuals with DS (Mendonca et al., 2013). Having prior knowledge of the athlete, their communication skills and level of understanding is also key to making appropriate adjustments.

Exercise testing specifically for individuals with intellectual impairment

Acknowledging the problems when choosing the most appropriate tests for the intellectually impaired population associated with balancing the psychometric validity against adapting to the needs of the population, researchers have developed batteries of tests specifically for this group. The most commonly used battery is EUROFIT, which has been used to evaluate many of the Special Olympics programmes and has been shown to discriminate between severity of intellectual impairment, gender and age (Skowroński et al., 2009). However, other studies have reported some limitations, with not all athletes being able to engage with the tasks (e.g., Salaun and Berthouze-Aranda, 2012). Building on this previous work (Oppewal and Hilgenkamp, 2020) focussed on tests that had good psychometric standards and available reference data to use with adults with intellectual impairment, and built the ID-fitscan battery. This consists of tests of body composition (BMI, waist circumference), muscular endurance (chair stand), strength (grip strength), static balance (one-leg stance), dynamic balance (gait speed) and muscular endurance (5× chair stand). The recommended tests are used in the general population, but this project demonstrated that they can be used with adults with intellectual impairment without adaptation and with the added advantage of then being able to compare the results with available reference data.

Researchers have also developed a physical fitness battery for use with individuals with DS: the SAMU Disability Fitness Battery (SAMU-DISFIT) (Cabeza-Ruiz et al., 2019). This study examined the reliability and feasibility of eight field-based tests in the flexibility, cardiorespiratory, musculoskeletal and motor domains and concluded that the recommended tests are fit for purpose. The tests chosen for inclusion had proven acceptable for use with the DS population and were simple to explain or demonstrate. Hilgenkamp et al. (2012) developed a test battery explicitly for older (50+) adults with intellectual impairment, including walking speed, muscle strength (grip), muscle endurance (30-s chair stand) and cardiorespiratory endurance (10-m shuttle walking). Again, tests were chosen through a rigorous review of previous research in the general population, simplicity of presentation and tested on a large sample (N = 1050). The tests were found feasible to administer and valid, but the authors suggested caution with the interpretation of maximal and submaximal $\dot{V}O_2$max estimates for this population.

These test batteries demonstrate that fitness tests across the range of domains can be used with this population, and there is a growing evidence base for their validity and reliability; however, the majority of studies have concentrated on those with less severe intellectual impairment, and many of these tests remain unproven in their application to those with more severe intellectual impairment and multiple impairments.

Testing and classification in Paralympic sport

Exercise testing is very important for developing optimal training programmes and monitoring progress, but in Paralympic sports there is another very important goal for which exercise testing is important: classification. A part of Paralympic classification is to understand the impact of the impairment on sports performance and measure the extent of that impact (Tweedy et al., 2016). Within intellectual impairment Paralympic testing, a system has been developed which assesses the impact of both generic 'sports intelligence' and 'sport specific' intelligence. The generic component consists of cognitive tests which assess skills that are implicated in all sports performances, e.g., reaction time (Tweedy et al., 2016; Van Biesen, Mactavish et al., 2016).

The sports-specific component relates to those cognitive skills which have been identified as having significance for that specific sport. The specificity of the measures of eligibility for each sport is important, as sports are impacted differently by the impairment. For example, one of the most important determinants of performance in running is pacing, which is defined as 'the goal-directed distribution of energy over a pre-determined exercise task, a process of decision-making regarding how and when to expend energy' (Edwards and Polman, 2013; Smits et al., 2014). It is highly reliant on cognitive functioning, specifically self-regulatory skills, as it demands the ability to anticipate, plan, monitor, adapt and learn from experience (Elferink-Gemser and Hettinga, 2017). In studies of pacing behaviour of athletes with and without intellectual impairment in middle-distance running, it was found that athletes with intellectual impairment were less able to execute successful pacing strategies (Van Biesen, Hettinga et al., 2016) and to consistently pace themselves at targets of submaximal performance (Van Biesen et al., 2017) compared to athletes without intellectual impairment. Similarly, researchers have found that in sports which require both technical and tactical proficiency underpinned by complex cognitive skills, e.g., table tennis, that individuals with intellectual impairment show significantly lower levels of proficiency compared to their able-bodied counterparts (Van Biesen et al., 2012).

Conclusion

The ability to accurately and appropriately measure the fitness of individuals with intellectual impairment has important consequences across the spectrum of sport and exercise, from recreational participation aimed at increased health and well-being to elite competition where athletes with intellectual impairment compete alongside other Paralympians.

References

AAIDD. (2010). *Intellectual Disability, Definition, Classification and Systems of Support* (11th ed.). Washington, DC: AAIDD.

American College of Sports Medicine. (2017). *ACSM's Guidelines for Exercise Testing and Prescription (American College of Sports Medicine)* (10th ed.). LWW.

Blomqvist, S., et al. (2013). Adolescents with intellectual disability have reduced postural balance and muscle performance in trunk and lower limbs compared to peers without intellectual disability. *Research in Developmental Disabilities*, 34(1), 198–206. doi: 10.1016/j.ridd.2012.07.008

Bremer, E. and Cairney, J. (2019). Reliable and feasible fitness testing for children on the Autism spectrum. *Research Quarterly for Exercise and Sport*, 90(4), 497–506. doi: 10.1080/02701367.2019.1623367

Cabeza-Ruiz, R., et al. (2019). Feasibility and reliability of a physical fitness test battery in individuals with down syndrome. *International Journal of Environmental Research and Public Health*, 16(15). doi: 10.3390/ijerph16152685

Edwards, A. M. and Polman, R. C. J. (2013). Pacing and awareness: Brain regulation of physical activity. *Sports Medicine*, 43(11), 1057–1064. doi: 10.1007/s40279-013-0091-4

Elferink-Gemser, M. T. and Hettinga, F. J. (2017). Pacing and self-regulation: Important skills for talent development in endurance sports. *International Journal of Sports Physiology and Performance*, 12(6), 831–835. doi: 10.1123/ijspp.2017-0080

Esposito, P., et al. (2017). Reaction time and fine motor dexterity in adults with intellectual disabilities. *American Journal of Occupational Therapy*, 71(4), 7111500043p1–7111500043p1. doi: 10.5014/ajot.2017.71S1-PO4100

Frey, G. C. and Chow, B. (2006). Relationship between BMI, physical fitness, and motor skills in youth with mild intellectual disabilities. *International Journal of Obesity*, 30, 861–867. doi: 10.1038/sj.ijo.0803196

Hilgenkamp, T. I. M., et al. (2012). Physical activity levels in older adults with intellectual disabilities are extremely low. *Research in Developmental Disabilities*, 33(2), 477–483. doi: 10.1016/j.ridd.2011.10.011

Hilgenkamp, T. I. M., van Wijck, R. and Evenhuis, H. M. (2010). Physical fitness in older people with ID-Concept and measuring instruments: A review. *Research in Developmental Disabilities*, 31(5), 1027–1038. doi: 10.1016/j.ridd.2010.04.012

Kinnear, D., et al. (2018). Prevalence of physical conditions and multimorbidity in a cohort of adults with intellectual disabilities with and without down syndrome: Cross-sectional study. *BMJ Open*, 8(2), 1–10. doi: 10.1136/bmjopen-2017-018292

Maïano, C., et al. (2019). Do exercise interventions improve balance for children and adolescents with down syndrome? A systematic review. *Physical Therapy*, 99(5), 507–518. doi: 10.1093/ptj/pzz012

Mendonca, G. V., Pereira, F. D. and Fernhall, B. (2013). Heart rate recovery and variability following combined aerobic and resistance exercise training in adults with and without down syndrome. *Research in Developmental Disabilities*, 34(1), 353–361. doi: 10.1016/j.ridd.2012.08.023

Nader-Grosbois, N. (2014). Self-perception, self-regulation and metacognition in adolescents with intellectual disability. *Research in Developmental Disabilities*, 35(6), 1334–1348. doi: 10.1016/j.ridd.2014.03.033

Oppewal, A., et al. (2013). Cardiorespiratory fitness in individuals with intellectual disabilities: A review. *Research in Developmental Disabilities*, 34(10), 3301–3316. doi: 10.1016/j.ridd.2013.07.005

Oppewal, A., et al. (2015). Physical fitness is predictive for a decline in the ability to perform instrumental activities of daily living in older adults with intellectual disabilities: Results of the HA-ID study. *Research in Developmental Disabilities*, 41–42, 76–85. doi: 10.1016/j.ridd.2015.05.002

Oppewal, A. and Hilgenkamp, T. I. M. (2019). Physical fitness is predictive for 5-year survival in older adults with intellectual disabilities. *Journal of Applied Research in Intellectual Disabilities*, 32(4), 958–966. doi: 10.1111/jar.12589

Oppewal, A. and Hilgenkamp, T. I. M. (2020). Adding meaning to physical fitness test results in individuals with intellectual disabilities. *Disability and Rehabilitation*, 42(10), 1406–1413. doi: 10.1080/09638288.2018.1527399

Sakalidis, K. E., et al. (2021). The impact of cognitive functions and intellectual impairment on pacing and performance in sports. *Psychology of Sport and Exercise*, 52(November), 0–43. doi: 10.1016/j.psychsport.2020.101840

Salaun, L. and Berthouze-Aranda, S. E. (2012). Physical fitness and fatness in adolescents with intellectual disabilities. *Journal of Applied Research in Intellectual Disabilities*, 25(3), 231–239. doi: 10.1111/j.1468-3148.2012.00659.x

Skowroński, W., Horvat, M., Nocera, J., Roswal, G. and Croce, R. (2009). Eurofit special: European fitness battery score variation among individuals with intellectual disabilities. *Adapted Physical Activity Quarterly*, 26(1), 54–67. doi: 10.1123/apaq.26.1.54

Smits, B. L. M., Pepping, G. J. and Hettinga, F. J. (2014). Pacing and decision making in sport and exercise: The roles of perception and action in the regulation of exercise intensity. *Sports Medicine*, 44(6), 763–775.

Tomlinson, C., Campbell, A., Hurley, A., Fenton, E. and Heron, N. (2020). Sport pre-participation screening for asymptomatic atlantoaxial instability in patients with down syndrome. *Clinical Journal of Sport Medicine*, 30(4), 293–295. doi: 10.1097/JSM.0000000000000642

Tweedy, S. M., Mann, D. and Vanlandewijck, Y. C. (2016). Research needs for the development of evidence-based systems of classification for physical, vision, and intellectual impairments. In Van Biesen, D., et al. (2010). The ability of elite table tennis players with intellectual disabilities to adapt their service/return. *Adapted Physical Activity Quarterly*, 27(3), 242–257. doi: 10.1123/apaq.27.3.242

Van Biesen, D., Hettinga, F. J., McCulloch, K. and Vanlandewijck, Y. C. (2017). Pacing ability in elite runners with intellectual impairment. *Medicine and Science in Sports and Exercise*, 49(3), 588–594. doi: 10.1249/MSS.0000000000001115

Van Biesen, D., Hettinga, F. J., McCulloch, K., and Vanlandewijck, Y. (2016). Pacing profiles in competitive track races: Regulation of exercise intensity is related to cognitive ability. *Frontiers in Physiology*, 7 (December), 1–10. doi: 10.3389/fphys.2016.00624

Van Biesen, D., Mactavish, J., McCulloch, K. and Vanlandewijck, Y. C. (2016). Cognitive profile of young well-trained athletes with intellectual disabilities. *Research in Developmental Disabilities*, 53–54, 377–390. doi: 10.1016/j.ridd.2016.03.004

Van Biesen, D., Mactavish, J., Pattyn, N. and Vanlandewijck, Y. (2012). Technical proficiency among table tennis players with and without intellectual disabilities. *Human Movement Science*, 31(6), 1517–1528. doi: 10.1016/j.humov.2012.07.004

Wouters, M., Evenhuis, H. M. and Hilgenkamp, T. I. M. (2017). Systematic review of field-based physical fitness tests for children and adolescents with intellectual disabilities. *Research in Developmental Disabilities*, 61, 77–94. doi: 10.1016/j.ridd.2016.12.016

Wouters, M., Evenhuis, H. M. and Hilgenkamp, T. I. M. (2019). Physical fitness of children and adolescents with moderate to severe intellectual disabilities. *Disability and Rehabilitation*, 42(18), 2542–2552. doi: 10.1080/09638288.2019.1573932

Part XIII
Specific populations

13.1 Testing the master athlete

R. C. Richard Davison and Paul M. Smith

Many sporting organisations define a master athlete as an individual older than 35 years of age, who either trains for or takes part in athletic competitions often specifically designed for older participants. Many of these athletes are experienced competitors who continue their athletic pursuits after their sports careers have ended, often transferring from another sport. Others include individuals who return to sport after extended periods of inactivity or simply participate and train sporadically for enjoyment and health benefits (Tayrose et al., 2015). At the elite level these athletes, both men and women, show remarkably well-maintained performance into their mid-50s for all sports (Balmer et al., 2005; Baker and Tang, 2010).

Trends for sport participation in younger age groups are generally in decline, and activity of older age groups of the general population are either flat or are, at best, increasing very slightly. However, over the last 50 years, the size of competitive age-group competitions has grown significantly, with elite masters-level competition flourishing (van Uffelen et al., 2015). For example, the Sydney 2009 World Masters Games attracted a record 28,676 competitors. This is more than double the number of competitors that took part in the Sydney 2000 Olympic Games. Other indicators of increased participation include an increase in the proportion of over 40-year-old male finishers in the 'Ironman Switzerland' from 23% to 48% in the period 1995–2010 (Stiefel et al., 2014). Participation rates in the marathon show that master athletes now make up ~55% (Lepers and Cattagni, 2012) of the total field, growing to ~70% of the field in ultra-marathons (Knechtle et al., 2012).

Possibly stemming from increased participation, age-categorised record performances have improved significantly over the last 50 years. For example, Ed Whitlock set a number of running world records in his later life, the most recent being the oldest person to complete the marathon in under 4 h (age 85; 3 h, 56 min, 34 s) and was estimated to have a $\dot{V}O_2max$ close to 50 ml·kg^{-1}·min^{-1} in his 80s (Lepers and Stapley, 2016). Remarkably, Robert Marchand set new world records for 1-h track cycling of 26.927 km at the age of 102 and then at 105 yr of age set a record of 22.547 km. Examples from other sports demonstrate significant improvements in master athletes' times, much greater than comparative improvements for younger counterparts (Akkari et al., 2015).

DOI: 10.4324/9781003045281-63

Therefore, the likelihood of conducting physiological assessments on an older (master) athlete is high and possibly increasing. The aim of this chapter is to highlight and address additional considerations required when conducting standard tests described elsewhere in this book. These considerations fall into two key areas:

1. Additional safety considerations related to the increased probability of underlying medical conditions with age;
2. Adaptations to protocols and methodology to accommodate the age-related declines in physiological function with age.

Safety and risks of exercise for the older athlete

Linked to the content of this sub-chapter, we also direct the reader to complementary information contained within Chapter 3.1. The risk of sudden cardiac death (SCD) or acute myocardial infarction (AMI) is much higher in older exercisers, particularly recreational athletes, and this declines significantly with increasing levels of exercise frequency (Mittleman and Mostofsky, 2011), duration and intensity. The relative risk of SCD within 30 min of vigorous exercise for highly athletic populations is about 10.9, with the relative risk of AMI of 5.9 (Chugh and Weiss, 2015). One must consider this risk in light of the prevalence of SCD and AMI in the general sedentary population, which is about 50 times higher than those who are regular exercisers. In addition, the burden of SCD during sport across all age groups represents a small proportion (5%–6%) of sudden deaths in the general population (Chugh and Weiss, 2015).

Data from the UK suggest that myocardial disease typically accounts for 40% of SCD in all athletes, being more prevalent in older athletes. The predominant causes were idiopathic left ventricular hypertrophy (LVH) and/or fibrosis and arrhythmogenic right ventricular cardiomyopathy (ARVC) (Finocchiaro et al., 2016). The majority of athletes died during exertion (61%), and only a minority of subjects (8%) had a family history of sudden death. Unfortunately, we do not know the relationship between age and circumstances of death, but many of the fatalities at rest are related to sudden arrhythmic death syndrome (SADS), which is more common in the younger athlete. The older athlete is more likely to die during exercise with coronary artery disease (CAD) as the predominant cause of SCD (Chugh and Weiss, 2015; Finocchiaro et al., 2016). The significantly lower prevalence of arrhythmias in the older population suggests that pre-participation electrocardiogram (ECG) screening may be of limited use although data from Jensen-Urstad et al. (1998) suggest that abnormal arrhythmias are highly prevalent in elderly (>70 yr of age) lifelong strenuous exercisers. Indeed, the European Society of Cardiology updated their ECG screening criteria in 2010 to distinguish training-related and training-unrelated changes (Corrado et al., 2010). Morrison et al. (2016) suggested that while cardiac screening protocols do exist around the world, researchers have not yet systematically and extensively evaluated them, particularly for their suitability for master athletes.

Following are a number of considerations and safeguards that the exercise physiologist should consider prior to conducting any physiological testing of master athletes. The purpose of this list is to guide the exercise physiologist in the development of appropriate protocols for their laboratory, and thus there is not an expectation that every item is included for every athlete – a pragmatic risk-stratified approach is required.

1. Age

    The older the athlete, regardless of current activity level, the higher risk of a potential complication resulting from physiological testing.

2. Exercise history

    If an athlete is already exercising and/or training, one should pose pertinent questions about frequency and overall weekly duration of exercising/training; i.e., is training >3 h per week? Further, does an athlete's habitual exercise/training include high-intensity efforts (i.e., intervals performed in the severe domain), and is the athlete competing on a regular basis?

3. Health history

    Employ the PAR-Q+ questionnaire and consider quantifying relative risk according to the European Society of Cardiology Systemic Coronary Risk Evaluation (SCORE). Since most deaths in the older athlete are from CAD, there needs to be a consideration of the known risk factors and symptoms (e.g., presence of angina, syncope or pre-syncope during or after exertion, or unusual fatigue, dyspnoea and/or palpitations). The use of the online SCORE assessment is an additional diagnostic resource, which can help detect CAD in master athletes.

4. Consider pre-screening ECG

    The European Society of Cardiology (ESC) 2005 criteria for resting ECG is effective at specifically detecting high-risk cardiac conditions in master athletes (Panhuyzen-Goedkoop et al., 2020). To prevent a high false-positive rate with physiologically normal training-related changes, an experienced sport cardiologist will be best suited for the assessment of high-risk athletes. However, resting ECG screening is likely to result in a considerable number of false negatives; thus, should not be routine nor accepted as a single source of information to assess risk.

5. Ensure that normal safety measures are in place, i.e., suitably trained test administrators with knowledge of emergency first aid and effective use of an automatic external defibrillator (AED)

    Unfortunately, in a high proportion (approximately two-thirds) of sports-related SCD, no cardiopulmonary resuscitation (CPR) was administered

(Marijon et al., 2011), which undoubtedly contributed to the final (fatal) outcome. Therefore, it is important that appropriately trained staff with knowledge of AED use are present for all testing.

Even with master athletes there is a low risk of SCD or AMI with exercise, and with the appropriate pre-checks, continuous monitoring and emergency procedures in place, overall risk of significant cardiac events and fatalities during physiological exercise testing are extremely low and, thankfully, rare. Thus, we would direct institutional ethics committees to, with appropriate safeguards in place, accept that the routine testing of master athletes can be conducted with minimal risk to the participant.

Recommendations for exercise testing adaptations

With an athlete's increasing age, the main adaptation linked to exercise testing will be to adjust an exercise test protocol to accommodate reductions in physical capacity. All physiological functions decline with age within the master category, and this rate of decline is highly individualistic and modified by activity levels (Pollock et al., 2015).

Existing research confirms that all physiological systems decline with age. Each of these systems will decline at subtly different rates, influenced by the activity and training an individual habitually undertakes. Therefore, an observable change in performance of any individual sport will be influenced both by the predominance of a specific physiological system(s) and the typical/habitual training of that system(s).

A number of research studies have quantified the impact of age on the rate of decline in function and performance across a variety of sports. However, few studies have specifically considered the impact of ageing on the design and implementation of a testing protocol. This raises the question of the suitability of an otherwise standard testing protocol as one ages.

On average, for variables like $\dot{V}O_2max$ (Pollock et al., 2015) and peak aerobic power (Balmer et al., 2005), the decline for master athletes is in the range of 8%–15% per decade. Elite athletes in many sports appear able to maintain relatively high levels of performance well into their 50s. However, despite debate about the nature of decline, it is likely that a reduction in physiological performance will exhibit an exponential fall from about the age of 35 yr, a pattern that is evident in the performances for most sports. Further, events that require strength and/or anaerobic power experience the greatest rates of decline with age (Baker and Tang, 2010).

With this in mind, a starting exercise intensity, along with adjustments to the rate of subsequent ramp or step increments, ensures that these do not have a dramatic effect on the duration of a test. This will ensure the rate of change of measured physiological variable responses will be equitable between athletes, reducing the likely (negative) impact on the validity of specific test measures.

Measurement of $\dot{V}O_2max$

Absolute $\dot{V}O_2max$ declines with age and, even in lifelong exercisers, while a rate of functional decline may be slowed, it cannot be completely halted (Degens et al., 2013; Valenzuela et al., 2020). Interestingly, and counterintuitively, for some components that contribute to measurable $\dot{V}O_2max$, observed rates of decline are similar between highly active and sedentary individuals. This is particularly noticeable for ventilatory function (Degens et al., 2013), where an age-related rate of decline is similar for most individuals. Such adverse changes will impact on function and performance and therefore should be considered in the context of the safe and effective design and implementation of testing methodologies. Due to these age-related functional reductions, older men and women are likely to perceive higher levels of exertional breathlessness.

Virtually all cardiopulmonary exercise testing (CPET) systems increase ventilatory dead space, which adds to the increasing physiological dead space related to increasing age. This may result in a disproportionate impact with older athletes. Further, many CPET systems will slightly increase the resistance to flow during inspiration and expiration. While this is meant to be negligible and imperceptible, a recent study has demonstrated variability between different systems (Beltrami et al., 2021), which could potentially impact more on the exercise tolerance of the older athlete, who naturally possesses reduced respiratory muscle strength and performance. Commonly a masters athlete may identify that a CPET system face mask or mouth piece causes acute dyspnoea, and it is likely that this effect may become increasingly evident at higher relative or maximal exercise intensities. Indeed, it was recently demonstrated that increasing the mechanical (ventilatory) constraint during moderate constant-load exercise in older adults did not increase the sensation of breathlessness (Molgat-Seon et al., 2019).

References

Akkari, A., Machin, D. and Tanaka, H. (2015). Greater progression of athletic performance in older masters athletes. *Age Ageing*, 44(4), 683–686.

Baker, A. B. and Tang, Y. Q. (2010). Aging performance for masters records in athletics, swimming, rowing, cycling, triathlon, and weightlifting. *Experimental Aging Research*, 36(4), 453–477.

Balmer, J., et al. (2005). Age-related changes in maximal power and maximal heart rate recorded during a ramped test in 114 cyclists age 15–73 years. *Journal of Aging and Physical Activity*, 13, 125–136.

Beltrami, F. G., et al. (2021). Current limits for flowmeter resistance in metabolic carts can negatively affect exercise performance. *Physiological Reports*, 9(7), e14814. doi: https://doi.org/10.14814/phy2.14814

Chugh, S. S. and Weiss, J. B. (2015). Sudden cardiac death in the older athlete. *Journal of the American College of Cardiology*, 65(5), 493–502.

Corrado, D., et al. (2010). Recommendations for interpretation of 12-lead electrocardiogram in the athlete. *European Heart Journal*, 31(2), 243–259. doi: 10.1093/eurheartj/ehp473

Degens, H., et al. (2013). Relationship between ventilatory function and age in master athletes and a sedentary reference population. *Age*, 35(3), 1007–1015. doi: 10.1007/s11357-012-9409-7

Finocchiaro, G., et al. (2016). Etiology of sudden death in sports: Insights from a United Kingdom Regional Registry. *Journal of the American College of Cardiology*, 67(18), 2108–2115. doi: 10.1016/j.jacc.2016.02.062

Jensen-Urstad, K., et al. (1998). High prevalence of arrhythmias in elderly male athletes with a lifelong history of regular strenuous exercise. *Heart*, 79(2), 161–164. doi: 10.1136/hrt.79.2.161

Knechtle, B., et al. (2012). Age-related changes in 100-km ultra-marathon running performance. *Age*, 34(4), 1033–1045.

Lepers, R. and Cattagni, T. (2012). Do older athletes reach limits in their performance during marathon running? *Age*, 34(3), 773–781.

Lepers, R. and Stapley, P. J. (2016). Master athletes are extending the limits of human endurance. *Frontiers in Physiology*, 7, 613.

Marijon, E., et al. (2011). Sports-related sudden death in the general population. *Circulation*, 124(6), 672–681. doi: 10.1161/CIRCULATIONAHA.110.008979

Mittleman, M. A. and Mostofsky, E. (2011). Physical, psychological and chemical triggers of acute cardiovascular events. *Circulation*, 124(3), 346–354. doi: 10.1161/CIRCULATIONAHA.110.968776

Molgat-Seon, Y., et al. (2019). Manipulation of mechanical ventilatory constraint during moderate intensity exercise does not influence dyspnoea in healthy older men and women. *The Journal of Physiology*, 597(5), 1383–1399. doi: https://doi.org/10.1113/JP277476

Morrison, B. N., et al. (2016). Cardiovascular pre-participation screening and risk assessment in the masters athlete: International recommendations and a Canadian perspective. *BC Medical Journal*, 58(4), 196–202.

Panhuyzen-Goedkoop, N. M., et al. (2020). ECG criteria for the detection of high-risk cardiovascular conditions in master athletes. *European Journal of Preventive Cardiology*, 27(14), 1529–1538. doi: 10.1177/2047487319901060

Pollock, R. D., et al. (2015). An investigation into the relationship between age and physiological function in highly active older adults. *Journal of Physiology*, 593(3), 657–680; discussion 680.

Stiefel, M., Knechtle, B. and Lepers, R. (2014). Master triathletes have not reached limits in their Ironman triathlon performance. *Scandinavian Journal of Medicine and Science in Sports*, 24(1), 89–97.

Tayrose, G. A., et al. (2015). The masters athlete: A review of current exercise and treatment recommendations. *Sports Health*, 7(3), 270–276.

van Uffelen, J., Jenkin, C., Westerbeek, H., Biddle, S. and Eime, R. (2015). *Active and healthy ageing through sport*. Australian Government.

Valenzuela, P. L., et al. (2020). Acute ketone supplementation and exercise performance: A systematic review and meta-analysis of randomized controlled trials. *International Journal of Sports Physiology and Performance*, 1–11.

13.2 Testing considerations for children

Craig A. Williams, Melitta McNarry, and Keith Tolfrey

Specific physiological testing guidelines for children and young people should be established instead of adopting those for adults due to age-specific ethics considerations, including the ability to provide informed consent; differences in body size, with implications for the appropriate methodological approaches and physiological interpretations; and the impact of growth and maturation on exercise responses.

We delimit the definition of a child or young person as anyone who has not reached their 18th birthday. These guidelines are recommendations for valid and reliable techniques in measuring physical and physiological parameters in children and young people and can be adopted for the purpose of testing in a sport and/or research context.

Assessment of maturation

Techniques for assessing biological maturity range in practicality, accuracy, required expertise, ethical viability and their ability to capture the continuous nature of this process that all young people experience (Malina et al., 2004). Two methods common to exercise physiology are the use of secondary sexual characteristics (Tanner, 1962) and the estimation of age at peak height velocity (maturity offset; Mirwald et al., 2002). The different stages of sexual maturity can either be self-assessed by children and adolescents, with varying degrees of accuracy and reliability (Matsudo and Matsudo, 1994; Taylor et al., 2001), or by a clinician, which is invasive and unlikely to be popular with study participants. This categorises the individual into one of five maturity levels ranging from prepubertal to adult maturation (see online supplementary material).

Use of maturity offset is increasingly common in the paediatric literature due to only requiring measures of stature, body mass, leg length and chronological age, subsequently used in sex-specific regression equations available online (wwwapps. usask.ca/kin-growthutility/phv_ui.php). The accuracy of the original equations has been questioned, with the equations subsequently simplified and updated for boys and girls (Moore et al., 20158):

Girls' maturity offset (years from PHV) = $-7.709133 + (0.0042232 \times$ (age $\times$ height)); $R^2 = 0.898$, SEE $= 0.528$

DOI: 10.4324/9781003045281-64

Boys' maturity offset (years from PHV) = −7.999994 + (0.0036124 (age × height)); $R^2 = 0.896$, SEE = 0.542

Concerns about the accuracy of this technique in exercise-trained young people and those who are early or late maturers (Koziel and Malina, 2018) are also acknowledged. For a more detailed overview, please refer to Malina (2017).

Anthropometry and body composition

The size, location and rates of change of skeletal muscle and adipose tissue are frequently measured or estimated in paediatric exercise physiology. Use of advanced technologies, such as quantitative magnetic resonance imaging (qMRI), dual energy x-ray absorptiometry (DXA), air displacement plethysmography (ADP), ultrasound and bioelectric impedance analysis (BIA), are more prevalent in contemporary laboratories; they all require considerable expertise and expense to obtain meaningful, consistent and accurate measurements within a paediatric population that is growing, developing and maturing (Simoni et al., 2020).

Critical to the use and understanding of these data are population-specific software derived from studies conducted with young people, which must at least take into account maturity, age, sex and ethnic differences in fat-free mass (Fomon et al., 1982). The meticulous measurement of body mass, stature, skinfolds and circumferences (Cameron, 2012) is vital, again with adjustments to ensure their interpretation reflects population-specific differences (see Chapter 3.4).

Sex, maturity and ethnic-specific equations have been published to estimate percent body fat (%BF) from skinfolds (e.g., Wendel et al., 2017), which are sample specific and should be used with caution because of changes in tissue density during childhood (Roemmich et al., 1997). Nevertheless, the prediction equations can be used if an estimation of percent body fat is desired, providing the participant characteristics match those in Table 13.2.1.

If body composition is the primary research outcome, qMRI, DXA or ADP is recommended (see also Chapter 3.14), but for secondary outcomes, field-based estimations can be used judiciously if they are well matched to the population characteristics and the validity is available in the literature.

Laboratory-based exercise tests

Ergometry

Cycle ergometer or treadmill tests are most common in children. Most children report being more comfortable on a cycle ergometer than on a treadmill (LeMura et al., 2001), and the quality of the data obtained for measures subject to movement artefact, such as electrocardiograms and blood pressure, is superior during cycle-based exercise (Takken et al., 2017). However, children may prematurely stop cycle tests due to local peripheral muscle fatigue, potentially limiting true maximal efforts. Conversely, despite its greater commonality with habitual movements, some children may adopt an unnatural gait on a treadmill and hold the handrail, which should be strongly discouraged, as it alters physiological responses (Ellestad, 2003).

Mostly due to differences in posture and the exercising muscle mass, cycle and treadmill exercise results are not directly comparable, with treadmill exercise eliciting a greater maximal oxygen uptake ($\dot{V}O_2$max), stroke volume, heart rate and cardiac output (Forbregd et al., 2019). Recently, a wider range of ergometers have been used in children, including rowing ergometers, arm cranks and swim benches. Whilst beneficial regarding sport specificity, it is important that any ergometers used are appropriately adapted for children and that the load is accurately applied and measured to enable the interpretation.

Aerobic performance (cardiorespiratory fitness)

The criterion measure of aerobic performance is $\dot{V}O_2$max using specialised respiratory gas analysis equipment (see Chapter 3.6). Following suitable preliminary pilot

Table 13.2.1 Sex, maturity and ethnic-specific equations for estimation of percent body fat (%BF) from skinfolds

	Non-African American	*African American*
Two-skinfold prediction equations		
Boys		
Tanner 1–3	(13.12 × log Sum 2SF) −15.46 × Log Height) + 64.58	(14.73 × log Sum 2SF) −10.55 × Log Height) + 64.82
Tanner 4–5	(13.12 × log Sum 2SF) −13.27 × Log Height) + 50.92	(14.73 × log Sum 2SF) −25.95 × Log Height) + 110.54
All[a]	(14.28 × log Sum 2SF) −21.50 × Log Height) + 90.69	(14.28 × log Sum 2SF) −19.23 × Log Height) + 78.29
Girls		
All	(13.95 × log Sum 2SF) −18.09 × Log Height) + 77.17	(13.95 × log Sum 2SF) −18.09 × Log Height) + 75.40
Four-skinfold prediction equations		
Boys		
Tanner 1–3	(12.41 × log Sum 4SF) −16.90 × Log Height) + 66.78	(14.68 × log Sum 4SF) −16.90 × Log Height) + 58.32
Tanner 4–5	(12.41 × log Sum 4SF) −16.90 × Log Height) + 64.94	(14.68 × log Sum 4SF) −16.90 × Log Height) + 58.32
All[a]	(12.74 × log Sum4) −21.47×Log Height) + 87.82	(14.68 × log Sum 4SF) −21.47 × Log Height) + 79.82
Girls		
All	(13.99 × log Sum 4SF) −21.42 × Log Height) + 85.65	(13.99 × log Sum 4SF) −14.69 × Log Height) + 51.04

[a] Simplified equation that does not require Tanner staging; Tanner = secondary sexual characteristic levels of biological maturity; sum 2SF = sum of triceps and subscapular skinfolds; sum 4SF = sum of triceps, biceps, subscapular and suprailiac skinfolds; Log = natural logarithm.

work with a sub-sample of the target population and familiarisation, our experience has supported a comfortable fixed treadmill speed or cycling cadence for the young person, with progressive increments in gradient or resistive load, respectively, until running or cycling cannot be sustained (i.e., volitional exhaustion). Paediatric exercise test considerations may include more extensive familiarisation with the ergometers and laboratory environment, appreciation of the young person's size – particularly for treadmill safety rails or harnesses and cycle ergometer seat and handlebar height and crank length – and expired gas mouth pieces and face masks. The timing of the increments will depend on whether other measures are required (heart rate or blood lactate) and if these need to demonstrate a physiological steady state (e.g., 1 or ≥3 min) (Zakrzewski and Tolfrey, 2012). Until quite recently, $\dot{V}O_2$max was expressed as peak $\dot{V}O_2$ for young people who did not demonstrate a plateau in oxygen consumption at the volitional termination of exercise, supported by secondary physiological measures (e.g., maximal heart rate or respiratory exchange ratio). However, this has been challenged with the suggestion that an extra 'verification' exercise bout be completed at a constant work rate in excess (110% ± 5%) of the final work rate from the initial test protocol (Barker et al., 2011). Finally, despite Tanner (1949) warning exercise physiologists not to adjust $\dot{V}O_2$max using a ratio scaling technique with total body mass (i.e., ml·kg^{-1}·min^{-1}) because it was 'theoretically fallacious', this practice has still continued, although the limitations have recently been reiterated (Armstrong and Welsman, 2020). Time will tell whether active muscle mass or even total fat-free mass will be used as recommended. For readers looking for exemplar protocols for measuring $\dot{V}O_2$max:

- Treadmill – fixed speed (preferred comfortable jogging 5–12 km·h^{-1}) with 1% gradient increases each minute; alternatively increases in gradient only increased once maximum running speed is obtained.
- Cycling – fixed cadence (preferred comfortable pace 50–80 revs·min^{-1}) with 10–25 W increases each minute.
- Faster cadences can offset lighter loads when cycling to avoid local muscular fatigue in the legs.

Anaerobic performance testing

Anaerobic testing protocols for children are less well developed than aerobic tests with no 'gold-standard' measure (Ingle and Tolfrey, 2013) and significant variations in methodologies used. The most widely used measure remains the Wingate test, commonly conducted on a cycle ergometer for 30 s, although other exercise modalities and test durations can be used (Chia et al., 1997; McNarry et al., 2011). The Wingate test allows the determination of peak power, mean power and fatigue index. These power metrics are influenced by the load applied; a load of 75 g and 45 g·kg^{-1} body mass are recommended for lower and upper body Wingate tests, respectively. A rolling start is advisable to avoid issues with overcoming flywheel inertia, which are likely to be greater in younger and/or smaller children.

A limitation of the Wingate test is that it is not a truly anaerobic test, with a significant aerobic contribution that depends on the exercise modality, age and training status (Chia et al., 1997; McNarry et al., 2011).

More recently, the 30-m over-ground sprint has been used as a measure of anaerobic performance, requiring participants to complete up to three all-out sprints from a standing start, with the force-velocity-power relationship subsequently derived. Whilst reported to be reliable and applicable to sporting contexts in children (Runacres et al., 2019), the associated biomechanical model is not overly accessible for practitioners.

Isokinetic strength testing

Isokinetic dynamometry is the gold-standard method of assessing muscle strength (Santos et al., 2013), with the knee the most widely studied joint due to ease of evaluation, and the knee extensor strength potentially representing total strength of the lower extremities (Muñoz-Bermejo et al., 2019). Provided appropriate standards are followed to ensure the correct positioning and stabilising of the child, isokinetic dynamometry is safe (Fagher et al., 2016) and allows the investigation of a range of angular velocities during both eccentric and concentric movements (Iga et al., 2006). There is little consensus regarding the optimal testing protocol, although a familiarisation session is essential. A variety of velocities have been used, ranging from 60 to 180 degrees·s^{-1}, with up to 90 s rest periods between efforts and three to ten maximal efforts typically utilised.

Field testing for fitness/performance

Field-based tests offer indirect estimations of health- and skill-related physical fitness in a manner that is easier and cheaper to administer than laboratory tests and are appropriate for population-level studies (Tabacchi et al., 2019). There are numerous physical fitness testing batteries, with the EUROFIT being the most widely used in children, for which both norm and criterion-referenced scales are available (Kemper and Mechelen, 1996). Criterion-referenced scales provide levels that all children are expected to achieve rather than percentile values for each test, which can result in inappropriate peer comparisons that fail to account for the influence of growth and maturation. Whilst field-based tests are potentially useful for large cohort studies, it is important to highlight that such tests do not provide equivalent information to physiological tests in a laboratory. Indeed, there has been significant controversy regarding field-based tests in recent years regarding their validity and reliability (Armstrong and Welsman, 2019; Tomkinson et al., 2019).

References

Armstrong, N. and Welsman, J. (2019). Twenty-metre shuttle run: (Mis)representation, (mis)interpretation and (mis)use. *British Journal of Sports Medicine*, 53(19), 1199.

Armstrong, N. and Welsman, J. (2020). Traditional and new perspectives on youth cardiorespiratory fitness. *Medicine and Science in Sports and Exercise*, 52, 2563–2573.

Barker, A. R., Williams, C. A., Jones, A. M. and Armstrong, N. (2011). Establishing maximal oxygen uptake in young people during a ramp cycle test to exhaustion. *British Journal of Sports Medicine*, 45, 498–503.

Cameron, N. (2012). The measurement of human growth. In N. Cameron and B. Bogin (eds.), *Human Growth and Development* (2nd ed.), pp. 487–513. Cambridge, USA: Academic Press.

Chia, M., Armstrong, N. and Childs, D. (1997). The assessment of children's anaerobic performance using modifications of the Wingate Anaerobic Test. *Pediatric Exercise Science*, 9(1), 80–89.

Ellestad, M. (2003). *Stress Testing*. Oxford: Oxford University Press.

Fagher, K., Fritzson, A. and Drake, A. M. (2016). Test-retest reliability of isokinetic knee strength measurements in children aged 8 to 10 years. *Sports Health*, 8(3), 255–259.

Fomon, S. J., Haschke, F., Ziegler, E. E. and Nelson, S. E. (1982). Body composition from birth to age 10 years. *American Journal of Clinical Nutrition*, 35, 1169–1175.

Forbregd, T. R., Aloyseus, M. A., Berg, A. and Greve, G. (2019). Cardiopulmonary capacity in children during exercise testing: The differences between treadmill and upright and supine cycle ergometry. *Frontiers in Physiology*, 10, 1440.

Fransen, J., Bush, S., Woodcock, S., Novak, A., Deprez, D., Baxter-Jones, A. D. G., Vaeyens, R. and Lenoir, M. (2018). Improving the prediction of maturity from anthropometric variables using a maturity ratio. *Pediatric Exercise Science*, 30, 296–307.

Iga, J., George, K., Lees, A. and Reilly, T. (2006). Reliability of assessing indices of isokinetic leg strength in pubertal soccer players. *Pediatric Exercise Science*, 18(4), 436–445.

Ingle, L. and Tolfrey, K. (2013). The variability of high intensity exercise tests in pre-pubertal boys. *International Journal of Sports Medicine*, 34(12), 1063–1069.

Kemper, H. C. G. and Mechelen, W. V. (1996). Physical fitness testing of children: A European perspective. *Pediatric Exercise Science*, 8(3), 201–214.

Koziel, S. M. and Malina, R. M. (2018). Modified maturity offset prediction equations: Validation in independent longitudinal samples of boys and girls. *Sports Medicine*, 48, 221–236.

LeMura, L. M., von Duvillard, S. P., Cohen, S. L., Root, C. J., Chelland, S. A., Andreacci, J., et al. (2001). Treadmill and cycle ergometry testing in 5- to 6-year-old children. *European Journal of Applied Physiology*, 85(5), 472–478.

Malina, R. M. (2017). Assessment of biological maturation. In N. Armstrong and W. van Mechelen (eds.), *Oxford Textbook of Children's Sport and Exercise Medicine* (3rd ed.), pp. 3–11. Oxford, UK: Oxford University Press.

Malina, R. M., Bouchard, C. and Bar-Or, O. (2004). *Growth, Maturation and Physical Activity* (2nd ed.). Champaign, USA: Human Kinetics.

Matsudo, S. M. M. and Matsudo, V. K. R. (1994). Self-assessment and physician assessment of sexual maturation in Brazilian boys and girls: Concordance and reproducibility. *American Journal of Human Biology*, 6, 451–455.

McNarry, M. A., Welsman, J. R. and Jones, A. M. (2011). The influence of training and maturity status on girls' responses to short-term, high-intensity upper- and lower-body exercise. *Applied Physiology of Nutrition and Metabolism*, 36(3), 344–352.

Mirwald, R. L., Baxter-Jones, A. D., Bailey, D. A. and Beunen, G. P. (2002). An assessment of maturity from anthropometric measurements. *Medicine and Science in Sports and Exercise*, 34, 689–694.

Muñoz-Bermejo, L., Pérez-Gómez, J., Manzano, F., Collado-Mateo, D., Villafaina, S. and Adsuar, J. C. (2019). Reliability of isokinetic knee strength measurements in children: A systematic review and meta-analysis. *PLoS One*, 14(12), e0226274.

Roemmich, J. N., Clark, P. A., Weltman, A. and Rogol, A. D. (1997). Alterations in growth and body composition during puberty: I. Comparing multicompartment body composition models. *Journal of Applied Physiology*, 83, 927–935.

Runacres, A., Bezodis, N. E., Mackintosh, K. A. and McNarry, M. A. (2019). The reliability of force-velocity-power profiling during over-ground sprinting in children and adolescents. *Journal of Sports Sciences*, 37(18), 2131–2137.

Santos, A. N., Pavão, S. L., Avila, M. A., Salvini, T. F. and Rocha, N. A. (2013). Reliability of isokinetic evaluation in passive mode for knee flexors and extensors in healthy children. *Brazilian Journal of Physical Therapy*, 17(2), 112–120.

Simoni, P., Guglielmi, R. and Gómez, M. P. A. (2020). Imaging of body composition in children. *Quantitative Imaging in Medicine and Surgery*, 10, 1661–1671.

Tabacchi, G., Lopez Sanchez, G. F., Nese Sahin, F., Kizilyalli, M., Genchi, R., Basile, M., et al. (2019). Field-based tests for the assessment of physical fitness in children and adolescents practicing sport: A systematic review within the ESA program. *Sustainability*, 11(24), 7187.

Takken, T., Bongers, B. C., van Brussel, M., Haapala, E. A. and Hulzebos, E. H. J. (2017). Cardiopulmonary exercise testing in pediatrics. *Annual American Thoracic Society*, 14(Supplement_1), S123–S128.

Tanner, J. M. (1949). Fallacy of per-weight and per-surface area standards and their relation to spurious correlation. *Journal of Applied Physiology*, 2, 1–15.

Tanner, J. M. (1962). *Growth of Adolescents* (2nd ed.). Oxford, UK: Blackwell Scientific.

Taylor, S. J. C., Whincup, P. H., Hindmarsh, P. C., Lampe, F., Odoki, K. and Cook, D. G. (2001). Performance of a new pubertal self-assessment questionnaire: A preliminary study. *Paediatric and Perinatal Epidemiology*, 15, 88–94.

Tomkinson, G. R., Lang, J. J., Léger, L. A., Olds, T. S., Ortega, F. B., Ruiz, J. R., et al. (2019). Response to criticisms of the 20 m shuttle run test: Deflections, distortions and distractions. *British Journal of Sports Medicine*, 53(19), 1200–1201.

Wendel, D., Weber, D., Leonard, M. B., Magge, S. N., Kelly, A., Stallings, V. A., Pipan, M. Stettler, N. and Zemel, B. S. (2017). Body composition estimation using skinfolds in children with and without health conditions affecting growth and body composition. *Annals of Human Biology*, 44, 108–120.

Zakrzewski, J. K. and Tolfrey, K. (2012). Comparison of fat oxidation over a range of intensities during treadmill and cycling exercise in children. *European Journal of Applied Exercise Physiology*, 112, 163–171.

13.3 Testing the female athlete

Kirsty M. Hicks, Anthony C. Hackney, Michael Dooley, and Georgie Bruinvels

Practitioners often pay close attention to the effect of circadian, diurnal and ultradian rhythms on exercise and health in athletes. However, in female athletes, the menstrual cycle, which is an infradian rhythm, is sometimes overlooked. The menstrual cycle is an essential biological rhythm during which ovarian sex hormones, specifically oestrogen and progesterone, fluctuate. These hormones exert biological effects on several body systems, including the reproductive, immune, cardiovascular, neuromuscular and musculoskeletal systems (e.g., Enns and Tiidus, 2010; Ansdell et al., 2019). Consequently, the cyclical pattern of changes in hormonal concentrations can result in a plethora of systemic physiological and psychological alterations, which can affect exercise responses. Despite these potential effects, most practitioners do not consider the influence of the menstrual cycle. Therefore, this chapter presents a systematic framework for working with female athletes by providing insight into the implementation and interpretation of screening and monitoring tools (Figure 13.3.1). Screening tools, including questionnaires and/or interviews, are designed to obtain medical and family history and identify any pre-existing conditions and risks which might precede medical conditions, whereas monitoring is a systematic, continuous process of collecting and analysing data to detect changes from the individual's 'baseline'.

The menstrual cycle

Menstrual cycle length is calculated from the first day of a menstrual bleed to the first day of the next menstrual bleed. Due to large inter- and intra-individual variability, the length of a menstrual cycle can range from 21 to 35 days. Consistent deviations from this range might indicate an irregularity (e.g., <21 days polymenorrhoea, >35 days oligomenorrhoea). Hormonal fluctuations throughout the menstrual cycle create three distinct hormonal milieu: the early follicular (low oestrogen and progesterone), late follicular (high oestrogen and low progesterone) and mid-luteal (high oestrogen and high progesterone) phases. However, significant hormonal shifts occur when transitioning between phases, which might be symptomatic. Another essential time point is ovulation – a fundamental marker of a eumenorrheic cycle, which occurs approximately 36 h following the surge in luteinizing hormone.

DOI: 10.4324/9781003045281-65

Testing the female athlete 369

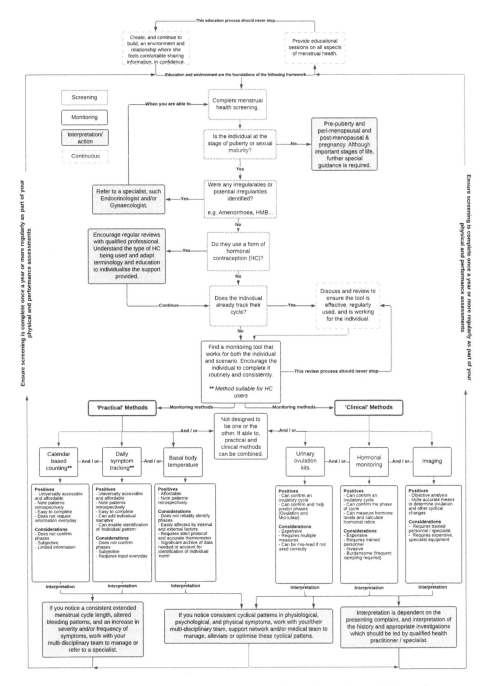

Figure 13.3.1 The implementation and interpretation of screening and monitoring tools.

The fluctuations in sex hormones can be altered by pregnancy, by chronological age and through the use of hormonal contraceptives. Although puberty, pregnancy and menopause are vital stages of the female life span, they are beyond the scope of this chapter. Secondary to birth control, hormonal contraceptives are used by both recreational and elite athletes to manipulate the menstrual cycle and manage dysfunction or unwanted symptoms. Approximately 50% of elite female athletes use a form of hormonal contraceptive. Of note, the extent and process in which hormonal contraceptives alter fluctuations in sex hormones must be understood, as they vary substantially with each type, and even brand, of hormonal contraceptive (Elliott-Sale et al., 2020).

Screening

Screening can be used for the identification and prevention of medical issues. It is also for establishing performance-related implications. There are a range of different symptoms and irregularities that females of a reproductive age can experience, such as amenorrhoea (no periods), heavy menstrual bleeding and premenstrual symptoms. Information regarding whether these might be present and if action is required (e.g., referral to specialist) can be obtained through menstrual history screening. This can be done through a questionnaire and/or an interview. The screening process will also highlight the potential need for, and focus of, education, in addition to identifying the best form(s) of monitoring. At a minimum, screening should be repeated once a year. The frequency can be increased if history or monitoring indicates (e.g., amenorrhoea).

Monitoring

Monitoring day-to-day physical, physiological and psychological changes across the menstrual cycle can provide insight into menstrual health and identify any potential perturbations. There are several methods of monitoring, some of which provide more discernment than others, but typically at a greater financial and logistical cost.

Practical methods are easy and affordable to implement. Calendar-based counting is the simplest tool, only requiring logging bleed days. From these data, menstrual cycle length can be calculated alongside bleeding patterns. Calendar-based counting is also required to support other monitoring tools (e.g., basal body temperature, urinary ovulation kits). If appropriate, calendar-based counting can be modified to narrate physical, physiological, pathological and psychological symptoms, e.g., cervical mucus, breast tenderness, menstrual cramps, bloating, mood, fatigue and physical performance. Over time (more than three cycles) consistent monitoring can be used, retrospectively and pre-emptively, to identify menstrual patterns and associations. Unfortunately, due to the subjective nature of these monitoring tools, physiological confirmation of menstrual phases and/ or ovulation is not possible. Alternatively, tracking basal body temperature can infer ovulation and, with calendar-based counting, menstrual phases. Twenty-four hours prior to ovulation, basal body temperature reaches its thermal nadir, followed by a 0.2°–0.5°C post-ovulatory rise, which plateaus and then returns preceding menstruation.

Clinical monitoring methods can provide further insight into menstrual health, pathology and performance associations. In tandem with calendar-based counting, urinary ovulation can be used to confirm an ovulatory cycle. Generally, ~5 days before predicted ovulation, the individual tests their urine daily until the luteinizing hormone surge preceding ovulation is detected. Hormonal concentrations can be measured directly or indirectly through body fluid. Knowing the concentration of these hormones can allow for specific phase verification and detect hormonal deficiencies, which could indicate menstrual irregularities such as luteal-phase deficiency, and prompt further investigations. This could include a physical examination by appropriately trained and qualified practitioners.

Interpretation

For practical monitoring methods, at least 3 months of menstrual cycle monitoring is required to establish a 'baseline'. From this archive of data, irregularities such as heavy menstrual bleeding, amenorrhoea or premenstrual symptoms can be identified. If menstrual irregularities are identified, a multidisciplinary team approach should be applied, with potential referral to a specialist. Where patterns or associations between hormonal changes and physical performance and/or readiness are observed (e.g., mood changes, fatigability or clumsiness), a multidisciplinary team approach should also be applied.

Considerations

As noted, the menstrual cycle can be manipulated via hormonal contraceptives. Users of hormonal contraceptives still experience cyclical symptoms and underlying bleeding irregularities; therefore, screening, monitoring and appropriate management in these female athletes remain important. Furthermore, practitioners should be mindful that hormonal contraceptive use might mask an underlying pathology. Not all tools are suitable for all types and brands of hormonal contraceptives; consequently, terminology, screening and monitoring tools should be individualised and appropriate for their choice of hormonal contraceptive.

Performance testing

Performance tests are often carried out several times per season/year to monitor progression, evaluate changes in performance, identify the athletes' strengths and weaknesses and facilitate individualisation of training programmes. These tests should be standardised to minimise variation and support the detection of 'true' changes in performance. Whilst many female athletes cite unwanted symptoms associated with specific times in their menstrual cycle, which might affect perceived readiness and ability to perform, to date, research is inconclusive on the effect of the menstrual cycle on performance per se. A large literature review reported that, on average, performance across the menstrual cycle is trivially reduced during the early follicular phase compared with other phases of the menstrual cycle (McNulty et al., 2020). Thus, to further standardise female athlete testing, it is recommended that the menstrual cycle phase is recorded, and, where possible, replicated for the next performance test(s). If an aim is to establish any potential effect of an individual's menstrual cycle on their performance, systematic monitoring over at least three cycles is needed along with appropriate verification of phases. While specific forms of hormonal contraception aim to create a more stable hormone milieu, the physiological and psychological response remains variable between individuals; therefore, this should still be taken into consideration when conducting performance test(s). Monitoring and screening procedures can facilitate the inclusion of the menstrual cycle and hormonal contraceptive use to standardise testing procedures. Currently, there is not enough evidence to recommend specific types of performance tests to be conducted at certain phases of the menstrual cycle, since athletes must be able to perform on any day of the cycle.

Summary

The menstrual cycle can affect physical readiness and highlight potential health issues; therefore, screening menstrual history and monitoring changes in the menstrual cycle are imperative actions when providing support to all female athletes. Due to large intra- and inter-variability in the menstrual cycle and the common use of hormonal contraceptives, the screening and monitoring tools and subsequent interpretation must be tailored to the individual. The implementation and progression of this process needs to be accompanied by ongoing education. When conducting performance tests, it is recommended that the individual's phase of the menstrual cycle or the use of, and response to, hormonal contraception, are captured and, where possible, replicated. Definitions and terminology were omitted from this chapter due to space; however, it is imperative that practitioners take the time to understand and use correct terminology and definitions (see Elliott-Sale et al. [2020] and Hackney [2016] for recommendations).

References

Ansdell, P., et al. (2019). Menstrual cycle-associated modulations in neuromuscular function and fatigability of the knee extensors in eumenorrheic women. *Journal of Applied Physiology*, 126(6), 1701–1712.

Elliott-Sale, K. J., et al. (2020). The effects of oral contraceptives on exercise performance in women: A systematic review and meta-analysis. *Sports Medicine*, 50(10), 1785–1812.

Enns, D. and Tiidus, P. (2010). The influence of estrogen on skeletal muscle. *Sports Medicine*, 40(1), 41–58.

Hackney, A. C. (ed.). (2016). *Sex Hormones, Exercise and Women: Scientific and Clinical Aspects*. Cham, Switzerland: Springer International Publishing.

McNulty, K. L., et al. (2020). The effects of menstrual cycle phase on exercise performance in eumenorrheic women: A systematic review and meta-analysis. *Sports Medicine*, 1–15.

Part XIV
Environmental-specific issues

14.1 Performing at altitude

Mike Stembridge and Charles R. Pedlar

For over 100 years, we have known that exposure to high altitude presents a significant challenge to the human body, particularly during exercise (West et al., 2007). Due to the nature of our atmosphere, the partial pressure of oxygen falls (hypoxia) as we ascend, such that by 5000 m above sea level (severe altitude), there is approximately half the amount of oxygen in the air as at sea level. Given that even mild elevations (500–900 m) can result in a decrease in aerobic performance (Gore et al., 1996), optimal preparation for any event held above sea level is essential. This chapter will summarise our current understanding of how to prepare for performance at altitude and provide guidance for the safe ascent to higher elevations.

Pre-ascent testing

The ability to accurately predict who will retain performance at high altitude is highly desirable. Paradoxically, those with the highest aerobic fitness experience the greatest decrement upon ascent (Young et al., 1985). The majority of approaches developed thus far require exposing an individual to simulated altitude (normobaric or hypobaric hypoxia) and examining the magnitude of arterial oxygen desaturation. Those who demonstrate a greater desaturation during hypoxic exercise experience the largest decrease in maximal oxygen consumption ($\dot{V}O_2$max) at high altitude (Gavin et al., 1998). The magnitude of decrease in $\dot{V}O_2$max and time trial performance at altitude also correlates with oxygen desaturation observed during race pace time trials performed in normoxia (Chapman et al., 1999). Given that the transition to a steeper portion of the haemoglobin dissociation curve occurs at ~90% saturation (Figure 14.1.1), athletes who present with <91% saturation during exercise at sea level are most likely to experience larger declines in performance at altitude (Chapman, 2013). Where blood gas analysers are not available, pulse oximetry (SpO_2) is a cost-effective alternative. SpO_2 sensors can be negatively affected by motion artefact during exercise, but with careful placement provide a non-invasive means of indirectly assessing oxygen saturation. For athletes with low saturation, modifications to training intensity or match play approach may be needed, or enhanced acclimatisation strategies applied to attempt to reduce the drop in performance.

DOI: 10.4324/9781003045281-67

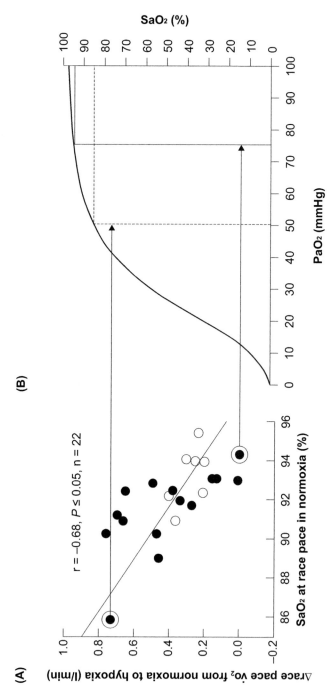

Figure 14.1.1 Panel A shows the change in race pace oxygen consumption at sea level vs. high altitude, with the most and least desaturated athlete highlighted with a circle. Arrows to Panel B depict where these two athletes will sit on the oxygen dissociation curve, demonstrating that a relatively small difference in oxygen saturation (~8%) is the result of ~22 mmHg (31%) lower PaO_2 due to the location on the steep portion of the curve.

Source: Adapted from Chapman et al. (2011).

Predictive tests have previously been developed to estimate the likelihood of severe illness associated with high altitude exposure in mountaineers (e.g., cerebral and pulmonary oedema), and these have recently been applied to athletic cohorts (Pla et al., 2020). Like the example in Figure 14.1.1, the test developed by Richalet et al. (2012) involves measuring oxygen saturation during a submaximal bout of exercise (30% of normoxic $\dot{V}O_2max$) performed in hypoxia (fraction of inspired oxygen [FiO_2] = 0.115) with the additional measurement of heart rate and ventilatory responses. These physiological variables are combined with age, gender, migraine or altitude illness history and endurance training status to calculate a predictive severe high altitude illness score ($SHAI_{score}$), with a score >3 associated with impaired performance. It should be noted that large inter-individual variability in rates of acclimatisation means single-measurement approaches need to guide, but not dictate, preparation.

Pre-ascent preparation

Athletes who experience exercise-induced hypoxemia in normoxia have consistently been shown to demonstrate a reduced ventilatory drive during exercise (Dempsey et al., 1984) and in response to hypoxia at rest (Harms and Stager, 1995). A number of studies have aimed to increase the hypoxic ventilatory response (HVR) before departure using hypoxic exposure (FiO_2 = 0.163) during sleeping hours (8–10 h) for 20 days (Townsend et al., 2002). Although HVR increased, performance remained unchanged. Exercise training in hypoxia over the course of 3 wk has been shown to increase peak power output in hypoxia compared to the same training regime in normoxia, but there were no differences in $\dot{V}O_2max$, suggesting the enhanced performance was independent to ventilatory adaptation (Roels et al., 2007). Therefore, whilst it is possible to modify components of the ventilatory response to exercise and hypoxia, whether these have a direct effect on performance is somewhat unanswered. Although it is beyond the scope of this chapter, it is important to note that there has also been the suggestion that exercise-induced arterial hypoxemia may be more prevalent in females than in males (Dominelli and Sheel, 2019), suggesting females may be more susceptible to performance decrements at high altitude, but this area warrants further investigation.

Whether competing or training at high altitude, the accelerated erythropoiesis stimulated by hypoxia requires adequate iron stores. Therefore, testing for iron status prior to a period of altitude exposure can identify those who could benefit from iron supplementation. Those who are iron deficient (<20 and < 30 ng/ml serum ferritin level for females and males, respectively) demonstrate a lower erythropoietic response to altitude (Okazaki et al., 2019), but oral supplementation can enhance the production of red blood cells (Garvican-Lewis et al., 2018).

Safety and monitoring

Acute hypoxia experienced in the laboratory is safe but should be used with caution, especially in combination with exercise. Transient hypotension following exercise can increase the risk of syncope, which will be exacerbated by arterial hypoxemia. Local guidance on the degree of hypoxia should be followed, but acute exposures of >5000 m (FiO_2 = ~11.5) are unlikely to be tolerated for prolonged periods without the development of acute mountain sickness (AMS) and way beyond altitudes typically employed in a sporting context. AMS is the umbrella term for a range of symptoms that can occur upon exposure to high altitude, ranging from mild headache, nausea and tiredness to life-threatening cerebral and pulmonary oedema. Given symptoms usually appear over 2500 m, and the more severe aspects of the condition generally reserved for higher altitudes, the overall risk to athletes is low. Support staff should be mindful of the precautionary principles and methods for quantification of symptomology. Preventative steps are broadly characterised by a gradual ascent profile, taking 2–3 days to acclimatise once above 2500 m and limiting daily ascent to 300–500 m per day. Adequate hydration is emphasised, and a reduction in training intensity and volume should be considered upon initial exposure (Pedlar et al., 2011). The symptoms of AMS can be assessed using the Lake Louise Questionnaire (Roach et al., 2018) (see supplementary material), which calculates an AMS clinical functional score based on headache, gastrointestinal symptoms, fatigue and/or weakness and dizziness/light-headedness. Mild symptoms can be treated with over-the-counter analgesics, but more severe symptoms require medical intervention and immediate descent.

Summary

Competition at altitude can be undertaken safely, but endurance-based athletes can expect a decrease in performance from as low as 500 m above sea level. The magnitude of the decrement in performance is highly variable between individuals, but exercise physiologists have a number of tests available to identify more susceptible athletes. Where available, acute hypoxic exposure prior to departure for competition at altitude may enhance ventilatory acclimatisation and reduce the time required at terrestrial altitude for performance to improve.

References

Chapman, R. F. (2013). The individual response to training and competition at altitude. *British Journal of Sports Medicine*, 47(Suppl 1), i40–i44.

Chapman, R. F., Emery, M. and Stager, J. M. (1999). Degree of arterial desaturation in normoxia influences $\dot{V}O_2$max decline in mild hypoxia. *Medicine and Science in Sports and Exercise*, 31, 658–663.

Chapman, R. F., Stager, J. M., Tanner, D. A., Stray-Gundersen, J. and Levine, B. D. (2011). Impairment of 3000-m run time at altitude is influenced by arterial oxyhemoglobin saturation. *Medicine and Science in Sports and Exercise*, 43, 1649–1656.

Dempsey, J. A., Hanson, P. G. and Henderson, K. S. (1984). Exercise-induced arterial hypoxaemia in healthy human subjects at sea level. *Journal of Physiology*, 355, 161–175.

Dominelli, P. B. and Sheel, A. W. (2019). Exercise-induced arterial hypoxemia; some answers, more questions. *Applied Physiology, Nutrition, and Metabolism*, 44, 571–579.

Garvican-Lewis, L. A., Vuong, V. L., Govus, A. D., Peeling, P., Jung, G., Nemeth, E., Hughes, D., Lovell, G., Eichner, D. and Gore, C. J. (2018). Intravenous iron does not augment the hemoglobin mass response to simulated hypoxia. *Medicine and Science in Sports and Exercise*, 50, 1669–1678.

Gavin, T. P., Derchak, P. A. and Stager, J. M. (1998). Ventilation's role in the decline in $\dot{V}O_2$max and SaO_2 in acute hypoxic exercise. *Medicine and Science in Sports and Exercise*, 30, 195–199.

Gore, C. J., Hahn, A. G., Scroop, G. C., Watson, D. B., Norton, K. I., Wood, R. J., Campbell, D. P. and Emonson, D. L. (1996). Increased arterial desaturation in trained cyclists during maximal exercise at 580 m altitude. *Journal of Applied Physiology (1985)*, 80, 2204–2210.

Harms, C. A. and Stager, J. M. (1995). Low chemoresponsiveness and inadequate hyperventilation contribute to exercise-induced hypoxemia. *Journal of Applied Physiology (1985)*, 79, 575–580.

Okazaki, K., Stray-Gundersen, J., Chapman, R. F. and Levine, B. D. (2019). Iron insufficiency diminishes the erythropoietic response to moderate altitude exposure. *Journal of Applied Physiology (1985)*, 127, 1569–1578.

Pedlar, C., Whyte, G., Kreindler, J., Hardman, S. and Levine, B. (2011). The BASES expert statement on human performance in hypoxia inducing environments: Natural and simulated altitude. *The Sport and Exercise Scientist*, 30, 6–7.

Pla, R., Brocherie, F., Le Garrec, S. and Richalet, J. P. (2020). Effectiveness of the hypoxic exercise test to predict altitude illness and performance at moderate altitude in high-level swimmers. *Physiological Reports*, 8, e14390.

Richalet, J. P., Larmignat, P., Poitrine, E., Letournel, M. and Canoui-Poitrine, F. (2012). Physiological risk factors for severe high-altitude illness: A prospective cohort study. *American Journal of Respiratory and Critical Care Medicine*, 185, 192–198.

Roach, R. C., Hackett, P. H., Oelz, O., Bartsch, P., Luks, A. M., MacInnis, M. J., Baillie, J. K. and Lake Louise, AMSSCC. (2018). The 2018 Lake Louise Acute Mountain Sickness Score. *High Altitude Medicine and Biology*, 19, 4–6.

Roels, B., Bentley, D. J., Coste, O., Mercier, J. and Millet, G. P. (2007). Effects of intermittent hypoxic training on cycling performance in well-trained athletes. *European Journal of Applied Physiology*, 101, 359–368.

Townsend, N. E., Gore, C. J., Hahn, A. G., McKenna, M. J., Aughey, R. J., Clark, S. A., Kinsman, T., Hawley, J. A. and Chow, C. M. (2002). Living high-training low increases hypoxic ventilatory response of well-trained endurance athletes. *Journal of Applied Physiology (1985)*, 93, 1498–1505.

West, J. B., Schoene, R. B., Milledge, J. S. and Ward, M. P. (2007). *High Altitude Medicine and Physiology*. London: Hodder Arnold.

Young, A. J., Cymerman, A. and Burse, R. L. (1985). The influence of cardiorespiratory fitness on the decrement in maximal aerobic power at high altitude. *European Journal of Applied Physiology and Occupational Physiology*, 54, 12–15.

14.2 Performing in the heat

Neil S. Maxwell, Carl A. James, and Ash G. B. Willmott

Tests of human endeavour have assessed exercise performance since the Ancient Greeks who visually inspected their Spartan athletes. Today's practitioners choose from a sophisticated array of physiological and performance-based tests. Hot environments exacerbate the physiological demands of exercise, often leading to performance impairments and/or a risk of heat-related illness (HRI). Consequently, there is an increasing need for practitioners to conduct heat stress testing and performance assessments, whilst considering the robustness, predictability, context and risk of protocols (Figure 14.2.1). This chapter aims to support evidence-based decision making of practitioners in selecting physiological tests for athletes who will perform in the heat.

Heat tolerance tests

Heat tolerance represents an individual's ability to mitigate or avoid extreme body temperature elevations when exercising in hot environments (Moran et al., 2004). Traditionally, heat tolerance tests (HTTs) have evaluated military personnel that have previously experienced an HRI (e.g., exertional heat stroke). The Israel Defense Force developed a 120-min walking HTT at 5 km·h^{-1} against a gradient of 2% in 40°C and 40% relative humidity (RH), with criteria for core temperature (T$_{core}$) and heart rate (HR) to indicate heat tolerance. However, the design of such military-based HTTs offers little specificity for athletes due to the exercise intensity and duration. Alternative protocols utilising cycling and running of greater relative intensities (~60%–70% maximal oxygen uptake [$\dot{V}O_2$max]) and shorter durations (30–90 min) offer greater sport specificity. Mee et al. (2015) developed a running HTT (30 min at 9 km·h^{-1} and 2% gradient, in 40°C and 40% RH) that is reliable and sensitive to heat adaptation following heat acclimation. Pooled data from 55 recreationally active males and females found average peak T$_{core}$ and HR values were 38.9 ± 0.5°C and 184 ± 16 b·min^{-1}. Thus, practitioners may identify whether an athlete responds better or worse than the average response, but the variability in these average responses indicates a continuum of heat tolerance, rather than dichotomising individuals as 'tolerant' or 'intolerant'. Practitioners should consider multiple criteria when choosing a test to evaluate heat tolerance and combine these with interventions to detect subsequent improvement (Figure 14.2.1).

DOI: 10.4324/9781003045281-68

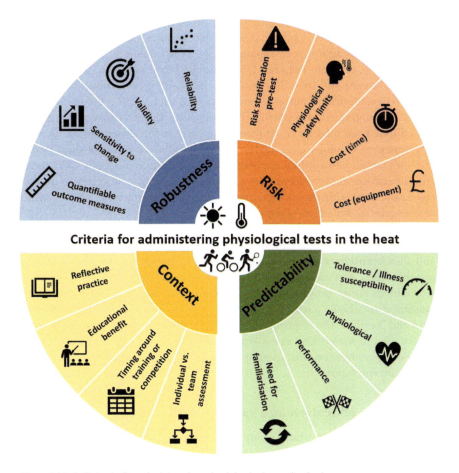

Figure 14.2.1 Criteria for administering physiological tests in the heat.

Exercise performance tests

The choice of exercise performance tests within heat stress is comparable to those undertaken in temperate conditions, albeit requiring additional safety monitoring (e.g., physiological safety limits) and data interpretation considerations (e.g., need for pacing familiarisation). Test choice is determined by whether the practitioner wishes to derive physiological or performance information. Graded exercise tests (GXTs), typically performed on treadmills, cycle or rowing ergometers, remain a valid and reliable method to assess endurance markers in heat stress, such as blood lactate threshold, economy/efficiency and $\dot{V}O_2$max. Conducting these tests in heat stress retains the predictive power for endurance running performance, where the composite measure of velocity at $\dot{V}O_2$max remains a strong individual predictor of 5-km running performance (James et al., 2017). Test design (i.e., stage duration, increments and gradient options) is adjustable, allowing greater sport specificity. The GXT in the heat can be separated into a discontinuous protocol of six to eight stages (e.g., 3 min exercise, 1 min rest for blood sampling, with 1 km·h^{-1} speed increments and fixed 1% gradient), followed by an incremental gradient protocol to volitional exhaustion (starting speed 2 km·h^{-1} below final prior speed, 1% or 1 min gradient increments). Fixed-intensity, time-to-exhaustion and preloaded time trials offer more representative exercise intensities and durations to GXTs, whilst retaining experimental control that allows for physiological evaluation. Arguably, free-paced time trials represent the only ecologically valid endurance assessment in heat stress, but are influenced by pacing strategies and are often associated with some of the highest body temperatures in athletes, which may surpass lab-based safety cut-off limits.

Practitioners should not overlook the value of heat familiarisation tests, especially for practicing interventions such as athlete cooling (e.g., ice vest/slurry) and allowing athletes to experience 'race pace sensations'. Anecdotally, athletes prioritise these experiences over the collection of data. Team sports can utilise intermittent sprint protocols on cycle ergometers (Hayes et al., 2013), non-/motorised treadmills (Gerrett et al., 2017) or in heated sports halls (Sunderland and Nevill, 2003) to prioritise the demands of the sport. Practitioners are encouraged to match heat stress conditions of the expected environment and the sport demands (i.e., duration/intensity) during testing for accurate performance interpretation.

Heat stress education and safety considerations

For all heat stress tests, practitioners should consider education for athletes and support staff to help recognise and treat HRI (see supplementary material). Education also facilitates the athlete's ownership and 'buy-in' for implementing testing. Heat alleviation practitioner guidelines (Gibson et al., 2020) may be disseminated using various communication methods (e.g., 'Hot Topics' seminars, narrated presentations, resource packs, infographics and/or animated videos). Challenges that heat stress testing brings include what and when to measure, non-negotiable physiological limits and their implications for competition. Therefore, resting, exercising and recovery monitoring of physiological (e.g., hydration status, T_{core}, HR and sweat rate) and perceptual (e.g., thermal comfort and sensation, ratings of perceived exertion and thirst; see supplementary material) responses are encouraged when implementing a heat stress test. A 'traffic light system' enables simple comparisons between athletes or time points to assess for changes in tolerance (e.g., heat sensitivity [L.hr^{-1}·°C^{-1}] = sweat rate/ΔT_{core}), performance and/or HRI risk (Table 14.2.1), still recognising a heat tolerance continuum exists. Perceptual data also offer behavioural insights, complementing physiological monitoring, where thermal comfort assesses how satisfied or dissatisfied an athlete is with the environment, and thermal sensation evaluates how hot or cold the environment feels.

Table 14.2.1 Traffic light system for the rating of heat tolerance

Risk	Peak T$_{CORE}$ (°C)	Change in T$_{CORE}$ from baseline (°C)	Sweat rate (L.hr^{-1})	Heat sensitivity (L.hr^{-1}.°C^{-1})
High	39.0	+2.0	1.5	0.8
Moderate	38.5	+1.5	2.0	1.3
Low	38.0	+1.0	2.5	2.5

Consideration of scientific principles (i.e., validity, reliability, sensitivity) of all measures is necessary for accurate data interpretation during single or repeated heat stress testing. These considerations are especially relevant following training interventions, such as heat acclimation, to interpret training effects (e.g., differences between T$_{core}$ measurement from tympanic or infrared thermal imagery vs. rectal thermometry [gold standard]) (Taylor et al., 2014). Utilising T$_{core}$ limits is not without constraints for performance interpretation in the heat (e.g., 5 km treadmill run may be completed, but 10 km potentially stopped), but may minimise HRI risks and should be agreed *a priori* as part of the risk assessment (i.e., maximal T$_{core}$ requiring activity cessation typically ranges between 39.2°C and 39.7°C).

Conclusion

Practitioners must decide which test provides the most relevant information. Figure 14.2.1 offers simple criteria to support this decision making, enabling athletes to prepare and compete safely and optimally in the heat.

References

Gerrett, N., Jackson, S., Yates, J. and Thomas, G. (2017). Ice slurry ingestion does not enhance self-paced intermittent exercise in the heat. *Scandinavian Journal of Medicine and Science in Sports*, 27, 1202–1212.

Gibson, O. R., James, C., Mee, J. A., Willmott, A., Turner, G., Hayes, M. and Maxwell, N. (2020). Heat alleviation strategies for athletic performance: A review and practitioner guidelines. *Temperature*, 7(1), 3–36.

Hayes, M., Smith, D., Castle, P. C., Watt, P., Ross, E. Z. and Maxwell, N. S. (2013). Peak power output provides the most reliable measure of performance in prolonged intermittent-sprint cycling. *Journal of Sport Sciences*, 31(5), 565–572.

James, C. A., Gibson, O. R., Willmott, A. G. B., Hayes, M., Schlader, Z., Flouris, A. and Maxwell, N. S. (2017). Defining the determinants of endurance running performance in the heat. *Temperature*, 4(3), 314–329.

Mee, J. A., Doust, J. and Maxwell, N. S. (2015). Repeatability of a running heat tolerance test. *Journal of Thermal Biology*, 49–50, 91–97.

Moran, D. S., Heled, Y., Still, L., Laor, A. and Shapiro, Y. (2004). Assessment of heat tolerance for post exertional heat stroke individuals. *Medical Science Monitor*, 10, CR252–CR257.

Sunderland, C. and Nevill, M. E. (2003). Effect of the menstrual cycle on performance of intermittent, high-intensity shuttle running in a hot environment. *European Journal of Applied Physiology*, 88(45), 345–352.

Taylor, N. A., Tipton, M. J. and Kenny, G. P. (2014). Considerations for the measurement of core, skin and mean body temperatures. *Journal of Thermal Biology*, 46, 72–101.

14.3 Performing in cold environments

Clare Eglin, Michael Tipton, and Heather Massey

Exposure to cold can impair performance and threaten life and remains one of the largest killers of sports people (Whyte and Tipton, 2020). Preparation for events such as the Polar Circle Marathon (air temperature −15°C) will necessitate exposure to similar conditions to optimise performance, clothing and risk mitigation. This chapter focuses on measurement of the physiological responses to cold; the impact of cold-induced vasoconstriction on some common physiological measures is also discussed. Whether cold exposure is undertaken for athlete preparation or research, it should be remembered that humans cool 4–5 times faster in cold water than in air at the same temperature (see Chapter 15.4). Therefore, thorough risk assessments should be undertaken, including appropriate withdrawal criteria and exclusions (Table 14.3.1, and see also supplementary material).

Measurement of the environment

The ambient environment should be measured adjacent to the participant. Wet bulb globe temperature (WBGT) includes measurement of convection (dry bulb temperature; T_{db}), evaporation (wet bulb temperature; T_w) and radiation (globe temperature; T_g):

$$\text{WBGT} = 0.7\,(T_w) + 0.2\,(T_g) + 0.1\,(T_{db})$$

In most laboratory scenarios, radiation is likely to be minimal and therefore T_{db} and relative humidity (RH) will suffice. RH can be measured using a humidity meter or calculated from the difference between T_w and T_{db}. If measuring wind speed, the anemometer should be positioned carefully, as the angle will influence the measurement.

Measurement of physiological responses

Core temperature

Core temperature (T_{core}) is normally about 37°C, a T_{core} of 36°C will invoke vigorous shivering, and 35°C is clinical hypothermia. T_{core} varies with measurement location (rectal warmest), time of day (peak 17:00 and trough 04:00) and

DOI: 10.4324/9781003045281-69

386 *Clare Eglin et al.*

Table 14.3.1 Suggested exclusion and withdrawal criteria for testing undertaken in cold environments

Risk	Exclusion Criteria*	Withdrawal Criteria*
General	Exercise-/cold-induced asthma Cold urticaria	
Hypothermia		Deep body temperature <35°C
Peripheral cold injury	Raynaud phenomenon Previous cold injuries	Skin temperature <8°C for 15 min or <4°C at any time
Cardiac event	Family history of sudden cardiac death Hypertension Cardiovascular disease	Appearance of cardiac irregularities on ECG

* Any other conditions or tests required by an independent medical officer.

menstrual cycle (lower in the follicular phase) and therefore should be controlled for in any experimental design (Taylor et al., 2014).

T_{core} can be measured using thermistors inserted into the rectum (T_{re}: 12–15 cm beyond the anal sphincter) or oesophagus (T_{oes}: inserted to the level of the heart), which are considered the best sites for measuring T_{core} in the cold (Taylor et al., 2014). T_{core} can also be estimated from gastrointestinal temperature (T_{gi}) measured by swallowing radio pills. Measurement of aural, tympanic, sublingual or axillary temperatures as indices of T_{core} are not recommended in the cold, as they are influenced by cooled T_{sk} and are unreliable (see supplementary material).

Skin temperature

Skin temperature (T_{sk}) can be measured using either conductive (thermistors and thermocouples) or radiative (infrared thermography) devices. The positioning of the thermistors will depend on the experimental conditions. Water immersion requires few sites, as T_{sk} will be clamped close to water temperature, whereas partial clothing in cold air will require more sites due to T_{sk} heterogeneity. Peripheral T_{sk} (e.g., finger and toe) should be monitored to prevent cold injuries; however, thermistors and thermocouples should not be used in extreme cold due to the risk of contact freezing. Telemetry systems such as iButtons give warmer T_{sk} compared to thermistors but are valid alternatives for field testing (Bach et al., 2015).

Mean T_{sk} ($\overline{T}_{sk}$) can be calculated from the unweighted mean or using formulae which take into consideration surface area, underlying muscle or distribution of cutaneous thermoreceptors (see supplementary material). Although the equation developed by Ramanathan (1964) is commonly used, it has not been validated for cold environments, clothed or exercising individuals or women. For clothed individuals resting or exercising in cool environments, 8–12 T_{sk} measurements are recommended.

Infrared thermography is a non-contact method of measuring T_{sk}, and to improve reproducibility, standardised procedures should be followed (Moreira et al., 2017). Infrared thermography and thermistors or thermocouples should not be used interchangeably to measure T_{sk}, as they do not have sufficient agreement – for example, infrared cameras may overestimate T_{sk} during rewarming following cold exposure, cannot measure T_{sk} under clothing and require dry skin. Whichever system is used, the sensitivity, dynamic response characteristics and data logging capability of the device should be appropriate for the experimental design (Taylor et al., 2014).

Mean body temperature

Mean body temperature ($\overline{T}_b$) is calculated from a weighted summation of T_{core} and $\overline{T}_{sk}$:

$$\overline{T}_b = = x T_{core} + (1-x) \overline{T}_{sk}$$

The weightings for mean body temperature are variable and subject to error (Taylor et al., 2014).

Shivering

Falling T_{sk} and T_{core} will initiate shivering, and whilst exercise often inhibits shivering, in severe conditions they can occur simultaneously up to a moderate level of exercise (oxygen consumption of 1.2 L·min^{-1}) (Whyte and Tipton, 2020). Maximal shivering is approximately 50% of maximal oxygen uptake and therefore can be assessed by measuring oxygen consumption (no correction is required for mechanical efficiency since shivering is 0% efficient). Electromyography (EMG; common sites: pectoralis major, trapezius, sternocleidomastoid and deltoideus) is useful for identifying the onset of shivering, but there are inter-individual variations in the order of muscle recruitment, and activation of deeper muscles is not measured. Shivering can also be assessed visually, for example, using the bedside shivering assessment scale (see supplementary material). It is recommended that shivering is assessed using a combination of techniques.

Thermal comfort and sensation

Visual analogue scales (VASs) of thermal sensation and thermal comfort are important additional measures, as depending on the preceding physiological state, the same T_{core} and $\overline{T}_{sk}$ may be perceived as uncomfortably cold or comfortably warm. Whole-body and peripheral thermal sensation and comfort in the cold will differ, and therefore both should be assessed.

Cutaneous blood flow

Cutaneous blood flow may be measured using methods such as laser Doppler (LD) flowmetry and laser speckle contrast imaging (LSCI). LSCI has good temporal and spatial resolution but is sensitive to movement artefact and is expensive.

LD flowmetry can be used during exercise; however, reproducibility can be poor due to the heterogeneity of skin perfusion and only 1 mm^3 of skin being sampled. Using a multifibre LD probe and reporting cutaneous vascular conductance (flux, mean arterial pressure) can reduce variability (see Davison et al., 2022).

An indirect index of vasomotor tone can be determined from the forearm-finger T_{sk} gradient, with a decline in finger T_{sk} indicating vasoconstriction. The onset of vasoconstriction can be identified from the inflection of forearm-finger T_{sk}, with a difference of 2°C indicating vasoconstrictor tone and 4°C intense vasoconstriction.

Consequences of cooling and peripheral vasoconstriction on measurement techniques

When peripherally vasoconstricted, capillary and venous sampling may yield a limited sample volume, which may also not be applicable to the systemic circulation. This may be overcome by arterialising the blood supply using a hot towel (~40°C for 3–5 min) or hand warming box or inserting a central line.

For accurate pulse oximetry readings, pulsatile flow is required, and therefore the measurement site should be warm. Caution should be taken when interpreting data from peripherally vasoconstricted or hypothermic participants, and alternative sites of measurement other than the finger should be considered. Potential sources of error in pulse oximetry are given in the supplementary material.

In cold hypoxic environments it can be difficult to determine if reductions in tissue oxygenation, as assessed by near-infrared spectroscopy (NIRS), occur due to reduced perfusion or reduced saturation or both. Coupling NIRS with measures of blood flow may help; however, care is needed to ensure the same vascular bed is measured. Maintaining contact pressure between the NIRS sensor and skin reduces shivering artefacts.

Shivering artefacts are common on electrocardiogram (ECG) traces and can prevent rhythm classification by obscuring wave forms, making interpretation difficult. Careful skin preparation will maximise the quality of the ECG recording. Alternatively, non-standard lead placements could be employed; however, the ECG should be marked to prevent diagnostic misinterpretation.

References

Bach, A. J. E., Stewart, I. B., Minett, G. M. and Costello, J. T. (2015). Does the technique employed for skin temperature assessment alter outcomes? A systematic review. *Physiological Measurement*, 36(9), R27–R51.

Moreira, D. G., Costellob, J. T., Britoc, C. J., Adamczykd, J. G., Ammere, K., Bachf, A. J. E., Costag, C. M. A., Eglinb, C., Fernandesh, A. A., Fernández-Cuevas, I., Ferreiraj, J. J. A., Formentik, D., Fournetl, D., Havenithm, G., Howelln, K., Jungo, A., Kennyp, G. P., Kolosovas-Machucaq, E. S., Maleyf, M. J., Merlar, A., Pascoes, D. D., Priego Quesadat, J. I., Schwartzu, R. G., Seixasv, A. R. D., Selfew, J., Vainerx, B. G. and Sillero-Quintana, M. (2017). Thermographic imaging in sports and exercise medicine: A Delphi study and consensus statement on the measurement of human skin temperature. *Journal of Thermal Biology*, 69, 155–162.

Ramanathan, N. L. (1964). A new weighting system for mean surface temperature of the human body. *Journal of Applied Physiology*, 1, 19(3), 531–533.

Taylor, N. A., Tipton, M. J. and Kenny, G. P. (2014). Considerations for the measurement of core, skin and mean body temperatures. *Journal of Thermal Biology*, 46, 72–101.

Whyte, G. and Tipton, M. J. (2020). The BASES expert statement on human performance and health in cold environments. *Sport and Exercise Scientist*, 66, 14–15.

14.4 Swimming in aquatic environments

Mitch Lomax and Heather Massey

Swimmers exercise in a unique environment. The increased hydrostatic pressure of water compared with air, coupled with the horizontal body position and periods of breath holding, affect physiological and biomechanical responses to swimming. On top of this, movements are slower in water, and heat exchange differs between the two mediums. Swimmers also exercise in a range of different environments. For example, commercial swimming pools operate within tightly regulated hygiene standards and water temperatures, whereas open-water swimming environments are naturally more variable. Here, factors such as air and water temperature, ambient and radiative temperatures, wetsuit use, wave profiles and fresh and saline water can vary enormously. These can impact safety requirements and will affect the physiological and biomechanical responses to swimming. This chapter will focus on the practical considerations for conducting physiological testing of swimmers in aquatic environments.

The testing environment

Swimming tests can be undertaken in indoor and outdoor swimming pools and flumes, rivers, lakes and seas (open water). If selecting an outside environment, practitioners will have to contend with a number of uncontrollable/semi-controllable factors, which may make testing problematic. In contrast, testing in an indoor swimming pool or flume will give the practitioner more control and extend the range of physiological measurements available; however, it might also reduce the ecological validity of measurements. Additionally, while some pool and flume testing techniques are transferable to open water, the greater distance and nature of open-water environments may limit the testing capability of equipment and the reproducibility of data (see supplementary material for an overview of testing equipment considerations).

The fluid dynamics of water also differ between environments, being either dynamic or quasi-static (Guignard et al., 2017). In a flume, the flowing water creates a dynamic aquatic environment, and a swimmer must maintain a stationary position by swimming against a flow of water directed at them from the front of the flume. This environment more closely resembles the dynamic fluid flow of a river current than that of a quasi-static environment. In contrast, the quasi-static

DOI: 10.4324/9781003045281-70

water mass of a swimming pool is more akin to that of a calm lake, and in both situations the swimmer pulls themselves through a relatively stable body of water (Guignard et al., 2017). Whether sea swimming is better replicated in a pool or flume will depend on the conditions to be replicated. For an overview of factors to consider when selecting the water environment for testing, see the supplementary material for this chapter.

Practitioners must also consider whether to tether the swimmer. When tethered, a swimmer is held in place by a belt connected to some form of pulley and weights. Weights are then added to the system until the swimmer can no longer maintain their position in the water. As tethering is best undertaken in a quasi-static water environment, the water flow should be switched off if using a flume. An advantage of tethering is that it requires less water space than free or untethered swimming and so may be attractive in a pool setting if space is limited. Importantly, maximal oxygen uptake ($\dot{V}O_2$max) and minute ventilation appear to be unaffected by tethering, whether swimming in a pool or flume (Bonen et al., 1980; Holmér et al., 1974). However, this is not the case for stroke kinematics, which do differ between pool and flume swimming (Guignard et al., 2017).

Measuring physiological responses in an aquatic environment

Despite the unique challenges posed by water, a number of physiological parameters can be measured. These include blood lactate, heart rate, perceptual measures, deep body temperature, expired gas (mainly for the determination of oxygen consumption [$\dot{V}O_2$]) and swimming economy. Additionally, specialised cameras, inertial measurement units, electromyography (EMG) equipment and measuring active drag (MAD) systems can be used for biomechanical analyses.

Traditionally, $\dot{V}O_2$ and $\dot{V}O_2$max have been assessed using the Douglas bag (or similar, e.g., meteorological balloons) technique (Bonen et al., 1980; Holmér et al., 1974). However, the development of aquatic-specific metabolic carts and snorkels have expanded the number of physiological parameters that can be measured (Lomax et al., 2019). Tables 14.4.1 and 14.4.2 provide examples of $\dot{V}O_2$max, economy and blood lactate testing protocols used in swimming. Typical $\dot{V}O_2$max values for trained swimmers and triathletes are 58 ml·kg^{-1}·min^{-1} and 53 ml·kg^{-1}·min^{-1}, respectively (Roels et al., 2005; Libicz et al., 2005).

Swimming with a snorkel or mouth piece and associated respiratory tubing may impede swimming performance, making the determination of $\dot{V}O_2$ impractical during swimming. In this situation, backward extrapolation (BE) of recovery $\dot{V}O_2$ can be used to predict end-swim $\dot{V}O_2$ (Montpetit et al., 1981). Briefly, BE requires swimmers to hold their breath after their last swimming stroke and release it only after they have inserted a mouth piece. They then breathe through the mouth piece connected to a Douglas bag rig or metabolic cart for up to 80 s in discrete 20-s bins. Regression is then used to predict end-swim $\dot{V}O_2$ (Montpetit et al., 1981).

Table 14.4.1 Example maximal oxygen uptake ($\dot{V}O_2$max) assessment protocols used in swimming. Where protocols are sufficiently similar, they have been amalgamated, and warm-ups are omitted. For specific reference, see supplementary material.

Pool or Flume	Details
Pool	3–7 × 200-m repeats or until exhaustion. Minimum 15–30 s rest between each. Starting speed based on % of season's best. Speed increments of 5%–10% or 0.05 $m·s^{-1}$ per repeat. Final repeat at maximal effort.
Pool	6 × 4 min discontinuous swimming at work levels consisting of 20, 26, 32, 38, 44 and 50 strokes·min^{-1}. 10 min recovery between each repeat.
Pool	4 min of maximal swimming.
Flume$_{UN}$	Progressive intensity test (GXT). Speed increased by 0.1–0.2 $m·min^{-1}$ until it cannot be maintained for 2 min.
Flume$_{UN}$	GXT. Speed increased by 0.05–0.10 $m·s^{-1}$ every 2 min until exhaustion. 15 min later, swimmers swim a verification test at 105% of end-test GXT speed until exhaustion.
Flume$_{UN}$	2 min of submaximal swimming followed by maximum velocity swimming until exhaustion. If exhaustion is not reached within 5 min, speed is increased by 0.1 $m·s^{-1}$ and swimming continued until exhaustion.
Flume$_T$	Increase the weight applied to the weight belt every 2, 3 or 4 min until the weight can no longer be supported by the swimmer unassisted for 2–3 min. Swims can be discontinuous in nature with 3–5 min rest periods.

Flume$_{UN}$: free/untethered swimming with flowing water.
Flume$_T$: tethered swimming with stationary water.
Water temperature varied between 25° and 29°C.

Measurement of basic swimming performance variables

Stroke rate, stroke length (i.e., distance covered per stroke), velocity, critical velocity and best effort performance tests provide useful information about swimming performance (Cardelli et al., 1999; Dekerle, 2006). These parameters are easier to measure than $\dot{V}O_2$ and blood lactate, as they do not require specialised equipment. All that is required is a stopwatch and a means of recording data over a known distance or time. Although velocity and stroking parameters can be recorded over any distance, measurement during a 'clean swimming zone' is recommended, as this eradicates any confounding impact of turns or dives. For example, if applying this to a 25-m pool, the first and last 5 m of each length can be excluded, with data collection occurring only during the middle 15 m per length. Basic stroke characteristics and performance variables and their calculations can be found within the supplementary material.

Summary

Practitioners must consider a number of factors before conducting physiological assessments in aquatic environments. These include the suitability of potential

Table 14.4.2 Example swimming economy and blood lactate ([La⁻]) assessment protocols used in swimming. For specific reference, see supplementary material.

Parameter	Details
Economy	Five or six 6-min submaximal (30%–70% $\dot{V}O_{2peak}$) swims, separated by 4 min of rest. Expired air is measured during the final 2 min of each stage and $\dot{V}O_2$ determined as the mean value per stage.
Two-speed lactate test	Same distance (typically 100 m to 400 m) swum twice. The first at 85%–90% race pace ([La⁻] should exceed 4 mmol l⁻¹) and the second at maximum effort. 20 min should separate each test (15 min active recovery, 5 min seated rest). [La⁻] is measured at minutes 1, 3 and 5 following swim 1 and at minutes 3, 5, 7, 10 and 12 (until peak occurs) following swim 2. Plot peak [La⁻] per repeat (y axis) vs. speed (x axis) and extend the linear line to predict speed at OBLA.
Step test	7 × 200-m on a 50-min cycle. Starting speed should be 70% of 200-m performance time with each subsequent repeat 5% faster. [La⁻] is measured after each repeat. One or two thresholds can be identified depending on the criteria adopted.
Step test	6 × 400 m: 3 × 400 m (separated by 60-s rest) at 85% maximum effort, rest 3 min after third swim; 1 × 400 m at 90% maximum effort, rest 6 min; 1 × 400 m at 95% effort, rest 20 min; 1 × 400 m at maximum effort. [La⁻] measured between minutes 2 and 3 of recovery following the third 400-m swim and during recovery minutes 5 and 6 for all other swims. One or two thresholds can be identified depending on the criteria adopted.
IAT	Multiple 200-m repeats until exhaustion. Each repeat is separated by 30 s rest with [La⁻] measured during this period, post-swim and then every 2 min thereafter until peak. Speed is increased by 0.05 m s⁻¹. IAT is defined as the interception of combined linear and exponential regressions on a [La⁻] (y axis)-velocity (x axis) curve.
MLSS	Three to five 30-min swims at different intensities, separated by 24 h rest. Starting speed is the speed associated with the IAT. If steady state or a decrease in [La⁻] occurs, speed should be increased by 2.5% per repeat until [La⁻] steady state cannot be maintained (reduce speed if no [La⁻] steady state occurs after swim 1 or exhaustion occurs before 30 min). [La⁻] is measured at minutes 10 and 30 per swim, and MLSS is defined as the [La⁻] that increases by no more than 1 mmol l⁻¹ during the final 20 min of the swim.
MLSS	2 × 30 min swims on separate days, one at 90% of maximal aerobic velocity and the other at 95% of maximal aerobic velocity. [La⁻] is measured every 400 m per swim. MLSS is defined as the highest [La⁻] that increased by no more than 1 mmol l⁻¹ during the final 20 min of swimming.

OBLA: Onset of blood lactate accumulation; IAT: individual anaerobic threshold; MLSS: maximal lactate steady state.
See companion website for references.

testing environments, the capability of potential equipment, the appropriateness of different testing protocols and their outcome measures and the test administrator expertise required.

References

Bonen, A., Wilson, B. A., Yarkony, M. and Belcastro, A. N. (1980). Maximal oxygen uptake during free, tethered, and flume swimming. *Journal of Applied Physiology: Respiratory and Environmental Exercise Physiology*, 48, 232–235.

Cardelli, C., Chollet, D. and Lerda, R. (1999). Analysis of the 100-m front crawl as a function of skill level in non-expert swimmers. *Journal of Human Movement Studies*, 36, 51–74.

Dekerle, J. (2006). The use of critical velocity in swimming: A place for critical stroke rate. *Portuguese Journal of Sport Sciences*, 6, 201–205.

Guignard, B., Rouard, A., Chollet, D., Ayad, O., Bonifazi, M., Vedova, D. D. and Seifert, L. (2017). Perception and action in swimming: Effects of aquatic environment on upper limb inter-segmental coordination. *Human Movement Science*, 55, 240–254.

Holmér, I., Lundin, A. and Eriksson, B. O. (1974). Maximum oxygen uptake during swimming and running by elite swimmers. *Journal of Applied Physiology*, 36, 711–714.

Libicz, S., Roels, B. and Millet, G. P. (2005). $\dot{V}O_2$ responses to intermittent swimming sets at velocity associated with $\dot{V}O_2$max. *Canadian Journal of Applied Physiology*, 30(5), 543–553.

Lomax, M., Mayger, B., Saynor, Z. L., Vine, C. and Massey, H. C. (2019). Practical considerations for assessing pulmonary gas exchange and ventilation during flume swimming using the MetaSwim metabolic cart. *Journal of Strength and Conditioning Research*, 33, 1941–1953.

Montpetit, R. R., Léger, L. A., Lavoie, J. M. and Cazorla, G. (1981). $\dot{V}O_2$peak during free swimming using the backward extrapolation of the O_2 recovery curve. *European Journal of Applied Physiology*, 47, 385–391.

Roels, B., Schmitt, L., Libicz, S., Bentley, D., Richalet, J.-P. and Millett, G. (2005). Specificity of $\dot{V}O_2$max and the ventilatory threshold in free swimming and cycle ergometry: Comparison between triathletes and swimmers. *British Journal of Sports Medicine*, 39, 965–968.

Part XV

Athlete health and wellbeing

15.1 The travelling athlete

Sarah Gilchrist and Luke Gupta

Contemporary training and competition for athletes often requires travel. The benefit of training in specific environments (e.g., training camps) and travel to overseas competition are an ever growing part of elite sport and are becoming more common in recreational athletes too (Waterhouse et al., 2004).

This chapter will outline considerations for the travelling athlete, including strategies to manage aspects of travel wellness (the maintenance of wellness following a period of travel; see Chapter 15.2 for 'wellness' reference) stemming from both short- and long-haul travel. It will also provide a description of the differences in travel fatigue and recommendations for methods of testing for time shift–associated symptoms and interventions to overcome them.

In planning travel around the demands of competition and training, it is important to separate the athlete's travel plan into four phases: preparation, during, arrival and return.

Overarching these phases, and underpinning travel wellness, are the typical responses to travel, of which two factors must be accounted for and managed accordingly: travel fatigue and jet lag. The former is a collective term for the physiological, psychological, emotional and environmental cost of short- or long-haul travel (e.g., dehydration, disorientation, weariness) and can be restored with generic recovery, e.g., rest, sleep and nutrition (Samuels, 2012). The latter, however, is an episodic physiological state that results from desynchronisation of the circadian rhythm caused by rapid long-distance transmeridian travel and varies to a greater or lesser extent, depending on the time zone shift (Samuels, 2012).

Jet lag manifests through several symptoms which can last a number of days, with the general rule for a rate of adjustment being 1 h per day for a number of days that is equal to the number of time zones crossed, or 2 h per day should an intervention be implemented (Roach and Sargent, 2019). Whether an athlete experiences general travel fatigue or more complicated time shift symptoms is difficult to decipher (Janse van Rensburg et al., 2020), but can largely be assumed using contextual information such as whether the travel is either short or long haul, whether time zones have been crossed and days since arrival in-country.

Short-haul travel can be classified as any flight travel period that takes up to 6.5 h to complete (Thornton et al., 2018). Whilst one-off short-haul travel jaunts

DOI: 10.4324/9781003045281-72

may not overly offset an athlete's circadian rhythm, frequent short-haul trips can have an adverse cumulative and chronic effect on an athlete's physiological, psychological and emotional state. Equally, the timing of short-haul travel can have a concomitant effect even if the journey itself is relatively short. This is where the disrupting influence of travel and travel scheduling on sleep (i.e., getting up earlier to catch transport) needs to be managed carefully, as they are crucial to athlete travel wellness.

With short-haul travel wellness, the signs and symptoms are often immunological, musculoskeletal or psychological and can be monitored via some of the methods described in the athlete wellbeing chapter (Chapter 15.2). The priority for the athlete is to monitor the accumulated fatigue, manage the impact and prevent the associated health consequences (Samuels, 2012).

Conversely jet lag symptoms are more persistent and need careful consideration and planning in order to manage and require resolution (in part or complete) for an athlete to be able to deliver effective training or an optimal performance in competition. For reference, Samuels (2012) described a simple algorithm highlighting the differences between short- and long-term travel effects on the athlete.

Assessing poor wellbeing induced by travel per se is challenging in the context of elite sport. As part of many sport programmes, existing monitoring protocols (see Chapter 15.2) include self-appraisals of more *general* wellbeing, and as a result distinguishing between travel and general wellbeing is difficult. Even though travel wellness symptoms have been well documented (see Reilly et al., 2007), when taken out of context, many of these symptoms are like those of poor wellbeing in general, e.g., fatigue, sleep disruption, low mood. Although not empirically supported, whether generic assessments of wellbeing are sufficient to capture the essence of travel wellness requires further research but are likely to suffice (see Figure 15.1.1).

Measuring travel fatigue and jet lag

Objectively, travel fatigue and jet lag are difficult to measure and can be expensive and disruptive to an athlete's training (Janes van Rensburg et al., 2020). Subjective measures are much more practical in helping to inform athletes, coaches and support staff of an athlete's overall experience of travel fatigue and jet lag and the impact of any planned intervention to overcome them, but are prone to time-of-day effects (see Waterhouse et al., 2005). An overview of measuring travel wellness can be seen in Figure 15.1.1.

The purpose of measuring travel fatigue and jet lag is two-fold: to ensure any subsequent travel intervention is targeted and individualised and to provide coaches and programme managers with information that can help make decisions regarding training scheduling and travel planning.

To physiologically quantify the extent by which an individual's circadian phase is misaligned or *lagging* relative to a new local time (following long-haul travel), precise measurement of an athlete's circadian phase is required both before and after travel (Arendt, 2009). However, circadian phase is difficult to measure in the field

(Reiter et al., 2020), and given its dynamicity that ensues after long-haul travel, an objective measure of circadian misalignment is rarely employed. Alternatively, circadian physiological assumptions from laboratory simulations are applied to estimate an individual's circadian phase and the rate of its adjustment following transition – the details of these assumptions have been detailed elsewhere (see Roach and Sargent, 2019).

It is important to note that these assumptions are limited in that they are considered to apply equally across all individuals, e.g., rate of adjustment. However, we know that jet lag is experienced differently between individuals, and therefore the earlier text provides an incomplete assessment of jet lag. As a result, *symptoms* of jet lag are typically assessed. While symptoms do not allow for circadian phase to be precisely pinpointed and circadian misalignment quantified, they do provide an indication of jet lag experience at a given time of day (Waterhouse et al., 2003). Standardised questionnaires have been employed previously to characterise athlete experiences over the course of a day and include the Liverpool John Moore's Jet Lag Questionnaire (see Waterhouse et al., 2005). Overall, capturing the subjective experience of jet lag coupled with an estimation of circadian phase realignment based off assumptions can help assess jet lag and therefore target management, such as light therapy, meal timing and exercise (see Roach and Sargent, 2019).

When managing jet lag for athletes, it is important to also consider the return leg of the journey. Managing the associated travel fatigue and jet lag associated with outbound travel typically takes precedence due to being in close proximity to competition. However, often athletes returning from competition are entering back into a subsequent training phase, and therefore return travel requires consideration. Return travel management strategies should allow for a successful re-entry into training.

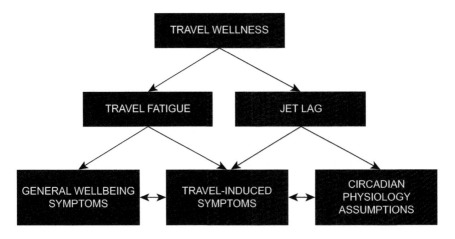

Figure 15.1.1 Components of measuring 'travel wellness'.

General considerations for travel

Of the various travel factor 'clusters' that impact on an athlete when travelling, circadian disruption factors predominate. Nonetheless, despite little supporting evidence (see Janse van Rensburg et al., 2020), other factors should also be considered in a travel wellness programme, for example, nutrition, hydration, hygiene, self-care, musculoskeletal health and deep vein thrombosis (risk is higher if travelling for more than 3 h by plane, train or car).

Summary

The travelling athlete should have a detailed travel plan ahead of any period of travel. This should include strategies for all aspects of the journey: preparation, during, arrival and return. In particular, athletes should pay attention to their ability to manage travel fatigue and circadian disruption and act accordingly in relation to being able to deliver performances at competition and training where travel is involved.

References

Arendt, J. (2009). Managing jet lag: Some of the problems and possible new solutions. *Sleep Medicine Reviews*, 13(4), 249–256.

Janse van Rensburg, D., Jansen van Rensburg, A., Fowler, P., Fullagar, H., Stevens, D., Halson, S., Bender, A., Vincent, G., Claassen-Smithers, A., Dunican, I., Roach, G. D., Sargent, C., Lastella, M. and Cronje, T. (2020). How to manage travel fatigue and jet lag in athletes? A systematic review of interventions. *British Journal of Sports Medicine*, 54(16), 960–968. doi: 10.1136/bjsports-2019-101635

Reilly, T., Atkinson, G., Edwards, B., Waterhouse, J., Åkerstedt, T., Davenne, D., Lemmer, B. and Wirz-Justice, A. (2007). Coping with jet-lag: A position statement for the European College of Sport Science. *European Journal of Sport Science*, 7(1), 1–7. doi: 10.1080/17461390701216823

Reiter, A. M., Sargent, C. and Roach, G. D. (2020). Finding DLMO: Estimating dim light melatonin onset from sleep markers derived from questionnaires, diaries and actigraphy. *Chronobiology International*, 1–13.

Roach, G. D. and Sargent, C. (2019). Interventions to minimize jet lag after westward and eastward flight. *Frontiers in Physiology*, 10, 927.

Samuels, C. H. (2012). Jet lag and travel fatigue: A comprehensive management plan for sport medicine physicians and high-performance support teams. *Clinical Journal of Sports Medicine*, 22(3), 268–273.

Thornton, H. R., Miller, J., Taylor, L., Sargent, C., Lastella, M. and Fowler, P. M. (2018). Impact of short-compared to long-haul international travel on the sleep and wellbeing of national wheelchair basketball athletes. *Journal of Sports Sciences*, 36(13), 1476–1484.

Waterhouse, J., Nevill, A., Edwards, B., Godfrey, R. and Reilly, T. (2003). The relationship between assessments of jet lag and some of its symptoms. *Chronobiology International*, 20(6), 1061–1073.

Waterhouse, J., Nevill, A., Finnegan, J., Williams, P., Edwards, B., Kao, S. Y. and Reilly, T. (2005). Further assessments of the relationship between jet lag and some of its symptoms. *Chronobiology International*, 22(1), 121–136.

Waterhouse, J., Reilly, T. and Edwards, B. (2004). The stress of travel. *Journal of Sports Sciences*, 22, 946–966.

15.2 Athlete wellbeing

Sarah Gilchrist and Emma Neupert

Monitoring athletes' responses to training and competition is a fundamental aspect of supporting an athlete and coach. What is monitored, the process of data collection, reporting and subsequent decision making are of vital significance to informing training programmes (Halson, 2014). This chapter aims to define athlete 'wellbeing', ascertain why daily monitoring of an athlete's wellbeing is important and provide information on what daily wellbeing markers can be monitored.

To avoid athlete maladaptation, monitoring daily athlete wellbeing in sport is important due to the high training loads and limited recovery periods athletes often face. Wellbeing, however, is a nebulous term that is arguably often misapplied. 'Wellbeing' has been conflated with other terms such as wellness and welfare, leading to confusion surrounding what constructs 'best' represent athlete wellbeing, how they might be measured and if they are useful for training and performance (Lundqvist, 2011). Indeed, it appears that the theoretical framework that underpins the use of some wellbeing measures is often absent (Jeffries et al., 2020). Therefore, for the purposes of clarity within this chapter, an operational definition of wellbeing is given as the state of thriving or doing well in sport (Giles et al., 2020). Within this chapter, athlete wellbeing is limited to assessing an athlete's *physiological* response to training. In particular, their ability to consistently and effectively execute training and performances. In short, they are 'doing well' in their daily response to the training programme. For more specific information on 'overreaching and overtraining' see Chapter 15.4.

Key to the collation of athlete monitoring data, at whatever stage of athletic development, is that we 1) ask the right questions with methodological rigour and 2) any data collected informs decision making around the training programme. Monitoring permits the description of patterns of behaviour and habits in response to a training programme. Further, athlete wellbeing monitoring is critical to injury and illness prevention and rehabilitation from such occurrences.

A holistic approach to athlete wellbeing monitoring is recommended and should include physical, psychological, performance and medical markers. A broad variety of metrics which purport to measure athlete wellbeing have been discussed in the literature (Duignan et al., 2020; McGuigan et al., 2020). Some of the most commonly employed physical metrics can be classified into objective

DOI: 10.4324/9781003045281-73

and subjective markers of internal load, and these markers are focused on in this chapter (Impellizzeri et al., 2019).

Subjective measures

Subjective measures that are frequently employed in sport include informal monitoring via the trained coaching 'eye', the value of which should not be underestimated (Crowcroft et al., 2020). Asking athletes to report their rating of perceived exhaustion (RPE) of training sessions can also provide a valuable indicator of athletic wellbeing over time (Wallace et al., 2009).

Psychometric questionnaires such as ARSS (Kölling et al., 2020) and REST-Q Sport (Kellmann and Kallus, 2016) can further enhance the scientific rigour of subjective monitoring (Jeffries et al., 2020). There is, however, a trend in applied settings to employ custom single-item questions, typically encompassing sleep health, muscle soreness, fatigue and recovery (Gastin et al., 2013). Custom questions should, however, be assessed for reliability/validity; otherwise, it is unclear if they measure what they purport to (Jeffries et al., 2020).

Objective measures

Objective measurements of daily wellbeing may include (but are not limited to) sleep health, hydration, body mass, countermovement jump and heart rate, the detailed methodology of which is beyond the scope of this chapter (see also Chapter 15.4), but a brief outline is described next.

Sleep is the physiological and psychological balance point for all, in that there is no system in the human body that is not significantly impaired by a lack of, or enhanced by, good sleep. Therefore, monitoring of sleep is important for the assessment of an athlete's general health, ability to deliver training and perform in competition. Through subjective and objective field measures, sport science and medicine practitioners can now measure athletes' sleep and waking movement behaviour in free-living settings. There are a myriad of sleep measurement techniques from the laboratory (e.g., polysomnography) to the field (e.g., actigraphy). Preliminary investigations can be adequately performed using the Sleep Health Questionnaire, an easy-to-use, single-use questionnaire (Allen et al., 2018).

Hydration can be monitored through urine colour charts or refractometry (Oppliger and Bartok, 2002). Basic weighing pre- and post-training session with a comparison against fluid ingested will help provide a guide to hydration status. A good gauge of an athlete's response to the training programme is through their body mass. Is it consistent? It is decreasing or increasing in relation to anthropometric measures (not appropriate to be completed daily, but certainly regularly throughout the training programme)? For consistency, weigh the athlete in minimal clothing at the same time each day.

A key marker of daily wellbeing, potential illness and recovery is heat rate. Methods such as resting, exercising or recovery heart rate, or heart rate variability provide data that can be used to inform the coach regarding an athlete's response to training and their overall wellbeing (Buchheit, 2014).

Finally, neuromuscular fatigue has also been assessed via countermovement jumps. Instead of using jump height alone, it is recommended to assess measures derived from the jump, such as time to peak power and eccentric and concentric power (Gathercole et al., 2015).

The key to any monitoring process is to be consistent and use reliable and valid methodologies. Failure to address content validity in particular will leave practitioners unable to infer meaning from their measures. Always monitor at the same time of day and ensure equipment is calibrated. Where changes are seen in athlete wellbeing data, this should be discussed with the relevant personnel, e.g., medic, to ensure the athlete can train safely and effectively. Further, it is crucial that the coaching team and athletes buy in to any wellbeing monitoring that occurs. This helps to ensure that the data are collected via positive athlete engagement, with any adverse findings appropriately managed. To avoid any misperceptions, there should be a clearly articulated rationale and identified need that underpins any athlete monitoring system, which is shared within the sporting organisation (Saw et al., 2017).

In summary, a range of measures can be used to assess daily athlete wellbeing. Such information should, however, not be used in isolation, as only in conjunction with the coaching insights, performance data, technical and tactical information and training load can a more holistic picture of athlete wellbeing be constructed.

References

Allen, S. F., Elder, G. J., Longstaff, L. F., Gotts, Z. M., Sharman, R., Akram, U. and Ellis, J. G. (2018). Exploration of potential objective and subjective daily indicators of sleep health in normal sleepers. *Nature and Science of Sleep*, 10, 303–312.

Buchheit, M. (2014). Monitoring training status with HR measures: Do all roads lead to Rome? *Frontiers in Physiology*, 5 Feb.

Crowcroft, S., Slattery, K., McCleave, E. and Coutts, A. J. (2020). Do athlete monitoring tools improve a coach's understanding of performance change? *International Journal of Sports Physiology and Performance*, 15(6), 847–852.

Duignan, C., Doherty, C., Caulfield, B. and Blake, C. (2020). Single-item self-report measures of team-sport athlete wellbeing and their relationship with training load: A systematic review. *Journal of Athletic Training*, 55(9), 944–953.

Gastin, P. B., Meyer, D. and Robinson, D. (2013). Perceptions of wellness to monitor adaptive responses to training and competition in elite Australian football. *The Journal of Strength and Conditioning Research*, 27(9), 2518–2526.

Gathercole, R., Sporer, B., Stellingwerff, T. and Sleivert, G. (2015). Alternative countermovement-jump analysis to quantify acute neuromuscular fatigue. *International Journal of Sports Physiology and Performance*, 10(1), 84–92.

Giles, S., Fletcher, D., Arnold, R., Ashfield, A. and Harrison, J. (2020). Measuring wellbeing in sport performers: Where are we now and how do we progress? *Sports Medicine*, 50(7), 1255–1270.

Halson, S. L. (2014). Monitoring training load to understand fatigue in athletes. *Sports Medicine*, 44(Suppl 2), S139–S147.

Impellizzeri, F. M., Marcora, S. M. and Coutts, A. J. (2019). Internal and external training load: 15 years on. *International Journal of Sports Physiology and Performance*, 14(2), 270–273.

Jeffries, A. C., Wallace, L., Coutts, A. J., McLaren, S. J., McCall, A. and Impellizzeri, F. M. (2020). Athlete-reported outcome measures for monitoring training responses: A systematic review of risk of bias and measurement property quality according to the COSMIN guidelines. *International Journal of Sports Physiology and Performance*, 15(9), 1203–1215.

Kellmann, M. and Kallus, K. W. (2016). Recovery-stress questionnaire for athletes: User manual. In M. Kellmann and K. W. Kallus (eds.), *The Recovery-Stress Questionnaires*. Frankfurt, Germany: Pearson.

Kölling, S., Schaffran, P., Bibbey, A., Drew, M., Raysmith, B., Nässi, A. and Kellmann, M. (2020). Validation of the Acute Recovery and Stress Scale (ARSS) and the Short Recovery and Stress Scale (SRSS) in three English-speaking regions. *Journal of Sports Sciences*, 38(2), 130–139.

Lundqvist, C. (2011). Well-being in competitive sports – the feel-good factor? A review of conceptual considerations of well-being. *International Review of Sport and Exercise Psychology*, 4(2), 109–127.

McGuigan, H., Hassmén, P., Rosic, N. and Stevens, C. J. (2020). Training monitoring methods used in the field by coaches and practitioners: A systematic review. *International Journal of Sports Science and Coaching*, 15(3), 439–451.

Oppliger, R. A. and Bartok, C. (2002). Hydration testing of athletes. *Sports Medicine*, 32(15), 959–971.

Saw, A. E., Kellmann, M., Main, L. C. and Gastin, P. B. (2017). Athlete self-report measures in research and practice: Considerations for the discerning reader and fastidious practitioner. *International Journal of Physiology and Performance (Epub)*, 12, S2–127, S2–135.

Wallace, L. K., Slattery, K. M. and Coutts, A. J. (2009). The ecological validity and application of the session-RPE method for quantifying training loads in swimming. *Journal of Strength and Conditioning Research*, 23(1), 33–38.

15.3 Training load

Shaun J. McLaren, Franco M. Impellizzeri, Aaron J. Coutts, and Matthew Weston

Training load is a multidimensional construct, which reflects the amount of physical training that an athlete completes or experiences. It is used to quantify an exercise stimulus based on its nature, frequency, volume and intensity (Impellizzeri et al., 2005, 2019). Within an athlete monitoring context, the term 'training load' is a construct label assigned to the above constitutive definition. This should not be confused with the mechanical definition of 'load'. Accordingly, training load can incorporate a variety of operational definitions and can be measured in numerous ways.

The training process framework categorises training load as having two distinct, multidimensional, sub-constructs: external and internal (Impellizzeri et al., 2005, 2019). External training load relates to an athlete's performance outputs, such as distance, power output, weight moved, etc. Internal training load is the relative, within-exercise biochemical (physiological and psychological) and biomechanical (e.g., stress-strain) stresses in response to, or caused by, external training load (Impellizzeri et al., 2005, 2019; Vanrenterghem et al., 2017). Importantly, external training load is the means by which internal training load is induced, but internal training load in combination with contextual factors (e.g., individual characteristics) is the primary stimulus of training-induced responses, which drive adaptations (Impellizzeri et al., 2005, 2019). As such, external training load is viewed as the dose for internal training load, while the latter is the dose for training response.

While training volume and frequency are easily measured, training intensity and training load are constructs for which there is no gold standard. They can, however, be quantified using various indicators or surrogate measures (i.e., proxies) based on operational definitions. Selecting these measures is challenging and should be based on conceptual, empirical and contextual merits. This includes a logical and theoretically sound basis, measurement properties (reliability, validity, sensitivity to change), sport and athlete specificity, feasibility (time efficiency, ease of administration, cost-effectiveness, scalability to groups, timely feedback) and the ability to provide meaningful information to those using the data (Starling and Lambert, 2018; Coutts, 2014; Robertson et al., 2017). There are many ways to quantify internal and external training load, with each method having strengths and limitations that depend on the context.

DOI: 10.4324/9781003045281-74

Internal training load

Banister's *Training Impulse* (TRIMP; Banister, 1991) was the first attempt to combine training volume and internal intensity (heart rate) into a single metric. The original TRIMP is the product of mean fractional elevation in session average heart rate (ΔHR), exercise duration and an arbitrary weighting factor based on the exponential ΔHR–blood lactate (B[La]) relationship from an incrementally graded exercise test (GXT; see Chapter 3.7). Since its advent, TRIMP has been subject to many alternatives and advancements, such as arbitrary and individualised weighted zones (Edwards, 1993; Lucía et al., 2003; Stagno et al., 2007) or the use of semi- and fully individualised ΔHR–B[La] weighting coefficients (Stagno et al., 2007; Manzi et al., 2009). The strengths and limitations of each TRIMP, along with calculation examples, can be found in the online supplementary material for this chapter.

The time spent at or above heart rate corresponding to 'high-intensity' activity can be a useful internal training metric, particularly with regard to aerobic fitness in intermittent sports (Jaspers et al., 2017; Fox et al., 2018). However, this is not strictly a measure of load, but rather an indicator of volume at a given intensity. The threshold is usually given as the second lactate or ventilatory threshold, but in the absence of a GXT, an arbitrary threshold of 90% maximum heart rate is sometimes used (Jaspers et al., 2017; Fox et al., 2018).

Measures such as heart rate recovery and post-exercise heart rate variability have also been categorised as internal training load (Orellana et al., 2019; Ruso-Álvarez et al., 2019). This is a misconception, however, because these are responses to internal training load, not internal training load itself. As a general rule, internal training load can always be prescribed and directly monitored or inferred from within exercise (Impellizzeri et al., 2019).

Heart rate provides a valid indicator of cardiorespiratory demands and the physiological aspects of internal training load in endurance-type activities. Technological advancements of the past two decades have also made the processing and analysis of raw data much more efficient (i.e., beat-to-beat or 5-s intervals). The validity of any training load indicator depends upon the context, however (Impellizzeri et al., 2019). Heart rate is clearly not valid for quantifying the internal training load of resistance training, for example. It may also underestimate demands of activities involving short intermittent bouts of high-intensity exercise (Coutts et al., 2003; Impellizzeri et al., 2005). Further, the use of heart rate monitors (and the associated data processing) may not always be feasible, or even prohibited in competition.

Foster and colleagues (Foster, 1998; Foster et al., 1996, 2001) proposed a method to quantify internal training load based on an application of Borg's *r*ating of *p*erceived *e*xertion (RPE; Borg, 1998) (see also Chapter 3.8). The so-called *s*ession-*RPE* method (sRPE) requires athletes to provide a retrospective, post-exercise cognitive appraisal of the typical effort they perceived throughout the session. This score is then multiplied by session duration (in minutes and excluding inactive time) to provide *sRPE t*raining *l*oad (sRPE-TL).

We recommend that sRPE be collected using non-modified versions of Borg's category-ratio (CR) 10 or 100 scales (CR10® and CR100®, respectively; Borg, 1998; Borg and Borg, 2010). A detailed overview of the RPE scales and the appropriate data collection procedures can be found in Chapter 3.8 and elsewhere (Borg and Borg, 2010; McLaren et al., 2021). Example calculations for sRPE-TL along with the strengths and limitations of each method are provided in the online supplementary material for this chapter.

RPE has undergone decades of psychophysics development (Borg, 1998; Borg and Borg, 2001) and validation as a measure of exercise intensity (Chen et al., 2002; Lea et al., 2018). Both sRPE and sRPE-TL have also demonstrated strong construct validity and reliability in athletes (Haddad et al., 2017; McLaren et al., 2018b). A strength of sRPE is therefore the ability to provide an accurate quantification of internal training load (psycho-physiological) across a range of activities and modalities. This measure is cost-free, making it feasible and accessible. However, perceived exertion and the rating process are complex neurological and psychobiological processes. If the appropriate standardised data collection procedures are deviated from, it is likely that error (data inaccuracy) will ensue (Pageaux, 2016). More detail on sources of error and bias, and how to mitigate them in the applied environment, can be found elsewhere (McLaren et al., 2021).

A further drawback of sRPE as an internal training load indicator is its gestalt nature (Hutchinson and Tenenbaum, 2006) – with generalisation comes oversimplification and a loss of specificity about the nature of the stimulus (Weston et al., 2015). Differential RPE (i.e., separate ratings for respiratory and muscular perceived exertion) might help overcome this issue (Weston et al., 2015; McLaren et al., 2016, 2017), although the use of these measures as a true internal training load indicator (combined with volume) is not yet well understood (McLaren et al., 2018a).

The training process framework has recently been extended to biomechanical components of internal training load (Vanrenterghem et al., 2017). This relates to the mechanical stresses experienced by different tissues of the musculoskeletal system. The measurement of these stresses – which occur at a tissue-specific, structure-specific or whole-body level – is extremely difficult, however (Verheul et al., 2020), particularly outside a laboratory setting and during exercise. Consequently, this important and emerging area of training load monitoring is not yet well understood or applied. We refer readers to relevant review articles for a more in-depth discussion of quantifying biomechanical internal training load in sports (Vanrenterghem et al., 2017; Verheul et al., 2020). It is important to remind that within the context of athlete monitoring, biomechanical variables should not be thought of as single, direct measures of training load – an overarching multidimensional construct – but as plausible indicators of a multidimensional sub-construct (internal training load) that must align to an appropriate operatorial definition.

External training load

The traditional measurement of external training load was made through counts of activities and distances using manual and semi-automated methods.

This technique is still extremely useful for endurance sports, as well as track and field sports and resistance exercise, where training is often prescribed in such a manner (e.g., number of laps, lengths, reps or throws, total running, rowing or cycling miles, the mass of objects). This is clearly limited in complex and stochastic sports such as the football codes, however. Nonetheless, early attempts to quantify external training load in soccer were sought using manual notation on the retrospective analysis of video footage (Reilly and Thomas, 1976). Semi-automated tracking and notation systems soon became a staple in these sports (Di Salvo et al., 2017) and still feature today (Castellano et al., 2014), although these methods are often limited to competition stadia only and for teams at the elite level (who can afford the technology).

The development of technology throughout the past 3–4 decades has paved the way for more detailed external training load measurement in sports. In cycling, for example, bike-mounted strain gauges and micro computers can provide athletes with real-time quantification of power output and other external kinetic and kinematic variables such as cadence (Passfield et al., 2017). In resistance training, linear position transducers and accelerometers have made it possible to track bar displacement, from which kinetic and kinematic variables such as velocity can be calculated (Weakley et al., 2021).

One of the biggest technological breakthroughs has been the spatiotemporal measurement of displacement-based kinetic and kinematic variables through technologies such as *g*lobal *p*ositioning, *l*ocal *p*ositioning and *m*icro*e*lectromechanical *s*ystems (GPS, LPS and MEMS, respectively) worn at either the foot, wrist, hip or scapula. Positional systems measure instantaneous velocity and acceleration of the unit as a whole – via the Doppler shift for GPS and positional differentiation for LPS – while MEMS devices measure instantaneous acceleration, rotation and magnetism in the three principal axes of movement. When bespoke algorithms are applied to data, some devices offer the ability to detect sporting events with reasonable accuracy, such as tackles, kicks, throws, scrums and lineouts (rugby) and shots (racquet and bat; Chambers et al., 2015).

The validity, accuracy and inter-/intra-device reliability of the technology used to measure external training load depends on the systems used, the metric being quantified and the activity/sport to which it applies. Regarding positional systems, locomotor data are more accurate 1) at lower velocities and magnitudes of acceleration, 2) for longer distances involving less change of direction, 3) at sampling frequencies >5 Hz and 4) for LPS when compared to GPS (Scott et al., 2016; Malone et al., 2017; Hoppe et al., 2018). Data also show less error when a clear overhead is present, with some stadia and built-up areas (e.g., cities) causing signal loss. This also means that GPS-derived data are not possible indoors, and practitioners must rely on MEMS- and LPS-derived data in these sports or training scenarios.

With access to more detailed data comes more challenges for practitioners to consider. As well as measurement properties, signal quality, data processing and smoothing, minimum effort durations and threshold cut-offs (e.g., high-speed running or high-intensity acceleration) are important technical considerations

(Malone et al., 2017). In the age of technology, it is also easy to fall into the trap of collecting an overabundance of external training load metrics and letting these data become the focus of feedback (Coutts, 2014). This is counterintuitive to the theory of training and defeats the purpose of training load monitoring. Therefore, a contemporary and somewhat hidden challenge of external training load monitoring is the ability to adopt a parsimonious selection of variables that have a well-justified theoretical basis. As the *internal* training load determines the training outcome, we recommend, when possible, to include it when monitoring athletes (Impellizzeri et al., 2019). External training load can then provide useful context for 'how' the internal training load may have been accrued.

Using and interpreting data in practice

The purpose of training load monitoring is to provide an objective quantification of the training process that can be used to aid decision making. The adjustment, planning and progression of training is a subjective decision based on generic training principles, however (Impellizzeri et al., 2020b). This process is best achieved through available evidence, professional knowledge and experience of coaches and practitioners. Training load data serve only as a feedback loop and objective means of process control. Training load alone should not be used to determine how appropriate training was or if athletes are tolerating the demands. This is based on the assumption that sports performance and health can be improved by optimising the balance between training load (i.e., dose) and associated consequences (i.e., response). Quantifying both training load and the training response (or outcome) is therefore vital for decision making, with the relationship between these two constructs providing useful insights. Even still, practitioners should be mindful of being data driven and instead strive to be data informed (Gamble et al., 2020).

Applying additional calculations to training load data should be approached with caution. The use of indices and ratios are among the most common pitfalls in this area. The acute–chronic workload ratio (ACWR) is an example of such a metric, which was implemented without proper validation and promoted as a modifiable prognostic indicator of injury risk in the absence of any evidence of causation (Impellizzeri et al., 2020a; Impellizzeri et al., 2021). This is an improper use of training load monitoring and endorses an overreliance on data. There can be no magic thresholds, red flag indicators or target values for training load. Use and interpretation depend entirely on the context, the individual athlete and the information required by the coach to adjust the training plan.

References

Banister, E. W. (1991). Modelling elite athletic performance. In J. D. MacDougall, H. A. Wenger and H. J. Green (eds.), *Physiological Testing of Elite Athletes*, pp. 403–424. Champaign, IL: Human Kinetics.

Borg, G. (1998). *Borg's Perceived Exertion and Pain Scales*. Champaign, IL: Human Kinetics.

Borg, G. and Borg, E. (2001). A new generation of scaling methods: Level-anchored ratio scaling. *Psychologica*, 28(1), 15–45.

Borg, G. and Borg, E. (2010). *The Borg CR Scales® Folder*. Hasselby, Sweden: Borg Perception.

Castellano, J., Alvarez-Pastor, D. and Bradley, P. S. (2014). Evaluation of research using computerised tracking systems (Amisco® and Prozone®) to analyse physical performance in elite soccer: A systematic review. *Sports Medicine*, 44(5), 701–712.

Chambers, R., et al. (2015). The use of wearable microsensors to quantify sport-specific movements. *Sports Medicine*, 45, 1065–1081.

Chen, M. J., Fan, X. and Moe, S. T. (2002). Criterion-related validity of the Borg ratings of perceived exertion scale in healthy individuals: A meta-analysis. *Journal of Sports Sciences*, 20(11), 873–899.

Coutts, A. J. (2014). In the age of technology, Occam's Razor still applies. *International Journal of Sports Physiology and Performance*, 9(5), 741–741.

Coutts, A. J., Reaburn, P. and Abt, G. (2003). Heart rate, blood lactate concentration and estimated energy expenditure in a semi-professional rugby league team during a match: A case study. *Journal of Sports Sciences*, 21(2), 97–103.

Di Salvo, V., et al. (2017). Validation of Prozone®: A new video-based performance analysis system. *International Journal of Performance Analysis in Sport*, 6(1), 108–119.

Edwards, S. (1993). *The Heart Rate Monitor Book*. New York, NY: Polar Electro Oy.

Foster, C. (1998). Monitoring training in athletes with reference to overtraining syndrome. *Medicine and Science in Sports and Exercise*, 30(7), 1164–1168.

Foster, C., et al. (1996). Athletic performance in relation to training load. *Wisconsin Medical Journal*, 95(6), 370–374.

Foster, C., et al. (2001). A new approach to monitoring exercise training. *Journal of Strength and Conditioning Research*, 15(1), 109–115.

Fox, J. L., et al. (2018). The association between training load and performance in team sports: A systematic review. *Sports Medicine*, 48(12), 2743–2774.

Gamble, P., Chia, L. and Allen, S. (2020). The illogic of being data-driven: Reasserting control and restoring balance in our relationship with data and technology in football. *Science and Medicine in Football*, 4(4), 338–341.

Haddad, M., et al. (2017). Session-RPE method for training load monitoring: Validity, ecological usefulness, and influencing factors. *Frontiers in Neuroscience*, 11, 113–14.

Hoppe, M. W., et al. (2018). Validity and reliability of GPS and LPS for measuring distances covered and sprint mechanical properties in team sports. *PLoS One*, 13(2), e0192708.

Hutchinson, J. C. and Tenenbaum, G. (2006). Perceived effort: Can it be considered gestalt? *Psychology of Sport and Exercise*, 7(5), 463–476.

Impellizzeri, F. M., et al. (2020a). Acute:chronic workload ratio: Conceptual issues and fundamental pitfalls. *International Journal of Sports Physiology and Performance*, 15(6), 907–913.

Impellizzeri, F. M., et al. (2020b). Training load and its role in injury prevention, Part I: Back to the future. *Journal of Athletic Training*, 55(9), 885–892.

Impellizzeri, F. M., et al. (2021). What role do chronic workloads play in the acute to chronic workload ratio? Time to dismiss ACWR and its underlying theory. *Sports Medicine*, 51(3), 581–592.

Impellizzeri, F. M., Marcora, S. M. and Coutts, A. J. (2019). Internal and external training load: 15 years on. *International Journal of Sports Physiology and Performance*, 14(2), 270–273.

Impellizzeri, F. M., Rampinini, E. and Marcora, S. M. (2005). Physiological assessment of aerobic training in soccer. *Journal of Sports Sciences*, 23(6), 583–592.

Jaspers, A., et al. (2017). Relationships between training load indicators and training outcomes in professional soccer. *Sports Medicine*, 47(3), 533–544.

Lea, J., et al. (2018). Criterion-related validity of ratings of perceived exertion during resistance exercise in healthy participants: A meta-analysis. In: M. H. Murphy, C. A. G. Boreham, G. De Vito and E. Tsolakidis (eds.), *Proceedings of the 23rd annual Congress of the European College of Sport Science*, Dublin, Ireland, 4–7 July, pp. 212.4.

Lucía, A., et al. (2003). Tour de France versus Vuelta a Espana: Which is harder? *Medicine and Science in Sports and Exercise*, 35(5), 872–878.

Malone, J. J., et al. (2017). Unpacking the black box: Applications and considerations for using GPS devices in sport. *International Journal of Sports Physiology and Performance*, 12(Suppl 2), S218–S226.

Manzi, V., et al. (2009). Relation between individualized training impulses and performance in distance runners. *Medicine and Science in Sports and Exercise*, 41(11), 2090–2096.

McLaren, S. J., Coutts, A. J. and Impellizzeri, F. M. (2021). Perception of effort and subjective monitoring. In D. N. French and L. Torres-Ronda (eds.), *NSCAs Essentials of Sport Science*, pp. 231–254. Champaign, IL: Human Kinetics.

McLaren, S. J., et al. (2016). The sensitivity of differential ratings of perceived exertion as measures of internal load. *International Journal of Sports Physiology and Performance*, 11(3), 404–406.

McLaren, S. J., et al. (2017). A detailed quantification of differential ratings of perceived exertion during team-sport training. *Journal of Science and Medicine in Sport*, 20(3), 290–295.

McLaren, S. J., et al. (2018a). Differential training loads and individual fitness responses to pre-season in professional rugby union players. *Journal of Sports Sciences*, 36(21), 2438–2446.

McLaren, S. J., et al. (2018b). The relationships between internal and external measures of training load and intensity in team sports: A meta-analysis. *Sports Medicine*, 48(3), 641–658.

Orellana, J. N., Nieto-Jiménez, C. and Ruso-Álvarez, J. F. (2019). Recovery slope of heart rate variability as an indicator of internal training load. *Health*, 11(2), 211–221.

Pageaux, B. (2016). Perception of effort in exercise science: Definition, measurement and perspectives. *European Journal of Sport Science*, 16(8), 885–894.

Passfield, L., et al. (2017). Knowledge is power: Issues of measuring training and performance in cycling. *Journal of Sports Sciences*, 35(14), 1426–1434.

Reilly, T. and Thomas, V. (1976). A motion analysis of work-rate in different positional roles in professional football match-play. *Journal of Human Movement Studies*, 2, 87–97.

Robertson, S., et al. (2017). Consensus on measurement properties and feasibility of performance tests for the exercise and sport sciences: A Delphi study. *Sports Medicine – Open*, 3(1), 2.

Ruso-Álvarez, J. F., et al. (2019). Utility of the 'RMSSD-slope' to assess the internal load in different sports situations. *Health*, 11(6), 683–691.

Scott, M. T. U., Scott, T. J. and Kelly, V. G. (2016). The validity and reliability of global positioning systems in team sport: A brief review. *Journal of Strength and Conditioning Research*, 30(5), 1470–1490.

Stagno, K. M., Thatcher, R. and van Someren, K. A. (2007). A modified TRIMP to quantify the in-season training load of team sport players. *Journal of Sports Sciences*, 25(6), 629–634.

Starling, L. T. and Lambert, M. I. (2018). Monitoring rugby players for fitness and fatigue: What do coaches want? *International Journal of Sports Physiology and Performance*, 13(6), 777–782.

Vanrenterghem, J., et al. (2017). Training load monitoring in team sports: A novel framework separating physiological and biomechanical load-adaptation pathways. *Sports Medicine*, 47(11), 2135–2142.

Verheul, J., et al. (2020). Measuring biomechanical loads in team sports: From lab to field. *Science and Medicine in Football*, 4(3), 246–252.

Weakley, J., et al. (2021). Velocity-based training: From theory to application. *Strength and Conditioning Journal*, 43(2), 31–49.

Weston, M., et al. (2015). The application of differential ratings of perceived exertion to Australian Football League matches. *Journal of Science and Medicine in Sport*, 18(6), 704–708.

15.4 Overreaching and overtraining

Lee Bell and Alan Ruddock

Careful programming and manipulation of training and recovery are required for optimal performance. Functional overreaching (FOR) occurs after well-timed periods of relatively large training loads and adequate restoration. However, excessive training loads and insufficient recovery can result in non-functional overreaching (NFOR) or the overtraining syndrome (OTS).

- **FOR**: Short-term reduction in performance lasting several days to weeks with subsequent performance improvement after a period of recovery.
- **NFOR**: Performance decrease is observed over a period of several weeks to months with no subsequent performance improvement.
- **OTS**: Long-term maladaptation resulting in reduced performance capacity observed over a period of several weeks, months or years with no subsequent performance improvement.

(Definitions taken from Halson and Jeukendrup, 2004; Meeusen et al., 2013)

A robust, multifactorial testing battery is recommended to identify potential deleterious effects on training and performance. At the time of writing there is no single-standard test to guide decision making; practitioners should therefore develop an individualised battery of assessments based on the needs analysis of the sport and the individual athlete. We specifically suggest a combination of objective performance metrics and physiological responses to fixed-intensity exercise, alongside psychophysiological, subjective responses to evaluate the risk of long-term performance decline and maladaptation caused by NFOR/OTS. For a more general consideration of athlete wellbeing, see Chapter 15.2.

Diagnosis

Differentiation between NFOR and OTS is difficult (Kreher, 2016; ten Haaf, 2017), and it is unclear whether symptoms of impairment (performance changes, altered mood state, fatigue, etc.) worsen with OTS (Halson and Jeukendrup, 2004). However, the time taken to restore normal function, not the type or extremity of performance impairment, might differentiate NFOR from OTS (Meeusen et al., 2013) (see Figure 15.4.1.). The OTS diagnostic flowchart

DOI: 10.4324/9781003045281-75

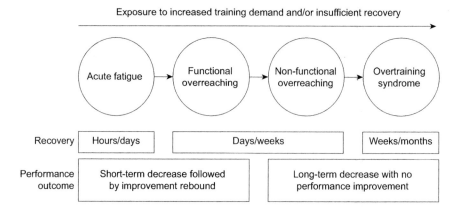

Figure 15.4.1 Schematic representation of performance outcomes.

presented in the *Joint Consensus Statement of the European College of Sport Science (ECSS) and the American College of Sports Medicine (ACSM)* (Meeusen et al., 2013) provides clinicians and practitioners with a step-by-step retrospective diagnostic tool. However, the nature of such a tool suggests it can only be utilised by those already considered to be at risk of OTS.

Symptoms

Athletes suffering from NFOR/OTS might not present with 'textbook symptoms'; instead, they could be asymptomatic, display a myriad of individualised symptoms or exhibit normal symptoms of acute fatigue. General symptoms of OTS can be categorised into *performance, physiological, endocrinological, immunological, biochemical* and *psychological* (Cadegiani et al., 2020).

Two-bout exercise protocol

The *two-bout exercise protocol* (Meeusen et al., 2004, 2010) might help to distinguish FOR from NFOR/OTS (Kreher, 2016) based on hypothalamic-pituitary-adrenal (HPA) axis dysfunction (Meeusen et al., 2010). The protocol involves two graded exercise tests to exhaustion with a 4-h rest between bouts (Meeusen et al., 2004) and involves measures of adrenocorticotropic hormone (ACTH) and prolactin (PRL), measured at four time points: baseline, immediately after completion of the first test, prior to the second test and immediately after the second test. Statistically significantly increased ACTH and PRL concentrations in NFOR appear to differentiate between athletes with OTS (Meeusen et al., 2010); however, further studies are required to establish valid and reliable boundaries (Cadegiani and Kater, 2017a).

Biochemical and hormonal assessment

Alterations to select hormones have been proposed as indicators of FOR/NFOR as well as OTS (Meeusen et al., 2013; Halson and Jeukendrup, 2004). These include decreased testosterone:cortisol in addition to blunted growth hormone (GH), luteinising hormone (LH), follicle-stimulating hormone (FSH) and insulin growth factor–binding protein 3 (IGF-BP3). Similarly, biochemical markers of various plasma catecholamines, immunological measurements and inflammatory markers appear to be sensitive to periods of elevated training load but are not able to reliably detect NFOR/OTS (Meeusen et al., 2013; Cadegiani and Kater, 2017b; Cadegiani et al., 2020). Much of the current research points to associations between alterations in select biochemical/hormonal markers and OTS, rather than experimental evidence. The EROS-DIAGNOSIS study proposes a series of novel diagnostic tools to identity OTS based on results from risk identification (energy intake, mood state and sleep quality metrics), followed by assessment of combined clinical and hormonal markers without the need to exclude confounding factors or the use of highly specialised medical or sports personnel, and therefore might provide an alternative to the diagnostic flowchart presented within the latest joint consensus guidelines (Cadegiani et al., 2020).

Performance measures

An important feature of NFOR/OTS is the inability to sustain exercise performance, and several studies have indicated NFOR using simulated or sport-specific performance testing such as incremental testing, time to exhaustion and competition performance (Halson and Jeukendrup, 2004). Dynamic performance testing, including squat jump (SJ) and countermovement jump (CMJ) height, might be sensitive to detecting fatigue prior to performance decrement, and as such could indicate acute changes in training load and fatigue, as well as alterations in neuromuscular characteristics prior to the onset of NFOR (Bell et al., 2020). Temporal changes to rate of force development, mean power and maximal force from jump testing have been observed during periods of increased training load; however, these cannot determine the transition from FOR to NFOR (Bell et al., 2020). Maximal strength via repetition maximum testing may also be used to identify changes in training state indicative of NFOR, with previous research demonstrating reduced maximal strength performance after periods of increased training load (Fry et al., 1994; Fry et al., 1998), likely due to impaired voluntary muscle activation.

Physiological measures

Heart rate variability (HRV) assesses autonomic regulation of the heart. In the presence of OTS, cardiac modulation shifts from parasympathetic to sympathetic dominance and may be a useful tool to identify tolerance to periods of elevated training load in endurance athletes (Halson and Jeukendrup, 2004; Aubert et al.,

2003), as well as during periods of resistance training (Kaikkonen et al., 2020). However, HRV assessment requires integration with other signs and symptoms of NFOR/OTS in order to be meaningful (Bosquet et al., 2008).

Psychological monitoring

Disturbances in mood state (reduced vigour, decreased mood, increased anxiety, etc.) are often reported in athletes suffering OTS and appear to be sensitive to periods of intensified training in both endurance and strength sports (Halson and Jeukendrup, 2004; Grandou et al., 2020). The *profile of mood states (POMS)* might be useful to modulate training load in and reduce the risk of OTS, as well as predict future occurrence and risk of OTS.

References

Aubert, A. E., Seps, B. and Beckers, F. (2003). Heart rate variability in athletes. *Sports Medicine*, 33, 889–919.

Bell, L., Ruddock, A., Maden-Wilkinson, T. and Rogerson, D. (2020). Overreaching and overtraining in strength sports and resistance training: A scoping review. *Journal of Sports Sciences*, 38(16), 1897–1912.

Bellinger, P. (2020). Functional overreaching in endurance athletes: A necessity or cause for concern. *Sports Medicine*, 50, 1059–1073.

Bosquet, L., Merkari, S., Arvisais, D. and Aubert, A. E. (2008). Is heart rate a convenient tool to monitor over-reaching? A systematic review of the literature. *British Journal of Sports Medicine*, 42(9), 709–714.

Buyse, L., Decroix, L., Timmermans, N., Barbé, K., Verrelst, R. and Meeusen, R. (2019). Improving the diagnosis of nonfunctional overreaching and overtraining syndrome. *Medicine and Science in Sports and Exercise*, 51(12), 2524–2530.

Cadegiani, F. A., da Silva, P. H. L., Abrao, T. C. P. and Kater, C. E. (2020). Diagnosis of overtraining syndrome: Results of the endocrine and metabolic responses on overtraining syndrome study: EROS-DIAGNOSIS. *Journal of Sports Medicine*. doi: 10.1155/2020/3937819

Cadegiani, F. A. and Kater, C. E. (2017a). Hormonal response to a non-exercise stress test in athletes with overtraining syndrome: Results from the Endocrine and metabolic Responses on Overtraining Syndrome (EROS): EROS-STRESS. *Journal of Science and Medicine in Sport*, 21(7), 648–653.

Cadegiani, F. A. and Kater, C. E. (2017b). Hormonal aspects of overtraining syndrome: A systematic review. *BMC Sports Science, Medicine and Rehabilitation*, 9, 14.

Fry, A. C., Kraemer, W. J. and Ramsey, L. T. (1998). Pituitary-adrenal-gonadal responses to high-intensity resistance exercise overtraining. *Journal of Applied Physiol*, 85(6), 2352–2359.

Fry, A. C., Kraemer, W. J., Van Borselen, F., Lynch, J. M., Marsit, J. L., Roy, E. P., et al. (1994). Performance decrements with high-intensity resistance exercise overtraining. *Medicine and Science in Sports and Exercise*, 26(9), 1165–1173.

Grandou, C., Wallace, L., Coutts, A. J., Bell, L. and Impellizzeri, F. (2020). Symptoms of overtraining in resistance exercise: International cross-sectional survey. *International Journal of Sports Physiology and Performance*, 17, 1–10.

Halson, S. and Jeukendrup, A. E. (2004). Does overtraining exist? *Sports Medicine*, 34(14), 967–981.

Kaikkonen, P., Hynynen, E., Hautala, A. and Ahtiainen, J. P. (2020). The effects of an intensive 2-wk resistance training period on strength performance and nocturnal heart rate variability. *International Journal of Physiology and Performance*, 1, 1–7.

Kreher, J. B. (2016). Diagnosis and prevention of overtraining syndrome: An opinion on education strategies. *Open Access Journal of Sports Medicine*, 7, 115–122.

Meeusen, R., Duclos, M., Foster, C., Fry, A., Gleeson, M., Nieman, D., Raglin, J., Rietjens, R., Steinacker, J. and Urhausen, A. (2013). Prevention, diagnosis, and treatment of the overtraining syndrome: Joint consensus statement of the European College of Sport Science and the American College of Sports Medicine. *Medicine and Science in Sports and Exercise*, 45(1), 186–205.

Meeusen, R., Nederhof, E., Buyse, L., Roelands, B., de Schutter, G. and Piacentini, M. F. (2010). Diagnosing overtraining in athletes using the two bout exercise protocol. *British Journal of Sports Medicine*, 44(9), 642–648.

Meeusen, R., Piacentini, M. F., Busschaert, B., Buyse, L., De Schutter, G. and Stray-Gundersen, J. (2004). Hormonal responses in athletes: The use of a two bout exercise protocol to detect subtle differences in (over)training status. *European Journal of Applied Physiology*, 91(2–3), 140–146.

Nederhof, E., Zwerver, J., Brink, M., Meeusen, R. and Lemmink, K. (2008). Different diagnostic tools in nonfunctional overreaching. *International Journal of Sports Medicine*, 29(7), 590–597.

ten Haaf, T., van Staveren, S., Oudenhoven, E., Piacentini, M. F., Meeusen, R., Roelands, B., Koenderman, L., Daanen, H. A. M., Foster, C. and de Koning, J. J. (2017). Prediction of functional overreaching from subjective fatigue and readiness to train after only 3 days of cycling. *International Journal of Sports Physiology and Performance*, 12(Suppl 2), S287–S289.

15.5 Exercise testing for the pregnant athlete

Victoria L. Meah, Amal Hassan, Lin Foo, Christoph Lees, and Marlize de Vivo

Pregnancy represents a period of profound physiological adaptation that is required to support foetal development without compromising maternal health (Figure 15.5.1). The multisystem adaptations of gestation present unique considerations for exercise performance.

The current national guidelines for physical activity during pregnancy recommend accumulating 150 min of moderate-intensity activity per week and performing strengthening activities twice per week (Department of Health and Social Care, 2019a, 2019b). When pregnant individuals meet these recommendations, regular physical activity provides significant clinical benefits. These include reduced odds of cardiometabolic complications (Davenport et al., 2018c), antenatal depression (Davenport et al., 2018a) and excessive gestational weight gain (Ruchat et al., 2018) without any increased risk of adverse foetal outcomes (Davenport et al., 2018b).

Elite athletes maintain a more strenuous training routine throughout pregnancy compared to recreationally active individuals. Consequently, pregnant athletes are advised to seek supervision from an obstetric care provider with knowledge of vigorous-intensity physical activity on maternal and foetal outcomes. However, there is a severe lack of evidence to support such advice. Guiding elite athletes through pregnancy therefore presents a challenge to coaches, sport scientists, team clinicians and obstetric healthcare providers. Standardisation of exercise testing during pregnancy is important to facilitate wider research in this area, as well as to maintain safety standards with this population. This chapter will focus on practical considerations for exercise testing in elite pregnant athletes.

Screening

A thorough clinical evaluation should be carried out in all pregnant athletes to rule out any medical or obstetrical reasons to stop or adapt activities (Bo et al., 2018). In pregnant individuals who develop certain conditions, acute and chronic physical activity may pose significant risks to maternal and/or foetal health (Meah et al., 2020). The Get Active for Pregnancy questionnaire is a screening tool that can be used to identify these contraindications to prenatal physical activity (Canadian Society for Exercise Physiology, 2021).

DOI: 10.4324/9781003045281-76

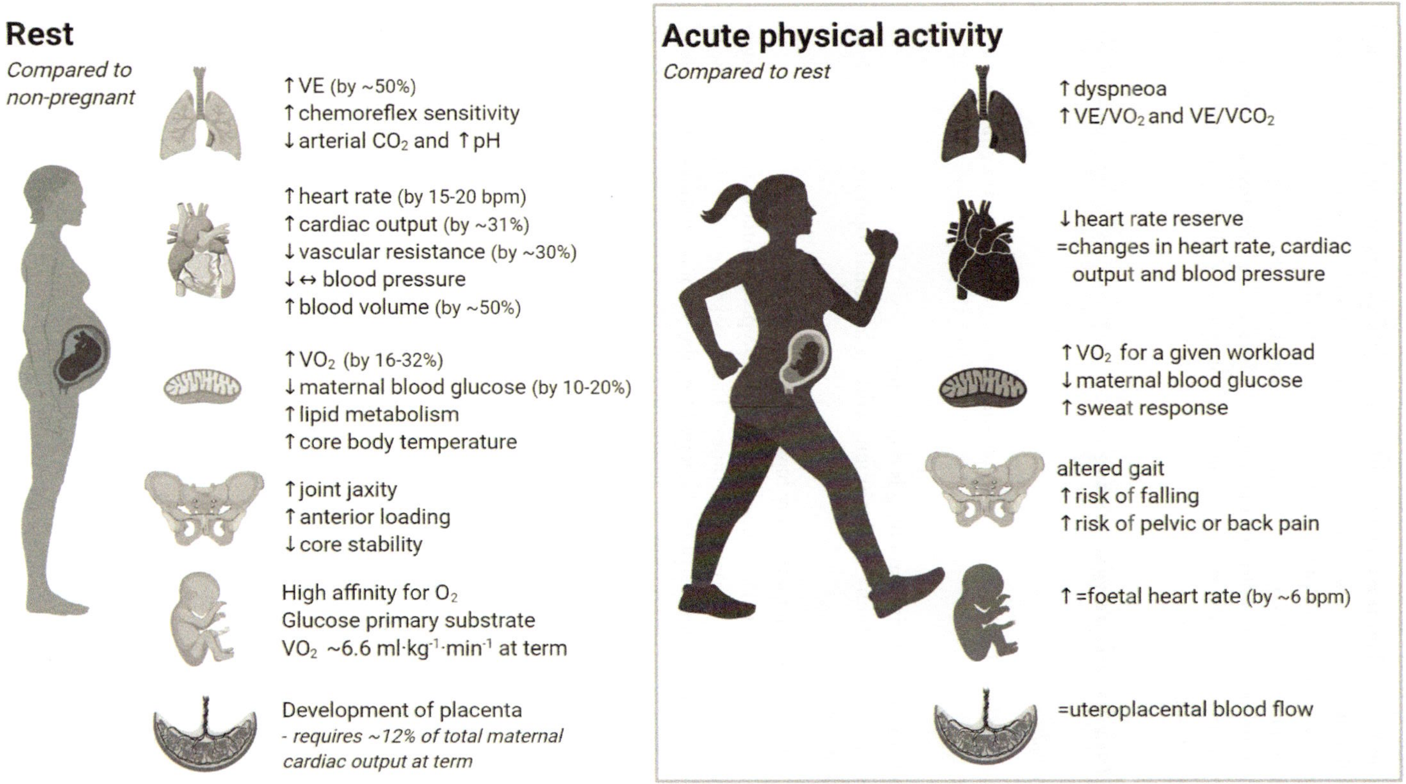

Rest
Compared to non-pregnant

↑VE (by ~50%)
↑chemoreflex sensitivity
↓arterial CO_2 and ↑pH

↑heart rate (by 15-20 bpm)
↑cardiac output (by ~31%)
↓vascular resistance (by ~30%)
↓↔ blood pressure
↑blood volume (by ~50%)

↑VO_2 (by 16-32%)
↓maternal blood glucose (by 10-20%)
↑lipid metabolism
↑core body temperature

↑joint laxity
↑anterior loading
↓core stability

High affinity for O_2
Glucose primary substrate
VO_2 ~6.6 ml·kg^{-1}·min^{-1} at term

Development of placenta
- requires ~12% of total maternal cardiac output at term

Acute physical activity
Compared to rest

↑dyspnoea
↑VE/VO_2 and VE/VCO_2

↓heart rate reserve
=changes in heart rate, cardiac output and blood pressure

↑VO_2 for a given workload
↓maternal blood glucose
↑sweat response

altered gait
↑risk of falling
↑risk of pelvic or back pain

↑=foetal heart rate (by ~6 bpm)

=uteroplacental blood flow

Figure 15.5.1 Physiological adaptation to healthy pregnancy at rest and altered responses or considerations for acute, submaximal physical activity in pregnant individuals.

VE, minute ventilation; CO_2, carbon dioxide; VO_2, oxygen consumption; O_2, oxygen; VCO_2, carbon dioxide production. Created with BioRender.com.

Participants must be fully informed of the purpose, procedures, risks and benefits, as well as their rights and expectations prior to completing exercise testing. Practitioners should ensure they have highlighted the pregnancy-specific risks and should inform participants of how adverse events and/or clinically meaningful results (e.g., resting blood pressure above 140/90 mmHg) will be handled. Practitioners should collect contact details of a maternity healthcare provider, and pregnant participants should be encouraged to inform their maternity healthcare provider of any exercise testing, enabling on-going advice about physical activity to be individual-specific.

Laboratory-based exercise testing

Pre-test considerations

Practitioners should prepare to complete an exercise test with a pregnant participant by:

- Ensuring pre-activity screening is completed.
- Ensuring an ambient environment with additional options for cooling, such as:
  - Pregnant participants may have a lower sweat threshold.
  - There are concerns regarding maternal hyperthermia in the first trimester and adverse foetal outcomes. These risks are unsubstantiated with moderate-vigorous physical activity in the second or third trimesters in ambient (Davenport et al., 2019) and temperate environments (Ravanelli et al., 2019).
- Ensuring a team of qualified and experienced personnel, including:
  - Exercise professional with relevant experience and/or accredited qualifications for antenatal physical activity.
  - Maternity healthcare provider with expertise in foetal monitoring for higher-risk participants.
- Creating clear health and safety protocols for risk mitigation and dealing with adverse events, such as falls, syncope, nausea or vomiting, or participant identification of reasons to cease exercise (Table 15.5.1).

In addition to usual pre-test procedures, pregnant participants should prepare to complete an exercise test by:

- Avoiding eating a heavy meal for 3 h prior to the test, instead eating a small snack containing 30–50 g of carbohydrate 1 h prior to the test;
- Wearing comfortable, light clothing with a supportive bra;
- Emptying their bladder immediately prior to the test to reduce the risk of urinary incontinence during activity.

Table 15.5.1 Physical reasons to stop antenatal activity and consult a healthcare provider

Persistent excessive shortness of breath prior to exertion or following exertion, does not resolve on rest
Severe chest pain
Regular and painful uterine contractions
Vaginal bleeding
Persistent loss of fluid from the vagina indicating rupture of the membranes
Persistent dizziness or faintness that does not resolve on rest
Abdominal pain
Amniotic fluid leakage indicating rupture of membranes
Headache
Muscle weakness affecting balance
Calf pain or swelling

Source: Adapted from Mottola et al. (2018) and American College of Obstetricians and Gynaecologists (2020).

Upon arrival for the exercise test, the practitioner should:

- Determine an individual's capability and preparedness by considering their activity background (i.e., exercise history), current physical activity status and intentions to engage in physical activity for the remainder of their pregnancy. This can be achieved through exploratory questions, validated questionnaires, and/or objective measures, although prior planning would be required for the latter. Such profiling of pregnant individuals allows practitioners to adapt tests accordingly (e.g., intensity, mode) and allows for tailored advice and feedback (De Vivo, 2017).
- Confirm that the participant is aware of the signs to cease exercise (Table 15.5.1).
- Obtain details of medication use and be aware of potential effects on responses to exercise.
- Identify musculoskeletal injuries or complaints (e.g., pelvic girdle pain, lower back pain) to offer modifications to exercise test modality.
- Inquire about hypotension in pregnancy (e.g., excessive fatigue or pre-syncopal symptoms) to identify any heightened risks of syncope during or upon cessation of activity.
- Confirm pre-exercise blood glucose is >4 mmol·L to prevent hypoglycaemia because of exercise (Hordern et al., 2012):
  - If pre-exercise blood glucose is ≤4 mmol·L, blood glucose can be increased through eating a snack prior to starting the test.
- Confirm that resting heart rate and blood pressure are <100 bpm and <140/90 mmHg, respectively:
  - Measurements should be made following >5 min of quiet, calm rest in a comfortable position (i.e., not resting on exercise equipment) with an

appropriately sized blood pressure cuff and automated sphygmomanometer validated for use in pregnancy.
- If resting heart rate or blood pressure is higher than these cut-off values, measurements should be repeated after a further 5 min of rest.
- If values remain elevated after this additional rest, the participant should not complete the exercise test and should be referred to their maternity healthcare provider for clinical evaluation.

Modality of exercise

Pregnancy results in an increase in hormonally mediated joint laxity and changes to axial, thoracic, pelvic and lower limb biomechanics, which shift the centre of gravity forwards, thus focusing load on the anterior chain. This can contribute to the experience of musculoskeletal pain in day-to-day life, as well as during and following physical activity. Specifically, up to three-quarters of pregnant individuals suffer from low back and/or pelvic girdle pain (Weis et al., 2018). Exercise modality should be adjusted to reduce the risk of worsening an individual's musculoskeletal pain simply because of participating. If any pregnant individual does suffer from day-to-day musculoskeletal pain, practitioners should offer non-weight-bearing options (e.g., recumbent cycle) where possible.

Changes to the centre of gravity alongside decreased abdominal strength, increased fluid retention in the lower limbs and increased joint laxity contribute to impaired balance during pregnancy, and individuals therefore have higher risks of falling (Mei et al., 2018). Falls, which can result in placental abruption, membrane rupture or foetal trauma, present the greatest risk of harm during physical activity for otherwise healthy individuals. All testing protocols should be chosen to specifically reduce this risk. These risks are also high in contact sports. Elite athletes performing in such activities are encouraged to refrain from participating when pregnant but to maintain non-contact training (Bo et al., 2018).

Pregnant individuals are more likely to use handrails when exercising on a treadmill; however, this can artificially improve performance. Encouragement for light touching for balance and not holding for support should be provided (Wowdzia and Davenport, 2020).

Maximal exercise testing

Maximal exercise tests, including the Bruce treadmill or ramp/cycling protocols to volitional fatigue (e.g., 3-min warm-up at 30 W, followed by increments of 20 W/minute), have previously been utilized in pregnant populations. However, pregnant individuals rarely achieve $\dot{V}O_2max$ (as per established attainment criteria) (Hesse et al., 2018), but in fact $\dot{V}O_2peak$. Adverse responses to maximal-effort exercise have been documented in high-level pregnant athletes (discussed in

'Foetal Monitoring'). As such, maximal exercise testing is not recommended unless completed in highly supervised settings.

Submaximal exercise testing

Submaximal exercise testing is preferred during pregnancy. For laboratory-based tests, previous research has utilised established (e.g., modified Balke treadmill or YMCA cycle protocols) and researcher-developed step/ramp protocols to pre-determined intensity thresholds. For the latter, calculation of a target threshold heart rate using heart rate reserve is recommended, as this accommodates for changes in resting heart rate across gestation (Meah et al., 2018).

Prediction of $\dot{V}O_2 peak$ during pregnancy through submaximal exercise testing is not without limitations. Specifically, resting $\dot{V}O_2$ increases during pregnancy; however, resting heart rate increases to a greater extent. The assumed linear relationship of $\dot{V}O_2$ and heart rate may be altered in pregnant individuals, and as a result, the accuracy of estimating maternal $\dot{V}O_2 peak$ using a heart rate-$\dot{V}O_2$ extrapolation may be reduced (Lotgering et al., 1992).

Field-based submaximal protocols, such as the 6-min walk test, have been shown to be feasible in late gestation, although their application to athletic performance is limited. Step and walking-based field test performance may also be reduced in pregnancy due to changes in gait (Mei et al., 2018), and this may be further impacted by the presence of low back or pelvic girdle pain.

Strength testing

Regular resistance exercise in pregnant athletes may maintain muscular strength and endurance, as well as contribute to favourable adaptations that reduce the risk of pregnancy complications (Mottola et al., 2018). There is a lack of evidence-based information regarding antenatal resistance training, and some individuals perceive a risk of harm from strenuous lifting. However, evidence of harm is not substantiated (Avery et al., 1999; Bgeginski et al., 2015; Petrov Fieril et al., 2016). No adverse maternal and foetal responses to acute resistance exercise of 10–15 repetitions up to 90% 10-repetition maximum have been reported (Avery et al., 1999; Meah et al., 2021). Strength testing in pregnancy is therefore feasible, although research in this area is limited.

Strength testing protocols used in pregnancy in a research environment utilized one- and ten-repetition maximum procedures established for the general population (Bgeginski et al., 2015; Avery et al., 1999; Meah et al., 2021). Protocols should take place on fixed machines, rather than using free weights to reduce the risk of injury from poor technique and/or falling. Using fixed-resistance machines may also improve signal acquisition for maternal heart rate and blood pressure measurement, as well as foetal monitoring if required.

Individuals who experience light-headedness or symptoms of urinary incontinence, vaginal prolapse or diastasis incompetence while using the Valsalva manoeuvre during resistance exercise should avoid the breath-hold. Additionally, all exercises in the supine position should be avoided after the first trimester.

Maternal monitoring

The following measures should be taken at a minimum:

- Continuous heart rate – intensity can be identified using Table 15.5.2.
- Blood pressure – pre-, during and post-exercise at a minimum (continuous where possible).
- Talk test – individuals exercising at a comfortable intensity can maintain a conversation. If not possible, the intensity may be reduced.
  - The rating of perceived exertion can be used for a subjective measure of participant effort; however, there is a poor correlation to exercising heart rate in pregnant populations, and targets require adjustment (Da Silva et al., 2020).
- Peripheral oxygen saturation – with a reading of <80% as a reason for test cessation.

Foetal monitoring

In an otherwise healthy pregnancy, acute exercise does not adversely affect foetal heart rate or uteroplacental blood flow (Skow et al., 2019). However, adverse foetal responses to maternal exercise, including foetal heart rate decelerations (drop by 15 bpm from baseline), foetal bradycardia (<100 bpm ≥3 min), foetal tachycardia (>160 bpm) and reduced uteroplacental blood flow, can occur in individuals

Table 15.5.2 Heart rate ranges and corresponding intensities of physical activity in individuals with uncomplicated pregnancies

Maternal Age (yr)	Intensity	Heart Rate Range (beats·min−1)
<29	Light	102–124
	Moderate*	125–146
	Vigorous**	147–169
≥30	Light	101–120
	Moderate*	121–141
	Vigorous*	142–162

* Moderate-intensity physical activity is equivalent to 40%–59% heart rate reserve.

** Vigorous-intensity physical activity is equivalent to 60%–80% heart rate reserve. There is limited evidence regarding physical activity at the upper end of the vigorous-intensity heart rate ranges; pregnant clients wishing to be active at this intensity (or beyond) should consult their healthcare professional.

Source: Adapted from Mottola et al. (2018).

with complications (Meah et al., 2020), but have also been observed in elite athletes during strenuous activity.

Specifically, longer duration (>40 min) and higher intensity (>90% max) exercise may result in transient impacts on foetal wellbeing in an otherwise healthy pregnancy (Carpenter et al., 1988; Erkkola et al., 1992; Manders et al., 1997). Of particular importance, foetal bradycardia and reduced uterine and umbilical blood flow have been observed in pregnant elite athletes and highly active females in response to exercise >90% maximal heart rate (Salvesen et al., 2012; Szymanski and Satin, 2012).

Exercise tests including pregnant athletes should include foetal monitoring using ultrasound or foetal heart cardiotocography by a suitably trained individual. Care should be taken to ensure quality recording without maternal movement artefact. Exercise testing should be stopped if any adverse responses are seen (foetal distress or umbilical or uterine blood flow <50% of baseline measurement), and conservative measures such as putting the participant into a left lateral tilt position could be carried out. Continued monitoring until return to normal values is essential. Adverse responses are considered transient if <3 min in duration and do not require follow-up; however, prolonged observations may be suggestive of complications, and participants should be referred to their healthcare provider.

Post-test considerations

Following an adequate cool-down, pregnant participants should rest in a comfortable seated position for a minimum of 5 min until heart rate and blood pressure are close to resting values (within 10 bpm/mmHg and not exceeding pre-exercise cut-offs). Pregnant participants should rehydrate during recovery, and practitioners should monitor for pre-syncopal symptoms. Post-exercise blood glucose levels should be checked, intervening (e.g., reclining, offering a carbohydrate-rich snack) where necessary.

Reporting and results

When comparing preconception and pregnancy performance in exercise testing, researchers must consider resting adaptations at the time of assessment (Figure 15.1.1). The delta change (change from rest to a given workload) provides opportunity for comparisons if repeated tests are completed across gestation. When reporting outcomes of exercise tests, it is recommended that:

- All maternal monitoring measures should be reported (i.e., heart rate, blood pressure, peripheral oxygen saturation, subjective measure of exertion);
- Where $\dot{V}O_2peak$ is measured or estimated, this parameter should be reported in absolute values (L·min) due to changes in body habitus during pregnancy;
- Adverse responses during or following exercise are detailed in academic publications;
- Modifications to tests should be detailed to inform future protocols.

Considerations for the pregnant athlete

Elite pregnant athletes can feel a loss of identity and body control and face fears about return to performance (Martinez-Pascual et al., 2017). Adequate support is required from a multidisciplinary team to ensure that these concerns do not develop into mental health complications.

Data help to ensure that elite pregnant athletes maintain a safe, consistent exercise regimen throughout pregnancy and can experience a successful return to competition following birth (Kardel, 2005). In contrast, the 'no pain, no gain' mentality that can be associated with elite performance raises concerns during pregnancy (Pivarnik et al., 2016). If observed, the pregnant athlete should be supported to alter their focus and be advised to pay attention to the physical symptoms to cease exercise (Table 15.5.1). A rapid return to high-intensity training in the postpartum period can result in higher risks of pelvic floor dysfunction, abdominal weakness and pelvic girdle pain (Erdener and Budgett, 2016), and appropriate support is required (Donnelly et al., 2020).

The incidence of eating disorders is higher in competitive athletes compared to the general population. As such, there is a higher likelihood of pregnant athletes with symptomatic eating disorders. Recent guidelines state that these individuals should be considered at high risk of pregnancy complications and require close monitoring by a multidisciplinary team (Bo et al., 2018). Consequently, exercise testing, particularly assessments of anthropometry, are not recommended in pregnant athletes with a symptomatic eating disorder.

For a pregnant athlete who develops significant health complications, one must seek advice from an obstetric healthcare provider. Where activity modification or restriction is indicated, this should be strictly followed for both maternal and foetal wellbeing. Psychological support may help adjustment to activity restriction (like injury rehabilitation).

Application of exercise testing in the pregnant athlete

Elite athletes do not have adequate resources, information or support regarding training during pregnancy (Darroch et al., 2016). As indicators of foetal distress have been observed during strenuous exertion in elite performers, exercise testing is critical to ascertain whether intensity thresholds for foetal wellbeing exist. Using these data, individualised training programmes for elite pregnant athletes could be determined across gestation.

There remains a severe lack of evidence-based knowledge for elite pregnant athletes, including poor understanding of the impact of regular high-intensity and high-volume training on pregnancy outcomes. This presents a significant challenge to coaches, sport scientists and obstetric healthcare providers who support elite athletes through pregnancy. Increasing research (observational, cohort or case studies) in exercise performance across gestation is therefore critical to understanding both the antenatal and performance outcomes of elite pregnant athletes.

References

American College of Obstetricians and Gynecologists. (2020). Committee opinion, number 804: Physical activity and exercise during pregnancy and the postpartum period. *Obstetrics and Gynecology*, 135, e178–e188.

Avery, N. D., Stocking, K. D., Tranmer, J. E., Davies, G. A. and Wolfe, L. A. (1999). Fetal responses to maternal strength conditioning exercises in late gestation. *Canadian Journal of Applied Physiology*, 24, 362–376.

Bgeginski, R., Almada, B. P. and Martins Kruel, L. F. (2015). Cardiorespiratory responses of pregnant and nonpregnant women during resistance exercise. *Journal of Strength and Conditioning Research*, 29, 596–603.

Bo, K., Artal, R., Barakat, R., Brown, W. J., Davies, G. A. L., Dooley, M., Evenson, K. R., Haakstad, L. A. H., Kayser, B., Kinnunen, T. I., Larsen, K., Mottola, M. F., Nygaard, I., Van Poppel, M., Stuge, B. and Khan, K. M. (2018). Exercise and pregnancy in recreational and elite athletes: 2016/2017 evidence summary from the IOC expert group meeting, Lausanne. Part 5: Recommendations for health professionals and active women. *British Journal of Sports Medicine*, 52, 1080–1085.

Canadian Society for Exercise Physiology. (2021). *Get Active for Pregnancy Questionnaire*. www.csep.ca/getactivequestionnaire-pregnancy/CSEP-PATH_GAQ_P_Guidelines.pdf (accessed 5 May 2021).

Carpenter, M. W., Sady, S. P., Hoegsberg, B., Sady, M. A., Haydon, B., Cullinane, E. M., Coustan, D. R. and Thompson, P. D. (1988). Fetal heart rate response to maternal exertion. *Journal of the American Medical Association*, 259, 3006–3009.

Darroch, F., Giles, A. R. and Mcgettigan-Dumas, R. (2016). Elite female distance runners and advice during pregnancy: Sources, content, and trust. *Women in Sport and Physical Activity Journal*, 24, 170.

Da Silva, D. F., Mohammad, S., Hutchinson, K. A. and Adamo, K. B. (2020). Cross-validation of ratings of perceived exertion derived from heart rate target ranges recommended for pregnant women. *International Journal of Exercise Science*, 13, 1340–1351.

Davenport, M. H., Mccurdy, A. P., Mottola, M. F., Skow, R. J., Meah, V. L., Poitras, V. J., Jaramillo Garcia, A., Gray, C. E., Barrowman, N., Riske, L., Sobierajski, F., James, M., Nagpal, T., Marchand, A. A., Nuspl, M., Slater, L. G., Barakat, R., Adamo, K. B., Davies, G. A. and Ruchat, S. M. (2018a). Impact of prenatal exercise on both prenatal and postnatal anxiety and depressive symptoms: A systematic review and meta-analysis. *British Journal of Sports Medicine*, 52, 1376–1385.

Davenport, M. H., Meah, V. L., Ruchat, S. M., Davies, G. A., Skow, R. J., Barrowman, N., Adamo, K. B., Poitras, V. J., Gray, C. E., Jaramillo Garcia, A., Sobierajski, F., Riske, L., James, M., Kathol, A. J., Nuspl, M., Marchand, A. A., Nagpal, T. S., Slater, L. G., Weeks, A., Barakat, R. and Mottola, M. F. (2018b). Impact of prenatal exercise on neonatal and childhood outcomes: A systematic review and meta-analysis. *British Journal of Sports Medicine*, 52, 1386–1396.

Davenport, M. H., Ruchat, S. M., Poitras, V. J., Jaramillo Garcia, A., Gray, C. E., Barrowman, N., Skow, R. J., Meah, V. L., Riske, L., Sobierajski, F., James, M., Kathol, A. J., Nuspl, M., Marchand, A. A., Nagpal, T. S., Slater, L. G., Weeks, A., Adamo, K. B., Davies, G. A., Barakat, R. and Mottola, M. F. (2018c). Prenatal exercise for the prevention of gestational diabetes mellitus and hypertensive disorders of pregnancy: A systematic review and meta-analysis. *British Journal of Sports Medicine*, 52, 1367–1375.

Davenport, M. H., Yoo, C., Mottola, M. F., Poitras, V. J., Jaramillo Garcia, A., Gray, C. E., Barrowman, N., Davies, G. A., Kathol, A., Skow, R. J., Meah, V. L., Riske, L.,

Sobierajski, F., James, M., Nagpal, T. S., Marchand, A. A., Slater, L. G., Adamo, K. B., Barakat, R. and Ruchat, S. M. (2019). Effects of prenatal exercise on incidence of congenital anomalies and hyperthermia: A systematic review and meta-analysis. *British Journal of Sports Medicine*, 53, 116–123.

Department of Health and Social Care. (2019a). *UK Chief Medical Officers' Physical Activity Guidelines*. https://assets.publishing.service.gov.uk/government/uploads/system/uploads/attachment_data/file/832868/ukchief-medical-officers-physical-activity-guidelines.pdf (accessed 5 May 2021).

Department of Health and Social Care. (2019b). *Physical Activity in Pregnancy Infographic Guidance*. https://assets.publishing.service.gov.uk/government/uploads/system/uploads/attachment_data/file/829894/5-physical-activity-for-pregnant-women.pdf (Accessed 5 May 2021).

De Vivo, M. (2017). *Predicting and Understanding Physical Activity Behaviour during Pregnancy: A Multiphase Investigation*. Ph.D., Canterbury Christ Church University, Canterbury, UK.

Donnelly, G. M., Rankin, A., Mills, H., M, D. E. V., Goom, T. S. and Brockwell, E. (2020). Infographic: Guidance for medical, health and fitness professionals to support women in returning to running postnatally. *British Journal of Sports Medicine*, 54, 1114–1115.

Erdener, U. and Budgett, R. (2016). Exercise and pregnancy: Focus on advice for the competitive and elite athlete. *British Journal of Sports Medicine*, 50, 567.

Erkkola, R. U., Pirhonen, J. P. and Kivijarvi, A. K. (1992). Flow velocity waveforms in uterine and umbilical arteries during submaximal bicycle exercise in normal pregnancy. *Obstetetrics and Gynecology*, 79, 611–615.

Hesse, C. M., Tinius, R. A., Pitts, B. C., Olenick, A. A., Blankenship, M. M., Hoover, D. L. and Maples, J. M. (2018). Assessment of endpoint criteria and perceived barriers during maximal cardiorespiratory fitness testing among pregnant women. *Journal of Sports Medicine and Physical Fitness*, 58, 1844–1851.

Hordern, M. D., Dunstan, D. W., Prins, J. B., Baker, M. K., Singh, M. A. and Coombes, J. S. (2012). Exercise prescription for patients with type 2 diabetes and pre-diabetes: A position statement from Exercise and Sport Science Australia. *Journal of Science and Medicine in Sport*, 15, 25–31.

Kardel, K. R. (2005). Effects of intense training during and after pregnancy in top-level athletes. *Scandanavian Journal of Medicine and Science in Sports*, 15, 79–86.

Lotgering, F. K., Struijk, P. C., Van Doorn, M. B. and Wallenburg, H. C. (1992). Errors in predicting maximal oxygen consumption in pregnant women. *Journal of Applied Physiology*, 72, 562–567.

Manders, M. A., Sonder, G. J., Mulder, E. J. and Visser, G. H. (1997). The effects of maternal exercise on fetal heart rate and movement patterns. *Early Human Development*, 48, 237–247.

Martinez-Pascual, B., Alvarez-Harris, S., Fernandez-De-Las-Penas, C. and Palacios-Cena, D. (2017). Pregnancy in Spanish elite sportswomen: A qualitative study. *Women Health*, 57, 741–755.

Meah, V. L., Backx, K., Davenport, M. H. and International Working Group on Maternal, H. (2018). Functional hemodynamic testing in pregnancy: Recommendations of the International Working Group on Maternal Hemodynamics. *Ultrasound in Obstetetrics and Gynecology*, 51, 331–340.

Meah, V. L., Davies, G. A. and Davenport, M. H. (2020). Why can't I exercise during pregnancy? Time to revisit medical 'absolute' and 'relative' contraindications: Systematic review of evidence of harm and a call to action. *British Journal of Sports Medicine*, 54, 1395–1404.

Meah, V. L., Strynadka, M. C., Steinback, C. D. and Davenport, M. H. (2021). Cardiac responses to prenatal resistance exercise with and without the valsalva maneuver. *Medicine and Science in Sports and Exercise*, 53, 1260–1269.

Mei, Q., Gu, Y. and Fernandez, J. (2018). Alterations of pregnant gait during pregnancy and post-partum. *Scientific Reports*, 8, 2217.

Mottola, M. F., Davenport, M. H., Ruchat, S. M., Davies, G. A., Poitras, V. J., Gray, C. E., Jaramillo Garcia, A., Barrowman, N., Adamo, K. B., Duggan, M., Barakat, R., Chilibeck, P., Fleming, K., Forte, M., Korolnek, J., Nagpal, T., Slater, L. G., Stirling, D. and Zehr, L. (2018/2019). Canadian guideline for physical activity throughout pregnancy. *British Journal of Sports Medicine*, 52, 1339–1346.

Petrov Fieril, K., Glantz, A. and Fagevik Olsen, M. (2016). Hemodynamic responses to single sessions of aerobic exercise and resistance exercise in pregnancy. *Acta Obstetricia et Gynecologica Scandinavica*, 95, 1042–1047.

Pivarnik, J. M., Szymanski, L. M. and Conway, M. R. (2016). The elite athlete and strenuous exercise in pregnancy. *Clin Obstet Gynecol*, 59, 613–619.

Ravanelli, N., Casasola, W., English, T., Edwards, K. M. and Jay, O. (2019). Heat stress and fetal risk: Environmental limits for exercise and passive heat stress during pregnancy: A systematic review with best evidence synthesis. *British Journal of Sports Medicine*, 53, 799–805.

Ruchat, S. M., Mottola, M. F., Skow, R. J., Nagpal, T. S., Meah, V. L., James, M., Riske, L., Sobierajski, F., Kathol, A. J., Marchand, A. A., Nuspl, M., Weeks, A., Gray, C. E., Poitras, V. J., Jaramillo Garcia, A., Barrowman, N., Slater, L. G., Adamo, K. B., Davies, G. A., Barakat, R. and Davenport, M. H. (2018). Effectiveness of exercise interventions in the prevention of excessive gestational weight gain and postpartum weight retention: A systematic review and meta-analysis. *British Journal of Sports Medicine*, 52, 1347–1356.

Salvesen, K. A., Hem, E. and Sundgot-Borgen, J. (2012). Fetal wellbeing may be compromised during strenuous exercise among pregnant elite athletes. *British Journal of Sports Medicine*, 46, 279–283.

Skow, R. J., Davenport, M. H., Mottola, M. F., Davies, G. A., Poitras, V. J., Gray, C. E., Jaramillo Garcia, A., Barrowman, N., Meah, V. L., Slater, L. G., Adamo, K. B., Barakat, R. and Ruchat, S. M. (2019). Effects of prenatal exercise on fetal heart rate, umbilical and uterine blood flow: A systematic review and meta-analysis. *British Journal of Sports Medicine*, 53, 124–133.

Szymanski, L. M. and Satin, A. J. (2012). Strenuous exercise during pregnancy: Is there a limit? *American Journal of Obstetrics and Gynecology*, 207, 179 e1–6.

Weis, C. A., Barrett, J., Tavares, P., Draper, C., Ngo, K., Leung, J., Huynh, T. and Landsman, V. (2018). Prevalence of low back pain, pelvic girdle pain, and combination pain in a pregnant Ontario population. *J Obstet Gynaecol Can*, 40, 1038–1043.

Wowdzia, J. B. and Davenport, M. H. (2020). Cardiopulmonary exercise testing during pregnancy. *Birth Defects Research*, 113, 248–264.

15.6 Methods in exercise immunology

Nicolette C. Bishop and Neil P. Walsh

Keeping those who are physically active free from infectious illness is a major priority for athletes to be able to reach their performance potential. Absence from training due to illness is a key contributor in athlete underperformance (Raysmith and Drew, 2016), and respiratory infections are a particular issue (Walsh et al., 2011a). While it is undoubtable that a high-performance environment can provide an ideal opportunity for pathogen transmission (for example, through close contact with others, long-haul travel and less-than-ideal hygiene practices such as sharing drink bottles, towels and utensils), this phenomenon is more prevalent in endurance and team sports than in sprint and power events (Timpka et al., 2017) and has been associated with the negative impact of physiological and psychological stress on immune function (Walsh et al., 2011b). As such, there is much interest in methods for monitoring infection burden (incidence, symptom severity and duration) and assessing immune function in this population.

Considerations before testing

Unlike other aspects of performance testing, there is no current standard or established exercise protocol to challenge immune function. An individual's immune response to an acute exercise challenge, be it interval, continuous, aerobic or power, is transient and depends on several aspects, not least the intensity and duration of the test itself. In this regard, responses to acute exercise protocols on their own, while useful for investigating mechanisms for research, will not provide much meaningful data on the integrity of an individual's immune defences and therefore risk for infection. It is the response at rest that is more useful in this situation, and this will depend on current training status, training volume and any underlying medical conditions. To add a further layer of complexity, there is not an established one-stop in vivo or in vitro outcome measure of immune status that is easily applicable to athletes where testing is often in field settings. As such, outcome measures tend to focus on particular aspects of immune function, and one often chooses a measurement tool(s) according to convenience, practicality and cost. Added to this, most immune functions exhibit a circadian rhythm, and so for monitoring purposes tests must be performed at the same time of day. Immune outcome measures are also notoriously variable, both within and between individuals.

DOI: 10.4324/9781003045281-77

For this reason, when assessing immune function in athletes, an individualised (rather than cohort) approach is best, whereby you gain some indication of what is 'normal' for that individual over time. This way deviations are easier to pick up and allow alterations to training to be made to minimise the risk of developing an infection, or at the very least, to reduce the severity and duration of symptoms, allowing a faster return to training.

Given the multitude of ways of assessing infection symptoms and immune function, many of which are beyond the scope of this chapter, here we describe key considerations and processes of data collection and suggest common methods of analysis and interpretation considered valid currently in the field of exercise immunology. We present relevant information in three subsections: assessing illness and infection, assessing mucosal immune function and assessing systemic immune function. For a detailed discussion of the methods suggested, readers are directed to the International Society of Exercise Immunology Consensus Statements (Walsh et al., 2011b; Bermon et al., 2017).

Assessing illness and infection

Monitoring symptoms of respiratory infections is usually performed using subjective self-report of either unstandardised health logs, standardised symptom questionnaires or physician assessment of the common cold. Swab testing of the oral mucosa (inside the mouth and back of the throat) can be performed and assessed using polymerase chain reaction techniques to amplify the presence of viral DNA and allows detection of the specific viral strains, but this is costly and requires specific expertise. It is also common practice now to assess for the presence of allergy, as this causes similar symptoms to respiratory infections but would require a different management strategy.

Collecting symptom data

There are two main standardised questionnaires used by exercise immunologists: the Jackson Common Cold Questionnaire (Jackson et al., 1958) and the Wisconsin Upper Respiratory Symptom Survey (WURSS; www.fammed.wisc.edu/wurss/). These are designed to be completed daily, and many sports incorporate modified versions of these into a training log for their own purposes. The Jackson Questionnaire was developed from the symptoms experienced by over 1000 volunteers in the 6 days after nasal inoculation with nasal common cold secretions collected from donors. It incorporates eight clinical symptoms: sneezing, headache, feeling generally unwell, runny nose, blocked nose, sore throat, cough and chilliness. These eight symptoms are scored on a 4-point scale from 0 (no symptom) to 3 (severe symptom) and summed to determine a total daily symptom score.

Table 15.6.1 summarises an example of a completed Jackson questionnaire and associated scoring. Jackson's criteria for a common cold included a total symptom score of ≥14 during the 6-day monitoring period and a 'yes' answer to the dichotomous question, 'do you think you are suffering from a common cold?'

For the early detection of a common cold, a total symptom score of ≥6 on 2 consecutive days (equating to three moderate or two severe symptoms each day) and a 'yes' answer to the dichotomous question is a reasonable practical recommendation. Common cold duration is recorded as the number of consecutive days with total symptom score ≥6; peak symptom severity and total symptom score for each episode are also frequently reported. The International Society of Exercise Immunology Consensus Statements provide important guidance for exercise both during and after respiratory infection (Walsh et al., 2011a; Bermon et al., 2017).

The WURSS is also widely used by researchers and practitioners. It was developed and validated against the Jackson Questionnaire, physician-verified common cold incidence and nasal inoculation with rhinovirus in ~400 participants (Barrett et al., 2002, 2005, 2006). It also considers the impact of common cold symptoms on an individual's quality-of-life measures. In addition to the original 44-question version there is a 21-question validated version, and influenza-like illness symptoms of headache, body aches and fever are included on a 24-question version. The WURSS is longer than the eight-question Jackson Questionnaire, so it is worth considering the time burden of daily completion if looking to use one of these questionnaires on a longer-term basis. An 11-question version and a version specifically for children are currently being validated.

Table 15.6.1 Case study example of a completed Jackson Common Cold Questionnaire

1 Do you think you are suffering from a common cold **today?**

   [X] YES   [ ] NO

2 For each sign of illness, please cross **one** box that describes how you feel **today**:

	Not at All (0)	Mild (1)	Moderate (2)	Severe (3)	Score
Sneezing			X		2
Headache			X		2
Feeling generally unwell		X			1
Runny nose		X			1
Blocked nose	X				0
Sore throat			X		2
Cough	X				0
Chilliness	X				0
				Total score	8

The original Jackson criteria for a common cold included a total symptom score of ≥14 during the 6-day monitoring period and a 'yes' answer to the dichotomous question, 'do you think you are suffering from a common cold?' However, in a practical sense, confirming a common cold after 6-day reporting is not helpful, as most athletes will be recovering after this time. Instead, we suggest a reasonable practical recommendation is a total symptom score of ≥6 on 2 consecutive days (equating to three moderate or two severe symptoms each day) and a 'yes' answer to the dichotomous question 'do you think you are suffering from a common cold?'

Assessing mucosal immune function

Immune markers in mucosal secretions, particularly saliva and tears, are of interest to exercise immunologists, particularly those working in the field environment. The process involved in collecting these fluids is non-invasive, convenient, practical, low cost and because as many as 95% of all infections are thought to be initiated at the mucosal surfaces (Bosch et al., 2002). This highlights the important role mucosal immunity plays in defence against opportunistic infections such as the common cold.

Salivary secretory IgA (SIgA) production is the major effector function of the mucosal immune system and acts with innate mucosal defences such as defensins, alpha-amylase, lactoferrin and lysozyme to provide the 'first line of defence' against pathogens and antigens presented at the mucosa. Falls in secretion rate of salivary markers of mucosal immunity have been implicated as a potential risk factor for subsequent episodes of respiratory infection in athletes; however, concentration and secretion of saliva markers are notoriously open to several influences, not least time of day, not taking hydration or saliva flow into consideration and unwittingly stimulating saliva flow through sight or smell of food when collecting the sample; this changes the composition of the saliva as well as the volume. Moreover, concentrations of mucosal markers of immune function are highly varied both within and between individuals. For this reason, to assess meaningful changes in mucosal immunity, the normal healthy (i.e., in the absence of infection) range for an individual must first be established. This is best assessed using weekly sample collection.

Collecting saliva samples

Saliva samples are usually collected 'passively', either via cotton swab or by dribbling into a sterile tube. Passive collection into cotton swabs is used to minimise the risk of gingival bleeding that is sometimes associated with the expectoration method of saliva collection. However, care is needed to ensure that the sample volume is optimal since there are issues with the reliability of SIgA determination from cotton swab collections in sample volumes of less than 200 µl and more than 2 ml (Li and Gleeson, 2004). Furthermore, SIgA concentrations from cotton swabs are often lower than those collected by passive dribbling (Strazdins et al., 2005). The choice of collection method may also depend on the subject population; studies of children and the elderly may prefer to use swab collections because they are rated positively for both comfort and acceptability compared with passive dribbling (Strazdins et al., 2005). Larger sterile tubes are useful for those with limited hand mobility.

The volume of saliva is also a key consideration and should be accounted for. Concentrations of antimicrobial proteins are diluted in higher volumes of saliva, giving an artefactual lower concentration. Likewise, a decrease in saliva volume will concentrate the proteins, giving higher values. Saliva volume can be accounted for by either collecting a fixed volume of saliva in a graduated tube (e.g., 1 ml) or by measuring the volume of saliva collected over a fixed period of time (e.g., 2 min). A standard protocol for collecting saliva samples is provided next; this can also be used for the collection of saliva for hormone analysis. Analysis of saliva antimicrobial proteins can be performed using commercially available enzyme-linked immunosorbent assays (ELISAs); these are widely available for SIgA, lysozyme, lactoferrin, defensins and α-amylase.

Protocol for collecting saliva samples using the passive dribble method:

1. Provide the participant with a small (approximately 100 ml) cup of plain water to wash the mouth and remove any contaminants 2–5 min prior to collection.
2. Give the participant the unopened sterile screw-top tube and ask them to unscrew the lid.
3. Ask the participant to swallow to empty the mouth and sit with their head tilted slightly forward.
4. Ask the participant to make minimal facial movement and expectorate saliva as it collects under their tongue every 20 s either for the duration of a timed collection (normally 2 min) or until the 1 ml of saliva is collected, as marked on the tube.
5. If using a timed collection, at the end of the collection period, the participant must expectorate any saliva in the mouth into the collection tube, replace the tube lid and pass the closed tube to you.
6. Store the saliva samples at −20°C or −80°C for analysis.
7. When analysing, thaw completely at room temperature. When defrosted, centrifuge for 2 min at 12,000 rpm in a micro centrifuge and use the clear supernatant in your analysis.

Assessing systemic immune function

There are a multitude of methods to assess both innate (non-specific, first line of defence) and adaptive (specific response) immune cell phenotypes and functions; however, the majority are not practical or feasible to be used in a field setting. For this reason, we only summarise key techniques here; a detailed overview of methods is provided in Bermon et al. (2017).

Immune cell numbers

Basic assessment of numbers of total immune cells (white blood cells or leukocytes) and the differential count of the key cells (neutrophils, lymphocytes, monocytes) can be derived from a full blood count in ethylenediaminetetraacetic acid (EDTA)–treated whole blood using a haematology analyser. If you do not have an analyser in your organisation, many hospital pathology labs offer this service.

Flow cytometry

More detailed assessment of immune cell types and their receptors can be determined using flow cytometry. This is a method of single-cell analysis, whereby the cell population is suspended in a clear saline solution and funnelled through a nozzle to create a stream of single cells. The cells flow past a set of laser sources, and as the light hits each cell, it is scattered in different directions; this gives an indication of the cell morphology. Light scattered in a forward direction ('forward scatter') gives an indication of cell size; bigger cells will cause more scattering. Light scattered sideways ('side scatter') gives an indication of volume of cytoplasmic granules inside of the cell. The degree of scattering is detected, converted into an electrical signal and visualised by the cytometer software; hence, populations of cells with similar properties are clustered together. As the three main circulating immune cell types (neutrophils, monocytes and lymphocytes) differ in size and granularity, plotting forward scatter against side scatter allows the identification of these different cell populations (Figure 15.6.1). Specific cell subpopulations within these populations can be subsequently identified by 'tagging' receptors on the surface of the cells using fluorescent emitting chemicals (fluorochromes) joined to antibodies, which then bind to cell surface receptors. Once excited by the laser, each fluorochrome emits light at a specific wavelength and is gathered by the flow cytometer's detectors.

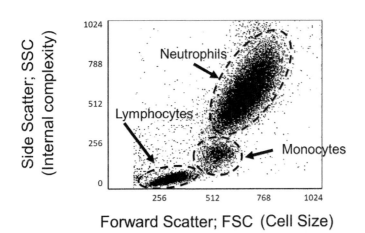

Cell Type	Size (Forward Scatter, FSC)	Complexity /'granularity' (Side Scatter, SSC)
Lymphocytes	small	Low
Monocytes	medium	Low
Neutrophils	medium-large	High

Figure 15.6.1 Cell morphology can be used to identify the three main immune cell populations in whole blood. Forward scatter (FSC) gives an indication of size, and side scatter (SSC) gives an indication of a cell's internal complexity. The cytometer plots FSC against SSC to provide a visual image of the three distinctive white blood cell populations.

Do not be put off by all-singing and all-dancing flow cytometers; simple and useful information can be gathered using just a few cell markers, and this technique is more accessible than ever, with several bench-top analysers now available – some even have an automated set-up. Flow cytometer manufacturers (e.g., Becton Dickinson, Beckman Coulter, Bio-Rad) provide excellent advice and training.

Immune cell functional responses

In vitro measures of systemic immune function rely on challenging immune cells with a stimulus (e.g., a plant-derived mitogen, a vaccine or other antigen) designed to elicit a response that closely mimics the response in vivo. This can be in whole blood or in cells separated from the blood and incubating them in the presence of a synthetic media enriched in serum (typically foetal calf serum [FCS]) or from a human participant. Using the participant's serum (autologous serum) can provide very useful information about how the immune cells might respond when challenged in vivo. Often the cell supernatant is collected before and after stimulation to provide information about soluble mediators (e.g., cytokines important in antiviral defence) that have been synthesised and released by the cells. The cells themselves can be harvested and changes in cell surface receptor expression assessed using flow cytometry. Alternatively, many techniques based on this principle can be used to assess other cell functions, including cell proliferation (e.g., Nieman et al., 1995; Bishop et al., 2005), the ability of cytotoxic cells to attack target cells and/or the ability of phagocytic cells to engulf foreign particles (Meaney et al., 2016).

Conclusion

In this chapter we have outlined key approaches and methods of data collection and analysis used in exercise immunology. There are a multitude of methods performed in research settings, but assessing symptoms and mucosal immune function are probably most useful and feasible for practical and field settings. In these situations, frequent resting collections are needed (e.g., daily symptoms, weekly saliva) to gain the most meaningful data, and several steps need to be taken to standardise longitudinal saliva collections. This will provide practical data to prompt early management intervention to maintain athlete health and facilitate a swift return to training.

References

Barrett, B., Brown, R., Mundt, M., Safdar, N., Dye, L., Maberry, R. and Alt, J. (2005). The Wisconsin Upper Respiratory Symptom Survey is responsive, reliable, and valid. *Journal of Clinical Epidemiology*, 58(6), 609–617.

Barrett, B., Brown, R., Voland, R., Maberry, R. and Turner, R. (2006). Relations among questionnaire and laboratory measures of rhinovirus infection. *European Respiratory Journal*, 28(2), 358–363.

Barrett, B., Locken, K., Maberry, R., Schwamman, J., Brown, R., Bobula, J. and Stauffacher, E. A. (2002). The Wisconsin Upper Respiratory Symptom Survey (WURSS): A new research instrument for assessing the common cold. *Journal of Family Practice*, 51(3), 265.

Bermon, S., Castell, L. M., Calder, P. C., Bishop, N. C., Blomstrand, E., Mooren, F. C., Krüger, K., Kavazis, A. N., Quindry, J. C., Senchina, D. S., Nieman, D. C., Gleeson, M., Pyne, D. B., Kitic, C. M., Close, G. L., Larson-Meyer, D. E., Marcos, A., Meydani, S. N., Wu, D., Walsh, N. P. and Nagatom, R. (2017). Consensus statement immunonutrition and exercise. *Exercise Immunology Review*, 23, 8–50.

Bishop, N. C., Walker, G. J., Bowley, L. A., Evans, K. F., Molyneux, K., Wallace, F. A. and Smith, A. C. (2005). Lymphocyte responses to influenza and tetanus toxoid in vitro following intensive exercise and carbohydrate ingestion on consecutive days. *Journal of Applied Physiology*, 99(4), 1327–1335.

Bosch, J. A., Ring, C., de Geus, E. J., Veerman, E. C. and Amerongen, A. V. (2002). Stress and secretory immunity. *International Review of Neurobiology*, 52, 213–253.

Jackson, G. G., Dowling, H. F., Spiesman, I. G. and Boand, A. V. (1958). Transmission of the common cold to volunteers under controlled conditions. I: The common cold as a clinical entity. *American Medical Association Archives of Internal Medicine*, 101(2), 267–278.

Li, T. L. and Gleeson, M. (2004). The effect of collection methods on unstimulated salivary immunoglobulin A, total protein, amylase and cortisol. *Bulletin of Physical Education*, 36, 17–30.

Meaney, M. P., Nieman, D. C., Henson, D. A., Jiang, Q. and Wang, F. Z. (2016). Measuring granulocyte and monocyte phagocytosis and oxidative burst activity in human blood. *Journal of Visualized Experiments*, 115, 54264.

Nieman, D. C., Brendle, D., Henson, D. A., Suttles, J., Cook, V. D., Warren, B. J., Butterworth, D. E., Fagoaga, O. R. and Nehlsen-Cannarella, S. L. (1995). Immune function in athletes versus nonathletes. *International Journal of Sports Medicine*, 16(5), 329–333.

Raysmith, B. and Drew, M. (2016). Performance success or failure is influenced by weeks lost to injury and illness in elite Australian track and field athletes: A 5-year prospective study. *Journal of Science and Medicine in Sport*, 19(10), 778–783.

Strazdins, L., Meyerkort, S., Brent, V., D'Souza, R. M., Broom, D. H. and Kyd, J. M. (2005). Impact of saliva collection methods on sIgA and cortisol assays and acceptability to participants. *Journal of Immunological Methods*, 307(1–2), 167–171.

Timpka, T., Jacobsson, J., Bargoria, V., Périard, J. D., Racinais, S., Ronsen, O., Halje, K., Andersson, C., Dahlström, Ö., Spreco, A., Edouard, P. and Alonso, J. M. (2017). Pre-participation predictors for championship injury and illness: Cohort study at the Beijing 2015 International Association of Athletics Federations World Championships. *British Journal of Sports Medicine*, 51(4), 271–276.

Walsh, N. P., Gleeson, M., Pyne, D. B., Nieman, D. C., Dhabhar, F. S., Shephard, R. J., Oliver, S. J., Bermon, S. and Kajeniene, A. (2011a). Position statement. Part two: Maintaining immune health. *Exercise Immunolology Review*, 17, 64–103.

Walsh, N. P., Gleeson, M., Shephard, R. J., Gleeson, M., Woods, J. A., Bishop, N. C., Fleshner, M., Green, C., Pedersen, B. K., Hoffman-Goetz, L., Rogers, C. J., Northoff, H., Abbasi, A. and Simon, P. (2011b). Position statement. Part one: Immune function and exercise. *Exercise Immunology Review*, 17, 6–63.

Index

Page numbers in *italic* indicate a figure and page numbers in **bold** indicate a table on the corresponding page

5-0-5 agility test: in basketball 246–247; in fencing 327–328; in netball 240, **241**
30-15 intermittent test: in basketball 246; in fencing 327; in netball **241**, 242; in rugby 236

absolute reliability 37
accident handling 22–23
accreditation 1, 5, 6, 55
acute-chronic workload ratio (ACWR) 409
acute mountain sickness 378
acute myocardial infarction 356
adverse events reporting 17
aerobic capacity *see also* VO₂max: fencing 326; paediatric exercise testing 363–365; table tennis 261; wheeled para-sport 339–340
agility: ambulant para-athletes 343–344, *344*; basketball player 246–247; netball 240, **241**; table tennis 263, *263*
alactic anaerobic performance 261–262
allometric cascade 45
altitude and exercise testing 375–378; pre-ascent testing 375–377, *376*
amateur boxing *see* boxing
ambulant para-athletes 333–338; 20-m linear sprint 343; 20 x 20 m repeated sprint test 345; aerobic capacity 339–340; agility test 343–344, *344*; anaerobic capacity assessment 342; ataxia 336; athetosis 336; box test *344*, 344–345; critical power (CP) 342; critical speed (CS) 342; fan drill *344*, 345; field-based testing 342–345; general considerations 333–334; hypertonia 336; impairment-specific considerations 335–338;

intellectual impairment 337–338; laboratory-based assessment 339–342; leg length differences 335–336; limb deficiency 335–336; lower body impairments 334–335; short stature 336–337; speed 342–343; step and ramp tests 340, **341**; testing and classification 349–350; upper body impairments 334; vision impairment 338; Wingate Anaerobic Test (WanT) 342
anaerobic capacity: ambulant para-athletes 342; canoeing 200; cycling 189–191, *190*, *192*; fencing 326; kayaking 200; table tennis 261–262
anthropometry 69; children 362
arm span 71
arterialised venous blood sampling 115
artistic gymnastics *see* gymnastics
ataxia 336
athetosis 336
athlete *see also* pregnant athlete: travelling 397–400; wellbeing 401–403
autonomic dysreflexia 339

back squat test: curling 285; squash 256
BASES 6, 55; Code of Conduct 5, 19, 24; promoting safety culture 25
basketball 244–248; 5-0-5 agility test 246–247; 30-15 intermittent fitness test 246; agility 246–247; neuromuscular assessment 244–245; physiological demands 244; speed 246; testing 244–248, **248**; testing feedback and monitoring 247–248; upper body strength 247; vertical jump test 245; Y-shaped reactive agility test 247

bench press in curling 285
Bergström needle 118, *119*, 120–121
biathlon skiing *see* skiing
blood sampling/sample 24, 112–116; arterialised venous blood sampling 115; capillary blood sampling 115; pre-sampling standardisation 112–114; safety issues 116; treatment after collection 115–116; venous blood sampling 114–115
body: scaling techniques for 42–46; surface law 44
body composition: boxing 322; children 362; and dual energy x-ray absorptiometry 148–150; laboratory-based exercise tests 362–365; race car drivers 292, 293; rugby 234–235; squash 256
body impairments: lower body 334–335; upper body 334
bone density 147, **147–148**, *149*, *150*, 150–151
bone mineral density 142
Borg 6-20 RPE scale 96, 100
bouldering *see* sport climbing
boxing 321–323; body mass and composition testing 322; movement assessment 322; physiological assessment 322–323, **323**; physiological assessment protocols 322–323; physiological demands 321; strength assessments 322
box test for ambulant para-athletes *344*, 344–345
brain-to-muscle pathway 126, *127*
breath-by-breath method of gas analysis 84–85
British Association of Sport and Exercise Sciences *see* BASES
broad jump test in curling 287

calibration of equipment 55–59, **57**, *58*, 147
canoeing 197–200; field-based testing 199–200; incremental step test **198**, 198–199; indoor anaerobic capacity testing 200; indoor sprint testing 199; laboratory-based physiological assessment 198–199; laboratory training zone certification and verification 200; sport-specific outdoor testing 200
capillary blood sampling 115
cardiomyopathy 51–52
cardiopulmonary exercise testing (CPET) 359

cardiorespiratory fitness 363–365
Cart and Load Effort Rating Scale (CALER) 100
change of direction speed test in squash 256, *257*
children as research participants *see* paediatric exercise testing
Children's Effort Rating Table (CERT) 100
circadian phase 398–399
climbing *see* sport climbing
Code of Conduct (BASES) 5, 19, 24
coefficient of variation (CV) 38
cold environments and measurement of physiological responses 385–388, **386**; core temperature 385–386; cutaneous blood flow 387–388; mean body temperature 387; shivering 387, 388; skin temperature 386–387; thermal comfort and sensation 387
compatibility limits (CL) 38
competency, professional 5–8
complaints, handling of 17
conchotome forceps 120, 121
confidentiality of data 15–16
consent for exercise testing 14–15; children 15, 17; informed consent 14–15; photographic images 16
cooling and measurement of physiological responses 388
core temperature measurement 385–386
countermovement jump (CMJ) test 415; basketball player 245; cricket 270–271; netball 239; squash 256–257
court based sports *see* wheeled para-sport
cricket 269–273; 2-km time trial 272; countermovement jump test 270–271; isometric holds test 270; isometric mid-thigh pull test 270; recommended standards for players 269, **273**; run-2 test 271–272, *272*; skinfold measurement 269; sprints 271
critical power (CP) 86, 90–93, **91**; ambulant para-athletes 342; cycling 191–192, *193*; sport climbing 300, **301**, *301*; triathlon 170
critical speed (CS): ambulant para-athletes 342; distance running 164; in swimming 175
cross-country skiing *see* skiing
curling 283–288; anthropometry 283; back squat test 285; balance 287–288; bench press 285; broad jump test 287; energy systems 283–284, **284**; FABER test 285; flexibility 284–285, **285**; modified

Thomas test 284, *286*; prone hold test 287; single-leg squat 287; strength and power 285–287
cutaneous blood flow measurement 387–388
cycling: anaerobic power reserve 189–191, *190, 192*; critical power (CP) 191–192, *193*; efficiency 194; lactate threshold 193–194; Lamberts submaximal cycling test 195; peak power output (PPO) 189–190, *195*; performance determinants 188–189; power-duration relationship in cycling 191–192, *192*; power-to-weight ratio 188; trial duration 191, *193*

data: confidentiality and usage 15–16; monitoring and reporting 16–17; withdrawal of by participant 16
data fatigue 34
data intelligence 31–35, **33**; collection 32; feedback 33–34; interpretation and visualisation 32–33; pitfalls 34–35
delta efficiency in cycling 194–195
deoxygenation in speed skating 202–203
Douglas bag method of gas analysis 31, 81–83, **83**, 391
Down syndrome 347, 348, 349
dual emission x-ray absorptiometry (DEXA) 184
dual energy x-ray absorptiometry (DXA) 142–153; and body composition 148–150, *149, 150*; calibration 147; cross calibration 152; indications and contraindications 143–145, **144**; interpretation and reporting 150–151; longitudinal scans 151–152; precision and least significant change 151–152; pre-scan standardisation 145–146, **146**; radiation dose 143; scan acquisition and analysis 147–150; technology 142–143; training requirements 153
dynamic lung function 63, *64*, 65
dynamometer: in fencing 326, **327**; isokinetic 128

echocardiography for pre-participation evaluation 52
efficiency in cycling 194–195
elastic similarity 44
electrocardiogram 357; for pre-participation evaluation 51–52

electromyography 126, *127*, *128*, **129**, 130–133
environment, measurement of 385
equipment: calibration 55–59, **57**, *58*; calibration sample quality 56; control test 56; documentation 59; maintenance of 59; user training 59
ergometry, children 362–363
Eston-Parfitt (E-P) scale 100, *100*
ethics *see* research ethics
ethics committee 10–12, 16
EUROFIT fitness test battery 348–349, 365
European Society of Cardiology Systemic Coronary Risk Evaluation (SCORE) 357
evidence-based practice 8
evoked twitch parameters in neuromuscular system 130
exercise immunology 430–436; assessing illness and infection 431–432; assessing mucosal immune function 433–434; systemic immune function assessment 434–436
exercise-induced asthma 61, 63
exercise-induced fatigue 125
exercise intensity domains 86–88, **88**, 161, *161*
exercise performance and lung function 61
exercise testing: adaptations for master athlete 358; ethics of 10–18; at high altitude 375–378; intellectual impaired individuals 347–350; international safeguards for children 26–27, 28; during pregnancy 418–426; safeguarding in 25–28, **26–27**
explosive broad jump test in table tennis 263
expression of force 126
external training load 405, 407–409

FABER test in curling 285
fan drill test *344*, 345
fatigue 122, 125, 397–399, 403
female athlete exercise testing 368–372; hormonal contraceptives 371; monitoring 370–371; performance testing 371–372; screening 370
fencing 325–328; 5-0-5 agility test 327–328; 30-15 intermittent test 327; aerobic capacity 326; anaerobic capacity 326; field-based testing 326–328, **327**; in-line lunge test 327; ioskinetic dynamometry 326, **327**; laboratory-based assessment

326; multiple sprints 326; repeated sprint ability (RSA) test 327; treadmill test 326
field-based testing 136–141; *see also* specific sport; data interpretation 139–140; developing protocols 138–139; evaluating demands of the sport 136–138, *137*; feedback strategies 140–141; identifying fitness attributes 138; organizing testing programmes 139; six-step process 136–141, *137*
field hockey 227–232; endurance tests 230; field-based testing 227; performance data 227, **228–229**; repeated sprint ability 231; shuttle dribble test *231*, 232; shuttle sprint test 230, *231*; skills 232; slalom sprint test 230, *231*; speed and ability 230
finger strength in sport climbing 299, *299*
first lactate threshold (LT1) **88**, 169, 171, 323, **323**
fitness to practice 6, 7
flow cytometry 434–435, *435*
force, measuring in neuromuscular system 128–130
forearm strength in sport climbing 298–300
fraction of expired nitric oxide 66
Functional Movement Screen (FMS) 76, 77–78; in motorsports 293; in table tennis 264
functional movement screening 76; tests 76, 77–79; uses 77
functional overreaching (FOR) 413

gas exchange threshold (GET) 88, 90
Get Active for Pregnancy questionnaire 418
girth measurement 72–73, **73**
global positioning systems (GPS) 408
golf 277–281; athlete golfer attributes 277; considerations for physiological measurement 280–281; performance demands 277–278; physical screening 280; physiological assessment 278–279, **279**
graded exercise testing 96–97, 381–382
gross efficiency in cycling 194
gymnastics 309–311; field-based assessment 310, **311**; laboratory-based assessment 310, **311**

hazard identification **20**, 20–21
Health and Safety at Work Act (1974) 19

Health and Safety Executive (HSE) on risk assessment 21–22
health and safety management 19–24; emergency procedures 23; hazard identification **20**, 20–21; hygiene 22; incidents and accidents 22–23; insurance and personal indemnity 24; risk assessment 21–22, **23**; standard operating procedures 24
heart rate: measurement 402–403; in race car drivers 291; variability 415–416
heat-related illness 380
heat stress 381–383
heat tolerance tests 380, *381*
heavy-intensity exercise domain 87, **88**, 90–92, **91**
high altitude and exercise testing 375–378
hormones and overtraining 415
hot environments and exercise tests 380–383, **383**
Human Tissue Authority 11
hydration measurement 402
hypertonia 336
hypoxia 377–378
hypoxic ventilatory response 377

illness and infection assessment 431–432
immune cell functional responses 436
immune cell numbers 434
immunology 430–436
impairments 335–338; impaired muscle power 335
incidents, handling 22–23
incremental step test **198**, 198–199
indoor anaerobic capacity testing for canoeing and kayaking 200
indoor sprint testing in canoeing and kayaking 199
informed consent 15, 17
Informed Consent Form (ICF) 13, 15
infrared thermography 386–387
in-line lunge test 327
insurance and personal indemnity 24
intellectual impairment 337–338, 347–350
inter-disciplinary teams 7–8
intermittent endurance capacity test for table tennis 262, *262*
internal training load 405–407
International Safeguards 28
interval shuttle run test 262, *262*
intraclass correlation coefficient (ICC) 37–38, 40
isokinetic dynamometers 128

isokinetic dynamometry in fencing 326, **327**
isokinetic strength testing 109; children 365; protocol 109
isometric holds test in cricket 270
isometric mid-thigh pull test: cricket 270; netball 239–240, **241**, *241*
isometric strength test (1RM) in motorsports 294–295
isometric strength testing 108–109; protocol 109
isotonic (isoinertial) strength testing 106–107; considerations for 107–108; protocol 107

Jackson Common Cold Questionnaire 431–432, **432**
jet lag 397–399
judo 315–319; laboratory-based assessment 315–316; lower body muscle power 315; Special Judo Fitness Test 316, **318**, 319; specific tests 316–319; strength endurance test 316, **317**

kayaking 197–200; field-based testing 199–200; indoor anaerobic capacity testing 200; indoor sprint testing 199; laboratory-based physiological assessment 198–199; laboratory training zone certification 200; laboratory training zone verification 200; sport-specific outdoor testing 200

lactate testing: distance runner 161–162; rower 186
lactate threshold (LT) 86–90, *89*, 161; cycling 193–194; in triathlon 168–169
lactate turnpoint 90, 161
Lamberts submaximal cycling test 195
Landing Error Scoring System (LESS) 77, 78–79
landmine-punch throw profile 322
laser Doppler (LD) flowmetry 387–388
laser speckle contrast imaging (LSCI) 387–388
lead climbing *see* sport climbing
lean mass index 234–235
leg length differences 335–336
license to practice 6
limb deficiency 335–336
local positioning systems (LPS) 408
long distance running: field-based performance testing 164; physiological assessment 159–165; submaximal aerobic assessment 160–162

long-distance triathlons 171
long-track speed skating *see* speed skating
low energy availability (LEA) 144
lower body impairments 334–335
lung function: airway inflammation 66; assessment and interpretation 61–68; functional residual capacity 65; residual volume 65; static lung volumes 65

master athlete 355–359; exercise testing adaptations 358; pre-participation evaluation 52–53; safety and exercise risks 356–358; $\dot{V}O_2$max measurement 358–359
maximal aerobic power ($\dot{V}O_2$max) assessment: distance running 160–163; fencing 326; on-kinetics assessment 163–164; table tennis 261; in triathlon 169–70
maximal expiratory pressure (MEP) 131–132
maximal inspiratory pressure (MIP) 67
maximal lactate steady state (MLSS) 90, 92; in rowing 185
maximal sprint speed in distance running 164
maximal steady state (MSS) 86, 90–92, *91*
maximal voluntary contraction (MVC) 126
maximal voluntary ventilation 61
maximum leg strength test for squash 256
mean body temperature 387
measurement error 37–38; in surface anthropometry 73–74
menstrual cycle 368, *369*, 370–372
metabolic threshold testing 86–93; lactate threshold (LT) 86–90; maximal steady state (MSS) 86, 90–92, *91*; value of 92–93
micro-biopsy needle biopsy 118, 120
microelectromechanical systems (MEMS) 408
middle distance running: field-based performance testing 164; physiological assessment 159–165; submaximal aerobic assessment 160–162
moderate-intensity exercise domain 86–90, **88**, 93
modified Edgren side-step test 263, *263*
modified Thomas test in curling 284, *286*
motor evoked potentials (MEPs) 131–132
motorsports 291–295; body composition of race car drivers 292, *293*; cardiovascular testing 293–294; cognitive demands 292–293; heat impact 291–292;

movement screening 293; neck strength testing 294–295; physiological assessment 293–295; physiological demands of race car drivers 291–293; sleep tracking 295; strength demands 292; strength testing 294–295; sweat testing 294
mouth pressure 66–67
movement quality tests (MQTs) 76
mucosal immune function assessment 433–434
multidisciplinary teams 7–8
muscle biopsy 118–122; procedure 120–121; risks and safety 122; tissue treatment after collection 121–122
muscle compound action potential 130–131
M-wave in neuromuscular system 130–131

netball 238–242; 5-0-5 agility test 240, **241**; 10-m speed test 240, **241**; 30-15 intermittent fitness test **241**, 242; countermovement jump test 239; isometric mid-thigh pull test 239–240, *241*; single-leg hop test 238–239; testing 238–242, **241**
neuromuscular fatigue 403
neuromuscular system assessment 125–133; applications of 125–126; data acquisition 133; evoked twitch parameters 130; expression of force 126; measuring force *126, 128*, 128–130, **129**; methods 126–133; motor and lumbar evoked potentials 131–132; surface electromyography 132–133; voluntary activation 131, *132*
non-court based sports *see* wheeled para-sport
non-functional overreaching (NFOR) 413–416, *414*; biochemical and hormonal assessment 415; performance measures 415; physiological measures 415–416; psychological monitoring 416; two-bout exercise protocol 414
non-isometric growth 44–45

older athlete *see* master athlete
one-repetition maximum (1-RM) test 106, 107, **108**
overreaching 413–416
overtraining syndrome (OTS) 413–416, *414*; biochemical and hormonal assessment 415; performance measures 415; physiological measures 415–416; pyschological monitoring 416; two-bout exercise protocol 414
oxygenation in speed skating 202–203
oxygen uptake (VO_2): and body scaling 42, 44; measurement 81–83; ratings of perceived exertion (RPE) 97–98; scaling 42, 45

paediatric exercise testing 361–365; aerobic performance 363–365; anaerobic performance 364–365; anthropometry and body composition 362; biologic maturation assessment 361–362; cardiorespiratory fitness 363–365; field-based testing 365; informed assent 15, 17; international safeguards **26–27**, 28; isokinetic strength testing 365; pre-participation evaluation 51–52
para-athletes *see* ambulant para-athletes
Paralympic sport testing and classification 349–350
Participant Information and Consent Form (PICF) 15
Participant Information Sheet (PIS) 13, 15
passive range of movement, impaired 335
pathological fatigue 122
peak power output (PPO) in cycling 189–190, *195*
perceptually regulated exercise testing (PRET) 98
percutaneous needle biopsy 118–120
personal protective equipment (PPE) 13
PGE (pulmonary gas exchange) variables 81
photographic images and confidentiality 16
power-duration relationship in cycling 191–192, *192*
power relationships 14
power-to-weight ratio in cycling 188
practice-based evidence 8
pre-ascent testing 375–377, *376*
pregnant athlete 418–426, *419*, **421**; exercise modality 422; foetal monitoring 424–425; laboratory-based assessment 420–423; maternal monitoring 424, **424**; maximal exercise testing 422–423; reporting results 425; screening during 418, 420; strength testing 423–425; submaximal exercise testing 423
pre-participation evaluation (PPE) 51–53
professional boxing *see* boxing
professional competency 5–8
professional development 6–7
prone hold test 287

pulmonary gas exchange (PGE): breath-by-breath method 84–85; Douglas bag technique 81–83, **83**; measurement 81–85
pulse oximetry 375
punch force 322

quantitative movement tests (QMTs) 76
quickness of action in table tennis 264

race car driving *see* motorsports
rate of force development (RFD) 108, 300
rating of perceived exhaustion 402
ratings of perceived exertion (RPE) 96–101, 406–407; in children 100; influencing factors 98–99; and physiological markers 97, **97**; predicting oxygen uptake ($\dot{V}O_2$) 97–98; recommendations for effective use 101; and relative measures of exercise intensity 96–97; scale 100; strength training 99–100
ratio standards 42–43
reactive strength index in squash 257
recovery from exercise 125–126
recruitment 13–14
reflective practice 7
relative reliability 37
reliability 36–37; absolute 37; analysis application of 38, *39*, 40, **40**; estimate uncertainty and magnitude interpretation 38; relative 37
repeated observations 36
repeated sprint ability (RSA) test: fencing 327; field hockey 231; squash 256, *257*
Reporting of Injuries, Diseases and Dangerous Occurrences Regulations (RIDDOR) 23
research ethics 10–18; minimisation of risk 13; power relationships 14; recruitment 13–14; risk *versus* benefits 12
respiratory gas analysis 81–85; breath-by-breath method 84–85; Douglas bag technique 81–83, **83**
respiratory muscle function: abnormal 61, **62–63**; assessment and interpretation 61–68; fraction of expired nitric oxide 66; mouth pressure 66–67; single breath gas transfer 65–66; spirometry 63, *64*, 65
rifle carriage in biathlon skiing 211
risk assessment 12–13, **23**; five-step approach 21–22

risk of relative energy deficiency in sports (RED-S) 142, 144
rock climbing *see* sport climbing
roller-ski assessments 213–214, **214**
rowing: ergometer for 184, 186; field-based testing 186–187; laboratory-based physiological assessment 186–187; lactate analyzers 186; performance determinants 184–185; seven-stroke power test 185; step test 185
rugby 234–236; body composition testing 234–235; body strength and power 235; data analysis and interpretation 236; high-intensity intermittent running capacity 236; sprinting and speed 235–236
run-2 test 271–272, *272*
running economy: distance running 160, *161*, 161–162, **163**; triathlon 170

saliva collection in exercise immunology 433–434
salivary secretory IgA 433
SAMU Disability Fitness Battery 349
scaling 42; allometric cascade 45; allometry 43–44; elastic similarity 44; non-isometric growth impacting 44–45; ratio standards 42–43; surface law 44; techniques 42–46
second lactate threshold (LT2) **88**, 161, 169, 171, 323, **323**
segmometer 70
self-paced $\dot{V}O_2$peak test (SPV) 98
SEM *see* standard error of measurement (SEM)
session-RPE method (sRPE) 406–407
shivering 387, 388
short distance triathlons 171
short stature 336–337
short-track speed skating *see* speed skating
shuttle dribble test *231*, 232
shuttle sprint test 230, *231*
single breath gas transfer 65–66
single-leg hop test 238–239
single-leg squat in curling 287
skeletal muscle biopsy 118–122
skiing 208–215; energetic demands 208, 210; incremental submaximal assessments 213, **214**; laboratory-based testing 211–213, *212*; maximal assessments 213–214, **214**; pacing 210; techniques 208, *209*, 210–211; terrain 210; testing protocols 211–214

skinfold calipers 70
skinfold location 71
skinfold measurement 71, **72**; children 362, **363**; cricket 269; rugby 234; squash player 256
skin temperature measurement 386–387
slalom sprint test 230, *231*
sleep measurement 402
sleep tracking in motorsports 295
soccer 221–225; agility 223; fitness testing 222–223, **225**; indirect field-based tests 222; linear sprinting tests 223; monitoring 223–224; reliability analysis 38, *39*, 40, **40**
Special Judo Fitness Test 316, **318**, 319
speed: ambulant para-athletes 243, **343**; table tennis 263, *263*
speed skating 202–205; exercise testing 203; pacing and tactics 204; performance analysis 205; physiological challenges 202–203; training and monitoring 203–204
spirometry 63, *64*, 65
sport climbing: anthropometric data 297–298; critical force 300, **301**, *301*; finger strength 299, *299*; forearm strength 298–300; physiological assessment 297–304; rate of force development (RFD) 300; two-repetition max pull up 302; upper body muscular endurance 304; upper body powerslap 302–304, *303*, **303–304**; upper body strength 300–304; whole-body exhaustive climbing 298–300
sprint test: ambulant para-athletes 343; cricket 271; fencing 326; rugby player 235–236
squash 253–259; body composition testing 256; change of direction speed test 256, *257*; countermovement jump test 256–257; data interpretation 257–259; maximum leg strength test 256; physical characteristics 253–255, *254*; physical demands 253; physical performance test 255–256; physical profile 257, *258*, 259; reactive strength index 257; repeated sprint ability 256, *257*; specificity of testing 255; testing 255–257, *257*
squat jump 322, 415
standard error of measurement (SEM) 37–38
standard operating procedures 24

standing broad jump test in table tennis 263
stepped-angle treadwall test in sport climbing 298
strength testing 106–110; isokinetic strength 109; isometric testing 108–109; isotonic (isoinertial) strength testing 106–107; motorsports 294–295; in pregnant athlete 423–425; and RPE 99–100; rugby player 235
stretch stature 70–71
submaximal aerobic exercise testing 160–162
sudden cardiac death (SCD) 51–53, 356
superimposed twitch (SIT) 131, *132*
surface anthropometry 69–75; data interpretation 74; measurement error 73–74; prerequisites 69–70; procedures 70–73; recommended equipment 70
surface electromyography 132–133
surface law 44
sweat testing in motorsports 294
swimming 390–394; 3-minute all-out test 175, **178**; 7 x 200-m step test 174–175, **177**; 12 x 25-m all-out test 176, **179**; 400-m time trial **179**; critical speed testing 175, **178**; dry-land testing 181; physiological measurement 391–394, **392**, **393**; pool-based testing 173–176; testing environment 390–391; test selection 174, *174*, **177–180**; tethered 176, *176*, **180**, 181
systemic immune function assessment 434–436

table tennis 260–264; aerobic capacity 261; alactic anaerobic performance 261–262; explosive power 263; field-based testing 262–264; Functional Movement Screen (FMS) 264; intermittent endurance capacity 262–263; laboratory-based tests 261–262; modified Edgren side-step test 263, *263*; normative physiological values 261, **264**; physiological demands 260, **261**; quickness of action 264; speed and agility test 263, *263*; standing broad jump test 263
teams: inter-disciplinary 7–8; multidisciplinary 7–8
technical error of measurement (TEM) 73–74
test-retest designs 36–37

thermal comfort and sensation measurement 387
training load 405–409; data interpretation 409; external 405, 407–409; internal 405–407
travel fatigue 397–399
travelling athletes 397–400
treadmill calibration **57**
treadmill test: children 362–363; distance runner 160–162; fencing 326
*Triaining Imp*ulse (TRIMP) 406
triathlon: critical power (CP) 170; health profiling 171; physiological assessment 168–171; running economy 170; short- and long-distance 171; $\dot{V}O_2$max 169–170
two-bout exercise protocol 414
two-trial (test-retest) design 36–37
typical error 37

upper body impairments 334
upper body powerslap 302–304, *303*, **303–304**
upper body strength in sport climbing 300–304

vasoconstriction and measurement of physiological responses in cool environments 388
venous blood sampling 114–115
vertical jump test in basketball 245
vision impairment 338
$\dot{V}O_2$max: at high altitude 375; of master athletes 358–359; paediatric exercise testing 363–365; in rowing 185; swimming 392
voluntary activation in neuromuscular system 131, *132*

weighing scales 77
wellbeing of athletes 401–403; objective measures 402–403; subjective measures 402
wet bulb globe temperature 385
wheelchair tennis 345
wheeled para-sport 339–345
whole-body exhaustive climbing 298–300
Wingate Anaerobic Test (WanT) 342, 364–365
Wisconsin Upper Respiratory Symptom Survey (WURSS) 431–432